Contemporary Artificial Intelligence

Contemporary Artificial Intelligence

Richard E. Neapolitan

Xia Jiang

CRC Press
Taylor & Francis Group
Boca Raton London New York

CRC Press is an imprint of the
Taylor & Francis Group, an **informa** business

A CHAPMAN & HALL BOOK

CRC Press
Taylor & Francis Group
6000 Broken Sound Parkway NW, Suite 300
Boca Raton, FL 33487-2742

Printed in the United States of America on acid-free paper
Version Date: 20120612

International Standard Book Number: 978-1-4398-4469-4 (Hardback)

Library of Congress Cataloging-in-Publication Data

Neapolitan, Richard E.
    Contemporary artificial intelligence / Richard E. Neapolitan, Xia Jiang.
      p. cm.
    Includes bibliographical references and index.
    ISBN 978-1-4398-4469-4 (hardback)
    1. Artificial intelligence. I. Jiang, Xia, 1967- II. Title.

Q335.N425 2012
006.3--dc23
                                                2012017897

Visit the Taylor & Francis Web site at
http://www.taylorandfrancis.com

and the CRC Press Web site at
http://www.crcpress.com

Contents

Preface

Over the years my view of an artificial intelligence (AI) course has changed significantly. I used to view it as a course that should discuss our efforts to develop an artificial entity that can learn and make decisions in a complex, changing environment, affect that environment, and communicate its knowledge and choices to humans; that is, an entity that can think. I would therefore, cover the weak AI methods that failed to scale up. However, as strong methods that solved challenging problems in limited domains became more predominant, my course increasingly concerned these methods. I would cover backward chaining, forward chaining, planning, inference in Bayesian networks, normative decision analysis, evolutionary computation, decision tree learning, Bayesian network learning, supervised and unsupervised learning, and reinforcement learning. I would show useful applications of these methods. These techniques have come to be as important to a computer science student's repertoire as techniques such as divide-and-conquer, greedy methods, branch-and-bound, etc. Yet a student would not see them unless the student took an AI course. So my AI course evolved into a course that undergraduate students would take either concurrently or following an analysis of algorithms course, and would cover what I viewed as important problem-solving strategies that have emerged from the field of AI. I feel such a course should be a standard component of every computer science curriculum just like data structures and analysis of algorithms.

No text satisfied my needs for the course I taught for two reasons:

1. AI is a vast field that has included the development of many and varied techniques in the past 50 years. Current texts tried to include most of what has been going on rather than simply providing useful methods and algorithms.

2. No current text was accessible to students at a mainstream university like Northeastern Illinois University. I had this same problem with my analysis of algorithms course, and was the reason I wrote *Foundations of Algorithms*.

So I taught the course using my own Bayesian network texts and class notes. I finally decided to turn these notes into this textbook so professors at other mainstream universities could provide a similar course. This text is not meant to be an encyclopedia or history of AI, but rather is meant to be a text that can be covered in one semester; and, in the amount of time one semester allows, provide the student with what I consider the most useful techniques that have emerged from AI. These techniques include the following:

1. Logic-based methods

2. Probability-based methods

3. Evolutionary computation and methods based on swarm intelligence

4. Language understanding

The text clearly reflects my own bias. I have not discussed neural networks, fuzzy logic, support vector machines, and many other endeavors in AI. I also do not include searching because most searching techniques appear in data structures and algorithms texts. Almost half the text is about probabilistic methods. This is perhaps partially due to the fact that I know these methods best because they are my own area of research, but also due to the fact that I view them as most important (that is why they are my area of research).

I have written the material in the order I teach it. So I recommend simply covering the chapters from first to last. If there is not time to cover the entire book, I recommend leaving out Sections 8.3 through 8.7 where I have explored more advanced topics in decision analysis, and Section 12.3 which concerns causal learning. Sections marked with a ★ contain material that is inherently more difficult than the other material in the text. However, they do cover important topics and should not be skipped if the students have the sophistication to grasp them.

I thank Dawn Holmes and Kevin Korb for reading the manuscript and providing useful comments. I also thank Prentice Hall for allowing me to include excerpts from my text *Learning Bayesian Networks*, and Morgan Kaufmann for allowing me to include excerpts from my texts *Probabilistic Methods for Financial and Marketing Informatics* and *Probabilistic Methods for Bioinformatics*. Finally, I thank Relu I. Jianu for designing an attractive and thought-provoking cover.

Richard E. Neapolitan
RE-Neapolitan@neiu.edu

About the Authors

Richard E. Neapolitan is a professor of computer science at Northeastern Illinois University. His research interests include probability and statistics, expert systems, cognitive science, and applications of probabilistic modeling to fields such as medicine, biology, and finance. Dr. Neapolitan is a prolific author and has published in the most prestigious journals in the broad area of reasoning under uncertainty. He has previously written five books, including the seminal 1990 Bayesian network text *Probabilistic Reasoning in Expert Systems*; *Learning Bayesian Networks* (2004); *Foundations of Algorithms* (1996, 1998, 2003, 2010), which has been translated into three languages; *Probabilistic Methods for Financial and Marketing Informatics* (2007); and *Probabilistic Methods for Bioinformatics* (2009). His approach to textbook writing is innovative; his books have the reputation for making difficult concepts easy to understand while still remaining thought-provoking.

Xia Jiang is an assistant professor in the Department of Biomedical Informatics at the University of Pittsburgh. She has over 13 years of teaching and research experience in Bayesian network modeling, machine learning, and algorithm design. She is the co-author of the book *Probabilistic Methods for Financial and Marketing Informatics* (2007). Dr. Jiang is currently focusing on developing novel algorithms/systems that improve the computational efficiency of large data analysis, and network modeling of cancer genome data.

Chapter 1

Introduction to Artificial Intelligence

In 1990, I (Richard Neapolitan) was relatively new to the field of **Artificial Intelligence** (**AI**). At the *6th Conference on Uncertainty in Artificial Intelligence*, which was held at MIT, I met Eugene Charniak, who at the time was a well-known researcher in AI. During a conversation while strolling along the campus, I said, "I heard that the Japanese are applying fuzzy logic to AI." Gene responded "I don't believe the Japanese have been any more successful at AI than us." This comment substantiated that which I had already begun to realize, namely that AI seemed to be a dismal failure.

Dr. Charniak's comment was correct in 1990 and it is still correct today. If we consider AI to be the development of an artificial entity such as the Terminator in the movie by the same name or HAL in the classic sci-fi movie *Space Odyssey*, then we have not developed anything close. The Terminator and HAL are artificial entities that can learn and make decisions in a complex, changing environment, affect that environment, and communicate their knowledge and choices to humans. We have no such entities.

So why does the field of AI persist, and why was this book written? In their efforts to develop artificial intelligence, researchers looked at the behavior/reasoning of intelligent entities such as humans, and developed algorithms based on that behavior. These algorithms have been used to solve many interesting problems, including the development of systems that behave intelligently in limited domains. Such systems includes ones that can perform medical diagnosis, diagnose problems with software, make financial decisions, navigate a difficult terrain, monitor the possible failure of a space shuttle, recognize speech, understand text, plan a trip, track a target, learn an individual's preferences from the preferences of similar individuals, learn the causal relationships among genes, and learn which genes affect a phenotype. This book concerns these algorithms and applications. Before discussing the content of this book further, we provide a brief history of AI.

1.1 History of Artificial Intelligence

We start by discussing early efforts to define artificial intelligence.

1.1.1 What Is Artificial Intelligence?

Abandoning the philosophical question of what it means for an artificial entity to think or have intelligence, Alan Turing [1950] developed an empirical test of artificial intelligence, which is more appropriate to the computer scientist endeavoring to implement artificial intelligence on a computer. The **Turing test** is an operational test; that is, it provides a concrete way to determine whether the entity is intelligent. The test involves a human interrogator who is in one room, another human being in a second room, and an artificial entity in a third room. The interrogator is allowed to communicate with both the other human and the artificial entity only with a textual device such as a terminal. The interrogator is asked to distinguish the other human from the artificial entity based on answers to questions posed by the interrogator. If the interrogator cannot do this, the Turing test is passed and we say that the artificial entity is intelligent.

Note that the Turing test avoids physical interaction between the interrogator and the artificial entity; the assumption is that physical interaction is not necessary for intelligence. For example, HAL in the movie *Space Odyssey* is simply an entity with which the crew communicates, and HAL would pass the Turing test. If the interrogator is provided with visual information about the artificial entity so that the interrogator can test the entity's ability to perceive and navigate in the world, we call the test the **total Turing test**. The Terminator in the movie of the same name would pass this test.

Figure 1.1 The Chinese room experiment.

Searle [1980] took exception to the Turing test with his **Chinese room** thought experiment. The experiment proceeds as follows. Suppose that we have successfully developed a computer program that appears to understand Chinese. That is, the program takes sentences written with Chinese characters as input, processes the characters, and outputs sentences written using Chinese characters. See Figure 1.1. If it is able to convince a Chinese interrogator that it is a human, then the Turing test would be passed.

Searle asks "Does the program literally *understand* Chinese, or is it only simulating the ability to understand Chinese?" To address this question, Searle proposes that he could sit in a closed room holding a book with an English version of the program, and adequate paper and pencils to carry out the instructions of the program by hand. The Chinese interrogator could then provide Chinese sentences through a slot in the door, and Searle could process them using the program's instructions and send Chinese sentences back through the same slot. Searle says that he has performed the exact same task as the computer that passed the Turing test. That is, each is following a program that simulates intelligent behavior. However, Searle notes that he does not speak Chinese. Therefore, because he does not understand Chinese, the reasonable conclusion is that the computer does not understand Chinese either. Searle argues that if the computer is not understanding the conversation, then it is not thinking, and therefore it does not have an intelligent mind.

Searle formulated the philosophical position known as **strong AI**, which is as follows:

> The appropriately programmed computer really is a mind, in the sense that computers given the right programs can be literally said to understand and have other cognitive states.

— Searle, 1980

Based on his Chinese room experiment, Searle concludes that strong AI is not possible. He states that "I can have any formal program you like, but I still understand nothing." Searle's paper resulted in a great deal of controversy and discussion for some time to come (See, for example, [Harnad, 2001]).

The position that computers could appear and behave intelligently, but not necessarily understand, is called **weak AI**. The essence of the matter is whether a computer could actually have a mind (strong AI) or could only simulate a mind (weak AI). This distinction is of greater concern to the philosopher who is discussing the notion of consciousness [Chalmers, 1996]. Perhaps facetiously, a philosopher could even argue that emergentism might take place in the Chinese room experiment, and a mind might arise from Searle performing all his manipulations. Practically speaking, none of this is of concern to the computer scientist. If the program for all purposes behaves as if it is intelligent, computer scientists have achieved their goal.

1.1.2   Emergence of AI

Initial efforts at AI involved modeling the neurons in the brain. An artificial neuron is treated as a binary variable that is switched to either *on* or *off*. This notion was first proposed in [McCulloch and Pitts, 1943], and was furthered by Donald Hebb [1949] when he developed **Hebbian learning** for **neural networks**. In 1951, Marvin Minsky and Dean Edmonds built SNARC, the first neural network computer.

Following this accomplishment and Turing's development of the Turing test, researchers became increasingly interested in the study of neural networks and intelligent systems, resulting in John McCarthy[1] organizing a 2-month workshop involving interested researchers at Dartmouth University in 1956. He coined the term *Artificial Intelligence* at that workshop. Attendees included Minsky, Claude Shannon (the developer of information theory), and many others. AI emerged as a new discipline whose goal was to create computer systems that could learn, react, and make decisions in a complex, changing environment.

1.1.3   Cognitive Science and AI

Cognitive science is the discipline that studies the mind and its processes. It concerns how information is represented and processed by the mind. It is an interdisciplinary field spanning philosophy, psychology, artificial intelligence, neuroscience, linguistics, and anthropology, and emerged as its own discipline somewhat concurrently with AI. Cognitive science involves empirical studies of the mind, whereas AI concerns the development of an artificial mind. However, owing to their related endeavors, each field is able to borrow from the other.

---

[1] John McCarthy developed the LISP programming language for AI applications and is considered by many to be the father of AI.

1.1.4 Logical Approach to AI

Most of the early successes of AI were based on modeling human logic. In 1955–1956 Allen Newell and Herbert Simon developed a program called the **Logic Theorist** that was intended to mimic the problem-solving skills of a human being and is considered the first artificial intelligence program. It was able to prove 38 of the first 52 theorems in Whitehead and Russell's *Principia Mathematica*, and find shorter proofs for some of them [McCorduck, 2004]. In 1961, Newell and Simon forwarded the **General Problem Solver (GPS)**, which was a program intended to work as a universal problem solver machine. Its reasoning was based on means-end analysis and the way humans handled goals and sub-goals while solving a problem. GPS was able to solve simple problems like the Towers of Hanoi, but did not scale up owing to combinatorial explosion. In 1959, Gelernter developed the **Geometry Theorem Prover** [Gelernter, 1959], which was able to prove theorems in elementary Euclidean plane geometry.

McCarthy [1958] describes a hypothetical program called the **Advice Taker**. This program was unlike previous efforts, in that it was designed to accept new axioms about the environment, and reason with them without being reprogrammed.

> The main advantages we expect the advice taker to have is that its behaviour will be improvable merely by making statements to it, telling it about its symbolic environment and what is wanted from it. To make these statements will require little if any knowledge of the program or the previous knowledge of the advice taker. One will be able to assume that the advice taker will have available to it a fairly wide class of immediate logical consequences of anything it is told and its previous knowledge. This property is expected to have much in common with what makes us describe certain humans as having common sense. We shall therefore say that a program has common sense if it automatically deduces for itself a sufficiently wide class of immediate consequences of anything it is told and what it already knows.
>
> — McCarthy, 1958

The Advice Taker advanced an important notion in AI, namely the notion of separating the representation of the world (the knowledge) from the manipulation of the representation (the reasoning).

In order to obtain a manageable grasp on developing an entity that could reason intelligently relative to all aspects of its world, researchers developed microworlds. The most well-known of these is the **blocks world** [Winograd, 1972]; [Winston, 1973], which is discussed in Section 3.2.2.1. This world consists of a set of blocks placed on a table. A robot then has the task of manipulating the blocks in various ways.

These early successes in AI led researchers to be very optimistic about its future. The following is a well-known quote:

It is not my aim to surprise or shock you – but the simplest way I can summarize is to say that there are now in the world machines that think, that learn and that create. Moreover, their ability to do these things is going to increase rapidly until – in a visible future – the range of problems they can handle will be coextensive with the range to which the human mind has been applied.

— Simon, 1957

However, systems that could prove theorems containing a limited number of facts and systems that behaved well in a microworld failed to scale up to systems that could prove theorems involving many facts and ones that interact with complex worlds. One reason for this is combinatorial explosion. There are relatively few objects in a microworld, and therefore there are not many possible actions. As the number of objects increases, the complexity of the search can increase exponentially. Another difficulty is in representing a complex world rather than a simple microworld.

1.1.5 Knowledge-Based Systems

The initial AI efforts just described concerned the development of all-purpose intelligent programs, which worked in limited domains and solved relatively simple problems. However, these programs failed to scale up to handling difficult problems. Such methods are called **weak methods** because of their failure to scale up (not to be confused with weak AI discussed earlier). With HAL and the terminator nowhere in sight, many researchers turned their efforts to developing useful systems that solved difficult problems in specialized domains. These systems used powerful, domain-specific knowledge and are called **knowledge-based systems**. Because they often perform the task of an expert, another term for many such systems is **expert systems**. Ordinarily, they follow the approach McCarthy specified for the Advice Taker. That is, the knowledge is represented by rules about the particular domain, and the reasoning consists of general-purpose algorithms that manipulate the rules. The details of how this is done appear in Section 2.3.1.

Successful knowledge-based systems include DENDRAL [Lindsay et al., 1980], a system for analyzing mass spectrograms in chemistry; XCON [McDermott, 1982], a system for configuring VAX computers; and ACRONYM [Brooks, 1981], a vision support system.

Initially, knowledge-based systems were based on logic, performed exact inference, and arrived at categorical conclusions. However, in many domains, in particular medicine, we cannot be certain of our conclusions.

Why are categorical decisions not sufficient for all of medicine? Because the world is too complex! Although many decisions may be made straightforwardly, many are too difficult to be prescribed in any simple matter. When many factors may enter into a decision, when these factors may themselves be uncertain, when some factors may become unimportant depending on other factors, and when there is a significant cost associated with gathering information that may not actually be required for the decision, then the rigidity of the flowchart makes it an inappropriate decision-making instrument.

— Szolovits and Pauker, 1978

Researchers searched for ways to incorporate uncertainty in the rules in their knowledge-based systems. The most notable such effort was the incorporation of **certainty factors** in the MYCIN system [Buchanan and Shortliffe, 1984]. MYCIN is a medical expert system for diagnosing bacterial infections and prescribing treatments for them. Certainty factors are described in the introduction to Chapter 5.

1.1.6 Probabilistic Approach to AI

Neapolitan [1989] shows that the rule-based representation of uncertain knowledge and reasoning is not only cumbersome and complex, but also does not model how humans reason very well. Pearl [1986] made the more reasonable conjecture that humans identify local probabilistic causal relationships between individual propositions and reason with these relationships. At this same time researchers in decision analysis [Shachter, 1986] were developing influence diagrams, which provide us with a normative decision in the face of uncertainty. In the 1980s, researchers from cognitive science (e.g., Judea Pearl), computer science (e.g., Peter Cheeseman and Lotfi Zadeh), decision analysis (e.g., Ross Shachter), medicine (e.g., David Heckerman and Gregory Cooper), mathematics and statistics (e.g., Richard Neapolitan and David Spiegelhalter) and philosophy (e.g., Henry Kyburg) met at the newly formed *Workshop on Uncertainty in Artificial intelligence* (now a conference) to discuss how to best perform uncertain inference in artificial intelligence. The texts *Probabilistic Reasoning in Intelligent Systems* [Pearl, 1988] and *Probabilistic Reasoning in Expert Systems* [Neapolitan, 1989] integrated many of the results of these discussions into the field we now call **Bayesian networks**. Bayesian networks have arguably become the standard for handling uncertain inference in AI, and many AI applications have been developed using them. Section 8.8 lists some of them.

1.1.7 Evolutionary Computation and Swarm Intelligence

A separate area of artificial called **evolutionary computation** [Frazer, 1958]; [Holland, 1975]; [Koza, 1992]; [Fogel, 1994] emerged simultaneously with the efforts discussed so far. Evolutionary computation endeavors to obtain approximate solutions to problems such as optimization problems using the evolutionary mechanisms involved in natural selection as its paradigm.

A related area of recent research concerns swarm intelligence. Many species perform complex tasks when working as a group, even though each member of the group seemingly exhibits little intelligence. For example, an ant colony is quite effective at finding the shortest path between its nest and some source of food, while an individual ant has no ability to accomplish this task. **Swarm intelligence** is intelligent collective behavior that emerges when some group of autonomous, non-intelligent entities interact. Using swarm intelligence as a model, researchers developed algorithms that solve many practical problems [Kennedy and Eberhart, 2001]; [Dorigo and Gambardella, 1997].

1.1.8   A Return to Creating HAL

The knowledge-based approach, the probabilistic approach, and evolutionary computation have resulted in many useful systems that behave intelligently or solve problems in specialized domains. Examples were provided at the beginning of this introduction. Nevertheless, some of the early researchers in AI, including John McCarthy [2007] and Marvin Minsky [2007], felt that AI should quit focusing on developing systems that perform specialized tasks well and return to developing systems that think. In 2004, they held their first symposium on **human-level AI** [Minsky et al., 2004].

In 2007, the related field called **Artificial General Intelligence (AGI)** [Goertzel and Pennachin, 2007] appeared, and now has its own journal titled the *Journal of Artificial General Intelligence.* Researchers in AGI are searching for a program that can learn and make decisions in any arbitrary environment.

Another current effort at developing a thinking entity is the work of Gerry Edelman. Edelman [2006] explains the development and organization of higher brain functions in terms of a process known as **neuronal group selection**. He calls this model **neural Darwinism**. Based on this model, he has developed a number of robot-like brain-based devices (BBDs) that interact with real-world environments [Edelman, 2007]. However, they are able to navigate only in limited domains.

1.2   Contemporary Artificial Intelligence

The efforts of the human-level AI community, the AGI community, and Gerry Edelman are all vitally important if we hope to someday have an intelligent entity that reasons in a changing, complex environment. However, the approach taken in this text is to focus on the strong AI methods, which have resulted in developing systems that successfully solve interesting and important problems in specialized domains. We call this a *contemporary* approach for an artificial intelligence text.

The early successes in AI were based on modeling logical reasoning. For example, suppose Mary knows that if someone completes 120 credit hours and passes the comprehensive exam, that person will graduate. Suppose she then learns that Joe completed 120 credit hours and that he did not graduate. She reasons logically that for sure he did not pass the comprehensive exam. AI models based on such logical reasoning is the focus of Part I of this text.

In the 1970s, it became increasingly apparent that many judgments made by humans involve uncertain or probabilistic inference. For example, suppose Mary knows that studying hard will greatly increase the chances of getting an

A on the exam; she also realizes that a smart person is more likely to get an A on the exam. She learns that Joe got an A. When Joe tells her that he did not study very hard, she reasons that Joe is probably smart. By 1990, the modeling of such probabilistic inference became commonplace in AI; such inference is the focus of Part II.

Intelligent behavior is not limited to human reasoning. Evolution itself seems pretty smart in that creatures better able to adapt to their environment tend to survive, with the result being the existence of humans themselves. Researchers in evolutionary computation have solved interesting problems based on a model of natural selection. The actions of non-intelligent entities acting in groups sometimes results in a type of emergent intelligence, called swarm intelligence, and useful algorithms have been developed based on this model. We call both these types of intelligence **emergent intelligence**. Algorithms based on emergent intelligence are discussed in Part III.

In Parts I and II we assume the system is created from knowledge extracted from humans, who are often experts in some domain. However, an important aspect of intelligence involves acquiring new knowledge from experience or data. Part IV concerns learning both logical and probabilistic models from data. Finally, Part V discusses an important endeavor in AI, namely natural language understanding.

Part I

Logical Intelligence

Chapter 2

Propositional Logic

Propositional logic concerns propositions/statements, which we assume to be true or false, and the deductive inference of the truth of other propositions from the ones whose truth states we assume to know. By **deductive inference** we mean a process by which the truth of the conclusion is demonstrated to necessarily follow from the truth of the premises. This variation of a classic example illustrates such a deduction:

Socrates is a man.

If Socrates is a man, then Socrates is mortal.

Therefore, Socrates is mortal.

$A = B$
$B = C$
$A = C$

If we assume we know that Socrates is a man and we believe that "if Socrates is a man, then Socrates is a mortal" is a true statement, then most of us would reason that Socrates is mortal. Propositional logic does not ask whether this line of reasoning makes sense. Rather, it mathematically models this and other common types of deductive inference that most of us agree make sense. When

13

we incorporate such inference in an artificial intelligence algorithm, we call the algorithm **logic-based.**

In Section 2.1 we provide the basic properties of propositional logic. Section 2.2 develops an inference method called resolution theorem proving, which is the strategy used in many automatic reasoning programs. Section 2.3 shows artificial intelligence applications of propositional logic.

2.1   Basics of Propositional Logic

Propositional logic is discussed starting with its syntax and its semantics.

2.1.1   Syntax

A **formal language** is a set of words or expressions that are obtained using an alphabet and rules. The **alphabet** for a formal language is the set of symbols from which each word is constructed. The set of **rules**, called the syntax of the language, specifies how elements of the alphabet are combined to construct words. These words are called **well-formed strings** of symbols.

Propositional logic consists of a formal language and semantics that give meaning to the well-formed strings, which are called **propositions**.

The alphabet of propositional logic contains the following symbols:

1. The letters of the English alphabet; that is, A, B, C, ..., Z, and each of these letters with an index (e.g., A_4).

2. The logical values True and False.

3. These special symbols:

   $\neg$ (NOT)

   $\wedge$ (AND)

   $\vee$ (OR)

   $\Rightarrow$ (IF-THEN)

   $\Leftrightarrow$ (IF AND ONLY IF)

   ( ) (GROUPING).

   The symbol $\neg$ is called a **unary connective** and the symbols $\wedge$, $\vee$, $\Rightarrow$, and $\Leftrightarrow$ are called **binary connectives**.

The rules for creating propositions are as follows:

1. All letters, all indexed letters, and the logical values True and False are propositions. They are called **atomic propositions**. .

2. If A and B are propositions, then so are $\neg A$, $A \wedge B$, $A \vee B$, $A \Rightarrow B$, $A \Leftrightarrow B$, and (A). They are called **compound propositions**.

The compound proposition $\neg A$ is called the **negation** of A, $A \wedge B$ is called the **conjunction** of A and B, and $A \vee B$ is called the **disjunction** of A and B.

Notice that we used italicized letters to refer to propositions. Such letters denote variables whose values can be propositions that are either atomic or compound. In this way we can recursively define compound propositions. These italicized letters are not part of the alphabet.

Example 2.1 Suppose P and Q are atomic propositions. Then applying Rule 2 once using the $\wedge$ connective, we have that P$\wedge$Q is a proposition. Applying Rule 2 to this compound proposition and the atomic proposition R using the $\vee$ connective, we have that P$\wedge$Q$\vee$R is a proposition. ∎

Mathematically, this is all there is to say about the formal language of propositional logic. However, propositional logic was developed to make statements about the real world and to reason with these statements. The next example illustrates such statements.

Example 2.2 Suppose the propositions P and Q stand for these statements about the world:

P: It is raining outside.

Q: The pavement is wet.

Then the following compound propositions stand for these statements about the world:

$\neg$P: It is not raining outside.

P$\wedge$Q: It is raining outside and the pavement is wet.

P$\vee$Q: It is raining outside or the pavement is wet.

P$\Rightarrow$Q: If it is raining outside, then the pavement is wet.

P$\Leftrightarrow$Q: It is raining outside if and only if the pavement is wet. ∎

Example 2.3 Let P, Q, and R stand for these statements about the world:

P: It is raining outside.

Q. The pavement is wet.

R: The sprinkler is on.

Then applying Rule 2 once using the $\vee$ connective, we have that P$\vee$R is a proposition. Applying Rule 2 a second time using the $\wedge$ connective, we obtain that Q$\wedge$P$\vee$R is a proposition. This proposition stands for the following statement about the world:

Q$\wedge$P$\vee$R: The pavement is wet and it is raining outside or the sprinkler is on. ∎

2.1.2   Semantics

When you saw Example 2.3, you may have asked which of the following is meant by the proposition Q∧P∨R:

1. It is *both* true that the pavement is wet *and* true that it is raining outside or the sprinkler is on.

2. It is *either* true that the pavement is wet and it is raining outside *or* true that the sprinkler is on.

Next we present the semantics of propositional logic, which answers this question.

The syntax of propositional logic is only concerned with developing propositions; it has nothing to do with attaching meaning to them. As mentioned previously, we need not even associate statements about the world with the propositions. The semantics of propositional logic gives meaning to the propositions. The semantics consists of rules for assigning either the value T (true) or F (false) to every proposition. Such an assignment is called the **truth value** of the proposition. If a proposition has truth value T, we say it is true; otherwise, we say it is false.

The **semantics** for propositional logic consist of the following rules:

1. The logical value True is always assigned the value T and the logical value False is always assigned the value F.

2. Every other atomic propositions is assigned a value T or F. The set of all these assignments constitutes a **model** or **possible world**. All possible worlds (assignments) are permissible.

3. The truth values obtained by applying each connective to arbitrary propositions are given by the following **truth tables**:

a:

A	$\neg A$
T	F
F	T

b:

A	B	$A \wedge B$
T	T	T
T	F	F
F	T	F
F	F	F

c:

A	B	$A \vee B$
T	T	T
T	F	T
F	T	T
F	F	F

d:

A	B	$A \Rightarrow B$
T	T	T
T	F	F
F	T	T
F	F	T

e:

A	B	$A \Leftrightarrow B$
T	T	T
T	F	F
F	T	F
F	F	T

4. The truth value for compound propositions such as P∧Q∨R are determined recursively using the above truth tables. This is done according to the following rules:

(a) The ( ) grouping has highest precedence i
an entire sub-proposition enclosed by ( ) i

(b) The precedence order for the connective

(c) Binary connectives that are the same a

We will show examples of applying Rule 4 shortly. ... ...
truth tables in Rule 3. Mathematically, the semantics for propos...
does no more than assign truth values to propositions. So, we could ha...
defined a semantics using different truth tables than those in Rule 3. However,
our purpose is to make statements about the real world and to reason with
those statements. So the semantics have been defined to reflect how humans
reason with statements in the world. Truth tables a through c agree readily
with our intuition. For example, we would only consider $A \wedge B$ true if both A
and B were true. However, Truth Table d, which concerns $A \Rightarrow B$, is not so
readily accessible. Consider the following propositions:

P: It is raining.

Q: Professor Neapolitan is 5 feet tall.

Suppose you look out the window and see that it is not raining, and you look
at Professor Neapolitan and note than he is almost 6 feet tall. So you know
both P and Q are false. Then, according to Truth Table d, Row 4, P⇒Q is
true. But how can raining imply that Neapolitan is 5 feet tall when we know
that he is not? First, we must be clear what a proposition denotes. Proposition
P denotes that it is currently raining. It has nothing to do with it raining at
some other time. Therefore, P⇒Q does not mean that if it rains some day, then
Neapolitan will be 5 feet tall. The implication only concerns the proposition
that there is rain at the present time, which is false.

The perceived difficulty with $A \Rightarrow B$ ordinarily concerns rows 3 and 4 of
Truth Table d. So, let's investigate whether the truth values in those rows agree
with our expectations. Suppose we learn $A \Rightarrow B$ is true. Then if we later learn
A is also true, we know we must be in row 1 of Truth Table d, which means B is
true. This is what we should expect. If we later learn that A is false, we know
we must be in row 3 or row 4, which means we do not know whether B is true
or false. This is also what we would expect. So the current assignments of truth
values agree with our expectations. Suppose now that we assign different truth
values to $A \Rightarrow B$ in rows 3 and 4. Assume first that we assign F to $A \Rightarrow B$ in
both these rows and leave the assignments in rows 1 and 2 unchanged. Then if
we know $A \Rightarrow B$ and B are both true, we must be in row 1, which means we
conclude that A is true. However, this mean B implies A, which is not what
we intended by $A \Rightarrow B$. Suppose instead we assign F to $A \Rightarrow B$ in row 3 but
not row 4. Then if we know $A \Rightarrow B$ is true and A is false, we must be in row
4, which means we conclude that B is false. However, this means that A being
false implies that B is false, which is not what we intended by $A \Rightarrow B$. A
similar difficulty results if we assign F to $A \Rightarrow B$ in row 4 but not row 3.

ussion like the one just presented lends intuition to the assignment of lues for $A \Leftrightarrow B$ in Truth Table e. It is left as an exercise to develop a discussion.

We now provide examples of evaluating the truth values of expressions.

Example 2.4 Consider the following proposition: Q∧P∨R. This is the proposition in Example 2.3. Because ∧ has precedence over ∨, the meaning of Q∧P∨R is the second statement shown at the beginning of this section, namely: It is *either* true that the pavement is wet and it is raining outside *or* true that the sprinkler is on.

A truth table shows which assignments of values to P, Q, and R make Q∧P∨R true. That is, it discloses us the possible worlds in which the proposition is true. The truth table is as follows:

Q	P	R	Q∧P	Q∧P∨R
T	T	T	T	T
T	T	F	T	T
T	F	T	F	T
T	F	F	F	F
F	T	T	F	T
F	T	F	F	F
F	F	T	F	T
F	F	F	F	F

The truth table is constructed by first listing all eight possible assignments of values to Q, P, and R; next computing the values of Q∧P using Truth Table b because ∧ has precedence over ∨; and finally computing the values of Q∧P∨R using Truth Table c. ∎

Example 2.5 Suppose we actually meant to say the first statement at the beginning of this section — namely, it is *both* true that the pavement is wet *and* true that it is raining outside or the sprinkler is on. Rule 4 above says that the ( ) connective has highest precedence. So we can write Q∧(P∨R) to make the first statement. A truth table for this proposition is as follows:

Q	P	R	P∨R	Q∧(P∨R)
T	T	T	T	T
T	T	F	T	T
T	F	T	T	T
T	F	F	F	F
F	T	T	T	F
F	T	F	T	F
F	F	T	T	F
F	F	F	F	F

Example 2.6 Suppose you read the following sign in the shoe store: *Your shoes may be returned within 30 days of the purchase date if they have not been worn.* Let's express this statement using propositional logic and investigate when it is true. Let the following propositions stand for these statements about the world:

P: Your shoes have been worn.

Q: It has been no more than 30 days since you purchased the shoes.

R: Your shoes may be returned.

Then the statement of the store's policy concerning your shoes is expressed logically as the following proposition:

$$\neg P \wedge Q \Rightarrow R.$$

A truth table for this proposition is as follows:

P	Q	R	¬P	¬P∧Q	¬P∧Q⇒R
T	T	T	F	F	T
T	T	F	F	F	T
T	F	T	F	F	T
T	F	F	F	F	T
F	T	T	T	T	T
F	T	F	T	T	F
F	F	T	T	F	T
F	F	F	T	F	T

This result may seem odd to you. The store owner's intent was to disallow shoes to be returned if they had been worn or if it has been more than 30 days. However, several of the possible worlds in which ¬P∧Q⇒R is true have P being T, which means the shoes have been worn, and/or Q being false, which means it has been more than 30 days. The only world that is disallowed is one in which P is false (your shoes have not been worn), Q is true (it has been no more than 30 days), and R is false (your shoes may not be returned). The problem is that the store owner, like humans often do, did not explicitly state that which was intended. The intent was to allow the shoes to be returned if and only if they were not worn and it has been no more than 30 days. If the store owner made this statement, then we would express the store owner's policy logically as follows:

$$\neg P \wedge Q \Leftrightarrow R.$$

It is left as an exercise to develop a truth table for this statement and show that the store owner's intent is properly modeled.   ∎

2.1.3 Tautologies and Logical Implication

We have the following definitions concerning propositions.

Definition 2.1 A proposition is called a **tautology** if and only if it is true in all possible worlds.♦

Definition 2.2 A proposition is called a **contradiction** if and only if it is false in all possible worlds.♦

Notice that we said "if and only if" in the previous definitions. Technically, if we did not, we would leave open the possibility that a proposition with some different properties could also be called a tautology. We did this to further make the point in Example 2.6. Henceforth, we will not be so precise when stating definitions. It is assumed that we mean "if and only if."

Example 2.7 The following truth table shows that $P \vee \neg P$ is a tautology.

P	¬P	P∨¬P
T	F	T
F	T	T

∎

Stated, either P must be true or ¬P must be true.

Example 2.8 The following truth table shows that $P \wedge \neg P$ is a contradiction.

P	¬P	P∧¬P
T	F	F
F	T	F

Stated, P and ¬P cannot both be true. ∎

The following definitions concern two important tautologies.

Definition 2.3 Given two propositions A and B, if $A \Rightarrow B$ is a tautology, we say that A **logically implies** B and we write $A \Rrightarrow B$.♦

Example 2.9 The following truth table shows that $A \wedge B \Rrightarrow A$:

A	B	$A \wedge B$	$A \wedge B \Rightarrow A$
T	T	T	T
T	F	F	T
F	T	F	T
F	F	F	T

Because $A \wedge B \Rightarrow A$ is true in all possible worlds, $A \wedge B \Rrightarrow A$. ∎

Example 2.10 The following truth table shows that $A \wedge (A \Rightarrow B) \Rrightarrow B$:

A	B	$A \Rightarrow B$	$A \wedge (A \Rightarrow B)$	$A \wedge (A \Rightarrow B) \Rightarrow B$
T	T	T	T	T
T	F	F	F	T
F	T	T	F	T
F	F	T	F	T

Because $A \wedge (A \Rightarrow B) \Rightarrow B$ is true in all possible worlds, $A \wedge (A \Rightarrow B) \Rrightarrow B$. ∎

Definition 2.4 Given two propositions A and B, if $A \Leftrightarrow B$ is a tautology, we say that A and B are **logically equivalent** and we write $A \equiv B$.♦

Example 2.11 The following truth table shows that $A \Rightarrow B \equiv \neg A \vee B$:

A	B	$\neg A$	$A \Rightarrow B$	$\neg A \vee B$	$A \Rightarrow B \Leftrightarrow \neg A \vee B$
T	T	F	T	T	T
T	F	F	F	F	T
F	T	T	T	T	T
F	F	T	T	T	T

Because $A \Rightarrow B \Leftrightarrow \neg A \vee B$ is a tautology, $A \Rightarrow B \equiv \neg A \vee B$. ∎

Notice in the previous example that $A \Rightarrow B$ and $\neg A \vee B$ have the same truth value in every possible world. This is a general result concerning logical equivalence, which we state in the following theorem.

Theorem 2.1 $A \equiv B$ if and only if A and B have the same truth value in every possible world.
Proof. The proof is left as an exercise. ∎

Table 2.1 shows some important logical equivalences, called *laws*. It is left as an exercise to establish them using truth tables. We can often simplify a logical expression using these laws due to the following theorem:

Theorem 2.2 Suppose we have a proposition A and a sub-proposition B within A. If in A we replace B by any proposition logically equivalent to B, we will obtain a proposition logically equivalent to A.
Proof. The proof is left as an exercise. ∎

Example 2.12 Suppose we have the following proposition:

$$\neg\neg P \wedge (Q \vee \neg Q)$$

We can simplify it is follows:

$$
\begin{aligned}
\neg\neg P \wedge (Q \vee \neg Q) \quad &\equiv \quad P \wedge (Q \vee \neg Q) \quad \text{due to the double negation law} \\
&\equiv \quad P \wedge \text{True} \quad\quad\; \text{due to the excluded middle law} \\
&\equiv \quad P \quad\quad\quad\quad\quad\;\; \text{due to the identity laws.}
\end{aligned}
$$

∎

Table 2.1 Some Well-Known Logical Equivalences

Logical Equivalence	Name	
$A \vee \neg A \equiv$ True	Excluded middle law	EM
$A \wedge \neg A \equiv$ False	Contradiction law	CL
$A \vee$ False $\equiv A$	Identity laws	IL
$A \wedge$ True $\equiv A$		
$A \wedge$ False $\equiv$ False	Domination laws	DL
$A \vee$ True $\equiv$ True		
$A \vee A \equiv A$	Idempotent laws	IL
$A \wedge A \equiv A$		
$A \wedge B \equiv B \wedge A$	Commutivity law	CL
$A \vee B \equiv B \vee A$		
$(A \wedge B) \wedge C \equiv A \wedge (B \wedge C)$	Associativity law	AL
$(A \vee B) \vee C \equiv A \vee (B \vee C)$		
$A \wedge (B \vee C) \equiv (A \wedge B) \vee (A \wedge C)$	Distributivity law	DL
$A \vee (B \wedge C) \equiv (A \vee B) \wedge (A \vee C)$		
$\neg(A \wedge B) \equiv \neg A \vee \neg B$	De Morgan's laws	DeML
$\neg(A \vee B) \equiv \neg A \wedge \neg B$		
$A \Rightarrow B \equiv \neg A \vee B$	Implication elimination	IE
$A \Leftrightarrow B \equiv A \Rightarrow B \wedge B \Rightarrow A$	If and only if elimination	IFFE
$A \Rightarrow B \equiv \neg B \Rightarrow \neg A$	Contraposition law	CL
$\neg\neg A \equiv A$	Double negation	DN

2.1.4   Logical Arguments

Now that we've laid some groundwork, we can return to our initial goal stated at the beginning of this chapter — namely, to mathematically model deductive inference. Recall the following example:

Socrates is a man.

If Socrates is a man, then Socrates is mortal.

Therefore, Socrates is mortal.

We said earlier that if we assume we know that Socrates is a man and we believe that "if Socrates is a man, then Socrates is mortal" is a true statement, then most of us would reason that Socrates is mortal. Let's see how proportional logic can model this inference. Let the following propositions stand for these statements about the world:

P: Socrates is man.

Q: Socrates is mortal.

Then the statement "if Socrates is a man, then Socrates is mortal" is modeled by this proposition:

$$P \Rightarrow Q.$$

If propositional logic models the way we reason, then the truth of P and P⇒Q should entail the truth of Q. We will show that it does, but first we formalize deductive inference using propositional logic.

An **argument** consists of a set of propositions, called the **premises**, and a proposition called the **conclusion**. We say that the premises **entail** the conclusion if in every model in which all the premises are true, the conclusion is also true. If the premises entail the conclusion, we say the argument is **sound**; otherwise we say it is a **fallacy**. We write arguments showing the list of premises followed by the conclusion as follows:

1. A_1

2. A_2

   $\vdots$

n. A_n
   B

We use the symbol $\models$ to denote "entails." So if the argument is sound we write

$$A_1, A_2, \ldots, A_n \models B,$$

and if it is a fallacy we write

$$A_1, A_2, \ldots, A_n \not\models B.$$

Example 2.13 The argument concerning Socrates is as follows:

1. P

2. P⇒Q
   Q

We have the following truth table concerning this argument:

P	Q	$P \Rightarrow Q$
T	T	T
T	F	F
F	T	T
F	F	T

Because every world in which P and P⇒Q are both true, Q is also true, the premises entail the conclusion and the argument is sound. So P, P⇒Q $\models$ Q. ∎

The following theorem concerns sound arguments and fallacies:

Theorem 2.3 Suppose we have an argument consisting of the premises $A_1, A_2, \ldots, A_n$ and the conclusion B. Then $A_1, A_2, \ldots, A_n \models B$ if and only if $A_1 \wedge A_2 \wedge \ldots \wedge A_n \Rightarrow B$.

Proof. The proof is left as an exercise. ∎

This theorem shows that, as we would expect, a sound argument is one in which the premises logically imply the conclusion.

Example 2.14 We showed that the argument in Example 2.13 is sound. Therefore, Theorem 2.3 says that we must have $P \wedge (P \Rightarrow Q) \Rrightarrow Q$. Example 2.10 already obtained this result because it showed that $A \wedge (A \Rightarrow B) \Rrightarrow B$ for arbitrary propositions A and B. ∎

Example 2.15 The following is a common idiom: "Where there is smoke there is fire." It is often used when one wants to conclude that an individual must be bad because bad statements are being made about the individual. Let's investigate doing inference with the literal statement itself. Let the following propositions stand for these statements about the world:

P: There is fire.

Q: There is smoke.

We can assume that fire always gives rise to smoke, but not the reverse. For example, there are friction smoke generators. So $P \Rightarrow Q$ is true but $Q \Rightarrow P$ is not true. Because $Q \Rightarrow P$ is not true, anyone who reasons using this idiom should not assume that $Q \Rightarrow P$ is true. Therefore, perhaps their reasoning is modeled by the following argument:

1. Q

2. $\underline{P \Rightarrow Q}$

   P

We have the following truth table concerning this argument:

P	Q	$P \Rightarrow Q$	$Q \wedge (P \Rightarrow Q)$	$Q \wedge (P \Rightarrow Q) \Rightarrow P$
T	T	T	T	T
T	F	F	F	T
F	T	T	T	F
F	F	T	F	T

Because $Q \wedge (P \Rightarrow Q) \Rightarrow P$ is not a tautology, we do not have $Q \wedge (P \Rightarrow Q) \Rrightarrow P$, which means the argument is a fallacy. So $Q, P \Rightarrow Q \nRightarrow Q$.

Smoke is an effect of fire but smoking also has other causes. In such a case, the presence of the effect makes the cause more probable but not certain. We will investigate probabilistically reasoning with causes and effects much more in Chapter 6. ∎

2.1.5 Derivation Systems

Although we can prove whether any argument is sound or a fallacy using truth tables, there are two difficulties with this process. First, the time complexity is exponential in terms of the number of premises. That is, if there are n premises, there are 2^n rows in the truth table needed to determine the soundness of the argument. Second, humans do not appear to perform deductive inference in this fashion. Consider the following example.

Example 2.16 Suppose we are trying to determine how Randi earns a living. We know that Randi either writes books or helps other people to write books. We also know that if Randi helps other people to write books, then she earns her living as an editor. Finally, we know that Randi does not write books.

Rather than using a truth table, we can reason as follows. Because Randi either writes books or helps other people to write books and because Randi does not write books, we can conclude Randi helps other people to write books. Because we now know Randi helps other people to write books, we can conclude that Randi earns her living as an editor. ∎

We used **inference rules** to reason deductively in the previous example. Let the following propositions stand for these statements about the world:

P: Randi writes books.

Q: Randi helps other people to write books.

R: Randi earns her living as an editor.

We knew $P \lor Q$ and $\neg P$. Using these two facts, we concluded Q. Drawing this conclusion from these facts makes use of the **disjunctive syllogism rule**. Next we concluded R because we knew Q and $Q \Rightarrow R$ were both true. This inference makes use of the **modus ponens rule**. A set of inference rules is called a **deduction system**. One such set appears in Table 2.2. A deduction system is **sound** if it only derives sound arguments. To show that the set of rules in Table 2.2 is sound we need show that each of them individually is sound. We can do this for each rule using a truth table.

Example 2.17 We establish the soundness of the modus tolens rule. Owing to Theorem 2.3 we need only show that $\neg B \land (A \Rightarrow B) \Rightarrow \neg A$. The following truth table establishes this result.

A	B	$\neg A$	$\neg B$	$A \Rightarrow B$	$\neg B \land (A \Rightarrow B)$	$\neg B \land (A \Rightarrow B) \Rightarrow \neg A$
T	T	F	F	T	F	T
T	F	F	T	F	F	T
F	T	T	F	T	F	T
F	F	T	T	T	T	T

Because $\neg B \land (A \Rightarrow B) \Rightarrow \neg A$ is a tautology, $\neg B \land (A \Rightarrow B) \Rightarrow \neg A$. ∎

Table 2.2 Inference Rules

Inference Rule	Name	
$A, B \vDash A \wedge B$	Combination rule	CR
$A \wedge B \vDash A$	Simplification rule	SR
$A \vDash A \vee B$	Addition rule	AR
$A, A \Rightarrow B \vDash B$	Modus ponens	MP
$\neg B, A \Rightarrow B \vDash \neg A$	Modus tolens	MT
$A \Rightarrow B, B \Rightarrow C \vDash A \Rightarrow C$	Hypothetical syllogism	HS
$A \vee B, \neg A \vDash B$	Disjunctive syllogism	DS
$A \Rightarrow B, \neg A \Rightarrow B \vDash B$	Rule of cases	RC
$A \Leftrightarrow B \vDash A \Rightarrow B$	Equivalence elimination	EE
$A \Rightarrow B, B \Rightarrow A \vDash A \Leftrightarrow B$	Equivalence introduction	EI
$A, \neg A \vDash B$	Inconsistency rule	IR
$A \wedge B \vDash B \wedge A$	"and" Commutivity rule	ACR
$A \vee B \vDash B \vee A$	"or" Commutivity rule	OCR
If $A_1, A_2, \ldots, A_n, B \vDash C$ then $A_1, A_2, \ldots, A_n \vDash B \Rightarrow C$	Deduction theorem	DT

It is left as an exercise to obtain the soundness of the other rules in Table 2.2. The next example derives a sound argument using these rules.

Example 2.18 We use the rules to derive the soundness of the argument in Example 2.16. Again let the following propositions stand for these statements about the world:

P: Randi writes books.

Q: Randi helps other people to write books.

R: Randi earns her living as an editor.

The following derivation determines Randi's occupation:

	Derivation	Rule
1	P∨Q	Premise
2	¬P	Premise
3	Q⇒R	Premise
4	Q	1, 2, DS
5	R	3, 4, MP

When we write "Premise" in the Rule column, we mean that the proposition is one of our premises. When, for example, we write "1, 2, DS" in row 4, we mean we are using the premises in rows 2 and 3 and the disjunctive syllogism rule to deduce Q. ∎

Consider the following quote from Sherlock Holmes concerning a murder case in the novel *A Study in Scarlet.*

> And now we come to the great question as to why. Robbery has not been the object of the murder, for nothing was taken. Was it politics, then, or was it a woman? That is the question which confronted me. I was inclined from the first to the latter supposition. Political assassins are only too glad to do their work and fly. This murder had, on the contrary, been done most deliberately, and the perpetrator had left his tracks all over the room, showing he had been there all the time.
>
> — A. Conan Doyle, *A Study in Scarlet*

The next example uses the rules in Table 2.2 to derive Holmes' conclusion based on this information.

Example 2.19 Let the following propositions stand for these statements about the world:

P: Robbery was the reason for the murder.

Q: Something was taken.

R: Politics was the reason for the murder.

S: A woman was the reason for the murder.

T: The murderer left immediately.

U: The murderer left tracks all over the room.

The following derivation determines the reason for the murder:

	Derivation	Rule
1	$\neg Q$	Premise
2	$P \Rightarrow Q$	Premise
3	$\neg P \Rightarrow R \vee S$	Premise
4	$R \Rightarrow T$	Premise
5	U	Premise
6	$U \Rightarrow \neg T$	Premise
7	$\neg P$	1, 2, MT
8	$R \vee S$	3 7, MP
9	$\neg T$	5, 6, MP
10	$\neg R$	4, 9, MT
11	S	8, 10, DS

So we conclude that a woman was the reason for the murder. ∎

A deduction system is **complete** if it can derive every sound argument. The set of rules in Table 2.2 is complete. However, it would not be complete if we removed the last rule called the *Deduction theorem*. Notice that this rule differs from the others. All the other rules concern arguments in which there are premises. The Deduction theorem is needed to derive arguments in which there are no premises. An argument without premises is simply a tautology.

Example 2.20 We derive that $\vDash A \vee \neg A$. Note that no premises appear before the $\vDash$ symbol. So this is an argument without premises, which is a tautology if it is sound. We use the rules in Table 2.2 to derive its soundness.

	Derivation	Rule	Comment
1	A	Assumption	We assume A.
2	$A \vee \neg A$	1, AR	
3	$A \Rightarrow A \vee \neg A$	1, 2, DT	We now discharge A.
4	$\neg A$	Assumption	We assume $\neg A$.
5	$\neg A \vee A$	4, AR	
6	$A \vee \neg A$	5, CR	
7	$\neg A \Rightarrow A \vee \neg A$	4, 6, DT	We now discharge $\neg A$.
8	$A \vee \neg A$	3, 7, RC	

Notice that to use the Deduction theorem, we first temporarily assume a proposition to be true (e.g., step 1), then we conclude that a second proposition is true (e.g., step 2), and finally we conclude that the assumed proposition implies the second proposition (e.g., step 3). At this point we *discharge* the assumed proposition because we do not really know it to be true. We just temporarily assumed this so as to derive an implication. ∎

2.2 Resolution

Although a logical human such as Sherlock Holmes might reason similar to our derivation in Example 2.19, it is not straightforward to convert this reasoning strategy to a computer program. Next we develop a different derivation strategy called **resolution theorem proving**. This is the strategy used in many automatic reasoning programs. First, we need to introduce normal forms.

2.2.1 Normal Forms

We start with some definitions.

Definition 2.5 A **literal** is a proposition of the form P or ¬P, where P is an atomic proposition other than True or False.◆

Definition 2.6 A **conjunctive clause** is a conjunction of literals.◆

Definition 2.7 A **disjunctive clause** is a disjunction of literals.◆

Definition 2.8 A proposition is in **disjunctive normal form** if it is the disjunction of conjunctive clauses.♦

Definition 2.9 A proposition is in **conjunctive normal form** if it is the conjunction of disjunctive clauses.♦

Example 2.21 The following propositions are in disjunctive normal form:

$$(P \wedge Q) \vee (R \wedge \neg P)$$
$$(P \wedge Q \wedge \neg R) \vee (S) \vee (\neg Q \wedge T).$$

The following proposition is not in disjunctive normal form because $R \vee S \wedge Q$ is not a conjunctive clause:

$$(P \wedge Q) \vee (R \vee S \wedge Q).$$

The following propositions are in conjunctive normal form:

$$(P \vee Q) \wedge (R \vee \neg P)$$
$$(P \vee Q \vee \neg R) \wedge (S) \wedge (\neg Q \vee T).$$

The following proposition is not in conjunctive normal form because $R \vee S \wedge Q$ is not a disjunctive clause:

$$(P \vee Q) \wedge (R \vee S \wedge Q).$$

■

Any proposition can be converted to a logically equivalent proposition in conjunctive (or disjunctive) normal form. Next we present an algorithm that accomplishes this task in the case of conjunctive normal form (the laws mentioned are the ones in Table 2.1). We use a straightforward pseudocode to show algorithms in this text. The keyword **var** is used to denote "pass by reference," which for our purposes means the variable is an output of the algorithm.

Algorithm 2.1 Conjunctive_Normal_Form
    Input: A proposition.
    Output: A logically equivalent proposition in conjunctive normal form.

Procedure *Conjuctive_Normal_form*(**var** *Proposition*);

remove all "⇔" symbols using the *if and only if elimination* law;
remove all "⇒" symbols using the *implication elimination* law;
repeat
    if there are any double negations
        remove then using the *double negation* law;
    if there are any negations of non-atomic propositions
        remove them using *DeMorgan's* laws;
until the only negations are single negations of atomic propositions;
repeat
    if there are any disjunctions in which one or more terms is a conjunction
        remove them using these laws:

$$A \vee (B \wedge C) \equiv (A \vee B) \wedge (A \vee C) \tag{2.1}$$

$$(A \wedge B) \vee C \equiv (A \vee C) \wedge (B \vee C); \tag{2.2}$$

until *Proposition* is in conjunctive normal form;   ◀

Equivalence 2.1 is the *Distributivity* law in Table 2.1 and Equivalence 2.2 can be derived from the *Commutivity* and *Distributivity* laws.

Example 2.22 We use Algorithm 2.1 to convert $\neg((P \Rightarrow Q) \wedge \neg R)$ to conjunctive normal form:

$$
\begin{aligned}
\neg((P \Rightarrow Q) \wedge \neg R) \quad &\equiv \neg((\neg P \vee Q) \wedge \neg R) && \text{implication elimination} \\
&\equiv \neg(\neg P \vee Q) \vee \neg\neg R && \text{DeMorgan's laws} \\
&\equiv \neg(\neg P \vee Q) \vee R && \text{double negation} \\
&\equiv (\neg\neg P \wedge \neg Q) \vee R && \text{DeMorgan's laws} \\
&\equiv (P \wedge \neg Q) \vee R && \text{double negation} \\
&\equiv (P \vee R) \wedge (\neg Q \vee R) && \text{Equiv. 2.2}
\end{aligned}
$$

■

Example 2.23 We use Algorithm 2.1 to convert $(P \wedge Q) \vee (R \wedge S)$ to conjunctive normal form:

$$
\begin{aligned}
(P \wedge Q) \vee (R \wedge S) \quad &\equiv ((P \wedge Q) \vee R) \wedge ((P \wedge Q) \vee S) && \text{Equiv. 2.1} \\
&\equiv (P \vee R) \wedge (Q \vee R) \wedge ((P \wedge Q) \vee S) && \text{Equiv. 2.2} \\
&\equiv (P \vee R) \wedge (Q \vee R) \wedge (P \vee S) \wedge (Q \vee S) && \text{Equiv. 2.2}
\end{aligned}
$$

■

2.2.2 Derivations Using Resolution

Next we develop a derivation system that uses a single rule called the resolution rule. We start with a theorem that provides us with a new strategy for showing that an argument is sound.

Theorem 2.4 Suppose we have the argument consisting of the premises $A_1, A_2, \ldots, A_n$ and the conclusion B. Then $A_1, A_2, \ldots, A_n \vDash B$ if and only if $A_1 \wedge A_2 \wedge \ldots \wedge A_n \wedge \neg B$ is a contradiction.
Proof. The proof is left as an exercise. ∎

Corollary 2.1 Suppose we have the argument consisting of the premises $A_1, A_2, \ldots, A_n$ and the conclusion B. Then $A_1, A_2, \ldots, A_n \vDash B$ if and only if $A_1, A_2, \ldots, A_n, \neg B \vDash$ False.
Proof. The proof follows from Theorem 2.4, the fact that a proposition is a contradiction if and only if it logically implies False, and Theorem 2.3. ∎

A soundness proof that uses Theorem 2.4 or Corollary 2.1 is called a **refutation**. In a refutation, we show that if we add the negation of B to the premises, we obtain a contradiction (i.e., a proposition that is false in all possible worlds). Because the premises are assumed to be true in the current world, the only way the entire conjunction can be false in this world is for $\neg B$ to be false, which means B is true.

Example 2.24 We derive the modus ponens rule ($A, A \Rightarrow B \vDash B$) using refutation and a truth table.

A	B	$\neg B$	$A \Rightarrow B$	$A \wedge (A \Rightarrow B) \wedge \neg B$
T	T	F	T	F
T	F	T	F	F
F	T	F	T	F
F	F	T	T	F

Because $A \wedge (A \Rightarrow B) \wedge \neg B$ is false in all possible worlds, it is a contradiction. Therefore, owing to Theorem 2.4, $A, A \Rightarrow B \vDash B$ ∎

In practice we do not prove soundness using refutation with a truth table. Rather we use a derivation system based on Corollary 2.1 that has a single inference rule. That rule is the statement of the next theorem. In what follows by **clause** we mean a disjunctive clause, which is a disjunction of literals.

Theorem 2.5 The following rule, called **resolution**, is sound:

$$(A \vee P), (B \vee \neg P) \vDash A \vee B,$$

where P is a literal and A and B are clauses.
Proof. The proof is left as an exercise. ∎

When we use the resolution rule, we say that we have **resolved** the clauses $A \lor$ P and $B \lor \neg$P, and that the **resolution** is on P. The clause $A \lor B$ is called the **resolvent**.

Example 2.25 We can resolve Q $\lor$ P and R $\lor$ $\neg$P to obtain the resolvent Q $\lor$ R. ∎

Example 2.26 We can resolve P $\lor$ $\neg$Q $\lor$ R and $\neg$S $\lor$ Q to obtain the resolvent P $\lor$ R $\lor$ $\neg$S. ∎

Example 2.27 If we resolve P and $\neg$P, we obtain an empty clause. Because P$, \neg$P $\vDash$ False, the resolvent of P and $\neg$P is False.

To obtain a soundness proof using the resolution rule, we first write each premise in the argument in conjunctive normal form using Algorithm 2.1. We then formulate the argument whose premises consist of each clause in each premise plus clauses obtained from the negation of the conclusion, and then we repeatedly use the resolution rule to derive False. Our argument has then been shown to be sound due to Corollary 2.1.

Example 2.28 To derive the modus ponens rule $(A, A \Rightarrow B \vDash B)$ we first write the premises in conjunctive normal form and make each clause a premise. Our resultant premises are as follows:

$$A, \neg A \lor B.$$

The conclusion is already in conjunctive normal form. Its negation is $\neg B$, which is added as a premise. Our argument then proceeds as follows:

	Derivation	Rule
1	A	Premise
2	$\neg A \lor B$	Premise
3	$\neg B$	Added premise derived from negation of conclusion
4	B	Resolvent of 1 and 2
5	False	Resolvent of 3 and 4

Because we have obtained False, we have a soundness proof due to Corollary 2.1. ∎

Notice that when we resolve $\neg B$ with B, we obtain the empty clause, which is logically equivalent to False. This result was shown in Example 2.27.

Example 2.29 To derive the hypothetical syllogism rule $(A \Rightarrow B, B \Rightarrow C \vDash A \Rightarrow C)$ we first write the premises in conjunctive normal form and make each clause a premise. Our resultant premises are as follows:

$$\neg A \lor B, \neg B \lor C.$$

We then write the conclusion in conjunctive normal form as follows:

$$\neg A \vee C.$$

Using DeMorgan's laws, the negation of the conclusion is $A \wedge \neg C$. Our premises based on the negation of the conclusion are therefore

$$A, \; \neg C.$$

Our argument then proceeds as follows:

	Derivation	Rule
1	$\neg A \vee B$	Premise
2	$\neg B \vee C$	Premise
3	A	Added premise derived from negation of conclusion
4	$\neg C$	Added premise derived from negation of conclusion
5	B	Resolvent of 1 and 3
6	$\neg B$	Resolvent of 2 and 4
7	False	Resolvent of 5 and 6

When using resolution to obtain a soundness proof, we must resolve clauses in some order. A human can choose an arbitrary order with the hope of getting to the conclusion. However, to write a program we need a strategy that results in specific steps. One such strategy is the *set of support strategy*. In this strategy the clauses are partitioned into two sets, the *auxiliary set* and the *set of support*. The auxiliary set is formed in such a way that no two clauses in that set resolve to False. Ordinarily, the set of premises is such a set, and therefore we let the auxiliary contain all the premises, while the set of support includes clauses obtained from the negation of the conclusion. We then perform all possible resolutions where one clause is from the set of support. The set of all resolvents obtained in this way are added to the set of support. We then perform all possible resolutions where one clause is from the new set of support. This step is repeated until we derive False or until no further resolutions are possible. The set of support strategy is complete. Next we apply the set of support strategy to the premises and conclusion in Example 2.19.

Example 2.30 Recall in Example 2.19 we had the following propositions:

P: Robbery was the reason for the murder.

Q: Something was taken.

R: Politics was the reason for the murder.

S: A woman was the reason for the murder.

T: The murderer left immediately.

U: The murderer left tracks all over the room.

Furthermore, we had these premises:

1	¬Q	Premise
2	P⇒Q	Premise
3	¬P⇒R∨S	Premise
4	R⇒T	Premise
5	U	Premise
6	U⇒ ¬T	Premise

We then concluded ¬S. We now use the set of support strategy for resolution to reach this same conclusion:

	Derivation	Rule
1	¬Q	Premise
2	¬P∨Q	Premise
3	P∨R∨S	Premise
4	¬R∨T	Premise
5	U	Premise
6	¬U∨¬T	Premise
7	¬S	Added premise derived from negation of conclusion
8	P∨R	Resolvent of 3 and 7
9	Q∨R	Resolvent of 2 and 8
10	R	Resolvent of 1 and 9
11	T	Resolvent of 4 and 10
12	¬U	Resolvent of 6 and 11
13	False	Resolvent of 5 and 12

∎

2.2.3   Resolution Algorithm

The following algorithm implements the set of support strategy for resolution that was illustrated in Example 2.30.

Algorithm 2.2 Set_of_Support_Resolution

> **Input:** A set *Premises* containing the premises in an argument; the *Conclusion* in the argument.
> **Output:** The value True if *Premises* entail *Conclusion*; False otherwise.

Function *Premises_Entail_Conclusion* (*Premises, Conclusion*);
Set_of_Support = clauses derived from the negation of *Conclusion*;
Auxiliary_Set = clauses derived from *Premises*;
New = { };
repeat
    Set_of_Support = *Set_of_Support* ∪ *New*;
    for each clause *C* in *Set_of_Support*
        for each clause *D* in *Auxiliary_Set* ∪ *Set_of_Support*
            Resolvents = set of clauses obtained by resolving *C* and *D*;
            if False ∈ *Resolvents*
                return True;
            else
                New = *New* ∪ *Resolvents*;
            endif
        endfor
    endfor
until *New* ⊆ *Set_of_Support*;
return False;

2.3 Artificial Intelligence Applications

2.3.1 Knowledge-Based Systems

A **knowledge-based system** is a system consisting of the following:

1. A data set called the **knowledge base** that contains knowledge about the domain of interest.

2. An **inference engine** that processes the knowledge to solve a problem.

Often knowledge-based systems are **expert systems**, which are systems that make the judgment or decisions of an expert. For example, a system that performs medical diagnosis and possibly recommends treatment options or further testing is a medical expert system.

Rather than discussing knowledge-based systems further in the abstract, we present an example of an application written without a knowledge base, note its shortcomings, and then show how a knowledge-based system addresses these shortcomings.

Example 2.31 Suppose Mary the botanist is trying to identify a plant based on information supplied to her over the Internet to her colleague Ralph. Because she cannot see the plant, she must ask the colleague questions in order to obtain the facts need to identify the plant. Plants are classified according to type, class, and family. Within a type there are many classes, and within a class there are many family. A portion of a tree representing the classification scheme appears in Figure 2.1. Each leaf of the tree contains a family and the description of

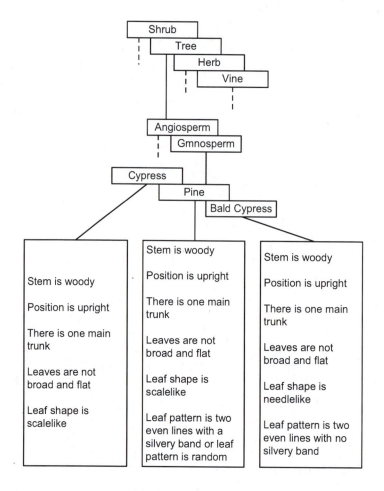

Figure 2.1 A portion of a classifcation tree for plants.

the family. To determine the family of the current plant, Mary could start by describing a cypress to Ralph. She could first ask if the stem was woody. If the answer were yes, she could ask if the position was upright. If the answer were no, she would conclude that the family was not cypress. She could then proceed to ask questions concerning pines. Although this procedure would work, there is a lot of redundancy in the questions. Because all trees have upright position, once Mary ascertained that the position was not upright, she would know that the type was not tree. So a better strategy would be to first ask questions that narrowed down the type. For instance, if Mary learned that the stem was woody and the position was upright, she would then ask of there was one main trunk. If the answer to this question was then yes, she would know that the type was tree. She would then ask questions that would determine the type of the plant. A portion of the **decision tree** (not to be confused with the decision trees introduced in Chapter 8) appears in Figure 2.2. The entire decision tree

Figure 2.2 A portion of a decision tree for identifying the family of a plant.

would be an expert system for determining the family of the plant. ■

There are two problems with the decision tree approach just introduced. First, experts systems are often developed by eliciting information or knowledge from an expert. It may be difficult for a botanist, for example, to identify the entire decision tree from the top down needed for a classification system. Second, even if the entire tree was developed, if a mistake were made and information needed to be added or delete it would be necessary to break edges in the tree and perhaps add new ones. So, the tree would need to be reconstructed each time it was necessary to change the knowledge in the system.

It seems that experts may have their knowledge locally organized among closely connected attributes. For example, Mary might know that all plants that have woody stems, stand upright, and have one main trunk are trees. We can express this knowledge as follows:

IF	stem is woody
AND	position is upright
AND	there is one main trunk
THEN	type is tree.

The preceding is an item of knowledge expressed as an **IF-THEN rule**. Often it is easier for a knowledge engineer (one whose specialty is creating expert systems) to elicit localized rules such as this from an expert than it is to elicit an entire system all at once. Mary might also know that all trees that have broad and flat leaves are gymnosperms. The rule representing this knowledge is

IF	type is tree
AND	leaves are broad and flat
THEN	class is gymnosperm.

The collection of all these items of knowledge, or rules, is called a **knowledge base**. The knowledge base that contains the knowledge in the decision tree in Figure 2.2 appears in Table 2.3. This is only a portion of a knowledge base for an expert system that determines the family of a plant. For a particular rule, the IF portion is called the **antecedent** of the rule and the THEN portion is called the **conclusion**. Each individual **clause** in the antecedent is called a **premise**.

The knowledge base is simply a collection of separate items of knowledge. It does not entail any particular way for using this knowledge. A mechanism that exploits the knowledge to solve a problem is called an **inference engine**. Next we discuss two well-known inference engines for rule-based systems.

2.3.1.1   Backward Chaining

Backward chaining is an inference engine that can use the rules in Table 2.3 to ask the same sequence of questions as in Figure 2.2. That is, if we wish to determine the family of the plant, backward chaining cycles through the rules until it finds one whose conclusion concerns family. Rule 1 in Table 2.3 is such a rule. If both premises in the rule are true, we know from the combination rule and modus ponens (Table 2.2) that the family is cypress. So backward chaining tries to determine whether these premises are true. How can it do this? By again using the rules. That is, to determine whether the class is gymnosperm, it again cycles through the rules looking for one whose conclusion determines the family. Rule 5 is such a rule. If Rule 5 can determine that the class is angiosperm, then the premises in Rule 1 are not all true, and backward chaining should go on to another rule to determine the family. So next, backward chaining tries to determine whether the premises in Rule 5 are true. To do this it cycles through the rules looking for one whose conclusion determines the type. Rule 9 is such a rule. Next, backward chaining tries to determine whether its premises are true by cycling through the rules looking for one that determines the properties of the stem. There is no such rule. This means that the user (in our example, Ralph) should be able to determine whether the current premise is true or

Table 2.3 A Subset of the Rules in an Expert System that Determines the Family of a Plant

1.	IF	class is gymnosperm
	AND	leaf shape is scalelike
	THEN	family is cypress.
2.	IF	class is gymnosperm
	AND	leaf shape is needlelike
	AND	pattern is random
	THEN	family is pine.
3.	IF	class is gymnosperm
	AND	leaf shape is needlelike
	AND	pattern is two even lines
	AND	silvery band is yes
	THEN	family is pine.
4.	IF	class is gymnosperm
	AND	leaf shape is needlelike
	AND	pattern is two even lines
	AND	silvery band is no
	THEN	family is bald cypress.
5.	IF	type is tree
	AND	broad and flat is yes
	THEN	class is angiosperm.
6.	IF	type is tree
	AND	broad and flat is no
	THEN	class is gymnosperm.
7.	IF	stem is green
	THEN	type is herb.
8.	IF	stem is woody
	AND	position is creeping
	THEN	type is vine.
9.	IF	stem is woody
	AND	position is upright
	AND	one main trunk is yes
	THEN	type is tree.
10.	IF	stem is woody
	AND	position is upright
	AND	one main trunk is no
	THEN	type is shrub.

false. So backward chaining asks Ralph whether the stem is woody. Notice that this is the same question asked first in Figure 2.2. If Ralph answers yes, backward chaining asks questions about the next premise in Rule 9. If he answers no, backward chaining looks for another rule that determines the type. Suppose Ralph answers yes to all the premises in Rule 9. Backward chaining then determines that the type is a tree, and goes back to Rule 5 to determine whether the other premises in Rule 5 are true. If it learns that the leaves are broad and flat, it the concludes that the class is angiosperm. Backward chaining then goes back to Rule 1 and, finding that the first premise is false, gives up on that rule and goes on to Rule 2 to determine the family. The algorithm proceeds in this manner until one of the rules eventually determines the family or it is learned that Ralph cannot supply enough information to solve the problem. This procedure is called **backward chaining** because of the way it backs up from rules that contain as their conclusion the information desired by the user, to rules containing premises that the user is asked to verify.

An algorithm for backward chaining follows. In a given clause, the feature in the clause is called an **attribute**. For example, the attribute in the clause "class is gymnosperm" is "class." The attribute, whose value is requested by the user, is the initial goal. Function *Backchain* tries to determine the value of that attribute by finding a rule whose conclusion concerns that attribute. When it finds such a rule, it tries to determine whether the premises in the rule are true. For each premise in the rule, *Backchain* calls itself recursively with the attribute in the premise being the next goal. Once the algorithm learns the value of an attribute, that fact is saved in a set of true assertions so that the algorithm does not try to determine that value again. For example, if the user says that the "stem is woody," that assertion is saved in the set of true assertions.

Algorithm 2.3 Backward_Chaining

    Input: The user's goal *Goal* and information requested of the user.
    Output: The value of the user's goal if it can be determined; otherwise "unknown."

    Function *Backchain(Goal)*;
    var *Assertion, Rule, Next_Goal, Premise, True_Assertion,*
        All_Premises_True;

    if there is an assertion in *Assertion_List* with *Goal* as its attribute
        Assertion = that assertion;
    else
        Assertion = Null;

if *Assertion* = Null
    Rule = first rule;
    while *Assertion* = Null and there are more rules
        if *Goal* = attribute in the conclusion of *Rule*
            All_Premises_True = False;
            Premise = first premise in the antecedent of *Rule*;
            repeat
                Next_Goal = attribute in *Premise*;
                True_Assertion = *Backchain(Next_Goal)*;
                if *Premise* = *True_Assertion*
                    Premise = next premise in the antecedent of *Rule*;
                    if *Premise* = Null
                        All_Premises_True = True;
                endif
            until *All_Premises_True* or *Premise* ≠ *True_Assertion*;
            if *All_Premises_True*
                Assertion = conclusion of *Rule*;
        endif
        Rule = next rule;
    endwhile
    if *Assertion* = Null
        prompt user for value of *Goal*;
        read Value;
        if *Value* ≠ Null
            Assertion = *Goal* "is" Value;
        else
            Assertion = *Goal* "is unknown";
        endif
        add *Assertion* to *Assertion_List*;
    endif
if *Goal* = *User_Goal*
    if *Assertion* = *Goal* "is unknown"
        write "You cannot answer enough questions to determine " *Goal*;
    else
        write *Assertion*;
    endif
endif
return *Assertion*;

At the top level Backchain is called as follows:

Empty(Assertion_List);   // Make the *Assertion_List* empty.
write "Enter your goal.";
read *User_Goal*;
Assertion = *Backchain(User_Goal)*;

Our backward chaining algorithm can be enhanced considerably. First, we should impose certain restrictions on the rules. One restriction is that the knowledge base should not contain rules that are circular. For example, if A, B, and C represent propositions, we should not have the following rules:

IF A THEN B IF B THEN C IF C THEN A.

Such a set of rules simply means that A, B, and C are always true simultaneously. The existence of such a set of rules in our knowledge base could cause the backward chaining algorithm to run in an infinite loop. Therefore an error check for cyclic rules should be included in the algorithm.

Another restriction on the rules is that there should not be contradictory rules. For example, we should not have the following two rules:

IF A THEN B IF A THEN NOT B.

A third rule restriction is best illustrated with an example. Suppose that we have the following two rules:

IF A AND B AND C THEN D IF A AND B THEN D.

The set of premises in the second rule is said to subsume the set of premises in the first rule. That is, if both A and B are true, we can conclude D regardless of the value of C. Therefore the first rule is superfluous and should be eliminated.

There exist other enhancements besides rule restrictions. One such enhancement is that we could allow the user to inquire as to why a question is being asked. For example, if the user wants to know why we are asking if stem is woody, the system could answer that it is because we are trying to determine the type of the plant (say, using Rule 9 in Table 2.3), and Rule 9 can tell us the type if we can determine the nature of the stem and other attributes. If the user then wanted to know why we need to know the type, the system could answer that it is because we are trying to determine the class of the plant (say, using Rule 5 in Table 2.3), and Rule 5 can tell us the class if we can determine the type and other attributes. The systems could continue in this manner as long as the user asks questions.

Computationally, backward chaining is inefficient compared to a simple implementation of the decision tree in Figure 2.2. However, our goal is to separate the control structure from the knowledge base. The reason for this is to permit items of knowledge to be added and deleted freely as the system is being developed. Once the knowledge base is fully developed, the system can be converted to a decision tree that can be used in practice.

2.3.1.2   Forward Chaining

Suppose our botanist Mary received an email containing a description of the plant, and her job was to deduce as much as possible from the description. For example, the email might state the following facts:

The stem is woody.

The position is upright.

There is one main trunk.

The leaves are not broad and flat.

She would not go through the questioning process shown in Figure 2.2. Rather she would apply her knowledge to deduce as much as possible. Because the stem is woody, the position is upright, and there is one main trunk, she would conclude the type is tree. Next, because the leaves are not broad and flat, she would conclude that the class is gymnosperm. This is all she could conclude from the facts in the email. We can accomplish the same result by applying an inference engine called **forward chaining** to the knowledge base. In forward chaining we start by putting all our true assertions in an assertion list. Then we cycle through the rules starting with the first one. If all the premises in a rule are in the assertion list (i.e. they are true), then the conclusion must be true and so we add the conclusion to the assertion list. Because a conclusion of one rule can be a premise in another rule, we must start over at the first rule each time we add a conclusion to the assertion list. An algorithm for forward chaining follows.

Algorithm 2.4 Forward_Chaining

> **Input:** A set *Assertion_List* of true assertions.
> **Output:** The set *Assertion_List* with all assertions that can be deduced by applying the rules to the input added to it.

> **Procedure** *Forward_Chain* (**var** *Assertion_List*);
> **var** *Rule*;
>
> *Rule* = first rule;
> **while** there are more rules
>   **if** all premises in *Rule* are in *Assertion_List*
>   and conclusion in *Rule* is not in *Assertion_List*
>   add conclusion of *Rule* to *Assertion_List*;
>   *Rule* = first rule;
>   **else**
>   *Rule* = next rule;
> **endwhile**

The above procedure can be made more efficient by sorting the rules before doing forward chaining. The sorting scheme is as follows. If rule A's conclusion is a premise in Rule B's antecedent, then we place rule A before rule B. Assuming we do not have circular rules, this is always possible. With the rules sorted in this manner, there is no need to return to the first rule when a conclusion is added to the true assertion list.

2.3.1.3   Using Forward Chaining in a Configuration System

A **configuration system** is one that arranges parts into some whole. For example, a system that arranges grocery items in grocery bags is a configuration system. Suppose we wish to create a robot that does this task. The set of rules in Table 2.4 is a portion of the rules the robot might use to perform this task. Note that these are action rules expressed using propositional logic. In an **action rule** if the premises are true, we take the action that makes the conclusion true. We will illustrate bagging groceries by applying forward chaining to these rules using the groceries in Table 2.5. The "bagged?" entry is set to "Yes" when an item is bagged.

Large items are bagged first, medium items next, and small items last. We assure that large items are bagged first by initially setting

$Step = $ Bag_large_items.

Next we look at the rules. Rules 1 and 2 both require the truth of the assertion "there is a bag with <6 large items." Because we have not gotten any bags yet, this assertion is not true. Rule 3 requires that "step is Bag_large_items" and that "there is a large item to be bagged." Because both these assertions are true, the rule triggers, and we start a fresh bag, Bag 1. We then return to the start of the rules, and again look for a rule whose premises are all true. Notice that the premises in each of rules 1 through 4 are all true. In this situation we say that there is a **conflict** as to which rule to trigger. A smart bagger would always put bottles on the bottom of the bag because a bottle could damage another item if placed on it. Rule 1 concerns bagging bottles. To makes sure this rule triggers we use a type of **conflict resolution** called specificity ordering.

Definition 2.10 Specificity Ordering. If the set of premises of one rule are a superset of the set of premises of another rule, then the first rule is triggered on the assumption that it is more specialized to the current situation.

We can efficiently implement specificity ordering by sorting the rules so that the rule with more premises appears first. This has been done in Table 2.4.

So rule 2 triggers because all the premises in the other three rules are subsets of the premises in rule 2. We therefore place the bottle of soda in Bag 1 and mark that the soda has been bagged. Looking at the rules again, we now notice that the premises in rules 2, 3, and 4 are all true. According to specificity ordering, rule 2 now triggers. So the detergent is placed in Bag 1 and the detergent is marked as having been bagged. Looking again at the rules, we see that only the premises in rule 4 are true. The rule therefore triggers to change the values of *Step* to Bag_medium_items. By using the variable *Step*, we separate the rules into disjoint subsets; only the rules in a given subset are active at any particular time. This is an example of conflict resolution called context limiting.

Definition 2.11 Context Limiting. Separate the rules into disjoint subsets. Only the rules in one subset are active at any particular time. The context is changed to a new context by a rule in the current context.

Table 2.4 A Subset of the Rules in a System for Bagging Groceries

1. IF   step is Bag_large_items
    AND   there is a large item to be bagged
    AND   there is a large bottle to be bagged
    AND   there is a bag with <6 items
    THEN   put the large bottle in the bag.

2. IF   step is Bag_large_items
    AND   there is a large item to be bagged
    AND   there is a bag with <6 items
    THEN   put the large item in the bag.

3. IF   step is Bag_large_items
    AND   there is a large item to be bagged
    THEN   start a fresh bag.

4. IF   step is Bag_large_items
    THEN   step is Bag_medium_items.

5. IF   step is Bag_medium_items
    AND   there is a medium item to be bagged
    AND   there is a bag with <10 medium items
    AND   that bag contains 0 large items
    AND   the medium item is frozen
    AND   the medium item is not in an insulated bag
    THEN   put the medium item in an insulated bag.

6. IF   step is Bag_medium_items
    AND   there is a medium item to be bagged
    AND   there is a bag with <10 medium items
    AND   that bag contains 0 large items
    THEN   put the medium item in the bag.

7. IF   step is Bag_medium_items
    AND   there is a medium item to be bagged
    THEN   start a fresh bag.

8. IF   step is Bag_medium_items
    THEN   step is Bag_small_items.

9. IF   step is Bag_small_items
    AND   there is a small item to be bagged
    AND   there is a bag that is not full
    THEN   put the small item in the bag.

10. IF   step is Bag_small_items
    AND   there is a small item to be bagged
    THEN   start a fresh bag.

11. IF   step is Bag_small_items
    THEN   halt.

Item	Container	Size	Frozen	Bagged?
Soda	Bottle	Large	No	No
Bread	Bag	Medium	No	No
Ice cream	Carton	Medium	Yes	No
Detergent	Box	Large	No	No
Eggs	Carton	Small	No	No
Popsicles	Insulated Bag	Medium	Yes	No

Table 2.5 A set of items to be bagged.

The rules for medium items will now trigger until there are no more medium items. Notice that we have written the rules so that a medium item is never placed in a bag with a large item. After the medium items are all bagged, the context is changed to the set of rules for bagging small items. We can place a small item in any available bag. After all small items are bagged, rule 11 halts execution.

There are other conflict resolution strategies, including the following:

Definition 2.12 Recency Ordering. The rule that has triggered most recently has the highest priority, or the rule that has triggered least recently has the highest priority. The choice depends on the particular application.

Definition 2.13 Priority Ordering. Order the rules according to the priority with which they should trigger.

2.3.1.4   Using Forward and Backward Chaining in a Diagnostic System

Diagnosis is the process of determining or analyzing the cause or nature of a problem. A **diagnostic system** is one that performs diagnosis. The classical example of diagnosis is medical diagnosis in which we are trying to determine the disease that is causing some manifestations. However, there are many other types of diagnoses. For example, an auto mechanic tries to diagnose the problem with an automobile. We illustrate a rule-based diagnostic system using this latter example.

Table 2.6 shows a subset of the rules in a system for diagnosing automobile problems. Suppose Melissa observes the following facts about her car:

The car does not start.

The engine does turn over.

There is gas in the fuel tank.

There is gas in the carburetor.

If we use forward chaining, rule 4 will trigger first because both its premises are true, and we will conclude that

Table 2.6 A Subset of the Rules in a System for Diagnosing Automobile Problems

1.	IF	the car does not start
	AND	the engine does not turn over
	AND	and the lights do not come on
	THEN	the problem is battery.
2.	IF	the car does not start
	AND	the engine does turn over
	AND	and the engine is getting enough gas
	THEN	the problem is spark plugs.
3.	IF	the car does not start
	AND	the engine does not turn over
	AND	the lights do come on
	THEN	the problem is the starter motor.
4.	IF	there is gas in the fuel tank
	AND	there is gas in the carburetor
	THEN	the engine is getting enough gas.

The engine is getting gas.

Now all three premises in rule 2 are true. So it will trigger and we will conclude that

The problem is spark plugs.

   Melissa may not observe that there is gas in the fuel tank or that there is gas in the carburetor. She might only notice that the car does not start but the engine does turn over. If this is the case, forward chaining will conclude nothing. Backward chaining better addresses this situation. Using goal-driven backward chaining, we start with each rule that concludes a problem and see if we can draw the conclusion in the rule. Suppose the user enters the following knowledge:

The car does not start.

The engine does turn over.

Rule 1 is tried first, but it does not trigger because one of its premises is false. Next, rule 2 is tried. Its first two premises are true, and there is a rule (rule 4) that concludes its third premise. So we backchain to rule 4 and check its premises. Neither of them is true and there is no rule for either of them. So we now prompt the user for their values. Melissa now knows to check these matters because she is prompted. Suppose she observes the following:

There is gas in the fuel tank.

there is gas in the carburetor.

Rule 4 now triggers and we conclude

The engine is getting enough gas.

We now return to rule 2 and conclude that

The problem is spark plugs.

An actual production system may use both forward chaining and backward chaining in turn. That is, it could first use forward chaining to conclude all that it can based on the user's initial knowledge. If that is not enough to make a diagnosis, it could then use goal-driven backward chaining.

In many complex diagnostic problems such as medical diagnosis, we cannot be sure of our conclusions. For example, based on a patient's manifestations, a physician may determine that is highly probable the patient has bronchitis, less probable that the patient has lung cancer, and only slightly probable that the patient has both diseases. To develop a diagnostic system that performs this type of reasoning, we need probability theory rather than logic. Section 6.7 shows such a system.

2.3.2   Wumpus World

The **wumpus** world is a simple environment that has components similar to those found in many real environments. A sample wumpus world appears in Figure 2.3. The world consists of a 4-by-4 grid. An agent begins in the lower left-hand corner. The agent can move up, down, left, or right. The agent's goal is to get to the square containing the gold, but there are dangers along the way. The only things the agent knows are its location and information it gathers as it moves from square to square. The specifics of the environment are as follows:

1. An evil wumpus is in one of the squares. If the agent enters that square, the wumpus will kill the agent.

2. There is a stench in each square adjacent to the square containing the wumpus. The agent perceives this stench if the agent enters this square.

3. Several of the squares contain pits. If the agent enters a square containing a pit, the agent will fall into the pit and die.

4. There is a breeze in any square adjacent to a pit. The agent perceives this breeze if the agent enters this square.

5. There is gold in one of the squares. The agent perceives the gold if the agent is in this square.

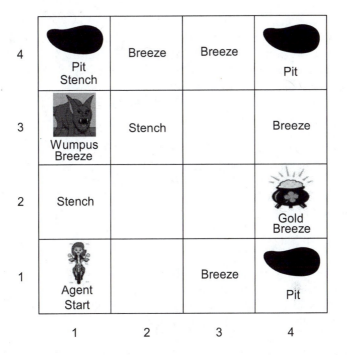

Figure 2.3 A wumpus world.

6. The agent has one arrow that it can shoot in any of the four directions. The arrow will go in a straight line. If it hits the wumpus, the wumpus will be killed and the agent will perceive a moan.

7. The agent's goal is to arrive, in as few moves as possible, at the square containing the gold and stop. If the agent dies along the way, the quest is over.

We can think of the wumpus world as a computer game in which the final score is $-n$ if the agent dies, 0 if the agent gives up without finding the gold, and n minus number of moves needed to find the gold if the agent eventually finds it (n is the maximum number of moves allowed). Suppose you were asked to play this game for the wumpus world in Figure 2.3. You do not see the entire grid. You are initially in square [1,1], and all you know is your location and that you have no perceptions. Let's discuss how you might reason logically to get to the gold. Because you have no perceptions, you conclude that squares [1,2] and [2,1] are both OK (safe). You move to square [1,2] (we index the column first), and you perceive a stench. So you conclude the wumpus is either in square [1,3] or square [2,2]. To be safe, you back up into square [1,1] and move to square [2,1]. Because there is no stench, you conclude the wumpus is not in square [2,2], which means it must be in square [1,3]. Because there are no perceptions, you conclude that squares [3,1] and [2,2] are both OK. You move to square [3,1], and you perceive a breeze. So to be safe, you back up into square [2,1]. Because you have already visited square [1,1], you move to square [2,2]. You continue in this manner until you reach the gold.

For the wumpus world in Figure 2.3 there is a path to the gold such that the agent needs to only visit squares that are known to be OK to reach it. In each occurrence of the world, the locations of the wumpus and pits are randomly generated. In some worlds, the agent will have to visit squares not known to be OK to proceed toward the gold but can still get to the gold, while in other occurrences it is impossible to reach the gold.

In general, a **goal** describes a situation or result that is desirable and toward which effort can be directed. Our agent's goal in the wumpus world is to arrive at the gold. Next, we develop a sequence of software agents designed to accomplish this goal.

2.3.2.1   The Environment

Suppose first that your task is to develop a wumpus world game that others can play on the computer. You would need to generate locations of the wumpus and the pits, and then store this information in a file we will call **environment**. You could implement this environment in a number of ways. For our discussion purposes, it is best to show it as a grid like the one in Figure 2.3. As the individual plays the game, you need to present perceptions in a given square when the individual enters the square. For example, if the individual enters square [4,2], you present G_{42} and B_{42}, where G_{42} denotes that there is gold in square [4,2] and B_{42} denotes that there is a breeze in square [4,2].

2.3.2.2   Software Agents

Suppose next that your task is to develop a software agent that searches for the gold in the environment you created. The agent performs moves in a sequence of time slots. Next we discuss different types of possible agents starting with the simplest type.

Reflex Agent   A **reflex agent** does not maintain any model of the world. It bases each move only on the perceptions it receives in each time slot. The agent needs the following two files:

1. Knowledge base

2. Action rules

In general, the **knowledge base**[1] contains information about the environment that the agent learns from its perceptions and by doing inference. In the case of a simple reflex agent, the knowledge base in each time slot is simply the

---

[1]Note that this usage of the term *knowledge base* is different from that forwarded in Section 2.3.1. Before, the knowledge base consisted of a set of rules used to deduce new items of information. Here we are saying the knowledge base consists of the items of information themselves.

Table 2.7 Action Rules for a Reflex Agent (Rules for when we are in the context of square [2,2] are shown.)

$$
\begin{array}{l}
\vdots \\
A_{22} \wedge W_{22} \Rightarrow \text{agent dies} \\
A_{22} \wedge P_{22} \Rightarrow \text{agent dies} \\
A_{22} \wedge G_{22} \Rightarrow \text{gold found, stop} \\
A_{22} \Rightarrow \text{shoot arrow randomly left, right, up, or down} \\
A_{22} \Rightarrow \text{move randomly left, right, up, or down} \\
\vdots
\end{array}
$$

set of perceptions in the time slot. The **action rules** contains rules determining the action the agent executes in each time slot. We use both context limiting and priority ordering to fire the rules. When the agent is, for example, in the context of square [2,2], only the rules for that square fire. The rules fire in the order in which they are listed. Because the agent's goal is to arrive at the gold and stop, we want the preference order for the rules to be aimed toward achieving this goal. Therefore, the first rule should be to stop if the agent is in the square with the gold. After that, based on only the current perceptions, the only action that is better than a random move is to shoot the arrow in an arbitrary direction. So that is our second rule. The third rule is a move in a random direction. Table 2.7 shows such action rules for a reflex agent. When action "move right" is executed, the agent's location for the next time slot is set to the square to the right of the current square. So if the agent is currently in square [2,2], the agent will be in square [3,2] in the next time slot. An algorithm showing the behavior of such an agent simply cycles through a sequence of time slots and in each time slot fires the first rule in the current context whose premises are all true. An algorithm for such an agent follows.

Algorithm 2.5 Reflex_Agent

> **Procedure** $Reflex$;
> A_{11} = True;
> **repeat**
> > $Knowledge\_Base$ = set of perceptions in this time slot;
> > fire action rules $Rules_{ij}$ such that A_{ij} = True;
> **until** stop is executed or agent is dead;

A Model-Based Agent   A **model-based agent** maintains a model of the world in its knowledge base. The perceptions in each time slot are added to the knowledge base rather than replacing what is in it. Furthermore, the agent maintains a set of **deduction rules** that it uses to deduce new facts to also add to the knowledge base in each time slot. Table 2.8 shows the deduction rules for square [2,2]. There would be a set of such rules for every square. When the agent enters a square, its new perceptions are added to the knowledge base, and the deduction rules are applied to the knowledge base to draw all possible conclusions and add these conclusions to the knowledge base. This can be done in an automated way using resolution as discussed in Section 2.2, or by using forward chaining to add new facts to the knowledge base, followed by backward chaining to deduce which squares are OK.

However, for the sake of illustration, we show how the knowledge base is updated using the inference rules in Table 2.2 rather than using an automated method. Suppose the agent has already visited square [1,2], backed up into square [1,1], and is about to visit square [2,1]. Assuming the agent has deduced all that is possible, Figure 2.4(a) shows the state of the knowledge base at this point in time. The question marks by the wumpus in squares [1,3] and [2,2] mean that the knowledge base contains the following information:

$$W_{13} \vee W_{22}.$$

After the agent moves into square [2,1] and does not perceive a stench or a breeze, we reason as follows:

1. Using $\neg S_{21}$, rule $\neg S_{21} \Rightarrow \neg W_{11} \wedge \neg W_{31} \wedge \neg W_{22}$ and *modus ponens*, we conclude

$$\neg W_{11} \wedge \neg W_{31} \wedge \neg W_{22}.$$

2. Using $\neg W_{11} \wedge \neg W_{31} \wedge \neg W_{22}$ and *and elimination*, we conclude

$$\neg W_{11}, \ \neg W_{31}, \ \neg W_{22}.$$

3. Using $\neg B_{21}$, rule $\neg B_{21} \Rightarrow \neg P_{11} \wedge \neg P_{31} \wedge \neg P_{22}$ and *modus ponens*, we conclude

$$\neg P_{11} \wedge \neg P_{31} \wedge \neg P_{22}.$$

4. Using $\neg P_{11} \wedge \neg P_{31} \wedge \neg P_{22}$ and *and elimination*, we conclude

$$\neg P_{11}, \ \neg P_{31}, \ \neg P_{22}.$$

5. Using $\neg W_{31}, \ \neg P_{31}, \ \neg W_{22}, \ \neg P_{22}$, and *and introduction*, we conclude

$$\neg W_{31} \wedge \neg P_{31}, \ \neg W_{22} \wedge \neg P_{22}.$$

6. Using $\neg W_{31} \wedge \neg P_{31}, \ \neg W_{22} \wedge \neg P_{22}$, rules $\neg W_{31} \wedge \neg P_{31} \Rightarrow OK_{31}, \ \neg W_{22} \wedge \neg P_{22} \Rightarrow OK_{22}$, and *modus ponens*, we conclude

$$OK_{31}, \ OK_{22}.$$

7. Using $W_{13} \vee W_{22}, \ \neg W_{22}$, and *disjunctive syllogism*, we conclude

$$W_{13}.$$

Figure 2.4(b) show the state of the knowledge base after these conclusions are added to it.

After a model-based agent adds conclusions to the knowledge base, it must decide on its action. Next we discuss two ways of doing this.

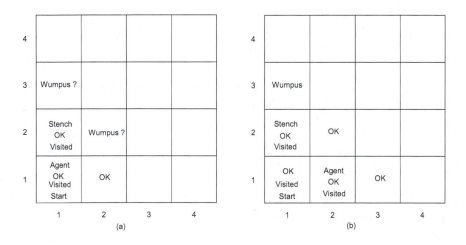

Figure 2.4 The state of the knowledge right before the agent moves to square [2,1] appears in (a), and its state after that move and inference is completed appears in (b).

Table 2.8 Deduction Rules for Square [2,2]

$$\vdots$$

1. $S_{22} \Rightarrow W_{12} \vee W_{21} \vee W_{32} \vee W_{23}$
2. $\neg S_{22} \Rightarrow \neg W_{12} \wedge \neg W_{21} \wedge \neg W_{32} \wedge \neg W_{23}$
3. $B_{22} \Rightarrow P_{12} \vee P_{21} \vee P_{32} \vee P_{23}$
4. $\neg B_{22} \Rightarrow \neg P_{12} \wedge \neg P_{21} \wedge \neg P_{32} \wedge \neg P_{23}$
5. $\neg W_{22} \wedge \neg P_{22} \Rightarrow OK_{22}$

$$\vdots$$

Rule-Based Agent A **rule-based, model-based agent** determines its next action according to a set of rules like a reflex agent. So like a reflex agent it needs a knowledge base and action rules. However, it also needs a set of deduction rules, which it uses to update the knowledge base in each time slot. The deduction rules appear in Table 2.8. So the agent needs the following files:

1. Knowledge base

2. Deduction rules

3. Action rules

As was the case for the reflex agent, we use context limiting and priority ordering to fire the action rules. However, now the agent has a much larger knowledge base (all the perceptions and everything that could be deduced). Given this knowledge, a reasonable set of action rules and strategy for prioritizing them is as follows:

1. If the gold is in the current square, stop.

2. If the wumpus or a pit is in the current square, die.

3. If there is an adjacent square that is OK and unvisited, move to that square.

4. If there is an adjacent square that is OK and has not been visited in one of the last six time slots, move to that square.

5. If the wumpus is located left, right, up, or down, shoot the arrow in that direction.

6. If the wumpus is possibly located left, right, up, or down, shoot the arrow in that direction.

7. If there is an adjacent square that is not known to not be OK, move to that square.

In rule 4 we require that there be an adjacent square that has not been recently visited to avoid going back and forth repeatedly when there are still possible successful paths to explore. Again we use context limiting to only fire the rules pertinent to the current square, and we use priority ordering as just described. The algorithm follows.

Algorithm 2.6 Rule_Based_Agent

> **Procedure** *Rule_Based*;
> A_{11} = true;
> **repeat**
> > *Knowledge_Base* = *Knowledge_Base* $\cup$ set of new perceptions;
> > using *Deduction_Rules* and *Knowledge_Base*,
> > > add all possible deductions to *Knowledge_Base*;
> > > fire action rules *Rules*$_{ij}$ such that A_{ij} = true;
> **until** stop is executed or agent is dead;

Planning Agent   A **plan** is a sequence of actions aimed at achieving a goal. Our rule-based agent decides on each move individually in each time slot based on reasonable criteria; it does not plan a sequence of moves. A **planning, model-based agent** develops a plan for executing a sequence of moves. Next we describe such an agent.

The agent's goal is to the reach the gold, and only an unvisited square could possibly contain the gold. So a reasonable sub-goal would be to arrive at an unvisited, OK square. Furthermore, we would want to do this in as few moves as possible and only go through OK squares (called a **safe** route). Our agent's plan is therefore to find such a safe route if one exists. This can be accomplished with a **breadth-first tree search** as illustrated in Figure 2.5.

Figure 2.5(a) shows a possible current state of knowledge of the environment, and Figure 2.5(b) shows the breadth-first tree search that finds a shortest safe

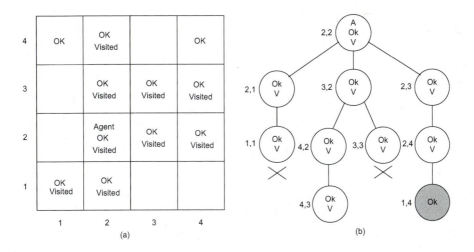

Figure 2.5 A possible state of knowledge is in (a) and a breadth-first tree that determines a shortest route to an unvisited, OK square based on that knowledge is in (b).

route to an unvisited OK square. The root (level 0) of the tree contains the agent's location. At level 1 of the tree we visit OK squares adjacent to the root. At level 2 of the tree we visit OK squares adjacent to level 1 squares, at level 3 we visit OK squares adjacent to level 2 squares, and so on. We only visit OK squares that are not already in the tree. We prune a node in the tree whenever there are no eligible squares adjacent to it. We continue until there are no nodes to expand (there is no possible safe route to an unvisited, OK square), or until we reach an unvisited, OK square. The node concerning square [1,1] at level 2 is pruned because the only OK square adjacent to it is square [2,1] which is already in the tree when square [1,1] is visited. The node concerning square [3,3] is also pruned because the only OK squares adjacent to it are already in the tree (by the time we investigate expanding that node). The shortest safe route to an unvisited, OK square is found to be one leading to square [1,4].

If there is no safe route to an unvisited, OK square, the agent's next course of action could be to plan a shortest safe route to a square which has a good chance of enabling the agent to kill the wumpus. If that is not possible, the agent could look for a shortest safe route to an unvisited square that is not known to not be OK. Finally, the agent could like for a shortest route to an unvisited square that is not known to not be OK, which only goes through squares that are not known to be not OK. If this is not possible, the agent should give up as there is no way to reach the gold.

The algorithm follows.

Algorithm 2.7 Planning_Agent

> **Procedure** *Planning*;
> A_{11} = true;
> **repeat**
> > *Knowledge_Base* = *Knowledge_Base* ∪ set of new perceptions;
> > using *Deduction_Rules* and *Knowledge_Base*,
> > > add all possible deductions to *Knowledge_Base*;
> > **if** there is a current plan
> > > perform next action in that plan;
> > **else**
> > > develop a new plan if possible and execute first action in the plan;
> > **if** the current square contains the gold
> > > stop;
> > **else** if the current square contains the wumpus or a pit
> > > die;
> **until** stop is executed or agent is dead or there is no plan;

2.3.2.3   More Complex Wumpus World

We presented a very simple version of the wumpus world. Both the environment and the tasks required of the agent could be made more complex. For example, the agent could be required to turn and face a direction before moving in that direction, or the agent could be required to pick up the gold and return back to square [1,1] in order to succeed. The environment could include several squares containing gold or containing a wumpus, or the wumpus could be allowed to move.

2.4   Discussion and Further Reading

In the **procedural approach** to **system design**, the steps that accomplish the desired task are hard-coded in the program. We would be using this approach if we directly coded the decision tree in Figure 2.2. In the **declarative approach**, the knowledge is separated from the reasoning. This is the approach taken when we used forward chaining and backward chaining to reason with rules, and when we developed wumpus algorithms that reasoned with knowledge bases. Boden [1977] provides an early discussion of the two approaches, while Newell [1981] discusses the problem of representation and knowledge. The two approaches are contrasted further in [Brooks, 1991], [Nillson, 1991], and [Shaparau et al., 2008].

XCON [McDermott, 1982] was a system that operated in a fashion similar to our grocery bagger. The system configured Digital Equipment Corporation's VAX computers. Since then propositional logic has been used to actually design computer hardware. For example, Norwick et al. [1993] discuss the design of a high-performance cache controller.

Yob [1975] developed the wumpus world. The version of the wumpus world shown here is based on one that appeared in [Russell and Norvig, 1995].

Williams et al. [2003] develop an agent similar to the wumpus that plans actions and diagnosis faults for NASA aircraft. Besides running programs, this agent uses the **circuit-based approach**, which is to transmit signals in hardware circuits instead of running standard computer programs [Rosenschein, 1985].

EXERCISES

Section 2.1

Exercise 2.1 Determine which of the following are propositions:

1. $\neg P \wedge Q \wedge R$.

2. $\neg P \wedge Q \wedge \wedge R$.

3. $\neg \neg P \wedge Q \Rightarrow R$.

4. $\neg (\neg P \wedge Q) \Rightarrow R$.

5. $\neg (\neg P \wedge) Q \Rightarrow R$.

Exercise 2.2 Write the following statements about the real world as propositions. Use the atomic propositions shown.

1. If Joe is in his office, we will tell Joe the news; otherwise we will leave him a message.

   P: Joe is in his office.

   Q: We will tell Joe the news.

   R: We will leave Joe a message.

2. If the operation succeeds and if Mary follows the doctor's instructions, she will be fine.

   P: The operation succeeds.

   Q: Mary follows the doctor's instructions.

   R: Mary will be fine.

3. An employee is eligible for a 3-week vacation if 1) the employee is a non-union worker who does not receive vacation pay and who has been with the company for at least a year; or 2) the employee is a union worker who has been with the company at least 6 months.

   P: The employee is eligible for a 3-week vacation.

   Q: The employee is a non-union worker.

R: The employee does not receive vacation pay.

S: The employee has been with the company for at least a year.

T: The employee is a union worker.

U: The employee has been with the company for at least 6 months.

Exercise 2.3 Develop truth tables for the following propositions:

1. ¬P∧Q∨R.

2. P∧Q∨R⇒S.

3. ¬(¬P ∧ Q) ⇒R.

4. (P∨(¬(Q∨R) ∧ ¬P)

Exercise 2.4 Consider the following statement, which often appears on a sign in a liquor store: *You must be 21 years old to purchase liquor.*

1. Express this statement as a proposition using logic. Develop the truth table for the proposition.

2. Does the truth table for this proposition entail what the store owner intended?

3. Create a new statement that you feel expresses what the store owner intended.

4. Express the new statement as a proposition and develop a truth table for the proposition. Check whether the truth table entails what the store owner intended.

Exercise 2.5 Determine whether each of the following propositions is a tautology, contradiction, or neither.

1. P∨Q∧¬P.

2. (P ∨ Q) ∧ ¬P.

3. (P ∧ Q) ∧ ¬P.

Exercise 2.6 Simplify the following propositions using the laws in Table 2.1.

1. R⇒Q∧ ((P ∧ ¬Q) ∨ (P ⇒ Q)) .

2. ¬P∧R∧¬(P∧¬(P∨Q)).

Exercise 2.7 Derive the following argument using the inference rules in Table 2.2.

$$P \lor Q, \ P \Rightarrow R, \ Q \Rightarrow R \ \vDash R.$$

Exercise 2.8 Consider the following argument. It was either Joe or Amit who stole the laptop. Joe was out of town when it was stolen. If Joe was out of town, he could not have been at the scene of the crime. If Joe was not at the scene of the crime, he could not have stolen the laptop. Therefore, Amit must have stolen the laptop. Using the inference rules in Table 2.2, derive this argument. Use these atomic propositions:

P: Joe stole the laptop.

Q: Amit stole the laptop.

R: Joe was out of town.

S: Joe was not at the scene of the crime.

Section 2.2

Exercise 2.9 Write the following proposition in conjunctive normal form:

$$P \lor Q \Rightarrow R \land (R \Rightarrow P).$$

Exercise 2.10 Derive the modus tolens rule using refutation and a truth table.

Exercise 2.11 Derive the modus tolens rule using the resolution rule.

Exercise 2.12 Use the set of support strategy for the argument in Exercise 2.8.

Section 2.3

Exercise 2.13 Finish bagging the groceries in Table 2.5.

Exercise 2.14 Create a rule base for a mini-classification system. For example, the system could determine the type of an animal or a mineral based on its description; or it could determine the drink for patron of a bar based on the individual's particular preferences.

Exercise 2.15 Create rule base for a mini-configuration system. The system could be an enhancement of the grocery bagger. For example, consideration could be given to placing crushable items such as potato chips on the top.

Exercise 2.16 Create a rule base for a mini-diagnostic system. For example, the system could determine the problem with an automobile or a DVD player.

Exercise 2.17 Consider the wumpus world in Figure 2.3. Show the first 5 moves and the state of the knowledge base after each move for each of the following types of agents (note that the answers may not be unique):

1. The reflex agent described in the text.

2. The rule-based agent described in the text.

3. The planning agent described in the text.

Exercise 2.18 Write a program that generates environments for the wumpus world and presents perceptions to an agent. Write a program for an agent that tries to find the gold in each world. Your agent need not be exactly like any of those presented in the text. For example, it could be a planning agent that likes to take more risk by visiting a closer square not known to be not OK over a more distant unvisited OK square.

Chapter 3

First-Order Logic

All fish are mortal.
I am mortal.
Therefore, I am a fish???

Chapter 2 started with a variation of a classic example concerning Socrates. Traditionally, the example actually proceeds as follows:

All humans are mortal.

Socrates is a human.

Therefore, Socrates is mortal.

The reasoning here is that every entity in the set of humans is mortal, Socrates is in that set, and so Socrates is mortal. Propositional logic is only concerned with propositions that are true or false; it does not address properties of sets of objects. First-order logic, also called predicate calculus, models reasoning with sets of objects.

Section 3.1 discusses the basic properties of first-order logic, while Section 3.2 shows artificial intelligence applications of first-order logic.

3.1   Basics of First-Order Logic

Like propositional logic, first-order logic consists of a formal language with a syntax and semantics that give meaning to the well-formed strings. We start by discussing its syntax and semantics.

3.1.1   Syntax

The alphabet of first-order logic contains the following symbols:

1. Constants: A constant is a symbol like 'Socrates', 'John', 'B', and '1'.

2. Predicates: The symbols 'True' and 'False' and other symbols like 'married', 'love', and 'brother'.

3. Functions: Symbols like 'mother', 'weight', and 'height'.

4. Variables: A variable is a lower-case alphabetic character like x, y, or z.

5. Operators: $\neg, \vee, \wedge, \Rightarrow, \Leftrightarrow$.

6. Quantifiers: The symbols $\forall$ (for all) and $\exists$ (there exists).

7. Grouping symbols: The open and closed parentheses and the comma.

The constant, predicate, and function symbols are called **non-logical symbols**. Traditionally, philosophers/logicians assumed the existence of a fixed, infinite set of non-logical symbols. According to this approach, there is only one language of first-order logic. In modern artificial intelligence applications, we specify non-logical symbols that are appropriate to the application. This specified set is called a **signature**.

The rules for creating well-formed strings are as follows:

1. A term is one of the following:

   (a) A constant symbol

   (b) A variable symbol

   (c) A function symbol followed by one or more terms separated by commas and enclosed in parentheses

2. An atomic formula is one of the following:

   (a) A predicate symbol

   (b) A predicate symbol followed by one or more terms separated by commas and enclosed in parentheses

   (c) Two terms separated by the = symbol

3. A formula is one of the following:

(a) An atomic formula

(b) The operator ¬ followed by a formula

(c) Two formulas separated by ∨, ∧, ⇒, or ⇔

(d) A quantifier following by a variable followed by a formula

4. A sentence is a formula with no free variables.

Rule 4 bears clarification. Consider the following formulas:

$$\forall x\ love(x, y) \qquad \forall x\ tall(x). \tag{3.1}$$

We discuss shortly what formulas like this mean. Currently, we present them to clarify the definition of a sentence. A variable in a formula is **free** if it is not quantified by the ∀ or the ∃ symbol; otherwise it is **bound**. The formula on the left in Expression 3.1 contains the free variable y and therefore is not a sentence, whereas the formula on the right does not contain any free variables and therefore is a sentence.

Mathematically, this is all there is to say about the formal language of first-order logic. However, like propositional logic, first-order logic was developed to make statements about the real world and to reason with these statements. The next examples illustrate such statements.

Example 3.1 As discussed more formally in the next section, in first-order logic we have a **domain of discourse**. This domain is a set and each element in the set is called an **entity**. Each constant symbol identifies one entity in the domain. For example, if we are considering all individuals living in a certain home, our constant symbols could be their names. If there are five such individuals, the constant symbols might be 'Mary', 'Fred', 'Sam', 'Laura', and 'Dave'.   ∎

Example 3.2 A predicate denotes a relationship among a set of entities or a property of a single entity. For example,

married(Mary,Fred)

denotes that Mary and Fred are married, and

young(Sam)

denotes that Sam is young. The number of arguments in a predicate is called its **arity**. The predicate 'married' has arity two while the predicate 'young' has arity one.   ∎

Example 3.3 If our application is considering the five individuals mentioned in Example 3.1, and we are only concerned with discussing whether any of them are married and whether any of them are young, then our signature would consist of the constant symbols 'Mary', 'Fred', 'Sam', 'Laura', and 'Dave' and the predicates 'married' and 'young', where 'married' has arity two and 'young' has arity one.   ∎

Example 3.4 A function denotes a mapping from some subset of entities to a single entity. For example, if the value of

$$\text{mother(Laura)}$$

is 'Mary', this means that Mary is the mother of Laura. If the value of

$$\text{sum(2,3)}$$

is 5, this means that the sum of 2 and 3 is 5.   ∎

Example 3.5 The operators $\neg, \vee, \wedge, \Rightarrow$, and $\Leftrightarrow$ have the same meaning they have in propositional logic. For example,

$$\neg\text{married(Mary,Fred)}$$

denotes that Mary and Fred are not married. The formula

$$\neg\text{married(Mary,Fred)} \wedge \text{young(Sam)}$$

denotes that Mary and Fred are not married and that Sam is young.   ∎

Example 3.6 The equality operator is used to denote that two terms refer to the same entity. For example,

$$\text{Mary} = \text{mother(Laura)}$$

denotes that Mary and mother(Laura) refer to the same entity. That is, Mary is the mother of Laura.   ∎

Example 3.7 The quantifier $\forall$ denotes that some formula is true for all entities in the domain of discourse. For example, suppose our domain consists of the five individuals named Mary, Fred, Sam, Laura, and Dave. The formula

$$\forall x \; \text{young}(x)$$

denotes that Mary, Fred, Sam, Laura, and Dave are all young.   ∎

Example 3.8 The quantifier $\exists$ denotes that some formula is true for at least one entity in the domain. Suppose again that our domain consists of the five individuals named Mary, Fred, Sam, Laura, and Dave. The formula

$$\exists x \; \text{young}(x)$$

denotes that at least one of Mary, Fred, Sam, Laura, and Dave is young.   ∎

3.1.2   Semantics

In first-order logic we first specify a signature, which determines the language. Given a language, a **model** has the following components:

1. A nonempty set D of **entities** called a **domain of discourse**.

2. An **interpretation**, which consists of the following:

   (a) An entity in D is assigned to each of the constant symbols. Ordinarily, every entity is assigned to a constant symbol.

   (b) For each function, an entity is assigned to each possible input of entities to the function.

   (c) The predicate 'True' is always assigned the value T, and the predicate 'False' is always assigned the value F.

   (d) For every other predicate, the value T or F is assigned to each possible input of entities to the predicate.

Example 3.9 Suppose our application is considering the five individuals mentioned in Example 3.1, and we are only concerned with discussing whether any of them are married and whether any of them are young. Our signature can be as follows:

1. Constant Symbols = {Mary, Fred, Sam, Laura, Dave }.

2. Predicate Symbols = {married, young}. The predicate 'married' has arity two and the predicate 'young' has arity one.

One particular model has these components:

1. The domain of discourse D is the set of these five particular individuals.

2. The interpretation is as follows:

   (a) A different individual is assigned to each of the constant symbols.

   (b) The truth value assignments are given by these tables:

x	Mary	Fred	Sam	Laura	Dave
young(x)	F	F	T	T	T

x \ y	Mary	Fred	Sam	Laura	Dave
Mary	F	T	F	F	F
Fred	T	F	F	F	F
Sam	F	F	F	F	F
Laura	F	F	F	F	F
Dave	F	F	F	F	F

married(x, y)

■

Example 3.10 Suppose our application is considering the three individuals named Dave, Gloria, and Ann, and we are concerned with discussing the mother of each individual and whether each individual loves the other. Our signature can be as follows:

1. Constant Symbols = {Dave, Gloria, Ann}.

2. Predicate Symbols = {love}. The predicate 'love' has arity two.

3. Function symbols = {mother}. The function 'mother' has arity one.

One particular model has these components:

1. The domain of discourse D is the set of these three particular individuals.

2. The interpretation is as follows:

   (a) A different individual is assigned to each of the constant symbols.

   (b) The truth value assignments are given by this table:

y x	Dave	Gloria	Ann
Dave	F	F	F
Gloria	T	F	T
Ann	T	T	F

$$\text{love}(x, y)$$

   (c) The function assignments are given by this table:

x	Dave	Gloria	Ann
mother(x)	Gloria	Ann	-

Notice that no assignment is made for the mother of Ann. Technically, every entity must be assigned a value by a function. If Ann's mother is not one of the entities, we can simply use a dummy symbol like the dash (-) as our assignment. In practice, we do not ordinarily reason with first-order logic by completely specifying a model. So we need not concern ourselves with this nuance. Note further that a binary predicate need not be symmetric. Gloria loves Dave but Dave does not love Gloria. ■

Once a model is specified, the truth values of all sentences are assigned according to the following rules:

1. The truth values for sentences developed with the symbols $\neg, \wedge, \vee, \Rightarrow$, and $\Leftrightarrow$ are assigned in the same way as done in propositional logic.

2. The truth value for two terms connected by the = symbol is T if both terms refer to the same entity; otherwise it is F.

3. The truth value for $\forall x$ p(x) has value T if p(x) has value T for every assignment to x of an entity in the domain D; otherwise it has value F.

4. The truth value for $\exists x$ p(x) has value T if p(x) has value T for at least one assignment to x of an entity in the domain D; otherwise it has value F.

5. The operator precedence is as follows: $\neg, =, \wedge, \vee, \Rightarrow, \Leftrightarrow$.

6. The quantifiers have precedence over the operators.

7. Parentheses change the order of the precedence.

Example 3.11 Suppose our application is considering the four individuals Socrates, Plato, Zeus, and Fido, and we are interested in discussing whether they are human, mortal, and have legs. Our signature can be as follows:

1. Constant Symbols = {Socrates, Plato, Zeus, Fido}.

2. Predicate Symbols = {human, mortal, legs}. All predicates have arity one.

Let the model have these components:

1. D is the set of these four particular individuals.

2. The interpretation is as follows:

   (a) A different individual is assigned to each of the constant symbols.

   (b) The truth value assignments are given by these tables:

x	Socrates	Plato	Zeus	Fido
human(x)	T	T	F	F

x	Socrates	Plato	Zeus	Fido
mortal(x)	T	T	F	T

x	Socrates	Plato	Zeus	Fido
legs(x)	T	T	T	T

Then we have the following:

1. The sentence

$$\text{human(Zeus)} \wedge \text{human(Fido)} \vee \text{human(Socrates)}$$

has value T because $\wedge$ takes precedence over $\vee$.

2. The sentence

$$\text{human(Zeus)} \wedge (\text{human(Fido)} \vee \text{human(Socrates)})$$

has value F because we changed the order of precedence with the parentheses.

3. The sentence
$$\forall x \ \text{human}(x)$$
has value F because human(Zeus) = F and human(Fido) = F.

4. The sentence
$$\forall x \ \text{mortal}(x)$$
has value F because mortal(Zeus) = F.

5. The sentence
$$\forall x \ \text{legs}(x)$$
has value T because $\text{legs}(x) = \text{T}$ for every assignment to x.

6. The sentence
$$\exists x \ \text{human}(x)$$
has value T because human(Socrates) = T and human(Plato) = T.

7. The sentence
$$\forall x \ (\text{human}(x) \Rightarrow \text{mortal}(x))$$
has value T. The following table shows this:

x	human(x)	mortal(x)	human$(x) \Rightarrow$ mortal(x)
Socrates	T	T	T
Plato	T	T	T
Zeus	F	F	T
Fido	F	T	T

■

Example 3.12 Suppose we have the model and interpretation in Example
3.10. Recall that the truth value assignments in that interpretation are given
by this table:

x \ y	Dave	Gloria	Ann
Dave	F	F	F
Gloria	T	T	T
Ann	T	T	F

$$\text{love}(x, y)$$

Then we have the following:

1. The sentence
$$\exists x \; \forall y \; \text{loves}(x, y)$$
has value T because love(Gloria,y) has value T for every value of y. This sentence means that there is someone who loves everybody. It is true because Gloria loves everyone.

2. The sentence
$$\forall x \; \exists y \; \text{loves}(x, y)$$
has value F because love(Dave,y) does not have value T for any value of y. This sentence means that everyone loves someone. It is false because Dave does not love anyone. ■

3.1.3 Validity and Logical Implication

The notions of a tautology and a fallacy in propositional logic extend to first-order logic. We have the definitions that follow.

Definition 3.1 If sentence s has value T under interpretation I, we say that I satisfies s, and we write $I \vDash s$. A sentence is **satisfiable** if there is some interpretation under which it has value T.◆

Example 3.13 The sentence

$$\text{human(Socrates)}$$

is satisfied in any interpretation that assign T to human(Socrates). ■

Example 3.14 The sentence

$$\forall x \; \text{human}(x)$$

is satisfied in any interpretation that assign T to human(x) for every individual x in the domain of discourse. ■

If a formula contains free variables (and therefore is not a sentence), then an interpretation alone does not determine its truth value. We extend the definition of satisfiability to such formulas as follows.

Definition 3.2 A formula that contains free variables is **satisfied** by an interpretation if the formula has value T regardless of which individuals from the domain of discourse are assigned to its free variables.◆

Example 3.15 The formula

$$\text{loves}(\text{Socrates}, y)$$

is satisfied by any interpretation that assigns T to loves(Socrates, y) for every individual y in the domain of discourse. ■

Definition 3.3 A formula is **valid** if it is satisfied by every interpretation.◆

Clearly, every tautology is a valid formula. Other examples of valid statements follow.

Example 3.16 The sentence

$$\text{human(Socrates)} \lor \neg\text{human(Socrates)}$$

is valid. A simple truth table shows this.   ■

Example 3.17 The sentence

$$\forall x \ (\text{human}(x) \lor \neg\text{human}(x))$$

is valid.

■

Example 3.18 The formula

$$\text{loves(Socrates}, y) \lor \neg\text{loves(Socrates}, y)$$

is valid. Regardless of which individual in the domain of discourse is assigned to y, the formula is true in every interpretation. So it is valid.

Definition 3.4 A sentence is a **contradiction** if there is no interpretation that satisfies it.◆

Example 3.19 The sentence

$$\exists x \ (\text{human}(x) \land \neg\text{human}(x))$$

is not satisfiable under any interpretation and is therefore a contradiction. ■

Definition 3.5 Given two formulas A and B, if $A \Rightarrow B$ is valid, we say that A **logically implies** B and we write $A \Rrightarrow B$.◆

Example 3.20 It is left as an exercise to show that

$$\text{human(Socrates)} \land (\text{human(Socrates)} \Rightarrow \text{mortal(Socrates)}) \Rrightarrow \text{mortal(Socrates)}.$$

■

Definition 3.6 Given two formulas A and B, if $A \Leftrightarrow B$ is valid, we say that A is **logically equivalent to** B and we write $A \equiv B$.◆

Example 3.21 It is left as an exercise to show that

$$\text{human(Socrates)} \Rightarrow \text{mortal(Socrates)} \equiv \neg\text{human(Socrates)} \lor \text{mortal(Socrates)}.$$

■

It is left as an exercise to prove the following theorem concerning logical equivalence of quantified expressions.

Theorem 3.1 The following logical equivalences hold. (A and B are variables denoting arbitrary predicates. Furthermore, they could have other arguments besides x.):

1. $\neg \exists x\; A(x) \equiv \forall x\; \neg A(x)$

2. $\neg \forall x\; A(x) \equiv \exists x\; \neg A(x)$

3. $\exists x\; (A(x) \vee B(x)) \equiv \exists x\; A(x) \vee \exists x\; B(x)$

4. $\forall x\; (A(x) \wedge B(x)) \equiv \forall x\; A(x) \wedge \forall x\; B(x)$

5. $\forall x\; A(x) \equiv \forall y\; A(y)$

6. $\exists x\; A(x) \equiv \exists y\; A(y)$

Equivalences 1 and 2 are **DeMorgan's laws** for quantifiers. Intuitively, Equivalence 1 holds because if $A(x)$ is false for every x then it cannot be true for any x. The other equivalences can readily be made clear with similar intuitive explanations.

3.1.4 Derivation Systems

Similar to propositional logic, in first-order logic an **argument** consists of a set of formulas, called the **premises**, and a formula called the **conclusion**. We say that the premises **entail** the conclusion if in every model in which all the premises are true, the conclusion is also true. If the premises entail the conclusion, we say the argument is **sound**; otherwise we say it is a **fallacy**. A set of inference rules is called a **deduction system**. A deduction system is **sound** if it only derives sound arguments. A deduction system is **complete** if it can derive every sound argument. Gödel's famous first incompleteness theorem proves that in general there is no complete deduction system in first-order logic. However, its discussion is beyond the scope of this text. Briefly, Gödel showed that there are statements about the natural numbers that cannot be proved.

We write arguments showing the list of premises followed by the conclusion as follows:

1. A_1

2. A_2

   $\vdots$

n. $\underline{A_n}$

   B

If the argument is sound, we write

$$A_1, A_2, \ldots, A_n \models B,$$

and if it is a fallacy, we write

$$A_1, A_2, \ldots, A_n \not\models B.$$

Next we provide some sound inference rules for first-order logic. First, all the rules we developed for propositional logic (Table 2.2) can be applied in the first-order logic to formulas containing no variables.

Example 3.22 Consider the following argument:

1. man(Socrates)

2. man(Socrates) $\Rightarrow$ human(Socrates)
   man(Socrates)

We have the following derivation for this argument:

	Derivation	Rule
1	man(Socrates)	Premise
2	man(Socrates) $\Rightarrow$ human(Socrates)	Premise
3	human(Socrates)	1, 2, MP

■

The previous example is not very exciting because we just used the syntax of first-order logic to stand for statements that we could have represented using the syntax of propositional logic. Next we develop additional inference rules that only concern first-order logic.

3.1.4.1   Universal Instantiation

The **universal instantiation (UI) rule** is as follows:

$$\forall x\ A(x) \models A(t),$$

where t is any term. This rules says that if $A(x)$ has value T for all entities in the domain of discourse, then it must have value T for term t.

Example 3.23 Consider the following argument:

1. man(Socrates)

2. $\forall x\ \text{man}(x) \Rightarrow \text{human}(x)$
   human(Socrates)

We have the following derivation for this argument:

Derivation	Rule
1 man(Socrates)	Premise
2 $\forall x$ (man(x) $\Rightarrow$ human(x))	Premise
3 man(Socrates) $\Rightarrow$ human(Socrates)	2, UI
4 human(Socrates)	1, 3, MP

∎

Example 3.24 Consider the following argument:

1. $\forall x$ (father(Sam, x) $\Rightarrow$ son(x, Sam) $\vee$ daughter(x, Sam))

2. father(Sam, Dave)

3. ¬daughter(Dave, Sam)

   son(Dave, Sam)

We have the following derivation for this argument:

Derivation	Rule
1 $\forall x$ (father(Sam, x) $\Rightarrow$ son(x, Sam) $\vee$ daughter(x, Sam))	Premise
2 father(Sam, Dave)	Premise
3 ¬daughter(Dave, Sam)	Premise
4 father(Sam, Dave) $\Rightarrow$ son(Dave, Sam) $\vee$ daughter(Dave, Sam)	1, UI
5 son(Dave, Sam) $\vee$ daughter(Dave, Sam))	2, 4, MP
6 son(Dave, Sam)	3, 5, DS

∎

Note that t can be any term, including a variable. However, t cannot be a bound variable. For example, suppose we have the following formula:

$$\forall x \exists y \text{ father}(y, x).$$

We can use UI to conclude $\exists y$ father(y,Dave), meaning that Dave has a father. Furthermore, we can use UI to conclude $\exists y$ father(y, z), meaning that the entity that is the value of z has a father. However, we cannot use UI to conclude $\exists y$ father(y,y), which would mean that some entity is its own father.

3.1.4.2 Universal Generalization

The **universal generalization (UG) rule** is as follows:

$A(e)$ for every entity e in the domain of discourse $\models \forall x A(x)$.

This rule says that if $A(e)$ has value T for every entity e, then $\forall x A(x)$ has value T. The rule is ordinarily applied by showing that $A(e)$ has value T for an arbitrary entity e.

Example 3.25 Consider the following argument:

1. $\dfrac{\forall x \; (\text{study}(\; x) \Rightarrow \text{pass}(x))}{\forall x \; (\neg\text{pass}(\; x) \Rightarrow \neg\text{study}(x))}$

This argument says that if it is true that everyone who studies passes, then we can conclude that everyone who did not pass did not study. We will use UG and the deduction theorem (DT) to derive this argument:

	Derivation	Rule	Comment
1	$\forall x \; (\text{study}(\; x) \Rightarrow \text{pass}(x))$	Premise	
2	$\text{study}(\; e) \Rightarrow \text{pass}(e)$	UI	Substitute arbitrary entity e.
3	$\neg\text{pass}(e)$	Assumption	We assume $\neg\text{pass}(e)$.
4	$\neg\text{study}(e)$	2, 3, MT	
5	$\neg\text{pass}(e) \Rightarrow \neg\text{study}(e)$	DT	We discharge $\neg\text{pass}(e)$.
6	$\forall x \; \neg\text{pass}(x) \Rightarrow \neg\text{study}(x)$	UG	

∎

Notice in the previous example that we showed the conclusion had value T for an arbitrary entity e and then applied UG. If we only know that a formula has value T for a specific entity, we cannot use UG. For example, if we only know young(Dave) or young(e) where e represents a specific entity, we cannot use UG. An entity e introduced with Existential instantiation (which will be discussed shortly) is an example of a case where e represents a specific entity.

3.1.4.3   Existential Generalization

The **existential generalization (EG) rule** is as follows:

$$A(e) \; \vDash \; \exists x \; A(x),$$

where e is an entity in the domain of discourse. This rule says that if $A(e)$ has value T for some entity e, then $\exists x \; A(x)$ has value T.

Example 3.26 Consider the following argument:

1. man(Socrates)

2. $\dfrac{\forall x \; \text{man}(x) \Rightarrow \text{human}(x)}{\exists x \; \text{human}(x)}$

We have the following derivation for this argument:

	Derivation	Rule
1	man(Socrates)	Premise
2	$\forall x \; \text{man}(x) \Rightarrow \text{human}(x)$	Premise
3	man(Socrates) $\Rightarrow$ human(Socrates)	2, UI
3	human(Socrates)	1, 3, MP
4	$\exists x \; \text{human}(x)$	4, EG

■

The variable x may not appear as a free variable in A which we apply EG. For example, suppose we know that father(x,e) has value T for some entity e. We cannot conclude that $\exists x$ father(x, x) as this would mean there is some entity that is its own father. We would need to use another variable such as y and conclude that $\exists y$ father(x, y).

3.1.4.4   Existential Instantiation

The **existential instantiation (EI) rule** is as follows:

$$\exists x \; A(x) \; \vDash A(e)$$

for some entity e in the domain of discourse. This rule says that if $\exists x \; A(x)$ has value T, then $A(e)$ has value T for some entity e .

Example 3.27 Consider the following argument:

1. $\exists x$ man(x)

2. $\underline{\forall x \; \text{man}(x) \Rightarrow \text{human}(x)}$
   $\exists x$ human(x)

We have the following derivation for this argument:

	Derivation	Rule
1	$\exists x$ man(x)	Premise
2	$\forall x$ man(x) $\Rightarrow$ human(x)	Premise
3	man(e)	1, EI
4	man(e) $\Rightarrow$ human(e)	2, UI
5	human(e)	3, 4, MP
6	$\exists x$ human(x)	5, EG

■

The variable used in EI cannot appear elsewhere as a free variable. For example, suppose we conclude man(e) using EI. We cannot later conclude monkey(e) using EI, for this would mean e is both a man and a monkey. Rather, we must use a different variable such as f and conclude monkey(f).

3.1.5   Modus Ponens for First-Order Logic

The next example illustrates how difficult inference can be if we only have the inference rules developed so far.

Example 3.28 Consider the following argument:

1. mother(Mary,Scott)

2. sister(Mary,Alice)

3. $\forall x\ \forall y \forall z$ mother$(x,y) \wedge$ sister$(x,z) \Rightarrow$ aunt(z,y)

   aunt(Alice,Scott)

We have the following derivation for this argument:

	Derivation	Rule
1	mother(Mary,Scott)	Premise
2	sister(Mary,Alice)	Premise
3	$\forall x\ \forall y \forall z$ mother$(x,y) \wedge$ sister$(x,z) \Rightarrow$ aunt(z,y)	Premise
4	mother(Mary,Scott)$\wedge$sister(Mary,Alice)	1, 2, CR
5	$\forall y \forall z$ mother(Mary,y) $\wedge$ sister(Mary,z) $\Rightarrow$ aunt(z,y)	3, UI
6	$\forall z$ mother(Mary,Scott) $\wedge$ sister(Mary,z) $\Rightarrow$ aunt$(z$,Scott)	5, UI
7	mother(Mary,Scott) $\wedge$ sister(Mary,Alice) $\Rightarrow$ aunt(Alice,Scott)	6, UI
8	aunt(Alice,Scott)	4 , 6, MP

■

We applied universal instantiation three times to reach our desired conclusion in the previous example. It does not seem that a human would go to all this trouble to reach that conclusion. Rather, a human would simply substitute Mary for x, Scott for y, and Alice for z in the antecedent in Premise 3 in the argument and then conclude aunt(Alice,Scott). Next we develop a version of modus ponens tailored to first-order logic that reasons like this.

3.1.5.1   Unification

We need to first develop the notion of unification.

Definition 3.7 Suppose we have two sentences A and B. A **unification** of A and B is a substitution θ of values for some of the variables in A and B that make the sentences identical. The set of substitutions θ is called the **unifier.**◆

Example 3.29 Suppose that we have the two sentences loves(Dave, y) and loves(x,Gloria). Then

$$\theta = \{x/\text{Dave},\ y/\text{Gloria}\}$$

unifies the two sentences into the sentence loves(Dave, Gloria).   ■

Example 3.30 Suppose that we have the two sentences parents(Dave, y, z) and parents(y, Mary, Sam). Because the y variables in the two sentences are different variables, we rename the second y variable as x to obtain the sentence parents(x, Mary, Sam). Then

$$\theta = \{x/\text{Dave},\ y/\text{Mary},\ z/\text{Sam}\}$$

unifies the two sentences into the sentence parents(Dave,Mary,Sam).   ■

Example 3.31 We cannot unify the sentences parents(Dave, Nancy, z) and parents(y, Mary, Sam) because Nancy and Mary are both constants and therefore cannot be substituted.   ■

Example 3.32 Suppose that we have the two sentences parents(x, father(x), mother(Dave)) and parents(Dave, father(Dave), y). Then

$$\theta = \{x/\text{Dave}, \ y/\text{mother(Dave)}\}$$

unifies the sentences into the sentence parents(Dave, father(Dave), mother(Dave)).
                                                                                   ■

Example 3.33 Suppose that we have the two sentences father(x, Sam) and father(y, z). Then
$$\theta_1 = \{x/\text{Dave}, \ y/\text{Dave}, \ z/\text{Sam}\}$$

unifies the two sentences into the sentence father(Dave, Sam). Furthermore,

$$\theta_2 = \{x/y \ , \ z/\text{Sam}\}$$

unifies the two sentences into the sentence father(y, Sam).   ■

In the previous example, the second unifier is more general than the first because father(Dave, Sam) is an instance of father(y, Sam). We have the following definition concerning this relationship.

Definition 3.8 A unifier θ is a **most general unifier** if every other unifier θ' is an instance of θ in the sense that θ' can be derived by making substitutions in θ.◆

Unifier θ_2 in Example 3.33 is a most general unifier. The following algorithm returns a most general unifier of two sentences if they can be unified.

Algorithm 3.1 Unification

> **Input:** Two sentences A and B; an empty set of substitutions θ.
> **Output:** A most general unifier of the sentences if they can be unified; otherwise failure.

Procedure $unify(A, B, \textbf{var } \theta)$;
scan A and B from left to right
    until A and B disagree on a symbol or A and B are exhausted;
if A and B are not exhausted
    let x and y be the symbols where A and B disagree;
    if x is a variable
        $\theta = \theta \cup \{x/y\}$;
        $unify(subst(\theta, A), subst(\theta, B), \theta)$;
    else if y is a variable
        $\theta = \theta \cup \{y/x\}$;
        $unify(subst(\theta, A), subst(\theta, B), \theta)$;
    else
        $\theta = $ Failure;
    endif
endif

The preceding algorithm calls a procedure *subst*, which takes as input a set of substitutions θ and a sentence A and applies the substitutions in θ to A.

Example 3.34 Suppose A is the sentence parents(Dave, y, z) and $\theta = \{x/\text{Dave}, y/\text{Mary}, z/\text{Sam}\}$. Then $subst(A, \theta)$ results in A being the sentence parents(Dave, Mary, Sam). ∎

A variable cannot be replaced by a term containing the variable when we unify. For example, we cannot make the substitution $x/f(x)$. It is necessary to add a check for this (called the **occurs check**) before the recursive calls in procedure *unify*; the algorithm should return failure if it occurs.

3.1.5.2   Generalized Modus Ponens

Next we present a generalized modus ponens rule for first-order logic. When using this rule, we do not bother to use universal instantiation notation for the implication statement. Rather, it is implicitly assumed. For example, we write

$$\text{mother}(x, y) \Rightarrow \text{parent}(x, y)$$

instead of writing

$$\forall x \forall y \; \text{mother}(x, y) \Rightarrow \text{parent}(x, y).$$

Suppose we have sentences A, B, and C, and the sentence $A \Rightarrow B$, which is implicitly universally quantified for all variables in the sentence. The **generalized modus ponens (GMP)** rule is as follows:

$$A \Rightarrow B, \; C, \; unify(A, C, \theta) \vDash subst(B, \theta).$$

Example 3.35 Consider the argument in Example 3.28:

Table 3.1 Action Rules for a Reflex Agent in the Wumpus World Expressed Using First-Order Logic

$$\vdots$$

$\forall i \forall j \ A(i,j) \wedge W(i,j) \Rightarrow$ agent dies
$\forall i \forall j \ A(i,j) \wedge P(i,j) \Rightarrow$ agent dies
$\forall i \forall j \ A(i,j) \wedge G(i,j) \Rightarrow$ gold found, stop
$\forall i \forall j \ A(i,j) \Rightarrow$ shoot arrow randomly left, right, up, or down
$\forall i \forall j \ A(i,j) \Rightarrow$ move randomly left, right, up, or down

$$\vdots$$

1. mother(Mary,Scott)

2. sister(Mary,Alice)

3. $\forall x \ \forall y \forall z$ mother$(x,y) \wedge$ sister$(x,z) \Rightarrow$ aunt(z,y)

   aunt(Alice,Scott)

We have the following new derivation for this argument (in Step 3 universal quantification is implicitly assumed):

Derivation	Rule
1 mother(Mary,Scott)	Premise
2 sister(Mary,Alice)	Premise
3 mother$(x,y) \wedge$ sister$(x,z) \Rightarrow$ aunt(z,y)	Premise
4 mother(Mary,Scott) $\wedge$ sister(Mary,Alice)	1, 2, CR
5 $\theta = \{x/$Mary, $y/$Scott, $z/$Alice$\}$	*unify* antecedent in 3 and 4
6 aunt(Alice,Scott)	3 , 4, 5, GMP

∎

3.2 Artificial Intelligence Applications

Next we discuss some applications of first-order logic to artificial intelligence.

3.2.1 Wumpus World Revisited

In Section 2.3.2 we showed action rules and deduction rules for negotiating the wumpus world using propositional logic. We can express these rules much more concisely using first-order logic. For example, recall that Table 2.7 showed action rules for Square [2,2]. Using propositional logic we would need to express a set of rules like this for every square. However, using first-order logic we can express them all together as shown in Table 3.1. $A(i,j)$ is a predicate that is true if and only if the agent is in Square$[i,j]$. The other predicates have similar meaning.

It would be troublesome to state the inference rules in Table 2.8 in this same way because of the boundary conditions. For example, there is no square to the left of Square [1,2]. So a stench in this square implies that the wumpus is in one of three other squares rather than one of four. An alternative way to present the rules is to maintain a predicate Adjacent$(i, j, k.m)$ that is true if and only if Square$[i, j]$ is adjacent to Square$[k, m]$. We can then write rule 1 in Table 2.8 as follows:

$$\forall i \forall j \; S(i,j) \Rightarrow \exists k \exists m \; \text{Adjacent}(i,j,k,m) \wedge W(i,j).$$

We have suggested a couple of ways that first-order logic enables us to express rules for negotiating the wumpus world. There is no "right" way to accomplish this. The point is merely that first-order logic simplifies our task.

3.2.2   Planning

In Section 2.3.1.3 we used forward chaining with conflict resolution to guide a robot when bagging groceries. Our goal was to bag the groceries in a way that would serve the shopper best. For example, bottles were put on the bottom so other items did not get crushed. However, we did not need to identify a plan for achieving our goal. Forward chaining simply proceeded methodically performing actions in sequence without looking ahead. Recall from Section 2.3.2.2 that a plan is a sequence of actions aimed at achieving a goal. In that section we developed a planning agent for negotiating the wumpus world. Next we discuss planning further.

3.2.2.1   The Blocks World

In the **blocks world**, a number of blocks are resting on a table, and some of the blocks are stacked on top of each other. Figure 3.1 shows a possible configuration. Our robot has the task of moving blocks in sequence to achieve some goal. For example, our goal may be that "block **e** rests on block **b** and block **a** rests on block **e**." To enable the robot to achieve this we need provide it with a plan. If we start with the situation in Figure 3.1, one such plan is as follows.

1. Pick up block **d**

2. Put block **d** on the table

3. Pick up block **a**

4. Put block **a** on the table

5. Pick up block **e**

6. Put block **e** on block **b**

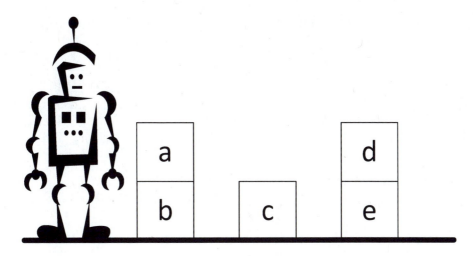

Figure 3.1 The blocks world.

7. Pick up block **a**

8. Put block **a** on block **e**

We want to develop an algorithm that will yield such a plan. First we use predicate calculus to describe the state of the world. To that end, we have the following predicates:

Predicate	Meaning
on(x,y)	Block x is on block y.
clear(x)	Block x has nothing on top of it.
gripping(x)	The robot is gripping block x; gripping(nothing) is true if robot is not gripping any block.
ontable(x)	Block x is on the table.

The state of the world in Figure 3.1 is described as follows:

ontable(**b**)

ontable(**c**)

ontable(**e**)

on(**a**,**b**)

on(**d**,**e**)

gripping(nothing)

Table 3.2 Action Rules for the Blocks World

1. $\forall x$ pickup$(x) \Rightarrow$ (gripping(nothing) $\wedge$ clear$(x) \Rightarrow$ gripping(x))
2. $\forall x$ putdown$(x) \Rightarrow$ (gripping$(x) \Rightarrow$ clear$(x) \wedge$ ontable$(x) \wedge$ gripping(nothing))
3. $\forall x \forall y$ stack$(x, y) \Rightarrow$ (gripping$(x) \wedge$ clear$(y) \Rightarrow$ gripping(nothing) $\wedge$ on(x, y))
4. $\forall x \forall y$ unstack$(x, y) \Rightarrow$
(on$(x, y) \wedge$ clear$(x) \wedge$ gripping(nothing)$\Rightarrow$ gripping $(x) \wedge$ clear(y))

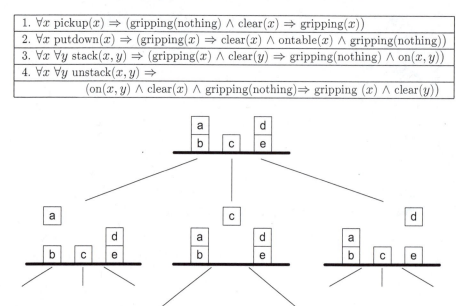

Figure 3.2 A portion of the state space tree when searching for a plan in the blocks world.

Next we need action rules for changing the state of the world. They are expressed in Table 3.2 using first-order logic.

These action rules mean that if we take the given action (make it true) stated as the premise of the rule, then the conclusion of the rule becomes true. For example, in rule 1 if we take the action to pickup(**a**), then if the robot is not gripping anything and **a** is clear, the robot will end up gripping **a**.

Now that we can describe the state of the world and the actions for changing, we can discuss developing a plan. One simple way to obtain a plan is to perform a breadth-first search of possible moves. When we arrive at the state that is our goal, the plan is the sequence of moves that led to that state. Figure 3.2 shows a portion of the search. The problem with this method is that it becomes computationally unfeasible for large problem instances. In Section 3.2.2.2 we discuss a way to address this problem.

The blocks world suffers from the **frame problem**, which concerns expressing using logic those aspects of the world that remain unchanged by an action that changes the world for the next time slot. The term **fluent** refers to an aspect of the world that changes over time, and the term **atemporal** refers to aspects that do not change. For example, suppose we perform unstack(**a,b**) for the world in Figure 3.1. Then the logical statement pertaining to this operation entails that the robot is grasping **a** and that there is nothing on **b**. However, it does not say anything about **c**, **d**, and **e**. They could be in the configuration shown in Figure 3.1 (the one we expect), but they could also be in any other configuration.

One way to address this problem is to include frame rules that tell us what aspects are not changed by the action. For example, we could have the following frame rule:

$$\forall x \ \forall y \ \forall z \ \text{unstack}(y, z) \Rightarrow (\text{ontable}(x) \Rightarrow \text{ontable}(x)).$$

This rule says that if x is on the table before we unstack y from z, then it is still on the table afterward.

3.2.2.2 PDDL and Macros

We use a version of **Planning Domain Definition Language** (PDDL) to address the frame problem. In our version of the language, each state is represented by a conjunction of fluents. For a given action, we list the **preconditions** (Pre), which are the conditions that must be true for an action to be applied; the **add list** (Add), which are the fluents that are added when the condition is applied; and the **delete list** (Del), which are the fluents that are deleted when the action is applied. For example, the unstack(x,y) action is represented as follows:

$$
\begin{array}{lll}
 & \text{Pre:} & \text{on}(x, y) \wedge \text{clear}(x) \wedge \text{gripping(nothing)} \\
\text{unstack}(x, y) & \text{Add:} & \text{gripping } (x) \wedge \text{clear}(y) \\
 & \text{Del:} & \text{on}(x, y) \wedge \text{gripping(nothing)}
\end{array}
$$

We then solve the frame problem but assuming a **frame axiom**, which is that all fluents that are not mentioned in the action description remain unchanged.

We can improve our breadth-first search by developing macro operators, which consists of sequences of actions that might often be performed. For example, suppose we often wish to invert two blocks when one rests on the other. The following macro accomplishes this:

$$
\begin{array}{lll}
 & \text{Pre:} & \text{on}(x, y) \wedge \text{clear}(x) \wedge \text{gripping(nothing)} \\
\text{invert}(x, y) & \text{Add:} & \text{on}(y, x) \wedge \text{clear}(y) \\
 & \text{Del:} & \text{on}(x, y) \wedge \text{clear}(x) \\
 & \text{Actions:} & \text{unstack}(x, y); \text{putdown}(x); \text{pickup}(y); \text{stack}(y, x)
\end{array}
$$

The Actions row shows the actions that comprise the macro. When searching, we not only search over the basic actions, but also over the macros.

Both a PDDL and macros were in the **Stanford University Institute Planning System** (STRIPS) [Fikes and Nilsson, 1971], which was developed by SRI International. STRIPS was used to plan the actions of the SHAKEY robot in the 1970s.

3.2.2.3   Backward Search

The breadth-first search strategy shown in Figure 3.2 is a **forward search** in that it starts with the current state of the world and looks forward trying to arrive at the desired state of the world. Alternatively, we could facilitate the search by performing a backward search. Similar to backward chaining, in a **backward search** we start with our goal, which is the desired state of the world, and proceed backwards. For example, suppose the world is as shown in Figure 3.1, and our goal is to invert blocks **a** and **b**. Then we start with the conditions on(**b,a**) and clear(**b**), and see what action could arrive at this state. The action is stack(**b,a**). Then we look at preconditions to this action. They are gripping(**b**) and clear(**a**). We next look at what actions could have led to these conditions, and continue in this fashion.

The backward search strategy was employed in the teleo-reactive planning strategy that was developed in [Nillson, 1994]. A **teleo-reactive program** is an agent control program that robustly directs an agent toward a goal while continuously taking into account the agent's changing perceptions of a dynamic environment. Teleo-reactive planning has been applied in a number of domains, including robot control [Benson, 1995], and for accelerator beamline tuning [Klein et al., 2000]. Katz [1997] extended the teleo-reactive paradigm for robotic agent task control using fuzzy logic [Zadeh, 1965].

3.3   Discussion and Further Reading

John McCarthy and Patrick Hayes identified the frame problem in their paper "Some Philosophical Problems from the Standpoint of Artificial Intelligence" [McCarthy and Hayes, 1969]. McCarthy proposed solving the problem by assuming that a minimal amount of changes has occurred. The Yale shooting problem [Hanks and McDermott, 1987] demonstrates that this solution is not always correct. Alternative solutions were then proposed, and in 1991, Reiter solved the problem with successor-state axioms.

EXERCISES

Section 3.1

Exercise 3.1 What is the arity of the predicate parents(x, y, z)? For example, we may have parents(Dave,Gloria,Mary).

Exercise 3.2 Describe the difference between a predicate and a function in first-order logic.

Exercise 3.3 Suppose our constant symbols are {Mary, Dave, Amit, Juan} and we have the following truth value assignment:

x	Mary	Dave	Amit	Juan
young(x)	F	F	T	T

x	Mary	Dave	Amit	Juan
happy(x)	T	T	T	T

Which of the following are true sentences:

1. $\forall x$ young(x).

2. $\exists x$ young(x).

3. $\forall x$ happy(x).

4. $\exists x$ happy(x).

Exercise 3.4 Suppose our constant symbols are {Mary, Fred, Sam, Laura, Dave} and we have the following truth value assignment:

x \\ y	Mary	Fred	Sam	Laura	Dave
Mary	F	T	F	T	F
Fred	T	T	F	F	F
Sam	F	T	F	F	F
Laura	F	T	F	T	F
Dave	F	T	F	F	F

loves(x, y)

Which of the following are true sentences:

1. $\exists x \, \forall y$ loves(x, y).

2. $\forall x \, \exists y$ loves(x, y).

3. $\exists y \, \forall x$ loves(x, y).

4. $\forall y \, \exists x$ loves(x, y).

Exercise 3.5 Prove Theorem 3.1.

Exercise 3.6 Derive the following argument:

1. $\forall x$ (father(Sam, x)$\wedge$father(x,Dave) $\Rightarrow$ grandfather(Sam, Dave)

2. father(Sam, Ralph)

3. father(Ralph, Dave)
   grandfather(Sam,Dave)

Exercise 3.7 Derive the following argument:

1. $\forall x$ (father(Sam, x)∧father(x,Dave) $\Rightarrow$ grandfather(Sam, Dave)

2. father(Sam, Ralph)

3. $\underline{\neg\text{grandfather(Sam, Dave)}}$
   ¬father(Ralph,Dave)

Exercise 3.8 Derive the following argument:

1. $\underline{\forall x \;(\text{study}(\;x) \vee \neg\text{pass}(x))}$
   $\forall x \; \neg(\text{pass}(\;x) \wedge \neg\text{study}(x))$

Exercise 3.9 Derive the following argument:

1. $\forall x$ (woman($\;x$) $\vee$ man(x))

2. $\underline{\neg\text{man(Jennifer)}}$
   $\exists x$ woman(x)

Exercise 3.10 Derive the following argument:

1. $\exists x$ (woman(x) $\vee$ man(x))

2. $\underline{\forall x \; \neg\text{man}(x)}$
   $\exists x$ woman(x)

Exercise 3.11 Show a unification of mother(Mary,x) and mother(z,Sam).

Exercise 3.12 Show a unification of children(Virginia,Eileen,x) and children(x, y,Ralph).

Exercise 3.13 Derive the following argument using GMP:

1. parent(Mary,Tom,Ralph)

2. ¬sister(Tom, Ralph)

3. $\underline{\forall x \forall y \forall z \; \text{parent}(x, y, z) \Rightarrow \text{brother}(y, z) \vee \text{sister}(y, z)}$
   brother(Tom,Ralph)

Section 3.2

Exercise 3.14 Write the rules in Table 2.8 using predicate calculus.

Exercise 3.15 Using PDDL, write a macro that takes as input two blocks x and y. If x is on y and nothing is on x, the result of the macro is that both x and y end up on the table.

Exercise 3.16 Using PDDL, develop a macro that takes as input three blocks x, y, and z. If x is on y and y is on z and nothing is on x, the effect of the macro is to invert all three blocks so that y is on x and z is on y.

Exercise 3.17 Using PDDL, write a macro that takes as input two blocks x and y. As long as neither block has a third block on it, the result of the macro is to end up with both x and y on the table.

Chapter 4

Certain Knowledge Representation

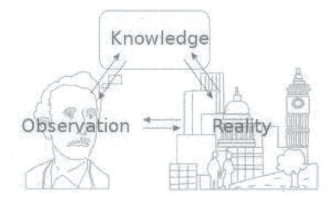

Recall the wumpus introduced in Section 2.3.2. The knowledge deduced by this wumpus consisted of simple facts about the environment such as whether there is a breeze in a particular square. Similarly, the knowledge deduced by the systems discussed in Section 2.3.1 consisted of simple facts such as the type of a plant or the bag location of a particular item. In these simply applications, there was little need to concern ourselves with an abstract representation of the knowledge. However, in more complex domains, this is not case. **Knowledge representation** is the discipline that represents knowledge in a manner that facilitates drawing inference from the knowledge. In philosophy, ontology is the study of the nature of existence and what is real. It concerns what entities can be said to exist, how they can be categorized, and the relationships among the categories. In artificial intelligence, an **ontology** is a representation of knowledge as a set of concepts and relationships that exist among those concepts.

---

[1]The picture on this page was obtained from https://commons.wikimedia.org/wiki/File: Knowledge, _observation_and_reality.svg under the GNU Free Documentation License.

We introduce an ontology for representing certain knowledge called a semantic net. Then we discuss frames that can be used to represent the knowledge in a semantic net. Finally, we introduce nonmonotonic inference, which is an inference method that allows us to retract conclusions in light of new evidence.

4.1   Taxonomic Knowledge

Often the entities with which we reason can be arranged in a hierarchical structure or **taxonomy**. We can represent this taxonomy using first-order logic. For example, suppose we want to represent the relationships among all animals and their properties. We could proceed as follows. First we represent subset (subcategory) information:

$\forall x$ bird$(x) \Rightarrow$animal(x)

$\forall x$ canary$(x) \Rightarrow$bird(x)

$\forall x$ ostrich$(x) \Rightarrow$bird(x)

$\vdots$

Then we represent set (category) membership of entities:

bird(Tweety)

shark(Bruce)

$\vdots$

Finally, we represent properties of the sets (categories) and entities:

$\forall x$ animal$(x) \Rightarrow$has_skin(x)

$\forall x$ bird$(x) \Rightarrow$can_fly(x)

$\vdots$

Note that the members of a subset inherit properties associated with its superset. For example, birds have skin because birds are a subset of animals and animals have skin.

4.1.1   Semantic Nets

It becomes cumbersome representing the taxonomy with first-order logic and the representation is not very transparent. A **semantic net** is a graph structure for representing the same taxonomy. Figure 4.1 shows a subset of the semantic net representing the taxonomy for all organisms. Both sets (categories) and entities are represented by nodes in the network. There are three types of edges:

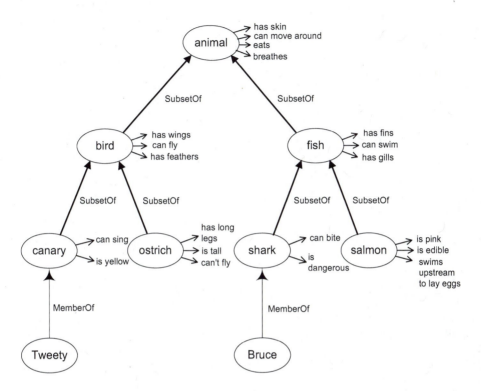

Figure 4.1 A semantic network.

1. An edge from a subset to a superset. For example, there is an edge from *bird* to *animal*.

2. An edge from an entity to the immediate set of which it is a member. For example, there is an edge from *Tweety* to *canary*.

3. An edge from an entity or set to one of its properties. For example, there is an edge from *bird* to *has wings* because birds have wings.

We have **inheritance** in a semantic network. That is, unless a node has an edge to a property, it inherits the property from its most recent ancestor that has an edge to that property. For example, the node *canary* does not have an edge to a property concerning flying. So it inherits that property from the node *bird*, which means canaries can fly. The node ostrich has an edge to the property that it can't fly; so it does not inherit that property from the node *bird*.

There are difficulties with the inheritance properties in semantic nets. Most notably, a node can inherit conflicting properties from two parent nodes. Consider the semantic network in Figure 4.2. Because Nixon is a Quaker, he inherits the property that he is a pacifist; and because he is a Republican, he inherits the conflicting property that he is not a pacifist. Because of this difficulty, some

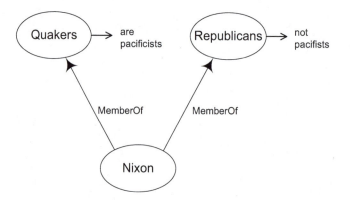

Figure 4.2 This semantic net entails the conflict that Nixon is a pacifist and is not a pacifist.

object-oriented programming languages such as Java do not allow multiple inheritance. Nonmonotonic logic, which is discussed in Section 4.3, addresses this difficulty by performing conflict resolution using prioritization.

4.1.2   Model of Human Organization of Knowledge

There is evidence that humans organize categorical knowledge in a semantic net. The semantic net in Figure 4.1 was taken from [Collins and Quillan, 1969]. That paper concerned reaction time studies in humans investigating how long it took humans to answer questions such as "is a canary yellow?" Their studies indicated that this question be answered more quickly than the question "can a canary fly?" In general, the closer the information is to the entity in the network, the more quickly the question can be answered. This supports the hypothesis that humans actually structure knowledge in this hierarchy because if fewer mental links needed to be traversed to retrieve the information, then the question should be answered more quickly. Exception handling supported this hypothesis. For example, subjects could answer "can an ostrich fly?" more quickly than they could answer "Does an ostrich have feathers?"

4.2   Frames

A **frame** is a data structure that can represent the knowledge in a semantic net. After showing the data structure, we present an example.

4.2.1   Frame Data Structure

The general structure of a frame is as follows:

```
(frame-name
     slot-name1: filler1;
     slot-name2: filler2;
          ⋮
)
```

Example 4.1 The first two frames of the frames representing the semantic net in Figure 4.1 are as follows:

(**animal**
     SupersetOf: **bird**;
     SupersetOf: **fish**;
     skin: has;
     mobile: yes;
     eats: yes;
     breathes: yes;
)

(**bird**
     SubsetOf: **animal**;
     SupersetOf: **canary**;
     SupersetOf: **ostrich**;
     wings: has;
     flies: yes;
     feathers: has;
)   ∎

Note in the previous example that we put frame names in bold face.

4.2.2   Planning a Trip Using Frames

Suppose a traveling salesperson is planning a round-trip that visits several cities. There are various components to the trip such as the means of travel, the cities visited, and the lodging, We develop frames to represent the components and show how they can be used to represent the plan for a trip.

We have the following general frames that are used to develop trips:

(**Trip**
     FirstStep: **TravelStep**;
     Traveler: human;
     BeginDate: date;
     EndDate: date;
     TotalCost: price;
)

```
(TripPart
      SupersetOf: TravelStep;
      SupersetOf: LodgingStay;
      BeginDate: date;
      EndDate: date;
      Cost: price;
      PaymentMethod: method;
)


(TravelStep
      SubsetOf: TripPart;
      Origin: city;
      Destination: city;
      OriginLodgingStay: LodgingStay;
      DestinationLodgingStay: LodgingStay;
      FormofTransportation: travelmeans;
      NextStep: TravelStep;
      PreviousStep: TravelStep;
)


(LodgingStay
      SubsetOf: TripPart;
      Place: city;
      Lodging: hotel;
      ArrivingTravelStep: TravelStep;
      DepartingTravelStep: TravelStep;
)
```

Note that TravelStep and LodgingStay are both subsets of TripPart. So they inherit the attributes in TripPart, namely BeginDate, EndDate, Cost, and PaymentMethod. Next we develop a simple trip that starts at the home city Chicago, visits Melbourne, and returns to Chicago.

```
(trip1
      MemberOf: Trip;
      FirstStep: TravelStep1;
      Traveler: Amit Patel;
      BeginDate: 06/22/2011;
      EndDate: 06/28/2011;
      TotalCost: $6000;
)
```

(TravelStep1
    MemberOf: **TravelStep**;
    BeginDate: 6/22/2011;
    EndDate: 6/23/2011;
    Cost: $1500;
    PaymentMethod: visa;
    Origin: Chicago;
    Destination: Melbourne;
    OriginLodgingStay: Null;
    DestinationLodgingStay: LodgingStay1;
    FormofTransportation: plane;
    NextStep: TravelStep2;
    PreviousStep: Null;
)

(TravelStep2
    MemberOf: **TravelStep**;
    BeginDate: 6/27/2011;
    EndDate: 6/28/2011;
    Cost: $2000;
    PaymentMethod: master card;
    Origin: Melbourne;
    Destination: Chicago;
    OriginLodgingStay: LodgingStay1;
    DestinationLodgingStay: Null;
    FormofTransportation: plane;
    NextStep: Null;
    PreviousStep: TravelStep1;
)

(LodgingStay1
    MemberOf: **LodgingStay**;
    BeginDate: 6/23/2011;
    EndDate: 6/27/2011;
    Cost: $2500;
    PaymentMethod: american express;
    Place: Melbourne;
    Lodging: Best Western;
    ArrivingTravelStep: TravelStep1;
    DepartingTravelStep: TravelStep2;
)

Figure 4.3 shows how the fillers in the frames link the frames into an organized plan for a trip. The previous example concerning planning a trip is based on a more complex example that appears in [Brachman and Levesque, 2004].

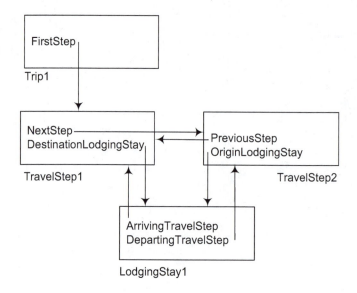

Figure 4.3 The links between the frames constituting a trip between Chicago and Melbourne.

4.3   Nonmonotonic Logic

Propositional logic and first-order logic arrive at certain conclusions and there is no mechanism for withdrawing or overriding conclusions. This is the **monotonicity** property. However, often conclusions reached by humans are only tentative, based on partial information, and they are retracted in the light of new evidence. For example, if we learn an entity is a bird, we conclude that it can fly. When we later learn that the entity is an ostrich, we withdraw the previous conclusion and deduce that the entity cannot fly. A logic that can systemize this reasoning is called **nonmonotonic**. We discuss such logic next. The other way to handle uncertain reasoning is to use probability theory, which is the focus of Part II of this text.

4.3.1   Circumscription

Circumscription was developed by McCarthy [1980] to formalize the assumption that everything is as expected unless we state otherwise. He introduced the notion by discussing the **cannibal-missionary** problem, which is as follows. Suppose there are three missionaries and three cannibals on one bank of a river, and they need to cross the river using a two-passenger boat. However, the number of cannibals on each bank can never outnumber the number of missionaries. McCarthy was not concerned with obtaining a solution to the problem, but rather with the following observation. Namely, there are a lot of details that are not stated. For example, does the boat have a leak that might make it sink, or, more relevantly, is there a bridge over which some individuals could walk to cross the river. There are many possible situations that could exist, but which are not stated, that could possibly affect the solution to the problem. The **circumscription assumption** is that no conditions change or are different than what is expected unless explicitly stated. In the current example, we assume that the only way to cross the river is by the two-passenger boat, and it will always make it reliably across.

Example 4.2 An example of a logical statement for circumscription is as follows:

$\forall x \ \text{bird}(x) \wedge \neg \ \text{abnormal}(x) \Rightarrow \text{flies}(x).$

The reasoner *circumscribes* the predicate *abnormal*, which means it is assumed to be false unless otherwise stated. So if we only know bird(Tweety), we deduce Tweety flies. However, suppose we include the following statement:

$\forall x \ \text{ostrich}(x) \Rightarrow \text{abnormal}(x).$

If we know both ostrich(Ralph) and bird(Ralph), we could not conclude that Ralph flies. ∎

Example 4.3 Suppose we have the following statements:

$\forall x \ \text{Quaker}(x) \wedge \neg \ \text{abnormal}_1(x) \Rightarrow \text{pacifist}(x)$

$\forall x \ \text{Republican}(x) \neg \ \text{abnormal}_2(x) \Rightarrow \neg \ \text{pacifist}(x)$

$\text{Republican(Nixon)} \wedge \text{Quaker(Nixon)}.$

Without knowing whether abnormal$_1$(Nixon) or abnormal$_2$(Nixon) is true, we would conclude that he is pacifist and that he is not a pacifist. In this case we could have the reasoner draw no conclusion about pacifism, or we could employ **prioritized circumscription** in which we give priority to being Quaker or to being a Republican. If we give the priority to the latter, we conclude that Nixon is not a pacifist. ∎

A formal description of circumscription appears in [Lifschitz, 1994].

4.3.2 Default Logic

Default logic employs rules of the form "in the absence of information to the contrary, assume...." Reiter [1980] provides a formalization of default logic and argues that default reasoning is of paramount importance to knowledge representation and reasoning. We provide an informal introduction next.

Default logic derives conclusions if they are consistent with the current state of the knowledge base. A typical rule in default logic is as follows:

$$\frac{\text{bird}(x)\colon \text{flies}(x)}{\text{flies}(x)} \quad .$$

This rule says that if bird(x) is true for a particular entity x, then we can conclude flies(x) for that entity as long as there is nothing in the knowledge base that contradicts flies(x). For example, if we learn bird(Tweety), then we can conclude flies(Tweety) as long as there is nothing in the knowledge base stating flies(Tweety) is not true. However, if $\neg$flies(Tweety) is in the knowledge base, then we cannot draw this conclusion.

The following is the general form of a default rule:

$$\frac{A\colon B_1, B_2, ..., B_n}{C} \quad ,$$

where A, B_i, and C are formulas in first-order logic. A is called the **prerequisite**; B_1, B_2, ..., and B_n are called the **consistent conditions**; and C is called the **consequent**. If any of the B_i can be proven false, then we cannot conclude C from A; otherwise we can.

A **default theory** is a pair (D, W), where D is a set of default rules and W is a set of sentences in first-order logic.

Example 4.4 The following is a default theory. Let D be as follows:

$$\frac{\text{bird}(x)\colon \text{flies}(x)}{\text{flies}(x)} \quad .$$

and

$$W = \{\text{bird(Tweety)}\}. \qquad \blacksquare$$

An **extension** of a default theory is a maximal set of consequences of the theory. That is, an extension consists of the statements in W and a set of conclusions that can be drawn using the rules such that no additional conclusions can be drawn. The only extension of the theory in Example 4.4 is as follows:

$$\{\text{bird(Tweety)}, \text{flies(Tweety)}\}.$$

Example 4.5 Let D be as follows:

$$\frac{\text{Quaker}(x)\colon \text{pacifist}(x)}{\text{pacifist}(x)}$$

$$\frac{\text{Republican}(x)\colon \neg\text{pacifist}(x)}{\neg\text{pacifist}(x)}$$

and

$W = \{\text{Quaker(Nixon)}, \text{Republican(Nixon)}\}$.

Then we have the following two extensions:

$\{\text{Quaker(Nixon)}, \text{Republican(Nixon)}, \text{pacifist(Nixon)}\}$

$\{\text{Quaker(Nixon)}, \text{Republican(Nixon)}, \neg\text{pacifist(Nixon)}\}$

As was the case for circumscription, prioritizing rules can give one of these extensions preference over the other. ∎

4.3.3 Difficulties

A difficulty with nonmonotonic logic is revising a set of conclusions when knowledge changes. For example, if we used sentence A to infer B, then removing A means we must remove B (unless B can be concluded from other sentences) and also removing every conclusion based on B. Truth maintenance systems ([Doyle, 1979]; [Goodwin, 1982]) were developed to address this problem.

Another problem with nonmonotonic logic is that it is difficult to base a decision on conclusions reached via this formalism. The conclusions are tentative and can be retracted in light of new evidence. For example, suppose we conclude a patient has metastatic cancer. What decision should we make that maximizes the benefit (utility) of the patient? We do not really know the likelihood of cancer; rather it is just our default conclusion based on current evidence. This problem is addressed using probability and maximum utility theory in Example 8.15.

4.4 Discussion and Further Reading

Initially artificial intelligence researchers were more interested in problem representation than knowledge representation [Amarel, 1968]. However, in the 1970s, researchers became interested in developing expert systems, which are knowledge based. Expert systems were introduced in Section 2.3.1, and in Section 2.4 we mentioned XCON [McDermott, 1982], which is a well-known early expert system. Another successful early expert systems was DENDRAL [Feigenbaum et al., 1971], which analyzed spectrographic data obtained from a substance, and then determined the substance's molecular structure. It performed as well as expert chemists.

Very-large-scale ontologies are being developed. Perhaps one of the most well-known is Cyc [Lenat, 1998], which is an artificial intelligence project started in 1984 by Douglas Lenat. The project's goal was to assemble a comprehensive ontology of common sense knowledge.

> OpenCyc is the open source version of the Cyc technology, the world's largest and most complete general knowledge base and common sense reasoning engine. OpenCyc contains the full set of (nonproprietary) Cyc terms as well as millions of assertions.

— http://www.cyc.com/cyc/opencyc/

Three methodologies for handling nonmonotonic inference, namely circumscription [McCarthy and Hayes, 1969], default logic [Reiter, 1991], and modal nonmonotonic logic [McDermott and Doyle, 1980], are discussed and compared in [Delgrande and Schaub, 2003].

EXERCISES

Section 4.1

Exercise 4.1 Develop a semantic set that represents some closed classification domain such as the set of all automobiles, or the set of all professional sports teams.

Exercise 4.2 Provide an explanation for why humans can answer the question "is a canary yellow?" more quickly than the question "can a canary fly?"

Section 4.2

Exercise 4.3 Example 4.1 showed two frames of the frames representing the semantic net in Figure 4.1. Create the remaining frames.

Exercise 4.4 In Section 4.2.2 we developed a plan for a trip between Chicago and Melbourne using frames. Again using frames, develop a plan for a trip that starts in Chicago, visits Los Angeles, visits Melbourne, and then returns to Chicago.

Section 4.3

Exercise 4.5 Ordinarily, football players are big. However, place kickers are usually small. Linemen are always big. Sam is both a place kicker and a lineman. Represent this situation using both circumscription and default logic. Should we give priority to Sam being a place kicker or a lineman?

Exercise 4.6 Consider the following piece of fictitious medical knowledge. Ordinarily, an influenza virus results in a temperature. However, if a person is young, swine flu does not result in a temperature. Joe is young and has swine flu. Try to represent this situation using both circumscription and default logic.

Part II

Probabilistic Intelligence

Chapter 5

Probability

As discussed in Chapter 2, it is reasonable to model a good deal of human reasoning under certainty using logic. This model led to the development of rule-based systems that use the inference engines forward chaining and backward chaining. For example, it is reasonable to postulate that Mary the botanist has the following rule or item of knowledge stored in her personal data bank of knowledge:

IF   stem is woody
THEN   type is tree.

Furthermore, if Mary were determining the family of a particular plant, it is plausible that she would reason in a way similar to the decision tree in Figure 2.2, which is the equivalent of backward chaining. That is, she would first ask questions that determined the type, then ones that determined the class, and finally ones that determined the family.

To handle uncertain reference, researchers tried staying in the logical framework by developing nonmonotonic logics. As discussed in Section 4.3.3, there are a number of difficulties with this approach. Another avenue explored by researchers was to remain in the rule-based or logical framework when modeling uncertain inference, but to augment the rules with numeric certainty factors [Buchanan and Shortliffe, 1984] or likelihood ratios [Duda et al., 1976]. For example, the MYCIN system [Buchanan and Shortliffe, 1984] was designed to diagnose bacterial infection while reasoning under uncertainty. A typical rule in MYCIN is as follows:

IF	the organism grows in clumps
AND	the organism grows in chains
AND	the organism grows in pairs
THEN	the organism is streptococcus with certainty .7

The **certainty factor** (in this case .7) is a number between -1 and 1. Certainty factors greater than 0 increase our belief in the conclusion, and ones less than 0 decrease our belief. So if we find that the organism grows in clumps, chains, and pairs, we become .7 certain that it is streptococcus. Suppose now that a second rule makes us .6 certain that the organism is streptococcus. We need to find the combined certainty due to these two rules. Two certainty factors are combined using the following formula:

$$C_{12} = \begin{cases} C_1 + C_2(1 - |C_1|) & C_1 \text{ and } C_2 \text{ both positive or both negative} \\ \dfrac{C_1 + C_2}{1 - \min(|C_1|, |C_2|)} & \text{one of } C_1 \text{ and } C_2 \text{ positive, the other negative} \end{cases}$$

So when $C_1 = .7$ and $C_2 = .6$, we have that

$$C_{12} = C_1 + C_2(1 - |C_1|) = .7 + .6(1 - |.7|) = .88.$$

If the second rule disconfirms streptococcus with $C_2 = -.6$, we have that

$$C_{12} = \frac{C_1 + C_2}{1 - \min(C_1, C_2)} = \frac{.7 + (-.6)}{1 - \min(|.7|, |-.6|)} = .25.$$

The scheme works okay when each rule by itself describes a relationship between the antecedent and the conclusion. However, consider the following now-classical example introduced in [Pearl, 1986]. Suppose that in the past few years, Mr. Holmes has noticed that frequently earthquakes have caused his burglar alarm to sound. The burglar alarm concerns his home but it is wired sound in his office, which is some distance from his home. Presently, he is sitting in his office, and the burglar alarm sounds. He then rushes home, assuming that there is a good chance that his residence has been burglarized. On the way home, he hears on the radio that there has been an earthquake. He then reasons that the earthquake may well have triggered the alarm, and therefore it is much less likely that he has been burglarized. Psychologists call this type of reasoning **discounting**.

Let's try to model this situation using rules. Denote the following propositions:

A: Mr. Holmes' burglar alarm sounds.

B: Mr. Holmes' residence is burglarized.

E: There is an earthquake.

Using the rule-based approach, we might assign the following certainty factors:

IF   A
THEN   B with certainty .8

IF   E
THEN   B with certainty −.4

When Mr. Holmes learns that his alarm has sounded, he becomes .8 certain that he has been burglarized. When he later learns of the earthquake, he combines the certainty factor .8 with the certainty factor −.4 as follows:

$$\frac{.8 + (-.4)}{1 - \min(|.8|, |-.4|)} = .67.$$

So his certainty in having been burglarized is reduce to .67.

A difficulty with this model is that E only decreases the certainty in B when we already know A. That is, if the alarm had not sounded, Mr. Holmes would not conclude that it is extremely unlikely that he has been burglarized today (i.e. more unlikely than on any other day) after he heard there was an earthquake. So we cannot have the rule above concerning earthquakes. Instead, we need rules with multiple premises in the antecedent as follows:

IF   A ∧ E
THEN   B with certainty .67

IF   A ∧ ¬E
THEN   B with certainty .85

Note that when we know A and ¬E, the certainty is higher than when we know only A because we know for sure the other cause is not present. If we wanted to represent additional causes such as an individual being seen lurking around the house, we would need to consider more combinations of assertions in the antecedent.

Another problem with this rule-based approach is that it only allows us to do inference in one direction. That is, if we wanted to model how Mr. Holmes would reason if he learned that he had been burglarized, we would need the following additional rule:

IF   B
THEN   A with certainty .7

There is no clear connection between the certainty factor in this rule and the rules that do inference in the other direction.

In addition to being cumbersome and complex, this rule-based representation of uncertain knowledge and reasoning does not seem to model how humans reason very well. That is, it seems unreasonable to postulate that a human mind has millions of rules, each representing a possibly complex uncertain relationship. Neapolitan [1989] discusses this matter in more detail. Pearl [1986] made the more reasonable conjecture that humans identify local probabilistic causal relationships between individual propositions, and that the change in the certainty of one proposition changes our certainty in a related one, which in turn changes our certainty in propositions related to that one. If Mr. Holmes' knowledge is structured with causal edges between propositions, we can represent his knowledge with a causal network, and we can model his reasoning by traversing links in this network. Regardless of how well this model represents human reasoning, it helped give rise to the field we now call *Bayesian networks*, which has arguably become the most important architecture for reasoning with uncertainty in artificial intelligence. We discuss the causal network representation of Mr. Holmes' reasoning and introduce Bayesian networks in the next chapter. In this chapter we review probability. Bayesian networks are based on probability theory.

5.1 Probability Basics

After defining probability spaces, we discuss conditional probability, independence and conditional independence, and Bayes' theorem.

5.1.1 Probability Spaces

You may recall using probability in situations such as drawing the top card from a deck of playing cards, tossing a coin, or drawing a ball from an urn. We call the process of drawing the top card or tossing a coin an **experiment**. Probability theory has to do with experiments that have a set of distinct **outcomes**. The set of all outcomes is called the **sample space** or **population**. Mathematicians ordinarily say sample space, while social scientists ordinarily say population. We will say sample space. In this simple review, we assume that the sample space is finite. Any subset of a sample space is called an **event**. A subset containing exactly one element is called an **elementary event**.

Example 5.1 Suppose we have the experiment of drawing the top card from an ordinary deck of cards. Then the set

$$\mathsf{E} = \{\text{jack of hearts, jack of clubs, jack of spades, jack of diamonds}\}$$

is an event, and the set

$$\mathsf{F} = \{\text{jack of hearts}\}$$

is an elementary event.   ∎

The meaning of an event is that one of the elements of the subset is the outcome of the experiment. In the preceding example, the meaning of the event E is that the card drawn is one of the four jacks, and the meaning of the elementary event F is that the card is the jack of hearts.

We articulate our certainty that an event contains the outcome of the experiment with a real number between 0 and 1. This number is called the **probability** of the event. When the sample space is finite, a probability of 0 means we are certain the event does not contain the outcome, whereas a probability of 1 means we are certain it does. Values in between represent varying degrees of belief. The following definition formally defines probability for a finite sample space.

Definition 5.1 Suppose we have a sample space Ω containing n distinct elements; that is,

$$\Omega = \{e_1, e_2, \ldots, e_n\}.$$

A function that assigns a real number $P(E)$ to each event $E \subseteq \Omega$ is called a **probability function** on the set of subsets of Ω if it satisfies the following conditions:

1. $0 \leq P(e_i) \leq 1$ for $1 \leq i \leq n$

2. $P(e_1) + P(e_2) + \ldots + P(e_n) = 1$

3. For each event that is not an elementary event, $P(E)$ is the sum of the probabilities of the elementary events whose outcomes are in E. For example, if

$$E = \{e_3, e_6, e_8\},$$

then

$$P(E) = P(e_3) + P(e_6) + P(e_8)$$

The pair (Ω, P) is called a **probability space.**◆

Because probability is defined as a function whose domain is a set of sets, we should write $P(\{e_i\})$ instead of $P(e_i)$ when denoting the probability of an elementary event. However, for the sake of simplicity, we do not do this. In the same way, we write $P(e_3, e_6, e_8)$ instead of $P(\{e_3, e_6, e_8\})$.

The most straightforward way to assign probabilities is to use the **Principle of Indifference**, which says that outcomes are to be considered equiprobable if we have no reason to expect one over the other. According to this principle, when there are n elementary events, each has probability equal to $1/n$.

Example 5.2 Let the experiment be tossing a coin. Then the sample space is

$$\Omega = \{\text{heads}, \text{tails}\},$$

and, according to the Principle of Indifference, we assign

$$P(\text{heads}) = P(\text{tails}) = .5.$$

■

We stress that there is nothing in the definition of a probability space that says we must assign the value of .5 to the probabilities of heads and tails. We could assign $P(\text{heads}) = .7$ and $P(\text{tails}) = .3$. However, if we have no reason to expect one outcome over the other, we give them the same probability.

Example 5.3 Let the experiment be drawing the top card from a deck of 52 cards. Then Ω contains the faces of the 52 cards, and, according to the Principle of Indifference, we assign $P(e) = 1/52$ for each $e \in \Omega$. For example,

$$P(\text{jack of hearts}) = \frac{1}{52}.$$

The event

$$E = \{\text{jack of hearts, jack of clubs, jack of spades, jack of diamonds}\}$$

means that the card drawn is a jack. Its probability is

$$\begin{aligned}
P(E) &= P(\text{jack of hearts}) + P(\text{jack of clubs}) + \\
&\quad P(\text{jack of spades}) + P(\text{jack of diamonds}) \\
&= \frac{1}{52} + \frac{1}{52} + \frac{1}{52} + \frac{1}{52} = \frac{1}{13}.
\end{aligned}$$

∎

We have Theorem 5.1 concerning probability spaces. Its proof is left as an exercise.

Theorem 5.1 Let (Ω, P) be a probability space. Then

1. $P(\Omega) = 1$.

2. $0 \leq P(\mathsf{E}) \leq 1$ for every $\mathsf{E} \subseteq \Omega$.

3. For every two subsets E and F of Ω such that $\mathsf{E} \cap \mathsf{F} = \varnothing$,

$$P(\mathsf{E} \cup \mathsf{F}) = P(\mathsf{E}) + P(\mathsf{F}),$$

where $\varnothing$ denotes the empty set.

Example 5.4 Suppose we draw the top card from a deck of cards. Denote by Queen the set containing the four queens and by King the set containing the four kings. Then

$$P(\mathsf{Queen} \cup \mathsf{King}) = P(\mathsf{Queen}) + P(\mathsf{King}) = \frac{1}{13} + \frac{1}{13} = \frac{2}{13}$$

because $\mathsf{Queen} \cap \mathsf{King} = \varnothing$. Next, denote by Spade the set containing the 13 spades. The sets Queen and Spade are not disjoint, so their probabilities are not additive. However, it is not hard to prove that, in general,

$$P(\mathsf{E} \cup \mathsf{F}) = P(\mathsf{E}) + P(\mathsf{F}) - P(\mathsf{E} \cap \mathsf{F}).$$

So

$$P(\text{Queen} \cup \text{Spade}) = P(\text{Queen}) + P(\text{Spade}) - P(\text{Queen} \cap \text{Spade})$$
$$= \frac{1}{13} + \frac{1}{4} - \frac{1}{52} = \frac{4}{13}.$$

∎

5.1.2 Conditional Probability and Independence

We start with a definition.

Definition 5.2 Let E and F be events such that $P(\mathsf{F}) \neq 0$. Then the **conditional probability** of E given F, denoted $P(\mathsf{E}|\mathsf{F})$, is given by

$$P(\mathsf{E}|\mathsf{F}) = \frac{P(\mathsf{E} \cap \mathsf{F})}{P(\mathsf{F})}. \blacklozenge$$

We can gain intuition for this definition by considering probabilities that are assigned using the Principle of Indifference. In this case, $P(\mathsf{E}|\mathsf{F})$, as defined previously, is the ratio of the number of items in $\mathsf{E} \cap \mathsf{F}$ to the number of items in F. We show this as follows: Let n be the number of items in the sample space, n_F be the number of items in F, and n_EF be the number of items in $\mathsf{E} \cap \mathsf{F}$. Then

$$\frac{P(\mathsf{E} \cap \mathsf{F})}{P(\mathsf{F})} = \frac{n_\mathsf{EF}/n}{n_\mathsf{F}/n} = \frac{n_\mathsf{EF}}{n_\mathsf{F}},$$

which is the ratio of the number of items in $\mathsf{E} \cap \mathsf{F}$ to the number of items in F. As far as the meaning is concerned, $P(\mathsf{E}|\mathsf{F})$ is our belief that event E contains the outcome (i.e., E occurs) when we already know that event F contains the outcome (i.e. F occurred).

Example 5.5 Again, consider drawing the top card from a deck of cards. Let Jack be the set of the four jacks, RedRoyalCard be the set of the six red royal cards,[1] and Club be the set of the thirteen clubs. Then

$$P(\text{Jack}) = \frac{4}{52} = \frac{1}{13}$$

$$P(\text{Jack}|\text{RedRoyalCard}) = \frac{P(\text{Jack} \cap \text{RedRoyalCard})}{P(\text{RedRoyalCard})} = \frac{2/52}{6/52} = \frac{1}{3}$$

$$P(\text{Jack}|\text{Club}) = \frac{P(\text{Jack} \cap \text{Club})}{P(\text{Club})} = \frac{1/52}{13/52} = \frac{1}{13}.$$

∎

Notice in the previous example that $P(\text{Jack}|\text{Club}) = P(\text{Jack})$. This means that finding out the card is a club does not change the likelihood that it is a jack. We say that the two events are independent in this case, which is formalized in the following definition.

---

[1] A royal card is a jack, queen, or king.

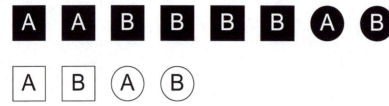

Figure 5.1 Using the Principle of Indifference, we assign a probability of 1/13 to each object.

Definition 5.3 Two events E and F are **independent** if one of the following holds:

1. $P(E|F) = P(E)$ and $P(E) \neq 0$, $P(F) \neq 0$

2. $P(E) = 0$ or $P(F) = 0$◆

Notice that the definition states that the two events are independent even though it is in terms of the conditional probability of E given F. The reason is that independence is symmetric. That is, if $P(E) \neq 0$ and $P(F) \neq 0$, then $P(E|F) = P(E)$ if and only if $P(F|E) = P(F)$. It is straightforward to prove that E and F are independent if and only if $P(E \cap F) = P(E)P(F)$.

If you have previously studied probability, you should have already been introduced to the concept of independence. However, a generalization of independence, called **conditional independence**, is not covered in many introductory texts. This concept is important to the applications discussed in this book. We discuss it next.

Definition 5.4 Two events E and F are **conditionally independent** given G if $P(G) \neq 0$ and one of the following holds:

1. $P(E|F \cap G) = P(E|G)$ and $P(E|G) \neq 0$, $P(F|G) \neq 0$

2. $P(E|G) = 0$ or $P(F|G) = 0$◆

Notice that this definition is identical to the definition of independence except that everything is conditional on G. The definition entails that E and F are independent once we know that the outcome is in G. The next example illustrates this.

Example 5.6 Let Ω be the set of all objects in Figure 5.1. Using the Principle of Indifference, we assign a probability of 1/13 to each object. Let Black be the set of all black objects, White be the set of all white objects, Square be the set of all square objects, and A be the set of all objects containing an A. We then have that

$$P(A) = \frac{5}{13}$$

$$P(A|\text{Square}) = \frac{3}{8}.$$

So A and **Square** are not independent. However,

$$P(A|\text{Black}) = \frac{3}{9} = \frac{1}{3}$$

$$P(A|\text{Square} \cap \text{Black}) = \frac{2}{6} = \frac{1}{3}.$$

We see that A and **Square** are conditionally independent given **Black**. Furthermore,

$$P(A|\text{White}) = \frac{2}{4} = \frac{1}{2}$$

$$P(A|\text{Square} \cap \text{White}) = \frac{1}{2}.$$

So A and **Square** are also conditionally independent given **White**. ∎

Next, we discuss an important rule involving conditional probabilities. Suppose we have n events $E_1, E_2, \ldots, E_n$ such that

$$E_i \cap E_j = \varnothing \qquad \text{for } i \neq j$$

and

$$E_1 \cup E_2 \cup \ldots \cup E_n = \Omega.$$

Such events are called **mutually exclusive and exhaustive**. Then the **Law of Total Probability** says that for any other event F,

$$P(F) = P(F \cap E_1) + P(F \cap E_2) + \cdots + P(F \cap E_n). \tag{5.1}$$

You are asked to prove this rule in the exercises. If $P(E_i) \neq 0$, then

$$P(F \cap E_i) = P(F|E_i)P(E_i).$$

Therefore, if $P(E_i) \neq 0$ for all i, the law is often applied in the following form:

$$P(F) = P(F|E_1)P(E_1) + P(F|E_2)P(E_2) + \cdots + P(F|E_n)P(E_n). \tag{5.2}$$

Example 5.7 Suppose we have the objects discussed in Example 5.6. Then, according to the Law of Total Probability,

$$P(A) = P(A|\text{Black})P(\text{Black}) + P(A|\text{White})P(\text{White})$$

$$= \left(\frac{1}{3}\right)\left(\frac{9}{13}\right) + \left(\frac{1}{2}\right)\left(\frac{4}{13}\right) = \frac{5}{13}.$$

∎

5.1.3   Bayes' Theorem

We can compute conditional probabilities of events of interest from known probabilities using the following theorem.

Theorem 5.2 (**Bayes**) Given two events E and F such that $P(E) \neq 0$ and $P(F) \neq 0$, we have

$$P(E|F) = \frac{P(F|E)P(E)}{P(F)}. \tag{5.3}$$

Furthermore, given n mutually exclusive and exhaustive events $E_1, E_2, \ldots, E_n$ such that $P(E_i) \neq 0$ for all i, we have for $1 \leq i \leq n$,

$$P(E_i|F) = \frac{P(F|E_i)P(E_i)}{P(F|E_1)P(E_1) + P(F|E_2)P(E_2) + \cdots P(F|E_n)P(E_n)}. \tag{5.4}$$

Proof. To obtain Equality 5.3, we first use the definition of conditional probability as follows:

$$P(E|F) = \frac{P(E \cap F)}{P(F)} \qquad \text{and} \qquad P(F|E) = \frac{P(F \cap E)}{P(E)}.$$

Next we multiply each of these equalities by the denominator on its right side to show that

$$P(E|F)P(F) = P(F|E)P(E)$$

because they both equal $P(E \cap F)$. Finally, we divide this last equality by $P(F)$ to obtain our result.

To obtain Equality 5.4, we place the expression for F, obtained using the Law of Total Probability (Equality 5.2), in the denominator of Equality 5.3. ■

Both of the formulas in the preceding theorem are called **Bayes' theorem** because the original version was developed by Thomas Bayes, published in 1763. The first enables us to compute $P(E|F)$ if we know $P(F|E)$, $P(E)$, and $P(F)$; the second enables us to compute $P(E_i|F)$ if we know $P(F|E_j)$ and $P(E_j)$ for $1 \leq j \leq n$. The next example illustrates the use of Bayes' theorem.

Example 5.8 Let Ω be the set of all objects in Figure 5.1, and assign each object a probability of $1/13$. Let A be the set of all objects containing an A, B be the set of all objects containing a B, and Black be the set of all black objects. Then, according to Bayes' theorem,

$$
\begin{aligned}
P(\text{Black}|\text{A}) &= \frac{P(\text{A}|\text{Black})P(\text{Black})}{P(\text{A}|\text{Black})P(\text{Black}) + P(\text{A}|\text{White})P(\text{White})} \\
&= \frac{\left(\frac{1}{3}\right)\left(\frac{9}{13}\right)}{\left(\frac{1}{3}\right)\left(\frac{9}{13}\right) + \left(\frac{1}{2}\right)\left(\frac{4}{13}\right)} = \frac{3}{5},
\end{aligned}
$$

which is the same value we get by computing $P(\text{Black}|\text{A})$ directly.   ■

In the previous example we can just as easily compute $P(\text{Black}|\text{A})$ directly. We will see a useful application of Bayes' theorem in Section 5.4.

5.2   Random Variables

In this section we present the formal definition and mathematical properties of a random variable. In Section 5.4 we show how they are developed in practice.

5.2.1   Probability Distributions of Random Variables

Definition 5.5 Given a probability space (Ω, P), a **random variable** X is a function whose domain is $\Omega.\blacklozenge$

The range of X is called the **space** of X.

Example 5.9 Let Ω contain all outcomes of a throw of a pair of six-sided dice, and let P assign $1/36$ to each outcome. Then Ω is the following set of ordered pairs:

$$\Omega = \{(1,1), (1,2), (1,3), (1,4), (1,5), (1,6), (2,1), (2,2), \ldots, (6,5), (6,6)\}.$$

Let the random variable X assign the sum of each ordered pair to that pair, and let the random variable Y assign *odd* to each pair of odd numbers and *even* to a pair if at least one number in that pair is an even number. The following table shows some of the values of X and Y.

e	$X(e)$	$Y(e)$
$(1,1)$	2	odd
$(1,2)$	3	even
...	...	...
$(2,1)$	3	even
...	...	...
$(6,6)$	12	even

The space of X is $\{2,3,4,5,6,7,8,9,10,11,12\}$, and that of Y is $\{$odd,even$\}$.
∎

For a random variable X, we use $X = x$ to denote the subset containing all elements $e \in \Omega$ that X maps to the value of x. That is,

$$X = x \quad \text{represents the event} \quad \{e \text{ such that } X(e) = x\}.$$

Note the difference between X and x: small x denotes any element in the space of X, whereas X is a function.

Example 5.10 Let Ω, P, and X be as in Example 5.9. Then

$$X = 3 \quad \text{represents the event} \quad \{(1,2), (2,1)\} \text{ and}$$

$$P(X = 3) = \frac{1}{18}.$$

Notice that

$$\sum_{x \in space(X)} P(X = x) = 1.$$

Example 5.11 Let Ω, P, and Y be as in Example 5.9. Then

$$\sum_{y \in space(Y)} P(Y = y) = P(Y = odd) + P(Y = even)$$

$$= \frac{9}{36} + \frac{27}{36} = 1.$$

∎

We call the values of $P(X = x)$ for all values x of X the **probability distribution** of the random variable X. When we are referring to the probability distribution of X, we write $P(X)$.

We often use x alone to represent the event $X = x$, and so we write $P(x)$ instead of $P(X = x)$ when we are referring to the probability that X has value x.

Example 5.12 Let Ω, P, and X be as in Example 5.9. Then if $x = 3$,

$$P(x) = P(X = x) = \frac{1}{18}.$$

∎

If we want to refer to all values of, for example, the random variables X, we sometimes write $P(X)$ instead of $P(X = x)$ or $P(x)$.

Example 5.13 Let Ω, P, and X be as in Example 5.9. Then for all values of X

$$P(X) > 1.$$

∎

Given two random variables X and Y, defined on the same sample space Ω, we use $X = x, Y = y$ to denote the subset containing all elements $e \in \Omega$ that are mapped both by X to x and by Y to y. That is,

$X = x, Y = y$ represents the event

$$\{e \text{ such that } X(e) = x\} \cap \{e \text{ such that } Y(e) = y\}.$$

Example 5.14 Let Ω, P, X, and Y be as in Example 5.9. Then

$X = 4, Y = odd$ represents the event $\{(1,3), (3,1)\}$,

and so

$$P(X = 4, Y = odd) = 1/18.$$

∎

We call $P(X = x, Y = y)$ the **joint probability distribution** of X and Y. If $\mathsf{A} = \{X, Y\}$, we also call this the joint probability distribution of A. Furthermore, we often just say *joint distribution* or *probability distribution*.

For brevity, we often use x, y to represent the event $X = x, Y = y$, and so we write $P(x, y)$ instead of $P(X = x, Y = y)$. This concept extends to three or more random variables. For example, $P(X = x, Y = y, Z = z)$ is the joint probability distribution function of the random variables X, Y, and Z, and we often write $P(x, y, z)$.

Example 5.15 Let Ω, P, X, and Y be as in Example 5.9. Then, if $x = 4$ and $y = $ odd,
$$P(x, y) = P(X = x, Y = y) = 1/18.$$

∎

Similar to the case of a single random variable, if we want to refer to all values of, for example, the random variables X and Y, we sometimes write $P(X, Y)$ instead of $P(X = x, Y = y)$ or $P(x, y)$.

Example 5.16 Let Ω, P, X, and Y be as in Example 5.9. It is left as an exercise to show that for all values of x and y, we have
$$P(X = x, Y = y) < 1/2.$$

For example, as shown in Example 5.14,
$$P(X = 4, Y = \text{odd}) = 1/18 < 1/2.$$

We can restate this fact as follows: for all values of X and Y, we have that
$$P(X, Y) < 1/2.$$

∎

If, for example, we let $\mathsf{A} = \{X, Y\}$ and $\mathsf{a} = \{x, y\}$, we use
$$\mathsf{A} = \mathsf{a} \qquad \text{to represent} \qquad X = x, Y = y,$$
and we often write $P(\mathsf{a})$ instead of $P(\mathsf{A} = \mathsf{a})$.

Example 5.17 Let Ω, P, X, and Y be as in Example 5.9. If $\mathsf{A} = \{X, Y\}$, $\mathsf{a} = \{x, y\}$, $x = 4$, and $y = $ odd, then
$$P(\mathsf{A} = \mathsf{a}) = P(X = x, Y = y) = 1/18.$$

∎

Recall the Law of Total Probability (Equalities 5.1 and 5.2). For two random variables X and Y, these equalities are as follows:
$$P(X = x) = \sum_y P(X = x, Y = y). \tag{5.5}$$

$$P(X = x) = \sum_{y} P(X = x | Y = y) P(Y = y). \qquad (5.6)$$

It is left as an exercise to show this.

Example 5.18 Let Ω, P, X, and Y be as in Example 5.9. Then, owing to Equality 5.5,

$$
\begin{aligned}
P(X = 4) &= \sum_{y} P(X = 4, Y = y) \\
&= P(X = 4, Y = odd) + P(X = 4, Y = even) = \frac{1}{18} + \frac{1}{36} = \frac{1}{12}.
\end{aligned}
$$

■

Example 5.19 Again, let Ω, P, X, and Y be as in Example 5.9. Then, due to Equality 5.6,

$$
\begin{aligned}
P(X = 4) &= \sum_{y} P(X = x | Y = y) P(Y = y) \\
&= P(X = 4 | Y = odd) P(Y = odd) + \\
&\quad P(X = 4 | Y = even) P(Y = even) \\
&= \frac{2}{9} \times \frac{9}{36} + \frac{1}{27} \times \frac{27}{36} = \frac{1}{12}.
\end{aligned}
$$

■

In Equality 5.5 the probability distribution $P(X = x)$ is called the **marginal probability distribution** of X relative to the joint distribution $P(X = x, Y = y)$ because it is obtained using a process similar to adding across a row or column in a table of numbers. This concept also extends in a straightforward way to three or more random variables. For example, if we have a joint distribution $P(X = x, Y = y, Z = z)$ of X, Y, and Z, the marginal distribution $P(X = x, Y = y)$ of X and Y is obtained by summing over all values of Z. If $A = \{X, Y\}$, we also call this the **marginal probability distribution** of A.

The next example reviews the concepts covered so far concerning random variables.

Example 5.20 Let Ω be a set of 12 individuals, and let P assign $1/12$ to each individual. Suppose the genders, heights, and wages of the individuals are as follows:

Case	Gender	Height (inches)	Wage ($)
1	female	64	30,000
2	female	64	30,000
3	female	64	40,000
4	female	64	40,000
5	female	68	30,000
6	female	68	40,000
7	male	64	40,000
8	male	64	50,000
9	male	68	40,000
10	male	68	50,000
11	male	70	40,000
12	male	70	50,000

Let the random variables G, H, and W, respectively, assign the gender, height, and wage of an individual to that individual. Then the probability distributions of the three random variables are as follows (recall that, for example, $P(g)$ represents $P(G = g)$).

g	$P(g)$
female	1/2
male	1/2

h	$P(h)$
64	1/2
68	1/3
70	1/6

w	$P(w)$
30,000	1/4
40,000	1/2
50,000	1/4

The joint distribution of G and H is as follows:

g	h	$P(g, h)$
female	64	1/3
female	68	1/6
female	70	0
male	64	1/6
male	68	1/6
male	70	1/6

The following table also shows the joint distribution of G and H and illustrates that the individual distributions can be obtained by summing the joint distribution over all values of the other variable.

g \ h	64	68	70	Distribution of G
female	1/3	1/6	0	1/2
male	1/6	1/6	1/6	1/2
Distribution of H	1/2	1/3	1/6	

The table that follows shows the first few values in the joint distribution of G, H, and W. There are eighteen values in all, many of which are 0.

g	h	w	$P(g, h, w)$
female	64	30,000	1/6
female	64	40,000	1/6
female	64	50,000	0
female	68	30,000	1/12
...	...	...	...

∎

We close with the **chain rule** for random variables, which says that given n random variables $X_1, X_2, \ldots, X_n$, defined on the same sample space Ω,

$$P(x_1, x_2, \ldots, x_n) = P(x_n | x_{n-1}, x_{n-2}, \ldots, x_1) \cdots \times P(x_2 | x_1) \times P(x_1)$$

whenever $P(x_1, x_2, \ldots, x_n) \neq 0$. It is straightforward to prove this rule using the rule for conditional probability.

Example 5.21 Suppose we have the random variables in Example 5.20. Then, according to the chain rule for all values g, h, and w of G, H, and W,

$$P(g, h, w) = P(w | h, g) P(h | g) P(g).$$

There are eight combinations of values of the three random variables. The table that follows shows that the equality holds for two of the combinations.

g	h	w	$P(g, h, w)$	$P(w\|h, g)P(h\|g)P(g)$
female	64	30,000	$\frac{1}{6}$	$\left(\frac{1}{2}\right)\left(\frac{2}{3}\right)\left(\frac{1}{2}\right) = \frac{1}{6}$
female	64	40,000	$\frac{1}{12}$	$\left(\frac{1}{2}\right)\left(\frac{1}{3}\right)\left(\frac{1}{2}\right) = \frac{1}{12}$

It is left as an exercise to show that the equality holds for the other six combinations. ∎

5.2.2 Independence of Random Variables

The notion of independence extends naturally to random variables.

Definition 5.6 Suppose we have a probability space (Ω, P) and two random variables X and Y defined on Ω. Then X and Y are **independent** if, for all values x of X and y of Y, the events $X = x$ and $Y = y$ are independent. When this is the case, we write

$$I_P(X, Y),$$

where I_P stands for independent in P.♦

Example 5.22 Let Ω be the set of all cards in an ordinary deck, and let P assign 1/52 to each card. Define random variables as follows:

Variable	Value	Outcomes Mapped to This Value
R	r_1	All royal cards
	r_2	All nonroyal cards
S	s_1	All spades
	s_2	All nonspades

Then the random variables R and S are independent. That is,

$$I_P(R, S).$$

To show this, we need show for all values of r and s that

$$P(r|s) = P(r).$$

The following table shows that this is the case.

s	r	$P(r)$	$P(r|s)$
s_1	r_1	$\frac{12}{52} = \frac{3}{13}$	$\frac{3}{13}$
s_1	r_2	$\frac{40}{52} = \frac{10}{13}$	$\frac{10}{13}$
s_2	r_1	$\frac{12}{52} = \frac{3}{13}$	$\frac{9}{39} = \frac{3}{13}$
s_2	r_2	$\frac{40}{52} = \frac{10}{13}$	$\frac{30}{39} = \frac{10}{13}$

■

The concept of conditional independence also extends naturally to random variables.

Definition 5.7 Suppose we have a probability space (Ω, P) and three random variables X, Y, and Z defined on Ω. Then X and Y are **conditionally independent** given Z if for all values x of X, y of Y, and z of Z, whenever $P(z) \neq 0$, the events $X = x$ and $Y = y$ are conditionally independent given the event $Z = z$. When this is the case, we write

$$I_P(X, Y|Z). \blacklozenge$$

Example 5.23 Let Ω be the set of all objects in Figure 5.1, and let P assign $1/13$ to each object. Define random variables S (for shape), L (for letter), and C (for color) as follows:

Variable	Value	Outcomes Mapped to This Value
L	l_1	All objects containing an A
	l_2	All objects containing a B
S	s_1	All square objects
	s_2	All circular objects
C	c_1	All black objects
	c_2	All white objects

Then L and S are conditionally independent given C. That is,

$$I_P(L, S|C).$$

To show this, we need to show for all values of l, s, and c that

$$P(l|s, c) = P(l|c).$$

There are a total of eight combinations of the three variables. The table that follows shows that the equality holds for two of the combinations:

c	s	l	$P(l|s,c)$	$P(l|c)$
c_1	s_1	l_1	$\frac{2}{6} = \frac{1}{3}$	$\frac{3}{9} = \frac{1}{3}$
c_1	s_1	l_2	$\frac{4}{6} = \frac{2}{3}$	$\frac{6}{9} = \frac{2}{3}$

It is left as an exercise to show that it holds for the other combinations. ∎

Independence and conditional independence can also be defined for sets of random variables.

Definition 5.8 Suppose we have a probability space (Ω, P) and two sets A and B containing random variables defined on Ω. Let a and b be sets of values of the random variables in A and B, respectively. The sets A and B are said to be **independent** if, for all values of the variables in the sets a and b, the events A = a and B = b are independent. When this is the case, we write

$$I_P(\mathsf{A}, \mathsf{B}),$$

where I_P stands for independent in P.♦

Example 5.24 Let Ω be the set of all cards in an ordinary deck, and let P assign $1/52$ to each card. Define random variables as follows:

Variable	Value	Outcomes Mapped to This Value
R	r_1	All royal cards
	r_2	All nonroyal cards
T	t_1	All tens and jacks
	t_2	All cards that are neither tens nor jacks
S	s_1	All spades
	s_2	All nonspades

Then the sets $\{R, T\}$ and $\{S\}$ are independent. That is,

$$I_P(\{R, T\}, \{S\}). \tag{5.7}$$

To show this, we need to show for all values of r, t, and s that

$$P(r, t|s) = P(r, t).$$

There are eight combinations of values of the three random variables. The table that follows shows that the equality holds for two of the combinations.

s	r	t	$P(r,t|s)$	$P(r,t)$
s_1	r_1	t_1	$\frac{1}{13}$	$\frac{4}{52} = \frac{1}{13}$
s_1	r_1	t_2	$\frac{2}{13}$	$\frac{8}{52} = \frac{2}{13}$

It is left as an exercise to show that it holds for the other combinations. ∎

When a set contains a single variable, we do not ordinarily show the braces. For example, we write Independency 5.7 as

$$I_P(\{R,T\}, S).$$

Definition 5.9 Suppose we have a probability space (Ω, P) and three sets A, B, and C containing random variables defined on Ω. Let a, b, and c be sets of values of the random variables in A, B, and C, respectively. Then the sets A and B are said to be **conditionally independent** given the set C if, for all values of the variables in the sets a, b, and c, whenever $P(c) \neq 0$, the events A = a and B = b are conditionally independent given the event C = c. When this is the case, we write

$$I_P(A, B|C).\blacklozenge$$

Example 5.25 Suppose we use the Principle of Indifference to assign probabilities to the objects in Figure 5.2, and we define random variables as follows:

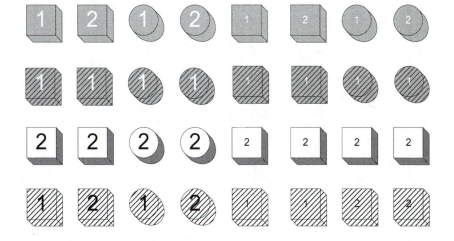

Figure 5.2 Objects with five properties.

Variable	Value	Outcomes Mapped to This Value
V	v_1	All objects containing a 1
	v_2	All objects containing a 2
L	l_1	All objects covered with lines
	l_2	All objects not covered with lines
C	c_1	All gray objects
	c_2	All white objects
S	s_1	All square objects
	s_2	All circular objects
F	f_1	All objects containing a number in a large font
	f_2	All objects containing a number in a small font

It is left as an exercise to show for all values of v, l, c, s, and f that

$$P(v, l | s, f, c) = P(v, l | c).$$

So we have

$$I_P(\{V, L\}, \{S, F\} | C).$$

∎

5.3   Meaning of Probability

When one does not have the opportunity to study probability theory in depth, one is often left with the impression that all probabilities are computed using ratios. Next, we discuss the meaning of probability in more depth and show that this is not how probabilities are ordinarily determined.

5.3.1   Relative Frequency Approach to Probability

A classic textbook example of probability concerns tossing a coin. Because the coin is symmetrical, we use the Principle of Indifference to assign

$$P(\mathsf{Heads}) = P(\mathsf{Tails}) = .5.$$

Suppose that instead we toss a thumbtack. It can also land one of two ways. That is, it could land on its flat end, which we will call *heads*, or it could land with the edge of the flat end and the point touching the ground, which we will call *tails*. Because the thumbtack is not symmetrical, we have no reason to apply the Principle of Indifference and assign probabilities of .5 to both outcomes. How then should we assign the probabilities? In the case of the coin, when we assign $P(\text{heads}) = .5$, we are implicitly assuming that if we tossed the coin a large number of times it would land heads about half the time. That is, if we tossed the coin 1000 times, we would expect it to land heads about 500 times. This notion of repeatedly performing the experiment gives us a method for computing (or at least estimating) the probability. That is, if we repeat an experiment many times, we are fairly certain that the probability of an outcome is about equal to the fraction of times the outcome occurs. For example, a student tossed a thumbtack 10,000 times and it landed heads 3761 times. So

$$P(\text{heads}) \approx \frac{3761}{10,000} = .3761.$$

Indeed, in 1919, Richard von Mises used the limit of this fraction as the definition of probability. That is, if n is the number of tosses and S_n is the number of times the thumbtack lands heads, then

$$P(\text{heads}) \equiv \lim_{n \to \infty} \frac{S_n}{n}.$$

This definition assumes that a limit actually is approached. That is, it assumes that the ratio does not fluctuate. For example, there is no reason *a priori* to assume that the ratio is not .5 after 100 tosses, .1 after 1000 tosses, .5 after 10,000 tosses, .1 after 100,000 tosses, and so on. Only experiments in the real world can substantiate that a limit is approached. In 1946, J. E. Kerrich conducted many such experiments using games of chance in which the Principle of Indifference seemed to apply (e.g., drawing a card from a deck). His results indicated that the relative frequency does appear to approach a limit and that this limit is the value obtained using the Principle of Indifference.

This approach to probability is called the **relative frequency approach to probability**, and probabilities obtained using this approach are called **relative frequencies**. A **frequentist** is someone who feels this is the only way we can obtain probabilities. Note that, according to this approach, we can never know a probability for certain. For example, if we tossed a coin 10,000 times and it landed heads 4991 times, we would estimate

$$P(\text{heads}) \approx \frac{4991}{10,000} = .4991.$$

On the other hand, if we used the Principle of Indifference, we would assign $P(\text{Heads}) = .5$. In the case of the coin, the probability might not actually be .5 because the coin might not be perfectly symmetrical. For example, Kerrich [1946] found that the six came up the most in the toss of a die and that one came up the least. This makes sense because, at that time, the spots on the die were hollowed out of the die, so the die was lightest on the side with a six. On the other hand, in experiments involving cards or urns, it seems we can be certain of probabilities obtained using the Principle of Indifference.

Example 5.26 Suppose we toss an asymmetrical six-sided die, and in 1000 tosses we observe that each of the six sides comes up the following number of times.

Side	Number of Times
1	250
2	150
3	200
4	70
5	280
6	50

So we estimate $P(1) \approx .25$, $P(2) \approx .15$, $P(3) \approx .2$, $P(4) \approx .07$, $P(5) \approx .28$, and $P(6) \approx .05$.   ∎

Repeatedly performing an experiment (so as to estimate a relative frequency) is called **sampling**, and the set of outcomes is called a **random sample** (or simply a **sample**). The set from which we sample is called a **population**.

Example 5.27 Suppose our population is all males in the United States between the ages of 31 and 85, and we are interested in the probability of such males having high blood pressure. Then, if we sample 10,000 males, this set of males is our sample. Furthermore, if 3210 have high blood pressure, we estimate

$$P(\text{High Blood Pressure}) \approx \frac{3210}{10,000} = .321.$$

∎

Technically, we should not call the set of all current males in this age group the population. Rather, the theory says that there is a propensity for a male in this group to have high blood pressure and that this propensity is the probability. This propensity might not be equal to the fraction of current males in the group who have high blood pressure. In theory, we would have to have an infinite number of males to determine the probability exactly. The current set of males in this age group is called a **finite population**. The fraction of them with high blood pressure is the probability of obtaining a male with high blood pressure when we sample him from the set of all males in the age group. This latter probability is simply the ratio of males with high blood pressure.

When doing statistical inference, we sometimes want to estimate the ratio in a finite population from a sample of the population, and at other times we want to estimate a propensity from a finite sequence of observations. For example, TV raters ordinarily want to estimate the actual fraction of people in a nation watching a show from a sample of those people. On the other hand, medical scientists want to estimate the propensity with which males tend to have high blood pressure from a finite sequence of males. One can create an infinite sequence from a finite population by returning a sampled item back to the population before sampling the next item. This is called **sampling with replacement**. In practice, it is rarely done, but ordinarily the finite population is so large that statisticians make the simplifying assumption that it is done. That is, they do not replace the item but still assume that the ratio is unchanged for the next item sampled.

In sampling, the observed relative frequency is called the **maximum likelihood estimate (MLE)** of the probability (limit of the relative frequency) because it is the estimate of the probability that makes the observed sequence most probable when we assume that the trials (repetitions of the experiment) are probabilistically independent.

Another facet of von Mises' relative frequency approach is that a random process is generating the sequence of outcomes. According to von Mises' theory, a **random process** is defined as a repeatable experiment for which the infinite sequence of outcomes is assumed to be a random sequence. Intuitively, a **random sequence** is one that shows no regularity or pattern. For example, the finite binary sequence 1011101100 appears random, whereas the sequence 1010101010 does not, because it has the pattern 10 repeated five times. There is evidence that experiments such as coin tossing and dice throwing are indeed random processes. In 1971, Iversen et al. ran many experiments with dice indicating the sequence of outcomes is random. It is believed that unbiased sampling also yields a random sequence and is therefore a random process. See [van Lambalgen, 1987] for a formal treatment of random sequences.

5.3.2   Subjective Approach to Probability

If we tossed a thumbtack 10,000 times and it landed heads 6000 times, we would estimate $P(\text{heads})$ to be .6. Exactly what does this number approximate? Is there some probability, accurate to an arbitrary number of digits, of the thumbtack landing heads? It seems not. Indeed, as we toss the thumbtack, its shape will slowly be altered, changing any propensity for landing heads. As another example, is there really an exact propensity for a male in a certain age group to have high blood pressure? Again, it seems not. So it seems that, outside of games of chance involving cards and urns, the relative frequency notion of probability is only an idealization. Regardless, we obtain useful insights concerning our beliefs from this notion. For example, after the thumbtack lands heads 6000 times out of 10,000 tosses, we believe it has about a .6 chance of landing heads on the next toss, and we bet accordingly. That is, we would consider it fair to win $0.40 if the thumbtack landed heads and to lose $1 − $0.40 = $0.60 if the thumbtack landed tails. Because the bet is considered fair, the opposite position, namely, to lose $0.40 if the thumbtack landed heads and to win $0.60 if it landed tails, would also be considered fair. Hence, we would take either side of the bet. This notion of a probability as a value that determines a fair bet is called a **subjective approach to probability**, and probabilities assigned within this frame are called **subjective probabilities** or **beliefs**. A **subjectivist** is someone who feels we can assign probabilities within this framework. More concretely, in this approach the **subjective probability** of an uncertain event is the fraction p of units of money we would agree it is fair to give (lose) if the event does not occur in exchange for the promise to receive (win) $1 - p$ units if it does occur.

Example 5.28 Suppose we estimate that $P(\text{heads}) = .6$. This means that we would agree it is fair to give $0.60 if heads does not occur for the promise to receive $0.40 if it does occur. Notice that if we repeated the experiment 100 times and heads did occur 60% of the time (as we expected), we would win $60(\$0.40) = \$24$ and lose $40(\$0.60) = \$24$. That is, we would break even.   ∎

Unlike the relative frequency approach to probability, the subjective approach allows us to compute probabilities of events that are not repeatable. A classic example concerns betting at the racetrack. To decide how to bet, we must first determine how likely we feel it is that each horse will win. A particular race has never run before and never will be run again, so we cannot look at previous occurrences of the race to obtain our belief. Rather, we obtain this belief from a careful analysis of the horses' overall previous performances, of track conditions, of jockeys, and so on. Clearly, not everyone will arrive at the same probabilities based on their analyses. This is why these probabilities are called *subjective*. They are particular to individuals. In general, they do not have objective values in nature on which we all must agree. Of course, if we did do an experiment such as tossing a thumbtack 10,000 times and it landed heads 6,000 times, most would agree that the probability of heads is about .6. Indeed, de Finetti [1937] showed that if we make certain reasonable assumptions about your beliefs, this would have to be your probability.

Before pursuing this matter further, we discuss a concept related to probability, namely, odds. Mathematically, if $P(E)$ is the probability of event E, then the **odds** $O(E)$ are defined by

$$O(E) = \frac{P(E)}{1 - P(E)}.$$

As far as betting, $O(E)$ is the amount of money we would consider it fair to lose if E did not occur in return for gaining \$1 if E did occur.

Example 5.29 Let E be the event that the horse Oldnag wins the Kentucky Derby. If we feel $P(E) = .2$, then

$$O(E) = \frac{P(E)}{1 - P(E)} = \frac{.2}{1 - .2} = .25.$$

This means we would consider it fair to lose \$0.25 if the horse did not win in return for gaining \$1 if it did win.

If we state the fair bet in terms of probability (as discussed previously), we would consider it fair to lose \$0.20 if the horse did not win in return for gaining \$0.80 if it did win. Notice that with both methods, the ratio of the amount won to the amount lost is 4, so they are consistent in the way they determine betting behavior. ∎

At the racetrack, the betting odds shown are the odds against the event. That is, they are the odds of the event not occurring. If $P(E) = .2$ and $\neg E$ denotes that E does not occur, then

$$O(\neg E) = \frac{P(\neg E)}{1 - P(\neg E)} = \frac{.8}{1 - .8} = 4,$$

and the odds shown at the racetrack are 4 to 1 against E. If you bet on E, you will lose \$1 if E does not occur and win \$4 if E does occur. Note that these are the track odds based on the betting behavior of all participants. If you believe $P(E) = .5$, for you the odds against E are 1 to 1 (even money), and you should jump at the chance to get 4 to 1.

Some individuals are uncomfortable at being forced to consider wagering to assess a subjective probability. There are other methods for ascertaining these probabilities. One of the most popular is the following, which was suggested by Lindley in 1985. This method says an individual should liken the uncertain outcome to a game of chance by considering an urn containing white and black balls. The individual should determine for what fraction of white balls the individual would be indifferent between receiving a small prize if the uncertain event E happened (or turned out to be true) and receiving the same small prize if a white ball was drawn from the urn. That fraction is the individual's probability of the outcome. Such a probability can be constructed using binary cuts. If, for example, you were indifferent when the fraction was .8, for you $P(E) = .8$. If someone else were indifferent when the fraction was .6, for that individual $P(E) = .6$. Again, neither individual is right or wrong.

It would be a mistake to assume that subjective probabilities are only important in gambling situations. Actually, they are important in all the applications discussed in this book. In the next section we illustrate interesting uses of subjective probabilities.

See [Neapolitan, 1989] for more on the two approaches to probability presented here.

5.4   Random Variables in Applications

Although it is mathematically elegant to first specify a sample space and then define random variables on the space, in practice this is not what we ordinarily do. In practice some single entity or set of entities has features, the states of which we want to determine but that we cannot determine for certain. So we settle for determining how likely it is that a particular feature is in a particular state. An example of a single entity is a jurisdiction in which we are considering introducing an economically beneficial chemical that might be carcinogenic. We would want to determine the relative risk of the chemical versus its benefits. An example of a set of entities is a set of patients with similar diseases and symptoms. In this case, we would want to diagnose diseases based on symptoms. As mentioned in Section 5.3.1, this set of entities is called a *population*, and technically it is usually not the set of all currently existing entities, but rather is, in theory, an infinite set of entities.

In these applications, a random variable represents some feature of the entity being modeled, and we are uncertain as to the value of this feature. In the case of a single entity, we are uncertain as to the value of the feature for that entity, whereas in the case of a set of entities, we are uncertain as to the value of the feature for some members of the set. To help resolve this uncertainty, we develop probabilistic relationships among the variables. When there is a set of entities, we assume the entities in the set all have the same probabilistic relationships concerning the variables used in the model. When this is not the case, our analysis is not applicable. In the case of the scenario concerning introducing a chemical, features may include the amount of human exposure and the carcinogenic potential. If these are our features of interest, we identify the random variables *HumanExposure* and *CarcinogenicPotential*. (For simplicity, our illustrations include only a few variables. An actual application ordinarily includes many more than this.) In the case of a set of patients, features of interest might include whether or not diseases such as lung cancer are present, whether or not manifestations of diseases such as a chest X-ray are present, and whether or not causes of diseases such as smoking are present. Given these features, we would identify the random variables *ChestXray*, *LungCancer*, and *SmokingHistory*, respectively.

After identifying the random variables, we distinguish a set of mutually exclusive and exhaustive values for each of them. The possible values of a random variable are the different states that the feature can take. For example, the state of *LungCancer* could be *present* or *absent*, the state of *ChestXray* could be *positive* or *negative*, and the state of *SmokingHistory* could be *yes* or *no*, where *yes* might mean the patient has smoked one or more packs of cigarettes every day during the past 10 years.

After distinguishing the possible values of the random variables (i.e., their spaces), we judge the probabilities of the random variables having their values. However, in general, we do not directly determine values in a joint probability distribution of the random variables. Rather, we ascertain probabilities concerning relationships among random variables that are accessible to us. We can then reason with these variables using Bayes' theorem to obtain probabilities of events of interest. The next example illustrates this idea.

Example 5.30 Suppose Sam plans to marry, and to obtain a marriage licence in the state in which he resides, one must take the blood test enzyme-linked immunosorbent assay (ELISA), which tests for the presence of human immunodeficiency virus (HIV). Sam takes the test and it comes back positive for HIV. How likely is it that Sam is infected with HIV? Without knowing the accuracy of the test, Sam really has no way of knowing how probable it is that he is infected with HIV.

The data we ordinarily have on such tests are the true positive rate (sensitivity) and the true negative rate (specificity). The true positive rate is the number of people who both have the infection and test positive divided by the total number of people who have the infection. For example, to obtain this number for ELISA, 10,000 people who were known to be infected with HIV were identified. This was done using the Western Blot, which is the gold standard test for HIV. These people were then tested with ELISA, and 9990 tested positive. Therefore, the true positive rate is .999. The true negative rate is the number of people who both do not have the infection and test negative divided by the total number of people who do not have the infection. To obtain this number for ELISA, 10,000 nuns who denied risk factors for HIV infection were tested. Of these, 9980 tested negative using the ELISA test. Furthermore, the 20 positive-testing nuns tested negative using the Western Blot test. So, the true negative rate is .998, which means that the false positive rate is .002. We therefore formulate the following random variables and subjective probabilities:

$$P(ELISA = positive | HIV = present) = .999 \qquad (5.8)$$

$$P(ELISA = positive | HIV = absent) = .002. \qquad (5.9)$$

You might wonder why we called these **subjective probabilities** when we obtained them from data. Recall that the frequentist approach says that we can never know the actual relative frequencies (objective probabilities); we can only estimate them from data. However, within the subjective approach, we can make our beliefs (subjective probabilities) equal to the fractions obtained from the data.

It might seem that Sam almost certainly is infected with HIV, as the test is so accurate. However, notice that neither the probability in Equality 5.8 nor the one in Equality 5.9 is the probability of Sam being infected with HIV. Because we know that Sam tested positive on ELISA, that probability is

$$P(HIV = present | ELISA = positive).$$

We can compute this probability using Bayes' theorem if we know $P(HIV = present)$. Recall that Sam took the blood test simply because the state required it. He did not take it because he thought for any reason he was infected with HIV. So, the only other information we have about Sam is that he is a male in the state in which he resides. Therefore if 1 in 100,000 men in Sam's state is infected with HIV, we assign the following subjective probability:

$$P(HIV = present) = .00001.$$

We now employ Bayes' theorem to compute

$P(present | positive)$

$$= \frac{P(positive | present) P(present)}{P(positive | present) P(present) + P(positive | absent) P(absent)}$$

$$= \frac{(.999)(.00001)}{(.999)(.00001) + (.002)(.99999)}$$

$$= .00497.$$

Surprisingly, we are fairly confident that Sam is not infected with HIV. ∎

A probability such as $P(HIV = present)$ is called a **prior probability** because, in a particular model, it is the probability of some event prior to updating the probability of that event, within the framework of that model, using new information. Do not mistakenly think it means a probability prior to any information. A probability such as $P(HIV = present | ELISA = positive)$ is called a **posterior probability** because it is the probability of an event after its prior probability has been updated, within the framework of some model, based on new information. In the previous example, the reason the posterior probability is small even though the test is fairly accurate, is that the prior probability is extremely low. The next example shows how dramatically a different prior probability can change things.

Example 5.31 Suppose Mary and her husband have been trying to have a baby and she suspects she is pregnant. She takes a pregnancy test that has a true positive rate of .99 and a false positive rate of .02. Suppose further that 20% of all women who take this pregnancy test are indeed pregnant. Using Bayes' theorem we then have

$$P(present|positive)$$

$$= \frac{P(positive|present)P(present)}{P(positive|present)P(present) + P(positive|absent)P(absent)}$$

$$= \frac{(.99)(.2)}{(.99)(.2) + (.02)(.8)}$$

$$= .92523.$$

∎

Even though Mary's test was less accurate than Sam's test, she probably is pregnant, whereas he probably is not infected with HIV. This is due to the prior information. There was a significant prior probability (.2) that Mary was pregnant, because only women who suspect they are pregnant on other grounds take pregnancy tests. Sam, however, took his test because he wanted to get married. We had no prior information indicating he could be infected with HIV.

In the previous examples, we obtained our beliefs (subjective probabilities) directly from the observed fractions in the data. Although this is often done, it is not necessary. In general, we obtain our beliefs from our information about the past, which means that these beliefs are a composite of all our experience rather than merely observed relative frequencies. The following is an example:

Example 5.32 Suppose you feel there is a .4 probability the NASDAQ will go up at least 1% today. This is based on your knowledge that, after trading closed yesterday, excellent earnings were reported by several big companies in the technology sector, and that U.S. crude oil supplies unexpectedly increased. Furthermore, if the NASDAQ does go up at least 1% today, you feel there is a .1 probability that your favorite stock NTPA will go up at least 10% today. If the NASDAQ does not go up at least 1% today, you feel there is only a .02 probability NTPA will go up at least 10% today. You have these beliefs because you know from the past that NTPA's performance is linked to overall performance in the technology sector. You checked NTPA after the close of trading, and you noticed it went up over 10%. What is the probability that the NASDAQ went up at least 1%? Using Bayes' theorem we have

$$P(NASDAQ = up\ 1\%|NTPA = up\ 10\%)$$

$$= \frac{P(up\ 10\%|up\ 1\%)P(up\ 1\%)}{P(up\ 10\%|up\ 1\%)P(up\ 1\%) + P(up\ 10\%|not\ up\ 1\%)P(not\ up\ 1\%)}$$

$$= \frac{(.1)(.4)}{(.1)(.4) + (.02)(.6)} = .769.$$

∎

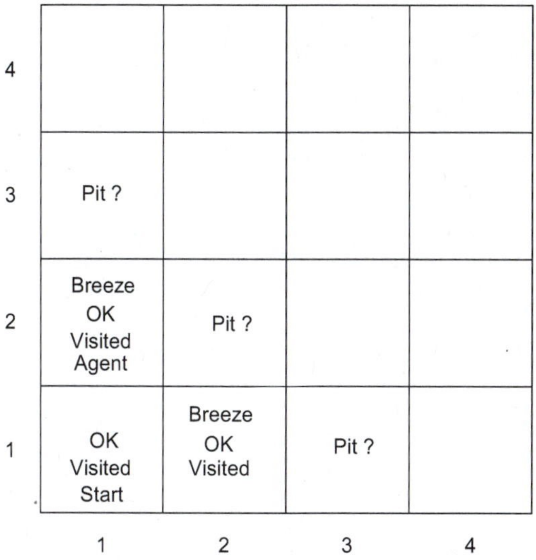

	1	2	3	4
4				
3	Pit ?			
2	Breeze OK Visited Agent	Pit ?		
1	OK Visited Start	Breeze OK Visited	Pit ?	

Figure 5.3 Current knowledge of the wumpus world after the agent' visits squares [2,1] and [1,2] and discovers breeezes in both of them.

In the previous three examples we used Bayes' theorem to compute posterior subjective probabilities from known subjective probabilities. In a rigorous sense, we can only do this within the subjective framework. That is, because strict frequentists say we can never know probabilities for certain, they cannot use Bayes' theorem. They can only do analyses such as the computation of a confidence interval for the value of an unknown probability based on the data. These techniques are discussed in any classic statistics text such as [Hogg and Craig, 1972]. Because subjectivists are the ones who use Bayes' theorem, they are often called **Bayesians**.

5.5 Probability in the Wumpus World

The wumpus world described in Section 2.3.2 involved uncertainty in that we did not know the location of the wumpus, gold, or any pits. However, we did not quantify this uncertainty numerically, and therefore could not use probability theory to reason in the world. Suppose now that we are able to quantify some of this uncertainty. Specifically, suppose that we assign a probability of .1 to a pit being located in each of these squares. This probability could be obtained from knowledge of how the game is generated (i.e., we could be told that a pit is assigned to each square with probability .1), or it could be based on your subjective judgment obtained from experience playing the game. Regardless, we can use probability theory to guide our decision. We show how next.

Suppose that the agent has moved to square [1,2] and [2,1], discovers breezes in both of them, and therefore currently has the knowledge shown in Figure 5.3.

The agent can give up or take a risk by visiting square [1,3] or [2,2]. A purely logical agent would make a random choice between them because neither one appears any more risky than the other. Let's see if a probabilistic agent can quantify this risk to help decide between the two.

Let P_{11} be a random variable whose value is p_{13} if there is a pit in square [1,1] and whose value is $\neg p_{13}$ otherwise. Random variables for breezes and other squares are defined similarly. Furthermore, let Brz denote the known facts about the breezes and Pit denote the known facts about the bits. That is,

$$Brz = \{\neg b_{11}, b_{12}, b_{21}\}$$

$$Pit = \{\neg p_{11}, \neg p_{12}, \neg p_{21}\}.$$

The agent's total knowledge consists of Brz and Pit. The agent would like to determine the probabilities of p_{13} and p_{22} conditional on this knowledge. To that end, by Bayes' theorem

$$
\begin{aligned}
P(p_{13}|Brz, Pit) &= \frac{P(Brz|p_{13}, Pit)P(p_{13}, Pit)}{P(Brz|p_{13}, Pit)P(p_{13}, Pit) + P(Brz|\neg p_{13}, Pit)P(\neg p_{13}, Pit)} \\
&= \frac{P(Brz|p_{13}, Pit)P(p_{13})}{P(Brz|p_{13}, Pit)P(p_{13}) + P(Brz|\neg p_{13}, Pit)P(\neg p_{13})}.
\end{aligned}
$$

We need to compute $P(Brz|p_{13}, Pit)$ and $P(Brz|\neg p_{13}, Pit)$. Owing to the Law of Total Probability, we have that

$$
\begin{aligned}
P(Brz|p_{13}, Pit) &= \sum_{P_{22}, P_{33}} P(Brz|p_{13}, Pit, P_{22}, P_{31})P(P_{22}, P_{31}|p_{13}, Pit) \\
&= \sum_{P_{22}, P_{33}} P(Brz|p_{13}, Pit, P_{22}, P_{31})P(P_{22})P(P_{31}) \\
&= P(Brz|p_{13}, Pit, p_{22}, p_{31})P(p_{22})P(p_{31}) + \\
&\quad P(Brz,|p_{13}, Pit, p_{22}, \neg p_{31})P(p_{22})P(\neg p_{31}) + \\
&\quad P(Brz|p_{13}, Pit, \neg p_{22}, p_{31})P(\neg p_{22})P(p_{31}) + \\
&\quad P(Brz|p_{13}, Pit, \neg p_{22}, \neg p_{31})P(\neg p_{22})P(\neg p_{31}) \\
&= (1)(.1)(.1) + (1)(.9)(.1) + (1)(.9)(.1) + (0)(.9)(.9) \\
&= .19.
\end{aligned}
$$

Note that the conditional probability of Brz is either 1 or 0, depending on whether we condition on pits being next to both square [1,2] and square [2,1] or we condition on no pit being next to at least one of them. It is left as an exercise to show in the same way that

$$P(Brz|\neg p_{13}, Pit) = .1.$$

Plugging these probabilities into Bayes' theorem, we now have that

$$
\begin{aligned}
P(p_{13}|Brz, Pit) &= \frac{P(Brz|p_{13}, Pit)P(p_{13})}{P(Brz|p_{13}, Pit)P(p_{13}) + P(Brz|\neg p_{13}, Pit)P(\neg p_{13})} \\
&= \frac{(.19)\,(.1)}{(.19)\,(.1) + (.1)(.9)} \\
&= .174.
\end{aligned}
$$

It is left as an exercise to show that $P(p_{22}|Brz, Pit) = .917$. So it is far less risky to visit square [1,3], which is what the agent should do next. Intuitively, there are two items of evidence indicating there is a pit in square [2,2] (breezes in both square [1,2] and square [2,1]), whereas there is only one item of evidence indicating there is a pit in square [1,3].

EXERCISES

Section 5.1

Exercise 5.1 Let the experiment be drawing the top card from a deck of 52 cards. Let Heart be the event a heart is drawn, and RoyalCard be the event a royal card is drawn.

1. Compute $P(\mathsf{Heart})$.

2. Compute $P(\mathsf{RoyalCard})$.

3. Compute $P(\mathsf{Heart} \cup \mathsf{RoyalCard})$.

Exercise 5.2 Prove Theorem 5.1.

Exercise 5.3 Example 5.5 showed that, in the draw of the top card from a deck, the event Jack is independent of the event Club. That is, it showed $P(\mathsf{Jack}|\ \mathsf{Club}) = P(\mathsf{Jack})$.

1. Show directly that the event Club is independent of the event Jack. That is, show $P(\mathsf{Club}|\mathsf{Jack}) = P(\mathsf{Club})$. Show also that $P(\mathsf{Jack} \cap \mathsf{Club}) = P(\mathsf{Jack})P(\mathsf{Club})$.

2. Show, in general, that if $P(\mathsf{E}) \neq 0$ and $P(\mathsf{F}) \neq 0$, then $P(\mathsf{E}|\mathsf{F}) = P(\mathsf{E})$ if and only if $P(\mathsf{F}|\mathsf{E}) = P(\mathsf{F})$, and each of these holds if and only if $P(\mathsf{E} \cap \mathsf{F}) = P(\mathsf{E})P(\mathsf{F})$.

Exercise 5.4 The complement of a set E consists of all the elements in Ω that are not in E and is denoted by $\overline{\mathsf{E}}$.

1. Show that E is independent of F if and only if $\overline{\mathsf{E}}$ is independent of F, which is true if and only if $\overline{\mathsf{E}}$ is independent of $\overline{\mathsf{F}}$.

2. Example 5.6 showed that, for the objects in Figure 5.1, A and Square are conditionally independent given Black and given White. Let B be the set of all objects containing a B, and Circle be the set of all circular objects. Use the result just obtained to conclude that A and Circle, B and Square, and B and Circle are each conditionally independent given either Black or White.

Exercise 5.5 Show that in the draw of the top card from a deck, the event E = $\{kh, ks, qh\}$ and the event F = $\{kh, kc, qh\}$ are conditionally independent given the event G = $\{kh, ks, kc, kd\}$. Determine whether E and F are conditionally independent given $\overline{\mathsf{G}}$.

Exercise 5.6 Prove the Law of Total Probability, which says that if we have n mutually exclusive and exhaustive events $\mathsf{E}_1, \mathsf{E}_2, \ldots, \mathsf{E}_n$, then for any other event F,
$$P(\mathsf{F}) = P(\mathsf{F} \cap \mathsf{E}_1) + P(\mathsf{F} \cap \mathsf{E}_2) + \cdots + P(\mathsf{F} \cap \mathsf{E}_n).$$

Exercise 5.7 Let Ω be the set of all objects in Figure 5.1, and assign each object a probability of 1/13. Let A be the set of all objects containing an A, and Square be the set of all square objects. Compute $P(\mathsf{A}|\mathsf{Square})$ directly and using Bayes' theorem.

Section 5.2

Exercise 5.8 Consider the probability space and random variables given in Example 5.20.

1. Determine the joint distribution of S and W, the joint distribution of W and H, and the remaining values in the joint distribution of S, H, and W.

2. Show that the joint distribution of S and H can be obtained by summing the joint distribution of S, H, and W over all values of W.

Exercise 5.9 Let a joint probability distribution be given. Using the Law of Total Probability, show that, in general, the probability distribution of any one of the random variables is obtained by summing over all values of the other variables.

Exercise 5.10 The chain rule says that for n random variables $X_1, X_2, \ldots, X_n$, defined on the same sample space Ω,
$$P(x_1, x_2, \ldots, x_n) = P(x_n | x_{n-1}, x_{n-2}, \ldots x_1) \cdots \times P(x_2 | x_1) \times P(x_1)$$
whenever $P(x_1, x_2, \ldots, x_n) \neq 0$. Prove this rule.

Exercise 5.11 Use the results in Exercise 5.4 (1) to conclude that it was only necessary in Example 5.22 to show that $P(r,t) = P(r,t|s_1)$ for all values of r and t.

Exercise 5.12 Suppose we have two random variables X and Y with spaces $\{x_1, x_2\}$ and $\{y_1, y_2\}$, respectively.

1. Use the results in Exercise 5.4 (1) to conclude that we need only show $P(y_1|x_1) = P(y_1)$ to conclude $I_P(X,Y)$.

2. Develop an example showing that if X and Y both have spaces containing more than two values, then we need to check whether $P(y|x) = P(y)$ for all values of x and y to conclude $I_P(X,Y)$.

Exercise 5.13 Consider the probability space and random variables given in Example 5.20.

1. Are H and W independent?

2. Are H and W conditionally independent given G?

3. If this small sample is indicative of the probabilistic relationships among the variables in some population, what causal relationships might account for this dependency and conditional independency?

Exercise 5.14 In Example 5.25, it was left as an exercise to show for all values v of V, l of L, c of C, s of S, and f of F that

$$P(v,l|s,f,c) = P(v,l|c).$$

Show this.

Section 5.3

Exercise 5.15 Kerrich [1946] performed experiments such as tossing a coin many times, and he found that the relative frequency did appear to approach a limit. That is, for example, he found that after 100 tosses, the relative frequency may have been .51; after 1000 tosses it may have been .508; after 10,000 tosses it may have been .5003; and after 100,000 tosses it may have been .50006. The pattern is that the 5 in the first place to the right of the decimal point remains in all relative frequencies after the first 100 tosses; the 0 in the second place remains in all relative frequencies after the first 1000 tosses; and so on. Toss a thumbtack at least 1000 times and see if you obtain similar results.

Exercise 5.16 Pick some upcoming event. It could be a sporting event or it could be the event that you will get an A in this course. Determine your probability of the event using Lindley's [1985] method of comparing the uncertain event to a draw of a ball from an urn. (See the discussion following Example 5.29.)

Section 5.4

Exercise 5.17 A forgetful nurse is supposed to give Mr. Nguyen a pill each day. The probability that the nurse will forget to give the pill on a given day is .3. If Mr. Nguyen receives the pill, the probability he will die is .1. If he does not receive the pill, the probability he will die is .8. Mr. Nguyen died today. Use Bayes' theorem to compute the probability that the nurse forgot to give him the pill.

Exercise 5.18 An oil well might be drilled on Professor Neapolitan's farm in Texas. Based on what has happened on similar farms, we judge the probability of oil being present to be .5, the probability of only natural gas being present to be .2, and the probability of neither being present to be .3. If oil is present, a geological test will give a positive result with probability .9; if only natural gas is present, it will give a positive result with probability .3; and if neither is present, the test will be positive with probability .1. Suppose the test comes back positive. Use Bayes' theorem to compute the probability that oil is present.

Section 5.5

Exercise 5.19 At the end of Section 5.5 it was left as an exercise to show that $P(Brz|\neg p_{13}, Pit) = .1$. Do this.

Exercise 5.20 At the end of Section 5.5 it was left as an exercise to show that $P(p_{22}|Brz, Pit) = .917$. Do this.

Exercise 5.21 In Section 5.5 we assumed that a pit is assigned to each square with probability of .1, and found that the probability that a pit is located in square [1,3] is less than the probability that a pit is located in square [2,2]. Investigate whether it is less probable that a pit is located in square [1,3] regardless of the value of this probability. If so, is it really necessary to make a subjective judgment of this probability to guide our decision?

Chapter 6

Uncertain Knowledge Representation

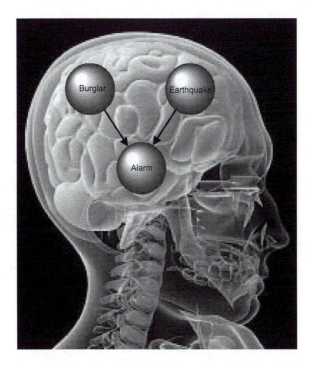

In the introduction to Chapter 5, we discussed the following situation. Suppose that in the past few years, Mr. Holmes has noticed that frequently earthquakes have caused his burglar alarm to sound. The burglar alarm concerns his home but it is wired sound in his office, which is some distance from his home. Presently, he is sitting in his office, and the burglar alarm sounds. He then rushes home, assuming that there is a good chance that his residence has been burglarized. On the way home, he hears on the radio that there has been

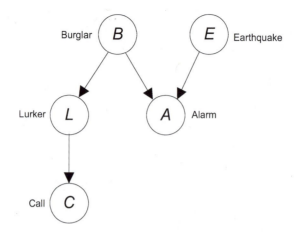

Figure 6.1 A causal network representing Mr. Holmes' knowledge.

an earthquake. He then reasons that the earthquake may well have triggered the alarm, and therefore it is much less likely that he has been burglarized. We now add more to the story. Suppose next that his neighbor Dr. Watson calls and says that he saw a suspicious-looking character lurking around Mr. Holmes' house. Mr. Holmes would then view this as additional evidence that he has indeed been burglarized and feel it is now more probable that he has been burglarized.

Pearl [1986] conjectured that uncertain knowledge is structured with causal edges between propositions, we can represent this knowledge with a causal network, and we can model uncertain reasoning by traversing links in this network. The model does not entail that the entire network exists at a cognitive level at any particular time. Rather, it says that a human develops individual causal links between pairs of propositions and recalls and reasons with these links as needed. For example, in the current situation, we have the following propositions:

A: Mr. Holmes' burglar alarm sounds.

B: Mr. Holmes' residence is burglarized.

E: There is an earthquake.

L: There is an individual lurking around the house.

C: Neighbor calls to report a lurker.

The **causal network model** says that Mr. Holmes has the following cognitive representation of the burglar-alarm situation: a burglar (B) usually causes his alarm (A) to sound; earthquakes (E) often cause his alarm to sound; and a burglar might lurk around the house (L) and be seen by the neighbor, causing the neighbor to call (C) to report the lurker. We call these causal relationships "causal edges." The causal network representation of this knowledge appears in Figure 6.1. When Mr. Holmes learns his alarm has sounded, he reasons along the edge between B and A in the direction of A to conclude he has probably been burglarized. When he later learns there has been an earthquake, he reasons along the edge between E and A in the direction of A to conclude that the earthquake explains away the alarm, and then he reasons along the edge between B and A in the direction of B to conclude that it is much less likely that he has been burglarized. When his neighbor calls (C) to report a lurker, he reasons along the edge between L and C in the direction of L to conclude there probably was a lurker, and then he reasons along the edge between L and B in the direction of B to infer that it is now more likely he has been burglarized.

Mr. Holmes uses these same causal links to reason in the other direction. For example, if Mr. Holmes learns (in his office) he has been burglarized, he reasons along the edge between B and A in the direction of A to conclude that his alarm probably sounded.

As noted in Chapter 5, regardless of how well this model represents human reasoning, it helped give rise to the field called *Bayesian networks*. This chapter introduces Bayesian networks. In Sections 6.1 and 6.2 we define Bayesian networks and discuss their properties. Section 6.3 shows how causal graphs often yield Bayesian networks. In Section 6.4 we discuss doing probabilistic inference using Bayesian networks. Section 6.5 introduces Bayesian networks containing continuous variables. Section 6.6 shows a technique for the determining the probability distributions needed in Bayesian networks. Finally, Section 6.7 shows a large-scale application of Bayesian networks.

6.1 Intuitive Introduction to Bayesian Networks

Recall that in Example 5.30, we computed the probability of Joe having the HIV virus, given that he tested positive for it. Specifically, we knew that

$$P(ELISA = positive | HIV = present) = .999$$

$$P(ELISA = positive | HIV = absent) = .002$$

$$P(HIV = present) = .00001.$$

We then employed Bayes' theorem to compute

$P(present | positive)$

$$= \frac{P(positive | present)P(present)}{P(positive | present)P(present) + P(positive | absent)P(absent)}$$

$$= \frac{(.999)(.00001)}{(.999)(.00001) + (.002)(.99999)}$$

$$= .00497.$$

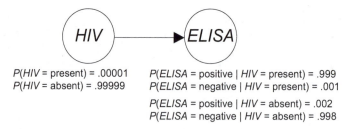

$P(HIV = \text{present}) = .00001$ $P(ELISA = \text{positive} \mid HIV = \text{present}) = .999$
$P(HIV = \text{absent}) = .99999$ $P(ELISA = \text{negative} \mid HIV = \text{present}) = .001$

$P(ELISA = \text{positive} \mid HIV = \text{absent}) = .002$
$P(ELISA = \text{negative} \mid HIV = \text{absent}) = .998$

Figure 6.2 A two-node Bayesian network.

We summarize the information used in this computation in Figure 6.2, which is a two-node/variable Bayesian network. Notice that it represents the random variables HIV and $ELISA$ by nodes in a directed acyclic graph (DAG) and the causal relationship between these variables with an edge from HIV to $ELISA$. That is, the presence of HIV has a causal effect on whether the test result is positive; so there is an edge from HIV to $ELISA$. Besides showing a DAG representing the causal relationships, Figure 6.2 shows the prior probability distribution of HIV and the conditional probability distribution of $ELISA$ given each value of its parent HIV. In general, Bayesian networks consist of a DAG, whose edges represent relationships among random variables that are often (but not always) causal; the prior probability distribution of every variable that is a root in the DAG; and the conditional probability distribution of every non-root variable given each set of values of its parents. We use the terms *node* and *variable* interchangeably in discussing Bayesian networks.

Let's illustrate a more complex Bayesian network by considering the problem of detecting credit card fraud (taken from [Heckerman, 1996]). Suppose that we have identified the following variables as being relevant to the problem:

Variable	What the Variable Represents
Fraud (F)	Whether the current purchase is fraudulent
Gas (G)	Whether gas has been purchased in the past 24 hours
Jewelry (J)	Whether jewelry has been purchased in the past 24 hours
Age (A)	Age of the card holder
Sex (S)	Sex of the card holder

These variables are all causally related. That is, a credit card thief is likely to buy gas and jewelry, and middle-aged women are most likely to buy jewelry, whereas young men are least likely to buy jewelry. Figure 6.3 shows a DAG representing these causal relationships. Notice that it also shows the conditional probability distribution of every non-root variable given each set of values of its parents. The Jewelry variable has three parents, and there is a conditional probability distribution for every combination of values of those parents. The DAG and the conditional distributions together constitute a Bayesian network.

You could have a few questions concerning this Bayesian network. First, you might ask, "What value does it have?" That is, what useful information can we obtain from it? Recall how we used Bayes' theorem to compute $P(HIV =$

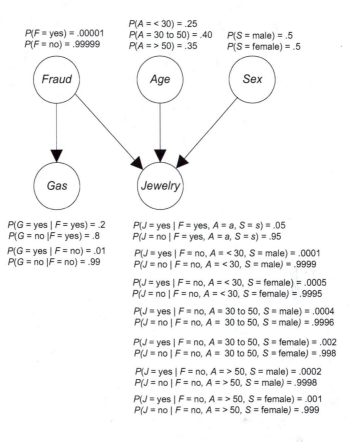

$P(F = yes) = .00001$
$P(F = no) = .99999$

$P(A = < 30) = .25$
$P(A = 30 \text{ to } 50) = .40$
$P(A = > 50) = .35$

$P(S = male) = .5$
$P(S = female) = .5$

$P(G = yes \mid F = yes) = .2$
$P(G = no \mid F = yes) = .8$

$P(G = yes \mid F = no) = .01$
$P(G = no \mid F = no) = .99$

$P(J = yes \mid F = yes, A = a, S = s) = .05$
$P(J = no \mid F = yes, A = a, S = s) = .95$

$P(J = yes \mid F = no, A = < 30, S = male) = .0001$
$P(J = no \mid F = no, A = < 30, S = male) = .9999$

$P(J = yes \mid F = no, A = < 30, S = female) = .0005$
$P(J = no \mid F = no, A = < 30, S = female) = .9995$

$P(J = yes \mid F = no, A = 30 \text{ to } 50, S = male) = .0004$
$P(J = no \mid F = no, A = 30 \text{ to } 50, S = male) = .9996$

$P(J = yes \mid F = no, A = 30 \text{ to } 50, S = female) = .002$
$P(J = no \mid F = no, A = 30 \text{ to } 50, S = female) = .998$

$P(J = yes \mid F = no, A = > 50, S = male) = .0002$
$P(J = no \mid F = no, A = > 50, S = male) = .9998$

$P(J = yes \mid F = no, A = > 50, S = female) = .001$
$P(J = no \mid F = no, A = > 50, S = female) = .999$

Figure 6.3 Bayesian network for detecting credit card fraud.

$present|ELISA = positive)$ from the information in the Bayesian network in Figure 6.2. Similarly, we can compute the probability of credit card fraud given values of the other variables in this Bayesian network. For example, we can compute $P(F = yes|G = yes, J = yes, A = < 30, S = female)$. If this probability is sufficiently high, we can deny the current purchase or require additional identification. The computation is not a simple application of Bayes' theorem as was the case for the two-node Bayesian network in Figure 6.2. Rather it is done using sophisticated inference algorithms.

Second, you might ask how we obtained the probabilities in the network. They can either be obtained from the subjective judgments of an expert in the area or be learned from data. (In Chapter 12 we discuss techniques for learning them from data.)

Finally, you could ask why we are including the variables for age and sex in the network when the age and sex of the card holder has nothing to do with whether the card has been stolen (fraud). That is, fraud has no causal effect on the card holder's age or sex, and vice versa. The reason we include these variables is because fraud, age, and sex all have a common effect, namely the

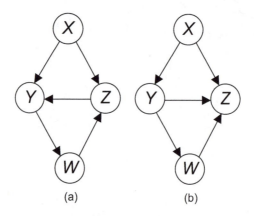

(a)   (b)

Figure 6.4 Both graphs are directed graphs; only the one in (b) is a directed acyclic graph.

purchasing of jewelry. So, when we know jewelry has been purchased, the three variables are rendered probabilistically dependent owing to *discounting*. This is just like the situation involving the burglar, the alarm, and the earthquake. For example, if jewelry has been purchased in the past 24 hours, it increases the likelihood of fraud. However, if the card holder is a middle-aged woman, the likelihood of fraud is lessened (discounted) because such women are prone to buying jewelry. That is, the fact that the card holder is a middle-aged woman explains the jewelry purchase. On the other hand, if the card holder is a young man, the likelihood of fraud is increased because such men are unlikely to purchase jewelry.

We have informally introduced Bayesian networks, their properties, and their usefulness. Next we formally develop their mathematical properties.

6.2   Properties of Bayesian Networks

After defining Bayesian networks, we show how they are ordinarily represented.

6.2.1   Definition of a Bayesian Network

First, let's review some graph theory. A **directed graph** is a pair (V, E), where V is a finite, nonempty set whose elements are called **nodes** (or vertices), and E is a set of ordered pairs of distinct elements of V. Elements of E are called **directed edges**, and if $(X, Y) \in \mathsf{E}$, we say there is an edge from X to Y. The graph in Figure 6.4 (a) is a directed graph. The set of nodes in that figure is

$$\mathsf{V} = \{X, Y, Z, W\},$$

and the set of edges is

$$\mathsf{E} = \{(X, Y), (X, Z), (Y, W), (W, Z), (Z, Y)\}.$$

A **path** in a directed graph is a sequence of nodes $[X_1, X_2, \ldots, X_k]$ such that $(X_{i-1}, X_i) \in E$ for $2 \leq i \leq k$. For example, $[X, Y, W, Z]$ is a path in the directed graph in Figure 6.4 (a). A **chain** in a directed graph is a sequence of nodes $[X_1, X_2, \ldots, X_k]$ such that $(X_{i-1}, X_i) \in E$ or $(X_i, X_{i-1}) \in E$ for $2 \leq i \leq k$. For example, $[Y, W, Z, X]$ is a chain in the directed graph in Figure 6.4 (b), but it is not a path. A **cycle** in a directed graph is a path from a node to itself. In Figure 6.4 (a) $[Y, W, Z, Y]$ is a cycle from Y to Y. However, in Figure 6.4 (b), $[Y, W, Z, Y]$ is not a cycle because it is not a path. A directed graph $\mathbb{G}$ is called a **directed acyclic graph** (DAG) if it contains no cycles. The directed graph in Figure 6.4 (b) is a DAG, whereas the one in Figure 6.4 (a) is not.

Given a DAG $\mathbb{G} = (V, E)$ and nodes X and Y in V, Y is called a **parent** of X if there is an edge from Y to X, Y is called a **descendent** of X and X is called an **ancestor** of Y if there is a path from X to Y, and Y is called a **nondescendent** of X if Y is not a descendent of X and Y is not equal to X.

We can now state the following definition.

Definition 6.1 Suppose we have a joint probability distribution P of the random variables in some set V and a DAG $\mathbb{G} = (V, E)$. We say that $(\mathbb{G}, P)$ satisfies the **Markov condition** if for each variable $X \in V$, X is conditionally independent of the set of all its nondescendents given the set of all its parents. Using the notation established in Chapter 5, Section 5.2.2, this means that if we denote the sets of parents and nondescendents of X by PA_X and ND_X, respectively, then

$$I_P(X, ND_X | PA_X).$$

If $(\mathbb{G}, P)$ satisfies the Markov condition, $(\mathbb{G}, P)$ is called a **Bayesian network.**◆

Example 6.1 Recall Chapter 5, Figure 5.1, which appears again as Figure 6.5. In Chapter 5, Example 5.23, we let P assign $1/13$ to each object in the figure, and we defined these random variables on the set containing the objects.

Variable	Value	Outcomes Mapped to This Value
L	l_1	All objects containing an A
	l_2	All objects containing a B
S	s_1	All square objects
	s_2	All circular objects
C	c_1	All black objects
	c_2	All white objects

We then showed that L and S are conditionally independent given C. That is, using the notation established in Chapter 2, Section 5.2.2, we showed

$$I_P(L, S | C).$$

Consider the DAG $\mathbb{G}$ in Figure 6.6. For that DAG we have the following.

Node	Parents	Nondescendents
L	C	S
S	C	L
C	$\varnothing$	$\varnothing$

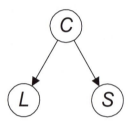

Figure 6.5 The random variables L and S are not independent, but they are conditionally independent given C.

Figure 6.6 The joint probability distribution of L, S, and C constitutes a Bayesian network with this DAG.

For $(\mathbb{G}, P)$ to satisfy the Markov condition, we need to have

$$I_P(L, S|C)$$
$$I_P(S, L|C).$$

Note that because C has no nondescendents, we do not have a conditional independency for C. Because independence is symmetric, $I_P(L, S|C)$ implies $I_P(L, S|C)$. Therefore, all the conditional independencies required by the Markov condition are satisfied, and $(\mathbb{G}, P)$ is a Bayesian network.　∎

Next we further illustrate the Markov condition with a more complex DAG.

Example 6.2 Consider the DAG $\mathbb{G}$ in Figure 6.7. If $(\mathbb{G}, P)$ satisfied the Markov condition with some probability distribution P of X, Y, Z, W, and V, we would have the following conditional independencies.

Node	Parents	Nondescendents	Conditional Independency
X	$\varnothing$	$\varnothing$	None
Y	X	Z, V	$I_P(Y, \{Z, V\}|X)$
Z	X	Y	$I_P(Z, Y|X)$
W	Y, Z	X, V	$I_P(W, \{X, V\}|\{Y, Z\})$
V	Z	X, Y, W	$I_P(V, \{X, Y, W\}|Z)$

∎

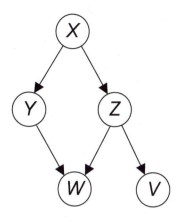

Figure 6.7 A DAG.

6.2.2   Representation of a Bayesian Network

A Bayesian network $(\mathbb{G}, P)$, by definition, is a DAG $\mathbb{G}$ and joint probability distribution P that together satisfy the Markov condition. Then why in Figures 6.2 and 6.3 do we show a Bayesian network as a DAG and a set of conditional probability distributions? The reason is that $(\mathbb{G}, P)$ satisfies the Markov condition if and only if P is equal to the product of its conditional distributions in $\mathbb{G}$. Specifically, we have the following theorem.

Theorem 6.1 $(\mathbb{G}, P)$ satisfies the Markov condition (and therefore is a Bayesian network) if and only if P is equal to the product of its conditional distributions of all nodes given their parents in G, whenever these conditional distributions exist.

Proof. The proof can be found in [Neapolitan, 2004]. ∎

Example 6.3 We showed that the joint probability distribution P of the random variables L, S, and C defined on the set of objects in Figure 6.5 constitutes a Bayesian network with the DAG $\mathbb{G}$ in Figure 6.6. Next we illustrate that the preceding theorem is correct by showing that P is equal to the product of its conditional distributions in $\mathbb{G}$. Figure 6.8 shows those conditional distributions. We computed them directly from Figure 6.5. For example, because there are nine black objects (c_1) and six of them are squares (s_1), we compute

$$P(s_1|c_1) = \frac{6}{9} = \frac{2}{3}.$$

The other conditional distributions are computed in the same way. To show that the joint distribution is the product of the conditional distributions, we need to show for all values of i, j, and k that

$$P(s_i, l_j, c_k) = P(s_i|c_k)P(l_j|c_k)P(c_k).$$

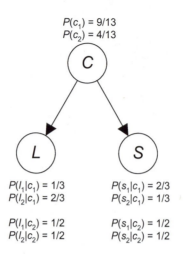

Figure 6.8 A Bayesian network representing the probability distribution P of the random variables L, S, and C defined on the set of objects in Figure 6.5.

There are a total of eight combinations. We show that the equality holds for one of them. It is left as an exercise to show that it holds for the others. To that end, we have directly from Figure 6.5 that

$$P(s_1, l_1, c_1) = \frac{2}{13}.$$

From Figure 6.8 we have

$$P(s_1|c_1)P(l_1|c_1)P(c_1) = \frac{2}{3} \times \frac{1}{3} \times \frac{9}{13} = \frac{2}{13}.$$

■

Owing to Theorem 6.1, we can represent a Bayesian network $(\mathbb{G}, P)$ using the DAG $\mathbb{G}$ and the conditional distributions. We do not need to show every value in the joint distributions. These values can all be computed from the conditional distributions. So we always show a Bayesian network as the DAG and the conditional distributions as we did in Figures 6.2, 6.3, and 6.8. Herein lies the representational power of Bayesian networks. If there are a large number of variables, there are many values in the joint distribution. However, if the DAG is sparse, there are relatively few values in the conditional distributions. For example, suppose all variables are binary, and a joint distribution satisfies the Markov condition with the DAG in Figure 6.9. Then there are $2^{10} = 1024$ values in the joint distribution, but only $2 + 2 + 8 \times 8 = 68$ values in the conditional distributions. Note that we are not even including redundant parameters in this count. For example, in the Bayesian network in Figure 6.8, it is not necessary to show $P(c_2) = 4/13$ because $P(c_2) = 1 - P(c_1)$. So we need only show $P(c_1) = 9/13$. If we eliminate redundant parameters, there are

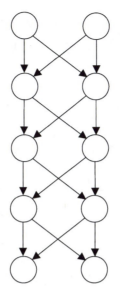

Figure 6.9 If all variables are binary and a joint distribution satisifes the Markov condition with this DAG, there are 1024 values in the joint distribution, but only 68 values in the conditional distributions.

only 34 values in the conditional distributions for the DAG in Figure 6.9 but still 1023 in the joint distribution. We see then that a Bayesian network is a structure for representing a joint probability distribution succinctly.

We cannot take just any DAG and expect a joint distribution to equal the product of its conditional distributions in the DAG. This is only true if the Markov condition is satisfied. Exercise 6.2 illustrates that this is the case in this exercise. It seems that we are left in a dilemma. That is, our goal is to succinctly represent a joint probability distribution using a DAG and conditional distributions for the DAG (a Bayesian network) rather than enumerating every value in the joint distribution. However, we do not know which DAG to use until we check whether the Markov condition is satisfied, and, in general, we would need to have the joint distribution to check this. A common way to resolve this dilemma is to construct a **causal DAG**, which is a DAG in which there is an edge from X to Y if X causes Y. The DAG concerning the burglar, the alarm, etc., and the DAGs in Figures 6.2 and 6.3 are causal; other DAGs shown so far in this chapter are not causal.

Next we discuss why a causal DAG should satisfy the Markov condition with the probability distribution of the variables in the DAG. A second way of obtaining the DAG is to learn it from data. This second way is discussed in Chapter 12.

6.3   Causal Networks as Bayesian Networks

We first formalize the notion of causality.

6.3.1   Causality

One dictionary definition of a cause is "the one, such as a person, an event, or a condition, that is responsible for an action or a result." Although useful, this definition is certainly not the last word on the concept of causation, which has been investigated for centuries (see, e.g., [Hume, 1748]; [Piaget, 1966]; [Eells, 1991]; [Salmon, 1997]; [Spirtes et al., 1993; 2000]; [Pearl, 2000]). This definition does, however, shed light on an operational method for identifying causal relationships. That is, if the action of making variable X take some value sometimes changes the value taken by variable Y, then we assume X is responsible for sometimes changing Y's value, and we conclude X is a cause[1] of Y. More formally, we say we **manipulate** X when we force X to take some value, and we say X **causes** Y if there is some manipulation of X that leads to a change in the probability distribution of Y. We assume that if manipulating X leads to a change in the probability distribution of Y, then X obtaining a value by any means whatsoever also leads to a change in the probability distribution of Y. So we assume that causes and their effects are statistically correlated. However, variables can be correlated without one causing the other.

A manipulation consists of a **randomized controlled experiment** (**RCE**) using some specific population of entities (e.g., individuals with chest pain) in some specific context (e.g., they currently receive no chest pain medication and they live in a particular geographical area). The causal relationship discovered is then relative to this population and this context.

Let's discuss how the manipulation proceeds. We first identify the population of entities we want to consider. Our random variables are features of these entities. Next we ascertain the causal relationship we want to investigate. Suppose we are trying to determine if variable X is a cause of variable Y. We then sample a number of entities from the population. For every entity selected, we manipulate the value of X so that each of its possible values is given to the same number of entities (if X is continuous, we choose the values of X according to a uniform distribution). After the value of X is set for a given entity, we measure the value of Y for that entity. The more the resultant data show a dependency between X and Y, the more the data support that X causes Y. The manipulation of X can be represented by a variable M that is external to the system being studied. There is one value m_i of M for each value x_i of X; the probabilities of all values of M are the same; and when M equals m_i, X equals x_i. That is, the relationship between M and X is deterministic. The data support that X causes Y to the extent that the data indicate $P(y_i|m_j) \neq P(y_i|m_k)$ for $j \neq k$. Manipulation is actually a special kind of causal relationship that we assume exists primordially and is within our control so that we can define and discover

---

[1] This notion of causality does not pertain to *token* causality, which concerns individual causal events rather than probabilistic relationships among variables.

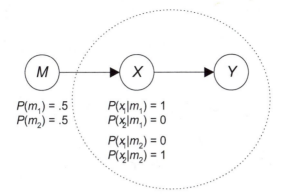

Figure 6.10 A causal DAG representing a manipulation experiment.

other causal relationships. The causal DAG representing the manipulation just discussed appears in Figure 6.10.

6.3.2 Causality and the Markov Condition

First, we more rigorously define a causal DAG. After that, we state the causal Markov assumption and argue why it should be satisfied.

6.3.2.1 Causal DAGs

We say X is a **cause** of Y if a manipulation of X results in a change in the probability distribution of Y. A **causal graph** is a directed graph containing a set of causally related random variables V such that for every $X, Y \in V$ there is an edge from X to Y if and only if X is a cause of Y, and there is no subset of variables W_{XY} of V such that if we knew the values of the variables in W_{XY}, a manipulation of X would no longer change the probability distribution of Y. If there is an edge from X to Y, we call X a **direct cause** of Y. Note that whether or not X is a direct cause of Y depends on the variables included in V. A causal graph is a **causal DAG** if the causal graph is acyclic (i.e., there are no causal feedback loops).

Example 6.4 Testosterone (T) is known to convert to dihydro-testosterone (D), and dihydro-testosterone is believed to be the hormone necessary for erectile function (E). A study in [Lugg et al., 1995] tested the causal relationship among these variables in rats. They manipulated testosterone to low levels and found that both dihydro-testosterone and erectile function declined. They then held dihydro-testosterone fixed at low levels and found that erectile function was low regardless of the manipulated value of testosterone. Finally, they held dihydro-testosterone fixed at high levels and found that erectile function was high regardless of the manipulated value of testosterone. So they learned that, in a causal graph containing only the variables T, D, and E, T is a direct cause

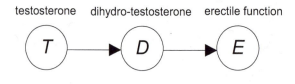

Figure 6.11 A causal DAG.

of D, and D is a direct cause of E; but, although T is a cause of E, it is not a direct cause. So the causal graph (DAG) is the one in Figure 6.11.   ∎

Notice that if the variable D were not in the DAG in Figure 6.11, T would be called a direct cause of E, and there would be an edge from T directly into E instead of the directed path through D. In general, our edges always represent only the relationships among the identified variables. It seems we can usually conceive of intermediate, unidentified variables along each edge. Consider the following example taken from [Spirtes et al., 1993; 2000], p. 42:

> If C is the event of striking a match, and A is the event of the match catching on fire, and no other events are considered, then C is a direct cause of A. If, however, we added B, the sulfur on the match tip achieved sufficient heat to combine with the oxygen, then we could no longer say that C directly caused A, but rather C directly caused B and B directly caused A. Accordingly, we say that B is a causal mediary between C and A if C causes B and B causes A.

Note that, in this intuitive explanation, a variable name is used to also stand for a value of the variable. For example, A is a variable whose value is *on-fire* or *not-on-fire*, and A is also used to represent that the match is on fire. Clearly, we can add more causal mediaries. For example, we could add the variable D, representing whether the match tip is abraded by a rough surface. C would then cause D, which would cause B, and so on. We could go much further and describe the chemical reaction that occurs when sulfur combines with oxygen.

Indeed, it seems we can conceive of a continuum of events in any causal description of a process. We see then that the set of observable variables is observer dependent. Apparently an individual, given myriad sensory input, selectively records discernible events and develops cause/effect relationships among them. Therefore, rather than assuming that there is a set of causally related variables out there, it seems more appropriate to only assume that, in a given context or application, we identify certain variables and develop a set of causal relationships among them.

6.3.2.2   Causal Markov Assumption

If we assume that the observed probability distribution P of a set of random variables V satisfies the Markov condition with the causal DAG $\mathbb{G}$ containing

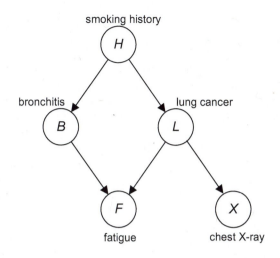

Figure 6.12 A causal DAG.

the variables, we say we are making the **causal Markov assumption**, and we call $(\mathbb{G}, P)$ a **causal network**. Why should we make the causal Markov assumption? To answer this question, we show several examples.

Example 6.5 Consider again the situation involving testosterone (T), dihydro-testosterone (D), and erectile function (E). Recall the manipulation study in [Lugg et al., 1995], which we discussed in Example 6.4. This study showed that if we instantiate D, the value of E is independent of the value of T. So there is experimental evidence that the Markov condition is satisfied for a three-variable causal chain. ∎

Example 6.6 A history of smoking (H) is known to cause both bronchitis (B) and lung cancer (L). Lung cancer and bronchitis both cause fatigue (F), but only lung cancer can cause a chest X-ray (X) to be positive. There are no other causal relationships among the variables. Figure 6.12 shows a causal DAG containing these variables. The causal Markov assumption for that DAG entails the following conditional independencies.

Node	Parents	Nondescendents	Conditional Independency
H	$\varnothing$	$\varnothing$	None
B	H	L, X	$I_P(B, \{L, X\}|H)$
L	H	B	$I_P(L, B|H)$
F	B, L	H, X	$I_P(F, \{H, X\}|\{B, L\})$
X	L	H, B, F	$I_P(X, \{H, B, F\}|L)$

Given the causal relationship in Figure 6.12, we would not expect bronchitis and lung cancer to be independent, because if someone had lung cancer it would make it more probable that the individual smoked (as smoking can cause lung cancer), which would make it more probable that another effect of smoking, namely bronchitis, was present. However, if we knew someone smoked, it would already be more probable that the person had bronchitis. Learning that the individual had lung cancer could no longer increase the probability of smoking (which is now 1), which means it cannot change the probability of bronchitis. That is, the variable H shields B from the influence of L, which is what the causal Markov condition says. Similarly, a positive chest X-ray increases the probability of lung cancer, which in turn increases the probability of smoking, which in turn increases the probability of bronchitis. So, a chest X-ray and bronchitis are not independent. However, if we knew the person had lung cancer, the chest X-ray could not change the probability of lung cancer and thereby change the probability of bronchitis. So B is independent of X conditional on L, which is what the causal Markov condition says. ∎

There are three situations in which a causal graph should not satisfy the Markov condition. The first one is when there is a causal feedback loop. For example, perhaps studying causes good grades, and good grades cause a student to study harder. When there is a causal feedback loop, our graph is not even a DAG.

The second situation is when a hidden common cause is present. The following example illustrates the problem with hidden common causes.

Example 6.7 Suppose we wanted to create a causal DAG containing the variables cold (C), sneezing (S), and runny nose (R). Because a cold can cause both sneezing and a runny nose and neither of these conditions can cause each other, we would create the DAG in Figure 6.13 (a). The causal Markov condition for that DAG would entail $I_P(S, R|C)$. However, if there were a hidden common cause of S and R as depicted in Figure 6.13 (b), this conditional independency would not hold because even if the value of C were known, S would change the probability of H, which in turn would change the probability of R. Indeed, there is at least one other cause of sneezing and runny nose, namely hay fever. So when making the causal Markov assumption, we must be certain that we have identified all common causes. ∎

The final situation is more subtle. It concerns the presence of *selection bias*. The following example illustrates this situation.

Example 6.8 The pharmaceutical company Merck had been marketing its drug finasteride as medication for men with benign prostatic hyperplasia (BPH). Based on anecdotal evidence, it seemed that there was a correlation between use of the drug and regrowth of scalp hair. Let's assume that Merck took a random sample from the population of interest and, based on that sample, determined that there is a correlation between finasteride use and hair regrowth. Assume further that there could be no hidden common causes of finasteride use and hair regrowth. Should Merck conclude that finasteride causes hair regrowth and therefore market it as a cure for baldness? Not necessarily. There is yet another possible causal explanation for this correlation. Suppose that our

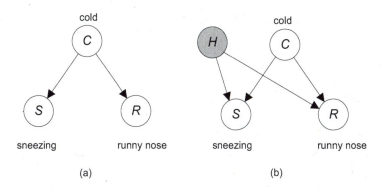

Figure 6.13 The causal Markov assumption would not hold for the DAG in (a) if there is a hidden common cause as depicted in (b).

sample (or even our entire population) consists of individuals who have some (possibly hidden) effect of both finasteride and *hair regrowth*.. For example, suppose finasteride (F) and apprehension about lack of hair regrowth (G) both cause hypertension[2], and our sample consists of individuals who have hypertension (T). We say a node is **instantiated** when we know its value for the entity currently being modeled. So we are saying the variable T is instantiated to the same value for every entity in our sample. This situation is depicted in Figure 6.14, where the cross through T means that the variable is instantiated. Usually, the instantiation of a common effect creates a dependency between its causes because each cause explains the occurrence of the effect, thereby making the other cause less likely. As noted earlier, psychologists call this *discounting*. So, if this were the case, discounting would explain the correlation between F and G[3]. This type of dependency is called **selection bias**.[4] ∎

In summary, we ordinarily can assume that the causal Markov assumption is justified for a causal graph if the following conditions are satisfied:

1. There are no hidden common causes. That is, all common causes are represented in the graph.

2. There are no causal feedback loops. That is, our graph is a DAG.

---

[2] There is no evidence that either finasteride or apprehension about the lack of hair regrowth causes hypertension. This example is only for the sake of illustration.

[3] Merck eventually did a RCE involving 1879 men aged 18 to 41 with mild to moderate hair loss of the vertex and anterior mid-scalp areas. Half of the men were given 1 mg of finasteride, whereas the other half were given 1 mg of placebo. The results indicated that finasteride does indeed cause hair regrowth. Merck now markets finasteride for hair regrowth under the label *propecia*.

[4] This could happen if our sample is a **convenience sample**, which is a sample in which the participants are selected at the convenience of the researcher. The researcher makes no attempt to ensure that the sample is an accurate representation of the larger population. In the context of the current example, this might be the case if it is convenient for the researcher to observe males hospitalized for hypertension.

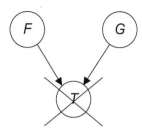

Figure 6.14 T is instantiated.

3. Selection bias is not present.

Note that, for the Markov condition to hold, there must be an edge from X to Y whenever there is a causal path from X to Y besides the ones containing variables in our graph. However, we did not stipulate this requirement above because it is entailed by the definition of a causal graph. Recall that in a causal graph there is an edge from X to Y if X is a direct cause of Y.

6.3.3   Markov Condition without Causality

We have argued that a causal DAG often satisfies the Markov condition with the joint probability distribution of the random variables in the DAG. This does not mean that the edges in a DAG in a Bayesian network must be causal. That is, a DAG can satisfy the Markov condition with the probability distribution of the variables in the DAG without the edges being causal. For example, we showed that the joint probability distribution P of the random variables L, S, and C defined on the set of objects in Figure 6.5 satisfies the Markov condition with the DAG $\mathbb{G}$ in Figure 6.6. However, we would not argue that the color of the objects causes their shape or the letter that is on them. As another example, if we reversed the edges in the DAG in Figure 6.11 to obtain the DAG $E \to DHT \to T$, the new DAG would also satisfy the Markov condition with the probability distribution of the variables, yet the edges would not be causal.

6.4   Inference in Bayesian Networks

As noted previously, a standard application of Bayes' theorem is inference in a two-node Bayesian network. Larger Bayesian networks address the problem of representing the joint probability distribution of a large number of variables. For example, Figure 6.3 represents the joint probability distribution of variables related to credit card fraud. Inference in this network consists of computing the conditional probability of some variable (or set of variables), given that other variables are instantiated to certain values. For example, we might want to compute the probability of credit card fraud, given that gas has been purchased, jewelry has been purchased, and the card holder is male. To accomplish

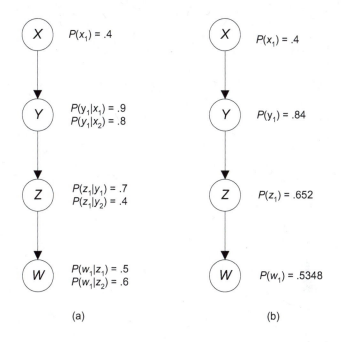

Figure 6.15 A Bayesian network appears in (a), and the prior probabilities of the variables in that network are shown in (b). Each variable has only two values, so only the probability of one is shown in (a).

this inference we need sophisticated algorithms. First, we show simple examples illustrating how one of these algorithms uses the Markov condition and Bayes' theorem to do inference. Then we reference papers describing some of the algorithms. Finally we show examples using the algorithms to do inference.

6.4.1 Examples of Inference

Next we present some examples illustrating how the conditional independencies entailed by the Markov condition can be exploited to accomplish inference in a Bayesian network.

Example 6.9 Consider the Bayesian network in Figure 6.15 (a). The prior probabilities of all variables can be computed using the Law of Total Probability:

$$P(y_1) = P(y_1|x_1)P(x_1) + P(y_1|x_2)P(x_2) = (.9)(.4) + (.8)(.6) = .84$$

$$P(z_1) = P(z_1|y_1)P(y_1) + P(z_1|y_2)P(y_2) = (.7)(.84) + (.4)(.16) = .652$$

$$P(w_1) = P(w_1|z_1)P(z_1) + P(w_1|z_2)P(z_2) = (.5)(.652) + (.6)(.348) = .5348.$$

These probabilities are shown in Figure 6.15 (b). Note that the computation for each variable requires information determined for its parent. We can therefore consider this method a message-passing algorithm in which each node passes its child a message needed to compute the child's probabilities. Clearly, this algorithm applies to an arbitrarily long linked list and to trees. ■

Example 6.10 Suppose now that X is instantiated for x_1. Because the Markov condition entails that each variable is conditionally independent of X given its parent, we can compute the conditional probabilities of the remaining variables by again using the Law of Total Probability (however, now with the background information that $X = x_1$) and passing messages down as follows:

$$P(y_1|x_1) = .9$$

$$
\begin{aligned}
P(z_1|x_1) &= P(z_1|y_1, x_1)P(y_1|x_1) + P(z_1|y_2, x_1)P(y_2|x_1) \\
&= P(z_1|y_1)P(y_1|x_1) + P(z_1|y_2)P(y_2|x_1) \quad // \text{ Markov condition} \\
&= (.7)(.9) + (.4)(.1) = .67
\end{aligned}
$$

$$
\begin{aligned}
P(w_1|x_1) &= P(w_1|z_1, x_1)P(z_1|x_1) + P(w_1|z_2, x_1)P(z_2|x_1) \\
&= P(w_1|z_1)P(z_1|x_1) + P(w_1|z_2)P(z_2|x_1) \\
&= (.5)(.67) + (.6)(1 - .67) = .533.
\end{aligned}
$$

Clearly, this algorithm also applies to an arbitrarily long linked list and to trees. ■

The preceding example shows how we can use downward propagation of messages to compute the conditional probabilities of variables below the instantiated variable. Next we illustrate how to compute conditional probabilities of variables above the instantiated variable.

Example 6.11 Suppose W is instantiated for w_1 (and no other variable is instantiated). We can use upward propagation of messages to compute the conditional probabilities of the remaining variables. First, we use Bayes' theorem to compute $P(z_1|w_1)$:

$$P(z_1|w_1) = \frac{P(w_1|z_1)P(z_1)}{P(w_1)} = \frac{(.5)(.652)}{.5348} = .6096.$$

Then, to compute $P(y_1|w_1)$, we again apply Bayes' theorem:

$$P(y_1|w_1) = \frac{P(w_1|y_1)P(y_1)}{P(w_1)}.$$

We cannot yet complete this computation because we do not know $P(w_1|y_1)$. We can obtain this value using downward propagation as follows:

$$P(w_1|y_1) = (P(w_1|z_1)P(z_1|y_1) + P(w_1|z_2)P(z_2|y_1).$$

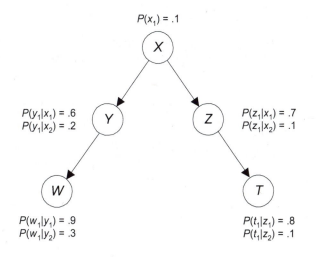

Figure 6.16 A Bayesian network. Each variable has only two possible values, so only the probability of one is shown.

After doing this computation, also computing $P(w_1|y_2)$ (because X will need this value) and then determining $P(y_1|w_1)$, we pass $P(w_1|y_1)$ and $P(w_1|y_2)$ to X. We then compute $P(w_1|x_1)$ and $P(x_1|w_1)$ in sequence:

$$P(w_1|x_1) = (P(w_1|y_1)P(y_1|x_1) + P(w_1|y_2)P(y_2|x_1)$$

$$P(x_1|w_1) = \frac{P(w_1|x_1)P(x_1)}{P(w_1)}.$$

It is left as an exercise to perform these computations. Clearly, this upward propagation scheme applies to an arbitrarily long linked list. ∎

The next example shows how to turn corners in a tree.

Example 6.12 Consider the Bayesian network in Figure 6.16. Suppose W is instantiated for w_1. We compute $P(y_1|w_1)$ followed by $P(x_1|w_1)$ using the upward propagation algorithm just described. Then we proceed to compute $P(z_1|w_1)$ followed by $P(t_1|w_1)$ using the downward propagation algorithm. This is left as an exercise. ∎

6.4.2   Inference Algorithms and Packages

By exploiting local independencies as we did in the previous subsection, Pearl [1986, 1988] developed a message-passing algorithm for inference in Bayesian networks. Based on a method originated in [Lauritzen and Spiegelhalter, 1988], Jensen et al. [1990] developed an inference algorithm that involves the extraction of an undirected triangulated graph from the DAG in a Bayesian network and the creation of a tree, whose vertices are the cliques of this triangulated

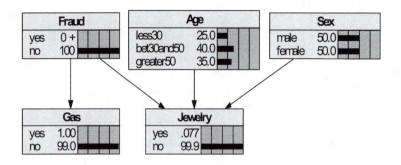

Figure 6.17 The fraud detection Bayesian network in Figure 6.3, implemented using Netica.

graph. Such a tree is called a **junction tree**. Conditional probabilities are then computed by passing messages in the junction tree. Li and D'Ambrosio [1994] took a different approach. They developed an algorithm that approximates finding the optimal way to compute marginal distributions of interest from the joint probability distribution. They call this **symbolic probabilistic inference** (SPI).

All these algorithms are worst-case nonpolynomial time. This is not surprising, as the problem of inference in Bayesian networks has been shown to be NP-hard [Cooper, 1990]. In light of this result, approximation algorithms for inference in Bayesian networks have been developed. One such algorithm, likelihood weighting, was developed independently in [Fung and Chang, 1990] and [Shachter and Peot, 1990]. It is proven in [Dagum and Luby, 1993] that the problem of approximate inference in Bayesian networks is also NP-hard. However, there are restricted classes of Bayesian networks that are provably amenable to a polynomial-time solution (see [Dagum and Chavez, 1993]). Indeed, a variant of the likelihood weighting algorithm, which is worst-case polynomial time as long as the network does not contain extreme conditional probabilities, appears in [Pradhan and Dagum, 1996].

Practitioners need not concern themselves with all these algorithms because a number of packages for doing inference in Bayesian networks have been developed. A few of them are shown here:

1. Netica (www.norsys.com/)

2. GeNIe (genie.sis.pitt.edu/)

3. HUGIN (/www.hugin.com/)

4. Elvira (www.ia.uned.es/~elvira/)

5. BUGS (www.mrc-bsu.cam.ac.uk/bugs/)

In this book we ordinarily use Netica to illustrate inference. Figure 6.17 shows the fraud detection network in Figure 6.3 implemented using Netica.

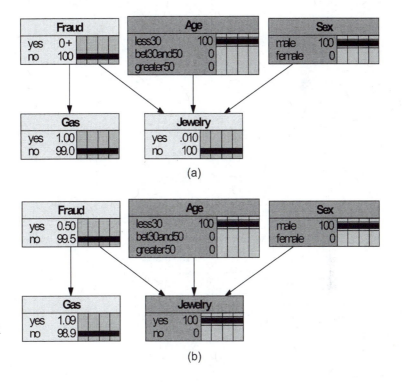

(a)

(b)

Figure 6.18 In (a) *Age* has been instantiated to *less*30 and *Sex* has been instantiated to *male*. In (b) *Age* has been instantiated to *less*30, *Sex* has been instantiated to *male*, and *Jewelry* has been instantiated to *yes*.

6.4.3   Inference Using Netica

Next we illustrate inference in a Bayesian network using Netica. Notice from Figure 6.17 that Netica computes and shows the prior probabilities of the variables rather than showing the conditional probability distributions. Probabilities are shown as percentages. For example, the fact that there is a .077 next to *yes* in the *Jewelry* node means

$$P(Jewelry = yes) = .00077.$$

This is the prior probability of a jewelry purchase in the past 24 hours being charged to any particular credit card.

After variables are instantiated, Netica shows the conditional probabilities of the other variables given these instantiations. In Figure 6.18 (a) we instantiated *Age* to *less*30 and *Sex* to *male*. So the fact that there is .010 next to *yes* in the *Jewelry* node means

$$P(Jewelry = yes|Age = less30, Sex = male) = .00010.$$

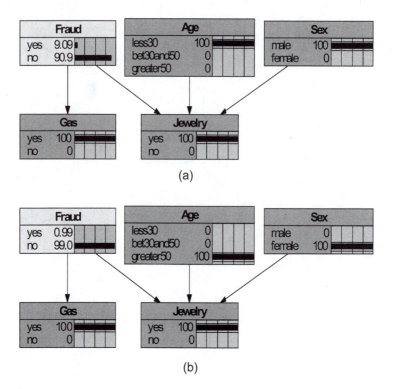

(a)

(b)

Figure 6.19 *Sex* and *Jewelry* have both been instantiated to *yes* in both (a) and (b). However, in (a) the card holder is a young man, whereas in (b) it is an older woman.

Notice that the probability of *Fraud* has not changed. This is what we would expect. First, the Markov condition says that *Fraud* should be independent of *Age* and *Sex*. Second, it seems they should be independent. That is, the fact that the card holder is a young man should not make it more or less likely that the card is being used fraudulently. Figure 6.18 (b) has the same instantiations as Figure 6.18 (a) except that we have also instantiated *Jewelry* to *yes*. Notice that the probability of *Fraud* has now changed. First, the jewelry purchase makes *Fraud* more likely to be *yes*. Second, the fact that the card holder is a young man means it is less likely the card holder would make the purchase, thereby making *Fraud* even more likely to be *yes*.

In Figures 6.19 (a) and 6.19 (b), *Gas* and *Jewelry* have both been instantiated to *yes*. However, in Figure 6.19 (a), the card holder is a young man, whereas in Figure 6.19 (b) it is an older woman. This illustrates discounting of the jewelry purchase. When the card holder is a young man, the probability of *Fraud* being *yes* is high (.0909). However, when it is an older woman, it is still low (.0099) because the fact that the card holder is an older woman explains the jewelry purchase.

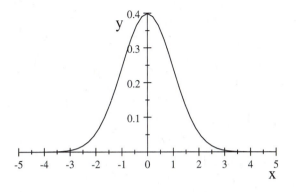

Figure 6.20 The standard normal density function.

6.5 Networks with Continuous Variables

So far in all our Bayesian networks the variables have been discrete. Next we discuss Bayesian networks that contain continuous variables.

6.5.1 Gaussian Bayesian Networks

Recall that the normal distribution is defined as follows:

Definition 6.2 The **normal density function with parameters** μ and σ, where $-\infty < \mu < \infty$ and $\sigma > 0$, is

$$\rho(x) = \frac{1}{\sqrt{2\pi}\sigma} e^{-\frac{(x-\mu)^2}{2\sigma^2}} \qquad -\infty < x < \infty, \qquad (6.1)$$

and is denoted $\text{NormalDen}(x; \mu, \sigma^2)$.

A random variables X that has this density function is said to have a **normal distribution.**◆

If the random variable X has the normal density function, then

$$E(X) = \mu \qquad \text{and} \qquad V(X) = \sigma^2,$$

where E denotes expected value and V denotes variance. The density function $\text{NormalDen}(x; 0, 1^2)$ is called the **standard normal density function**. Figure 6.20 shows this density function.

Gaussian Bayesian networks contain variables that are normally distributed. We motivate such networks with the following example.

Example 6.13 Suppose you are considering taking a job that pays $10 an hour and you expect to work 40 hours per week. However, you are not guaranteed

40 hours, and you estimate the number of hours actually worked in a week to be normally distributed with mean 40 and standard deviation 5. You have not yet fully investigated the benefits such as bonus pay and nontaxable deductions (e.g., contributions to a retirement program). However, you estimate these other influences on your gross taxable weekly income to also be normally distributed with mean 0 (that is, you feel they about offset) and standard deviation 30. Furthermore, you assume that these other influences are independent of your hours worked.

We define the following random variables:

Variable	What the Variable Represents
X	Hours worked in the week
Y	Salary obtained in the week

Based on the preceding discussion, X is distributed as follows:

$$\rho(x) = \text{NormalDen}(x; 40, 5^2).$$

A portion of your salary Y is a deterministic function of X. That is, you will receive $10x$ dollars if you work x hours. However, your gross salary may be greater or less than this based on the other influences we discussed. That is,

$$y = 10x + \varepsilon_Y,$$

where

$$\rho(\varepsilon_Y) = \text{NormalDen}(\varepsilon_Y; 0, 30^2).$$

Because the expected value of those other influences is 0,

$$E(Y|x) = 10x.$$

and because the variance of those other influences is 30^2,

$$V(Y|x) = 30^2.$$

So Y is distributed conditionally as follows:

$$\rho(y|x) = \text{NormalDen}(y; 10x, 30^2).$$

Therefore, the relationship between X and Y is represented by the Bayesian network in Figure 6.21. ∎

The Bayesian network we just developed is an example of a Gaussian Bayesian network. In general, in a Gaussian Bayesian network, the root is normally distributed, and each non-root Y is a linear function of its parents plus an error term ε_Y that is normally distributed with mean 0 and variance σ_Y^2. So if $X_1, X_2, \ldots$ and X_k are the parents of Y, then

$$Y = b_1 x_1 + b_2 x_2 + \cdots b_k x_k + \varepsilon_Y, \tag{6.2}$$

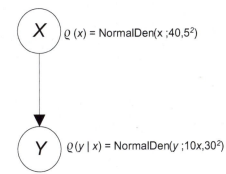

$\varrho(x) = \text{NormalDen}(x; 40, 5^2)$

$\varrho(y \mid x) = \text{NormalDen}(y; 10x, 30^2)$

Figure 6.21 A Gaussian Bayesian network.

where
$$\rho(\varepsilon_Y) = \text{NormalDen}(\varepsilon_Y; 0, \sigma_Y^2),$$
and Y is distributed conditionally as follows:
$$\rho(y|x) = \text{NormalDen}(y; b_1 x_1 + b_2 x_2 + \cdots b_k x_k, \sigma_Y^2).$$

The linear relationship in Equality 6.2 has been used in causal models in economics [Joereskog, 1982], in structural equations in psychology [Bentler, 1980], and in path analysis in sociology and genetics [Kenny, 1979], [Wright, 1921].

Pearl [1988] developed an exact inference algorithm for Gaussian Bayesian networks. It is described in [Neapolitan, 2004]. Most Bayesian network inference algorithms handle Gaussian Bayesian networks. Some use the exact algorithm; others discretize the continuous distribution and then do inference using discrete variables.

Example 6.14 Netica (www.norsys.com/) requires that we discretize continuous variables. However, HUGIN [Olesen et al., 1992] does exact inference in Gaussian Bayesian networks. Figure 6.22 shows the network in Figure 6.21 developed using HUGIN. The prior means and variances are shown under the DAG. Suppose now you just got your paycheck and it is only $300. Your spouse becomes suspicious that you did not work very many hours. So your spouse instantiates Y to 300 in the network. The updated mean and variance of X are shown in Figure 6.22 under the priors. It turns out that the expected value of the hours you worked is only about 32.64. ∎

6.5.2 Hybrid Networks

Hybrid Bayesian networks contain both discrete and continuous variables. Figure 6.23 shows a hybrid network, which will be discussed shortly. Methods for exact inference in hybrid Bayesian networks have been developed. For example, Shenoy [2006] develops a method that approximates general hybrid Bayesian

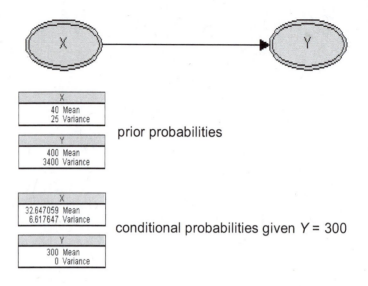

Figure 6.22 The Bayesian network in Figure 6.21, implemented in HUGIN.

networks by a mixture of Gaussian Bayesian networks. However, packages often deal with hybrid networks by discretizing the continuous distributions. HUGIN allows Gaussian variables to have discrete parents while still doing exact inference. It could, therefore, handle the Bayesian network in the following example.

Example 6.15 Recall the Bayesian network in Figure 6.3, which models fraudulent use of a credit card. Suppose that if jewelry is purchased, the cost of the jewelry is likely to be greater if the purchase was due to fraudulent use. We could model this situation using the hybrid Bayesian network in Figure 6.23. The variable *Cost* is normally distributed given each set of values of its discrete parents. Note that if $J = no$, the distribution is NormalDen$(s; 0, 0)$. This is the same as stating that

$$P(C = 0 | F = yes, J = no) = 0.$$

However, we showed the conditional probability distribution as a normal distribution to be consistent with the other distributions of C.   ∎

Example 6.16 The protein transcription factor produced by one gene can have a causal effect on the level of mRNA (called the gene expression level) of another gene. Researchers endeavor to learn these causal effects from data. Gene expression level is often set as the ratio of measured expression to a control level. So, values greater than 1 would indicate a relatively high expression level, whereas values less than 1 would indicate a relatively low expression level. Because gene expression levels are continuous, we could try learning a

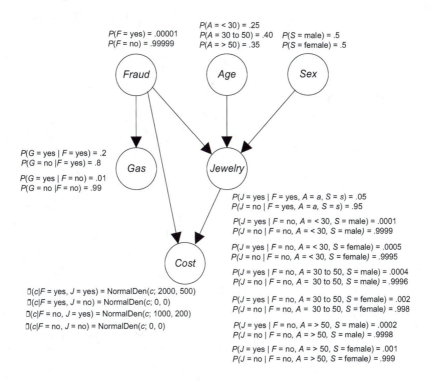

Figure 6.23 A hybrid Bayesian network modeling the situation in which the cost of the jewelry is likely to be higher if the purchase was fraudulent.

Gaussian Bayesian network. Another approach taken in [Segal et al., 2005] is to learn a network in which each variable is normally distributed given values of its parents. However, each parent has only two values, namely *high* and *low*, which determine the conditional distribution of the child. The value *high* represents all expression levels greater than 1, and the value *low* represents all expression levels less than or equal to 1. Such a network appears in Figure 6.24. The nodes in the network represent genes. This network is not exactly hybrid, because every variable is continuous. However, the conditional distributions are based on discrete values. ∎

6.6 Obtaining the Probabilities

So far we have simply shown the conditional probability distributions in the Bayesian networks we have presented. We have not been concerned with how we obtained them. For example, in the credit card fraud example, we simply stated that $P(Age = less30) = .25$. However, how did we obtain this and other probabilities? As mentioned at the beginning of this chapter, they can either be obtained from the subjective judgments of an expert in the area, or they can be learned from data. In Chapter 12 we discuss techniques for learning them

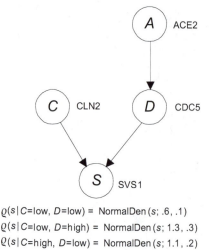

$\varrho(s\,|\,C{=}low,\ D{=}low)\ =\ \text{NormalDen}\,(s;\,.6,\,.1)$
$\varrho(s\,|\,C{=}low,\ D{=}high)\ =\ \text{NormalDen}\,(s;\,1.3,\,.3)$
$\varrho(s\,|\,C{=}high,\ D{=}low)\ =\ \text{NormalDen}\,(s;\,1.1,\,.2)$
$\varrho(s\,|\,C{=}high,\ D{=}high)\ =\ \text{NormalDen}\,(s;\,1.7,\,.4)$

Figure 6.24 A Bayesian network showing possible causal relationships among the expression levels of genes. Only the conditional probability distribution of the leaf is shown.

from data. Here, we show a technique for simplifying the process when a node has multiple parents

After discussing a problem in obtaining the conditional probabilities when a node has multiple parents, we present models that address this problem.

6.6.1   Difficulty Inherent in Multiple Parents

Suppose lung cancer, bronchitis, and tuberculosis all cause fatigue, and we need to model this relationship as part of a system for medical diagnosis. The portion of the DAG concerning only these four variables appears in Figure 6.25. We need to assess eight conditional probabilities for node F, one for each of the eight combinations of that node's parents. That is, we need to assess the following:

$$P(F = yes | B = no, T = no, L = no)$$

$$P(F = yes | B = no, T = no, L = yes)$$

$$\ldots$$

$$P(F = yes | B = yes, T = yes, L = yes).$$

It would be quite difficult to obtain these values either from data or from an expert physician. For example, to obtain the value of $P(F = yes | B = yes, T = yes, L = no)$ directly from data, we would need a sufficiently large population of individuals who are known to have both bronchitis and tuberculosis, but not

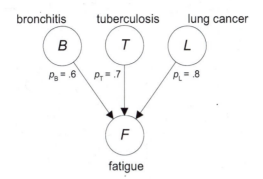

Figure 6.25 We need to assess eight conditional probabilities for node F.

lung cancer. To obtain this value directly from an expert, the expert would have to be familiar with the likelihood of being fatigued when two diseases are present and the third is not. Next, we show a method for obtaining these conditional probabilities in an indirect way.

6.6.2 Basic Noisy OR-Gate Model

The noisy OR-gate model concerns the case where the relationships between variables ordinarily represent causal influences, and each variable has only two values. The situation shown in Figure 6.25 is a typical example. Rather than assessing all eight probabilities, we assess the causal strength of each cause for its effect. The **causal strength** is the probability of the cause resulting in the effect whenever the cause is present. In Figure 6.25 we have shown the causal strength p_B of bronchitis for fatigue to be .6. *The assumption is that bronchitis will always result in fatigue unless some unknown mechanism inhibits this from taking place, and this inhibition takes place 40% of the time.* So 60% of the time, bronchitis will result in fatigue. Presently, *we assume that all causes of the effect are articulated in the DAG, and the effect cannot occur unless at least one of its causes is present.* In this case, mathematically we have

$$p_B = P(F = yes | B = yes, T = no, L = no).$$

The causal strengths of tuberculosis and lung cancer for fatigue are also shown in Figure 6.25. These three causal strengths should not be as difficult to ascertain as all eight conditional probabilities. For example, to obtain p_B from data, we only need a population of individuals who have lung bronchitis and do not have the other diseases. To obtain p_B from an expert, the expert need only ascertain the frequency with which bronchitis gives rise to fatigue.

We can obtain the eight conditional probabilities we need from the three causal strengths if we make one additional assumption. *We need to assume that the mechanisms that inhibit the causes act independently from each other.* For example, the mechanism that inhibits bronchitis from resulting in fatigue acts independently from the mechanism that inhibits tuberculosis from resulting in fatigue. Mathematically, this assumption is as follows:

$$
\begin{aligned}
P(F = no | B = yes, T = yes, L = no) &= (1 - p_B)(1 - p_T) \\
&= (1 - .6)(1 - .7) = .12.
\end{aligned}
$$

Note that in the previous equality we are conditioning on bronchitis and tuberculosis both being present and lung cancer being absent. In this case, fatigue should occur unless the causal effects of bronchitis and tuberculosis are both inhibited. Because we have assumed these inhibitions act independently, the probability that both effects are inhibited is the product of the probabilities that each is inhibited, which is $(1 - p_B)(1 - p_T)$.

In this same way, if all three causes are present, we have

$$
\begin{aligned}
P(F = no | B = yes, T = yes, L = yes) &= (1 - p_B)(1 - p_T)(1 - p_L) \\
&= (1 - .6)(1 - .7)(1 - .8) = .024.
\end{aligned}
$$

Notice that when more causes are present, it is less probable that fatigue will be absent. This is what we would expect. It is left as an exercise to compute the remaining six conditional probabilities needed for node F in Figure 6.25. The reason that we only need to compute eight conditional probabilities is because the variables are binary, and therefore we need only compute the probabilities that $F = no$. The probabilities that $F = yes$ are are uniquely determined by these. For example,

$$
P(F = yes | B = yes, T = yes, L = yes) = 1 - .024 = .976.
$$

Although we illustrated the model for three causes, it clearly extends to an arbitrary number of causes. We showed the assumptions in the model in italics when we introduced them. Next, we summarize them and show the general formula.

The **noisy OR-gate model** makes the following three assumptions:

1. **Causal inhibition:** This assumption entails that there is some mechanism which inhibits a cause from bringing about its effect, and the presence of the cause results in the presence of the effect if and only if this mechanism is disabled (turned off).

2. **Exception independence:** This assumption entails that the mechanism which inhibits one cause is independent of the mechanism that inhibits other causes.

3. **Accountability:** This assumption entails that an effect can happen only if at least one of its causes is present and is not being inhibited.

The **general formula for the noisy OR-gate model** is as follows: Suppose Y has n causes $X_1, X_2, \ldots, X_n$, all variables are binary, and we assume the noisy OR-gate model. Let p_i be the causal strength of X_i for Y. That is,

$$
p_i = P(Y = yes | X_1 = no, X_2 = no, \ldots X_i = yes, \ldots X_n = no).
$$

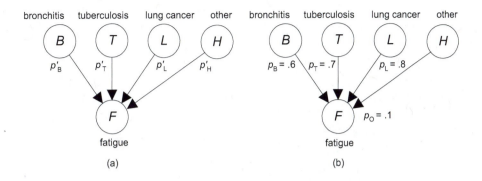

Figure 6.26 The probabilities in (a) are the causal strengths in the noisy OR-gate model. The probabilities in (b) are the ones we ascertain.

Then if X is a set of nodes that are instantiated to yes,

$$P(Y = no | \mathsf{X}) = \prod_{i \text{ such that } X_i \in \mathsf{X}} (1 - p_i).$$

6.6.3   Leaky Noisy OR-Gate Model

Of the three assumptions in the noisy OR-gate model, the assumption of accountability seems to be justified least often. For example, in the case of fatigue, there are certainly other causes of fatigue such as listening to a lecture by Professor Neapolitan. So the model in Figure 6.25 does not contain all causes of fatigue, and the assumption of accountability is not justified. It seems in many, if not most, situations we would not be certain that we have elaborated all known causes of an effect. Next, we show a version of the model that does not assume accountability. The derivation of the formula for this model is not simple and intuitive like the one for the basic noisy OR-gate model. So here we simply present the model without deriving it. The formula is derived in [Neapolitan and Jiang, 2007].

6.6.3.1   Leaky Noisy OR-Gate Formula

The leaky noisy OR-gate model assumes that all causes that have not been articulated can be grouped into one other cause H and that the articulated causes, along with H, satisfy the three assumptions in the noisy OR-gate model. This is illustrated for the fatigue example in Figure 6.26 (a). The probabilities in that figure are the causal strengths in the noisy OR-gate model. For example,

$$p'_B = P(F = yes | B = yes, T = no, L = no, H = no).$$

We could not ascertain these values because we do not know whether or not H is present. The probabilities in Figure 6.26 (b) are the ones we could ascertain. For each of the three articulated causes, the probability shown is the probability the effect is present given that the remaining two articulated causes are not present. For example,

$$p_B = P(F = yes | B = yes, T = no, L = no).$$

Note the difference in the probabilities p'_B and p_B. The latter one does not condition on a value of H, while the former one does. The probability p_0 is different from the other probabilities. It is the probability that the effect will be present given none of the articulated causes are present. That is,

$$p_0 = P(F = yes | B = no, T = no, L = no).$$

Note again that we are not conditioning on a value of H.

Our goal is to develop conditional probability distributions for a Bayesian network containing the nodes B, T, L, and F from the probabilities ascertained in Figure 6.26 (b). We show an example that realizes this goal after presenting the formula necessary to the task.

The **general formula for the leaky noisy OR-gate model** is as follows (a derivation appears in the next subsection): Suppose Y has n causes $X_1, X_2, \ldots, X_n$, all variables are binary, and we assume the leaky noisy OR-gate model. Let

$$p_i = P(Y = yes | X_1 = no, X_2 = no, \ldots X_i = yes, \ldots X_n = no) \tag{6.3}$$

$$p_0 = P(Y = yes | X_1 = no, X_2 = no, \ldots X_n = no). \tag{6.4}$$

Then if X is a set of nodes that are instantiated to yes,

$$P(Y = no | \mathsf{X}) = (1 - p_0) \prod_{i \text{ such that } X_i \in \mathsf{X}} \frac{1 - p_i}{1 - p_0}.$$

Example 6.17 Let's compute the conditional probabilities for a Bayesian network containing the nodes B, T, L, and F from the probabilities ascertained in Figure 6.26 (b). We have

$$
\begin{aligned}
P(F = no | B = no, T = no, L = no) &= 1 - p_0 \\
&= 1 - .1 = .9
\end{aligned}
$$

$$
\begin{aligned}
P(F = no | B = no, T = no, L = yes) &= (1 - p_0) \frac{1 - p_L}{1 - p_0} \\
&= 1 - .8 = .2
\end{aligned}
$$

$$
\begin{aligned}
P(F = no | B = no, T = yes, L = no) &= (1 - p_0) \frac{1 - p_T}{1 - p_0} \\
&= 1 - .7 = .3
\end{aligned}
$$

$$
\begin{aligned}
P(F = no | B = no, T = yes, L = yes) &= (1 - p_0) \frac{1 - p_T}{1 - p_0} \frac{1 - p_L}{1 - p_0} \\
&= \frac{(1 - .7)(1 - .8)}{1 - .1} = .067
\end{aligned}
$$

sushi chef

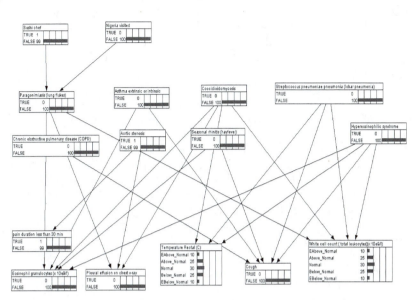

Figure 6.27 A small portion of the Bayesian network in Promedas. Courtesy of Bert Kappen, Promedas project.

It is left as an exercise to compute the remaining four conditional probabilities. ∎

6.6.4 Further Models

A generalization of the noisy OR-gate model to the case of more than two values appears in [Srinivas, 1993]. Diez and Druzdzel [2002] propose a general framework for canonical models, classifying them into three categories: deterministic, noisy, and leaky. They then analyze the most common families of canonical models, namely the noisy OR/MAX, the noisy AND/MIN, and the noisy XOR. Other models for succinctly representing the conditional distributions use the **sigmoid** function [Neal, 1992] and the **logit** function [McLachlan and Krishnan, 2008]. Another approach to reducing the number of parameter estimates is the use of **embedded Bayesian networks**, which is discussed in [Heckerman and Meek, 1997].

6.7 Large-Scale Application: Promedas

Bayesian networks have been applied successfully in many domains. Section 8.8 discusses many of these applications. Here we present perhaps the largest

sushi chef

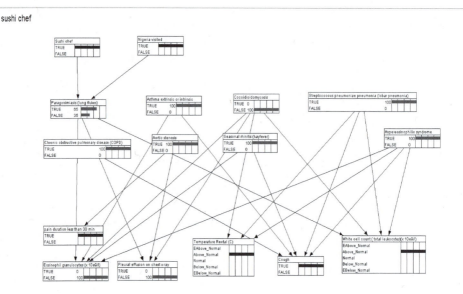

Figure 6.28 The Bayesian network in Figure 6.27 with some of the nodes instantiated. Courtesy of Bert Kappen, Promedas project.

deployed Bayesian network, namely Promedas.

> **Promedas** (PRObabilistic MEdical Diagnostic Advisory System) is a diagnostic decision support system used in health care. This computer program was developed by research groups of SNN Adaptive Intelligence, University of Nijmegen and University Medical Center Utrecht. Promedas produces a differential diagnosis using a set of patient findings such as history data, physical findings and laboratory data. The findings can be provided by an individual user or an Electronic Patient Records. For each diagnoses Promedas suggests additional tests that can be performed to make the differential diagnosis more precise.
>
> — http://www.promedas.nl/

A small part of the Bayesian network in Promedas appears in Figure 6.27. This figure shows a subset of diagnoses and some of the conditions that affect their prior probability. In addition, some tests are shown, whose probability is affected by these diagnoses. Connections between these diagnoses and other tests are suppressed, as well as connections between the shown tests and other diagnoses. Figure 6.28 shows as an application of this small subnetwork to a particular patient. This patient is a sushi chef who recently visited Nigeria. Both these facts affect his prevalence for lung flukes. His white blood cell count is above normal as is his rectal temperature. In addition, he coughs and at times has some unspecific pain. Based on these findings, Promedas computes the conditional probabilities for each of the diagnoses.

Promedas has been is used at Utrecht Academic Hospital in the Netherlands for about 2 years by about 100 doctors in the process of real decision making as an advisory tool. Based on their positive experiences, this hospital has decided to formally implement it in a new electronic patient dossier that will be installed in the hospital. Promedas is in a new commercial phase where the aim is to implement it in more hospitals.

EXERCISES

Section 6.2

Exercise 6.1 In Example 6.3 it was left as an exercise to show for all values of s, l, and c that

$$P(s, l, c) = P(s|c)P(l|c)P(c).$$

Show this.

Exercise 6.2 It is important to realize that we cannot take just any DAG and expect a joint distribution to equal the product of its conditional distributions in the DAG. This is only true if the Markov condition is satisfied. You will illustrate that this is the case in this exercise. Consider the joint probability distribution P in Example 6.1.

1. Show that probability distribution P satisfies the Markov condition with the DAG in Figure 6.29 (a) and that P is equal to the product of its conditional distributions in that DAG.

2. Show that probability distribution P satisfies the Markov condition with the DAG in Figure 6.29 (b) and that P is equal to the product of its conditional distributions in that DAG.

Show that probability distribution P does not satisfy the Markov condition with the DAG in Figure 6.29 (c) and that P is not equal to the product of its conditional distributions in that DAG.

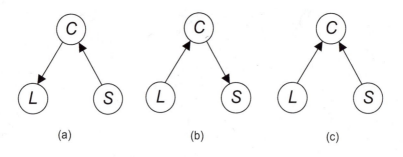

Figure 6.29 The probability distribution discussed in Example 6.1 satisfies the Markov condition with the DAGs in (a) and (b), but not with the DAG in (c).

Section 6.3

Exercise 6.3 Professor Morris investigated gender bias in hiring in the following way. He gave hiring personnel equal numbers of male and female résumés to review, and then he investigated whether their evaluations were correlated with gender. When he submitted a paper summarizing his results to a psychology journal, the reviewers rejected the paper because they said this was an example of fat-hand manipulation. Investigate the concept of fat-hand manipulation, and explain why the journal reviewers might have thought this.

Exercise 6.4 Consider the following piece of medical knowledge: tuberculosis and lung cancer can each cause shortness of breath (dyspnea) and a positive chest X-ray. Bronchitis is another cause of dyspnea. A recent visit to Asia could increase the probability of tuberculosis. Smoking can cause both lung cancer and bronchitis. Create a DAG representing the causal relationships among these variables. Complete the construction of a Bayesian network by determining values for the conditional probability distributions in this DAG, either based on your own subjective judgment or from data.

Exercise 6.5 Explain why, if we reverse the edges in the DAG in Figure 6.11 to obtain the DAG $E \rightarrow D \rightarrow T$, the new DAG also satisfies the Markov condition with the probability distribution of the variables.

Section 6.4

Exercise 6.6 Compute $P(x_1|w_1)$, assuming the Bayesian network in Figure 6.15.

Exercise 6.7 Compute $P(t_1|w_1)$, assuming the Bayesian network in Figure 6.16.

Exercise 6.8 Compute $P(x_1|t_2, w_1)$, assuming the Bayesian network in Figure 6.16.

Exercise 6.9 Using Netica, develop the Bayesian network in Figure 6.3, and use that network to determine the following conditional probabilities.

1. $P(F = yes|Sex = male)$. Is this conditional probability different from $P(F = yes)$? Explain why it is or is not.

2. $P(F = yes|J = yes)$. Is this conditional probability different from $P(F = yes)$? Explain why it is or is not.

3. $P(F = yes|Sex = male, J = yes)$. Is this conditional probability different from $P(F = yes|J = yes)$? Explain why it is or is not.

4. $P(G = yes|F = yes)$. Is this conditional probability different from $P(G = yes)$? Explain why it is or is not.

5. $P(G = yes|J = yes)$. Is this conditional probability different from $P(G = yes)$? Explain why it is or is not.

6. $P(G = yes|J = yes, F = yes)$. Is this conditional probability different from $P(G = yes|F = yes)$? Explain why it is or is not.

7. $P(G = yes|A = < 30)$. Is this conditional probability different from $P(G = yes)$? Explain why it is or is not.

8. $P(G = yes|A = < 30, J = yes)$. Is this conditional probability different from $P(G = yes|J = yes)$? Explain why it is or is not.

Section 6.5

Exercise 6.10 Using Netica, HUGIN, or some other Bayesian network software package, implement the Bayesian network in Figure 6.23. Using that network, compute the conditional probabilities in Exercise 6.9. Compare your answers to those obtained in Exercise 6.9.

Section 6.6

Exercise 6.11 It was left as an exercise to compute the remaining six conditional probabilities needed for node F in Figure 6.25 using the noisy OR-gate model. Do this.

Exercise 6.12 Assume the noisy OR-gate model and the causal strengths are those shown in Figure 6.30. Compute the probability $T = yes$ for all combinations of values of the parents.

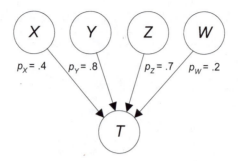

Figure 6.30 The noisy OR-gate model is assumed.

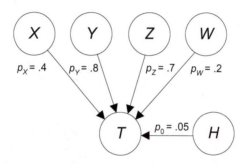

Figure 6.31 The leaky noisy OR-gate model is assumed.

Exercise 6.13 In Example 6.17 it was left as an exercise to compute the remaining four conditional probabilities assuming the leaky noisy OR-gate model. Do this.

Exercise 6.14 Assume the leaky noisy OR-gate model and the relevant probabilities are those shown in Figure 6.31. Compute the probability $T = yes$ for all combinations of values of the parents. Compare the results to those obtained in Exercise 6.12.

Chapter 7

Advanced Properties of Bayesian Network

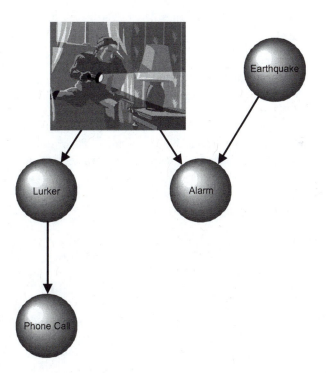

If Mr. Holmes' neighbor Dr. Watson called to report that he sees a lurker, Mr. Holmes would reason that there probably is a lurker; therefore he might be burglarized, which means his alarm might sound. However, if Mr. Holmes already knew there was a burglar as depicted above, then the phone call could not make a burglar more likely, which means the likelihood of the alarm sounding would not go up. This conditional independency, however, does not follow from the statement of the Markov condition. That is, the Markov condition only says that *Lurker* and *Alarm* are independent given *Burglar*; it does not say that *Phone Call* and *Alarm* are independent given *Burglar*. It turns out that certain conditional independencies such as this one are entailed by the Markov condition. That is, if the Markov condition is satisfied, they must hold. These entailed conditional independencies are discussed in Section 7.1.

Recall that we argued in Chapter 6 that if Mr. Holmes knew the alarm had sounded, then knowledge of the earthquake should bring down the probability of having been burglarized. This conditional dependency is not entailed by the Markov condition; that condition only entails independencies. However, it is entailed by another condition called *faithfulness*. This condition is introduced in Section 7.2.1. Finally, in Section 7.4 we discuss Markov blankets and Markov boundaries, which are sets of variables that render a given variable conditionally independent of all other variables.

7.1   Entailed Conditional Independencies

If $(\mathbb{G}, P)$ satisfies the Markov condition, then each node in $\mathbb{G}$ is conditionally independent of the set of all its nondescendents given its parents. Do these conditional independencies entail any other conditional independencies? That is, if $(\mathbb{G}, P)$ satisfies the Markov condition, are there any other conditional independencies that P must satisfy other than the one based on a node's parents? The answer is yes. Such conditional independencies are called *entailed conditional independencies*. Specifically, we say a DAG **entails a conditional independency** if every probability distribution that satisfies the Markov condition with the DAG must have the conditional independency. Before explicitly showing all the entailed conditional independencies, we illustrate that one would expect these conditional independencies.

7.1.1   Examples of Entailed Conditional Independencies

Suppose some distribution P satisfies the Markov condition with the DAG in Figure 7.1 (a). Then we know $I_P(C, \{F, G\} | B)$, because B is the parent of C, and F and G are nondescendents of C. Furthermore, we know $I_P(B, G | F)$ because F is the parent of B, and G is a nondescendent of B. These are the only conditional independencies, according to the statement of the Markov condition. However, can any other conditional independencies be deduced from them? For example, can we conclude $I_P(C, G | F)$? Let's first give the variables meaning and the DAG a causal interpretation to see if we would expect this conditional independency.

Suppose we are investigating the way that professors obtain citations, and the variables represent the following:

G: Graduate program quality
F: First job quality
B: Number of publications
C: Number of citations

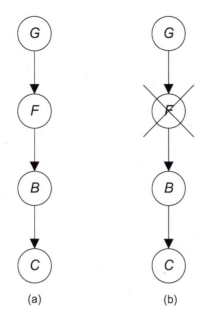

Figure 7.1 A causal DAG is shown in (a). The variable F is instantiated in (b).

Furthermore, suppose the DAG in Figure 7.1 (a) represents the causal relationships among these variables, and there are no hidden common causes.[1] Then it is reasonable to make the causal Markov assumption, and we would feel that the probability distribution of the variables satisfies the Markov condition with the DAG. Suppose we learn that Professor La Budde attended a graduate program (G) of high quality. We would now expect that his first job (F) may well be of high quality, which means that he should have a large number of publications (B), which in turn implies he should have a large number of citations (C). Therefore, we would not expect $I_P(C, G)$.

Suppose we next learn that Professor Pellegrini's first job (F) was of high quality. That is, we instantiate F to "high quality." The cross through the node F in Figure 7.1 (b) indicates it is instantiated. We would now expect his number of publications (B) to be large and, in turn, his number of citations (C) to be large. If Professor Pellegrini then tells us he attended a graduate program (G) of high quality, would we expect the number of citations to be even higher than we previously thought? It seems not. The graduate program's high quality implies that the number of citations is probably large, because it implies that the first job is probably of high quality. Once we already know that the first job is of high quality, the information concerning the graduate program should be irrelevant to our beliefs concerning the number of citations.

---

[1] We make no claim that this model accurately represents the causal relationships among the variables. See [Spirtes et al., 1993; 2000] for a detailed discussion of this problem.

Therefore, we would expect C to not only be conditionally independent of G given its parent B, but also its grandparent F. Either one seems to block the dependency between G and C that exists through the chain $[G, F, B, C]$. So, we would expect $I_P(C, G|F)$.

It is straightforward to show that the Markov condition does indeed entail $I_P(C, G|F)$ for the DAG $\mathbb{G}$ in Figure 7.1. We show this next. If $(\mathbb{G}, P)$ satisfies the Markov condition,

$$
\begin{aligned}
P(c|g, f) &= \sum_b P(c|b, g, f)P(b|g, f) \\
&= \sum_b P(c|b, f)P(b|f) \\
&= P(c|f).
\end{aligned}
$$

The first equality is due to the Law of Total Probability (in the background space that we know the values of g and f), the second equality is due to the Markov condition, and the last equality is again due to the Law of Total Probability.

If we have an arbitrarily long directed linked list of variables, and P satisfies the Markov condition with that list, in the same way as just illustrated we can show that for any variable in the list, the set of variables above it is conditionally independent of the set of variables below it given that variable. That is, the variable blocks the dependency transmitted through the chain.

Suppose now that P does not satisfy the Markov condition with the DAG in Figure 7.1 (a) because there is a common cause A of G and B. For the sake of illustration, let's say that A represents the following in the current example:

$$A: \quad \text{Ability}$$

Further, suppose there are no other hidden common causes, so we would now expect P to satisfy the Markov condition with the DAG in Figure 7.2 (a). Would we still expect $I_P(C, G|F)$? It seems not. For example, as before, suppose that we initially learn Professor Pellegrini's first job (F) was of high quality. This instantiation is shown in Figure 7.2 (b). We learn next that his graduate program (G) was of high quality. Given the current model, the fact that G is of high quality is indicative of his having high ability (A), which can directly affect his publication rate (B) and therefore his citation rate (C). So, we now would feel his citation rate (C) could be even higher than what we thought when we only knew his first job (F) was of high quality. This means we would not feel $I_P(C, G|F)$, as we did with the previous model. Suppose next that we know Professor Pellegrini's first job (F) was of high quality and that he has high ability (A). These instantiations appear in Figure 7.2 (c). In this case, his attendance at a high-quality graduate program (G) can no longer be indicative of his ability (A), and therefore it cannot affect our belief concerning his citation rate (C) through the chain $[G, A, B, C]$. That is, this chain is blocked at A. So, we would expect $I_P(C, G|\{A, F\})$. Indeed, it is possible to prove that the Markov condition does entail $I_P(C, G|\{A, F\})$.

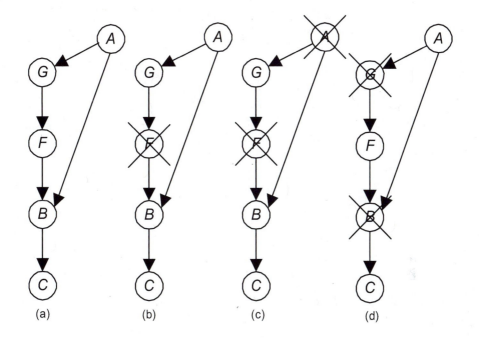

Figure 7.2 A causal DAG is shown in (a). The variable F is instantiated in (b). The variables A and F are instantiated in (c). The variables B and G are instantiated in (d).

Finally, consider the conditional independency $I_P(F, A|G)$. This independency is obtained directly by applying the Markov condition to the DAG in Figure 7.2 (a). So, we will not offer an intuitive explanation for it. Rather, we discuss whether we would expect the conditional independency to still exist if we also knew the state of B. Suppose we first learn that Professor Georgakis has a high publication rate (B) and attended a high-quality graduate program (G). These instantiations are shown in Figure 7.2 (d). We later learn she also has high ability (A). In this case, her high ability (A) could explain her high publication rate (B), thereby making it less probable she had a high-quality first job (F). As mentioned in Section 6.1, psychologists call this *discounting*. So, the chain $[A, B, F]$ is opened by instantiating B, and we would not expect $I_P(F, A|\{B, G\})$. Indeed, the Markov condition does not entail $I_P(F, A|\{B, G\})$. Note that the instantiation of C should also open the chain $[A, B, F]$. That is, if we know the citation rate (C) is high, then it is probable the publication rate (B) is high, and each of the causes of B can explain this high probability. Indeed, the Markov condition does not entail $I_P(F, A|\{C, G\})$, either.

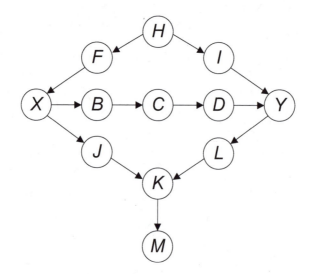

Figure 7.3 This DAG illustrates the chains that can transmit a dependency between X and Y.

7.1.2   d-Separation

Figure 7.3 shows the chains that can transmit a dependency between variables X and Y in a Bayesian network. To discuss these dependencies intuitively, we give the edges in that figure causal interpretations as follows:

1. The chain $[X, B, C, D, Y]$ is a causal path from X to Y. In general, there is a dependency between X and Y on this chain, and the instantiation of any intermediate cause on the chain blocks the dependency.

2. The chain $[X, F, H, I, Y]$ is a chain in which H is a common cause of X and Y. In general, there is a dependency between any X and Y on this chain, and the instantiation of the common cause H or either of the intermediate causes F and I blocks the dependency.

3. The chain $[X, J, K, L, Y]$ is a chain in which X and Y both cause K. There is no dependency between X and Y on this chain. However, if we instantiate K or M, in general a dependency would be created. We would then need to also instantiate J or L to render X and Y independent.

To render X and Y conditionally independent, we need to instantiate at least one variable on all the chains that transmit a dependency between X and Y. So, we would need to instantiate at least one variable on the chain $[X, B, C, D, Y]$, at least one variable on the chain $[X, F, H, I, Y]$, and, if K or M are instantiated, at least one other variable on the chain $[X, J, K, L, Y]$.

Now that we have discussed intuitively how dependencies can be transmitted and blocked in a DAG, we show precisely what conditional independencies are entailed by the Markov condition. To do this, we need the notion of *d-separation*, which we define shortly. First we present some preliminary concepts. We say there is a **head-to-head meeting** at X on a chain in a DAG $\mathbb{G}$ if the edges incident to X both have their arrows into X. For example, the chain $Y \leftarrow W \rightarrow X \leftarrow V$ has a head-to-head meeting at X. We say there is a **head-to-tail meeting** at X on a chain in a DAG $\mathbb{G}$ if precisely one of the edges incident to X has its arrows into X. For example, the chain $Y \leftarrow W \leftarrow X \leftarrow V$ has a head-to-tail meeting at X. We say there is a **tail-to-tail meeting** at X on a chain in a DAG $\mathbb{G}$ if neither of the edges incident to X has its arrows into X. For example, the chain $Y \leftarrow W \leftarrow X \rightarrow V$ has a tail-to-tail meeting at X. We now have the following definition:

Definition 7.1 Suppose we have a DAG $\mathbb{G} = (\mathsf{V}, \mathsf{E})$, a chain ρ in the DAG connecting two nodes X and Y, and a subset of nodes $\mathsf{W} \subseteq \mathsf{V}$. We say that the chain ρ is **blocked** by W if at least one of the following is true:

1. There is a node $Z \in \mathsf{W}$ that has a head-to-tail meeting on ρ.

2. There is a node $Z \in \mathsf{W}$ that has a tail-to-tail meeting on ρ.

3. There is a node Z, such that Z and all Z's descendents are not in W, that has a head-to-head meeting on ρ.◆

Example 7.1 For the DAG in Figure 7.3, the following are some examples of chains that are blocked and that are not blocked.

1. The chain $[X, B, C, D, Y]$ is blocked by $W = \{C\}$ because there is a head-to-tail meeting at C.

2. The chain $[X, B, C, D, Y]$ is blocked by $W = \{C, H\}$ because there is a head-to-tail meeting at C.

3. The chain $[X, F, H, I, Y]$ is blocked by $W = \{C, H\}$ because there is a tail-to-tail meeting at H.

4. The chain $[X, J, K, L, Y]$ is blocked by $W = \{C, H\}$ because there is a head-to-head meeting at K, and K and M are both not in W.

5. The chain $[X, J, K, L, Y]$ is not blocked by $W = \{C, H, K\}$ because there is a head-to-head meeting at K, and K is not in W.

6. The chain $[X, J, K, L, Y]$ is blocked by $W = \{C, H, K, L\}$ because there is a head-to-tail meeting at L. ■

We can now define d-separation.

Definition 7.2 Suppose we have a DAG $\mathbb{G} = (\mathsf{V}, \mathsf{E})$ and a subset of nodes $\mathsf{W} \subseteq \mathsf{V}$. Then X and Y are **d-separated** by W in $\mathbb{G}$ if every chain between X and Y is blocked by W. We write

$$I_{\mathbb{G}}(X, Y | \mathsf{W}).◆$$

Definition 7.3 Suppose we have a DAG $\mathbb{G} = (V, E)$ and three subsets of nodes $X, Y \subseteq V$, and W. We say X and Y are d-separated by W in $\mathbb{G}$ if for every $X \in X$ and $Y \in Y$, X and Y are d-separated by W. We write

$$I_\mathbb{G}(X, Y | W). \blacklozenge$$

As you might have already suspected, d-separation recognizes all the conditional independencies entailed by the Markov condition. Specifically, we have the following theorem.

Theorem 7.1 Suppose we have a DAG $\mathbb{G} = (V, E)$ and three subsets of nodes $X, Y,$ and $W \subseteq V$. Then $\mathbb{G}$ entails the conditional independency $I_P(X, Y | W)$ if and only if $I_\mathbb{G}(X, Y | W)$.

Proof. The proof can be found in [Neapolitan, 1989]. ∎

We stated the theorem for sets of variables, but clearly it holds for single variables. That is, if X contains a single variable X and Y contains a single variable Y, then $I_P(X, Y | W)$ is the same as $I_P(X, Y | W)$. We show examples of this simpler case next and investigate more complex sets in the exercises.

Example 7.2 Owing to Theorem 7.1, the following are some conditional independencies the Markov condition entails for the DAG in Figure 7.3.

Conditional Independency	Reason Conditional Independency Is Entailed
$I_P(X, Y | \{H, C\})$	$[X, F, H, I, Y]$ is blocked at H $[X, B, C, D, Y]$ is blocked at C $[X, J, K, L, Y]$ is blocked at K
$I_P(X, Y | \{F, D\})$	$[X, F, H, I, Y]$ is blocked at F $[X, B, C, D, Y]$ is blocked at D $[X, J, K, L, Y]$ is blocked at K
$I_P(X, Y | \{H, C, K, L\})$	$[X, F, H, I, Y]$ is blocked at H $[X, B, C, D, Y]$ is blocked at C $[X, J, K, L, Y]$ is blocked at L
$I_P(X, Y | \{H, C, M, L\})$	$[X, F, H, I, Y]$ is blocked at H $[X, B, C, D, Y]$ is blocked at C $[X, J, K, L, Y]$ is blocked at L

In the third row it is necessary to include L to obtain the independency because there is a head-to-head meeting at K on the chain $[X, J, K, L, Y]$, and $K \in \{H, C, K, L\}$. Similarly, in the fourth row, it is necessary to include L to obtain the independency because there is a head-to-head meeting at K on the chain $[X, J, K, L, Y]$, M is a descendent of K, and $M \in \{H, C, M, L\}$. ∎

Example 7.3 Owing to Theorem 7.1, the following are some conditional independencies the Markov condition does not entail for the DAG in Figure 7.3.

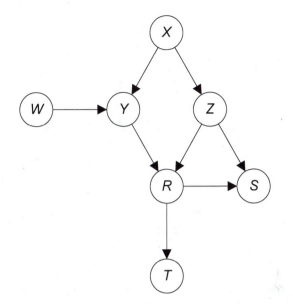

Figure 7.4 The Markov condition entails $I_P(W, X)$ for this DAG.

Conditional Independency	Reason Conditional Independency Is Not Entailed
$I_P(X, Y\|H)$	$[X, B, C, D, Y]$ is not blocked
$I_P(X, Y\|D)$	$[X, F, H, I, Y]$ is not blocked
$I_P(X, Y\|\{H, C, K\})$	$[X, J, K, L, Y]$ is not blocked
$I_P(X, Y\|\{H, C, M\})$	$[X, J, K, L, Y]$ is not blocked

■

Example 7.4 Owing to Theorem 7.1, the Markov condition entails the following conditional independency for the DAG in Figure 7.4.

Conditional Independency	Reason Conditional Independency Is Entailed
$I_P(W, X)$	$[W, Y, X]$ is blocked at Y
	$[W, Y, R, Z, X]$ is blocked at R
	$[W, Y, R, S, Z, X]$ is blocked at S

Note that $I_P(W, X)$ is the same as $I_P(W, X|\varnothing)$, where $\varnothing$ is the empty set, and Y, R, S, and T are all not in $\varnothing$.   ■

7.2   Faithfulness

Recall that a DAG entails a conditional independency if every probability distribution, which satisfies the Markov condition with the DAG, must have the conditional independency. Theorem 7.1 states that all and only d-separations

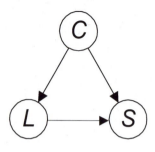

Figure 7.5 A complete DAG.

are entailed conditional independencies. Do not misinterpret this result. It does not say that if some particular probability distribution P satisfies the Markov condition with a DAG $\mathbb{G}$, then P cannot have conditional independencies that $\mathbb{G}$ does not entail. Rather, it only says that P must have all the conditional independencies that are entailed. We illustrate the difference next.

7.2.1   Unfaithful Probability Distributions

We show two examples of probability distributions that satisfy the Markov condition with a DAG and contain a conditional independency that is not entailed by the DAG.

Example 7.5 A complete DAG is a DAG in which there is an edge between every pair of nodes. Figure 7.5 shows a complete DAG $\mathbb{G}$ containing three nodes, C, L, and S. A complete DAG entails no conditional independencies. So, every probability distribution P of C, L, and S satisfies the Markov condition with the DAG in Figure 7.5.

Another way to look at this is to notice that the chain rule says that for every probability distribution P of C, L, and S, for all values c, l, and s,

$$P(c,l,s) = P(s|l,c)P(l|c)P(c).$$

So, P is equal to the product of its conditional distributions for the DAG in Figure 7.5, which means that, owing to Theorem 6.1, P satisfies the Markov condition with that DAG.

However, any probability distribution that has a conditional independency will have a conditional independency that is not entailed by the complete DAG $\mathbb{G}$. For example, consider the joint probability distribution P of C, L, and S discussed in Example 6.1. We showed that

$$I_P(L, S|C).$$

Therefore, this distribution has a conditional independency that is not entailed by $\mathbb{G}$.   ∎

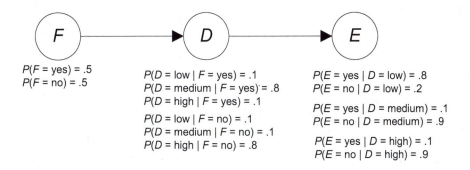

$P(F = yes) = .5$
$P(F = no) = .5$

$P(D = low \mid F = yes) = .1$
$P(D = medium \mid F = yes) = .8$
$P(D = high \mid F = yes) = .1$

$P(D = low \mid F = no) = .1$
$P(D = medium \mid F = no) = .1$
$P(D = high \mid F = no) = .8$

$P(E = yes \mid D = low) = .8$
$P(E = no \mid D = low) = .2$

$P(E = yes \mid D = medium) = .1$
$P(E = no \mid D = medium) = .9$

$P(E = yes \mid D = high) = .1$
$P(E = no \mid D = high) = .9$

Figure 7.6 For the distribution P in this Bayesian network, we have $I_P(E, F)$, but the Markov condition does not entail this conditional independency.

Example 7.6 Consider the Bayesian network in Figure 7.6. The only conditional independency entailed by the Markov condition for the DAG $\mathbb{G}$ in that figure is $I_P(E, F|D)$. So, Theorem 7.1 says that all probability distributions that satisfy the Markov condition with $\mathbb{G}$ must have $I_P(E, F|D)$, which means that the probability distribution P in the Bayesian network in Figure 7.6 must have $I_P(E, F|D)$. However, the theorem does not say that P cannot have other independencies. Indeed, it is left as an exercise to show that we have $I_P(E, F)$ for the distribution P in that Bayesian network. ∎

We purposefully assigned values to the conditional distributions in the network in Figure 7.6 to achieve $I_P(E, F)$. If we randomly assigned values, we would be almost certain to obtain a probability distribution that does not have this independency. That is, Meek [1995] proved that almost all assignments of values to the conditional distributions in a Bayesian network will result in a probability distribution that only has conditional independencies entailed by the Markov condition.

Could actual phenomena in nature result in a distribution like that in Figure 7.6? Although we made up the numbers in the network in that figure, we patterned them after something that actually occurred in nature. Let the variables in the figure represent the following:

Variable	What the Variable Represents
F	Whether the subject takes finasteride
D	Subject's dihydro-testosterone level
E	Whether the subject suffers from erectile dysfunction

As shown in Example 6.4, dihydro-testosterone seems to be the hormone necessary for erectile function. Recall from Example 6.8 that Merck performed a study indicating that finasteride has a positive causal effect on hair growth. Finasteride accomplishes this by inhibiting the conversion of testosterone to dihydro-testosterone, the hormone responsible for hair loss. Given this, Merck feared that dihydro-testosterone would cause erectile dysfunction. That is, ordinarily if X has a causal influence on Y and Y has a causal influence on Z, then

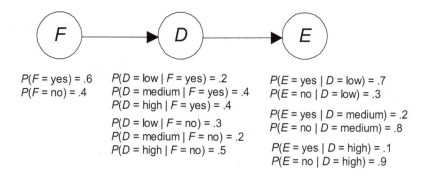

$P(F = \text{yes}) = .6$ $P(D = \text{low} \mid F = \text{yes}) = .2$ $P(E = \text{yes} \mid D = \text{low}) = .7$
$P(F = \text{no}) = .4$ $P(D = \text{medium} \mid F = \text{yes}) = .4$ $P(E = \text{no} \mid D = \text{low}) = .3$
                $P(D = \text{high} \mid F = \text{yes}) = .4$

                $P(D = \text{low} \mid F = \text{no}) = .3$ $P(E = \text{yes} \mid D = \text{medium}) = .2$
                $P(D = \text{medium} \mid F = \text{no}) = .2$ $P(E = \text{no} \mid D = \text{medium}) = .8$
                $P(D = \text{high} \mid F = \text{no}) = .5$

                                       $P(E = \text{yes} \mid D = \text{high}) = .1$
                                       $P(E = \text{no} \mid D = \text{high}) = .9$

Figure 7.7 The probability distribution in this Bayesian network is faithful to the DAG in the network.

X has a causal influence on Z through Y. However, in a manipulation study, Merck found that F does not appear to have a causal influence on E. That is, they learned $I_P(E, F)$. The explanation for this is that finasteride does not lower dihydro-testosterone levels beneath some threshold level, and that threshold level is all that is necessary for erectile function. The numbers we assigned in the Bayesian network in Figure 7.6 reflect these causal relationships. The value of F has no effect on whether D is *low*, and D must be *low* to make the probability that E is *yes* high.

7.2.2　Faithfulness Condition

The probability distribution in the Bayesian network in Figure 7.6 is said to be unfaithful to the DAG in that figure because it contains a conditional independency that is not entailed by the Markov condition. We have the following definition:

Definition 7.4 Suppose we have a joint probability distribution P of the random variables in some set V and a DAG $\mathbb{G} = (\mathsf{V}, \mathsf{E})$. We say that $(\mathbb{G}, P)$ satisfies the **faithfulness condition** if all and only the conditional independencies in P are entailed by $\mathbb{G}$. Furthermore, we say that P and $\mathbb{G}$ are faithful to each other.◆

Notice that the faithfulness condition includes the Markov condition because *only* conditional independencies in P can be entailed by $\mathbb{G}$. However, it requires more; that is, it requires that *all* conditional independencies in P must be entailed by $\mathbb{G}$. As noted previously, almost all assignments of values to the conditional distributions will result in a faithful distribution. For example, it is left as an exercise to show that the probability distribution P in the Bayesian network in Figure 7.7 is faithful to the DAG in that figure. We arbitrarily assigned values to the conditional distributions in the figure. However, owing to the result in [Meek, 1995] that almost all assignments of values to the con-

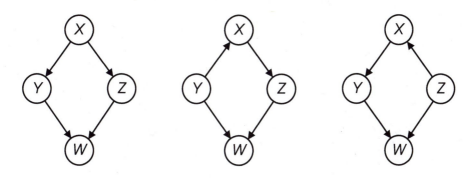

Figure 7.8 These DAGs are Markov equivalent, and there are no other DAGs that are Markov equivalent to them.

ditional distributions will lead to a faithful distribution, we were willing to bet the farm that this assignment would, too.

Is there some DAG faithful to the probability distribution in the Bayesian network in Figure 7.6? The answer is no, but it is beyond the scope of this book to show this. See [Neapolitan, 2004] for a proof of this fact. Intuitively, the DAG in Figure 7.6 represents the causal relationships among the variables, which means we should not be able to find a DAG that better represents the probability distribution.

7.3   Markov Equivalence

Many DAGs are equivalent in the sense that they have the same d-separations, which means they entail the same conditional independencies. For example, each of the DAGs in Figure 7.8 contains the d-separations $I_{\mathbb{G}}(Y, Z \mid X)$ and $I_{\mathbb{G}}(X, W \mid \{Y, Z\})$, and these are the only d-separations each has. After stating a formal definition of this equivalence, we give a theorem showing how it relates to probability distributions. Finally, we establish a criterion for recognizing this equivalence.

Definition 7.5 Let $\mathbb{G}_1 = (V, E_1)$ and $\mathbb{G}_2 = (V, E_2)$ be two DAGs containing the same set of variables V. Then $\mathbb{G}_1$ and $\mathbb{G}_2$ are called **Markov equivalent** if for every three mutually disjoint subsets $A, B, C \subseteq V$, A and B are d-separated by C in $\mathbb{G}_1$ if and only if A and B are d-separated by C in $\mathbb{G}_2$. That is,

$$I_{\mathbb{G}_1}(A, B|C) \Longleftrightarrow I_{\mathbb{G}_2}(A, B|C). \blacklozenge$$

Although the previous definition has only to do with graph properties, its application is in probability due to the following theorem:

Theorem 7.2 Two DAGs are Markov equivalent if and only if they entail the same conditional independencies.

Proof. The proof follows immediately from Theorem 7.1. ∎

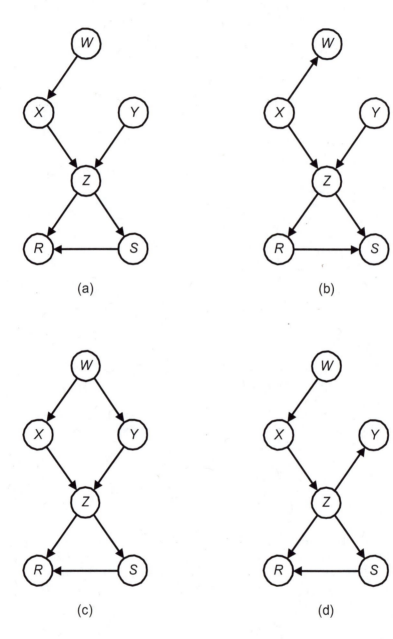

Figure 7.9 The DAGs in (a) and (b) are Markov equivalent. The DAGs in (c) and (d) are not Markov equivalent to the first two DAGs or to each other.

Corollary 7.1 Let $\mathbb{G}_1 = (V, E_1)$ and $\mathbb{G}_2 = (V, E_2)$ be two DAGs containing the same set of variables V. Then $\mathbb{G}_1$ and $\mathbb{G}_2$ are Markov equivalent if and only if for every probability distribution P of V, $(\mathbb{G}_1, P)$ satisfies the Markov condition if and only if $(\mathbb{G}_2, P)$ satisfies the Markov condition.

Proof. The proof is left as an exercise. ∎

The theorem that follows enables us to identify Markov equivalence. This theorem was first stated in [Pearl et al., 1989]. First we need this definition. We say there is an **uncoupled head-to-head meeting** at X on a chain in a DAG $\mathbb{G}$ if there is a head-to-head meeting $Y \rightarrow X \leftarrow Z$ at X and there is no edge between Y and Z.

Theorem 7.3 Two DAGs $\mathbb{G}_1$ and $\mathbb{G}_2$ are Markov equivalent if and only if they have the same links (edges without regard for direction) and the same set of uncoupled head-to-head meetings.

Proof. The proof can be found in [Neapolitan, 2004]. ∎

Example 7.7 The DAGs in Figures 7.9 (a) and 7.9 (b) are Markov equivalent because they have the same links and the only uncoupled head-to-head meeting in both is $X \rightarrow Z \leftarrow Y$. The DAG in Figure 7.9 (c) is not Markov equivalent to the first two because it has the link $W - Y$. The DAG in Figure 7.9 (d) is not Markov equivalent to the first two because, although it has the same links, it does not have the uncoupled head-to-head meeting $X \rightarrow Z \leftarrow Y$. Clearly, the DAGs in Figures 7.9 (c) and 7.9 (d) are not Markov equivalent to each other, either. ∎

Theorem 7.3 easily enables us to develop a polynomial-time algorithm for determining whether two DAGs are Markov equivalent. The algorithm would simply check whether the two DAGs have the same links and the same set of uncoupled head-to-head meetings. It is left as an exercise to write such an algorithm.

Furthermore, Theorem 7.3 gives us a simple way to represent a Markov equivalence class with a single graph. That is, we can represent a Markov equivalence class with a graph that has the same links and the same uncoupled head-to-head meeting as the DAGs in the class. Any assignment of directions to the undirected edges in this graph that does not create a new uncoupled head-to-head meeting or a directed cycle yields a member of the equivalence class.

Often there are edges other than uncoupled head-to-head meetings that must be oriented the same in Markov equivalent DAGs. For example, if all DAGs in a given Markov equivalence class have the edge $X \rightarrow Y$, and the uncoupled meeting $X \rightarrow Y - Z$ is not head-to-head, then all the DAGs in the equivalence class must have $Y - Z$ oriented as $Y \rightarrow Z$. So, we define a **DAG pattern** for a Markov equivalence class to be the graph that has the same links as the DAGs in the equivalence class and has oriented all and only the edges common to all the DAGs in the equivalence class. The directed links in a DAG pattern are called

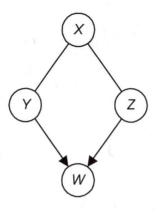

Figure 7.10 This DAG pattern represents the Markov equivalence class in Figure 7.8.

compelled edges. The DAG pattern in Figure 7.10 represents the Markov equivalence class in Figure 7.8. The DAG pattern in Figure 7.11 (b) represents the Markov equivalence class in Figure 7.11 (a). Notice that no DAG, which is Markov equivalent to each of the DAGs in Figure 7.11 (a), can have $W - U$ oriented as $W \leftarrow U$, because this would create another uncoupled head-to-head meeting.

7.4   Markov Blankets and Boundaries

A Bayesian network can have a large number of nodes, and the conditional probability of a given node can be affected by instantiating a distant node. However, it turns out that the instantiation of a set of close nodes can shield a node from the effect of all the other nodes. The next definition and theorem show this.

Definition 7.6 Let V be a set of random variables, P be their joint probability distribution, and $X \in V$. Then a **Markov blanket** M of X is any set of variables such that X is conditionally independent of all the other variables given M. That is,

$$I_P(X, V - (M \cup \{X\})|M).\blacklozenge$$

Theorem 7.4 Suppose $(\mathbb{G}, P)$ satisfies the Markov condition. Then for each variable X, the set of all parents of X, children of X, and parents of children of X is a Markov blanket of X.

Proof. Clearly the set of all parents of X, children of X, and parents of children of X d-separates X from the set of all other nodes in V. The proof, therefore, follows from Theorem 7.1. ∎

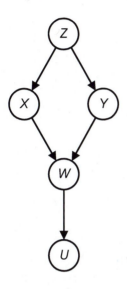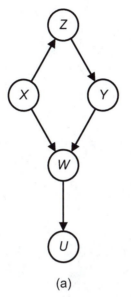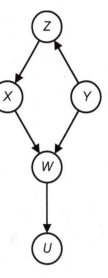

(a)

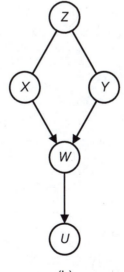

(b)

Figure 7.11 The DAG pattern in (b) represents the Markov equivalence class in (a).

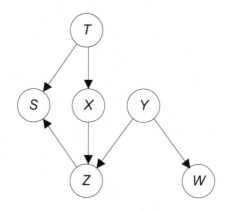

Figure 7.12 If P satisfies the Markov condition with this DAG, then $\{T, Y, Z\}$ is a Markov blanket of X.

Example 7.8 Suppose $(\mathbb{G}, P)$ satisfies the Markov condition where $\mathbb{G}$ is the DAG in Figure 7.12. Then, due to Theorem 7.4, $\{T, Y, Z\}$ is a Markov blanket of X. So, we have

$$I_P(X, \{S, W\}|\{T, Y, Z\}).$$

∎

Example 7.9 Suppose $(\mathbb{G}, P)$ satisfies the Markov condition where $\mathbb{G}$ is the DAG in Figure 7.12, and P has the following conditional independency:

$$I_P(X, \{S, T, W\}|\{Y, Z\}).$$

Then the Markov blanket $\{T, Y, Z\}$ is not minimal in the sense that its subset $\{Y, Z\}$ is also a Markov blanket of X. ∎

The last example motivates the definition that follows.

Definition 7.7 Let V be a set of random variables, P be their joint probability distribution, and $X \in \mathsf{V}$. Then a **Markov boundary** of X is any Markov blanket such that none of its proper subsets is a Markov blanket of X.♦

We have the following theorem.

Theorem 7.5 Suppose $(\mathbb{G}, P)$ satisfies the faithfulness condition. Then, for each variable X, the set of all parents of X, children of X, and parents of children of X is the unique Markov boundary of X.

Proof. The proof can be found in [Neapolitan, 2004]. ∎

Example 7.10 Suppose $(\mathbb{G}, P)$ satisfies the faithfulness condition where $\mathbb{G}$ is the DAG in Figure 7.12. Then, due to Theorem 7.5, $\{T, Y, Z\}$ is the unique Markov boundary of X. ∎

EXERCISES

Section 7.1

Exercise 7.1 Consider the DAG $\mathbb{G}$ in Figure 7.2 (a). Prove that the Markov condition entails $I_P(C, G|\{A, F\})$ for $\mathbb{G}$.

Exercise 7.2 Suppose we add another variable R, an edge from F to R, and an edge from R to C to the DAG $\mathbb{G}$ in Figure 7.2 (a). The variable R might represent the professor's initial reputation. State which of the following conditional independencies you would feel are entailed by the Markov condition for $\mathbb{G}$. For each that you feel is entailed, try to prove it actually is.

1. $I_P(R, A)$

2. $I_P(R, A|F)$

3. $I_P(R, A|\{F, C\})$

Exercise 7.3 Show that the Markov condition entails the following conditional independencies for the DAG in Figure 7.4.

1. $I_P(X, R|\{Y, Z\})$

2. $I_P(X, T|\{Y, Z\})$

3. $I_P(W, T|R)$

4. $I_P(Y, Z|X)$

5. $I_P(W, S|\{R, Z\})$

6. $I_P(W, S|\{Y, Z\})$

7. $I_P(W, S|\{Y, X\})$

Exercise 7.4 Show that the Markov condition does not entail the following conditional independencies for the DAG in Figure 7.4.

1. $I_P(W, X|Y)$

2. $I_P(W, T|Y)$

Exercise 7.5 State which of the following conditional independencies are entailed by the Markov condition for the DAG in Figure 7.4.

1. $I_P(W, S|\{R, X\})$

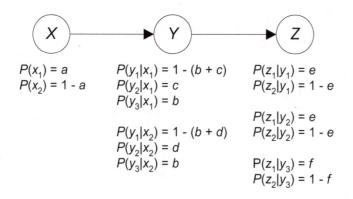

Figure 7.13 Any probability distribution P obtained by assigning values to the parameters in this network is not faithful to the DAG in the network because we have $I_P(X, Z)$.

2. $I_P(\{W, X\}, \{S, T\}|\{R, Z\})$

3. $I_P(\{Y, Z\}, T|\{R, S\})$

4. $I_P(\{X, S\}, \{W, T\}|\{R, Z\})$

5. $I_P(\{X, S, Z\}, \{W, T\}|R)$

6. $I_P(\{X, Z\}, W)$

7. $I_P(\{X, S\}, W)$

Exercise 7.6 Does the Markov condition entail $I_P(\{X, S\}, W|U)$ for any subset of variables U in the DAG in Figure 7.4?

Section 7.2

Exercise 7.7 Show $I_P(F, E)$ for the distribution P in the Bayesian network in Figure 7.6.

Exercise 7.8 Consider the Bayesian network in Figure 7.13. Show that for all assignments of values to a, b, c, d, e, and f that yield a probability distribution P, we have $I_P(X, Z)$. Such probability distributions are not faithful to the DAG in that figure because X and Z are not d-separated by the empty set. Note that the probability distribution in Figure 7.6 is a member of this family of distributions.

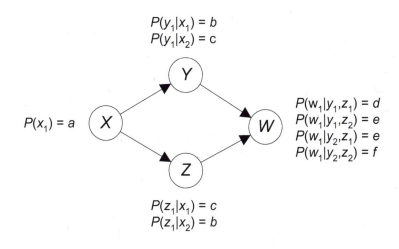

Figure 7.14 Any probability distribution P obtained by assigning values to the parameters in this network is not faithful to the DAG in the network because we have $I_P(X, W)$.

Exercise 7.9 Assign arbitrary values to the conditional distributions for the DAG in Figure 7.13, and see whether the resultant distribution is faithful to the DAG. Try to find an unfaithful distribution besides ones in the family shown in that figure.

Exercise 7.10 Consider the Bayesian network in Figure 7.14. Show that for all assignments of values to a, b, c, d, e, and f that yield a probability distribution P, we have $I_P(X, W)$. Such probability distributions are not faithful to the DAG in that figure because X and W are not d-separated by the empty set.

If the edges in the DAG in Figure 7.14 represent causal influences, X and W would be independent if the causal effect of X on W through Y negated the causal effect of X on W through Z. If X represents an individual's age, W represents the individual's typing ability, Y represents the individual's experience, and Z represents the individual's manual dexterity, do you feel X and W might be independent for this reason?

Exercise 7.11 Consider the Bayesian network in Figure 7.15. Show that for all assignments of values to a, b, c, d, e, f, and g that yield a probability distribution P, we have $I_P(X, Y|Z)$. Such probability distributions are not faithful to the DAG in that figure because X and Y are not d-separated by Z.

If the edges in the DAG in Figure 7.15 represent causal influences, X and Y would be independent given Z, if no discounting occurred. Try to find some causal influences that might behave like this.

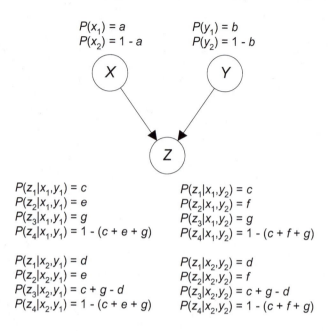

$P(x_1) = a$ $P(y_1) = b$
$P(x_2) = 1 - a$ $P(y_2) = 1 - b$

$P(z_1|x_1,y_1) = c$ $P(z_1|x_1,y_2) = c$
$P(z_2|x_1,y_1) = e$ $P(z_2|x_1,y_2) = f$
$P(z_3|x_1,y_1) = g$ $P(z_3|x_1,y_2) = g$
$P(z_4|x_1,y_1) = 1 - (c + e + g)$ $P(z_4|x_1,y_2) = 1 - (c + f + g)$

$P(z_1|x_2,y_1) = d$ $P(z_1|x_2,y_2) = d$
$P(z_2|x_2,y_1) = e$ $P(z_2|x_2,y_2) = f$
$P(z_3|x_2,y_1) = c + g - d$ $P(z_3|x_2,y_2) = c + g - d$
$P(z_4|x_2,y_1) = 1 - (c + e + g)$ $P(z_4|x_2,y_2) = 1 - (c + f + g)$

Figure 7.15 Any probability distribution P obtained by assigning values to the parameters in this network is not faithful to the DAG in the network, because we have $I_P(X, Y|Z)$.

Section 7.3

Exercise 7.12 Prove Corollary 7.1.

Exercise 7.13 Write an algorithm that determines whether two DAGs are Markov equivalent.

Section 7.4

Exercise 7.14 Apply Theorem 7.4 to find a Markov blanket for node Z in the DAG in Figure 7.12.

Exercise 7.15 Apply Theorem 7.4 to find a Markov blanket for node Y in Figure 7.4.

Chapter 8

Decision Analysis

In general, the information obtained by doing inference in a Bayesian network can be used to arrive at a decision, even though the Bayesian network itself does not recommend a decision. In this chapter, we extend the structure of a Bayesian network so that the network actually does recommend a decision. Such a network is called an influence diagram. Section 8.1 introduces decision trees, which are mathematically equivalent to influence diagrams, but which have difficulty representing large instances because their size grows exponentially with the number of variables. In Section 8.2 we discuss influence diagrams, whose size only grows linearly with the number of variables. When using decision trees and influence diagrams to model a monetary decision, the recommended decision is the one that maximizes the expected value of the monetary result. Most individuals would not make a monetary decision by simply maximizing expected values if the amounts of money involved were large compared to their total wealth. That is, most individuals are risk averse. So, in general, we need to model an individual's attitude toward risk when using decision analysis to recommend a decision. Section 8.3 shows how to do this using a personal utility function. Rather than assess a utility function, a decision maker may prefer to analyze the risk directly. In Section 8.4 we discuss risk profiles, which enable the decision maker to do this. Section 8.5 distinguishes good decisions from good outcomes. Both influence diagrams and decision trees require that we assess probabilities and outcomes. Sometimes assessing these values precisely can be a difficult and laborious task, and further refinement of these values would not affect our decision anyway. Section 8.6 shows how to measure the sensitivity of our decisions to the values of the probabilities. Often, before making a decision we have access to information, but at a cost. For example, before deciding to buy a stock, we may be able to purchase the advice of an investment analyst. In Section 8.7 we illustrate how to compute the value of information, which enables us to determine whether the information is worth the cost.

8.1   Decision Trees

After presenting some simple examples of decision trees, we discuss several issues regarding their use. Then we provide more complex examples.

8.1.1   Simple Examples

We start with the following example:

Example 8.1 Suppose your favorite stock NASDIP is downgraded by a reputable analyst, and it plummets from $40 to $10 per share. You feel this is a good buy, but there is a lot of uncertainty involved. NASDIP's quarterly earnings are about to be released, and you think they will be good, which should positively influence its market value. However, you also think there is a good chance the whole market will crash, which will negatively influence NASDIP's market value. In an attempt to quantify your uncertainty, you decide there is a .25 probability the market will crash, in which case you feel NASDIP will go to $5 by the end of the month. If the market does not crash, you feel that by the end of the month NASDIP will be either at $10 or at $20 depending on the earnings report. You think it is twice as likely it will be at $20 as at $10. So you assign a .5 probability to NASDIP being at $20 and a .25 probability to it being at $10 at the end of the month. Your decision now is whether to buy 100 shares of NASDIP for $1000 or to leave the $1000 in the bank where it will earn .005 interest in the next month.

One way to make your decision is to determine the expected value of your investment if you purchase NASDIP and compare that value to the amount of

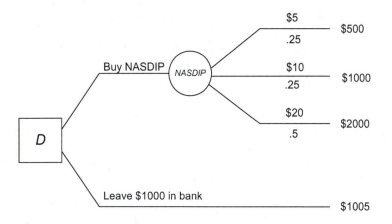

Figure 8.1 A decision tree representing the problem instance in Example 8.1.

money you would have if you put the money in the bank. Let X be a random variable, whose value is the worth of your $1000 investment in one month if you purchase NASDIP. If NASDIP goes to $5, your investment will be worth $500; if it stays at $10, your investment will be worth $1000; and if it goes to $20, it will be worth $2000. Therefore,

$$E(X) \quad = \quad .25(\$500) + .25(\$1000) + .5(\$2000)$$
$$= \quad \$1375,$$

where E denotes expected value. If you leave the money in the bank, your investment will be worth

$$1.005(\$1000) = \$1005.$$

If you are what is called an expected value maximizer, your decision would be to buy NASDIP because that decision has the larger expected value. ∎

The problem instance in the previous example can be represented by a decision tree. That tree is shown in Figure 8.1. A **decision tree** contains two kinds of nodes: **chance (or uncertainty) nodes** representing random variables and **decision nodes** representing decisions to be made. We depict these nodes as follows:

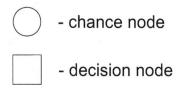

A **decision** represents a set of mutually exclusive and exhaustive actions the decision maker can take. Each action is called an **alternative** in the decision.

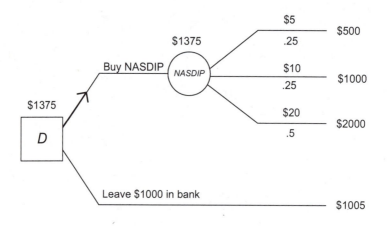

Figure 8.2 The solved decision tree given the decision tree in Figure 8.1.

There is an edge emanating from a decision node for each alternative in the decision. In Figure 8.1, we have the decision node D with two alternatives: "Buy NASDIP" and "Leave $1000 in bank." There is one edge emanating from a chance node for each possible outcome (value) of the random variable. We show the probability of the outcome on the edge and the utility of the outcome to the right of the edge. The **utility** of the outcome is the value of the outcome to the decision maker. When an amount of money is small relative to one's total wealth, we can usually take the utility of an outcome to be the amount of money realized given the outcome. Currently, we make this assumption. Handling the case where we do not make this assumption is discussed in Section 8.3. So, for example, if you buy 100 shares of NASDIP, and NASDIP goes to $20, we assume that the utility of this outcome to you is $2000. In Figure 8.1, we have the chance node $NASDIP$ with three possible outcome utilities, namely $500, $1000, and $2000. The **expected utility** EU of a chance node is defined to be the expected value of the utilities associated with its outcomes. The expected utility of a decision alternative is defined to be the expected utility of the chance node encountered if that decision is made. If there is certainty when the alternative is taken, the expected utility is the value of that certain outcome. So

$$EU(\text{Buy NASDIP}) = EU(NASDIP) \quad = \quad .25(\$500) + .25(\$1000) + .5(\$2000)$$
$$= \quad \$1375$$

$$EU(\text{Leave } \$1000 \text{ in bank}) = \$1005.$$

Finally, the expected utility of a decision node is defined to be the maximum of the expected utilities of all its alternatives. So

$$EU(D) = \max(\$1375, \ \$1005) = \$1375.$$

The alternative chosen is the one with the largest expected utility. The process of determining these expected utilities is called **solving the decision tree**.

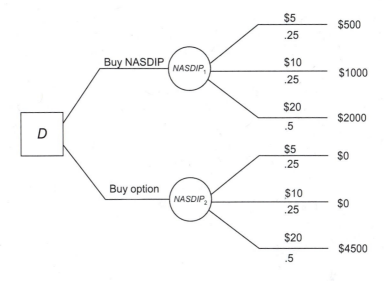

Figure 8.3 The decision tree modeling the investment decision concerning NASDIP when the other choice is to buy an option on NASDIP.

After solving it, we show expected utilities above nodes and an arrow to the alternative chosen. The solved decision tree, given the decision tree in Figure 8.1, is shown in Figure 8.2. The entire process of identifying the components of a problem, structuring the problem as a decision tree (or influence diagram), solving the decision tree (or influence diagram), performing sensitivity analysis (discussed in Chapter 6, Section 8.6), and possibly reiterating these steps is called **decision analysis**.

Example 8.2 Suppose you are in the same situation as in Example 8.1, except, instead of considering leaving your money in the bank, your other choice is to buy an option on NASDIP. The option costs $1000, and it allows you to buy 500 shares of NASDIP at $11 per share in one month. So if NASDIP is at $5 or $0 per share in one month, you would not exercise your option, and you would lose $1000. However, if NASDIP is at $20 per share in one month, you would exercise your option, and your $1000 investment would be worth

$$500(\$20 - \$11) = \$4500.$$

Figure 8.3 shows a decision tree representing this problem instance. From that tree, we have

$$
\begin{aligned}
EU(\text{Buy option}) = EU(NASDIP_2) &= .25(\$0) + .25(\$0) + .5(\$4500) \\
&= \$2250.
\end{aligned}
$$

Recall that EU(Buy NASDIP) is only $1375. So our decision would be to buy the option. It is left as an exercise to show the solved decision tree.

Notice that the decision tree in Figure 8.3 is symmetrical, whereas the one in Figure 8.2 is not. The reason is that we encounter the same uncertain event regardless of which decision is made. Only the utilities of the outcomes are different.   ∎

Before proceeding, we address a concern you may have. That is, you may be wondering how an individual could arrive at the probabilities of .25, .5, and .25 in Example 8.1. These probabilities are often not relative frequencies; rather, they are subjective probabilities that represent an individual's reasonable numeric beliefs. The individual arrives at them by a careful analysis of the situation. Methods for assessing subjective beliefs were discussed briefly in Chapter 2, Section 5.3.2 and are discussed in more detail in [Neapolitan, 1996]. Even so, you may argue that the individual surely must believe there are many more possible future values for a share of NASDIP than three. How can the individual claim the only possible values are $5, $10, and $20? You are correct. However, if further refinement of one's beliefs would not affect the decision, then it is not necessary to do so. So if the decision maker feels that a model containing more values would not result in a different decision, it is sufficient to use the model containing only the values $5, $10, and $20.

8.1.2   Solving More Complex Decision Trees

The general algorithm for solving decision trees is quite simple. There is a time ordering from left to right in a decision tree. That is, any node to the right of another node occurs after that node in time. The tree is solved as follows:

> Starting at the right,
> > proceed to the left
> > > passing expected utilities to chance nodes;
> > > passing maximums to decision nodes;
> > until the root is reached.

We now present more complex examples of modeling with decision trees.

Example 8.3 Suppose Nancy is a high roller, and she is considering buying 10,000 shares of ICK for $10 a share. This number of shares is so high that if she purchases them, it could affect market activity and bring up the price of ICK. She also believes the overall value of the Dow Jones Industrial Average will affect the price of ICK. She feels that in one month the Dow will be at either 10,000 or 11,000, and ICK will be at either $5 or $20 per share. Her other choice is to buy an option on ICK for $100,000. The option will allow her to buy 50,000 shares of ICK for $15 a share in one month. To analyze this problem instance, she constructs the following probabilities:

$$P(ICK = \$5 | \text{Decision} = \text{Buy ICK}, Dow = 11{,}000) = .2$$
$$P(ICK = \$5 | \text{Decision} = \text{Buy ICK}, Dow = 10{,}000) = .5$$
$$P(ICK = \$5 | \text{Decision} = \text{Buy option}, Dow = 11{,}000) = .3$$
$$P(ICK = \$5 | \text{Decision} = \text{Buy option}, Dow = 10{,}000) = .6.$$

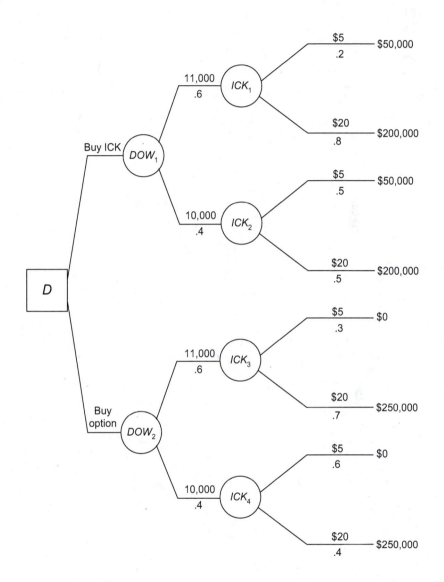

Figure 8.4 A decision tree representing Nancy's decision whether to buy ICK or an option on ICK.

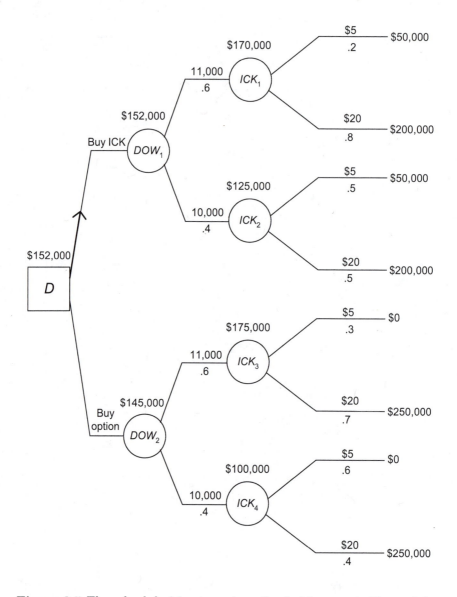

Figure 8.5 The solved decision tree given the decision tree in Figure 8.4.

Furthermore, she assigns

$$P(Dow = 11,000) = .6.$$

This problem instance is represented by the decision tree in Figure 8.4. Next we solve the tree:

$$EU(ICK_1) = (.2)(\$50,000) + (.8)(\$200,000) = \$170,000$$

$$EU(ICK_2) = (.5)(\$50,000) + (.5)(\$200,000) = \$125,000$$

$$EU(\text{Buy ICK}) = EU(DOW_1) = (.6)(\$170,000) + (.4)(\$125,000) = \$152,000$$

$$EU(ICK_3) = (.3)(\$0) + (.7)(\$250,000) = \$175,000$$

$$EU(ICK_4) = (.6)(\$0) + (.4)(\$250,000) = \$100,000$$

$$EU(\text{Buy option}) = EU(DOW_2) = (.6)(\$175,000) + (.4)(\$100,000) = \$145,000$$

$$EU(D) = \max(\$152,000, \ \$145,000) = \$152,000.$$

The solved decision tree is shown in Figure 8.5. The decision is to buy ICK. ∎

The previous example illustrates a problem with decision trees. That is, the representation of a problem instance by a decision tree grows exponentially with the size of the instance. Notice that the instance in Example 8.3 only has one more element in it than the instance in Example 8.2; that is, it includes that uncertainty about the Dow. Yet its representation is twice as large. So it is quite difficult to represent a large instance with a decision tree. We will see in the next section that influence diagrams do not have this problem. Before that, we show more examples.

Example 8.4 Sam has the opportunity to buy a 1996 Spiffycar automobile for $10,000, and he has a prospect who would be willing to pay $11,000 for the auto if it is in excellent mechanical shape. Sam determines that all mechanical parts except for the transmission are in excellent shape. If the transmission is bad, it will cost Sam $3000 to repair it, and he would have to repair it before the prospect would buy it. So he would only end up with $8000 if he bought the vehicle and its transmission was bad. He cannot determine the state of the transmission himself. However, he has a friend who can run a test on the transmission. The test is not absolutely accurate. Rather, 30% of the time it judges a good transmission to be bad and 10% of the time it judges a bad transmission to be good. To represent this relationship between the transmission and the test, we define the following random variables:

Variable	Value	When the Variable Takes This Value
Test	*positive*	Test judges the transmission to be bad.
	negative	Test judges the transmission to be good.
Tran	*good*	Transmission is good.
	bad	Transmission is bad.

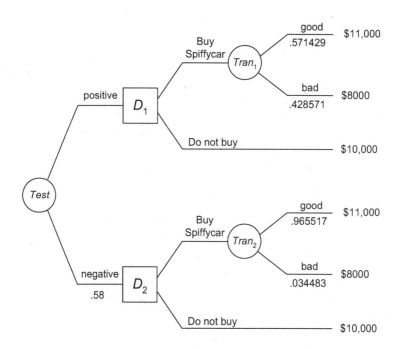

Figure 8.6 The decision tree representing the problem instance in Example 8.4.

The previous discussion implies that we have these conditional probabilities:

$$P(Test = positive|Tran = good) = .3$$

$$P(Test = positive|Tran = bad) = .9.$$

Furthermore, Sam knows that 20% of the 1996 Spiffycars have bad transmissions. That is,

$$P(Tran = good) = .8.$$

Sam is going to have his friend run the test for free, and then he will decide whether to buy the car.

This problem instance is represented in the decision tree in Figure 8.6. Notice first that, if he does not buy the vehicle, the outcome is simply $10,000. This is because the point in the future is so near that we can neglect interest as negligible. Note further that the probabilities in that tree are not the ones stated in the example. They must be computed from the stated probabilities. We do that next. The probability on the upper edge emanating from the *Test* node is the prior probability the test is positive. It is computed as follows (note that we use our abbreviated notation):

$$\begin{aligned} P(positive) &= P(positive|good)P(good) + P(positive|bad)P(bad) \\ &= (.3)(.8) + (.9)(.2) = .42. \end{aligned}$$

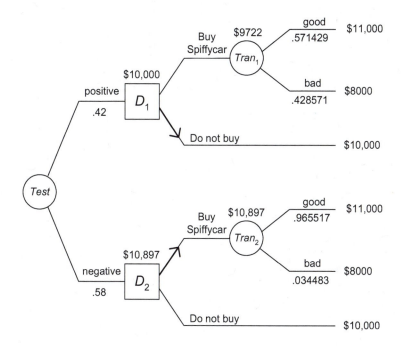

Figure 8.7 The solved decision tree given the decision tree in Figure 8.6.

The probability on the upper edge emanating from the $Tran_1$ node is the probability the transmission is good given the test is positive. We compute it using Bayes' theorem as follows:

$$P(good|positive) = \frac{P(positive|good)P(good)}{P(positive)}$$

$$= \frac{(.3)(.8)}{.42} = .571429.$$

It is left as an exercise to determine the remaining probabilities in the tree. Next, we solve the tree:

$$EU(Tran_1) = (.571429)(\$11,000) + (.428571)(\$8000) = \$9714$$

$$EU(D_1) = \max(\$9714, \$10,000) = \$10,000$$

$$EU(Tran_2) = (.965517)(\$11,000) + (.034483)(\$8000) = \$10,897$$

$$EU(D_2) = \max(\$10,897, \ \$10,000) = \$10,897.$$

We need not compute the expected value of the $Test$ node because there are no decisions to the left of it. The solved decision tree is shown in Figure 8.7. The decision is to not buy the vehicle if the test is positive and to buy it if the test is negative. ∎

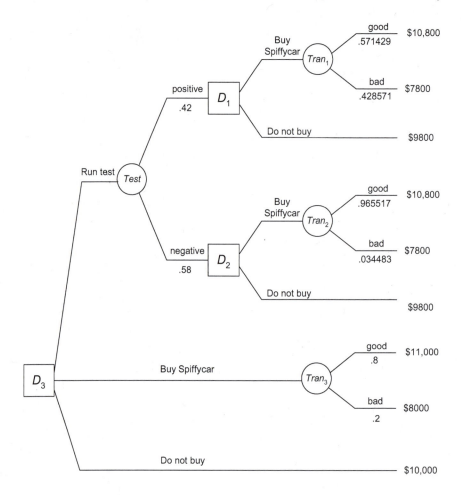

Figure 8.8 The decision tree representing the problem instance in Example 8.5.

The previous example illustrates another problem with decision trees. That is, the probabilities needed in a decision tree are not always the ones that are readily available to us. So we must compute them using the Law of Total Probability and Bayes' theorem. We will see that influence diagrams do not have this problem either. More examples follow.

Example 8.5 Suppose Sam is in the same situation as in Example 8.4, except that the test is not free. Rather, it costs $200. So Sam must decide whether to run the test, buy the car without running the test, or keep his $10,000. The decision tree representing this problem instance is shown in Figure 8.8. Notice that the outcomes when the test is run are all $200 less than their respective outcomes in Example 8.4. This is because it costs $200 to run the test. Note further that, if the vehicle is purchased without running the test, the probability of the transmission being good is simply its prior probability of .8. This is because no test was run. So our only information about the transmission is our prior information. Next, we solve the decision tree. It is left as an exercise to show that

$$EU(D_1) = \$9800$$

$$EU(D_2) = \$10,697.$$

Therefore,

$$EU(Test) = (.42)(\$9800) + (.58)(\$10,697) = \$10,320.$$

Furthermore,

$$EU(Tran_3) = (.8)(\$11,000) + (.2)(\$8000) = \$10,400.$$

Finally,

$$EU(D_3) = \max(\$10,320, \ \$10,400, \ \$10,000) = \$10,400.$$

So Sam's decision is to buy the vehicle without running the test. It is left as an exercise to show the solved decision tree. ∎

The next two examples illustrate cases in which the outcomes are not numeric.

Example 8.6 Suppose Leonardo has just bought a new suit, he is about to leave for work, and it looks like it might rain. Leonardo has a long walk from the train to his office. So he knows if it rains and he does not have his umbrella, his suit will be ruined. His umbrella will definitely protect his suit from the rain. However, he hates the inconvenience of lugging the umbrella around all day. Given that he feels there is a .4 probability it will rain, should he bring his umbrella? A decision tree representing this problem instance is shown in Figure 8.9.

Notice that the outcomes have numeric values, which are needed to solve the problem. We assigned those values as follows. Clearly, the ordering of the outcomes from worst to best is as follows:

1. suit ruined
2. suit not ruined, inconvenience
3. suit not ruined.

We assign a utility of 0 to the worst outcome and a utility of 1 to the best outcome. So

$$U(\text{suit ruined}) = 0$$

$$U(\text{suit not ruined}) = 1.$$

Then we consider lotteries (chance nodes) L_p in which Leonardo gets the outcome "suit not ruined" with probability p and outcome "suit ruined" with

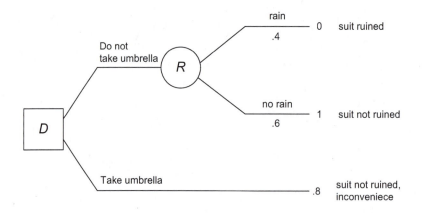

Figure 8.9 The decision tree representing the problem instance in Example 8.6.

probability $1 - p$. The utility of "suit not ruined, inconvenience" is defined to be the expected utility of the lottery L_p for which Leonardo would be indifferent between lottery L_p and being assured of "suit not ruined, inconvenience." We then have

U(suit not ruined, inconvenience)

$$\equiv \; EU(L_p)$$
$$= \; pU(\text{suit not ruined}) + (1 - p)U(\text{suit ruined})$$
$$= \; p(1) + (1 - p)0 = p.$$

Let's say Leonardo decides $p = .8$. Then

$$U(\text{suit not ruined, inconvenience}) = .8.$$

We now solve the decision in Figure 8.9.

$$EU(R) = (.4)(0) + (.6)(1) = .6$$

$$EU(D) = \max(.6, .8) = .8.$$

So the decision is to take the umbrella.   ∎

The method used to obtain numeric values in the previous example easily extends to the case where there are more than three outcomes. For example, suppose there was a fourth outcome "suit goes to cleaners" in between "suit not ruined, inconvenience" and "suit not ruined" in the preference ordering. We consider lotteries L_q in which Leonardo gets outcome "suit not ruined" with probability q and outcome "suit not ruined, inconvenience" with probability $1 - q$. The utility of "suit goes to cleaners" is defined to be the expected utility of the lottery L_q for which Leonardo would be indifferent between lottery L_q and being assured of "suit goes to cleaners." We then have

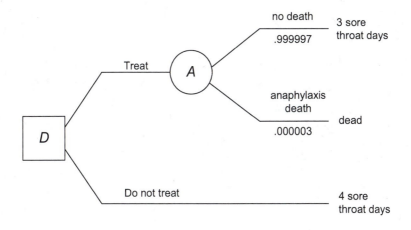

Figure 8.10 A decision tree representing Amit's decision concerning being treated for streptococcal infection.

U(suit goes to cleaners)

$$\equiv \quad EU(L_q)$$
$$= \quad qU(\text{suit not ruined}) + (1 - q)U(\text{suit not ruined, inconvenience})$$
$$= \quad q(1) + (1 - q)(.8) = .8 + .2q.$$

Let's say Leonardo decides $q = .6$. Then

$$U(\text{suit goes to cleaners}) = .8 + (.2)(.6) = .92.$$

Next, we give an example from the medical domain.[1]

Example 8.7 Amit, a 15-year-old high school student, has been definitively diagnosed with streptococcal infection, and he is considering having a treatment that is known to reduce the number of days with a sore throat from 4 to 3. He learns, however, that the treatment has a .000003 probability of causing death due to anaphylaxis. Should he have the treatment?

You may argue that, if he may die from the treatment, he certainly should not have it. However, the probability of dying is extremely small, and we daily accept small risks of dying in order to obtain something of value to us. For example, many people take a small risk of dying in a car accident in order to arrive at work. We see then that we cannot discount the treatment based solely on that risk. So what should Amit do? Next, we apply decision analysis to recommend a decision to him. Figure 8.10 shows a decision tree representing Amit's decision. To solve this problem instance, we need to quantify the outcomes in that tree. We can do this using **quality adjusted life expectancies**

---

[1] This example is based on an example in [Nease and Owens, 1997]. Although the information is not fictitious, some of it is controversial.

(QALE). We ask Amit to determine what one year of life with a sore throat is worth relative to one year of life without one. We will call such years "well years." Let's say he says it is worth .9 well years. That is, for Amit

1 year with sore throat   is equivalent to   .9 well years.

We then assume a **constant proportional trade-off**. That is, we assume the time trade-off associated with having a sore throat is independent of the time spent with one. The validity of this assumption and alternative models are discussed in [Nease and Owens, 1997]. Given this assumption, for Amit

t years with sore throat   is equivalent to $.9t$ well years.

The value .9 is called the **time-trade-off quality adjustment** for a sore throat. Another way to look at it is that Amit would give up .1 years of life to avoid having a sore throat for .9 years of life. Now, if we let t be the amount of time Amit will have a sore throat due to this infection, and l be Amit's remaining life expectancy, we define his quality **QALE** as follows:

$$QALE(l, t) = (l - t) + .9t.$$

From life expectancy charts, we determine Amit's remaining life expectancy is 60 years. Converting days to years, we have the following:

$$3 \text{ days} = .008219 \text{ years}$$

$$4 \text{ days} = .010959 \text{ years.}$$

Therefore, Amit's QALEs are as follows:

$$
\begin{aligned}
QALE(60 \text{ years}, 3 \text{ sore throat days}) &= 60 - .008219 + .9(.008219) \\
&= 59.999178
\end{aligned}
$$

$$
\begin{aligned}
QALE(60 \text{ years}, 4 \text{ sore throat days}) &= 60 - .010959 + .9(.010959) \\
&= 59.998904.
\end{aligned}
$$

Figure 8.11 shows the decision tree in Figure 8.10 with the actual outcomes augmented with QALEs. Next, we solve that tree.

$$
\begin{aligned}
EU(Treat) = EU(A) &= (.999993)(59.999178) + (.000003)(0) \\
&= 59.998758
\end{aligned}
$$

$$EU(\text{Do not treat}) = 59.998904$$

$$EU(D) = \max(59.998758, \ 59.998904) = 59.998904.$$

So the decision is to not treat, but just barely.   ■

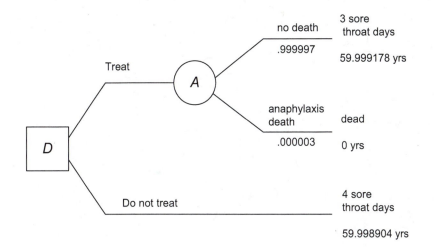

Figure 8.11 The decision tree in Figure 8.10 with the actual outcomes augmented by QALEs.

Example 8.8 This example is an elaboration of the previous one. Actually, Streptococcus infection can lead to rheumatic heart disease (RHD), which is less probable if the patient is treated. Specifically, if we treat a patient with Streptococcus infection, the probability of rheumatic heart disease is .000013, while if we do not treat the patient, the probability is .000063. Rheumatic heart disease would be for life. So Amit needs to take all this into account. First, he must determine time trade-off quality adjustments both for having rheumatic heart disease alone and for having it along with a sore throat. Suppose he determines the following:

$$1 \text{ year with RHD} \quad \text{is equivalent to} \quad .15 \text{ well years.}$$

$$1 \text{ year with sore throat and RHD} \quad \text{is equivalent to} \quad .1 \text{ well years.}$$

We then have

$$QALE(60 \text{ years, RHD, 3 sore throat days}) = .15\left(60 - \frac{3}{365}\right) + .1\left(\frac{3}{365}\right)$$
$$= 8.999589$$

$$QALE(60 \text{ years, RHD, 4 sore throat days}) = .15\left(60 - \frac{4}{365}\right) + .1\left(\frac{4}{365}\right)$$
$$= 8.999452.$$

We have already computed QALEs for 3 or 4 days with only a sore throat in the previous example. Figure 8.12 shows the resultant decision tree. We solve that decision tree next.

$$EU(RHD_1) = (.000013)(8.999569) + (.999987)(59.999178)$$
$$= 59.998515$$

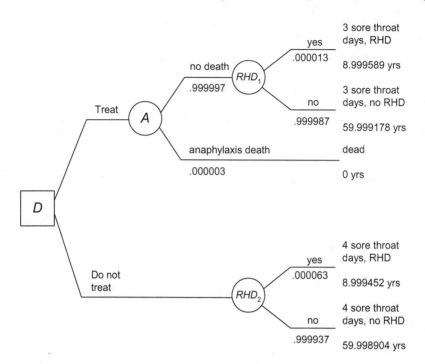

Figure 8.12 A decision tree modeling Amit's decision concerning being treated for streptococcal infection when rheumatic heart disease is considered.

$$
\begin{aligned}
EU(\text{Treat}) = EU(A) \ &= \ (.999997)(59.998515) + (.000003)(0) \\
&= \ 59.998335
\end{aligned}
$$

$$
\begin{aligned}
EU(\text{Do not treat}) \ &= \ EU(RHD_2) \\
&= \ (.000063)(8.999452) + (.999937)(59.998904) \\
&= \ 59.995691
\end{aligned}
$$

$$
EU(D) = \max(59.998335, \ 59.995691) = 59.998335.
$$

So now the decision is to treat, but again just barely.   ■

You may argue that, in the previous two examples, the difference in the expected utilities is negligible because the number of significant digits needed to express it is far more than the number of significant digits in Amit's assessments. This argument is reasonable. However, the utilities of the decisions are so close because the probabilities of both anaphylaxis death and rheumatic heart disease are so small. In general, this situation is not always the case. It is left as an exercise to rework the previous example with the probability of rheumatic heart disease being .13 instead of .000063.

Another consideration in medical decision making is the financial cost of the treatments. In this case, the value of an outcome is a function of both the QALE and the financial cost associated with the outcome.

8.2 Influence Diagrams

In Section 8.1, we noted two difficulties with decision trees. First, the representation of a problem instance by a decision tree grows exponentially with the size of the instance. Second, the probabilities needed in a decision tree are not always the ones that are readily available to us. Next, we present an alternative representation of decision problem instances, namely influence diagrams, which do not have either of these difficulties. First, we only discuss representing problem instances with influence diagrams. Then in Section 8.2.2 we discuss solving influence diagrams.

8.2.1 Representing with Influence Diagrams

An **influence diagram** contains three kinds of nodes: **chance (or uncertainty) nodes** representing random variables; **decision nodes** representing decisions to be made; and one **utility node**, which is a random variable whose possible values are the utilities of the outcomes. We depict these nodes as follows:

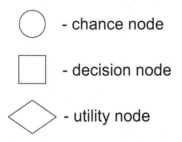

The edges in an influence diagram have the following meaning:

Value of the node is probabilistically dependent on the value of the parent.

Value of the parent is known at the time the decision is made; hence the edge represents sequence.

Value of the node is deterministically dependent on the value of the parent.

The chance nodes in an influence diagram satisfy the Markov condition with the probability distribution. That is, each chance node X is conditionally independent of the set of all its nondescendents given the set of all its parents.

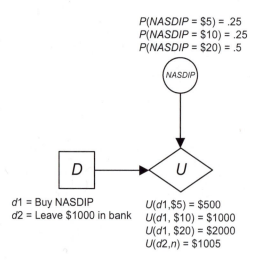

P(NASDIP = $5) = .25
P(NASDIP = $10) = .25
P(NASDIP = $20) = .5

d1 = Buy NASDIP
d2 = Leave $1000 in bank

U(d1,$5) = $500
U(d1, $10) = $1000
U(d1, $20) = $2000
U(d2,n) = $1005

Figure 8.13 An influence diagram modeling your decision whether to buy NASDIP.

So an influence diagram is actually a Bayesian network augmented with decision nodes and a utility node. There must be an ordering of the decision nodes in an influence diagram based on the order in which the decisions are made. The order is specified using the edges between the decision nodes. For example, if we have the order

$$D_1, D_2, D_3,$$

then there are edges from D_1 to D_2 and D_3 and an edge from D_2 to D_3.

To illustrate influence diagrams, we next represent the problem instances, in the examples in the section on decision trees by influence diagrams.

Example 8.9 Recall Example 8.1 in which you felt there was a .25 probability NASDIP will be at $5 at month's end, a .5 probability it will be at $20, and a .25 probability it will be at $10. Your decision is whether to buy 100 shares of NASDIP for $1000 or to leave the $1000 in the bank where it will earn .005 interest. Figure 8.13 shows an influence diagram representing this problem instance. Notice a few things about that diagram. There is no edge from D to NASDIP because your decision as to whether to buy NASDIP has no effect on its performance. (We assume your 100 shares are not enough to affect market activity.) There is no edge from NASDIP to D because at the time you make your decision, you do not know NASDIP's value in one month. There are edges from both NASDIP and D to U because your utility depends both on whether NASDIP goes up and whether you buy it. Notice that if you do not buy it, the utility is the same regardless of what happens to NASDIP. This is why we write $U(d2, n) = \$1005$. The variable n represents any possible value of NASDIP. ∎

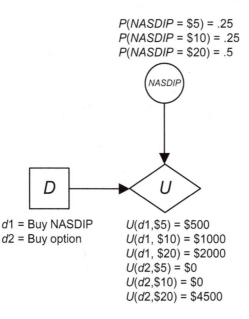

$P(NASDIP = \$5) = .25$
$P(NASDIP = \$10) = .25$
$P(NASDIP = \$20) = .5$

$d1$ = Buy NASDIP
$d2$ = Buy option

$U(d1,\$5) = \$500$
$U(d1, \$10) = \$1000$
$U(d1, \$20) = \$2000$
$U(d2,\$5) = \$0$
$U(d2,\$10) = \$0$
$U(d2,\$20) = \$4500$

Figure 8.14 An influence diagram modeling your decision whether to buy NASDIP when the other choice is to buy an option.

Example 8.10 Recall Example 8.2, which concerned the same situation as in Example 8.1, except that your choices were either to buy NASDIP or to buy an option on NASDIP. Recall further that if NASDIP was at $5 or $0 per share in one month, you would not exercise your option and you would lose your $1000; and if NASDIP was at $20 per share in one month, you would exercise your option and your $1000 investment would be worth $4500. Figure 8.14 shows an influence diagram representing this problem instance. Recall that when we represented this instance with a decision tree (Figure 8.3), that tree was symmetrical because we encountered the same uncertain event regardless of which decision was made. This symmetry manifests itself in the influence diagram in that the value of the utility node U depends on the value of the chance node NASDIP regardless of the value of the decision node D. ∎

Example 8.11 Recall Example 8.3 in which Nancy was considering either buying 10,000 shares of ICK for $10 a share or an option on ICK for $100,000 that would allow her to buy 50,000 shares of ICK for $15 a share in one month. Recall further that she believed that in one month the Dow would be either at 10,000 or at 11,000, and ICK would be either at $5 or at $20 per share. Finally, recall that she assigned the following probabilities:

$$P(ICK = \$5|Dow = 11{,}000, \text{Decision} = \text{Buy ICK}) = .2$$
$$P(ICK = \$5|Dow = 11{,}000, \text{Decision} = \text{Buy option}) = .3$$

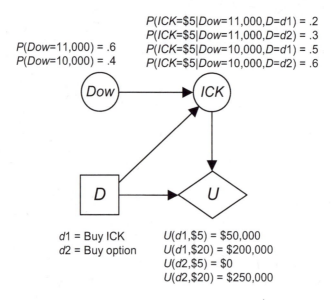

$P(Dow=11,000) = .6$
$P(Dow=10,000) = .4$

$P(ICK=\$5|Dow=11,000,D=d1) = .2$
$P(ICK=\$5|Dow=11,000,D=d2) = .3$
$P(ICK=\$5|Dow=10,000,D=d1) = .5$
$P(ICK=\$5|Dow=10,000,D=d2) = .6$

$d1$ = Buy ICK
$d2$ = Buy option

$U(d1,\$5) = \$50,000$
$U(d1,\$20) = \$200,000$
$U(d2,\$5) = \$0$
$U(d2,\$20) = \$250,000$

Figure 8.15 An influence diagram modeling Nancy's decision concerning buying ICK or an option on ICK.

$$P(ICK = \$5|Dow = 10,000, \text{Decision} = \text{buy ICK}) = .5$$
$$P(ICK = \$5|Dow = 10,000, \text{Decision} = \text{Buy option}) = .6$$

$$P(Dow = \$11,000) = .6.$$

Figure 8.15 shows an influence diagram representing this problem instance. Notice that the value of ICK depends not only on the value of the Dow, but also on the decision D. This is because Nancy's purchase can affect market activity. Note further that this instance has one more component than the instance in Example 8.10, and we needed to add only one more node to represent it with an influence diagram. So the representation grew linearly with the size of the instance. By contrast, recall that when we represented the instances with decision trees, the representation grew exponentially. ∎

Example 8.12 Recall Example 8.4 in which Sam had the opportunity to buy a 1996 Spiffycar automobile for $10,000, and he had a prospect who would be willing to pay $11,000 for the auto if it were in excellent mechanical shape. Recall further that if the transmission were bad, Sam would have to spend $3000 to repair it before he could sell the vehicle. So he would only end up with $8000 if he bought the vehicle and its transmission was bad. Finally, recall he had a friend who could run a test on the transmission, and we had the following:

$$P(Test = positive|Tran = good) = .3$$
$$P(Test = positive|Tran = bad) = .9$$

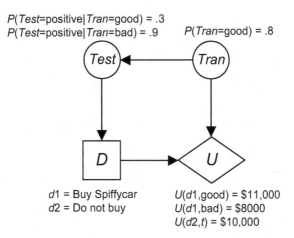

P(Test=positive|Tran=good) = .3
P(Test=positive|Tran=bad) = .9   P(Tran=good) = .8

d1 = Buy Spiffycar   U(d1,good) = $11,000
d2 = Do not buy   U(d1,bad) = $8000
                          U(d2,t) = $10,000

Figure 8.16 An influence diagram modeling Sam's decision concerning buying the Spiffycar.

$$P(Tran = good) = .8.$$

Figure 8.16 shows an influence diagram representing this problem instance. Notice that there is an arrow from $Tran$ to $Test$ because the value of the test is probabilistically dependent on the state of the transmission, and there is an arrow from $Test$ to D because the outcome of the test will be known at the time the decision is made. That is, D follows $Test$ in sequence. Note further that the probabilities in the influence diagram are the ones we know. We did not need to use the Law of Total Probability and Bayes' theorem to compute them, as we did when we represented the instance with a decision tree.   ■

Example 8.13 Recall Example 8.5 in which Sam was in the same situation as in Example 8.4 except that the test was not free. Rather, it costs $200. So Sam had to decide whether to run the test, buy the car without running the test, or keep his $10,000. Figure 8.17 shows an influence diagram representing this problem instance. Notice that there is an edge from R to D because decision R is made before decision D. Note further that there is an edge from D to T because the test T is run only if we make decision $r1$.   ■

Next, we show a more complex instance, which we did not represent with a decision tree.

Example 8.14 Suppose Sam is in the same situation as in Example 8.13, but with the following modifications. First, Sam knows that 20% of the Spiffycars were manufactured in a plant that produced lemons and 80% of them were manufactured in a plant that produced peaches. Furthermore, he knows 40% of the lemons have good transmissions and 90% of the peaches have good transmissions. Also, 5% of the lemons have fine alternators, and 80% of the peaches

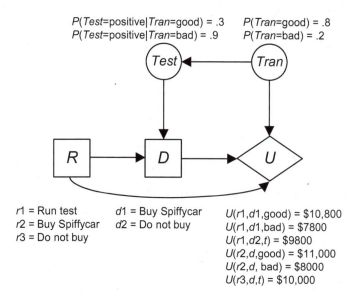

P(*Test*=positive|*Tran*=good) = .3   P(*Tran*=good) = .8
P(*Test*=positive|*Tran*=bad) = .9   P(*Tran*=bad) = .2

r1 = Run test   d1 = Buy Spiffycar   U(r1,d1,good) = $10,800
r2 = Buy Spiffycar   d2 = Do not buy   U(r1,d1,bad) = $7800
r3 = Do not buy   U(r1,d2,t) = $9800
                                            U(r2,d,good) = $11,000
                                            U(r2,d, bad) = $8000
                                            U(r3,d,t) = $10,000

Figure 8.17 An influence diagram modeling Sam's decision concerning buying the Spiffycar when he must pay for the test.

have fine alternators. If the alternator is faulty (not fine), it will cost Sam $600 to repair it before he can sell the vehicle. Figure 8.18 shows an influence diagram representing this problem instance. Notice that the set of chance nodes in the influence diagram constitutes a Bayesian network. For example, *Tran* and *Alt* are not independent, but they are conditionally independent given *Car*. ∎

We close with a large problem instance in the medical domain.

Example 8.15 This example is taken from [Nease and Owens, 1997]. Suppose a patient has a non-small-cell carcinoma of the lung. The primary tumor is 1 cm in diameter, a chest X-ray indicates the tumor does not abut the chest wall or mediastinum, and additional workup shows no evidence of distant metastases. The preferred treatment in this situation is a thoracotomy. The alternative treatment is radiation. Of fundamental importance in the decision to perform a thoracotomy is the likelihood of mediastinal metastases. If mediastinal metastases are present, a thoracotomy would be contraindicated because it subjects the patient to a risk of death with no health benefit. If mediastinal metastases are absent, a thoracotomy offers a substantial survival advantage as long as the primary tumor has not metastasized to distant organs.

We have two tests available for assessing the involvement of the mediastinum. They are computed tomography (CT scan) and mediastinoscopy. This problem instance involves three decisions. First, should the patient undergo a CT scan? Second, given this decision and any CT results, should the patient undergo mediastinoscopy? Third, given these decisions and any test results, should the patient undergo a thoracotomy?

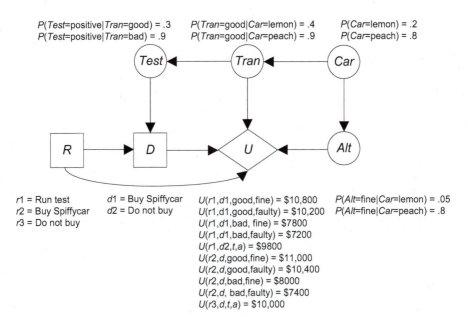

P(Test=positive|Tran=good) = .3   P(Tran=good|Car=lemon) = .4   P(Car=lemon) = .2
P(Test=positive|Tran=bad) = .9   P(Tran=good|Car=peach) = .9   P(Car=peach) = .8

r1 = Run test   d1 = Buy Spiffycar   U(r1,d1,good,fine) = $10,800   P(Alt=fine|Car=lemon) = .05
r2 = Buy Spiffycar   d2 = Do not buy   U(r1,d1,good,faulty) = $10,200 P(Alt=fine|Car=peach) = .8
r3 = Do not buy   U(r1,d1,bad, fine) = $7800
                                             U(r1,d1,bad,faulty) = $7200
                                             U(r1,d2,t,a) = $9800
                                             U(r2,d,good,fine) = $11,000
                                             U(r2,d,good,faulty) = $10,400
                                             U(r2,d,bad,fine) = $8000
                                             U(r2,d, bad,faulty) = $7400
                                             U(r3,d,t,a) = $10,000

Figure 8.18 An influence diagram modeling Sam's decision concerning buying the Spiffycar when the alternator may be faulty.

The CT scan can detect mediastinal metastases. The test is not absolutely accurate. Rather, if we let $MedMet$ be a variable whose values are *present* and *absent* depending on whether or not mediastinal metastases are present and $CTest$ be a variable whose values are *cpos* and *cneg* depending on whether or not the CT scan is positive, we have

$$P(CTest = cpos|MedMet = present) = .82$$
$$P(CTest = cpos|MedMet = absent) = .19.$$

The mediastinoscopy is an invasive test of mediastinal lymph nodes for determining whether the tumor has spread to those nodes. If we let $Mtest$ be a variable whose values are *mpos* and *mneg* depending on whether or not the mediastinoscopy is positive, we have

$$P(MTest = mpos|MedMet = present) = .82$$
$$P(MTest = mpos|MedMet = absent) = .005.$$

The mediastinoscopy can cause death. If we let E be the decision concerning whether to have the mediastinoscopy, $e1$ be the choice to have it, $e2$ be the choice not to have it, and $MedDeath$ be a variable whose values are *mdie* and *mlive* depending on whether the patient dies from the mediastinoscopy, we have

$$P(MedDeath = mdie|E = e1) = .005$$
$$P(MedDeath = mdie|E = e2) = 0.$$

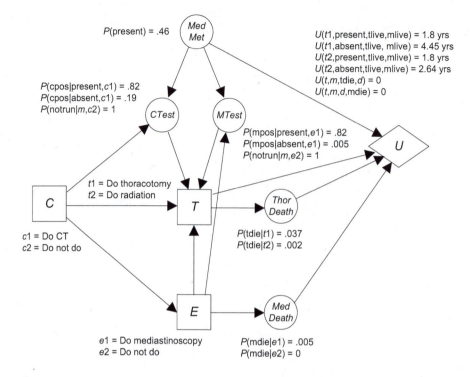

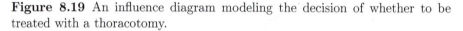

Figure 8.19 An influence diagram modeling the decision of whether to be treated with a thoracotomy.

The thoracotomy has a greater chance of causing death than the alternative treatment of radiation. If we let T be the decision concerning which treatment to have, $t1$ be the choice to undergo a thoracotomy, $t2$ be the choice to undergo radiation, and $Thordeath$ be a variable whose values are $tdie$ and $tlive$ depending on whether the patient dies from the treatment, we have

$$P(ThorDeath = tdie|T = t1) = .037$$
$$P(ThorDeath = tdie|T = t2) = .002.$$

Finally, we need the prior probability that mediastinal metastases are present. We have

$$P(MedMet = present) = .46.$$

Figure 8.19 shows an influence diagram representing this problem instance. Note that we considered quality adjustments to life expectancy (QALE) and financial costs to be insignificant in this example. The value node is only in terms of life expectancy. ∎

8.2.2 Solving Influence Diagrams

We first illustrate how influence diagrams can be solved by presenting some examples. Then we show solving influence diagrams using the package Netica.

8.2.3 Techniques for Solving Influence Diagrams

Next, we show how to solve influence diagrams.

Example 8.16 Consider the influence diagram in Figure 8.13, which was developed in Example 8.9. To solve the influence diagram, we need to determine which decision choice has the largest expected utility. The expected utility of a decision choice is the expected value E of U given the choice is made. We have

$$
\begin{aligned}
EU(d1) &= E(U|d1) \\
&= P(\$5|d1)U(d1, \$5) + P(\$10|d1)U(d1, \$10) + P(\$20|d1)U(d1, \$20) \\
&= (.25)(\$500) + (.25)(\$1000) + (.5)(\$2000) \\
&= \$1375
\end{aligned}
$$

$$
\begin{aligned}
EU(d2) &= E(U|d2) \\
&= P(\$5|d2)U(d2, \$5) + P(\$10|d2)U(d2, \$10) + P(\$20|d2)U(d2, \$20) \\
&= (.25)(\$1005) + (.25)(\$1005) + (.5)(\$1005) \\
&= \$1005.
\end{aligned}
$$

The utility of our decision is therefore

$$
\begin{aligned}
EU(D) &= \max(EU(d1), EU(d2)) \\
&= \max(\$1375, \ \$1005) = \$1375,
\end{aligned}
$$

and our decision choice is $d1$. ∎

Notice in the previous example that the probabilities do not depend on the decision choice. This is because there is no edge from D to $NASDIP$. In general, this is not always the case, as the next example illustrates.

Example 8.17 Consider the influence diagram in Figure 8.15, which was developed in Example 8.11. We have

$$
\begin{aligned}
EU(d1) &= E(U|d1) \\
&= P(\$5|d1)U(d1, \$5) + P(\$20|d1)U(d1, \$20) \\
&= (.32)(\$50,000) + (.68)(\$200,000) \\
&= \$152,000
\end{aligned}
$$

$$
\begin{aligned}
EU(d2) &= E(U|d2) \\
&= P(\$5|d2)U(d2, \$5) + P(\$20|d2)U(d2, \$20) \\
&= (.42)(\$0) + (.58)(\$250,000) \\
&= \$145,000
\end{aligned}
$$

$$
\begin{aligned}
EU(D) &= \max(EU(d1), EU(d2)) \\
&= \max(\$152{,}000, \ \$145{,}000) = \$152{,}000,
\end{aligned}
$$

and our decision choice is $d1$. You may wonder where we obtained the values of $P(\$5|d1)$ and $P(\$5|d2)$. Once we instantiate the decision node, the chance nodes comprise a Bayesian network. We then call a Bayesian network inference algorithm to compute the needed conditional probabilities. For example, that algorithm would do the following computation:

$$
\begin{aligned}
P(\$5|d1) &= P(\$5|11{,}000, d1)P(11{,}000) + P(\$5|10{,}000, d1)P(10{,}000) \\
&= (.2)(.6) + (.5)(.4) = .32.
\end{aligned}
$$

Henceforth, we will not usually show the computations done by the Bayesian network inference algorithm. We will only show the results. ∎

Example 8.18 Consider the influence diagram in Figure 8.16, which was developed in Example 8.12. Because there is an arrow from $Test$ to D, the value of $Test$ will be known when the decision is made. So we need to determine the expected value of U given each value of $Test$. We have

$$
\begin{aligned}
EU(d1|positive) &= E(U|d1, positive) \\
&= P(good|d1, positive)U(d1, good) + \\
&\quad P(bad|d1, positive)U(d1, bad) \\
&= (.571429)(\$11{,}000) + (.428571)(\$8000) \\
&= \$9714
\end{aligned}
$$

$$
\begin{aligned}
EU(d2|positive) &= E(U|d2, positive) \\
&= P(good|d2, positive)U(d2, good) + \\
&\quad P(bad|d2, positive)U(d2, bad) \\
&= (.571429)(\$10{,}000) + (.428571)(\$10{,}000) \\
&= \$10{,}000
\end{aligned}
$$

$$
\begin{aligned}
EU(D|positive) &= \max(EU(d1|positive), EU(d2|positive)) \\
&= \max(\$9714, \ \$10{,}000) = \$10{,}000,
\end{aligned}
$$

and our decision choice is $d2$. As in the previous example, the needed conditional probabilities are obtained from a Bayesian network inference algorithm.

It is left as an exercise to compute $EU(D|negative)$. ∎

Example 8.19 Consider the influence diagram in Figure 8.17, which was developed in Example 8.13. Now we have two decisions: R and D. Because there is an edge from R to D, decision R is made first, and the EU of this decision is the one we need to compute. We have

$$
\begin{aligned}
EU(r1) &= E(U|r1) \\
&= P(d1, good|r1)U(r1, d1, good) + P(d1, bad|r1)U(r1, d1, bad) + \\
&\quad P(d2, good|r1)U(r1, d2, good) + P(d2, bad|r1)U(r1, d2, bad).
\end{aligned}
$$

We need to compute the conditional probabilities in this expression. Because D and $Tran$ are not dependent on R (decision R only determines the value of decision D in the sense that decision D does not take place for some values of R), we no longer show $r1$ to the right of the conditioning bar. We have

$$
\begin{aligned}
P(d1, good) &= P(d1|good)P(good) \\
&= [P(d1|positive)P(positive|good) + \\
&\quad P(d1|negative)P(negative|good)]P(good) \\
&= [(0)P(positive|good) + (1)P(negative|good)]\, P(good) \\
&= P(negative|good)P(good) \\
&= (.7)(.8) = .56.
\end{aligned}
$$

The second equality above is obtained because D and $Tran$ are independent conditional on $Test$. The values of $P(d1|positive)$ and $P(d1|negative)$ were obtained by first computing expected utilities as in Example 8.18 and then by setting the conditional probability to 1 if the decision choice is the one that maximizes expected utility and to 0 otherwise. It is left as an exercise to show that the other three probabilities are .02, .24, and .18, respectively. We therefore have

$$
\begin{aligned}
EU(r1) &= E(U|r1) \\
&= P(d1, good)U(r1, d1, good) + P(d1, bad)U(r1, d1, bad) + \\
&\quad P(d2, good)U(r1, d2, good) + P(d2, bad)U(r1, d2, bad) \\
&= (.56)(\$10{,}800) + (.02)(\$7800) + (.24)(\$9800) + (.18)(\$9800) \\
&= \$10{,}320.
\end{aligned}
$$

It is left as an exercise to show

$$EU(r2) = \$10{,}400$$

$$EU(r3) = \$10{,}000.$$

So

$$
\begin{aligned}
EU(R) &= \max(EU(r1), EU(r2), EU(r2)) \\
&= \max(\$10{,}320,\ \$10{,}400,\ \$10{,}000) = \$10{,}500,
\end{aligned}
$$

and our decision choice is $r2$. ∎

Example 8.20 Next, we show another method for solving the influence diagram in Figure 8.17, which, although it may be less elegant than the previous method, corresponds more to the way decision trees are solved. In this method, with decision R fixed at each of its choices, we solve the resultant influence diagram for decision D, and then we use these results to solve R.

First, fixing R at $r1$, we solve the influence diagram for D. The steps are the same as those in Example 8.18. That is, because there is an arrow from

$Test$ to D, the value of $Test$ will be known when the decision is made. So we need to determine the expected value of U given each value of $Test$. We have

$$
\begin{aligned}
EU(d1|r1, positive) &= E(U|r1, d1, positive) \\
&= P(good|positive)U(r1, d1, good) + \\
&\quad P(bad|positive)U(r1, d1, bad) \\
&= (.571429)(\$11{,}000) + (.429571)(\$8000) \\
&= \$9522
\end{aligned}
$$

$$
\begin{aligned}
EU(d2|r1, positive) &= E(U|r1, d2, positive) \\
&= P(good|positive)U(r1, d2, good) + \\
&\quad P(bad|positive)U(r1, d2, bad) \\
&= (.571429)(\$9800) + (.429571)(\$9800) \\
&= \$9800
\end{aligned}
$$

$$
\begin{aligned}
EU(D|r1, positive) &= \max(EU(d1|r1, positive), EU(d2|r1, positive)) \\
&= \max(\$9522, \ \$9800) = \$9800
\end{aligned}
$$

$$
\begin{aligned}
EU(d1|r1, negative) &= E(U|r1, d1, negative) \\
&= P(good|negative)U(r1, d1, good) + \\
&\quad P(bad|negative)U(r1, d1, bad) \\
&= (.965517)(\$10{,}800) + (.034483)(\$7800) \\
&= \$10{,}697
\end{aligned}
$$

$$
\begin{aligned}
EU(d2|r1, negative) &= E(U|r1, d2, negative) \\
&= P(good|negative)U(r1, d2, good) + \\
&\quad P(bad|negative)U(r1, d2, bad) \\
&= (.965517)(\$9800) + (.034483)(\$9800) \\
&= \$9800
\end{aligned}
$$

$$
\begin{aligned}
EU(D|r1, negative) &= \max(EU(d1|r1, negative), EU(d2|r1, negative)) \\
&= \max(\$10{,}697, \ \$9800) = \$10{,}697.
\end{aligned}
$$

As before, the conditional probabilities are obtained from a Bayesian network inference algorithm. Once we have the expected utilities of D, we can compute the expected utility of R as follows:

$$
\begin{aligned}
EU(r1) &= EU(D|r1, positive)P(positive) + EU(D|r1, negative)P(negative) \\
&= \$9800(.42) + \$10{,}697(.58) \\
&= \$10{,}320.
\end{aligned}
$$

Note that this is the same value we obtained using the other method. We next proceed to compute $EU(r2)$ and $EU(r3)$ in the same way. It is left as an exercise to do so. ∎

The second method illustrated in the previous example extends readily to an algorithm for solving influence diagrams. The algorithm solves the influence diagram by converting it to the decision tree corresponding to the influence diagram. For example, if we had three decision nodes D, E, and F in that order, we would first instantiate D to its first decision choice $d1$. This amounts to focusing on the subtree (of the corresponding decision tree) emanating from decision $d1$. Then, we would instantiate E to its first decision choice $e1$. This amounts to focusing on the subtree emanating from decision $e1$. Because F is our last decision, we would then solve the influence diagram for decision F. Next, we would compute the expected utility of E's first decision choice $e1$. After doing this for all of E's decision choices, we would solve the influence diagram for decision E. We would then compute the expected utility of D's first decision choice. This process would be repeated for each of D's decision choices. It is left as an exercise to write an algorithm that implements this method.

Olmsted [1983] developed a way to evaluate an influence diagram without transforming it to a decision tree. The method operates directly on the influence diagram by performing arc reversal/node reduction operations. These operations successively transform the diagram, ending with a diagram with only one utility node that holds the utility of the optimal decision. The method appears in [Shachter, 1986]. Tatman and Schachter [1990] use supervalue nodes, which simplify the construction of influence diagrams and subsequent sensitivity analysis. Another method for evaluating influence diagrams is to use variable elimination, which is described in [Jensen, 2001].

8.2.4 Solving Influence Diagrams Using Netica

Next we show how to solve an influence diagram using the software package Netica.

Example 8.21 Recall that Figure 8.15 showed an influence diagram representing the problem instance in Example 8.11. Figure 8.20 shows that influence diagram developed using Netica. A peculiarity of Netica is that node values must start with a letter. So we placed an "n" before numeric values. Another unfortunate feature is that both chance and decision nodes are depicted as rectangles.

The values shown at the decision node D are the expected values of the decision alternatives. We see that

$$E(d1) = 1.520 \times 10^5 = 152{,}000$$

$$E(d2) = 1.450 \times 10^5 = 145{,}000.$$

So the decision alternative that maximizes expected value is $d1$. ∎

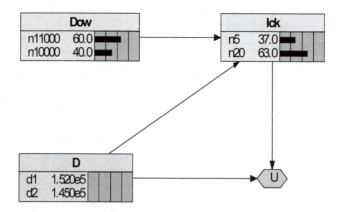

Figure 8.20 The influence diagram in Figure 8.15 developed using Netica.

Example 8.22 Recall that Figure 8.18 showed an influence diagram representing the problem instance in Example 8.14. Figure 8.21 (a) shows that influence diagram developed using Netica. We see that the decision alternative of "Run Test" that maximizes expected utility is to run the test. After running the test, the test will come back either positive or negative, and we must then decide whether or not to buy the car. The influence diagram updated to running the test and the test coming back positive appears in Figure 8.21 (b). We see that in this case the decision alternative that maximizes expected utility is to not buy the car. The influence diagram updated to running the test and the test coming back negative appears in Figure 8.21 (c). We see that in this case the decision alternative that maximizes expected utility is to buy the car. ∎

Example 8.23 Recall that Figure 8.19 showed an influence diagram representing the problem instance in Example 8.15. Figure 8.22 (a) shows that influence diagram developed using Netica. We see that the decision alternative of "CT Scan" that maximizes expected utility is $c1$, which is to do the scan. After doing the scan, the scan will come back either positive or negative, and we must then decide whether or not to do the mediastinoscopy. The influence diagram updated to doing the CT scan and the scan coming back positive appears in Figure 8.22 (b). We see that in this case the decision alternative that maximizes expected utility is to do the mediastinoscopy. The influence diagram updated to then doing the mediastinoscopy and the test coming back negative appears in Figure 8.22 (c). We see that in this case the decision alternative that maximizes expected utility is to do the thoracotomy. ∎

In the previous example, it is not surprising that the decision alternative that maximizes expected utility is to do the CT scan because that scan has no cost. Suppose instead that there is a financial cost of $1000 involved in doing the scan. Because the utility function is in terms of years of life, to perform a decision analysis we must convert the $1000 to units of years of life (or vice

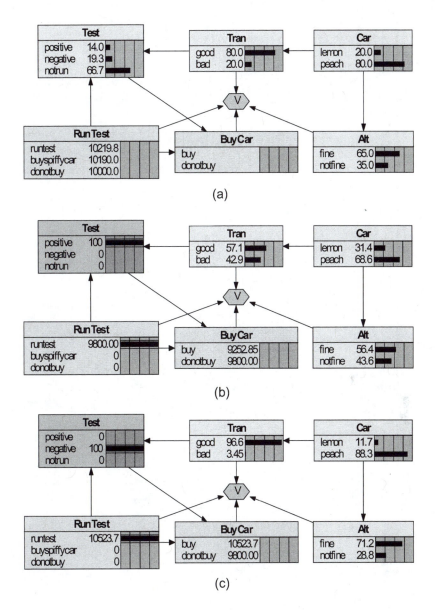

Figure 8.21 The influence diagram in Figure 8.18 developed using Netica
appears in (a). The influence diagram updated to running the test and the test
coming back positive appears in (b). The influence diagram updated to running
the test and the test coming back negative appears in (c).

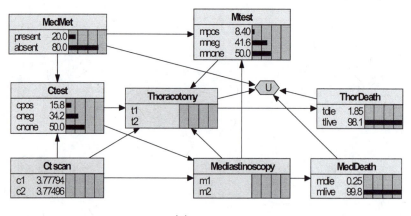

(a)

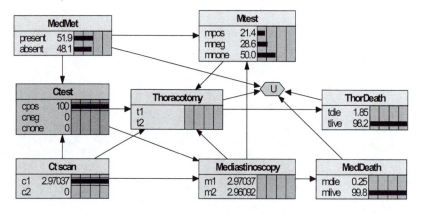

(b)

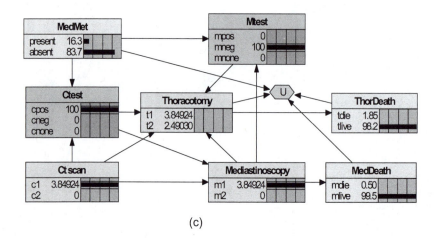

(c)

Figure 8.22 The influence diagram in Figure 8.19 developed using Netica appears in (a). The influence diagram updated to doing the CT scan and the scan coming back positive appears in (b). The influence diagram updated to then doing the mediastinoscopy and the test coming back negative appears in

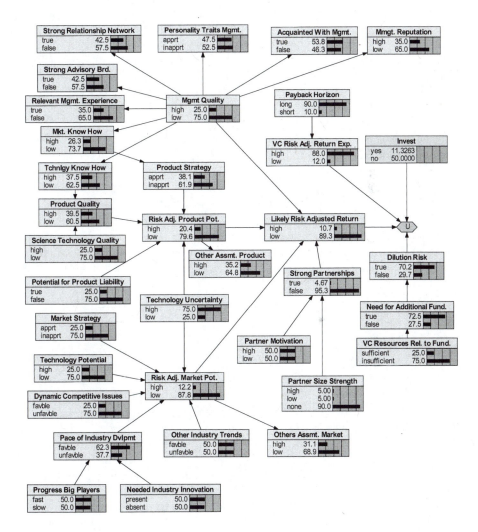

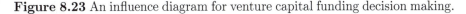

Figure 8.23 An influence diagram for venture capital funding decision making.

versa). Let's say the decision maker decides $1000 is equivalent to .01 years of life. It is left as an exercise to determine whether in this case the decision alternative that maximizes expected utility is still to do the CT scan.

Example 8.24 Start-up companies often do not have access to sufficient capital, but if they could obtain that capital, they may have the potential for good long-term growth. If a company is perceived as having such potential, investors can hope to obtain above-average returns by investing in such companies. Money provided by investors to start-up firms is called **venture capital (VC)**. Wealthy investors, investment banks, and other financial institutions typically provide venture capital funding. Venture capital investment can be very risky. A study in [Ruhnka et al., 1992] indicates that 40% of backed ventures fail. Therefore, careful analysis of a new firm's prospects is warranted before deciding whether to back the firm. Venture capitalists are experts who analyze a firm's prospects. Kemmerer et al. [2006] performed an in-depth interview of an expert venture capitalist and elicited a causal (Bayesian) network from that expert. They then refined the network, and finally assessed the conditional probability distributions for the network with the help of the venture capitalist. As discussed in [Shepherd and Zacharakis, 2002], such models often outperform the venture capitalist, whose knowledge was used to create them. Figure 8.23 shows the expert system resulting from their study. This application is discussed in detail in [Neapolitan and Jiang, 2007].   ■

8.3   Modeling Risk Preferences

Recall that in Example 8.1, we chose the alternative with the largest expected value. Surely, a person who is very risk averse might prefer the sure $1005 over the possibility of ending up with only $500. However, many people maximize expected value when the amount of money is small relative to their total wealth. The idea is that in the long run they will end up better off by so doing. When an individual maximizes expected value to reach a decision, the individual is called an **expected value maximizer**. On the other hand, given the situation discussed in Example 8.1, most people would not invest $100,000 in NASDIP because that is too much money relative to their total wealth. In the case of decisions in which an individual would not maximize expected value, we need to model the individual's attitude toward risk in order to use decision analysis to recommend a decision. One way to do this is to use a **utility function**, which is a function that maps dollar amounts to utilities. We discuss such functions next.

8.3.1   Exponential Utility Function

The **exponential utility function** is given by

$$U_r(x) = 1 - e^{-x/r}.$$

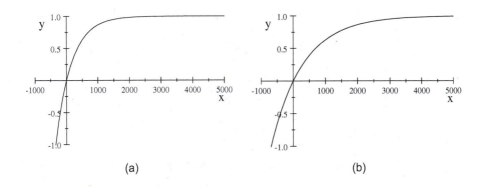

Figure 8.24 The $U_{500}(x) = 1 - e^{-x/500}$ function is in (a), while the $U_{1000}(x) = 1 - e^{-x/1000}$ function is in (b).

In this function the parameter r, called the **risk tolerance**, determines the degree of risk-aversion modeled by the function. As r becomes smaller, the function models more risk-averse behavior. Figure 8.24 (a) shows $U_{500}(x)$, while Figure 8.24 (b) shows $U_{1000}(x)$. Notice that both functions are concave (opening downward), and the one in Figure 8.24 (b) is closer to being a straight line. The more concave the function is, the more risk averse is the behavior modeled by the function. To model risk neutrality (i.e., simply being an expected value maximizer), we would use a straight line instead of the exponential utility function, and to model risk seeking behavior we would use a convex (opening upward) function. Chapter 5 showed many examples of modeling risk-neutrality. Here, we concentrate on modeling risk-averse behavior.

Example 8.25 Suppose Sam is making the decision in Example 8.1, and Sam decides his risk tolerance r is equal to 500. Then for Sam,

$EU(\text{Buy NASDIP})$

$$
\begin{aligned}
&= EU(NASDIP) \\
&= .25U_{500}(\$500) + .25U_{500}(\$1000) + .5U_{500}(\$2000) \\
&= .25\left(1 - e^{-500/500}\right) + .25\left(1 - e^{-1000/500}\right) + .5\left(1 - e^{-2000/500}\right) \\
&= .86504
\end{aligned}
$$

$$EU(\text{Leave \$1000 in bank}) = U_{500}(\$1005) = 1 - e^{-1005/500} = .86601.$$

So Sam decides to leave the money in the bank. ∎

Example 8.26 Suppose Sue is less risk averse than Sam, and she decides that her risk tolerance r equals 1000. If Sue is making the decision in Chapter 5, Example 8.1, then for Sue,

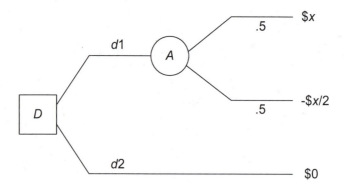

Figure 8.25 You can assess the risk tolerance r by determining the largest value of x for which you would be indifferent between $d1$ and $d2$.

$EU(\text{Buy NASDIP})$

$$= EU(NASDIP)$$
$$= .25U_{1000}(\$500) + .25U_{1000}(\$1000) + .5U_{1000}(\$2000)$$
$$= .25\left(1 - e^{-500/1000}\right) + .25\left(1 - e^{-1000/1000}\right) + .5\left(1 - e^{-2000/1000}\right)$$
$$= .68873$$

$$EU(\text{Leave \$1000 in bank}) = U_{1000}(\$1005) = 1 - e^{-1005/1000} = .63396.$$

So Sue decides to buy NASDIP.   ■

8.3.2 Assessing r

In the previous examples we simply assigned risk tolerances to Sam and Sue. You should be wondering how an individual arrives at her or his personal risk tolerance. Next, we show a method for assessing it.

One way to determine your personal value of r in the exponential utility function is to consider a gamble in which you will win $\$x$ with probability $.5$ and lose $-\$x/2$ with probability $.5$. Your value of r is the largest value of x for which you would choose the lottery over obtaining nothing. This is illustrated in Figure 8.25.

Example 8.27 Suppose we are about to toss a fair coin. I (Richard Neapolitan) would certainly like the gamble in which I win $10 if a heads occurs and lose $5 if a tails occurs. If we increased the amounts to $100 and $50, or even to $1000 and $500, I would still like the gamble. However, if we increased the amounts to $1,000,000 and $500,000, I would no longer like the gamble because I cannot afford a 50% chance of losing $500,000. By going back and forth like this (similar to a binary cut), I can assess my personal value of r. For me, r is about equal to $50,000. (Professors do not make all that much money.)   ■

You may inquire as to the justification for using this gamble to assess r. Notice that for any r,

$$.5\left(1 - e^{-r/r}\right) + .5\left(1 - e^{-(-r/2)/r}\right) = .0083$$

and

$$1 - e^{-0/r} = 0.$$

We see that for a given value of the risk tolerance r, the gamble in which one wins $\$r$ with probability .5 and loses $-\$r/2$ with probability .5 has about the same utility as receiving \$0 for certain. We can use this fact and then work in reverse to assess r. That is, we determine the value of r for which we are indifferent between this gamble and obtaining nothing.

8.4 Analyzing Risk Directly

Some decision makers may not be comfortable assessing personal utility functions and making decisions based on such functions. Rather, they may want to directly analyze the risk inherent in a decision alternative. One way to do this is to use the variance as a measure of spread from the expected value. Another way is to develop risk profiles. We discuss each technique in turn.

8.4.1 Using the Variance to Measure Risk

We start with an example.

Example 8.28 Suppose Patricia is going to make the decision modeled by the decision tree in Figure 8.26. If Patricia simply maximizes expected value, it is left as an exercise to show that

$$\begin{align} E(d1) &= \$1220 \\ E(d2) &= \$1200. \end{align}$$

So $d1$ is the decision alternative that maximizes expected value. However, the expected values by themselves tell us nothing of the risk involved in the alternatives. Let's also compute the variance of each decision alternative. If we choose alternative $d1$, then

$$\begin{align} P(2000) &= .8 \times .7 = .56 \\ P(1000) &= .1 \\ P(0) &= .8 \times .3 + .1 = .34. \end{align}$$

Notice that there are two ways \$0 could be obtained. That is, outcomes $a1$ and $c1$ could occur with probability $.8 \times .3$, and outcome $a2$ could occur with probability .1. We then have that

$$Var(d1)$$

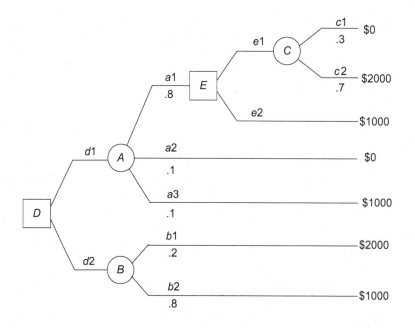

Figure 8.26 The decision tree discussed in Example 8.28.

$$= (2000 - 1220)^2 P(2000) + (1000 - 1220)^2 P(1000) + (0 - 1220)^2 P(0)$$
$$= (2000 - 1220)^2 \times .56 + (1000 - 1220)^2 \times .1 + (0 - 1220)^2 \times .34$$
$$= 851,600$$

$$\sigma_{d1} = \sqrt{851,600} = 922.82.$$

It is left as an exercise to show that

$$Var(d2) = 160,000$$
$$\sigma_{d2} = 400.$$

So if we use the variance as our measure of risk, we deem $d1$ somewhat more risky, which means if Patricia is somewhat risk averse, she might choose $d2$. ∎

Using the variance alone as the measure of risk can sometimes be misleading. The next example illustrates this.

Example 8.29 Now suppose Patricia is going to make the decision modeled by the decision tree in Figure 8.27. It is left as an exercise to show that

$$E(d1) = \$2900$$
$$Var(d1) = 32,490,000$$
$$\sigma_{d1} = 5700$$

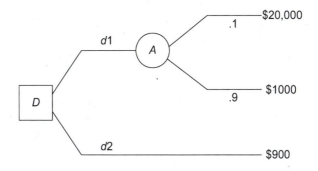

Figure 8.27 The decision tree discussed in Example 8.28.

and

$$E(d2) \;=\; \$900$$
$$Var(d2) \;=\; 0$$
$$\sigma_{d2} \;=\; 0.$$

If Patricia uses only the variance as her measure of risk, she might choose alternative $d2$ because $d1$ has such a large variance. Yet alternative $d1$ is sure to yield more return than alternative $d2$. This is a case of deterministic dominance, which is discussed in Section 8.4.3.   ∎

We see that the use of the variance alone as our measure of risk can be very misleading.

8.4.2   Risk Profiles

The expected value and variance are summary statistics, and, therefore, we lose information if all we report are these values. Alternatively, for each decision alternative, we could report the probability of all possible outcomes if the alternative is chosen. A graph that shows these probabilities is called a **risk profile**.

Example 8.30 Consider again Patricia's decision, which was discussed in Example 8.28. In that example, we computed the probability of all possible outcomes for each decision. We used those results to create the risk profiles in Figure 8.28. From these risk profiles, Patricia can see that there is a good chance she could end up with nothing if she chooses alternative $d1$, but she also has a good chance of obtaining $2000. On the other hand, the least she could end up with is $1000 if she chooses alternative $d2$, but probably this is all she will obtain.   ∎

A **cumulative risk profile** shows for each amount x the probability that the payoff will be less than or equal to x if the decision alternative is chosen. A

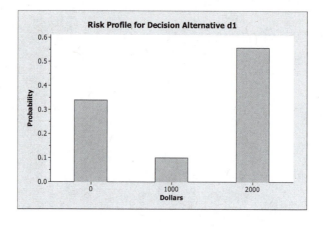

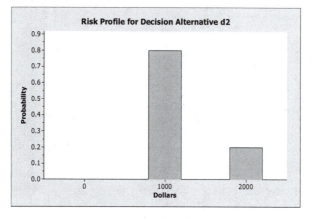

Figure 8.28 Risk profiles for the decision in Example 8.28.

cumulative risk profile is a cumulative distribution function. Figure 8.29 shows the cumulative risk profiles for the decision in Example 8.28.

8.4.3 Dominance

Some decisions do not require the use of utility functions or risk profiles because one decision alternative dominates the other for all decision makers. We discuss dominance next.

8.4.3.1 Deterministic Dominance

Suppose we have a decision that can be modeled using the decision tree in Figure 8.30. If we choose alternative $d1$, the least amount of money we will realize is $4, whereas if we choose alternative $d2$, the most amount of money we will realize is $3. Assuming that maximizing wealth is the only consideration in this decision, there is then no reasonable argument one can offer for choosing $d2$ over $d1$, and

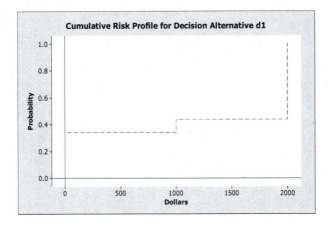

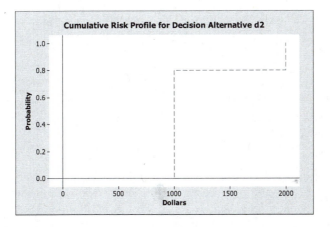

Figure 8.29 Cumulative risk profiles for the decision in Example 8.28.

we say $d1$ deterministically dominates $d2$. In general, decision alternative $d1$ **deterministically dominates** decision alternative $d2$ if the utility obtained from choosing $d1$ is greater than the utility obtained from choosing $d2$ regardless of the outcomes of chance nodes. When we observe deterministic dominance, there is no need to compute expected utility or develop a risk profile.

8.4.3.2 Stochastic Dominance

Suppose we have a decision that can be modeled using the decision tree in Figure 8.31. If the outcomes are $a1$ and $b2$, we will realize more money if we choose $d1$, while if the outcomes are $a2$ and $b1$, we will realize more money if we choose $d2$. So there is no deterministic dominance. However, the outcomes are the same for both decisions, namely $6 and $4, and, if we choose $d2$, the probability is higher that we will receive $6. So again, assuming that maximizing wealth is the only consideration in this decision, there is no reasonable argument for choosing $d1$

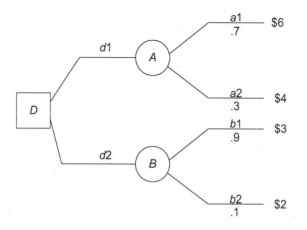

Figure 8.30 Decision alternative *d*1 deterministically dominates decision alternative *d*2.

over *d*2, and we say alternative *d*2 stochastically dominates alternative *d*1.

A different case of stochastic dominance is illustrated by the decision tree in Figure 8.32. In that tree, the probabilities are the same for both chance nodes, but the utilities for the outcomes of *B* are higher. That is, if *b*1 occurs, we realize $7, while if *a*1 occurs, we realize only $6, and if *b*2 occurs, we realize $5, while if *a*2 occurs, we realize only $4. So again, assuming that maximizing wealth is the only consideration in this decision, there is no reasonable argument for choosing *d*1 over *d*2, and we say alternative *d*2 stochastically dominates alternative *d*1.

Although it often is not hard to recognize stochastic dominance, it is a bit tricky to define the concept. We do so next in terms of cumulative risk profiles. We say that alternative *d*2 **stochastically dominates** alternative *d*1 if the cumulative risk profile $F_2(x)$ for *d*2 lies under the cumulative risk profile $F_1(x)$ for *d*1 for at least one value of x and does not lie over it for any values of x. That is, for at least one value of x,

$$F_2(x) < F_1(x),$$

and for all values of x,

$$F_2(x) \leq F_1(x).$$

This is illustrated in Figure 8.33. Why should this be the definition of stochastic dominance? Look again at Figure 8.33. There is no value of x such that the probability of realizing $$x$ or less is smaller if we choose *d*1 than if we choose *d*2. So there is no amount of money that we may want or require that would make *d*1 the better choice.

Figure 8.34 shows two cumulative risk profiles that cross, which means we do not have stochastic dominance. Now the decision alternative chosen can depend on an individual's preference. For example, if the amounts are in units of $100, and Mary needs at least $400 to pay her rent or else be evicted, she

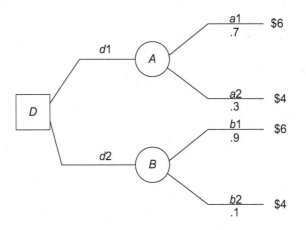

Figure 8.31 Decision alternative $d2$ stochastically dominates decision alternative $d1$.

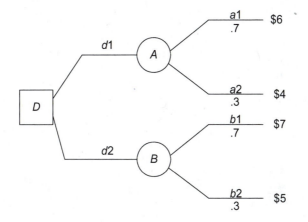

Figure 8.32 Decision alternative $d2$ stochastically dominates decision alternative $d1$.

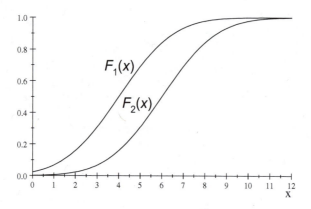

Figure 8.33 If $F_1(x)$ is the cumulative risk profile for $d1$ and $F_2(x)$ is the cumulative risk profile for $d2$, then $d2$ stochastically dominates $d1$.

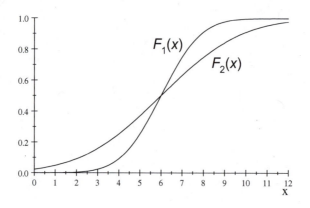

Figure 8.34 There is no stochastic dominance.

may choose alternative $d1$. On the other hand, if Sam needs at least $800 to pay his rent or else be evicted, he may choose alternative $d2$.

8.5   Good Decision versus Good Outcome

Suppose Scott and Sue are each about to make the decision modeled by the decision tree in Figure 8.32, Scott chooses alternative $d1$, and Sue chooses alternative $d2$. Suppose further that outcomes $a1$ and $b2$ occur. So Scott ends up with $6, and Sue ends up with $5. Did Scott make a better decision than Sue? We just claimed that there is no reasonable argument for choosing $d1$ over $d2$. If we accept that claim, we cannot now conclude that Scott made the better decision. Rather, Scott made a **bad decision with a good outcome**, while Sue made a **good decision with a bad outcome**. The quality of a decision must be judged based on the information available when the decision is made, not on outcomes realized after the decision is made. I (Richard Neapolitan) amusingly remember the following story from my youth. When my Uncle Hershell got out of the army, he used his savings to buy a farm in Texas next to his parents' farm. The ostensible reason was that he wanted to live near his parents and resume his life as a farmer. Somewhat later, oil was discovered on his farm, and Hershell became wealthy as a result. After that, my dad used to say, "Everyone thought Hershell was not too bright when he wasted money on a farm with such poor soil, but it turns out he was shrewd like a fox."

8.6   Sensitivity Analysis

Both influence diagrams and decision trees require that we assess probabilities and outcomes. Sometimes assessing these values precisely can be a difficult and laborious task. For example, it would be difficult and time consuming to determine whether the probability that the S&P 500 will be above 1500 in January 2008 is .3 or .35. Sometimes further refinement of these values would not affect our decision anyway. Next, we discuss **sensitivity analysis**, which is an analysis of how the values of outcomes and probabilities can affect our decision. In a **one-way sensitivity analysis**, we analyze the sensitivity to a single probability.

Example 8.31 Suppose that currently IBM is at $10 a share, and you feel there is a .5 probability it will be go down to $5 by the end of the month and a .5 probability it will go up to $20. You have $1000 to invest, and you will either buy 100 shares of IBM or put the money in the bank and earn a monthly interest rate of .005. Although you are fairly confident of your assessment of the outcomes, you are not very confident of your assessment of the probabilities. In this case, you can represent your decision using the decision tree in Figure 8.35. Notice in that tree that we represented the probability of IBM going up by a variable p. We then have

$$E(\text{Buy IBM}) = p(2000) + (1 - p)(500)$$

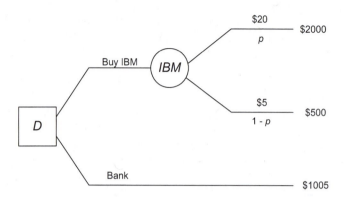

Figure 8.35 As long as p is greater than .337, buying IBM maximizes expected value.

$$E(\text{Bank}) = \$1005.$$

We will buy IBM if $E(\text{Buy IBM}) > E(\text{Bank})$, which is the case if

$$p(2000) + (1 - p)(500) > 1005.$$

Solving this inequality for p, we have

$$p > .337.$$

We have determined how sensitive our decision is to the value of p. As long as we feel that the probability of IBM going up is at least equal to .337, we will buy IBM. We need not refine our probabilistic assessment further. ∎

In a **two-way sensitivity analysis**, we simultaneously analyze the sensitivity of our decision to two quantities. The next example shows such an analysis.

Example 8.32 Suppose you are in the same situation as in the previous example, except you are confident in your assessment of the probability of the Dow going up, but you are not confident in your assessment of the probabilities of your stock going up dependent on whether the Dow goes up or down. Specifically, you model your decision using the decision tree in Figure 8.36. We then have

$$E(\text{Buy IBM}) = .4(q \times 2000 + (1 - q) \times 500) + .6(r \times 2000 + (1 - r) \times 500)$$

$$E(\text{Bank}) = 1005.$$

We will buy IBM if $E(\text{Buy IBM}) > E(\text{Bank})$, which is the case if

$$.4(q \times 2000 + (1 - q) \times 500) + .6(r \times 2000 + (1 - r) \times 500) > 1005.$$

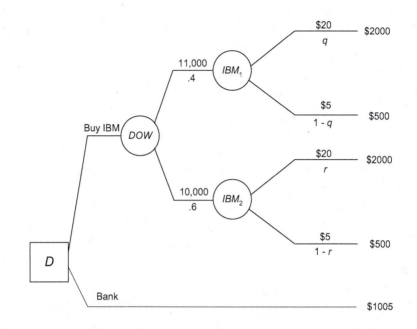

Figure 8.36 For this decision we need to do a two-way sensitivity analysis.

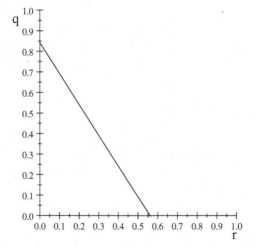

Figure 8.37 The line $q = 101/120 - 3r/2$. As long as (r, q) is above this line, the decision that mazimizes expected value in Example 8.32 is to buy IBM.

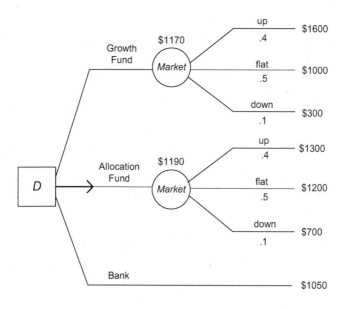

Figure 8.38 Buying the allocation fund maximizes expected value.

Simplifying this inequality, we obtain

$$q > \frac{101}{120} - \frac{3r}{2}.$$

The line $q = 101/120 - 3r/2$ is plotted in Figure 8.37. Owing to the previous inequality, the decision that maximizes expected value is to buy IBM as long as the point (r, q) lies above that line. For example, if $r = .6$ and $q = .1$ or $r = .3$ and $q = .8$, this would be our decision. However, if $r = .3$ and $q = .1$, it would not. ■

8.7   Value of Information

Figure 8.38 shows a decision tree concerning a choice between two mutual funds and putting the money in the bank. It is left as an exercise to show that, given these values, the decision that maximizes expected value is to buy the allocation fund and

$$E(D) = E(\text{allocation fund}) = \$1190.$$

This is shown in Figure 8.38. Before making a decision, we often have the chance to consult with an expert in the domain which the decision concerns. Suppose in the current decision we can consult with an expert financial analyst who is perfect at predicting the market. That is, if the market will go up, the analyst will say it will go up; if it will be flat, the analyst will say it will be flat; and if it will go down, the analyst will say it will go down. We should be willing to pay for this information, but not more than the information is worth.

Next, we show how to compute the expected value (worth) of this information, which is called the expected value of perfect information.

8.7.1 Expected Value of Perfect Information

To compute the expected value of perfect information, we add another decision alternative, which is to consult the perfect expert. Figure 8.39 shows the decision tree in Figure 8.38 with that alternative added. Next, we show how the probabilities for that tree were obtained. Because the expert is perfect, we have

$$P(\text{Expert} = \text{says up} \mid \text{Market} = \text{up}) = 1$$

$$P(\text{Expert} = \text{says flat} \mid \text{Market} = \text{flat}) = 1$$

$$P(\text{Expert} = \text{says down} \mid \text{Market} = \text{down}) = 1.$$

We therefore have

$P(\text{up} \mid \text{says up})$

$$= \frac{P(\text{says up} \mid \text{up})P(\text{up})}{P(\text{says up} \mid \text{up})P(\text{up}) + P(\text{says flat} \mid \text{up})P(\text{flat}) + P(\text{says down} \mid \text{down})P(\text{down})}$$

$$= \frac{1 \times .4}{1 \times .4 + 0 \times .5 + 0 \times .1} = 1.$$

It is not surprising that this value is 1, as the expert is perfect. This value is the far right and uppermost probability in the decision tree in Figure 8.39. It is left as an exercise to compute the other probabilities and solve the tree. We see that

$$E(\text{Consult Perfect Analyst}) = \$1345.$$

Recall that without consulting this analyst, the decision alternative that maximizes expected utility is to buy the allocation fund and

$$E(D) = E(\text{allocation fund}) = \$1190.$$

The difference between these two expected values is the **expected value of perfect information (EVPI)**. That is,

$$
\begin{aligned}
EVPI &= E(\text{Consult Perfect Analyst}) - E(D) \\
&= \$1345 - \$1190 = \$155.
\end{aligned}
$$

This is the most we should be willing to pay for the information. If we pay less than this amount, we will have increased our expected value by consulting the expert, while if we pay more, we will have decreased our expected value.

We showed decision trees in Figures 8.38 and 8.39 so that you could see how the expected value of perfect information is computed. However, as is usually the case, it is much easier to represent the decisions using influence diagrams. Figure 8.40 shows the decision tree in Figure 8.38 represented as an influence diagram and solved using Netica. Figure 8.41 shows the decision tree in Figure 8.39 represented as an influence diagram and solved using Netica. We

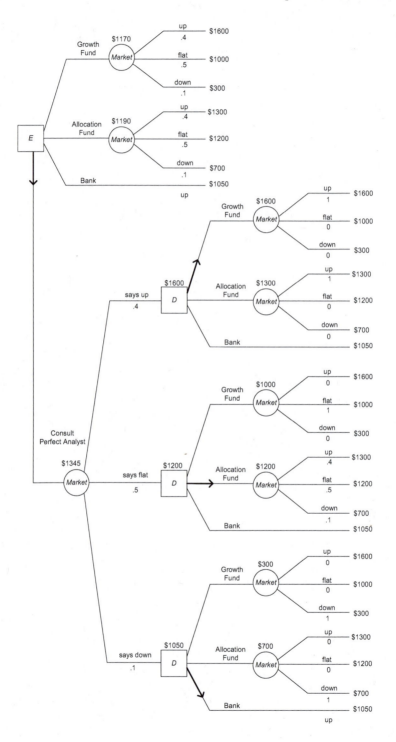

Figure 8.39 The maximum expected value without consulting the perfect expert is $1190, while the expected value of consulting that expert is $1345.

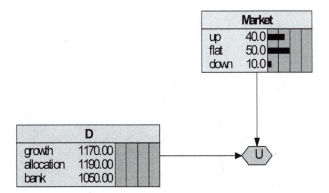

Figure 8.40 The decision tree in Figure 8.38 represented as an influence diagram and solved using Netica.

P(says up | up) = 1 P(says up | flat) = 0 P(says up | down) = 0
P(says flat | up) = 0 P(says flat | flat) = 1 P(says flat | down) = 0
P(says down | up) = 0 P(says down | flat) = 0 P(says down | down) = 1

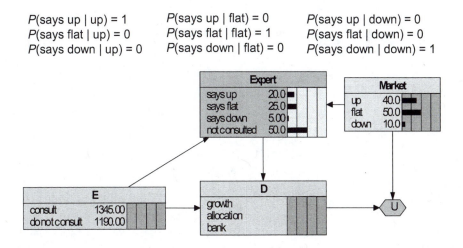

Figure 8.41 The decision tree in Figure 8.39 represented as an influence diagram and solved using Netica.

have added the conditional probabilities of the Expert node to that diagram. (Recall that Netica does not show conditional probabilities.) Notice that we can obtain the EVPI directly from the values listed at decision node E in the influence diagram in Figure 8.41. That is,

$$
\begin{aligned}
EVPI &= E(\text{consult}) - E(\text{do not consult}) \\
&= \$1345 - \$1190 = \$155.
\end{aligned}
$$

8.7.2   Expected Value of Imperfect Information

Real experts and tests ordinarily are not perfect. Rather, they are only able to give estimates that are often correct. Let's say we have a financial analyst who has been predicting market activity for 30 years and has had the following results:

1. When the market went up, the analyst said it would go up 80% of the time, would be flat 10% of the time, and would go down 10% of the time.

2. When the market was flat, the analyst said it would go up 20% of the time, would be flat 70% of the time, and would go down 10% of the time.

3. When the market went down, the analyst said it would go up 20% of the time, would be flat 20% of the time, and would go down 60% of the time.

We therefore estimate the following conditional probabilities for this expert:

$$
\begin{aligned}
P(\text{Expert} = \text{says up} \mid \text{Market} = \text{up}) &= .8 \\
P(\text{Expert} = \text{says flat} \mid \text{Market} = \text{up}) &= .1 \\
P(\text{Expert} = \text{says down} \mid \text{Market} = \text{up}) &= .1 \\
P(\text{Expert} = \text{says up} \mid \text{Market} = \text{flat}) &= .2 \\
P(\text{Expert} = \text{says flat} \mid \text{Market} = \text{flat}) &= .7 \\
P(\text{Expert} = \text{says down} \mid \text{Market} = \text{flat}) &= .1 \\
P(\text{Expert} = \text{says up} \mid \text{Market} = \text{down}) &= .2 \\
P(\text{Expert} = \text{says flat} \mid \text{Market} = \text{down}) &= .2 \\
P(\text{Expert} = \text{says down} \mid \text{Market} = \text{down}) &= .6.
\end{aligned}
$$

Figure 8.42 shows the influence diagram in Figure 8.40 with the additional decision alternative that we can consult this imperfect expert. We also show the conditional probabilities of the Expert node in that diagram. The increased expected value we realize by consulting such an expert is called the **expected value of imperfect information (EVII)**. It is given by

$$
\begin{aligned}
EVII &= E(\text{consult}) - E(\text{do not consult}) \\
&= \$1261.50 - \$1190 = \$71.50.
\end{aligned}
$$

This is the most we should pay for this expert's information.

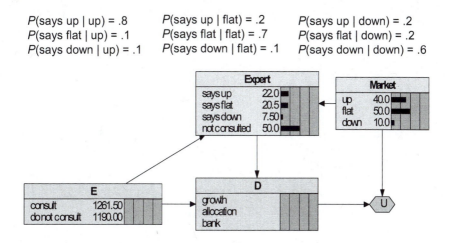

P(says up | up) = .8   P(says up | flat) = .2   P(says up | down) = .2
P(says flat | up) = .1   P(says flat | flat) = .7   P(says flat | down) = .2
P(says down | up) = .1   P(says down | flat) = .1   P(says down | down) = .6

Figure 8.42 An influence diagram that enables us to compute the expected value of imperfect information.

8.8 Discussion and Further Reading

The analysis methodology presented in this and the previous chapter for recommending decisions is called **normative decision analysis** because the methodology prescribes how people should make decisions rather than describes how people do make decisions. In 1954, L. Jimmie Savage developed axioms concerning an individual's preferences and beliefs. If an individual accepts these axioms, Savage showed that the individual must prefer the decisions obtained using decision analysis. Tversky and Kahneman [1981] conducted a number of studies showing that individuals do not make decisions consistent with the methodology of decision analysis. That is, their studies indicate that decision analysis is not a descriptive theory. Kahneman and Tversky [1979] developed **prospect theory** to describe how people actually make decisions when they are not guided by decision analysis. In 2002, Dan Kahneman won the Nobel Prize in economics for this effort. An alternative descriptive theory of decision making is **regret theory** [Bell, 1982].

We only briefly introduced notions like risk preferences and sensitivity analysis. There are many more considerations. For example, the exponential utility function is a **constant risk-aversion utility function** because one's total wealth does not affect the decision obtained using the function. A **decreasing risk-averse utility function** can obtain a different decision depending on one's total wealth. In sensitivity analysis we can model sensitivity to the values of the outcomes besides the probabilities. These matters and more are discussed in texts such as [Clemen, 1996] and [Neapolitan and Jiang, 2007].

The previous three chapters have introduced Bayesian networks and influence diagrams. These architectures have been applied successfully in a number of domains. A representative list follows. The list is by no means meant to be exhaustive. Some of these applications use dynamic Bayesian networks and dynamic influence diagrams, which will be introduced in Section 14.2.

8.8.1   Academics

1. The Learning Research and Development Center at the University of Pittsburgh developed Andes [VanLehn et al., 2005], an intelligent tutoring system for physics. Andes infers a student's plan as the student works on a physics problem, and it assesses and tracks the student's domain knowledge over time.

2. Royalty et al. [2002] developed POET, which is an academic advising tool that models the evolution of a student's transcripts.

8.8.2   Business and Finance

1. Demirer et al. [2007] developed a portfolio risk analyzer.

2. Lander and Shenoy [1999] modeled real options using an influence diagram, that also provides a plan. That is, it not only recommends the decision alternative to make today, but also recommends the decision to make in the future after new information is obtained.

3. Kemmer et al. [2006] developed an influence diagram for venture capital decision making.

4. Data Digest (www.data-digest.com) modeled and predicted customer behavior in a variety of business settings.

8.8.3   Capital Equipment

Knowledge Industries, Inc. (KI) (www.kic.com) developed a relatively large number of applications during the 1990s. Most of them are used in internal applications by their licensees and are not publicly available. KI applications in capital equipment include locomotives, gas-turbine engines for aircraft and land-based power production, the space shuttle, and office equipment.

8.8.4   Computer Games

Valadares [2002] developed a computer game that models the evolution of a simulated world.

8.8.5   Computer Vision

1. The Reading and Leeds Computer Vision Groups developed an integrated traffic and pedestrian model-based vision system. Information concerning this system can be found at www.cvg.cs.rdg.ac.uk/~imv.

2. Huang et al. [1994] developed a computer vision system that analyzed freeway traffic using dynamic Bayesian networks.

3. Pham et al. [2002] developed a face detection system.

8.8.6 Computer Software

1. Microsoft Research (research.microsoft.com) has developed a number of applications. Since 1995, Microsoft Office's AnswerWizard has used a naive-Bayesian network to select help topics based on queries. Also since 1995, there are about ten troubleshooters in Windows that use Bayesian networks. See [Heckerman et al., 1994].

2. Burnell and Horvitz [1995] describe a system, which was developed by UT-Arlington and American Airlines (AA), for diagnosing problems with legacy software, specifically the Sabre airline reservation system used by AA. Given the information in a dump file, this diagnostic system identifies which sequences of instructions may have led to the system error.

8.8.7 Medicine

1. "Promedas is the biggest and fastest probabilistic medical diagnostic network in the World based on medical expert knowledge, acquired from the literature by our medical specialists. More than 3500 diagnoses and 47,000 network connections provide a diagnosis in seconds." - http://www.promedas.nl/. See the site just referenced for a demonstration of Promedas, which is based on a Bayesian network.

2. Heckerman et al. [1992] describe Pathfinder, which is a system that assists community pathologists with the diagnosis of lymph node pathology. Pathfinder has been integrated with videodiscs to form the commercial system Intellipath.

3. Nicholson [1996] modeled the stepping patterns of the elderly to diagnose falls using a dynamic Bayesian network.

4. Onisko [2001] describes Hepar II, which is a system for diagnosing liver disorders.

5. Ogunyemi et al. [2002] developed TraumaSCAN, which assesses conditions arising from ballistic penetrating trauma to the chest and abdomen. It accomplishes this by integrating three-dimensional geometric reasoning about anatomic likelihood of injury with probabilistic reasoning about injury consequences.

6. Galán et al. [2002] created NasoNet, which is a system that performs diagnosis and prognosis of nasopharyngeal cancer (cancer concerning the nasal passages).

8.8.8   Natural Language Processing

Koehler [1998] developed Symtext, a natural language understanding system for
encoding free text medical data. Related work appears in [Meystre and Haug, 2005]
and [Christensen et al., 2009].

8.8.9   Planning

1. Dean and Wellman [1991] applied dynamic Bayesian networks to planning
   and control under uncertainty.

2. Cozman and Krotkov [1996] developed quasi-Bayesian strategies for efficient plan generation.

8.8.10   Psychology

Glymour [2001] discusses applications to cognitive psychology.

8.8.11   Reliability Analysis

1. Torres-Toledano and Sucar [1998] developed a system for reliability analysis in power plants.

2. The Centre for Software Reliability at Agena Ltd. (www.agena.co.uk) developed TRACS (Transport Reliability Assessment and Calculation System), which is a tool for predicting the reliability of military vehicles.
   The tool is used by the United Kingdom's Defense Research and Evaluation Agency (DERA) to assess vehicle reliability at all stages of the design
   and development lifecycle. TRACS is described in [Strutt and Hall, 2003].
   The TRACS tool was built using the SERENE tool and the Hugin API
   (www.hugin.dk), and it was written in VB using the MSAccess database
   engine. The SERENE method was used to develop the Bayesian network
   structure and generate the parameters. TRACS and other Bayesian network systems developed by Agena. Ltd. are described in a paper available
   at http://www.agenarisk.com/resources/apps_bayesian_networks.pdf.

8.8.12   Scheduling

MITRE Corporation (www.mitre.org) developed a system for real-time weapons
scheduling for ship self-defense. Used by the United States Navy (NSWC-DD),
the system can handle multiple target, multiple weapon problems in under two
seconds on a Sparc laptop.

8.8.13   Speech Recognition

1. Bilmes [2000] applied dynamic Bayesian multinets to speech recognition.

2. Nefian et al. [2002] developed a system for audio-visual speech recognition
   using dynamic Bayesian networks.

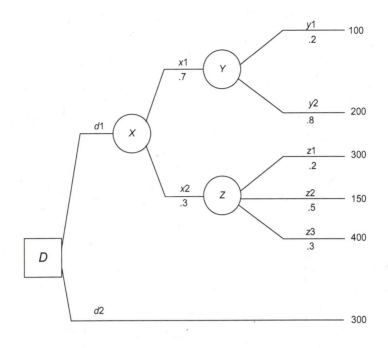

Figure 8.43 A decision tree.

8.8.14 Vehicle Control and Malfunction Diagnosis

1. Horvitz et al. [1992] describe Vista, which is a decision-theoretic system used at NASA Mission Control Center in Houston. The system uses Bayesian networks to interpret live telemetry, and it provides advice on the likelihood of alternative failures of the space shuttle's propulsion systems. It also considers time criticality and recommends actions of the highest expected utility. Furthermore, the Vista system employs decision-theoretic methods for controlling the display of information to dynamically identify the most important information to highlight.

2. Morjaia et al. [1993] developed a system for locomotive diagnostics.

EXERCISES

Section 8.1

Exercise 8.1 Solve the decision tree in Figure 8.43.

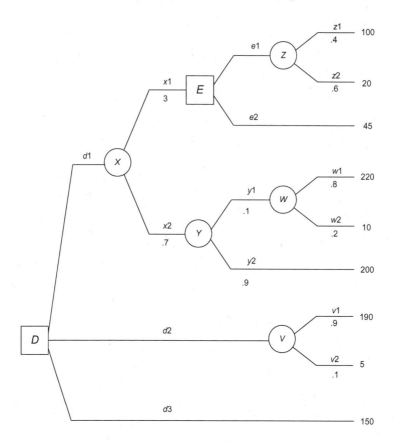

Figure 8.44 A decision tree with two decisions.

Exercise 8.2 Solve the decision tree in Figure 8.44.

Exercise 8.3 Show the solved decision tree given the decision tree in Figure 8.3.

Exercise 8.4 Compute the conditional probabilities in the decision tree in Figure 8.6 from the conditional probabilities given in Example 8.4.

Exercise 8.5 Show $EU(D_1) = \$9800$ and $EU(D_2) = \$10,697$ for the decision tree in Figure 8.8.

Exercise 8.6 Consider Example 8.6. Suppose Leonardo has the opportunity to consult the weather forecast before deciding on whether to take his umbrella. Suppose further that the weather forecast says it will rain on 90% of the days it actually does rain and on 20% of the days it does not rain. That is,

$$P(Forecast = \text{rain}|R = \text{rain}) = .9$$

$$P(Forecast = \text{rain}|R = \text{no rain}) = .2.$$

As before, suppose Leonardo judges that

$$P(R = \text{rain}) = .4.$$

Show the decision tree representing this problem instance assuming the utilities in Example 8.6. Solve that decision tree.

Exercise 8.7 Consider again Example 8.6. Assume that if it rains, there is a .7 probability the suit will only need to go to the cleaners, and a .3 probability it will be ruined. Assume again that

$$P(R = \text{rain}) = .4.$$

Assess your own utilities for this situation, show the resultant decision tree, and solve that decision tree.

Exercise 8.8 Consider Example 8.8. Assume that your life expectancy from birth is 75 years. Assess your own QALEs for the situation described in that example, show the resultant decision tree, and solve that decision tree.

Exercise 8.9 Suppose Jennifer is a young, potential capitalist with $1000 to invest. She has heard glorious tales of many who have made fortunes in the stock market. So she decides to do one of three things with her $1000. (1) She could buy an option on Techjunk that would allow her to buy 1000 shares of Techjunk for $22 a share in one month. (2) She could use the $1000 to buy shares of Techjunk. (3) She could leave the $1000 in the bank earning .07 annually. Currently, Techjunk is selling for $20 a share. Suppose further she feels there is a .5 chance the NASDAQ will be at 2000 in two months and a .5 chance it will be at 2500. If it is at 2000, she feels there is a .3 chance Techjunk will be at $23 a share and a .7 chance it will be at $15 a share. If the NASDAQ is at 2500, she feels there is a .7 chance Techjunk will be at $26 a share and a .3 chance it will be $20 a share. Show a decision tree that represents this decision, and solve that decision tree.

Let $P(NASDAQ = 2000) = p$ and $P(NASDAQ = 2500) = 1 - p$. Determine the maximal value of p for which the decision would be to buy the option. Is there any value of p for which the decision would be to buy the stock?

Exercise 8.10 This exercise is based on an example in [Clemen, 1996]. In 1984, Penzoil and Getty Oil agreed to a merger. However, before the deal was closed, Texaco offered Getty a better price. So Gordon Getty backed out of the Penzoil deal and sold to Texaco. Penzoil immediately sued, won the case, and was awarded $11.1 billion. A court order reduced the judgment to $2 billion, but interest and penalties drove the total back up to $10.3 billion. James Kinnear, Texaco's chief executive officer, said he would fight the case all the way up to the U.S. Supreme Court because, he argued, Penzoil had not followed Security and Exchange Commission regulations when negotiating with

Getty. In 1987, just before Penzoil was to begin filing liens against Texaco, Texaco offered to give Penzoil $2 billion to settle the entire case. Hugh Liedke, chairman of Penzoil, indicated that his advisors told him a settlement between $3 billion and $5 billion would be fair.

What should Liedke do? Two obvious choices are (1) he could accept the $2 billion or (2) he could turn it down. Let's say that he is also considering counteroffering $5 billion. If he does, he judges that Texaco will either accept the counteroffer with probability .17, refuse the counteroffer with probability .5, or counter back in the amount of $3 billion with probability .33. If Texaco does counter back, Liedke will then have the decision of whether to refuse or accept the counteroffer. Liedke assumes that if he simply turns down the $2 billion with no counteroffer, if Texaco refuses his counteroffer, or if he refuses their return counteroffer, the matter will end up in court. If it does go to court, he judges that there is .2 probability Penzoil will be awarded $10.3 billion, a .5 probability they will be awarded $5 billion, and a .3 probability they will get nothing.

Show a decision tree that represents this decision, and solve that decision tree.

What finally happened? Liedke simply refused the $2 billion. Just before Penzoil began to file liens on Texaco's assets, Texaco filed for protection from creditors under Chapter 11 of the federal bankruptcy code. Penzoil then submitted a financial reorganization plan on Texaco's behalf. Under the plan, Penzoil would receive about $4.1 billion. Finally, the two companies agreed on $3 billion as part of Texaco's financial reorganization.

Section 8.2

Exercise 8.11 Represent the problem instance in Exercise 8.6 with an influence diagram. Hand solve the influence diagram. Using Netica or some other software package, construct and solve the influence diagram.

Exercise 8.12 Represent the problem instance in Exercise 8.7 with an influence diagram. Hand solve the influence diagram. Using Netica or some other software package, construct and solve the influence diagram.

Exercise 8.13 Represent the problem instance in Exercise 8.9 with an influence diagram. Hand solve the influence diagram. Using Netica or some other software package, construct and solve the influence diagram.

Exercise 8.14 Represent the problem instance in Exercise 8.10 with an influence diagram. Hand solve the influence diagram. Using Netica or some other software package, construct and solve the influence diagram.

Exercise 8.15 After Example 8.23, we noted that it was not surprising that the decision alternative that maximizes expected utility is to do the CT scan because that scan has no cost. Suppose instead that there is a financial cost of $1000 involved in doing the scan. Let's say the decision maker decides $1000 is equivalent to .01 years of life. Using Netica or some other software package, construct an influence diagram representing this problem instance, and determine whether in this case the decision alternative that maximizes expected utility is still to do the CT scan.

Section 8.3

Exercise 8.16 Using the technique illustrated in Example 8.27, assess your personal risk tolerance r.

Exercise 8.17 Using the value of r assessed in the previous exercise, determine the decision that maximizes expected utility for the decision in Example 8.1..

Section 8.4

Exercise 8.18 Compute the variance of the decision alternatives for the decision in Example 8.2. Plot risk profiles and cumulative risk profiles for the decision alternatives. Discuss whether you find the variance or the risk profiles more helpful in determining the risk inherent in each alternative.

Exercise 8.19 Compute the variance of the decision alternatives for the decision in Example 8.3. Plot risk profiles and cumulative risk profiles for the decision alternatives. Discuss whether you find the variance or the risk profiles more helpful in determining the risk inherent in each alternative.

Exercise 8.20 Compute the variance of the decision alternatives for the decision in Example 8.5. Plot risk profiles and cumulative risk profiles for the decision alternatives. Discuss whether you find the variance or the risk profiles more helpful in determining the risk inherent in each alternative.

Section 8.5

Exercise 8.21 Does one of the decision alternatives in the decision tree in Figure 8.45 deterministically dominate? If so, which one?

Exercise 8.22 Does one of the decision alternatives in the decision tree in Figure 8.46 stochastically dominate? If so, which one? Create cumulative risk profiles for the decision alternatives.

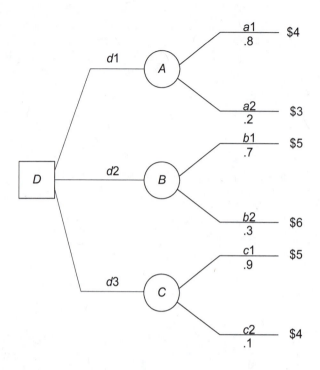

Figure 8.45 A decision tree.

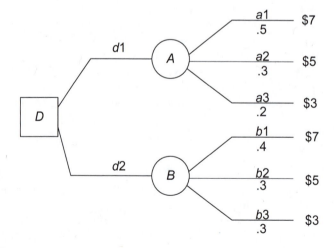

Figure 8.46 A decision tree.

Section 8.6

Exercise 8.23 Suppose that currently Lucent is at $3 a share, and you feel there is a .6 probability it will be go down to $2 by the end of the month and a .4 probability it will go up to $5. You have $3000 to invest, and you will either buy 1000 shares of Lucent or put the money in the bank and earn a monthly interest rate of .004. Although you are fairly confident of your assessment of the outcomes, you are not very confident of your assessment of the probabilities. Let p be the probability Lucent will go down. Determine the largest value of p for which you would decide to buy Lucent.

Exercise 8.24 Suppose you are in the same situation as in the previous exercise, except you feel that the value of Lucent will be affected by the overall value of the NASDAQ in one month. Currently, the NASDAQ is at 2300, and you assess that it will either be at 2000 or 2500 at the end of the month. You feel confident assessing the probabilities of your stock going up dependent on whether the NASDAQ goes up or down, but you are not confident assessing the probability of the NASDAQ going up or down. Specifically, you feel the probability of Lucent going up if the NASDAQ goes up is .8 and the probability of Lucent going up given the NASDAQ goes down is .3. Let p be the probability the NASDAQ will go up. Determine the smallest value of p for which you would decide to buy Lucent.

Exercise 8.25 Suppose you are in the same situation as in the previous exercise, except you are confident in your assessment of the probability of the NASDAQ going up, but you are not confident in your assessment of the probabilities of your stock going up dependent on whether the NASDAQ goes up or down. Specifically, you feel the probability that the NASDAQ will go up is .7. Let p be the probability of Lucent going up given the NASDAQ goes up, and let q be the probability of Lucent going up given the NASDAQ goes down. Do a two-way sensitivity analysis on p and q.

Section 8.7

Exercise 8.26 Suppose we have the decision tree in Figure 8.39, except the growth fund will be at $1800, $1100, and $200 if the market is, respectively, up, flat, or down, while the allocation fund will be at $1400, $1000, or $400.

1. Compute the expected value of perfect information by hand.

2. Model the problem instance as an influence diagram using Netica, and determine the expected value of perfect information using that influence diagram.

Exercise 8.27 Suppose we have the same decision as in the previous example, except we can consult an expert who is not perfect. Specifically, the expert's accuracy is as follows:

$$P(\text{Expert} = \text{says up} \mid \text{Market} = \text{up}) \;=\; .7$$
$$P(\text{Expert} = \text{says flat} \mid \text{Market} = \text{up}) \;=\; .2$$
$$P(\text{Expert} = \text{says down} \mid \text{Market} = \text{up}) \;=\; .1$$
$$P(\text{Expert} = \text{says up} \mid \text{Market} = \text{flat}) \;=\; .1$$
$$P(\text{Expert} = \text{says flat} \mid \text{Market} = \text{flat}) \;=\; .8$$
$$P(\text{Expert} = \text{says down} \mid \text{Market} = \text{flat}) \;=\; .1.$$

Model the problem instance as an influence diagram using Netica, and determine the expected value of consulting the expert using that influence diagram.

Exercise 8.28 Consider the decision problem discussed in Exercise 8.10. Represent the problem with an influence diagram using Netica, and, using that influence diagram, determine the EVPI concerning Texaco's reaction to a $5 billion counteroffer.

Exercise 8.29 Recall Chapter 2, Exercise 5.18, in which Professor Neapolitan has the opportunity to drill for oil on his farm in Texas. It costs $25,000 to drill. Suppose that if he drills and oil is present, he will receive $100,000 from the sale of the oil. If only natural gas is present, he will receive $30,000 from the sale of the natural gas. If neither is present, he will receive nothing. The alternative to drilling is to do nothing, which would definitely result in no profit, but he will not have spent the $25,000.

1. Represent the decision problem with an influence diagram, and solve the influence diagram.

2. Now include a node for the test discussed in Exercise 5.18, and determine the expected value of running the test.

Part III

Emergent Intelligence

Chapter 9

Evolutionary Computation

Evolution is the process of change in the genetic makeup of populations. **Natural selection** is the process by which organisms which have traits that better enable them to adapt to environmental pressures will tend to survive and reproduce in greater numbers than other similar organisms, thereby increasing the existence of those favorable traits in future generations.

Evolutionary computation endeavors to obtain approximate solutions to problems such as optimization problems using the evolutionary mechanisms involved in natural selection as its paradigm. The four areas of evolutionary computation are genetic algorithms, genetic programming, evolutionary programming, and evolutionary strategies. The first two areas are discussed in detail. First we briefly review genetics to provide a proper context for the motivation for these algorithms.

9.1   Genetics Review

This brief review assumes that you have seen this material before. For an introduction to genetics, see [Griffiths et al., 2007] or [Hartl and Jones, 2006].

An **organism** is an individual form of life such as a plant or animal. A **cell** is the basic structural and functional unit of an organism. **Chromosomes** are the carriers of biologically expressed hereditary characteristics. A **genome** is a complete set of chromosomes in an organism. The human genome contains 23 chromosomes. A **haploid cell** contains one genome; that is, it contains one set of chromosomes. So a human haploid cell contains 23 chromosomes. A **diploid cell** contains two genomes; that is, it contains two sets of chromosomes. Each chromosome in one set is matched with a chromosome in the other set. This pair of chromosomes is called a **homologous pair**. Each chromosome in the pair is called a **homolog**. So a human diploid cell contains $2 \times 23 = 46$ chromosomes. One homolog comes from each parent.

A **somatic cell** is one of the cells in the body of the organism. A **haploid organism** is an organism whose somatic cells are haploid. A **diploid organism** is an organism whose somatic cells are diploid. Humans are diploid organisms.

A **gamete** is a mature sexual reproductive cell that unites with another gamete to become a **zygote**, which eventually grows into a new organism. A gamete is always haploid. The gamete produced by a male is called a **sperm**, whereas the gamete that is produced by the female is called an **egg**. **Germ cells** are precursors of gametes. They are diploid.

In diploid organisms, each adult produces a gamete, the two gametes combine to form a zygote, and the zygote grows to become a new adult. This process is called **sexual reproduction**. Unicellular haploid organisms commonly reproduce asexually by a process called **binary fission**. The organism simply splits into two new organisms. So, each new organism has the exact same genetic content as the original organism. Some unicellular haploid organisms reproduce sexually by a process called **fusion**. Two adult cells first combine to form what is called a **transient diploid meiocyte**. The transient diploid meiocyte contains a homologous pair of chromosomes, one from each parent. A child can obtain a given homolog from each parent. So the children are not genetic copies of the parents. For example, if the genome size is 3, there are $2^3 = 8$ different chromosome combinations that a child could have.

Chromosomes consist of the compound **deoxyribonucleic acid (DNA)**. DNA is composed of four basic molecules called **nucleotides**. Each nucleotide contains a pentose sugar (deoxyribose), a phosphate group, and a purine or pyrimidine base. The **purines**, adenine (A) and guanine (G), are similar in structure, as are the **pyrimidines**, cytosine (C) and thymine (T). DNA is a macromolecule composed of two complementary strands, each strand consisting of a sequence of nucleotides. The strands are joined together by hydrogen bonds between pairs of nucleotides. Adenine always pairs with thymine, and guanine always pairs with cytosine. Each such pair is called a **canonical base pair**

A A G T C C G

··· | | | | | | | ···

T T C A G G C

Figure 9.1 A section of DNA.

(bp), and A, G, C, and T are called **bases**.

A section of DNA is depicted in Figure 9.1. You may recall from your biology course that the strands twist around each other to form a right-handed double helix. However, for our computational purposes, we need only consider them as character strings as shown in Figure 9.1.

A **gene** is a section of a chromosome, often consisting of thousands of base pairs, but the size of genes varies a great deal. Genes are responsible for both the structure and the processes of the organism. The **genotype** of an organism is its genetic makeup, while the **phenotype** of an organism is its appearance resulting from the interaction of the genotype and the environment.

An **allele** is any of several forms of a gene, usually arising through mutation. Alleles are responsible for hereditary variation.

Example 9.1 The bey2 gene on chromosome 15 is responsible for eye color in humans. There is one allele for blue eyes, which we call BLUE, and one for brown eyes, which we call BROWN. As is the case for all genes, an individual gets one allele from each parent. The BLUE allele is **recessive**. This means that if an individual receives one BLUE allele and one BROWN allele, that individual will have brown eyes. The only way the individual could have blue eyes would be for the individual to have two BLUE alleles. We also say that the brown allele is **dominant**. ∎

Because a human gamete has 23 chromosomes and each of these chromosomes can come from either genome, there are $2^{23} = 8{,}388{,}608$ different genetic combinations a parent could pass on to his or her offspring. Actually, there are many more than this, for the following reason. During **meiosis** (the cell division that produces gametes), each chromosome duplicates itself and aligns with its homolog. The duplicates are called **chromatids**. Often there is an exchange of corresponding segments of genetic material between the homologous chromatids facing each other. This exchange is called **crossing-over** and is illustrated in Figure 9.2.

Sometimes during cell division, errors occur during the DNA replication process. These errors are called **mutations**. Mutations can occur in either somatic cells or germ cells. It is believed that mutations in germ cells are the source of all variation in evolution. On the other hand, mutations in a somatic cell could affect the organism (e.g., cause cancer) but would have no effect on the offspring.

In a **substitution mutation**, one nucleotide is simply replaced by another.

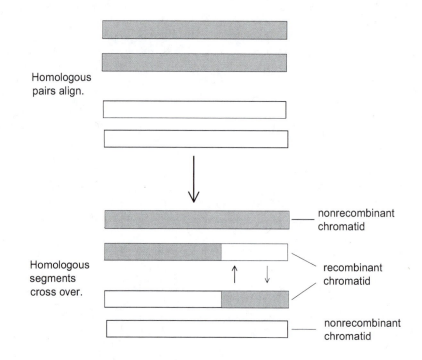

Figure 9.2 An illustration of crossing-over.

An **insertion mutation** occurs when a section of DNA is added to a chromosome; a **deletion mutation** occurs when a section of DNA is removed from a chromosome.

Evolution is the process of change in the genetic makeup of populations. It is believed that the changes in genetic makeup are due to mutations. As noted earlier, **natural selection** is the process by which organisms that have traits that better enable them to adapt to environmental pressures such as predators, changes in climate, or competition for food or mates will tend to survive and reproduce in greater numbers than other similar organisms, thereby increasing the existence of those favorable traits in future generations. So, natural selection can result in an increase in the relative frequencies of alleles that impart to the individual these favorable traits. The process of the change in allele relative frequencies due only to chance is called **genetic drift**. There is some disagreement in the scientific community as to whether natural selection or genetic drift is more responsible for evolutionary change [Li, 1997].

9.2   Genetic Algorithms

First we describe the basic genetic algorithm; then we provide two applications.

9.2.1   Algorithm

Genetic algorithms use fusion in haploid organisms as a model. Candidate solutions to a problem are represented by haploid **individuals** in a population. Each individual has one chromosome. The alphabet for the chromosome is not A, G, C, and T as in actual organisms, but rather consists of characters that represent solutions. In each generation, a certain number of fit individuals are allowed to reproduce. Individuals representing better solutions are more fit. The chromosomes from two fit individuals then line up and exchange genetic material (substrings of the problem solution) by **crossing-over**. Furthermore, **mutations** possibly occur. This results in the next generation of individuals. The process is repeated until some terminal condition is met.

Algorithm 9.1 Genetic_Algorithm

> **Procedure** *Generate_Populations*;
> $t = 0$;
> initialize population P_0;
> **repeat**
> > evaluate fitness of each individual in population P_t;
> > Select individuals for reproduction based on fitness;
> > Perform crossover and mutation on the selected individuals;
> > $t = t + 1$;
> **until** terminal condition is met;

When selecting individuals based on fitness, we do not necessarily simply choose the most fit individuals. Rather, we may employ both exploitation and exploration. In general, when evaluating candidate regions of a search space to investigate, by **exploitation** we mean to exploit knowledge already obtained by concentrating on regions that look good, while by **exploration** we mean looking for new regions without regard for how good they currently appear. In the case of choosing individuals, we could explore by choosing a random individual with probability ε and exploit by choosing a fit individual with probability $1 - \varepsilon$.

9.2.2   Illustrative Example

Suppose our goal is to find the value of x that maximizes

$$f(x) = \sin\left(\frac{x\pi}{256}\right) \qquad \text{in the interval } 0 \le x \le 255,$$

where x is restricted to being an integer. Of course the sine function has its maximum value of 1 at $\pi/2$, which means $x = 128$ maximizes the function. So there is no practical reason to develop an algorithm to solve this problem. However, we develop a genetic algorithm for solving it to illustrate the various aspects of such algorithms. The following steps are used to develop the algorithm.

Table 9.1 Initial Population of Individuals along with Their Fitnesses

Individual	x	$f(x)$	normed $f(x)$	cumulative normed $f(x)$
1 0 1 1 1 1 0 1	189	.733	.144	.144
1 1 0 1 1 0 0 0	216	.471	.093	.237
0 1 1 0 0 0 1 1	99	.937	.184	.421
1 1 1 0 1 1 0 0	236	.243	.048	.469
1 0 1 0 1 1 1 0	174	.845	.166	.635
0 0 1 0 0 0 1 1	74	.788	.155	.790
0 0 1 0 0 0 1 1	35	.416	.082	.872
0 0 1 1 0 1 0 1	53	.650	.128	1.000

1. Decide on an alphabet to represent solutions to the problem. Because candidate solutions are simply integers in the range 0 to 255, we can represent each individual (candidate solution) using 8 bits. For example, the integer 189 is represented as

$$1\ 0\ 1\ 1\ 1\ 1\ 0\ 1.$$

2. Decide on how many individuals make up a population. In general, there can be thousands of individuals. In this simple example, we will use 8 individuals.

3. Decide how to initialize the population. Often this is done at random. We will generate 8 numbers at random from the range 0 to 255. Possible initial values appear in Table 9.1.

4. Decide on how to evaluate fitness. Because our goal is to maximize $f(x) = \sin(x\pi/256)$, the fitness of individual x is simply the value of this function.

5. Decide on which individuals to select for reproduction. We will combine exploration with exploitation as follows. The fitnesses are normalized by dividing each fitness by the sum of all the fitnesses, which is 5.083, to yield normalized fitnesses. In this way, the normalized fitnesses add to 1. These normalized fitnesses are then used to determine cumulative fitness values, which provide a wedge on a roulette wheel for each individual based on its fitness. This is shown in Table 9.1. For example, the second individual has a normalized fitness of .093 and that individual is assigned the wedge corresponding to the interval $(.144, .237]$, which has width .093. We then generate a random number from the interval $(0, 1]$. That number will fall in the range assigned to precisely one individual, and this is the individual chosen. This process is performed 8 times.

   Suppose the individuals chosen for reproduction are the ones appearing in Table 9.2. Note that an individual can appear more than once, and the likelihood of how often it appears depends on its fitness.

6. Determine how to perform crossovers and mutations. First, we randomly pair individuals, resulting in 4 pairs. For each pair, we randomly select

Table 9.2 Individuals Chosen for Reproduction

Individual
0 1 1 0 0 0 1 1
0 0 1 1 0 1 0 1
1 1 0 1 1 0 0 0
1 0 1 0 1 1 1 0
0 1 0 0 1 0 1 0
1 0 1 0 1 1 1 0
0 1 1 0 0 0 1 1
1 0 1 1 1 1 0 1

Table 9.3 Parents and Children Resulting from Crossover

Parents	Children	x	$f(x)$
0 1 1¹ |0 0 0|²1 1	0 1 1¹ |1 0 1|²1 1	119	.994
0 0 1 |1 0 1| 0 1	0 0 1 |0 0 0| 0 1	33	.394
1¹ |1 0 1 1|²0 0 0	1¹ |0 1 0 1|²0 0 0	168	.882
1 |0 1 0 1| 1 1 0	1 |1 0 1 1| 1 1 0	222	.405
0 1 |²0 0 1 0 1 1¹|0	1 0 |²0 0 1 0 1 1¹|0	138	.992
1 0 |1 0 1 1 1|0	0 1 |1 0 1 1 1|0	110	.976
0 1 1 0 0¹|0 1 1|²	0 1 1 0 0¹|1 0 1|²	101	.946
1 0 1 1 1 |1 0 1|	1 0 1 1 1 |0 1 1|	187	.749

two points along the individuals. Genetic material between the crossover points is exchanged. Table 9.3 shows possible results. Note that if the second point appears before the first point in the individual, crossover is performed by wrapping around. The third pair of individuals in Table 9.3 illustrates this case. Based on the values in Tables 9.1 and 9.3, the average fitness before crossover is .635, while that after crossover is .792. Furthermore, after crossover, two individuals have fitnesses above .99.

Next we determine how to perform mutations. For each bit in each individual, we decide at random whether to flip the bit (change 0 to 1 or 1 to 0). Mutation probabilities are commonly in the range .01 to .001.

7. Decide when to terminate. We could terminate when some maximum number of generations is attained, or when some allotted amount of time has expired, or when the fitness of the most fit individual reaches a certain level, or when one of these conditions is met. For example, in this example, we could terminate when either 10,000 generations are produced or when

the fitness exceeds .999.

Note that Steps 2, 3, 5, and 7 above are **generic** in the sense that we can apply the strategies mentioned to most problems.

9.2.3   Traveling Salesperson Problem

The Traveling Salesperson Problem is a well-known NP-hard problem. **NP-hard problems** are a class of problems for which no one has ever developed a polynomial-time algorithm, but no one has ever shown that such an algorithm is not possible.

Suppose a salesperson is planning a sales trip to n cities. Each city is connected to some of the other cities by a road. To minimize travel time, we want to find a shortest route (called a **tour**) that starts at the salesperson's home city, visits each of the cities once, and ends up at the home city. The problem of determining a shortest tour is the **Traveling Salesperson Problem (TSP)**. Note that the starting city is irrelevant to the shortest tour.

The TSP problem is represented by a **weighted directed graph** in which the **vertices** represent the cities and the weights on the **edges** represent road lengths. In general, the graph in an instance of TSP need not be **complete**, which is a graph in which there is an edge from every vertex to every other vertex. Furthermore, if the edges $v_i \rightarrow v_j$ and $v_j \rightarrow v_i$ are both in the graph, their weights need not be the same. Besides application to transportation scheduling, TSP has been applied to problems such as scheduling of a machine to drill holes in a circuit board and DNA sequencing.

Next we show three genetic algorithms for TSP.

9.2.3.1   Order Crossover

Order crossover is presented first. Only the steps that are different from those that appear Section 9.2.2 are shown.

1. Decide on an alphabet to represent solutions to the problem. A straightforward representation of a solution to TSP is to label the vertices 1 through n and list the vertices in the order visited. For example, if there are 9 vertices, [2 1 3 9 5 4 8 7 6] represents that we visit vertex v_1 after v_2, v_3 after v_2,..., and v_2 after v_6. Again, the starting vertex is irrelevant.

4. The fitness is the length of the tour, where tours with shorter lengths are more fit.

6. Determine how to perform crossovers and mutations. As before, individuals are randomly paired and, for each pair, two points are randomly selected along the individuals. Call the segment between those points the **pick**. We must make sure the results of a crossover are legitimate tours, which means each city must be listed only once. So, we cannot simply exchange picks. In **order crossover**, the pick in the child has the same value as the pick in the parent, whereas the non-pick area is filled in from

Table 9.4 An Example of Order Crossover

Parents	Other Parent Template	Children
p_1: 2 1 3^1|9 5 4|^{2}8 7 6	6 8 7 1 3 2 from p_2	c_1: 6 8 7^1|9 5 4|^{2}1 3 2
p_2: 5 3 2 |6 8 9| 7 1 4	5 4 7 2 1 3 from p_1	c_2: 5 4 7 |6 8 9| 2 1 3

values in the other parent, omitting values that are not already present, in the order in which those values appear in the other parent, starting from the other parent's pick. These values are called its **template**. Table 9.4 illustrates this. Notice that child c_1 has value [9 5 4]" for the pick just as parent p_1. The pick for parent p_2 is [6 8 9]. The template from this parent is constructed by starting at site 6 and in sequence listing all cities that are not in [9 5 4]. This is done with wrap-around. So the template is [6 8 7 1 3 2]. These values are copied in order into the non-pick area of child c_2.

If the graph is not complete, we would need to check whether the new child represents an actual tour, and if it does not reject the crossover.

As far as mutations, we cannot just mutate a site by changing a given vertex to another vertex because a vertex would then appear twice. We could mutate by interchanging two vertices or reversing the order of a subset of vertices. However, if the graph is not complete, we must make certain that the result represents an actual tour.

9.2.3.2 Nearest Neighbor Crossover

The **Nearest Neighbor Algorithm** (**NNA**) for TSP is an example of a greedy algorithm. A greedy algorithm arrives at a solution by making a sequence of choices, each of which simply looks best at the moment. NNA starts with an arbitrary vertex to initiate a tour, and then repeatedly adds the closest unvisited vertex to the partial tour until a tour is completed. NNA assumes the graph is complete; otherwise it may not result in a tour. The algorithm follows.

Algorithm 9.2 Nearest_Neighbor

> **Procedure** *Generate_Tour*(**var** *tour*);
> *tour* = $[v_i]$ where v_i is chosen at random;
> **repeat**
>> add unvisited vertex to *tour*
>> that is closest to current last vertex in *tour*;
>
> **until** all vertices are in *tour*;

Figure 9.3 (a) shows an instance of TSP where the undirected edges represent that there is a directed edge with the given weight in both directions, Figure 9.3 (b) shows the shortest tour, Figure 9.3 (c) shows the tour obtained

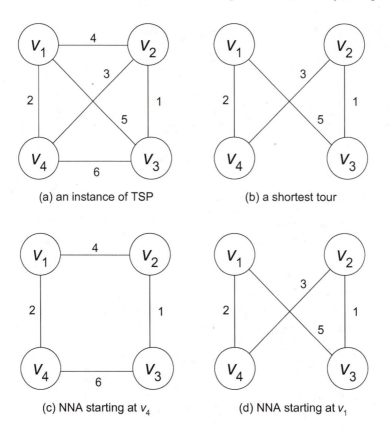

Figure 9.3 An instance of TSP illustrating the nearest neighbor algorithm.

when we apply NNA starting at v_4, and Figure 9.3 (d) shows the tour obtained when we apply NNA starting at v_1. Note that this latter tour is the optimal one.

Next we present **Nearest Neighbor Crossover (NNX)**, which was developed in [Süral et al., 2010]. The steps shown are the ones used by those researchers when evaluating the algorithm.

1. Decide on an alphabet to represent solutions to the problem. The representation is the same as that for order crossover which appears at the beginning of Section 9.2.3.1

2. Decide on how many individuals make up a population. Population sizes of 50 and 100 were used.

3. One technique tried was to initialize the entire initial population at random. A second technique was to initialize half of the population at random and the other half using a hybrid technique involving NNX and GEA (discussed next).

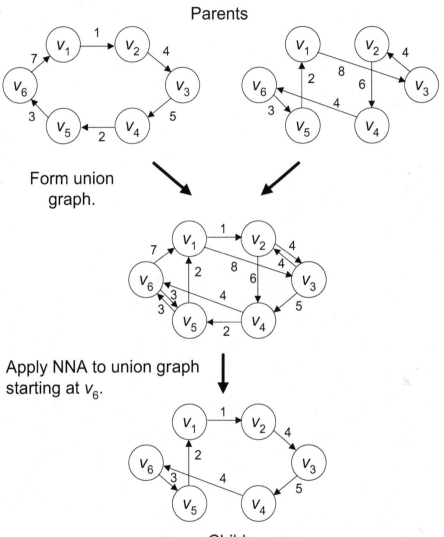

Figure 9.4 The union graph is formed and then the NNA is applied to that graph starting a vertex v_6.

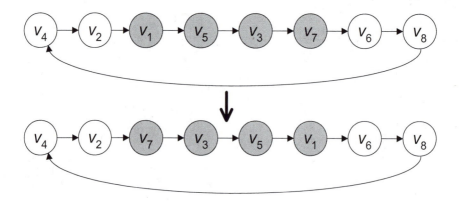

Figure 9.5 A mutation in which the subpath connecting vertices v_1 and v_7 is reversed.

4. Decide on how to evaluate fitness. The fitness is the same as that for order crossover.

5. Decide on which individuals to select for reproduction. The top 50% of individuals ordered according to fitness are allowed to reproduce. Four copies of each of these individuals are put in a pool. Then pairs of parents are randomly selected without replacement from the pool.

6. Determine how to perform crossovers and mutations. In NNX, two parents produce only one child. So the process is not really crossover; nevertheless, we call it that. The parents first combine to form a union graph, which is a graph containing the edges in both parents. This process is illustrated in Figure 9.4. Then NNA is applied to the union graph. This is also shown in Figure 9.4. In that figure we applied NNA starting with vertex v_6, and we obtained a child that is more fit than either parent. It is left as an exercise to show that if we start at v_1, this does not happen. If we start at v_3, we reach a dead-end at v_1 and do not obtain a tour. If the chosen vertex does not result in a tour, we can try other vertices until one does. If no starting vertex results in a tour, we can make other edges in the complete graph eligible for our tour.

Note that because four copies of each parent are used and each pair of parents produce one offspring, the child generation is twice as large as the number of parents allowed to reproduce. However, because only half of the parents are allowed to do so, the size of the population stays the same in each generation.

Mutations are performed as follows. Two vertices are selected at random, and the subpath connecting the two vertices is reversed. This is illustrated in Figure 9.5, where the vertices selected are v_1 and v_7. There are two versions of mutation. In version **M1**, the mutation is applied only to the best offspring in each generation. In version **M2**, it is applied to all offspring.

As a variation, a stochastic version of NNX would choose the next edge incident to the current vertex probabilistically. The chance of being chosen would be inversely proportional to the length of the edge. It is possible to increase population diversity by doing this and thereby increase the portion of the search space investigated. However, Süral et al. [2010] found that this stochastic technique performed significantly worse than the deterministic version, and did not include this in their final testing, which we discuss shortly.

6. Decide when to terminate. The algorithm terminates when the average fitness in two successive generations is the same or when 500 generations are produced.

NNA and NNX are very similar to Dikstra's algorithm for the Shortest Paths Problem (see, e.g., [Neapolitan and Naimipour, 2010]), and like that algorithm take $\theta(n^2)$ time, where n is the number of vertices.

9.2.3.3 Greedy Edge Crossover

In the **Greedy Edge Algorithm** (**GEA**), we first sort the edges in nondecreasing sequence. We then greedily add edges to the tour, starting with the first edge, while making certain that no vertex has more than two edges touching it and that no cycle smaller than n is created. GEA assumes the graph is complete; otherwise it may not result in a tour. The algorithm follows.

Algorithm 9.3 Greedy_Edge

> **Procedure** *Generate_Tour*(**var** *tour*);
> Sort the edges in nondecreasing order;
> $tour = \varnothing$;   // The tour is represented by a set of edges.
> **repeat**
>   **if** adding next edge to *tour* does not result in
>   a vertex having two edges touching it
>   **and** does not create a cycle smaller than n
>   add the edge to *tour*;
> **until** there are $n - 1$ edges in *tour*;

Figure 9.6 illustrates GEA using the same instance of GEA as in Figure 9.3. The Greedy edge crossover algorithm (GEX) (also in [Süral et al., 2010]) has all the same steps as NNX except the 6th step which we show next.

6. Determine how to perform crossovers and mutations. As in NNX, in GEX the parents first combine to form a union graph. Then GEA is applied to the edges in this union graph. If this process does not result in a tour, the remaining edges in a tour are obtained by applying GEA to the complete graph. This process, however, will result in little exploration

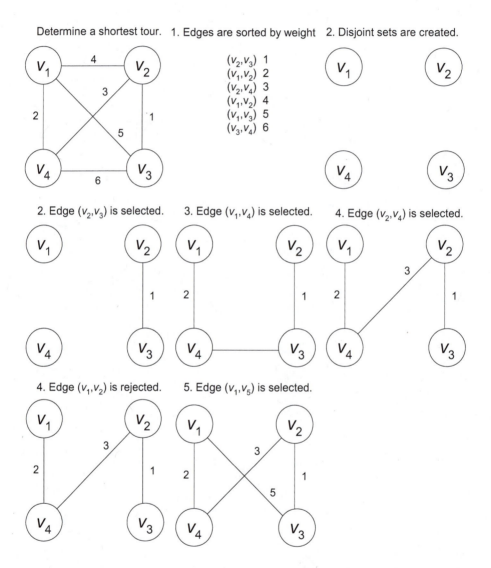

Figure 9.6 An instance of TSP illustrating the Greedy Edge Algorithm.

and therefore high edge preservation and possible early convergence to a low-quality solution. To increase exploration, the first half of the new tour can be taken from the union graph and the second half from the complete graph. In initial investigations, this version performed much better than the one that took as many edges as possible from the union graph. This is the version that was used in the evaluation discussed next.

NNA and NNX are very similar to Kruskal's algorithm for the Minimum Spanning Tree Problem (see, e.g., [Neapolitan and Naimipour, 2010]), and like that algorithm take $\theta(n^2 \log n)$ and $\theta(m \log m)$ time, where n is the number of vertices and m is the number of edges.

9.2.3.4   Evaluation

As is the case for many heuristic algorithms, genetic algorithms do not have provably correct properties. Therefore, we evaluate them by investigating their performance on a number of instances of the problem. Süral et al. [2010] did this as follows for NNX and GEX.

First, they obtained 10 instances of TSP from the TSPLIB, which represent distances between real cities and in which the distance is symmetric (the same in both directions). The largest instance had n (the number of cities) $= 226$. They investigated versions of NNX and GEX using no mutations, mutations M1 (discussed above), and mutations M2 (discussed above). Furthermore, they tried initialing the first population at random (R) and initializing using a hybrid technique (H) based on nearest neighbor and greedy edge heuristics. For each combination of mutation type and initialization type, they ran each of the algorithms 30 times on each of the 10 instances, making a total of 300 runs. The algorithm was coded in ANSIC and ran on a Pentium IV 1600 MHz machine with 256 MB RAM running RedHat Linux 8.0.

Table 9.5 shows the averages over all 300 runs. The headings in that table denote the following:

- Algorithm: The algorithm used.

- Mutation: The type of mutation used. "No M" denotes no mutations.

- Int. Pop.: Whether the population was initialized at random (R) or using hybrid initialization (H).

- Dev: Percent deviation of the final best solution from the optimal solution.

- #Gen: Number of generations until convergence.

- Time: Time in seconds until convergence.

We see from Table 9.5 that NNX performed much better than GEX, that mutation M2 performed the best of the mutations, and that hybrid initialization did not result in much better performance than random initialization. The researchers then investigated whether using NNX with various percentage usage

Table 9.5 Average Results over 30 Runs on Each of 10 Small Problem Instances where Population Size is 50

Algorithm	Mutation	Init. Pop.	Dev	#Gen	Time
	No M	R	3.10	45.39	0.38
		H	4.82	33.52	2.95
NNX	M1	R	1.67	40.21	0.62
		H	1.57	36.09	3.55
	M2	R	0.55	53.37	5.52
		H	0.55	43.53	8.11
	No M	R	12.54	17.35	48.23
		H	7.19	16.37	54.27
GEX	M1	R	4.36	60.44	208.70
		H	3.67	48.44	178.65
	M2	R	3.30	26.30	82.79
		H	3.01	25.83	90.58
	No M	R	8.15	42.50	73.25
		H	5.53	38.47	75.67
50% NNX	M1	R	1.92	66.04	113.81
50 % GEX		H	1.68	61.21	112.77
	M2	R	1.76	19.25	26.40
		H	1.61	20.68	34.19
	No M	R	7.23	41.16	13.39
		H	5.19	34.93	14.95
90% NNX	M1	R	1.84	55.60	19.14
10% GEX		H	1.67	46.93	20.16
	M2	R	0.51	37.13	19.26
		H	0.48	37.24	21.95
	no M	R	6,69	41.23	6.74
		H	5.06	33.04	8.93
95% NNX	M1	R	1.77	52.62	10.03
5% GEX		H	1.41	44.33	11.30
	M2	R	0.49	37.15	11.58
		H	0.44	36.19	14.88

Table 9.6 Average Results over 30 Replications of 10 Small Problem Instances where Population Size is 100 and the Initial Population is Generated at Random

Algorithm	Mutation	Dev	Time
	No M	5.40	18.4
NNX	M1	1.44	26.4
	M2	0.35	26.2

Table 9.7 Average Results over 10 Replications of 15 Large Problem Instances where Population Size is100 and Initial Population is Generated at Random

Algorithm	Mutation	Dev	Time
	No M	7.61	25.3
NNX	M1	4.94	65.0
	M2	4.70	1063.0

of GEX might improve performance. Table 9.5 also shows these results. When, for example, it says 50% NNX and 50% GEX, it means that 50% of the time the next population was generated using NNX and the other 50% of the time it was generated using GEX. Slight improvement over pure NNX was observed in the case of mutation M2 for the higher percentages of NNX usage.

Based on these results, the researchers concluded that using mixtures of the two algorithms was not worth the increased computational time. So further experiments were performed using only NNX by itself.

Using only NNX with random initialization but with a population size of 100, they obtained the results in Table 9.6. Note that for mutation M2, the average percent deviation is 0.35 and the average time is 26.2. Looking again at Table 9.5 we see that using this same combination with a population size of 50, the average percent deviation is 0.55 and the average time is 5.52. This increase in accuracy should be worth the increased time.

Next the researchers investigated larger instances from TSPLIB in which $318 \leq n \leq 1748$. Having concluded that hybrid initialization is also not worth additional time, they ran NNX 10 times on each of these instances with random initialization and a population size of 100. Table 9.7 shows the results. Curiously, on the large problem instances, mutation M2 did not do much better than mutation M2 but required substantially more computation time. Looking again at Table 9.6 we see that in the case of small instances M2 performed much better than M1 with little increased computational cost.

Simply testing a heuristic algorithm on a number of instances does not show if it as an advancement. We need to see how it fares relative to previously existing heuristic algorithms. Süral et al. [2010] compared NNX to the heuristic TSP algorithms Meta-RaPS [DePuy et al., 2005] and ESOM [Leung et al., 2004] using 10 benchmark TSP instances. Table 9.8 shows the results. Either NNX-M1 (mutation M1) or NNX-M2 (mutation M2) performed the best for every problem instance.

Table 9.8 A Comparison of NNX to Two Other Heurisic Algorithms for TSP for 10 Problem Instances

Problem	NNX-M1		NNX-M2		Meta-RaPS		ESOM3	
	Dev	Time[1]	Dev	Time[1]	Dev	Time[2]	Dev	Time[3]
ei101	0.93	8.7	0.82	14.3	NA	NA	3.43	NA
bier127	0.62	15.3	0.28	12.0	0.90	48	1.70	NA
pr136	2.87	18.4	0.37	35.2	0.39	73	4.31	NA
kroa200	1.78	87.3	0.32	98.6	1.07	190	2.91	NA
pr226	0.79	93.0	0.01	21.6	0.23	357	NA	NA
lin318	1.87	8.0	2.01	105	NA	NA	2.89	NA
pr439	3.44	10.0	1.48	240	3.30	2265	NA	NA
pcb442	4.75	15.0	3.18	270	NA	NA	7.43	NA
pcb1173	3.00	97.0	8.01	1230	NA	NA	9.87	200
vm1748	7.05	203	7.09	4215	NA	NA	7.27	475

[1] Pentium 4.16 GHz
[2] AMD Athlon 900 MHz
[3] SUN Ultra 5/270

9.3 Genetic Programming

Whereas in genetic algorithms the "chromosome" or "individual" represents a solution to a problem, in **genetic programing** the individual represents a program that solves a problem. The fitness function for the individual in some way measures how well the program solves the problem. We start with an initial population of programs, allow the more fit programs to reproduce by crossover, perform mutations on the population of children, and then repeat this process until some terminal condition is met. The high-level algorithm for this procedure is exactly the same as the one for genetic algorithms. However, we show it next for completeness.

Algorithm 9.4 Genetic_Programming

> **Procedure** *Generate_Populations*;
> $t = 0$;
> initialize population P_0;
> **repeat**
> >   evaluate fitness of each individual in population P_t;
> >   Select individuals for reproduction based on fitness;
> >   Perform crossover and mutation on the selected individuals;
> > $t = t + 1$;
> **until** terminal condition is met;

The individuals (programs) in a genetic program are represented by trees in which in each node is either a **terminal symbol** or a **function symbol**. If a node is a function symbol, it arguments are its children. As an example,

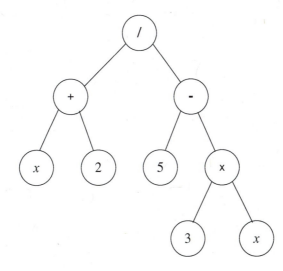

Figure 9.7 A tree representing Expression 9.1.

suppose have the following mathematical expression (program):

$$\frac{x+2}{5-3 \times x}. \tag{9.1}$$

Its tree structure representation appears in Figure 9.7.

9.3.1 Illustrative Example

A simple way to illustrate genetic programming is to show an application that learns a function $y = f(x)$ from pairs of points (x_i, y_i) known to satisfy the function. For example, suppose we have the pairs of points in Table 9.9.

These points were actually generated from the function

$$y = x^2/2.$$

However, we are assuming that we do not know this, and are trying to discover the function. Steps for developing a genetic program for this discovery problem are as follows:

1. Decide on the terminal set T. Let the terminal set include the symbol x and the integers between -5 and 5.

2. Decide on the function set F. Let the function set be the symbols $+$, $-$, $\times$, and $/$. Note that we could include other functions such as sin, cos, etc. if desired.

3. Decide on how many individuals make up a population. Our population size will be 600.

Table 9.9 We Want to Learn a Function that Describes the Relationship between x and y Based on These 10 Points.

x	y
0	0
.1	.005
.2	.020
.3	.045
.4	.080
.5	.125
.6	.180
.7	.245
.8	.320
.9	.405

4. Decide how to initialize the population. Each initial individual is created by a process called **growing the tree**. First, a symbol is randomly generated from $T \cup F$. If it is a terminal symbol, we stop and our tree consists of a single node containing this symbol. If it is a function symbol, we randomly generate children for the symbol. We continue down the tree, randomly generating symbols and stopping at terminal symbols. For example, the tree in Figure 9.7 would be obtained by the following random generation of symbols: First the symbol / is generated, followed by the values of + and − for its children. The children generated for + are x and 2. We stop at each of these children. The children generated for − are 5 and ×. We stop at the 5, and finally generate the children 3 and x for the ×.

5. Decide on a fitness function. The fitness function will be the square error. That is, the fitness of function $f(x)$ is as follows:

$$\sum_{i=1}^{10} (f(x_i) - y_i)^2,$$

where each (x_i, y_i) is a point in Table 9.9. Functions with smaller errors are more fit.

6. Decide on which individuals to select for reproduction. A 4 individual tournament selection process is used. In the **tournament selection process**, n individuals are randomly selected from the population. In this case, $n = 4$. We say that these n individuals enter a tournament in which the $n/2$ most fit of them win and the $n/2$ least fit lose. The $n/2$ winners are allowed to reproduce to produce $n/2$ children. These children replace the $n/2$ losers in the population for the next generation. In this case, the 2 winners reproduce twice to produce 2 children who replace the 2 losers.

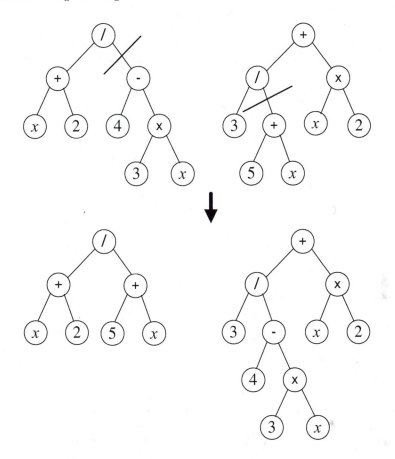

Figure 9.8 Crossover by exchanging subtrees.

A small tournament size results in low selection process, whereas a high tournament size results in high pressure.

7. Decide on how to perform crossovers and mutations. Crossover between two individuals will be performed by exchanging randomly selected subtrees. Such a crossover is illustrated in Figure 9.8. Mutations are performed by randomly selecting a node and replacing the subtree at that node by a growing a new subtree. Mutations are randomly performed on 5% of the offspring.

8. Decide when to terminate. Terminate when the square error of the most fit individual is 0 or when 100 generations have been produced.

Banzhaf et al. [1998] applied the technique just presented to the data in Table 9.9. The following shows the most fit individual in the first 4 generations:

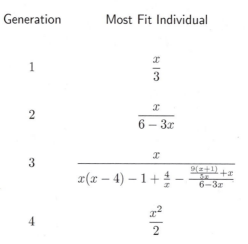

Generation	Most Fit Individual
1	$\dfrac{x}{3}$
2	$\dfrac{x}{6-3x}$
3	$\dfrac{x}{x(x-4)-1+\frac{4}{x}-\frac{\frac{9(x+1)}{5x}+x}{6-3x}}$
4	$\dfrac{x^2}{2}$

The most fit individual had expanded to a very large tree by generation 3 but shrunk back down to the correct solution (the function generating the data) by generation 4.

9.3.2   Artificial Ant

Consider the problem of developing a robotic ant that navigates along a trail of food. Figure 9.9 shows such a trail called the "Sante Fe trail." Each black square represents one pellet of food; there are 89 such squares. The ant starts at the square labeled "start" facing right, and its goal is to arrive at the square labeled "89" after visiting all 89 black squares (thereby eating all the food on the trail) in as few time steps as possible. Notice that there are a number of gaps along the trail. The problem with a time limit represents a challenging **planning problem**.

The ant has one sensor as follows:

food_ahead: Has value True of there is food in the square the ant is facing; otherwise has value False.

There are three different actions the ant can execute in each time slot:

right: The ant turns right by 90° (without moving).

left: The ant turns left by 90° (without moving).

move: The ant moves forward into the square it is facing. If the square contains food, the ant eats the food, thereby eliminating the food from the square and erasing it from the trail.

Koza [1992] developed the following genetic programming algorithm for this problem.

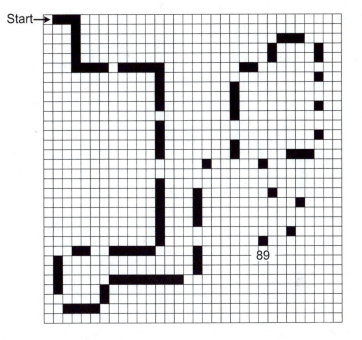

Figure 9.9 The Santa Fe trail. Each black square reprsents a pellet of food.

1. Decide on the terminal set T. The terminal set contains the actions the ant can take. That is,

$$T = \{right, left, move\}.$$

2. Decide on the function set F. The function set is as follows:

   (a) $if\_food\_ahead(instruction1, instruction2)$;
   (b) $do2(instruction1, instruction2)$;
   (c) $d03(instruction1, instruction2, instruction3)$;

   The first function executes $instruction1$ if $food\_ahead$ is true; otherwise it executes $instruction2$. The second function unconditionally executes $instruction1$ and $instruction2$. The third function unconditionally executes $instruction1$, $instruction2$, and $instruction3$. For example,

   $$do2(right, move)$$

   causes the ant to turn right and then move ahead.

3. Decide on how many individuals make up a population. The population size is 500.

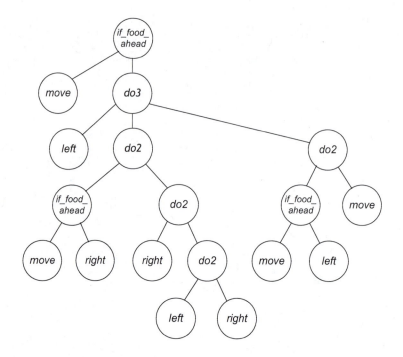

Figure 9.10 The individual in generation 22 with a fitness equal to 89.

4. Decide how to initialize the population. Each initial individual is created by *growing the tree* (See Section 9.3.1).

5. Decide on a fitness function. It is assumed that each action (right,left,move) takes one time step, and each individual is allowed 400 time steps. Each individual starts in the upper left-hand square facing east. Fitness is defined to be the number of food pellets consumed in the allotted time. So the maximum fitness is 89.

6. Decide on which individuals to select for reproduction.

7. Decide on how to perform crossovers and mutations. Crossover between two individuals will be performed by exchanging randomly selected subtrees. Such a crossover is illustrated in Figure 9.8. Mutations are performed by randomly selecting a node and replacing the subtree at that node by growing a new subtree. Mutations are randomly performed on 5% of the offspring.

8. Decide when to terminate. Terminate when one individual has a fitness of 89 or some maximum amount of iterations is reached.

In each iteration, each individual in the population (program) is run repeatedly until 400 time steps are performed. The individual's fitness is then evaluated. In one particular run, Koza [1992] obtained an individual with a fitness equal to 89 in the 22nd generation. That individual appears in Figure 9.10. The average fitness of individuals in generation 0 was 3.5, while the most fit individual in generation 0 had a fitness of 32.

9.3.3 Application to Financial Trading

An important decision facing everyone who invests in the stock and other financial markets is whether to buy, sell, or hold on a given day. There have been many efforts to develop automated systems that make this decision for us. Farnsworth et al. [2004] developed such a system using genetic programming. Their system makes an investment decision based on values of market indicators on a given day. We discuss that system next.

9.3.3.1 Developing the Trading System

First we show the eight steps using to create the system.

1. Decide on the terminal set T. The terminal symbols are the market indicators. The researchers tried and tested various indicators before deciding on the ones to include in the final system. We only present the final ones. They are as follows:

    (a) The S&P500 is a market index based on 500 leading companies in leading industries of the U.S. economy. For a given day, the indicator based on the S&P500 is as follows:

    $$\frac{S\&P500_{today} - S\&P500_{avg}}{S\&P500_{\sigma}},$$

    where $S\&P500_{today}$ is the value of the S&P500 on the current day, $S\&P500_{avg}$ is the average value over the past 200 days, and $S\&P500_{\sigma}$ is the standard deviation over the past 200 days.

    We denote this indicator simply as $SP500$.

    (b) The k-**day Exponential Moving Average** (EMA) for a security is a weighted average of the security over the past k days. The **Moving Average Convergence/Divergence** (**MACD**) of a security x is as follows:

    $$MACD(x) = 12\text{-day } EMA(x) - 26\text{-day } EMA(x).$$

    The MACD is considered a momentum indicator. When it is positive, traders say upside momentum is increasing; when it is negative, they say downside momentum is increasing.

    A second indicator used in this system is $MACD(S\&P500)$, which we denote simply as $MACD$.

    (c) The indicator $MACD9$ is the 9-day EMA of the MACD of the S&P500.

(d) Let $Diff$ be the difference of the number of advancing and declining securities. That **McClennan Oscillator** (**MCCL**) is as follows:

$$MCCL = 19\text{-day } EMA(Diff) - 39\text{-day } EMA(Diff).$$

Traders consider the market overbought when $MCCL > 100$ and oversold when $MCCL < -100$.

We denote this indicator simply as $MCCL$.

(e) The indicators $SP500lag$, $MACDlag$, $MACD9lag$, and $MCCLlag$ are the values of those indicators on the previous day.

(f) Other terminal symbols include real constants in the interval $[-1, 1]$.

All indicator values were normalized to the interval $[-1, 1]$.

2. Decide on the function set F. Function symbols include $+$, $-$, and $\times$, and the following control structures:

(a) if $x > 0$ then y else z. This structure is represented in the tree with the symbol IF having the children x, y, and z.

(b) if $x > w$ then y else z. This structure is represented in the tree with the symbol IFGT having the children x, w, y, and z.

3. Decide on how many individuals make up a population. Various population sizes were tried. Sizes below 500 were ineffectual, whereas ones around 2500 had good results.

4. Decide how to initialize the population. Each initial individual was created by growing the tree as discussed in Section 9.3.1. The maximum number of levels allowed was 4 and the maximum number of total nodes allowed was 24. This restriction was also enforced in future populations. The purpose of these limitations was to avoid **overfitting**, which occurs when the tree matches the training data very closely but has limited predictive value for unseen data.

5. Decide on a fitness function. Data was obtained on the S&P closing prices from April 4, 1983, to June 18, 2004. A given tree analyzes the first 4750 days of this data. The tree starts with $1 on the first day. If the tree returns a value greater than 0 on a given day, a buy signal is generated, otherwise a sell signal is generated. All the current money is always invested or withdrawn when there is a buy or a sell. There are no partial investments. If the tree was in the market on the previous day and a buy signal is generated, no action is taken. Similarly, if the tree was out of the market on the previous day and a sell signal is generated, no action is taken. When the 4750 days of trading are complete, the initial dollar is subtracted so that the final value represents profit. To further avoid overfitting, a fitness penalty proportional to the total number of transactions was imposed.

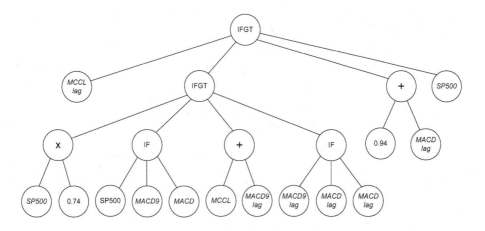

Figure 9.11 A tree that survived as most fit in one run and performed well in an evaluation.

6. Decide on which individuals to select for reproduction. The population is sorted according to fitness. The bottom 25% are "killed off" and replaced by more fit individuals.

7. Decide on how to perform crossovers and mutations. Crossover between two individuals is performed by exchanging randomly selected subtrees. **Node mutations** are done by randomly selecting a few nodes and randomly changing their values to nodes that take the same arguments. Mutations to function nodes change operations, and mutations to terminal nodes change indicator or constant values. **Tree mutations** are performed by randomly selecting a subtree and replacing it by a new random subtree.

   The top 10% of the population are left unchanged; 50% are randomly selected for crossover with individuals from the top 10%; 20% are selected for node mutations; 10% are selected for tree mutations; and 10% are killed and randomly replaced.

8. Decide when to terminate. The maximum number of generations was in the 300–500 range.

Figure 9.11 shows a tree that survived as the most fit tree in one particular run.

9.3.3.2 Evaluation

Recall that data was obtained on the S&P closing prices from April 4, 1983, to June 18, 2004, and the first 4750 days of these data were used to determine the fitness and thereby learn a system. The remaining 500 days were used to evaluate a system by computing its fitness based on these data. The system represented by the tree in Figure 9.11 had an evaluation fitness of 0.397. The **buy-and-hold** strategy in investing is simply to buy a security and hold on to it. Based on the evaluation data, the buy-and-hold strategy only had a fitness of 0.1098.

9.4   Discussion and Further Reading

The remaining two areas of evolutionary computation are evolutionary programming and evolution strategies. **Evolutionary programming** is similar to genetic algorithms in that it uses a population of candidate solutions to evolve into an answer to a specific problem. Evolutionary programming differs in that the concentration is on developing behavioral models of the observable systems interaction with the environment. Fogel [1994] presents this approach. **Evolution strategies** models problem solutions as species. Rechenberg [1994] says that the field of evolution strategies is based on the evolution of evolution. See [Kennedy and Eberhart, 2001] for a complete introduction to all four areas of evolutionary computation.

EXERCISES

Section 9.1

Exercise 9.1 Describe the difference between sexual reproduction in diploid organisms, binary fission in haploid organisms, and fusion in haploid organisms.

Exercise 9.2 Suppose a diploid organism has 10 chromosomes in one of its genomes.

1. How many chromosomes are in each of its somatic cells?

2. How many chromosomes are in each of its gametes?

Exercise 9.3 Suppose two adult haploid organisms reproduce by fusion.

1. How many children will be produced?

2. Will the genetic content of the children all be the same?

Exercise 9.4 Consider the eye color of a human being as determined by the bey2 gene. Recall that the allele for brown eyes is dominant. For each of the following parent allele combinations, determine the eye color of the individual.

Father	Mother
BLUE	BLUE
BLUE	BROWN
BROWN	BLUE
BROWN	BROWN

Section 9.2

Exercise 9.5 Consider Table 9.1. Suppose the fitnesses of the eight individuals are .61, .23, .85, .11, .27, .36, .55, and .44. Compute the normed fitnesses and the cumulative normed fitnesses.

Exercise 9.6 Suppose we perform basic crossover as illustrated in Table 9.3, the parents are 01101110 and 11010101, and the starting and ending points for crossover are 3 and 7. Show the two children produced.

Exercise 9.7 Implement the genetic algorithm for finding the value of x that maximizes $f(x) = \sin(x\pi/256)$, which is discussed in Section 9.2.2.

Exercise 9.8 Consider the instance of TSP in Figure 9.12. Assume the weights in both directions on an edge are the same. Find the shortest tour.

Exercise 9.9 Suppose we perform order crossover, the parents are 3 5 2 1 4 6 8 7 9 and 5 3 2 6 9 1 8 7 4, and the starting and ending points for the pick are 4 and 7. Show the two children produced.

Exercise 9.10 Consider the instance of TSP in Figure 9.12. Apply the nearest neighbor algorithm starting with each of the vertices. Do any of them yield the shortest tour?

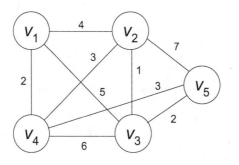

Figure 9.12 An instance of TSP.

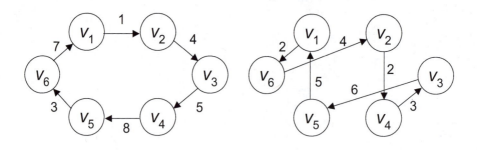

Figure 9.13 Two tours.

Exercise 9.11 Form the union graph of the two tours shown in Figure 9.13, and apply the Nearest Neighborhood Algorithm to the resultant graph starting at vertex v_5.

Exercise 9.12 Apply the Greedy Edge Algorithm to the instance of TSP in Figure 9.12. Does it yield a shortest tour?

Section 9.3

Exercise 9.13 Consider the two trees in Figure 9.8. Show the new trees that would be obtained if we exchanged the subtree starting with the "4" in the left tree with the subtree starting with the "+" in the right tree.

Exercise 9.14 Consider the individual (program) in Figure 9.10. Show the moves produced by that program when negotiating the Santa Fe trail for the first 10 time steps.

Exercise 9.15 Implement the genetic programming algorithm for the Santa Fe trail discussed in Section 9.3.2.

Chapter 10

Swarm Intelligence

Many species perform complex tasks when working as a group, even though each member of the group seemingly exhibits little intelligence. For example, an ant colony is quite effective at finding the shortest path between its nest and some source of food, while an individual ant has no ability to accomplish this task. As another example, many of us have been fascinated watching a flock of birds turn and maneuver as a single unit, while there is no apparent master plan guiding their behavior. Schools of fish likewise move in unison. **Swarm intelligence** is intelligent collective behavior that emerges when some group of autonomous, non-intelligent entities interact. The entities can be real (e.g., ants) or artificial (called swarm robots).

We discuss two forms of swarm behavior, namely the ant colony and the flock.

10.1   Ant System

First we discuss how real ants find the shortest path; then we develop artificial ants to solve the Traveling Salesperson Problem.

10.1.1   Real Ant Colonies

Real ants can find the shortest path between a food source and their nest [Beckers et al., 1992]. It is well-known that they accomplish this task by depositing pheromone. A **pheromone** is a secreted or excreted chemical factor that elicits a response in members of the same species. Each ant deposits a certain amount of pheromone while walking, and each ant is attracted to pheromone. This attraction makes it more probable that a given ant will follow a path rich in pheromone. This localized, individual behavior explains how the ants find the shortest path between their nest and a food source. Figure 10.1 illustrates this. Figure 10.1 (a) shows a straight line between the nest and the food, and the ants methodically going back and forth picking up food and depositing it in the nest. Suppose now that we deposit an obstacle in the path as shown in Figure 10.1 (b). On average, about half the ants will take the upper path and about half the ants will take the lower path, as depicted in Figure 10.1 (c). Because the upper path is shorter and has the same number of ants traversing it per unit time, it will accumulate more pheromone. This increase in pheromone will attract each ant, making it more probable that the ant will take the upper path in its next iteration. The path will become even richer in pheromone, and eventually all ants will take the upper path, as shown in Figure 10.1 (d).

10.1.2   Artificial Ants for Solving the TSP

Using the behavior of real ants as a model, we can develop colonies of artificial ants, known as **swarm robots** or **agents**, that solve interesting problems. Regardless of the application, these colonies have the following features in common:

1. There is no top-down central command guiding the agents' behavior.

2. Each agent is able to generate some change in the environment.

3. Each agent is able to sense some change in the environment.

Based on a method that appears in [Dorigo and Gambardella, 1997], we will develop a colony that solves the Travel Salesperson Problem (TSP). See Section 9.2.3 for a description of this problem. In the application considered here, there is an edge from every vertex to every other vertex; that is, the graph is complete.

Our colony has the following three properties that are borrowed from real ant colonies:

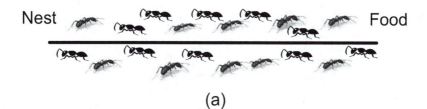

(a)

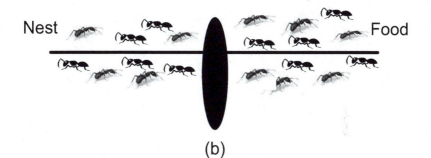

(b)

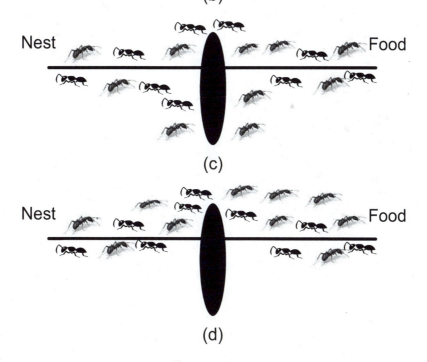

(c)

(d)

Figure 10.1 (a) Ants follow a path between their nest and food. (b) An obstacle appears on the path. (c) About half the ants follow the upper path and the other half the lower path. (d) Because pheromones deposit more quickly on the shorter path, eventually all ants choose this path.

1. Each agent prefers a path with a higher pheromone level.

2. Pheromone will accumulate at a faster rate on shorter paths.

3. The trails mediate the communication between the agents.

Additionally, our colony has the following properties that do not have a natural counterpart:

1. Each agent k has a working memory M_k that contains the vertices the agent has already visited. The memory is emptied at the beginning of each new tour, and is updated each time a vertex is visited.

2. Each agent knows how far away vertices are from the agent's current vertex.

Given these properties, there are many ways we could develop an algorithm for solving TSP. The one appearing in [Dorigo and Gambardella, 1997] proceeds as follows:

1. Deciding how to choose the next vertex:

   If agent k is currently at vertex r, the next vertex s is chosen from the vertices not in M_k according to the following rule:

$$s = \begin{cases} \underset{u \notin M_k}{\arg\max} \left[\tau(r,u) \times \{\eta(r,u)\}^{\beta} \right] & \text{if } p \leq p_0 \\ S & \text{otherwise.} \end{cases} \quad (10.1)$$

   The function $\tau(r,u)$ is the amount of pheromone currently on the edge (r,u); $\eta(r,u)$ is a heuristic function, which was chosen to be the inverse of the weight of edge (r,u); and β is a parameter that determines the relative importance placed on pheromone level versus closeness. S is a random variable selected according to the following probability distribution, which favors shorter edges with higher levels of pheromone:

$$p_{r,k}(s) = \begin{cases} \dfrac{\tau(r,s) \times \{\eta(r,s)\}^{\beta}}{\sum\limits_{u \notin M_k} \tau(r,u) \times \{\eta(r,u)\}^{\beta}} & \text{if } s \notin M_k \\ 0 & \text{otherwise.} \end{cases} \quad (10.2)$$

   The parameter p_0 is in the interval $[0,1]$ and is chosen according to the relative importance placed on exploitation versus exploration. The value of p is chosen at random according to the uniform distribution over $[0,1]$. If $p \leq p_0$, we perform exploitation by simply choosing the vertex with the best combination of shortness and pheromone level (top of Equality 10.1); Otherwise, we perform exploration by randomly choosing a vertex based on a probability distribution that favors shorter paths and higher pheromone levels (Equality 10.2).

2. Depositing pheromone:

   (a) Local pheromone updating:

   Every time an edge is chosen by an agent, the pheromone on the edge is updated according to the following updating formula:

   $$\tau(r, s) \leftarrow (1 - \alpha)\tau(r, s) + \alpha\tau_0,$$

   where α and τ_0 are parameters. Local updating is motivated by trail evaporation in real ants.

   (b) Global pheromone updating:

   When all agents complete a tour, each edge on the shortest tour ST has its pheromone level updated as follows:

   $$\tau(r, s) \leftarrow (1 - \alpha)\tau(r, s) + \alpha \, \Delta \, \tau(r, s),$$

   where

   $$\Delta \, \tau(r, s) = \frac{1}{length(ST)}.$$

   Global updating is like reinforcement learning, in that better solutions obtain more reinforcement.

We start with some number m of ants and perform some number t of iterations, where in each iteration all agents generate new tours. The starting vertex for each tour is chosen at random. We call this method the **ant colony system (ACS)**.

Dorigo and Gambardella [1997] compared ACS to methods that used simulated annealing (SA), elastic net (EN), self organizing map (SOM), and the farthest insertion heuristic (FI). In these comparisons they use the following values of the parameters:

$m = 20$

$t = 1250$

$\alpha = 0.1$

$\beta = 2$

$p_0 = 0.9$

$\tau_0 = \dfrac{1}{n \times L}$

L is the length of the tour produced by the nearest neighbor heuristic and n is the number of vertices.

The results of one of their comparisons appear in Table 10.1. ACS did quite well, having the shortest average tour length for 4 of the 5 problem instances.

Table 10.1 Comparison of Average Tour Length for Five 50-Vertex Problem Instances

Problem Instance	ACS	SA	EN	SOM	FI
1	**5.86**	5.88	5.98	6.06	6.03
2	6.05	**6.01**	6.03	6.25	6.28
3	**5.57**	5.65	5.70	5.83	5.85
4	**5.70**	5.81	5.86	5.87	5.96
5	**6.17**	6.33	6.49	6.70	6.71

Note: Results on SA, EN, and SOM are from [Durbin and Willshaw, 1987] and [Potvin 1993]. Results for FL and ACS are averages over 15 trials. The best average tour length is in bold.

Dorigo and Gambardella [1997] show results of further comparisons involving ACS and other methods.

Dorigo and Gambardella [1997] suggest several ways for improving the algorithm. One interesting possibility is parallization. Using this method, the same TSP would be solved on each processor by a smaller number of ants and the best tour found would be exchanged asynchronously among processors [Dorigo et al., 1996]. Another possible improvement would be to introduce specialized families of ants [Gambardella and Dorigo, 1995].

To apply the technique introduced here to a new problem, it is necessary to identify an appropriate representation of the problem in the form of a graph searched by many agents, and an appropriate heuristic that defines the distance between any two nodes on the graph.

10.2   Flocks

While intelligence in ants emerges through the medium of pheromone, birds, fish, and cows exhibit emergent intelligence without their members sharing any physical medium. Birds fly in flocks, fish swim in schools, and cows run in herds. The words *flock*, *school*, and *herd* are used for the different types of species, but the behavior is all the same, namely that the members of a group move in unison without any apparent central command. For the sake of focus, we will discuss flocks of birds.

Many of us have been fascinated by the coordinated movements of flocks of birds. The flock maneuvers as a single unit, changing direction almost instantaneously. Two immediate questions are (1) Why do they do this? and (2) How do they do this? Hamilton [1971] offered an evolutionary answer to the first question. This behavior is exhibited primarily in prey rather than predators. A bird near the edge of the flock is more likely to be caught by a predator. So a bird has a survival benefit in staying close to the center of the flock.

As to the second question, at one time, some researchers suggested that electromagnetic communication may be involved. However, current research suggests another mechanism. Breder [1954] performed experiments in which

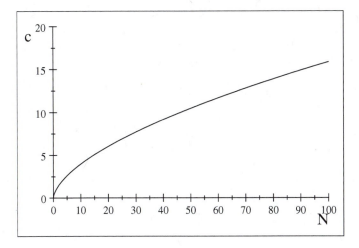

Figure 10.2 The attraction of a fish for a school as a function of the number N of fish in the school. In this example, $c = N^{0.6}$.

an isolated fish was separated from the school. The results showed that the attraction for the school by the isolated fish (as measured by the fish swimming toward the school) is given by the following formula:

$$c = kN^t,$$

where c and t are constant and N is the number of fish in the school. In one experiment, $k = 0.355$ and $t = 0.818$. Note that because $t < 1$, the attraction c increases as N increases; but for larger N, the effect of adding more fish to the school is less pronounced. This is illustrated in Figure 10.2 with $c = N^{0.6}$.

Partridge [1982] conducted experiments providing a physical description of the behavior of a school of fish. The **lateral line** in a fish is a sense organ used to detect movement and vibration in the surrounding water. In Partridge's experiment, blinded fish with intact lateral lines swam farther from their neighbors than fish with vision. However, sighted fish with lateral lines removed swam close to other fish but tended to collide with them. Fish with both sensory systems disabled did not stay with the school at all. These findings indicate that a fish uses local observations (vibration in the water) to avoid collisions and sight (possibly local) to stay with the school.

Based on considerations like these, Reynolds [1987] postulated that there is no leader or central control; rather, the flock's movements are determined by each individual bird (or fish) following simple rules in response to interactions with its neighbors. Using such rules, Reynolds developed a simulator of bird flocking. We describe Reynold's rules and the simulator next.

Reynolds [1987] defines a **flock** as a group of objects that exhibits generalized aligned, non-colliding, aggregate motion. A member of the flock is called a bird-oid or simply **boid**. A given boid reacts only to other boids in a small region around itself. Figure 10.3 shows such a region. The region is determined

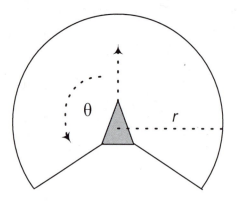

Figure 10.3 A boid's neighborhood. The parameter r is the radius of its circular neighborhood, and the parameter θ is the angle determining how much of the circle is included in the neighborhood.

by a parameter r, which is the radius of a circular neighborhood with center at the boid, and a parameter θ, which is an angle measured from the boid's direction of flight and which determines how much of the circle is included in the neighborhood. Boids outside the local neighborhood are ignored.

A boid uses the following three rules (in order of decreasing precedence) to guide its behavior based on the other boids in its neighborhood.

1. Collision avoidance: Avoid collisions with boids in its neighborhood

2. Velocity matching: Attempt to maintain the same velocity with boids in its neighborhood. Velocity is a vector consisting of both direction and speed

3. Flock Centering: Attempt to stay close to boids in its neighborhood

These three rules determine three steering behaviors that determine how a boid maneuvers based on the location and velocities of boids in its neighborhood. Figure 10.4 shows the behaviors. The arrow shows the direction in which the boid turns when it is in the given situation. Reynolds [1987] describes the details of how these behaviors are implemented and interact with each other in his simulator. The simulated flock model also enables the flock to avoid obstacle and go around them. The simulation can be viewed at http://www.red3d.com/cwr/boids/.

Another interesting behavior exhibited by flocks of birds is their ability to locate edibles from hundreds of feet in the air and swoop down to consume them. Heppner and Granander [1990] and Kennedy and Eberhard [1995] investigated the modeling of this behavior. Further mathematical models of flocking appear in [Jadbabaie et al., 2003] and [Vicsek et al., 1995].

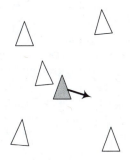

(a) Collision avoidance: steer to avoid collision with local boids.

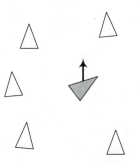

(b) Velocity matching: steer toward average direction of local boids.

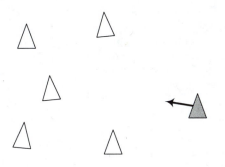

(c) Centering: steer toward average position of local boids.

Figure 10.4 The three local steering behaviors that result in the boids maintaining a cohesive flock.

10.3   Discussion and Further Reading

Kennedy and Eberhart [2001] discuss much of the initial research concerning swarm intelligence. However, further research in this area has proliferated in the past decade. For example, Campo et al. [2010] applied the pheromone strategy to collective foraging, which is a task in which a group of robots search for resources and exploit them. Robot foraging can be applied to search and rescue, mining, agriculture, and exploration of unknown environments. These researchers implement artificial ants that deposit pheromone inside a network of robots. The concentration of pheromone on a given robot allows it to decide whether it should be part of a particular path, and whether it should stop participating in path maintenance and switch to another task. Montes de Oca et al. [2011] developed a technique called incremental social learning to improve performance when the number of agents is large. In their technique, the population size grows over time. When a new agent is added to the population, its position is initialized using a "social learning" rule that is biased toward the best agent. Then the agent goes through a process of "individual learning" that consists of a local search procedure. Baldassarre et al. [2007] developed swarm robots that are able to dynamically change their structure according to environmental variability.

The flock model can be applied to many biological systems involving clustering and migration. Besides schools of fish and flock of birds, it can be applied to phenomena such as bacterial colony growth [Vicsek et al., 1995]. The model has also been applied to human behavior. For example, Latané [1981] developed **social impact theory** based on experiments concerning human behavior and groups of people. Such behavior includes various crowd effects, including how the number of people in a group in a restaurant affects tipping behavior and how the nervousness of an individual on-stage is a function of the number of people in the audience. **Behavioral finance** explains phenomena such as stock market bubbles and crashes by herding manifested in the collective irrationality of investors [Shiller, 2000]; [Hey and Morrone, 2004]. Goldstone and Janssen [2005] provide a computational model of how individual decisions lead to the emergence of group-level organizations.

EXERCISES

Section 10.1

Exercise 10.1 Explain why all the ants will eventually take the shorter path as illustrated in Figure 10.1.

Exercise 10.2 Consider the parameter β in Equality 10.1. Do larger values of β place more importance on pheromone level or closeness?

Exercise 10.3 Consider the parameter p_0 in Equality 10.1. Do larger values of p_0 place more importance on exploitation or exploration?

Exercise 10.4 Implement the ant colony system (ACS) discussed in Section 10.1.2. Investigate ways to improve it.

Section 10.2

Exercise 10.5 Recall from Section 10.2 that the attraction for a school by an isolated fish is given by the following formula $c = kN^t$, where c and t are constant and N is the number of fish in the school. Investigate the behavior of this function for $t < 1$ and for $t > 1$. When is the effect of adding another fish less pronounced as N increases, and when is it more pronounced?.

Exercise 10.6 Consider Reynolds' three rules for guiding the behavior of a boid, which appear in Section 10.2. For each rule, discuss the behavior of the boid if that rule was not present and the other two rules were present.

Part IV

Learning

Chapter 11

Learning Deterministic Models

In Part I (Logical Intelligence), we solved problems using models that represented deterministic relationships. For example, in Section 2.3.1, we introduced decision trees, and we showed how we could use a decision tree to determine the family of a plant from its properties. In Part II (Probabilistic Intelligence), we solved problems using models that represented probabilistic relationships. For example, in Section 6.7, we introduced Promedas, which produces a differential (probabilistic) diagnosis using a set of patient findings such as history data, physical findings, and laboratory data. In both parts, we constructed applications based on human knowledge that might be obtained from an expert in the application area.

In Part III we present methods for learning the models from data. The current chapter concerns learning deterministic models, while Chapters 12 and 13 address learning probabilistic models such as Bayesian networks. Chapter 14 introduces two related types of learning, namely unsupervised learning and reinforcement learning.

11.1 Supervised Learning

Artificial intelligence researchers have coined the type of learning discussed in this chapter as "supervised learning." **Supervised learning** involves learning a function from a training set. The function maps a variable x (which may be a vector) to a variable y, and the **training set** is a set of known values of (x, y) pairs. The variables in x are called the **predictors**, and the variable y is called the **target**. For example, American Express might be interested in learning the relationship between charges on an American Express card and the number of miles traveled by the card holder. The training set consists of pairs (x, y), where x is the number miles traveled by a given card holder in a given year and y is the amount of money charged that year by the card holder. As another example, we may wish to learn a way to determine the family of a plant from a vector of properties of the plant. In this case, the training set consists of pairs (x, y) where x is a vector of attributes of the a given plant and y is the known family of the plant. The function learned is called a **model** of the underlying system generating that data.

In the first example above, the variable y is continuous; whereas in the second, it is discrete. Next we discuss techniques for handling each of these situations.

11.2 Regression

Regression is a standard statistical technique for performing supervised learning when all variables are continuous. It was not developed by the artificial intelligence community, but rather traces its roots to Francis Galton in the 19th century [Bulmer, 2003]. Next, we briefly review linear regression, which is the simplest type of regression. You should consult a statistics text such as [Freedman et al., 2007] for a thorough coverage of regression.

11.2.1 Simple Linear Regression

In **simple linear regression**, we assume we have an independent random variable X and a dependent random variable Y such that

$$y = \beta_0 + \beta_1 x + \epsilon_x, \qquad (11.1)$$

where ϵ_x is a random variable, which depends on the value x of X, with the following properties:

1. For every value x of X, ϵ_x is normally distributed with 0 mean

Table 11.1 Miles and Dollars for 25 American Express Card Holders

Passenger	Miles (X)	Dollars (Y)
1	1211	1802
2	1345	2405
3	1422	2005
4	1687	2511
5	1849	2332
6	2026	2305
7	2133	3016
8	2253	3385
9	2400	3090
10	2468	3694
11	2699	3371
12	2806	3998
13	3082	3555
14	3209	4692
15	3466	4244
16	3643	5298
17	3852	4801
18	4033	5147
19	4267	5738
20	4498	6420
21	4533	6059
22	4804	6426
23	5090	6321
24	5233	7026
25	5439	6964

2. For every value x of X, ϵ_x has the same standard deviation σ

3. The random variables ϵ_x for all x are mutually independent

Note that these assumptions entail that the expected value of Y given a value x of X is given by

$$E(Y|X = x) = \beta_0 + \beta_1 x.$$

The idea is that the expected value of Y is a deterministic linear function of x. However, the actual value y of Y is not uniquely determined by the value of X because of a random error term ϵ_x.

Once we make these assumptions about two random variables, we use simple linear regression to try to discover the linear relationship shown in Equality 11.1 from a random sample of values of X and Y. To estimate the values of β_0 and β_1, we find the values of b_0 and b_1 that minimize the **Mean Square Error (MSE)**, which is

$$\frac{\sum_{i=1}^{n}[y_i - (b_0 + b_1 x_i)]^2}{n},$$

where n is the size of the sample, and x_i and y_i are the values of X and Y for the ith item in the sample. An example follows.

Example 11.1 This example is taken from [Aczel and Sounderpandian, 2002]. American Express suspected that charges on American Express cards increased with the number of miles traveled by the card holder. To investigate this matter, a research firm randomly selected 25 card holders and obtained the data shown in Table 11.1. Figure 11.1 shows a scatterplot of the data. We see that it appears that a linear relationship holds between Dollars (Y) and Miles (X).

    The values of b_0 and b_1 that minimize the MSE are our estimates of β_0 and β_1. We do not review how to find the minimizing values here. Any statistics package such as MINITAB, SAS, or SPSS has a linear regression module. If we use one such package to do a linear regression analysis based on the data in Table 11.1, we obtain that

$$b_0 = 274.8 \qquad\qquad b_1 = 1.26.$$

So the linear relationship is estimated to be

$$\begin{aligned} y &= b_0 + b_1 x \\ &= 274.8 + 1.26x. \end{aligned} \qquad (11.2)$$

                                                             ■

    Other information provided by a statistics package, when used to do the linear regression analysis in Example 11.1, includes the following:

Predictor	Coefficient	SE Coefficient	T	P
Constant	$b_0 = 274.8$	170.3	1.61	.12
x	$b_1 = 1.255$	.0497	25.25	0

Briefly, we discuss what each of these quantities means.

1. SE coefficient: This quantity, called the **standard error of the coefficient**, enables us to compute our confidence in how close our approximations are to the true values of β_0 and β_1 (assuming a linear relationship exists). Recall that for the normal density function, 95% of the mass falls in an interval whose endpoints are the mean $\pm$ 1.96 times the standard deviation. So if σ_0 is the SE coefficient for b_0, we can be 95% confident that

$$\beta_0 \in (b_0 - 1.96\sigma_0, b_0 + 1.96\sigma_0).$$

In Example 11.1, we can be 95% confident that

$$\begin{aligned} \beta_0 &\in (274.8 - 1.96 \times 170.3, 274.8 + 1.96 \times 170.3) \\ &= (-58.988, 608.588) \end{aligned}$$

$$\begin{aligned} \beta_1 &\in (1.255 - 1.96 \times .0497, 1.255 + 1.96 \times .0497) \\ &= (1.158, 1.352). \end{aligned}$$

Note that we can be much more confident in the estimate of β_1.

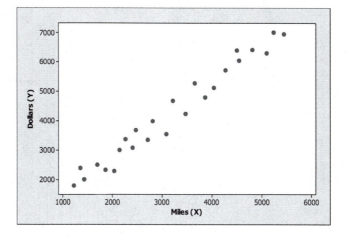

Figure 11.1 Scatterplot of dollars verses miles for 25 American Express card holders.

2. T: We have
$$T = \frac{\text{coefficient}}{\text{SE coefficient}}$$
The larger the value of T, the more confident we can be that the estimate is close to the true value. Notice in Example 11.1 that T is quite large for b_1 and not very large for b_0.

3. P: If the true value of the parameter (b_0 or b_1) is 0, then this is the probability of obtaining data more unlikely than the result. In Example 11.1, if $b_0 = 0$, then the probability of obtaining data more unlikely than the result is .12, while if $b_1 = 0$, the probability of obtaining data more unlikely than the result is 0. So we can be very confident that $b_1 \neq 0$, while we cannot be so confident that $b_0 \neq 0$. This means that the data strongly implies a linear dependence of Y on X, but it is not improbable that the constant is 0.

Note that even though regression involves using probability theory and random variables, we still classify it as deterministic learning because the function learned (e.g., Function 11.2) yields a unique value of y for each value of x rather than a probability distribution of y. So the model learned is deterministic.

11.2.2 Multiple Linear Regression

Multiple linear regression is just like simple linear regression except that there is more than one independent variable. That is, we assume we have m independent variables $X_1, X_2, \ldots, X_m$ and a dependent variable Y such that

$$y = b_0 + b_1 x_1 + b_2 x_2 + \ldots + b_m x_m + \epsilon_{x_1, x_2, \ldots, x_m},$$

where $\epsilon_{x_1, x_2, \ldots, x_n}$ is as described at the beginning of Section 11.2.1.

Table 11.2 Data on Miles Traveled, Number of Deliveries, and Travel Time in Hours

Driver	Miles (X_1)	Deliveries (X_2)	Travel Time (Y)
1	100	4	9.3
2	50	3	4.8
3	100	4	8.9
4	100	2	6.5
5	50	2	4.2
6	80	2	6.2
7	75	3	7.4
8	65	4	6.0
9	90	3	7.6
10	90	2	6.1

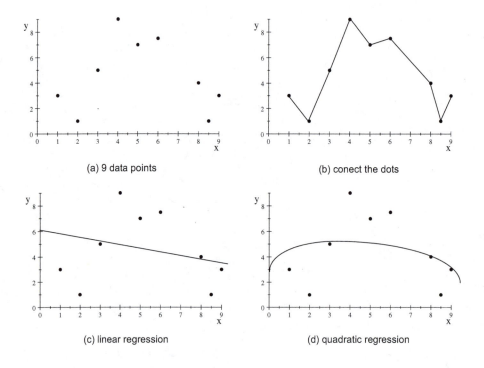

(a) 9 data points

(b) conect the dots

(c) linear regression

(d) quadratic regression

Figure 11.2 Nine data points are shown in (a) and models based in those data points appear in (c), (d), and (e).

Example 11.2 This example is taken from [Anderson et al., 2007]. Suppose a delivery company wants to investigate the dependence of drivers' travel time on miles traveled and number of deliveries. Assume we have the data in Table 11.2. We obtain the following results from a regression analysis based on these data:

$$b_0 = -.869$$
$$b_1 = .061$$
$$b_2 = .923.$$

So the linear relationship is estimated to be

$$y = -0.8689 + 0.061x_1 + 0.923x_2 + \epsilon_{x_1, x_2}.$$

Furthermore, we have the following:

Predictor	Coefficient	SE Coefficient	T	P
Constant	$b_0 = -.8687$	.9515	−.91	.392
Miles (X_1)	$b_1 = .061135$	.009888	6.18	0
Deliveries (X_2)	$b_2 = .9234$	.2211	4.18	.004

∎

11.2.3 Overfitting and Cross Validation

Our goal is to learn a model of the underlying system generating the data. Often we have several different models based on different learning techniques, and we want to choose the model that seems to fit the underlying system best. **Overfitting** occurs when a model describes the data well, but as a result describes the underlying relationship among the variables poorly. For example, suppose we have the 9 data points in Figure 11.2 (a). A straightforward model is one that fits the data exactly by connecting the data points with straight lines. We call the method that learns this model **connect the dots**. This model appears in Figure 11.2 (b). The MSE of the data for this model is clearly 0. However, the model may exhibit poor performance on unseen data. The linear regression model based on the same data appears in Figure 11.2 (c). Figure 11.2 (d) shows the model learned using quadratic regression. **Quadratic regression** is like linear regression except that we learn a quadratic function with the following form:

$$y = b_0 + b_1 x + b_2 x^2.$$

In this example, the connect the dots model has 18 scalar parameters, the linear regression model has two scalar parameters, and the quadratic regression model has three scalar parameters. In general, as we make a model more complex, we fit the data better, but often fit the underlying system worse. In order to avoid overfitting, we need techniques to evaluate the fit of the model to the underlying system. Next we discuss such techniques.

Table 11.3 MSE for Several Evaluation Methods and Several Model Learning Techniques

Method	Connect the Dots	Linear Regression	Quadratic Regression
Test Set	2.20	2.40	0.90
LOOCV	3.32	2.12	0.96
3-FoldCV	2.93	2.05	1.11

11.2.3.1   Test Set Method

In the **test set method**, we partition the data into a **training set** and a **test set**. For example, we can choose 30% of the data at random to be the test set and the remaining 70% to be the training set. We then learn a model from the training set and estimate the performance on unseen data using the test set. Using a 30%–70% split and the data in Figure 11.2 (a), the first row in Table 11.3 shows the MSE for the data items in the test set, relative to the model learned from the training set, for connect the dots, linear regression, and quadratic regression. Note that this result is based on one random draw, and a different random draw could show a different result. Based on this result, we would choose quadratic regression.

11.2.3.2   LOOCV Method

In **Leave-One-Out Cross Validation (LOOCV)**, we remove one of the n data items and train using the remaining $n-1$ data items. We then compute the error for the removed item relative to the model learned. After this process is repeated for all n data items, the MSE is computed. Using the LOOCV Method and the data in Figure 11.2 (a), the second row in Table 11.3 shows the MSE for connect the dots, linear regression, and quadratic regression. Based on this result, we would again choose quadratic regression.

11.2.3.3 k-Fold Cross Validation

In k-**Fold Cross Validation**, we divide the data into k partitions of the same size. For example, if $k = 3$ and there are 9 data items, then there are 3 data items in each partition. For each partition j we train using the data items in the remaining $k-1$ partitions, and we compute the error for each data item in partition j relative to the model learned. After this process is repeated for all k partitions, the MSE for all data items is computed. Using 3-FoldCV and the data in Figure 11.2 (a), the third row in Table 11.3 shows the MSE for connect the dots, linear regression, and quadratic regression. Based on this result, we would again choose the quadratic regression model. Note that Connect the Dots fared better than Linear Regression using the Test Set Method, but performed substantially worse using the other two methods. So based on all our results, linear regression would be chosen second.

Table 11.4 Data Concerning the Decision as to How to Spend a Saturday Afternoon.

Day	Outlook	Temp	Humidity	Wind	Activity
1	rain	hot	high	strong	stay home
2	overcast	cool	high	strong	stay home
3	overcast	cool	normal	strong	walk
4	rain	cool	normal	strong	stay home
5	sunny	cool	normal	strong	tennis
6	sunny	cool	normal	weak	tennis
7	rain	hot	normal	strong	stay home
8	sunny	hot	normal	weak	walk
9	sunny	mild	normal	strong	tennis
10	sunny	mild	high	weak	tennis
11	rain	mild	high	strong	stay home
12	overcast	mild	high	strong	walk
13	sunny	mild	high	strong	tennis
14	overcast	hot	high	strong	stay home

11.2.3.4 Learning Our Final Model

Once a learning technique is chosen, we learn a model from all the data using the technique. In the example just discussed, we would learn a model from all 9 data points using quadratic regression.

11.3 Learning a Decision Tree

A decision tree provides a function from the predictors to the target when all variables are discrete. We saw a decision tree in Figure 2.2 in Section 2.3.1. That decision tree predicted the family of a plant from attributes of the plant. In Section 2.3.1 we discussed how the decision tree could be constructed from rules identified by an expert. Another way to obtain a decision tree is to learn it from data. Next we present the ID3 algorithm [Quinlan, 1986] for doing this.

Suppose on each Saturday afternoon we either stay home, go for a walk, or play tennis. There are a several variables that could affect our decision, including the weather outlook, the temperature, the humidity, and the wind. Suppose further that we are pretty happy with our decisions on the past 14 Saturdays. However, we went to a lot of trouble to reach those decisions, and so we want to learn a decision tree from the data concerning those Saturdays. That data appears in Table 11.4.

Our goal is to learn a decision tree from these data that classifies all of these 14 instances correctly. Figures 11.3 and 11.4 show two such decision trees. The decision tree in Figure 11.4 is smaller than the one in Figure 11.3, and does not even contain the attribute *wind*. This result indicates that this variable is extraneous to the correct classification of those instances. In general, we do

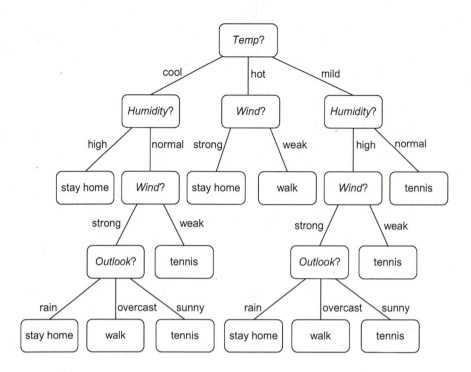

Figure 11.3 A decision tree that classifies the instances in Table 11.4 correctly.

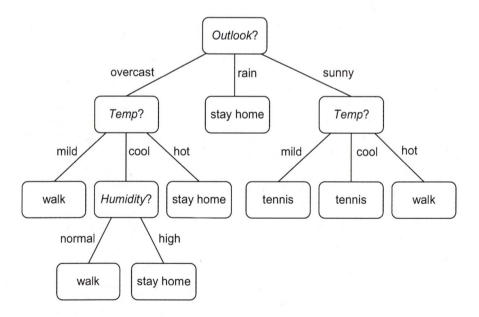

Figure 11.4 A parsimonious decision tree that classifies the instances in Table 11.4 correctly.

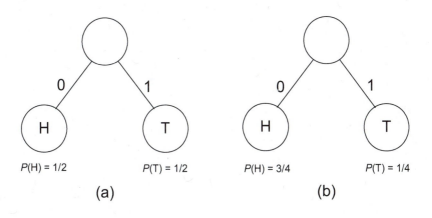

Figure 11.5 Binary trees representing binary codes.

not want to include extraneous attributes in our decision tree; we want the tree to be as parsimonious as possible. This is an example of the **Occam's Razor Principle**, which in this contest says that we should always look for the simplest model that fits the data. The ID3 algorithm, which we describe shortly, searches for the simplest decision tree.

11.3.1 Information Theory

Before presenting the algorithm, we need to review first information theory and then information gain.

Suppose we have a fair coin. Then if we denote the event that the coin lands heads by H, $P(H) = 1/2$. Suppose further that Joe tosses the coin and views the result, and Mary does not view it; then Joe knows the outcome of the toss, while Mary does not. If Joe informs Mary as to that outcome, how much information is he providing? If we let 0 represent H and 1 represent T, then Joe can tell Mary 0 if the outcome is H and 1 if it is T. Regardless, Joe can encode the outcome in 1 bit. So we say that Joe is providing Mary with one bit of information. Suppose next that the coin is weighted such that $P(H) = 1$. Then even if Mary does not view the outcome of the toss, she knows that it is H. Therefore, if Joe informs her as to the outcome, Joe is providing zero bits of information. Finally suppose $P(H) = 3/4$. This probability is between $1/2$ and 1; therefore it seems the report of an outcome of a toss should provide information in between the two extremes of $1/2$ and 1. However, Joe still needs to provide Mary with one bit of information to let her know for certain the outcome of the toss. So if we do the experiment just once, Joe must supply one bit of information unless we have the extreme probability of 1 or 0. Binary trees representing the binary code we identified for the probabilities of $1/2$ and $3/4$ appear in Figure 11.5.

Suppose next that we toss the fair coin twice, and Joe informs Mary as to the outcome of the tosses. If he reports 00 for HH, 01 for HT, 10 for TH, and

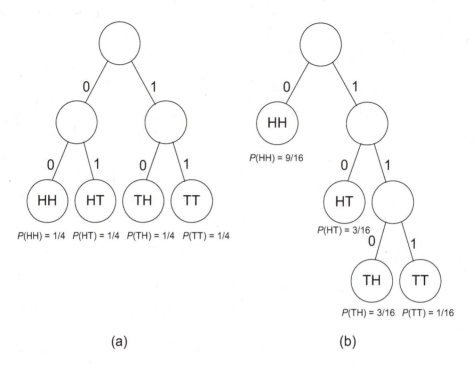

Figure 11.6 Binary trees corresponding to two optimal prefix codes.

11 for TT, then the binary tree in Figure 11.6 (a) represents this binary code. Clearly, Joe is now always supplying Mary with two bits of information. If we toss the coin that has $P(\text{H}) = 3/4$ twice, we could use the binary code in Figure 11.6 (a). However, on average, it is more efficient to use the code in Figure 11.6 (b). Using this code, the expected value of the number of bits needed to provide the result of the two tosses is equal to

$$1 \times \frac{9}{16} + 2 \times \frac{3}{16} + 3 \times \frac{3}{16} + 3 \times \frac{1}{16} = 1.6875. \qquad (11.3)$$

If we use the code in Figure 11.6 (a), two bits are always required, which means the expected value of the number of bits needed to provide the result of the two tosses is equal to 2.

The binary codes in Figure 11.6 are prefix codes. In a **prefix code**, no code word for one character constitutes the beginning of the code word for another character. For example, if 10 is the code word for HT, then 101 cannot be the code word for TH. An **optimal binary prefix code** for a probability distribution is a binary prefix code that yields the minimal expected value of the number of bits needed to report the outcome of the experiment. The binary code in Figure 11.6 (a) is an optimal binary prefix code if $p(\text{H}) = 1/2$, and the one in Figure 11.6 (b) is an optimal code if $P(\text{H}) = 3/4$. Huffman's algorithm, which appears in a standard algorithms text such as [Neapolitan and Naimipour, 2010], produces an optimal binary prefix code.

Suppose now that we repeat the experiment of tossing the coin n times. If we use an optimal binary prefix code to report the outcome of the n tosses, Shannon [1948] showed that the limit as $n \to \infty$ of the expected value of the number of bits needed to report the outcome of each toss is equal to

$$- (p_1 \log_2 p_1 + p_2 \log_2 p_2)$$

where $p_1 = P(\text{H})$ and $p_2 = P(\text{T})$. This value is called the **entropy** H associated with the given random variable.

If $p_1 = p_2 = 1/2$, then

$$H = - \left(\frac{1}{2} \log_2 \frac{1}{2} + \frac{1}{2} \log_2 \frac{1}{2} \right) = 1.$$

This result is expected because we know it always takes one bit to report the outcome of each toss, regardless of how many tosses we perform.

If $p_1 = 3/4$ and $p_2 = 1/4$, then

$$H = - \left(\frac{3}{4} \log_2 \frac{3}{4} + \frac{1}{4} \log_2 \frac{1}{4} \right) = .81128.$$

Equality 11.3 shows that if $n = 2$, then the expected number of the number of bits needed to report both outcomes is 1.6875, which means the expected value of the number of bits needed to report each outcome is $1.6875/2 = .843\,75$. This value is much closer to closer to H than 1 (the number of bits needed when $n = 1$). When $n = 3$, the expected value will be even closer to H, and in the limit it equals H.

If there are m outcomes to the experiment and p_i is the probability of the ith outcome, then the entropy associated with the given random variable is

$$- \sum_{i=1}^{m} p_i \log_2 p_i.$$

The entropy is maximized when all p_i are equal to $1/m$. In this case we are providing the most information when we report the outcome of the experiment. The entropy is minimized (equal to 0) when $p_i = 1$ for some i. In this case we are providing no information.

11.3.2 Information Gain and the ID3 Algorithm

Consider the probability distribution of *Outlook* in Table 11.4. Recall that our goal is determine the value of *Activity*. There are 6 days in which the value of *Activity* is to stay home, 3 days on which it is to walk, and 5 days on which it is to play tennis. The entropy associated with the probability distribution of *Activity* (as determined by the data) is therefore as follows:

$$
\begin{aligned}
H(Activity) &= - \left(\frac{6}{14} \log_2 \frac{6}{14} + \frac{3}{14} \log_2 \frac{3}{14} + \frac{5}{14} \log_2 \frac{5}{14} \right) \\
&= 1.531.
\end{aligned}
$$

Our goal is to get this entropy down to 0 as quickly as possible so we know the value of *Activity*. Notice that if we found out that the value of *Outlook* was rain we would know that the value of *Activity* was to stay home because we stayed home on every one of the 4 days it rained, and we would have achieved our goal. On the other hand, if we found out that the value of *Outlook* was sunny, the probability that the value of *Activity* is tennis would be 5/6 because we played tennis on 5 of the 6 days it was sunny, and we would be close to an entropy of 0. So it looks like we can possibly gain a lot of information by learning the value of *Outlook*. To formalize this notion, we compute the expected value of the entropy of *Activity* conditional on *Outlook*, which we denote as $EH_{Outlook}(Activity)$. To obtain this value, we first compute

$$H_{rain}(Activity) = -\left(\frac{4}{4}\log_2\frac{4}{4} + \frac{0}{4}\log_2\frac{0}{4} + \frac{0}{4}\log_2\frac{0}{4}\right) = 0$$

$$H_{sunny}(Activity) = -\left(\frac{5}{6}\log_2\frac{5}{6} + \frac{1}{6}\log_2\frac{1}{6} + \frac{0}{6}\log_2\frac{0}{6}\right) = .650$$

$$H_{overcast}(Activity) = -\left(\frac{2}{4}\log_2\frac{2}{4} + \frac{2}{4}\log_2\frac{2}{4} + \frac{0}{4}\log_2\frac{0}{4}\right) = 1.$$

By $H_{rain}(Activity)$ we mean the entropy of *Activity* given that it rains. We then have that

$$\begin{aligned}
EH_{Outlook}(Activity) &= H_{rain}(Activity)P(\text{rain}) + \\
&\quad H_{sunny}(Activity)P(\text{sunny}) + \\
&\quad H_{overcast}(Activity)P(\text{overcast}) \\
&= H_{rain}(Activity)\frac{4}{14} + \\
&\quad H_{sunny}(Activity)\frac{6}{14} + \\
&\quad H_{overcast}(Activity)\frac{4}{14} \\
&= 0 \times \frac{4}{14} + .650 \times \frac{6}{14} + 1 \times \frac{4}{14} \\
&= .564.
\end{aligned}$$

So we can expect to reduce the entropy of *Activity* from 1.531 to .564 if we learn the value of *Outlook*. We define this difference to be the **information gain** associated with *Outlook*. That is,

$$\begin{aligned}
Gain_{Outlook}(Activity) &= H(Activity) - EH_{Outlook}(Activity) \\
&= 1.531 - .564 = .967.
\end{aligned}$$

It is left as an exercise to compute the gain associated with the other three variables, and show that *Outlook* has the largest gain. The ID3 Algorithm therefore makes *Outlook* the top node in our decision tree. For each value of

Outlook, we then compute the gain associated with each of the other three variables. To that end,

$$
\begin{aligned}
EH_{\text{overcast},Temp}(Activity) &= H_{\text{overcast,cool}}(Activity)P(\text{cool}|\text{overcast}) + \\
&\quad H_{\text{overcast,mild}}(Activity)P(\text{mild}|\text{overcast}) + \\
&\quad H_{\text{overcast,hot}}(Activity)P(\text{hot}|\text{overcast}) \\
&= 1 \times \frac{1}{2} + 0 \times \frac{1}{4} + 0 \times \frac{1}{4} = \frac{1}{2}.
\end{aligned}
$$

So

$$
\begin{aligned}
Gain_{\text{overcast},Temp}(Activity) &= H_{\text{overcast}}(Activity) - EH_{\text{overcast},Temp}(Activity) \\
&= 1 - \frac{1}{2} = \frac{1}{2}.
\end{aligned}
$$

It is left an exercise to compute the gain associated with the other two variables, and show that *Temp* has the largest gain. So the ID3 Algorithm makes *Temp* the node touching the edge emanating from *Outlook* that is labeled overcast. When the value of *Outlook* is rain, the value of *Activity* is always to stay home. So we make "stay home" the node touching the edge emanating from *Outlook* that is labeled rain; this node is a leaf. It is left as an exercise to determine the remaining nodes in the tree.

We illustrated the ID3 algorithm; it now follows.

Algorithm 11.1 ID3
    Input: A data file whose records contains values of predictors and a target variable.
    Output: A decision tree.

    Function *Addnode(datafile, set_of_predictors)*;
    if every record in *datafile* has the same value V of *target*
        then **return** a node labeled with V;
    elseif *set_of_predictors* is empty
        then **return** a node labeled with disjunction of values of *target*
        in *datafile*;
    else
        choose *predictor* in *set_of_predictors* with largest gain;
        create a node *node* labeled with *predictor*;
        set_of_predictors = *set_of_predictors* − {*predictor*};
        for each value V of *predictor*
            datafile = data file consisting only of records where *predictor*
            has value V;
            newnode = *Addnode(datafile, set_of_predictors)*;
            create an edge from *node* to *newnode* labeled with V;
        endfor
        return *node*;
    endelse

Table 11.5 Performance of the ID3 Algorithm in a Chess Domain

Training Set Size	Fraction of Entire Universe	Errors in 10,000 trials
200	.0001	199
1000	.0007	33
5000	.0036	8
25,000	.0179	6
125,000	.0893	2

The global call to function *Addnode* is as follows:

$$root\_of\_tree = Addnode(datafile, set\_of\_predictors);$$

where *datafile* contains all the records and *set_of_predictors* contains all the predictors.

Although the ID3 Algorithm produces a parsimonious decision tree, the question remains as the whether the resultant tree performs well at classifying new instances. Quinlan [1983] evaluated the performance of ID3 on the problem of learning to classify boards in a chess-related game. The game involved white versus black, where white played with a king and a rook, and black played with a king and a knight. The goal was to learn to recognize boards that would lead to a loss for black within three moves. The predictors consisted of 23 properties of the board such as "there is an inability to move the king safely." There were 1,400,000 possible boards, of which 474,000 led to a loss for black within three moves. Results of the evaluation appear Table 11.5.

11.3.3　Overfitting

As discussed in Section 11.2.3, overfitting can occur when we learn a model from data. In the case of learning a decision tree, we can address overfitting by pruning the tree after learning it. Quinlan [1987] introduced several methods for pruning decision trees including **Reduced Error Pruning**, which we discuss next.

When we prune a node from a decision tree, we replace the node by the most common-occurring value of the target at that node. For example, suppose we are pruning the node on the branch labeled sunny that is a child of *Outlook* in the tree in Figure 11.4. Suppose further that we are pruning using the data file in Table 11.4. Of the 6 records that have *Outlook* equal to sunny, 5 have *Activity* equal to tennis. Therefore if we pruned the node labeled *Temp* that touches the edge labeled sunny, we would replace node *Temp* by a node labeled tennis.

In Reduced Error Pruning, the data set is partitioned into a training set and a test set. We learn a decision tree from the training set using an algorithm such as ID3, and then prune the tree using the test set. This is done by first determining the predictive accuracy of the tree for the test set. Next we individually prune each node in the tree, and determine the predictive accuracy with the node removed. We prune the node that increases the predictive accuracy the most. This procedure is followed until no node improves the predictive accuracy. The algorithm follows.

Algorithm 11.2 Reduced Error Pruning
   Input: A decision tree and a test data set.
   Output: A pruned decision tree.

   Procedure *Prune*(**var** *decision_tree, test_data*);
   repeat
        for each node in *decision_tree*
            determine how much pruning the node improves predictive
            accuracy on *test_data*;
            if pruning some node improves predictive accuracy
                prune the node that increases predictive accuracy the most;
        endfor
   until pruning no node improves predictive accuracy;

EXERCISES

Section 11.2

Exercise 11.1 Suppose we have the following data on 10 college students concerning their grade point averages (GPA) and scores on the graduate record exam (GRE):

Student	GPA	GRE
1	2.2	1400
2	2.4	1300
3	2.8	1550
4	3.1	1600
5	3.3	1400
6	3.3	1700
7	3.4	1650
8	3.7	1800
9	3.9	1700
10	4.0	1800

Using some statistical package such as MINITAB, do a linear regression for GRE in terms of GPA. Show the values of b_0 and b_1 and the values of the SE coefficient, T, and P for each of them. Show R^2. Do these results indicate a linear relationship between GRE and GPA? Does it seem that the constant term is significant?

Exercise 11.2 Suppose we have the same data as in Exercise 11.1, except we also have data on family income as follows:

Student	GPA	GRE	Income ($1000)
1	2.2	1400	44
2	2.4	1300	40
3	2.8	1550	46
4	3.1	1600	50
5	3.3	1400	40
6	3.3	1700	54
7	3.4	1650	52
8	3.7	1800	56
9	3.9	1700	50
10	4.0	1800	56

Using some statistical package such as MINITAB, do a linear regression for GRE in terms of GPA and income. Show the values of b_0, b_1, and b_2, and the values of the SE coefficient, T, and P for each of them. Show R^2. Does it seem that we have improved our predictive accuracy for the GRE by also considering income?

Exercise 11.3 Suppose we have the same data as in Exercise 11.1, except that we also have data on the students' American College Test (ACT) scores as follows:

Student	GPA	GRE	ACT
1	2.2	1400	22
2	2.4	1300	23
3	2.8	1550	25
4	3.1	1600	26
5	3.3	1400	27
6	3.3	1700	27
7	3.4	1650	28
8	3.7	1800	29
9	3.9	1700	30
10	4.0	1800	31

Using some statistical package such as MINITAB, do a linear regression for GRE in terms of GPA and ACT. Show the values of b_0, b_1, and b_2 and the values of the SE coefficient, T, and P for each of them. Show R^2. Does it seem that we have improved our predictive accuracy for GRE by also considering ACT score? If not, what do you think would be an explanation for this?

Exercise 11.4 Using the data in Exercise 11.3 and some statistical package such as MINITAB, do a linear regression for GPA in terms of ACT. Show the values of b_0 and b_1, and the values of the SE coefficient, T, and P for each of them. Show R^2. Relate this result to that obtained in Exercise 11.3.

Table 11.6 Test Data Concerning the Decision as to How to Spend a Saturday Afternoon

Day	Outlook	Temp	Humidity	Wind	Activity
1	rain	hot	high	strong	stay home
2	overcast	hot	high	weak	tennis
3	overcast	cool	high	strong	tennis
4	rain	cool	normal	weak	stay home
5	sunny	cool	high	strong	tennis
6	sunny	cool	normal	weak	tennis
7	rain	hot	normal	strong	stay home
8	sunny	hot	normal	strong	walk
9	sunny	hot	normal	strong	tennis
10	sunny	mild	high	weak	tennis
11	rain	mild	normal	strong	stay home
12	overcast	mild	high	weak	walk
13	sunny	mild	high	strong	tennis
14	overcast	hot	high	strong	stay home

Exercise 11.5 Consider again the data in Exercise 11.1. Investigate models learned from those data using connect the dots, linear regression, and quadratic regression. Evaluate the fit of each model using the test set method, LOOCV, and 3-fold cross-validation. Which model seems to fit the underlying system best?

Exercise 11.6 Suppose we have the data in Table 11.1. Investigate models learned from that data using connect the dots, linear regression, and quadratic regression. Evaluate the fit of each model using the test set method, LOOCV, and 3-fold cross-validation. Which model seems to fit the underlying system best?

Section 11.3

Exercise 11.7 Suppose we have a variable with two states x_1 and x_2, and $P(x_1) = .3$. Compute the entropy associated with the random variable.

Exercise 11.8 Suppose we have a variable with three states x_1, x_2, and x_3, and $P(x_1) = .3$, $P(x_2) = .5$. Compute the entropy associated with the random variable.

Exercise 11.9 In Section 11.3.2 it was left as an exercise to compute the gain associated with the variables $Temp$, $Humidity$, and $Wind$ based on the data in Table 11.4. Do this.

Exercise 11.10 In Section 11.3.2 it was left as an exercise to compute the gain associated with the variables *Humidity* and *Wind* given that the *Outlook* is overcast based on the data in Table 11.4. Do this.

Exercise 11.11 Suppose we have the test data in Table 11.6. Using Algorithm 11.2 and these test data, prune the decision trees in Figures 11.3 and 11.4.

Chapter 12

Learning Probabilistic Model Parameters

Until the early 1990s, the DAG in a Bayesian network was ordinarily hand-constructed by a domain expert. Then the conditional probabilities were assessed by the expert, learned from data, or obtained using a combination of both techniques. Eliciting Bayesian networks from experts can be a laborious and difficult process in the case of large networks. As a result, researchers developed methods that could learn the DAG from data. Furthermore, they formalized methods for learning the conditional probabilities from data. In a Bayesian network, the conditional probability distributions are called the **parameters**. In this chapter we address the problem of parameter learning. We only discuss learning discrete parameters. Neapolitan [2004] shows a method for learning the parameters in a Gaussian Bayesian network. In a Bayesian network the DAG is called the **structure.** In Chapter 13 we discuss structure learning.

12.1   Learning a Single Parameter

We can only learn parameters from data when the probabilities are relative frequencies, which were discussed in Section 5.3.1. So, this discussion pertains only to such probabilities. Although the method is based on rigorous mathematical results obtained by modeling an individual's subjective belief concerning a relative frequency, the method itself is quite simple. Here, we merely present the method. See [Neapolitan, 2004] for the mathematical development. After presenting a method for learning the probability of a binomial random variable, we extend the method to multinomial random variables. Finally, we provide guidelines for articulating our prior beliefs concerning probabilities.

12.1.1   Binomial Random Variables

We illustrate learning with a sequence of examples.

Example 12.1 Recall the discussion concerning a thumbtack at the beginning of Section 5.3.1. We noted that a thumbtack could land on its flat end, which we call "heads," or it could land with the edge of the flat end and the point touching the ground, which we call "tails." Because the thumbtack is not symmetrical, we have no reason to apply the Principle of Indifference and assign probabilities of .5 to both outcomes. So, we need data to estimate the probability of heads. Suppose we toss the thumbtack 100 times, and it lands heads 65 of those times. Then the maximum likelihood estimate (MLE) is

$$P(heads) \approx \frac{65}{100} = .65.$$

∎

In general, if there are s heads in n trials, the MLE of the probability is

$$P(heads) \approx \frac{s}{n}.$$

Using the MLE seems reasonable when we have no prior belief concerning the probability. However, it is not so reasonable when we do have prior belief. Consider the next example.

Example 12.2 Suppose you take a coin from your pocket, toss it 10 times, and it lands heads all those times. Then using the MLE, we estimate

$$P(heads) \approx \frac{10}{10} = 1.$$

After the coin landed heads 10 times, we would not bet as though we were certain that the outcome of the 11th toss will be heads. So, our belief concerning the $P(heads)$ is not the MLE value of 1. Assuming we believe the coins in our pockets are fair, should we instead maintain $P(heads) = .5$ after all 10 tosses landed heads? This might seem reasonable for 10 tosses, but it does not seem so reasonable if 1000 straight tosses landed heads. At some point we would start suspecting the coin was weighted to land heads. We need a method that incorporates one's prior belief with the data. The standard way to do this is for the probability assessor to ascertain integers a and b such that the assessor's experience is equivalent to having seen the first outcome (heads, in this case) occur a times and the second outcome occur b times in $m = a + b$ trials. Then the assessor's prior probabilities are

$$P(heads) = \frac{a}{m} \qquad P(tails) = \frac{b}{m}. \tag{12.1}$$

After observing s heads and t tails in $n = s + t$ trials, the assessor's posterior probabilities are

$$P(heads|s,t) = \frac{a+s}{m+n} \qquad P(tails|s,t) = \frac{a+t}{m+n}. \tag{12.2}$$

∎

This posterior probability is called the **maximum a posteriori probability (MAP)**. Note that we have used the symbol $=$ rather than $\approx$, and we have written the probability as a conditional probability rather than as an estimate. The reason is that this is a Bayesian technique, and Bayesians say that the value is their probability (belief) based on the data rather than saying it is an estimate of a probability (relative frequency).

We developed Equalities 12.1 and 12.2 based on intuitive grounds. The following theorem is a rigorous derivation of them.

Theorem 12.1 Suppose we are about to repeatedly toss a thumbtack (or perform any repeatable experiment with two outcomes). Suppose further we assume exchangeability, and we represent our prior belief concerning the probability of heads using a **beta distribution** with parameters a and b. Then our prior probabilities are given by Equality 12.1, and after observing s heads and t tails in $n = s + t$ trials, our posterior probabilities are given by Equality 12.2.
Proof. The proof can be found in [Neapolitan, 2004]. ∎

The preceding theorem assumes exchangeability. Briefly, the assumption of **exchangeability**, which was first developed by de Finetti in 1937, is that an individual assigns the same probability to all sequences of the same length containing the same number of each outcome. For example, the individual assigns the same probability to these two sequences of heads (H) and tails (T):

$$H, T, H, T, H, T, H, T, T, T \qquad \text{and} \qquad H, T, T, T, T, H, H, T, H, T.$$

Furthermore, the individual assigns the same probability to any other sequence of 10 tosses that has 4 heads and 6 tails.

Next, we show more examples. In these examples we only compute the probability of the first outcome because the probability of the second outcome is uniquely determined by it.

Example 12.3 Suppose you are going to repeatedly toss a coin from your pocket. Because you would feel it highly probable that the relative frequency is around .5, you might feel your prior experience is equivalent to having seen 50 heads in 100 tosses. Therefore, you could represent your belief with $a = 50$ and $b = 50$. Then $m = 50 + 50 = 100$, and your prior probability of heads is

$$P(heads) = \frac{a}{m} = \frac{50}{100} = .5.$$

After seeing 48 heads in 100 tosses, your posterior probability is

$$P(heads|48, 52) = \frac{a + s}{m + n} = \frac{50 + 48}{100 + 100} = .49.$$

The notation $48, 52$ on the right of the conditioning bar in $P(heads|48, 52)$ represents the event that 48 heads and 52 tails have occurred.   ■

Example 12.4 Suppose you are going to repeatedly toss a thumbtack. Based on its structure, you might feel it should land heads about half the time, but you are not nearly so confident as you were with the coin from your pocket. So, you might feel your prior experience is equivalent to having seen 3 heads in 6 tosses. Then your prior probability of heads is

$$P(heads) = \frac{a}{m} = \frac{3}{6} = .5.$$

After seeing 65 heads in 100 tosses, your posterior probability is

$$P(heads|65, 35) = \frac{a + s}{m + n} = \frac{3 + 65}{6 + 100} = .64.$$

■

Example 12.5 Suppose you are going to sample individuals in the United States and determine whether they brush their teeth. In this case, you might feel your prior experience is equivalent to having seen 18 individuals brush their teeth out of 20 sampled. Then your prior probability of brushing is

$$P(brushes) = \frac{a}{m} = \frac{18}{20} = .9.$$

After sampling 100 individuals and learning that 80 brush their teeth, your posterior probability is

$$P(brushes|80, 20) = \frac{a + s}{m + n} = \frac{18 + 80}{20 + 100} = .82.$$

■

You could feel that if we have complete prior ignorance as to the probability, we should take $a = b = 0$. However, consider the next example.

Example 12.6 Suppose we are going to sample dogs and determine whether or not they eat the potato chips we offer them. Because we have no idea whether a particular dog would eat potato chips, we assign $a = b = 0$, which means $m = 0 + 0 = 0$. Because we cannot divide a by m, we have no prior probability. Suppose next that we sample one dog, and that dog eats the potato chips. Our probability of the next dog eating potato chips is now

$$P(eats|1,0) = \frac{a+s}{m+n} = \frac{0+1}{0+1} = 1.$$

This belief is not very reasonable, because it means that we are certain that all dogs eat potato chips. Owing to difficulties such as this and more rigorous mathematical results, prior ignorance to a probability is usually modeled by taking $a = b = 1$, which means $m = 1 + 1 = 2$. If we use these values instead, our posterior probability when the first sampled dog was found to eat potato chips is given by

$$P(eats|1,0) = \frac{a+s}{m+n} = \frac{1+1}{2+1} = \frac{2}{3}.$$

∎

12.1.2 Multinomial Random Variables

The method just discussed readily extends to multinomial random variables. We have the following theorem.

Theorem 12.2 Suppose we are about to repeatedly perform an experiment with k outcomes $x_1, x_2, \ldots, x_k$. Suppose further we assume exchangeability, and we represent our prior belief concerning the probability of the k outcomes using a **Dirichlet distribution** with parameters $a_1, a_2, \ldots, a_k$. Then our prior probabilities are

$$P(x_1) = \frac{a_1}{m} \qquad P(x_2) = \frac{a_2}{m} \qquad \cdots \qquad P(x_k) = \frac{a_k}{m},$$

where $m = a_1 + a_2 + \cdots + a_k$. After seeing x_1 occur s_1 times, x_2 occur s_2 times, ..., and x_n occur s_n times in $n = s_1 + s_2 + \cdots + s_k$ trials, our posterior probabilities are as follows:

$$P(x_1|s_1, s_2, \ldots, s_k) = \frac{a_1 + s_1}{m + n}$$

$$P(x_2|s_1, s_2, \ldots, s_k) = \frac{a_2 + s_2}{m + n}$$

$$\vdots$$

$$P(x_k|s_1, s_2, \ldots, s_k) = \frac{a_k + s_k}{m + n}.$$

Proof. The proof can be found in [Neapolitan, 2004]. ∎

Notice that in Theorem 12.1 we represented our belief using a beta distribution, and in Theorem 12.2 we used a Dirichlet distribution. The beta distribution is the same as the Dirichlet distribution when there are only two parameters, and Theorem 12.1 is a special case of Theorem 12.2.

We ascertain the numbers $a_1, a_2, \ldots, a_k$ by equating our experience to having seen the first outcome occur a_1 times, the second outcome occur a_2 times, $\ldots$, and the last outcome occur a_k times.

Example 12.7 Suppose we have an asymmetrical, six-sided die, and we have little idea of the probability of each side coming up. However, it seems that all sides are equally likely. So, we assign

$$a_1 = a_2 = \cdots = a_6 = 3.$$

Then our prior probabilities are as follows:

$$P(1) = P(2) = \cdots = P(6) = \frac{a_i}{n} = \frac{3}{18} = .16667.$$

Suppose next we throw the die 100 times, with the following results:

Outcome	Number of Occurrences
1	10
2	15
3	5
4	30
5	13
6	27

We then have

$$P(1|10, 15, 5, 30, 13, 27) \quad = \quad \frac{a_1 + s_1}{m + n} = \frac{3 + 10}{18 + 100} = .110$$

$$P(2|10, 15, 5, 30, 13, 27) \quad = \quad \frac{a_2 + s_2}{m + n} = \frac{3 + 15}{18 + 100} = .153.$$

It is left as an exercise to compute the remaining four probabilities. ∎

12.2   Learning Parameters in a Bayesian Network

The method for learning parameters in a Bayesian network follows readily from the method for learning a single parameter. We illustrate the method with binomial variables. It extends readily to the case of multinomial variables (see [Neapolitan, 2004]). After showing the method, we discuss equivalent sample sizes.

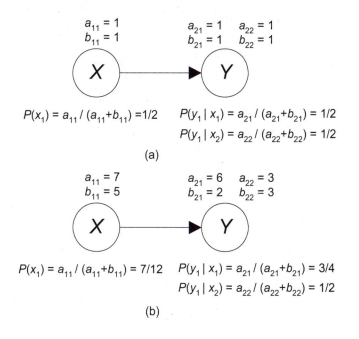

$P(x_1) = a_{11} / (a_{11}+b_{11}) = 1/2$ $P(y_1 | x_1) = a_{21} / (a_{21}+b_{21}) = 1/2$

$P(y_1 | x_2) = a_{22} / (a_{22}+b_{22}) = 1/2$

(a)

$P(x_1) = a_{11} / (a_{11}+b_{11}) = 7/12$ $P(y_1 | x_1) = a_{21} / (a_{21}+b_{21}) = 3/4$

$P(y_1 | x_2) = a_{22} / (a_{22}+b_{22}) = 1/2$

(b)

Figure 12.1 A Bayesian network for parameter learning appears in (a); the updated network based on the data in Figure 12.2 appears in (b).

12.2.1   Procedure for Learning Parameters

Consider the two-node network in Figure 12.1 (a). We call such a network a **Bayesian network for parameter learning**. For each probability in the network, there is a pair (a_{ij}, b_{ij}). The i indexes the variable; the j indexes the value of the parent(s) of the variable. For example, the pair (a_{11}, b_{11}) is for the first variable (X) and the first value of its parent (in this case there is a default of one parent value because X has no parent). The pair (a_{21}, b_{21}) is for the second variable (Y) and the first value of its parent, namely x_1. The pair (a_{22}, b_{22}) is for the second variable (Y) and the second value of its parent, namely x_2. We have attempted to represent prior ignorance as to the value of all probabilities by taking $a_{ij} = b_{ij} = 1$. We compute the prior probabilities using these pairs, just as we did when we were considering a single parameter. We have the following:

$$P(x_1) = \frac{a_{11}}{a_{11} + b_{11}} = \frac{1}{1+1} = \frac{1}{2}$$

$$P(y_1|x_1) = \frac{a_{21}}{a_{21} + b_{21}} = \frac{1}{1+1} = \frac{1}{2}$$

$$P(y_1|x_2) = \frac{a_{22}}{a_{22} + b_{22}} = \frac{1}{1+1} = \frac{1}{2}.$$

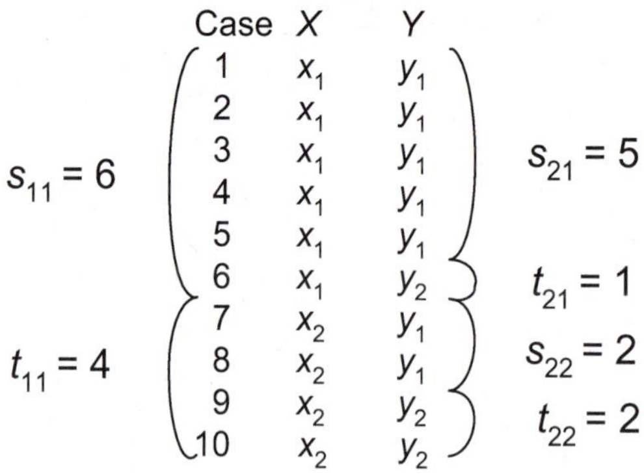

$$
\begin{array}{ccc}
\text{Case} & X & Y \\
1 & x_1 & y_1 \\
2 & x_1 & y_1 \\
3 & x_1 & y_1 \\
4 & x_1 & y_1 \\
5 & x_1 & y_1 \\
6 & x_1 & y_2 \\
7 & x_2 & y_1 \\
8 & x_2 & y_1 \\
9 & x_2 & y_2 \\
10 & x_2 & y_2
\end{array}
$$

$s_{11} = 6$

$t_{11} = 4$

$s_{21} = 5$

$t_{21} = 1$

$s_{22} = 2$

$t_{22} = 2$

Figure 12.2 Data on 10 cases.

When we obtain data, we use an (s_{ij}, t_{ij}) pair to represent the counts for the ith variable when the variable's parents have their jth value. Suppose we obtain the data in Figure 12.2. The values of the (s_{ij}, t_{ij}) pairs are shown in that figure. We have that $s_{11} = 6$ because x_1 occurs six times, and $t_{11} = 4$ because x_2 occurs four times. Of the six times that x_1 occurs, y_1 occurs five times and y_2 occurs one time. So, $s_{21} = 5$ and $t_{21} = 1$. Of the four times that x_2 occurs, y_1 occurs two times and y_2 occurs two times. So, $s_{22} = 2$ and $t_{22} = 2$. To determine the posterior probability distribution based on the data, we update each conditional probability with the counts relative to that conditional probability. Because we want an updated Bayesian network, we recompute the values of the (a_{ij}, b_{ij}) pairs. We therefore have the following:

$$
\begin{aligned}
a_{11} &= a_{11} + s_{11} = 1 + 6 = 7 \\
b_{11} &= b_{11} + t_{11} = 1 + 4 = 5
\end{aligned}
$$

$$
\begin{aligned}
a_{21} &= a_{21} + s_{21} = 1 + 5 = 6 \\
b_{21} &= b_{21} + t_{21} = 1 + 1 = 2
\end{aligned}
$$

$$
\begin{aligned}
a_{22} &= a_{22} + s_{22} = 1 + 2 = 3 \\
b_{22} &= b_{22} + t_{22} = 1 + 2 = 3.
\end{aligned}
$$

We then compute the new values of the parameters:

$$
P(x_1) = \frac{a_{11}}{a_{11} + b_{11}} = \frac{7}{7 + 5} = \frac{7}{12}
$$

$$
P(y_1 | x_1) = \frac{a_{21}}{a_{21} + b_{21}} = \frac{6}{6 + 2} = \frac{3}{4}
$$

$$
P(y_1 | x_2) = \frac{a_{22}}{a_{22} + b_{22}} = \frac{3}{3 + 3} = \frac{1}{2}.
$$

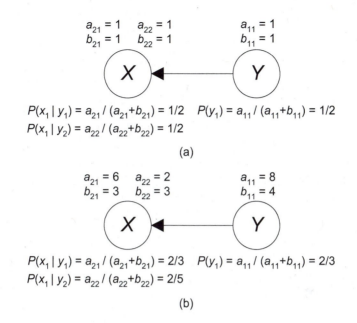

Figure 12.3 A Bayesian network initialized for parameter learning appears in (a); the updated network based on the data in Figure 12.2 appears in (b).

The updated network is shown in Figure 12.1 (b).

12.2.2 Equivalent Sample Size

There is a problem with the way we represented prior ignorance in the preceding subsection. Although it seems natural to set $a_{ij} = b_{ij} = 1$ to represent prior ignorance of all the conditional probabilities, such assignments are not consistent with the metaphor we used for articulating these values. Recall that we said the probability assessor is to choose values of a and b such that the assessor's experience is equivalent to having seen the first outcome occur a times in $a + b$ trials. Therefore, if we set $a_{11} = b_{11} = 1$, the assessor's experience is equivalent to having seen x_1 occur one time in two trials. However, if we set $a_{21} = b_{21} = 1$, the assessor's experience is equivalent to having seen y_1 occur one time out of the two times x_1 occurred. This is not consistent. First, we are saying x_1 occurred once; then we are saying it occurred twice. Aside from this inconsistency, we obtain odd results if we use these priors.

Consider the Bayesian network for parameter learning in Figure 12.3 (a). If we update that network with the data in Figure 12.2, we obtain the network in Figure 12.3 (b). The DAG in Figure 12.3 (a) is Markov equivalent to the one in Figure 12.1 (b). It seems that if we represent the same prior beliefs with equivalent DAGs, then the posterior distributions based on data should be the same. In this case we have attempted to represent prior ignorance as to all probabilities with the networks in Figure 12.1 (a) and Figure 12.3 (a). So, the posterior distributions based on the data in Figure 12.2 should be the same. However, from the Bayesian network in Figure 12.1 (b), we have

$$P(x_1) = \frac{7}{12} = .583,$$

whereas from the Bayesian network in Figure 12.3 (b) we have

$$
\begin{aligned}
P(x_1) &= P(x_1|y_1)P(y_1) + P(x_1|y_2)P(y_2) \\
&= \frac{2}{3} \times \frac{2}{3} + \frac{2}{5} \times \frac{1}{3} = .578.
\end{aligned}
$$

We see that we obtain different posterior probabilities. Such results are not only odd, but unacceptable because we have attempted to model the same prior belief with the Bayesian networks in Figures 12.1 (a) and 12.3 (a), but we end up with different posterior beliefs.

We can eliminate this difficulty by using a prior equivalent sample size. That is, we specify values of a_{ij} and b_{ij} that could actually occur in a prior sample that exhibit the conditional independencies entailed by the DAG. For example, given the network $X \rightarrow Y$, if we specify that $a_{21} = b_{21} = 1$, this means our prior sample must have x_1 occurring two times. So, we need to specify $a_{11} = 2$. Similarly, if we specify that $a_{22} = b_{22} = 1$, this means that our prior sample must have x_2 occurring two times. So, we need to specify $b_{11} = 2$. Note that we are not saying we actually have a prior sample. We are saying that the probability assessor's beliefs are represented by a prior sample. Figure 12.4 shows prior Bayesian networks using equivalent sample sizes. Notice that the values of a_{ij} and b_{ij} in these networks represent the following prior sample:

Case	X	Y
1	x_1	y_1
2	x_1	y_2
3	x_2	y_1
4	x_2	y_2

It is left as an exercise to show that if we update both the Bayesian networks in Figure 12.4 using the data in Figure 12.2, we obtain the same posterior probability distribution. This result is true, in general, when we use a prior equivalent sample size; the proof can be found in [Neapolitan, 2004]. Presently, we give a formal definition of a prior equivalent sample size.

Definition 12.1 Suppose we specify a Bayesian network for parameter learning in the case of binomial variables. If there is a number α such that for all i and j we have that

$$a_{ij} + b_{ij} = P(\mathsf{pa}_{ij}) \times \alpha,$$

where pa_{ij} denotes the jth instantiation of the parents of the ith variable, then we say the network has **prior equivalent sample size** α.♦

This definition is a bit hard to grasp by itself. The following theorem, whose proof can be found in [Neapolitan, 2004], yields a way to represent uniform prior distributions, which is often what we want to do.

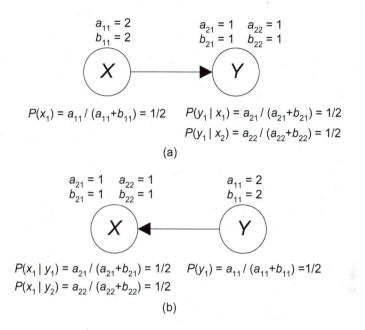

$$P(x_1) = a_{11} / (a_{11}+b_{11}) = 1/2 \quad P(y_1 | x_1) = a_{21} / (a_{21}+b_{21}) = 1/2$$
$$P(y_1 | x_2) = a_{22} / (a_{22}+b_{22}) = 1/2$$

(a)

$$P(x_1 | y_1) = a_{21} / (a_{21}+b_{21}) = 1/2 \quad P(y_1) = a_{11} / (a_{11}+b_{11}) = 1/2$$
$$P(x_1 | y_2) = a_{22} / (a_{22}+b_{22}) = 1/2$$

(b)

Figure 12.4 Bayesian networks for parameter learning containing prior equivalent sample sizes.

Theorem 12.3 Suppose we specify a Bayesian network for parameter learning in the case of binomial variables and assign for all i and j

$$a_{ij} = b_{ij} = \frac{\alpha}{2q_i}$$

where N is a positive integer and q_i is the number of instantiations of the parents of the ith variable. Then the resultant Bayesian network has equivalent sample size α, and the joint probability distribution in the Bayesian network is uniform.

Figure 12.4 (a) shows a Bayesian network for parameter learning obtained using Theorem 12.3 with $\alpha = 4$.

We developed the method for learning parameters in a Bayesian network in the case of binomial variables. It extends readily to multinomial variables. See [Neapolitan, 2004] for that extension.

12.3   Learning Parameters with Missing Data★

So far we have considered data sets in which every value of every variable is recorded in every case. Next, we consider the case where some data items might be omitted. How might they be omitted? A common way, and indeed a way that is relatively easy to handle, is that they are simply random omissions due to recording problems or some similar error. We present that case.

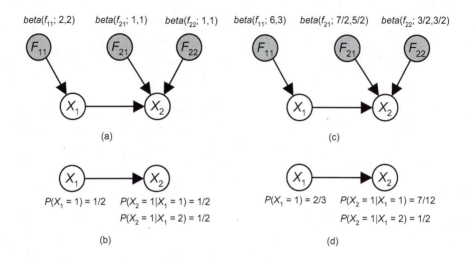

Figure 12.5 The network in (a) has been updated to the network in (c) using a first pass of the EM Algorithm.

First, we need to provide more formal notation than that used so far. Recall that in Theorem 12.1 we said that we were representing our prior belief concerning the probability of heads using a **beta distribution** with parameters a and b. Formally, this means we are considering the probability of heads a random variable F, and that this random variable has a beta distribution with parameters a and b. The beta density function is as follows:

$$beta(f : a, b) = \frac{\Gamma(a + b)}{\Gamma(a)\Gamma(b)} f^{a-1}(1 - f)^{b-1} \qquad 0 \le f \le 1.$$

The formal statement of Theorem 12.1 is that if

$$\rho(f) = beta(f : a, b)$$

then

$$\rho(f|\mathsf{D}) = beta(f : a + s, b + t), \tag{12.3}$$

where the data D consists of s occurrences of the first alternative and t occurrences of the second alternative.

Now we show how to update parameters based on data containing data items missing at random. Before discussing how to update based on such data, let's review how we update when no data items are missing. Figure 12.5 (a) shows a Bayesian network where now we have explicitly included random variables for the parameters. Such a network is called an **augmented Bayesian network**. We denote the set of all random variables F_{ij} in the network as F. Suppose we want to update that network with the data D in Table 12.1. Let s_{21} be the number of cases that have X_1 equal to 1 and X_2 equal to 1, and t_{21} be the

Table 12.1 Data on 5 Cases

Case	X_1	X_2
1	1	1
2	1	1
3	1	1
4	1	2
5	2	2

Table 12.2 Data on 5 Cases with Some Data Items Missing

Case	X_1	X_2
1	1	1
2	1	?
3	1	1
4	1	2
5	2	?

number of cases that have X_1 equal to 1 and X_2 equal to 2. We then have that

$$s_{21} = 3$$
$$t_{21} = 1.$$

Therefore,

$$\rho(f_{21}|\mathsf{D}) = beta(f_{21}; a_{21} + s_{21}, b_{21} + t_{21})$$
$$= beta(f_{21}; 1 + 3, 1 + 1)$$
$$= beta(f_{21}; 4, 2).$$

Suppose next that we want to update the network in Figure 12.5 (a) with the data D in Table 12.2. These data contain missing data items. We do not know the value of X_2 for cases 2 and 5. It seems reasonable to estimate the value of X_2 in these cases using $P(X_2 = 1|X_1 = 1)$. That is, because this probability equals $1/2$, we say X_2 has a $1/2$ occurrence of 1 in each of cases 2 and 5. So we replace the data D in Table 12.2 by the data D′ in Table 12.3. We then update

Table 12.3 Estimates of Missing Values

Case	X_1	X_2	# Occurences
1	1	1	1
2	1	1	1/2
2	1	2	1/2
3	1	1	1
4	1	2	1
5	2	1	1/2
5	2	2	1/2

our density functions using the number of occurrences listed in Table 12.3. So
we have

$$s'_{21} = 1 + \tfrac{1}{2} + 1 = \tfrac{5}{2} \tag{12.4}$$
$$t'_{21} = \tfrac{1}{2} + 1 = \tfrac{3}{2},$$

$$s'_{22} = \tfrac{1}{2} \tag{12.5}$$
$$t'_{22} = \tfrac{1}{2},$$

where s'_{21}, t'_{21}, s'_{22}, and t'_{22} denote the counts in data D' (shown in Table 12.3).
We then have

$$
\begin{aligned}
\rho(f_{21}|D') &= beta(f_{21}; a_{21} + s'_{21}, b_{21} + t'_{21}) \\
&= beta\left(f_{21}; 1 + \tfrac{5}{2}, 1 + \tfrac{3}{2}\right) \\
&= beta\left(f_{21}; \tfrac{7}{2}, \tfrac{5}{2}\right)
\end{aligned}
$$

and

$$
\begin{aligned}
\rho(f_{22}|D') &= beta(f_{21}; a_{22} + s'_{22}, b_{22} + t'_{22}) \\
&= beta\left(f_{21}; 1 + \tfrac{1}{2}, 1 + \tfrac{1}{2}\right) \\
&= beta\left(f_{21}; \tfrac{3}{2}, \tfrac{3}{2}\right).
\end{aligned}
$$

The updated network is shown in Figure 12.5 (c).

If we let S_{ij} and T_{ij} be random variables denoting the counts in the complete
data set, the method just outlined determines the expected value of these counts
relative to the joint probability distribution of X_1 and X_2 conditional on the data
and on the variables in F having their prior expected values. That is, if we set

$$
\begin{aligned}
f_{11} &= \frac{2}{2+2} = \frac{1}{2} \\
f_{21} &= \frac{1}{1+1} = \frac{1}{2} \\
f_{21} &= \frac{1}{1+1} = \frac{1}{2}
\end{aligned}
$$

then

$$\mathbf{f} = \{f_{11}, f_{21}, f_{22}\} = \{1/2, 1/2, 1/2\}$$

and

$$
\begin{aligned}
s'_{21} = E(S_{21}|D, \mathbf{f}) &= \sum_{h=1}^{5} 1 \times P(X_1^{(h)} = 1, X_2^{(h)} = 1|D, \mathbf{f}) \tag{12.6} \\
&= \sum_{h=1}^{5} P(X_1^{(h)} = 1, X_2^{(h)} = 1|\mathbf{x}^{(h)}, \mathbf{f}) \\
&= \sum_{h=1}^{5} P(X_1^{(h)} = 1, X_2^{(h)} = 1|x_1^{(h)}, x_2^{(h)}, \mathbf{f}) \\
&= 1 + \tfrac{1}{2} + 1 + 0 + 0 = \tfrac{5}{2}.
\end{aligned}
$$

In the preceding equality, $\mathbf{X}^{(h)} = \{X_1^{(h)}, X_2^{(h)}\}$ represents the value of the hth data item. Similarly,

$$t_{21}' = E(T_{21}|\mathsf{D}, \mathsf{f}) = 0 + \tfrac{1}{2} + 0 + 1 + 0 = \tfrac{3}{2}.$$

Furthermore,

$$
\begin{aligned}
s_{22}' = E(S_{22}|\mathsf{D}, \mathsf{f}) &= \sum_{h=1}^{5} 1 \times P(X_1^{(h)} = 1, X_2^{(h)} = 2|\mathsf{D}, \mathsf{f}) \\
&= \sum_{h=1}^{5} P(X_1^{(h)} = 1, X_2^{(h)} = 2|\mathbf{x}^{(h)}, \mathsf{f}) \\
&= \sum_{h=1}^{5} P(X_1^{(h)} = 1, X_2^{(h)} = 2|x_1^{(h)}, x_2^{(h)}, \mathsf{f}) \\
&= 0 + 0 + 0 + 0 + \tfrac{1}{2} = \tfrac{1}{2}
\end{aligned}
$$

and

$$t_{22}' = E(T_{22}|\mathsf{D}, \mathsf{f}) = 0 + 0 + 0 + 0 + \tfrac{1}{2} = \tfrac{1}{2}.$$

Note that these are the same values obtained in Equalities 12.4 and 12.5.

Using these expected values to estimate our density functions seems reasonable. However, note that our estimates are based only on our prior sample. They are not based on the data D. That is, we say X_2 has a $1/2$ occurrence of 1 in each of cases 2 and 5 because $P(X_2 = 1|X_1 = 1) = 1/2$ according to our prior sample. However, the data D *prefers* the event $X_1 = 1, X_2 = 1$ to the event $X_1 = 1, X_2 = 2$ because the former event occurs twice while the latter event occurs only once. To incorporate the data D in our estimates, we can now repeat the computation in Expression 12.6 using the probability distribution in the updated network (Figures 12.5 (c) and (d)). That is, if we set

$$
\begin{aligned}
f_{11} &= \frac{6}{6+3} = \frac{2}{3} \\
f_{21} &= \frac{7/2}{7/2+5/2} = \frac{7}{12} \\
f_{21} &= \frac{3/2}{3/2+3/2} = \frac{1}{2}
\end{aligned}
$$

then

$$\mathsf{f} = \{f_{11}, f_{21}, f_{22}\} = \{2/3, 7/12, 1/2\}$$

and

$$
\begin{aligned}
s'_{21} = E(S_{21}|D, f) &= \sum_{h=1}^{5} 1 \times P(X_1^{(h)} = 1, X_2^{(h)} = 1|D, f) \\
&= \sum_{h=1}^{5} P(X_1^{(h)} = 1, X_2^{(h)} = 1|x^{(h)}, f) \\
&= \sum_{h=1}^{5} P(X_1^{(h)} = 1, X_2^{(h)} = 1|x_1^{(h)}, x_2^{(h)}, f') \\
&= 1 + \tfrac{7}{12} + 1 + 0 + 0 = 2\tfrac{7}{12}.
\end{aligned}
$$

Similarly,

$$
t'_{21} = E(T_{21}|D, f) = 0 + \tfrac{5}{12} + 0 + 1 + 0 = 1\tfrac{5}{12}.
$$

We re-compute s'_{22} and t'_{22} in the same manner.

Clearly, we can keep repeating the previous two steps. Suppose we reiterate these steps, let $s_{ij}^{(v)}$ and $t_{ij}^{(v)}$ be the values of s'_{ij} and t'_{ij} after the vth iteration, and take the

$$
\lim_{v \to \infty} f_{ij} = \lim_{v \to \infty} \frac{a_{ij} + s_{ij}^{(v)}}{a_{ij} + s_{ij}^{(v)} + b_{ij} + t_{ij}^{(v)}}.
$$

Then under certain regularity conditions, the limit is a value of f that locally maximizes $\rho(f|D)$[1].

The procedure we have just described is an application of the EM Algorithm ([Dempster et al., 1977]; [McLachlan and Krishnan, 2008]). In this algorithm, the step in which we recompute s'_{ij} and t'_{ij} is called the **expectation step**, and the step in which we recompute the value of f is called the **maximization step** because we are approaching a local maximum.

The value of f that maximizes $\rho(f|D)$ is called the **maximum a posteriori probability (MAP)** value of f. We want to arrive at this value rather than at a local maximum. After presenting the algorithm, we discuss a way to avoid a local maximum.

Algorithm 12.1 EM-MAP-Determination

Input: Binomial augmented Bayesian network $(\mathbb{G}, \mathsf{F}, \rho)$ and data D containing some incomplete data items.

Output: Estimate f of the MAP value of the parameter set F.

Procedure $MAP(\ (\mathbb{G}, \mathsf{F}, \rho),\ \mathsf{D},\ \mathbf{var}\ f)$
for $i = 1$ **to** n
    for $j = 1$ **to** q_i
        assign f_{ij} a value in the interval $(0, 1)$;

---

[1] The maximizing values actually depend on the coordinate systems used to express the parameters. The ones given here correspond to the canonical coordinate system for the multinomial distribution (see, e.g., [Bernardo and Smith, 1994].).

repeat k times   // the number of iterations
    for $i = 1$ **to** n // expectation step
        for $j = 1$ **to** q_i
$$s'_{ij} = E(S_{ij}|D, f) = \sum_h P(X_i^{(h)} = 1, \mathsf{pa}_{ij}|x^{(h)}, f);$$
$$t'_{ij} = E(T_{ij}|D, f) = \sum_h P(X_i^{(h)} = 2, \mathsf{pa}_{ij}|x^{(h)}, f);$$
        endfor
    endfor
    for $i = 1$ **to** n // maximization step
        for $j = 1$ **to** q_i
$$f_{ij} = \frac{a_{ij} + s'_{ij}}{a_{ij} + s'_{ij} + b_{ij} + t'_{ij}};$$
        endfor
    endfor
endrepeat

Note that in the algorithm we initialized the algorithm by saying "assign f_{ij} a value in the interval $(0, 1)$" rather than setting $f_{ij} = a_{ij}/(a_{ij} + b_{ij})$ as we did in our illustration. We want to end up with the MAP value of f; however, in general, we could end up with a local maximum when starting with any particular configuration of f'. So we do not start at only one particular configuration. Rather, we use multiple restarts of the algorithm. The following is a multiple-restart strategy discussed in [Chickering and Heckerman, 1997]. We sample 64 prior configurations of the variables in F according to a uniform distribution. By a configuration of the variables, we mean an assignment of values to the variables. Next, we perform one expectation and one maximization step, and we retain the 32 initial configurations that yielded the 32 values of f with the largest values of $\rho(f|D)$. Then we perform two expectation and maximization steps, and we retain 16 initial configurations using this same rule. We continue in this manner, in each iteration doubling the number of expectation-maximization steps, until only one configuration remains. You may wonder how we could determine which values of f had the largest values of $\rho(f|D)$ when we do not know this density function. For any value of f we have

$$\rho(f|D) = \alpha\rho(D|f)\rho(f),$$

which means we can determine whether $\rho(f'|D)$ or $\rho(f''|D)$ is larger by comparing $\rho(D|f')\rho(f')$ and $\rho(D|f'')\rho(f'')$. To compute $\rho(D|f)\rho(f)$, we simply calculate $\rho(f)$ and determine $\rho(D|f) = \prod_{h=1}^M P(x^{(h)}|f)$ using a Bayesian network inference algorithm.

The **maximum likelihood estimate (MLE)** value of f is the value such that $P(D|f)$ is a maximum. Algorithm 12.1 can be modified to produce the ML value. We simply update as follows:

$$f_{ij} = \frac{s'_{ij}}{s'_{ij} + t'_{ij}}.$$

A parameterized EM algorithm, which has faster convergence, is discussed in [Bauer et al., 1997]. The EM Algorithm is not the only method for handling missing data items. Other methods include Monte Carlo techniques, in particular Gibb's sampling, which is discussed in Section 13.2.6.2.

EXERCISES

Section 12.1

Exercise 12.1 For some two-outcome experiment that you can repeat indefinitely (such as the tossing of a thumbtack), determine the number of occurrences a and b of each outcome that you feel your prior experience is equivalent to having seen. Determine the probability of the first outcome.

Exercise 12.2 Assume that you feel your prior experience concerning the relative frequency of smokers in a particular bar is equivalent to having seen 14 smokers and 6 nonsmokers.

1. You then decide to poll individuals in the bar and ask them if they smoke. What is your probability of the first individual you poll being a smoker?

2. Suppose that after polling 10 individuals, you obtain these data (the value 1 means the individual smokes and 2 means the individual does not smoke):
$$\{1, 2, 2, 2, 2, 2, 1, 2, 2, 2, 1\}.$$
What is your probability that the next individual you poll is a smoker?

3. Suppose that after polling 1000 individuals (it is a big bar), you learn that 312 are smokers. What is your probability that the next individual you poll is a smoker? How does this probability compare to your prior probability?

Exercise 12.3 Find a rectangular block (not a cube) and label the sides. Determine values of $a_1, a_2, \ldots, a_6$ that represent your prior probability concerning each side coming up when you throw the block.

1. What is your probability of each side coming up on the first throw?

2. Throw the block 20 times. Compute your probability of each side coming up on the next throw.

Exercise 12.4 Suppose that you are going to sample individuals who have smoked two packs of cigarettes or more daily for the past 10 years. You will determine whether each individual's systolic blood pressure is ≤ 100, 101–120, 121–140, 141–160, or ≥ 161. Determine values of $a_1, a_2, \ldots, a_5$ that represent your prior probability of each blood pressure range.

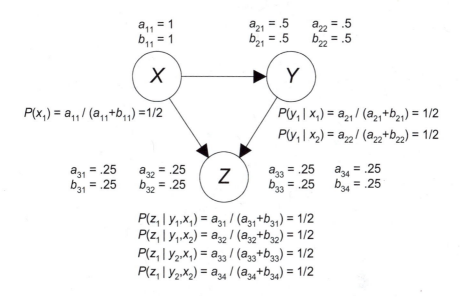

$$P(x_1) = a_{11}/(a_{11}+b_{11}) = 1/2$$

$$P(y_1 \mid x_1) = a_{21}/(a_{21}+b_{21}) = 1/2$$
$$P(y_1 \mid x_2) = a_{22}/(a_{22}+b_{22}) = 1/2$$

$$P(z_1 \mid y_1,x_1) = a_{31}/(a_{31}+b_{31}) = 1/2$$
$$P(z_1 \mid y_1,x_2) = a_{32}/(a_{32}+b_{32}) = 1/2$$
$$P(z_1 \mid y_2,x_1) = a_{33}/(a_{33}+b_{33}) = 1/2$$
$$P(z_1 \mid y_2,x_2) = a_{34}/(a_{34}+b_{34}) = 1/2$$

Figure 12.6 A Bayesian network for parameter learning.

1. Next, you sample such smokers. What is your probability of each blood pressure range for the first individual sampled?

2. Suppose that after sampling 100 individuals, you obtain the following results:

Blood Pressure Range	# of Individuals in This Range
≤ 100	2
101–120	15
121–140	23
141–160	25
≥ 161	35

Compute your probability of each range for the next individual sampled.

Section 12.2

Exercise 12.5 Suppose that we have the Bayesian network for parameter learning in Figure 12.6, and we have the following data:

Case	X	Y	Z
1	x_1	y_2	z_1
2	x_1	y_1	z_2
3	x_2	y_1	z_1
4	x_2	y_2	z_1
5	x_1	y_2	z_1
6	x_2	y_2	z_2
7	x_1	y_2	z_1
8	x_2	y_1	z_2
9	x_1	y_2	z_1
10	x_1	y_1	z_1
11	x_1	y_2	z_1
12	x_2	y_1	z_2
13	x_1	y_2	z_1
14	x_2	y_2	z_2
15	x_1	y_2	z_1

Determine the updated Bayesian network for parameter learning.

Exercise 12.6 Use the method in Theorem 12.3 to develop Bayesian networks for parameter learning with equivalent sample sizes 1, 2, 4, and 8 for the DAG in Figure 12.7.

Section 12.3

Exercise 12.7 In the text, we updated the augmented Bayesian network in Figure 12.5 (a) with the data **d** in Table 12.2 using two iterations of Algorithm 12.1. Starting with the results in the text, perform the next two iterations.

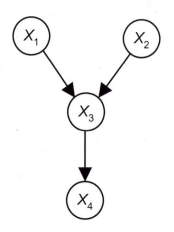

Figure 12.7 A DAG.

Chapter 13

Learning Probabilistic Model Structure

In the previous chapter we addressed the problem of parameter learning in a Bayesian network. In this chapter we discuss structure learning. Section 13.1 introduces the problem of Bayesian network structure learning from data. Sections 13.2 and 13.3 discuss two different techniques for learning that structure. Then Section 13.4 provides a large-scale example of structure learning. Next,

Table 13.1 Data on 12 Workers

Case	Sex	Height (inches)	Wage ($)
1	female	64	30,000
2	male	64	30,000
3	female	64	40,000
4	female	64	40,000
5	female	68	30,000
6	female	68	40,000
7	male	64	40,000
8	male	64	50,000
9	male	68	40,000
10	male	68	50,000
11	male	70	40,000
12	male	70	50,000

Section 13.5 introduces software packages for learning structure, and Section 13.6 shows how we can use Bayesian network structure learning to learn something about causal influences. Finally, Section 13.7 concerns class probability trees, which are used for learning structure when we have a single target variable.

13.1 Structure Learning Problem

Bayesian network **Structure learning** concerns learning the DAG in a Bayesian network from data. To accomplish this, we need to learn a DAG that satisfies the Markov condition with the probability distribution P that is generating the data. Note that we do not know P; all we know are the data. The process of learning such a DAG is called **model selection**.

Example 13.1 Suppose we want to model the probability distribution P of sex, height, and wage for American workers. We may obtain the data on 12 workers appearing in Table 13.1. We do not know the probability distribution P. However, from these data we want to learn a DAG that is likely to satisfy the Markov condition with P.   ■

If our only goal was simply learning some DAG that satisfied the Markov condition with P, our task would be trivial because, as discussed in Section 7.2.1, a probability distribution P satisfies the Markov condition with every complete DAG containing the variables over which P is defined. Recall that our goal with a Bayesian network is to represent a probability distribution succinctly. A complete DAG does not accomplish this because, if there are n binomial variables, the last variable in a complete DAG would require 2^{n-1} conditional distributions. To represent a distribution P succinctly, we need to find a sparse DAG (one containing few edges) that satisfies the Markov condition with P. Next we present methods for doing this.

13.2   Score-Based Structure Learning

In **score-based structure learning**, we assign a score to a DAG based on how well the DAG fits the data.

13.2.1   Bayesian Score

The **Bayesian score** is the probability of the data D given the DAG. We present this score shortly. First we need to discuss the probability of data.

13.2.1.1   Probability of Data

Suppose that we are going to toss the same coin two times in a row. Let X_1 be a random variable whose value is the result of the first toss, and let X_2 be a random variable whose value is the result of the second toss. If we know that the probability of heads for this coin is .5 and make the usual assumption that the outcomes of the two tosses are independent, we have

$$P(X_1 = heads, X_2 = heads) = \frac{1}{2} \times \frac{1}{2} = \frac{1}{4}.$$

This is a standard result. Suppose now that we are going to toss a thumbtack two times in a row. Suppose further we represent our prior belief concerning the probability of heads using a Dirichlet distribution with parameters a and b (as discussed in Section 12.1.1), and we represent prior ignorance of the probability of heads by taking $a = b = 1$. If the outcome of the first toss is heads, using the notation developed in Section 12.1.1, our updated probability of heads is

$$P(heads|1,0) = \frac{a+1}{a+b+1} = \frac{1+1}{1+1+1} = \frac{2}{3}.$$

Heads is more probable for the second toss because our belief has changed owing to heads occurring on the first toss. So, using our current notation in which we have identified two random variables, we have that

$$P(X_2 = heads|X_1 = heads) = P(heads|1,0) = \frac{2}{3},$$

and

$$
\begin{aligned}
P(X_1 = heads, X_2 = heads) &= P(X_2 = heads|X_1 = heads)P(X_1 = heads) \\
&= \frac{2}{3} \times \frac{1}{2} = \frac{1}{3}
\end{aligned}
$$

$$
\begin{aligned}
P(X_1 = heads, X_2 = tails) &= P(X_2 = tails|X_1 = heads)P(X_1 = heads) \\
&= \frac{1}{3} \times \frac{1}{2} = \frac{1}{6}
\end{aligned}
$$

$$P(X_1 = tails, X_2 = heads) = P(X_2 = heads|X_1 = tails)P(X_1 = tails)$$
$$= \frac{1}{3} \times \frac{1}{2} = \frac{1}{6}$$

$$P(X_1 = tails, X_2 = tails) = P(X_2 = tails|X_1 = tails)P(X_1 = tails)$$
$$= \frac{2}{3} \times \frac{1}{2} = \frac{1}{3}.$$

It might seem odd that the four outcomes do not have the same probability. However, recall that we do not know the probability of heads. Therefore, we learn something about the probability of heads from the result of the first toss. If heads occurs on the first toss, that probability goes up; if tails occurs, it goes down. So, two consecutive heads or two consecutive tails are more probable *a priori* than a head followed by a tail or a tail followed by a head.

This result extends to a sequence of tosses. For example, suppose we toss the thumbtack three times. Then, owing to the chain rule,

$$P(X_1 = heads, X_2 = tails, X_3 = tails)$$

$$= P(X_3 = tails|X_2 = tails, X_1 = heads)P(X_2 = tails|X_1 = heads)$$
$$\quad P(X_1 = heads)$$
$$= \frac{b+1}{a+b+2} \times \frac{b}{a+b+1} \times \frac{a}{a+b}$$
$$= \frac{1+1}{1+1+2} \times \frac{1}{1+1+1} \times \frac{1}{1+1} = .0833.$$

We get the same probability regardless of the order of the outcomes as long as the number of heads and tails is the same. For example,

$$P(X_1 = tails, X_2 = tails, X_3 = heads)$$

$$= P(X_3 = heads|X_2 = tails, X_1 = tails)P(X_2 = tails|X_1 = tails)$$
$$\quad P(X_1 = tails)$$
$$= \frac{a}{a+b+2} \times \frac{b+1}{a+b+1} \times \frac{b}{a+b}$$
$$= \frac{1}{1+1+2} \times \frac{2}{1+1+1} \times \frac{1}{1+1} = .0833.$$

We now have the following theorem:

Theorem 13.1 Suppose that we are about to repeatedly toss a thumbtack (or perform any repeatable experiment with two outcomes). Suppose further that we assume exchangeability, and we represent our prior belief concerning the probability of heads using a Dirichlet distribution with parameters a and b, where a and b are positive integers and $m = a + b$. Let D be data that consist of s heads and t tails in n trials. Then

$$P(\mathsf{D}) = \frac{(m-1)!}{(m+n-1)!} \times \frac{(a+s-1)!(b+t-1)!}{(a-1)!(b-1)!}.$$

Proof. Because the probability is the same regardless of the order in which the heads and tails occur, we can assume all the heads occur first. We therefore have (as before, the notation s, t on the right side of the conditioning bar means that we have seen s heads and t tails) the following:

$P(\mathsf{D})$

$$
\begin{aligned}
= {} & P(X_{s+t} = tails | s, t-1) \cdots P(X_{s+2} = tails | s, 1) P(X_{s+1} = tails | s, 0) \\
& P(X_s = heads | s-1, 0) \cdots P(X_2 = heads | 1, 0) P(X_1 = heads)
\end{aligned}
$$

$$
\begin{aligned}
= {} & \frac{b+t-1}{a+b+s+t-1} \times \cdots \frac{b+1}{a+b+s+1} \times \frac{b}{a+b+s} \times \\
& \frac{a+s-1}{a+b+s-1} \times \cdots \frac{a+1}{a+b+1} \times \frac{a}{a+b}
\end{aligned}
$$

$$
= \frac{(a+b-1)!}{(a+b+s+t-1)!} \times \frac{(a+s-1)!}{(a-1)!} \times \frac{(b+t-1)!}{(b-1)!}
$$

$$
= \frac{(m-1)!}{(m+n-1)!} \times \frac{(a+s-1)!(b+t-1)!}{(a-1)!(b-1)!}.
$$

The first equality is due to Theorem 12.1. This completes the proof. ∎

Example 13.2 Suppose that, before tossing a thumbtack, we assign $a = 3$ and $b = 5$ to model the slight belief that tails is more probable than heads. We then toss the coin ten times and obtain four heads and six tails. Owing to the preceding theorem, the probability of obtaining these data D is given by

$$
\begin{aligned}
P(\mathsf{D}) &= \frac{(m-1)!}{(m+n-1)!} \times \frac{(a+s-1)!(b+t-1)!}{(a-1)!(b-1)!} \\
&= \frac{(8-1)!}{(8+10-1)!} \times \frac{(3+4-1)!(5+6-1)!}{(3-1)!(5-1)!} = .00077.
\end{aligned}
$$

Note that the probability of these data is very small. This is because there are many possible outcomes (namely 2^{10}) of tossing a thumbtack ten times. ∎

Theorem 13.1 holds, even if a and b are not integers. We merely state the result here.

Theorem 13.2 Suppose we are about to repeatedly toss a thumbtack (or perform any repeatable experiment with two outcomes), we assume exchangeability, and we represent our prior belief concerning the probability of heads using a Dirichlet distribution with parameters a and b, where a and b are positive real numbers and $m = a + b$. Let D be data that consist of s heads and t tails in n trials. Then

$$
P(\mathsf{D}) = \frac{\Gamma(m)}{\Gamma(m+n)} \times \frac{\Gamma(a+s)\Gamma(b+t)}{\Gamma(a)\Gamma(b)}. \tag{13.1}
$$

Proof. The proof can be found in [Neapolitan, 2004]. ∎

In the preceding theorem Γ denotes the gamma function. When n is an integer ≥ 1, we have that

$$\Gamma(n) = (n-1)! \, .$$

So, the preceding theorem generalizes Theorem 13.1.

We developed the method for computing the probability of data for the case of binomial variables. It extends readily to multinomial variables. See [Neapolitan, 2004] for that extension.

13.2.1.2   Learning DAG Models Using the Bayesian Score

Next we show how we score a DAG model by computing the probability of the data given the model and how we use that score to learn a DAG model.

Suppose we have a Bayesian network for learning, as discussed in Section 12.2. For example, we might have the network in Figure 13.1 (a). Here we call such a network a **DAG model**. We can score a DAG model $\mathbb{G}$ based on data D by determining how probable the data are given the DAG model. That is, we compute $P(\mathsf{D}|\mathbb{G})$. The formula for this probability is the same as that developed in Theorem 13.2, except there is a term of the form in Equality 13.1 for each probability in the network. So, the probability of data D given the DAG model $\mathbb{G}_1$ in Figure 13.1 (a) is given by

$$P(\mathsf{D}|\mathbb{G}_1) = \frac{\Gamma(m_{11})}{\Gamma(m_{11} + n_{11})} \times \frac{\Gamma(a_{11} + s_{11})\Gamma(b_{11} + t_{11})}{\Gamma(a_{11})\Gamma(b_{11})} \times \quad (13.2)$$

$$\frac{\Gamma(m_{21})}{\Gamma(m_{21} + n_{21})} \times \frac{\Gamma(a_{21} + s_{21})\Gamma(b_{21} + t_{21})}{\Gamma(a_{21})\Gamma(b_{21})} \times$$

$$\frac{\Gamma(m_{22})}{\Gamma(m_{22} + n_{22})} \times \frac{\Gamma(a_{22} + s_{22})\Gamma(b_{22} + t_{22})}{\Gamma(a_{22})\Gamma(b_{22})} \, .$$

The data used in each term include only the data relevant to the conditional probability the term represents. This is exactly the same scheme that was used to learn parameters in Section 12.2. For example, the value of s_{21} is the number of cases that have J equal to j_2 and F equal to f_1.

Similarly, the probability of data D given the DAG model $\mathbb{G}_2$ in Figure 13.1 (b) is given by

$$P(\mathsf{D}|\mathbb{G}_2) = \frac{\Gamma(m_{11})}{\Gamma(m_{11} + n_{11})} \times \frac{\Gamma(a_{11} + s_{11})\Gamma(b_{11} + t_{11})}{\Gamma(a_{11})\Gamma(b_{11})} \times \quad (13.3)$$

$$\frac{\Gamma(m_{21})}{\Gamma(m_{21} + n_{21})} \times \frac{\Gamma(a_{21} + s_{21})\Gamma(b_{21} + t_{21})}{\Gamma(a_{21})\Gamma(b_{21})} \, .$$

Note that the values of a_{11}, s_{11}, and so on in Equality 13.3 are the ones relevant to $\mathbb{G}_2$ and are not the same values as those in Equality 13.2. We have not explicitly shown their dependence on the DAG model, for the sake of notational simplicity.

Example 13.3 Suppose we want to determine whether job status (J) has a causal effect on whether someone defaults on a loan (F). Furthermore, we articulate just two values for each variable as follows:

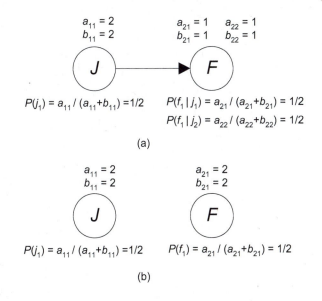

$$a_{11} = 2 \qquad\qquad a_{21} = 1 \qquad a_{22} = 1$$
$$b_{11} = 2 \qquad\qquad b_{21} = 1 \qquad b_{22} = 1$$

$$J \longrightarrow F$$

$$P(j_1) = a_{11} / (a_{11}+b_{11}) =1/2 \qquad P(f_1 \,|\, j_1) = a_{21} / (a_{21}+b_{21}) = 1/2$$
$$P(f_1 \,|\, j_2) = a_{22} / (a_{22}+b_{22}) = 1/2$$

(a)

$$a_{11} = 2 \qquad\qquad a_{21} = 2$$
$$b_{11} = 2 \qquad\qquad b_{21} = 2$$

$$J \qquad\qquad F$$

$$P(j_1) = a_{11} / (a_{11}+b_{11}) =1/2 \qquad P(f_1) = a_{21} / (a_{21}+b_{21}) = 1/2$$

(b)

Figure 13.1 The network in (a) models that J has a causal effect on F, whereas the network in (b) models that neither variable causes the other.

Variable	Value	When the Variable Takes This Value
J	j_1	Individual is a white-collar worker
	j_2	Individual is a blue-collar worker
F	f_1	Individual has defaulted on a loan at least once
	f_2	Individual has never defaulted on a loan

We represent the assumption that J has a causal effect on F with the DAG model $\mathbb{G}_1$ in Figure 13.1 (a) and the assumption that neither variable has a causal effect on the other with the DAG model $\mathbb{G}_2$ in Figure 13.1 (b). We assume that F does not have a causal effect on J, so we do not model this situation.

Suppose that next we obtain the data $\mathbf{D}$ in the following table:

Case	J	F
1	j_1	f_1
2	j_1	f_1
3	j_1	f_1
4	j_1	f_1
5	j_1	f_2
6	j_2	f_1
7	j_2	f_2
8	j_2	f_2

Then, owing to Equality 13.2,

$$P(\mathsf{D}|\mathbb{G}_1) = \frac{\Gamma(m_{11})}{\Gamma(m_{11}+n_{11})} \times \frac{\Gamma(a_{11}+s_{11})\Gamma(b_{11}+t_{11})}{\Gamma(a_{11})\Gamma(b_{11})} \times$$
$$\frac{\Gamma(m_{21})}{\Gamma(m_{21}+n_{21})} \times \frac{\Gamma(a_{21}+s_{21})\Gamma(b_{21}+t_{21})}{\Gamma(a_{21})\Gamma(b_{21})} \times$$
$$\frac{\Gamma(m_{22})}{\Gamma(m_{22}+n_{22})} \times \frac{\Gamma(a_{22}+s_{22})\Gamma(b_{22}+t_{22})}{\Gamma(a_{22})\Gamma(b_{22})}$$

$$= \frac{\Gamma(4)}{\Gamma(4+8)} \times \frac{\Gamma(2+5)\,\Gamma(2+3)}{\Gamma(2)\Gamma(2)} \times$$
$$\frac{\Gamma(2)}{\Gamma(2+5)} \times \frac{\Gamma(1+4)\,\Gamma(1+1)}{\Gamma(1)\Gamma(1)} \times$$
$$\frac{\Gamma(2)}{\Gamma(2+3)} \times \frac{\Gamma(1+1)\,\Gamma(1+2)}{\Gamma(1)\Gamma(1)}$$

$$= 7.2150 \times 10^{-6}.$$

Furthermore,

$$P(\mathsf{D}|\mathbb{G}_2) = \frac{\Gamma(m_{11})}{\Gamma(m_{11}+n_{11})} \times \frac{\Gamma(a_{11}+s_{11})\Gamma(b_{11}+t_{11})}{\Gamma(a_{11})\Gamma(b_{11})} \times$$
$$\frac{\Gamma(m_{21})}{\Gamma(m_{21}+n_{21})} \times \frac{\Gamma(a_{21}+s_{21})\Gamma(b_{21}+t_{21})}{\Gamma(a_{21})\Gamma(b_{21})} \times$$

$$= \frac{\Gamma(4)}{\Gamma(4+8)} \times \frac{\Gamma(2+5)\,\Gamma(2+3)}{\Gamma(2)\Gamma(2)} \times$$
$$\frac{\Gamma(4)}{\Gamma(4+8)} \times \frac{\Gamma(2+5)\,\Gamma(2+3)}{\Gamma(2)\Gamma(2)}$$

$$= 6.7465 \times 10^{-6}.$$

If our prior belief is that neither model is more probable than the other, we assign

$$P(\mathbb{G}_1) = P(\mathbb{G}_2) = .5.$$

Then, owing to Bayes' theorem,

$$P(\mathbb{G}_1|\mathsf{D}) = \frac{P(\mathsf{D}|\mathbb{G}_1)P(\mathbb{G}_1)}{P(\mathsf{D}|\mathbb{G}_1)P(\mathbb{G}_1) + P(\mathsf{D}|\mathbb{G}_2)P(\mathbb{G}_2)}$$
$$= \frac{7.2150 \times 10^{-6} \times .5}{7.2150 \times 10^{-6} \times .5 + 6.7465 \times 10^{-6} \times .5}$$
$$= .517$$

and

$$P(\mathbb{G}_2|\mathsf{D}) = \frac{P(\mathsf{D}|\mathbb{G}_2)P(\mathbb{G}_2)}{P(\mathsf{D})}$$

$$= \frac{6.7465 \times 10^{-6}(.5)}{7.2150 \times 10^{-6} \times .5 + 6.7465 \times 10^{-6} \times .5}$$

$$= .483.$$

We select (learn) DAG $\mathbb{G}_1$ and conclude that it is more probable that job status does have a causal effect on whether someone defaults on a loan. ∎

13.2.1.3 Learning DAG Patterns

The DAG $F \to J$ is Markov equivalent to the DAG in Figure 13.1 (a). Intuitively, we would expect it to have the same score. As long as we use a prior equivalent sample size (see Section 12.2.2), they will have the same score. This is discussed in [Neapolitan, 2004]. In general, we cannot distinguish Markov-equivalent DAGs based on data. So, we are actually learning Markov equivalence classes (DAG patterns) when we learn a DAG model from data.

13.2.1.4 Scoring Larger DAG Models

We illustrated Bayesian scoring using two variables. The general formula for the score when there are n variables and the variables are binomial is as follows.

Theorem 13.3 Suppose we have a DAG $\mathbb{G} = (\mathsf{V}, \mathsf{E})$ where V is a set of binomial random variables, we assume exchangeability, and we use a Dirichlet distribution to represent our prior belief for each conditional probability distribution of every variable in V. Suppose further we have data D consisting of a set of data items such that each data item is a vector of values of all the variables in V. Then

$$P(\mathsf{D}|\mathbb{G}) = \prod_{i=1}^{n} \prod_{j=1}^{q_i} \frac{\Gamma(N_{ij})}{\Gamma(N_{ij} + M_{ij})} \frac{\Gamma(a_{ij} + s_{ij})\Gamma(b_{ij} + t_{ij})}{\Gamma(a_{ij})\Gamma(b_{ij})} \tag{13.4}$$

where

1. n is the number of variables.

2. q_i is the number of different instantiations of the parents of X_i.

3. a_{ij} is our ascertained prior belief concerning the number of times X_i took its first value when the parents of X_i had their jth instantiation.

4. b_{ij} is our ascertained value prior belief concerning the number of times X_i took its second value when the parents of X_i had their jth instantiation.

5. s_{ij} is the number of times in the data that X_i took its first value when the parents of X_i had their jth instantiation.

6. t_{ij} is the number of times in the data that X_i took its second value when the parents of X_i had their jth instantiation.

7.

$$N_{ij} = a_{ij} + b_{ij}$$

$$M_{ij} = s_{ij} + t_{ij}.$$

Proof. The proof can be found in [Neapolitan, 2004]. ∎

Note that, other than n, all the variables defined in the previous theorem depend on $\mathbb{G}$, but we do not show that dependency for the sake of simplicity.

We call the $P(D|\mathbb{G})$, obtained using the assumptions in the previous theorem, the **Bayesian score assuming Dirichlet priors**, but ordinarily we only say **Bayesian score**. When we use a prior equivalent sample α such that the prior joint distribution is uniform as shown in Theorem 12.3 the score is called the **Bayesian Dirichlet equivalent uniform** (**BDeu**) score. When each hyperparameter $a_{ij} = b_{ij} = 1$, the score is called the **K2 score**.

We developed the method for computing the Bayesian score for the case of binomial variables. See [Neapolitan, 2004] for an extension to multinomial variables.

Geiger and Heckerman [1994] developed a Bayesian score for scoring Gaussian Bayesian networks. That is, each variable is assumed to be a function of its parents as shown in Equality 6.2 in Section 6.5.1.

13.2.2   BIC Score

The **Bayesian information criterion (BIC) score** is as follows:

$$BIC\,(\mathbb{G}:D) = \ln\left(P(D|\hat{P},\mathbb{G})\right) - \frac{d}{2}\ln m,$$

where m is the number of data items, d is the dimension of the DAG model, and $\hat{P}$ is the set of maximum likelihood values of the parameters. The dimension is the number of parameters in the model.

The BIC score is intuitively appealing because it contains (1) a term that shows how well the model predicts the data when the parameter set is equal to its ML value, and (2) a term that punishes for model complexity. Another nice feature of the BIC is that it does not depend on the prior distribution of the parameters, which means there is no need to assess one.

Example 13.4 Suppose we have the DAG models in Figure 13.1 and the data in Example 13.3. That is, we have the data D in the following table:

Case	J	F
1	j_1	f_1
2	j_1	f_1
3	j_1	f_1
4	j_1	f_1
5	j_1	f_2
6	j_2	f_1
7	j_2	f_2
8	j_2	f_2

For the DAG model in Figure 13.1 (a), we have that

$$\hat{P}(j_1) = \frac{5}{8} \qquad \hat{P}(f_1|j_1) = \frac{4}{5} \qquad \hat{P}(f_1|j_2) = \frac{1}{3}.$$

Because there are three parameters in the model, $d = 3$. We then have that

$P(D|\hat{P}, \mathbb{G}_1)$

$$
\begin{aligned}
&= \left[\hat{P}(f_1|j_1)\hat{P}(j_1)\right]^4 \left[\hat{P}(f_2|j_1)\hat{P}(j_1)\right] \left[\hat{P}(f_1|j_2)\hat{P}(j_2)\right] \left[\hat{P}(f_2|j_2)\hat{P}(j_2)\right]^2 \\
&= \left(\frac{4}{5}\frac{5}{8}\right)^4 \left(\frac{1}{5}\frac{5}{8}\right) \left(\frac{1}{3}\frac{3}{8}\right) \left(\frac{2}{3}\frac{3}{8}\right)^2 \\
&= 6.1035 \times 10^{-5}
\end{aligned}
$$

and therefore

$$
\begin{aligned}
BIC(\mathbb{G}_1 : D) &= \ln\left(P(D|\hat{P}, \mathbb{G}_1)\right) - \frac{d}{2}\ln m \\
&= \ln\left(6.1035 \times 10^{-5}\right) - \frac{3}{2}\ln 8 \\
&= -12.823.
\end{aligned}
$$

For the DAG model in Figure 13.1 (b) we have that

$$\hat{P}(j_1) = \frac{5}{8} \qquad \hat{P}(f_1) = \frac{5}{8}.$$

Because there are three parameters in the model, $d = 2$. We then have that

$P(D|\hat{P}, \mathbb{G}_2)$

$$
\begin{aligned}
&= \left[\hat{P}(f_1)\hat{P}(j_1)\right]^4 \left[\hat{P}(f_2|)\hat{P}(j_1)\right] \left[\hat{P}(f_1)\hat{P}(j_2)\right] \left[\hat{P}(f_2)\hat{P}(j_2)\right]^2 \\
&= \left(\frac{5}{8}\frac{5}{8}\right)^4 \left(\frac{3}{8}\frac{5}{8}\right) \left(\frac{5}{8}\frac{3}{8}\right) \left(\frac{3}{8}\frac{3}{8}\right)^2 \\
&= 2.5292 \times 10^{-5},
\end{aligned}
$$

and therefore

$$
\begin{aligned}
BIC\,(\mathbb{G}_2 : \mathsf{D}) &= \ln\left(P(\mathsf{D}|\hat{\mathsf{P}}, \mathbb{G}_2)\right) - \frac{d}{2}\ln m \\
&= \ln\left(2.529\,2 \times 10^{-5}\right) - \frac{2}{2}\ln 8 \\
&= -12.644.
\end{aligned}
$$

Note that although the data were more probable given $\mathbb{G}_1$, G_2 won because it is less complex. ∎

Looking at Examples 13.3 and 13.4, we see that the Bayesian score and the BIC can choose different DAG models. The reason is that the data set is small. In the limit they will both choose the same DAG model because the BIC is asymptotically correct. A scoring criterion for DAG models is called **asymptotically correct** if for a sufficiently large data set it chooses the DAG that maximizes $P(D|\mathbb{G})$.

13.2.3 Consistent Scoring Criteria

We have presented two methods for scoring DAG models. There are others, several of which are discussed in [Neapolitan, 2004]. The question remains as to the quality of these scores. The probability distribution generating the data is called the **generative distribution**. Our goal with a Bayesian network is to represent the generative distribution succinctly. A consistent scoring criterion will almost certainly do this if the data set is large. Specifically, we say a DAG **includes** a probability distribution P if every conditional independency entailed by the DAG is in P. A **consistent scoring criterion** for DAG models has the following two properties:

1. As the size of the data set approaches infinity, the probability approaches one that a DAG that includes P will score higher than a DAG that does not include P.

2. As the size of the data set approaches infinity, the probability approaches one that a smaller DAG that includes P will score higher than a larger DAG that includes P.

Both the Bayesian score and the BIC are consistent scoring criteria.

13.2.4 How Many DAGs Must We Score?

When there are not many variables, we can exhaustively score all possible DAGs. We then select the DAG(s) with the highest score. However, when the number of variables is not small, it is computationally unfeasible to find the maximizing DAGs by exhaustively considering all DAG patterns. That is, Robinson [1977] showed that the number of DAGs containing n nodes is given

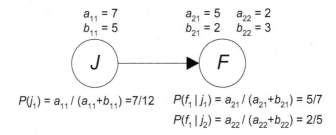

Figure 13.2 An updated Bayesian network for learning based on the data in Example 13.5.

by the following recurrence:

$$f(n) = \sum_{i=1}^{n} (-1)^{i+1} \binom{n}{i} 2^{i(n-i)} f(n-i) \qquad n > 2$$

$$f(0) = 1$$

$$f(1) = 1.$$

It is left as an exercise to show $f(2) = 3$, $f(3) = 25$, $f(5) = 29,000$, and $f(10) = 4.2 \times 10^{18}$. Furthermore, Chickering [1996] proved that for certain classes of prior distributions, the problem of finding a highest-scoring DAG is NP-hard. So, researchers developed heuristic DAG search algorithms. We discuss such algorithms in Section 13.2.7.

13.2.5 Using the Learned Network to Do Inference

Once we learn a DAG from data, we can then learn the parameters. The result will be a Bayesian network that we can use to do inference for the next case. The next example illustrates the technique.

Example 13.5 Suppose we have the situation and data in Example 13.3. Then, as shown in Example 13.3, we would learn the DAG in Figure 13.1 (a). Next we can update the conditional probabilities in the Bayesian network for learning in Figure 13.1 (a) using the preceding data and the parameter learning technique discussed in Section 12.2. The result is the Bayesian network in Figure 13.2.

Suppose now that we find out that Sam has $F = f_2$. That is, Sam has never defaulted on a loan. We can use the Bayesian network to compute the probability that Sam is a white-collar worker. For this simple network, we can just use Bayes' theorem as follows:

$$P(j_1|f_1) = \frac{P(f_1|j_1)P(j_1)}{P(f_1|j_1)P(j_1) + Pf_1|j_2)P(j_2)}$$

$$= \frac{(5/7)\,(7/12)}{(5/7)\,(7/12) + (2/5)\,(5/12)} = .714.$$

Table 13.2 Data on Five Cases with Some Data Items Missing

Case	X_1	X_2	X_3
1	1	1	2
2	1	?	1
3	?	1	?
4	1	2	1
5	2	?	?

The probabilities in the previous calculation are all conditional on the data D and the DAG that we select. However, once we select a DAG and learn the parameters, we do not bother to show this dependence. ∎

13.2.6   Learning Structure with Missing Data⋆

Suppose now our data set has data items missing at random. Table 13.2 shows such a data set. The straightforward way to handle this data set is to apply the law of total probability and sum over all the variables with missing values. That is, if D is the set of random variables for which we have values, and M is the set of random variables whose values are missing, for a given DAG $\mathbb{G}$,

$$P(\mathsf{D}|\mathbb{G}) = \sum_{\mathsf{M}} P(\mathsf{D},\mathsf{M}|\mathbb{G}). \qquad (13.5)$$

For example, if $\mathsf{X}^{(h)} = \{X_1^{(h)}, X_1^{(h)}, \dots X_n^{(h)}\}$ represents the value of the data for the hth case in Table 13.2, we have for the data set in that table that

$$\mathsf{D} = \{X_1^{(1)}, X_2^{(1)}, X_3^{(1)}, X_1^{(2)}, X_3^{(2)}, X_2^{(3)}, X_1^{(4)}, X_2^{(4)}, X_3^{(4)}, X_1^{(5)}\}$$

and

$$\mathsf{M} = \{X_2^{(2)}, X_1^{(3)}, X_3^{(3)}, X_2^{(5)}, X_3^{(5)}\}.$$

We can compute each term in the sum in Equality 13.5 using Equality 13.4. Because this sum is over an exponential number of terms relative to the number of missing data items, we can only use it when the number of missing items is not large. To handle the case of a large number of missing items, we need approximation methods. One approximation method is to use Monte Carlo techniques. We will use a Monte Carlo technique called Gibb's sampling to approximate the probability of data containing missing items. Gibb's sampling is one variety of an approximation method called Markov Chain Monte Carlo (MCMC). So first we review Markov chains and MCMC.

13.2.6.1   Markov Chains

This exposition is only for the purpose of review. If you are unfamiliar with Markov chains, you should consult a complete introduction as can be found in [Feller, 1968]. We start with the definition:

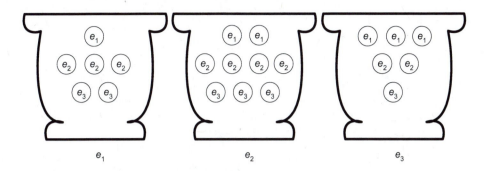

Figure 13.3 An urn model of a Markov chain.

Definition 13.1 A **Markov chain** consists of the following:

1. A set of outcomes (states) $e_1, e_2, \ldots$.

2. For each pair of states e_i and e_j a transition probability p_{ij} such that

$$\sum_j p_{ij} = 1.$$

3. A sequence of trials (random variables) $E^{(1)}, E^{(2)}, \ldots$ such that the outcome of each trial is one of the states, and

$$P(E^{(h+1)} = e_j | E^{(h)} = e_i) = p_{ij}.$$

∎

To completely specify a probability space we need to define initial probabilities $P(E^{(0)} = e_j) = p_j$, but these probabilities are not necessary to our theory and will not be discussed further.

Example 13.6 Any Markov chain can be represented by an urn model. One such model is shown in Figure 13.3. The Markov chain is obtained by choosing an initial urn according to some probability distribution, picking a ball at random from that urn, moving to the urn indicated on the ball chosen, picking a ball at random from the new urn, and so on. ∎

The transition probabilities p_{ij} are arranged in a matrix of transition probabilities as follows:

$$\mathbf{P} = \begin{pmatrix} p_{11} & p_{12} & p_{13} & \cdots \\ p_{21} & p_{22} & p_{23} & \cdots \\ p_{31} & p_{32} & p_{33} & \cdots \\ \vdots & \vdots & \vdots & \ddots \end{pmatrix}.$$

This matrix is called the **transition matrix** for the chain.

Example 13.7 For the Markov chain determined by the urns in Figure 13.3 the transition matrix is

$$\mathbf{P} = \begin{pmatrix} 1/6 & 1/2 & 1/3 \\ 2/9 & 4/9 & 1/3 \\ 1/2 & 1/3 & 1/6 \end{pmatrix}.$$

A Markov chain is called **finite** if it has a finite number of states. Clearly the chain represented by the urns in Figure 13.3 is finite. We denote by $p_{ij}^{(n)}$ **the probability of a transition from** e_i **to** e_j **in exactly** n **trials.** That is, $p_{ij}^{(n)}$ is the conditional probability of entering e_j at the nth trial given the initial state is e_i. We say e_j **is reachable from** e_i if there exists an $n \geq 0$ such that $p_{ij}^{(n)} > 0$. A Markov chain is called **irreducible** if every state is reachable from every other state.

Example 13.8 Clearly, if $p_{ij} > 0$ for every i and j, the chain is irreducible. ■

The state e_i has **period** $t > 1$ if $p_{ii}^{(n)} = 0$ unless $n = mt$ for some integer m, and t is the largest integer with this property. Such a state is called **periodic.** A state is **aperiodic** if no such $t > 1$ exists.

Example 13.9 Clearly, if $p_{ii} > 0$, e_i is aperiodic.   ■

We denote by $f_{ij}^{(n)}$ the probability that starting from e_i the first entry to e_j occurs at the nth trial. Furthermore, we let

$$f_{ij} = \sum_{n=1}^{\infty} f_{ij}^{(n)}.$$

Clearly, $f_{ij} \leq 1$. When $f_{ij} = 1$, we call $P_{ij}(n) \equiv f_{ij}^{(n)}$ the **distribution of the first passage** for e_j starting at e_i. In particular, when $f_{ii} = 1$, we call $P_i(n) \equiv f_{ii}^{(n)}$ the **distribution of the recurrence times** for e_i, and we define the **mean recurrence time** for e_i to be

$$\mu_i = \sum_{n=1}^{\infty} n f_{ii}^{(n)}.$$

The state e_i is called **persistent** if $f_{ii} = 1$ and **transient** if $f_{ii} < 1$. A persistent state e_i is called **null** if its mean recurrence time $\mu_i = \infty$ and otherwise it is called **non-null.**

Example 13.10 It can be shown that every state in a finite irreducible chain is persistent (see [Ash, 1970]), and that every persistent state in a finite chain is non-null (see [Feller, 1968]). Therefore every state in a finite irreducible chain is persistent and non-null.   ■

An aperiodic persistent non-null state is called **ergodic.** A Markov chain is called **ergodic** if all its states are ergodic.

Example 13.11 Owing to Examples 13.8, 13.9, and 13.10, if in a finite chain we have $p_{ij} > 0$ for every i and j, the chain is an irreducible ergodic chain. ∎

We have the following theorem concerning irreducible ergodic chains:

Theorem 13.4 In an irreducible ergodic chain, the limits

$$r_j = \lim_{n \to \infty} p_{ij}^{(n)} \tag{13.6}$$

exist and are independent of the initial state e_i. Furthermore, $r_j > 0$,

$$\sum_j r_j = 1, \tag{13.7}$$

$$r_j = \sum_i r_i p_{ij}, \tag{13.8}$$

and

$$r_j = \frac{1}{\mu_j},$$

where μ_j is the mean recurrence time of e_j.

The probability distribution

$$P(E = e_j) \equiv r_j$$

is called the **stationary distribution** of the Markov chain.

Conversely, suppose a chain is irreducible and aperiodic with transition matrix $\mathbf{P}$, and there exists numbers $r_j \geq 0$ satisfying Equalities 13.7 and 13.8. Then the chain is ergodic, and the r_js are given by Equality 13.6.

Proof. The proof can be found in [Feller, 1968]. ∎

We can write Equality 13.8 in the matrix/vector form

$$\mathbf{r}^T = \mathbf{r}^T \mathbf{P}. \tag{13.9}$$

That is,

$$\begin{pmatrix} r_1 & r_2 & r_3 & \cdots \end{pmatrix} = \begin{pmatrix} r_1 & r_2 & r_3 & \cdots \end{pmatrix} \begin{pmatrix} p_{11} & p_{12} & p_{13} & \cdots \\ p_{21} & p_{22} & p_{23} & \cdots \\ p_{31} & p_{32} & p_{33} & \cdots \\ \vdots & \vdots & \vdots & \ddots \end{pmatrix}.$$

Example 13.12 Suppose we have the Markov chain determined by the urns in Figure 13.3. Then

$$\begin{pmatrix} r_1 & r_2 & r_3 \end{pmatrix} = \begin{pmatrix} r_1 & r_2 & r_3 \end{pmatrix} \begin{pmatrix} 1/6 & 1/2 & 1/3 \\ 2/9 & 4/9 & 1/3 \\ 1/2 & 1/3 & 1/6 \end{pmatrix}. \tag{13.10}$$

Solving the system of equations determined by Equalities 13.7 and 13.10, we obtain

$$\begin{pmatrix} r_1 & r_2 & r_3 \end{pmatrix} = \begin{pmatrix} 2/7 & 3/7 & 2/7 \end{pmatrix}.$$

This means for n large, the probabilities of being in states e_1, e_2, and e_3 are respectively about 2/7, 3/7, and 2/7 regardless of the initial state. ∎

13.2.6.2　MCMC

Again our coverage is cursory. See [Hastings, 1970] for a more thorough introduction.

Suppose we have a finite set of states $\{e_1, e_2, \ldots e_s\}$, and a probability distribution $P(E = e_j) \equiv r_j$ defined on the states such that $r_j > 0$ for all j. Suppose further we have a function f defined on the states, and we wish to estimate

$$I = \sum_{j=1}^{s} f(e_j) r_j.$$

We can obtain an estimate as follows. Given we have a Markov chain with transition matrix $\mathbf{P}$ such that $\mathbf{r}^T = (\begin{array}{cccc} r_1 & r_2 & r_3 & \cdots \end{array})$ is its stationary distribution, we simulate the chain for trials $1, 2, \ldots M$. Then if k_i is the index of the state occupied at trial i and

$$I' = \sum_{i=1}^{M} \frac{f(e_{k_i})}{M}, \tag{13.11}$$

the **ergodic theorem** says that $I' \to I$ with probability 1 (See [Tierney, 1996].). So we can estimate I by I'. This approximation method is called **Markov Chain Monte Carlo (MCMC)**. To obtain more rapid convergence, in practice a "burn-in" number of iterations is used so that the probability of being in each state is approximately given by the stationary distribution. The sum in Expression 13.11 is then obtained over all iterations past the burn-in time. Methods for choosing a burn-in time and the number of iterations to use after burn-in are discussed in [Gilks et al., 1996].

It is not hard to see why the approximation converges. After a sufficient burn-in time, the chain will be in state e_j about r_j fraction of the time. So if we do M iterations after burn in, we would have

$$\sum_{i=1}^{M} f(e_{k_i})/M \approx \sum_{j=1}^{s} \frac{f(e_j) r_j M}{M} = \sum_{j=1}^{s} f(e_j) r_j.$$

To apply this method for a given distribution $\mathbf{r}$, we need to construct a Markov chain with transition matrix $\mathbf{P}$ such that $\mathbf{r}$ is its stationary distribution. Next we show two ways of doing this.

Metropolis-Hastings Method　Owing to Theorem 13.4, we see from Equality 13.9 that we need only find an irreducible aperiodic chain such that its transition matrix $\mathbf{P}$ satisfies

$$\mathbf{r}^T = \mathbf{r}^T \mathbf{P}. \tag{13.12}$$

It is not hard to see that if we determine values p_{ij} such that for all i and j,

$$r_i p_{ij} = r_j p_{ji}, \tag{13.13}$$

then the resultant $\mathbf{P}$ satisfies Equality 13.12. Toward determining such values, let $\mathbf{Q}$ be the transition matrix of an arbitrary Markov chain whose states are the members of our given finite set of states $\{e_1, e_2, \ldots e_s\}$, and let

$$\alpha_{ij} = \begin{cases} \dfrac{s_{ij}}{1 + \dfrac{r_i q_{ij}}{r_j q_{ji}}} & q_{ij} \neq 0, \, q_{ji} \neq 0 \\ \\ 0 & q_{ij} = 0 \text{ or } q_{ji} = 0 \end{cases}, \tag{13.14}$$

where s_{ij} is a symmetric function of i and j chosen so that $0 \leq \alpha_{ij} \leq 1$ for all i and j. We then take

$$\begin{align} p_{ij} &= \alpha_{ij} q_{ij} && i \neq j \tag{13.15} \\ p_{ii} &= 1 - \sum_{j \neq i} p_{ij}. \end{align}$$

It is straightforward to show that the resultant values of p_{ij} satisfy Equality 13.13. The irreducibility of $\mathbf{P}$ must be checked in each application.

Hastings [1970] suggests the following way of choosing $\mathbf{s}$: If q_{ij} and q_{ji} are both nonzero, set

$$s_{ij} = \begin{cases} 1 + \dfrac{r_i q_{ij}}{r_j q_{ji}} & \dfrac{r_j q_{ji}}{r_i q_{ij}} \geq 1 \\ \\ 1 + \dfrac{r_j q_{ji}}{r_i q_{ij}} & \dfrac{r_j q_{ji}}{r_i q_{ij}} \leq 1 \end{cases}. \tag{13.16}$$

Given this choice, we have

$$\alpha_{ij} = \begin{cases} 1 & q_{ij} \neq 0, \, q_{ji} \neq 0, \, \dfrac{r_j q_{ji}}{r_i q_{ij}} \geq 1 \\ \\ \dfrac{r_j q_{ji}}{r_i q_{ij}} & q_{ij} \neq 0, \, q_{ji} \neq 0, \, \dfrac{r_j q_{ji}}{r_i q_{ij}} \leq 1 \\ \\ 0 & q_{ij} = 0 \text{ or } q_{ji} = 0 \end{cases}. \tag{13.17}$$

If we make $\mathbf{Q}$ symmetric (that is, $q_{ij} = q_{ji}$ for all i and j), we have the method devised by Metropolis et al. (1953). In this case

$$\alpha_{ij} = \begin{cases} 1 & q_{ij} \neq 0, \, r_j \geq r_i \\ \\ r_j/r_i & q_{ij} \neq 0, \, r_j \leq r_i \\ \\ 0 & q_{ij} = 0 \end{cases}. \tag{13.18}$$

Note that with this choice if $\mathbf{Q}$ is irreducible, so is $\mathbf{P}$.

Example 13.13 Suppose $r^T = (\; 1/8 \quad 3/8 \quad 1/2 \;)$. Choose Q symmetric as follows:

$$Q = \begin{pmatrix} 1/3 & 1/3 & 1/3 \\ 1/3 & 1/3 & 1/3 \\ 1/3 & 1/3 & 1/3 \end{pmatrix}.$$

Choose s according to Equality 13.16 so that α has the values in Equality 13.18. We then have

$$\alpha = \begin{pmatrix} 1 & 1 & 1 \\ 1/3 & 1 & 1 \\ 1/4 & 3/4 & 1 \end{pmatrix}.$$

Using Equality 13.15 we have

$$P = \begin{pmatrix} 1/3 & 1/3 & 1/3 \\ 1/9 & 5/9 & 1/3 \\ 1/12 & 1/4 & 2/3 \end{pmatrix}.$$

Notice that

$$
\begin{aligned}
r^T P &= (\; 1/8 \quad 3/8 \quad 1/2 \;) \begin{pmatrix} 1/3 & 1/3 & 1/3 \\ 1/9 & 5/9 & 1/3 \\ 1/12 & 1/4 & 2/3 \end{pmatrix} \\
&= (\; 1/8 \quad 3/8 \quad 1/2 \;) = r^T,
\end{aligned}
$$

as it should. ∎

Once we have constructed matrices Q and α as discussed above, we can conduct the simulation as follows:

1. Given the state occupied at the kth trial is e_i, choose a state using the probability distribution given by the ith row of Q. Suppose that state is e_j.

2. Choose the state occupied at the $(k+1)$st trial to be e_j with probability α_{ij} and to be e_i with probability $1 - \alpha_{ij}$.

In this way, when state e_i is the current state, e_j will be chosen q_{ij} fraction of the time in Step (1), and of those times e_j will be chosen α_{ij} fraction of the time in Step (2). So overall, e_j will be chosen $\alpha_{ij} q_{ij} = p_{ij}$ fraction of the time (see Equality 13.15), which is what we want.

Gibb's Sampling Method Next we show another method for creating a Markov chain whose stationary distribution is a particular joint probability distribution. The method is called **Gibb's sampling**, and it concerns the case where we have n random variables $X_1, X_2, \ldots X_n$ and a joint probability distribution P of the variables (as in a Bayesian network). If we let $X = \{X_1, X_2, \ldots X_n\}$, we want to approximate

$$\sum_{x} f(x) P(x).$$

To approximate this sum using MCMC, we need to create a Markov chain whose set of states is all possible values of X, and whose stationary distribution is $P(\mathsf{x})$. We do this by choosing the value of X in the hth trial as follows:

Pick $x_1^{(h)}$ using the distribution $P(x_1|x_2^{(h-1)}, x_3^{(h-1)}, \ldots, x_n^{(h-1)})$.

Pick $x_2^{(h)}$ using the distribution $P(x_2|x_1^{(h)}, x_3^{(h-1)}, \ldots, x_n^{(h-1)})$.

$\vdots$

Pick $x_k^{(h)}$ using the distribution $P(x_k|x_1^{(h)}, \ldots, x_{k-1}^{(h)}, x_{k+1}^{(h-1)} \ldots, x_n^{(h-1)})$.

$\vdots$

Pick $x_n^{(h)}$ using the distribution $P(x_n|x_1^{(h)}, \ldots, x_{n-1}^{(h)})$.

Notice that in the kth step, all variables except $x_k^{(h)}$ are unchanged, and the new value of $x_k^{(h)}$ is drawn from its distribution conditional on the current values of all the other variables.

As long as all conditional probabilities are nonzero, the chain is irreducible. Next we verify that $P(\mathsf{x})$ is the stationary distribution for the chain. If we let $p(\mathsf{x}; \hat{\mathsf{x}})$ denote the transition probability from x to $\hat{\mathsf{x}}$ in each trial, we need to show that

$$P(\hat{\mathsf{x}}) = \sum_{\mathsf{x}} P(\mathsf{x})p(\mathsf{x}; \hat{\mathsf{x}}). \tag{13.19}$$

It is not hard to see that it suffices to show that Equality 13.19 holds for each each step of each trial. To that end, for the kth step we have

$$\sum_{\mathsf{x}} P(\mathsf{x})p_k(\mathsf{x}; \hat{\mathsf{x}})$$

$$= \sum_{x_1,\ldots x_n} P(x_1,\ldots,x_n)p_k(x_1,\ldots,x_n; \hat{x}_1,\ldots,\hat{x}_n)$$

$$= \sum_{x_k} P(\hat{x}_1,\ldots,\hat{x}_{k-1}, x_k, \hat{x}_{k+1},\ldots,\hat{x}_n)P(\hat{x}_k|\hat{x}_1,\ldots,\hat{x}_{k-1},\hat{x}_{k+1},\ldots,\hat{x}_n)$$

$$= P(\hat{x}_k|\hat{x}_1,\ldots,\hat{x}_{k-1},\hat{x}_{k+1},\ldots,\hat{x}_n)\sum_{x_k} P(\hat{x}_1,\ldots,\hat{x}_{k-1}, x_k, \hat{x}_{k+1},\ldots,\hat{x}_n)$$

$$= P(\hat{x}_k|\hat{x}_1,\ldots,\hat{x}_{k-1},\hat{x}_{k+1},\ldots\hat{x}_n)P(\hat{x}_1,\ldots\hat{x}_{k-1},\hat{x}_{k+1},\ldots\hat{x}_n)$$

$$= P(\hat{x}_1,\ldots\hat{x}_{k-1},\hat{x}_k,\hat{x}_{k+1},\ldots,\hat{x}_n)$$

$$= P(\hat{\mathsf{x}}).$$

The second step follows because $p_k(\mathsf{x}; \hat{\mathsf{x}}) = 0$ unless $\hat{x}_j = x_j$ for all $j \neq k$. See [Geman and Geman, 1984] for more on Gibb's sampling.

13.2.6.3 Learning with Missing Data Using Gibb's Sampling

The Gibb's sampling approach we use is called the **Candidate method** (See [Chib, 1995].). The approach proceeds as follows: Let D be the set of values of the variables for which we have values. By Bayes' theorem we have

$$P(\mathsf{D}|\mathbb{G}) = \frac{P(\mathsf{D}|\check{\mathsf{f}}^{(\mathbb{G})}, \mathbb{G})\rho(\check{\mathsf{f}}^{(\mathbb{G})}|\mathbb{G})}{\rho(\check{\mathsf{f}}^{(\mathbb{G})}|\mathsf{D}, \mathbb{G})}, \tag{13.20}$$

where $\check{\mathsf{f}}^{(\mathbb{G})}$ is an arbitrary assignment of values to the parameters in $\mathbb{G}$. To approximate $P(\mathsf{D}|\mathbb{G})$, we choose some value of $\check{\mathsf{f}}^{(\mathbb{G})}$, evaluate the numerator in Equality 13.20 exactly, and approximate the denominator using Gibb's sampling. For the denominator, we have

$$\rho(\check{\mathsf{f}}^{(\mathbb{G})}|\mathsf{D}, \mathbb{G}) = \sum_{\mathsf{m}} \rho(\check{\mathsf{f}}^{(\mathbb{G})}|\mathsf{D}, \mathsf{m}, \mathbb{G})P(\mathsf{m}|\mathsf{D}, \mathbb{G})$$

where M is the set of variables that has missing values.

To approximate this sum using Gibb's sampling, we do the following:

1. Initialize the state of the unobserved variables to arbitrary values yielding a complete data set D_1.

2. Choose some unobserved variable $X_i^{(h)}$ arbitrarily and obtain a value of $X_i^{(h)}$ using

$$P(x_i'^{(h)}|\mathsf{D}_1 - \{\check{x}_i^{(h)}\}, \mathbb{G}) = \frac{P(x_i'^{(h)}, \mathsf{D}_1 - \{\check{x}_i^{(h)}\}|\mathbb{G})}{\displaystyle\sum_{x_i^{(h)}} P(x_i^{(h)}, \mathsf{D}_1 - \{\check{x}_i^{(h)}\}|\mathbb{G})}$$

   where $\check{x}_i^{(h)}$ is the value of $X_i^{(h)}$ in D_1, and the sum is over all values in the space of $X_i^{(h)}$. The terms in the numerator and denominator can be computed using Equality 13.4.

3. Repeat Step (2) for all the other unobserved variables, where the complete data set used in the $(k+1)$st iteration contains the values obtained in the previous k iterations.

   This will yield a new complete data set D_2.

4. Iterate the previous two steps some number R times where the complete data set from the the jth iteration is used in the $(j+1)$st iteration. In this manner R complete data sets will be generated. For each complete data set D_j, compute

$$\rho(\check{\mathsf{f}}^{(\mathbb{G})}|\mathsf{D}_j, \mathbb{G})$$

   using Equality 12.3.

5. Approximate

$$\rho(\check{\mathsf{f}}^{(\mathbb{G})}|\mathsf{D}, \mathbb{G}) \approx \frac{\sum_{j=1}^{R} \rho(\check{\mathsf{f}}^{(\mathbb{G})}|\mathsf{D}_j, \mathbb{G})}{R}.$$

Although the Candidate method can be applied with any value of $\check{\mathsf{f}}^{(\mathbb{G})}$ of the parameters, some assignments lead to faster convergence. Chickering and Heckerman [1997] discuss methods for choosing the value.

13.2.7 Approximate Structure Learning

Recall from Section 13.2.4 that when the number of variables is not small, it is computationally unfeasible to find the maximizing DAGs by exhaustively considering all DAGs. Therefore, researchers have developed heuristic search algorithms. We discuss such algorithms next.

13.2.7.1 K2 Algorithm

We present an algorithm in which the search space is the set of all DAGs containing n nodes, where n is our number of random variables. In these algorithms, our goal is to find a DAG with maximum score, where our scoring criterion could be the Bayesian score, the BIC score, or some other score. Therefore, we will simply refer to the score as $score(\mathbb{G} : \mathsf{D})$, where D is our data.

If we use either the Bayesian score or the BIC score, the score for the entire DAG is a product of local scores for each node. For example, Theorem 13.3 obtains the result that the Bayesian score is given by

$$
P(\mathsf{D}|\mathbb{G}) = \prod_{i=1}^{n} \prod_{j=1}^{q_i^{\mathbb{G}}} \frac{\Gamma(N_{ij}^{\mathbb{G}})}{\Gamma(N_{ij}^{\mathbb{G}} + M_{ij}^{\mathbb{G}})} \frac{\Gamma(a_{ij}^{\mathbb{G}} + s_{ij}^{\mathbb{G}})\Gamma(b_{ij}^{\mathbb{G}} + t_{ij}^{\mathbb{G}})}{\Gamma(a_{ij}^{\mathbb{G}})\Gamma(b_{ij}^{\mathbb{G}})}.
$$

See Theorem 13.3 for the definition of the variables in this formula. Note that we have now explicitly shown their dependence on $\mathbb{G}$. Let $\mathsf{PA}_i^{\mathbb{G}}$ denote the parents of X_i in $\mathbb{G}$. For each node X_i, define

$$
score(X_i, \mathsf{PA}_i^{\mathbb{G}} : \mathsf{D}) = \prod_{j=1}^{q_i^{\mathbb{G}}} \frac{\Gamma(N_{ij}^{\mathbb{G}})}{\Gamma(N_{ij}^{\mathbb{G}} + M_{ij}^{\mathbb{G}})} \frac{\Gamma(a_{ij}^{\mathbb{G}} + s_{ij}^{\mathbb{G}})\Gamma(b_{ij}^{\mathbb{G}} + t_{ij}^{\mathbb{G}})}{\Gamma(a_{ij}^{\mathbb{G}})\Gamma(b_{ij}^{\mathbb{G}})}.
$$

This local score depends only on parameter values stored at X_i, and data values of X_i and nodes in $\mathsf{PA}_i^{\mathbb{G}}$, and the $P(\mathsf{D}|\mathbb{G})$ is the product of these local scores.

Cooper and Herskovits [1992] developed a greedy search algorithm that tries to maximize the score of the DAG by maximizing these local scores. That is, for each variable X_i, they locally find a value PA_i that approximately maximizes $score(X_i, \mathsf{PA}_i^{\mathbb{G}} : \mathsf{D})$. The single operation in this search algorithm is the addition of a parent to a node. The algorithm proceeds as follows: We assume an ordering of the nodes such that if X_i precedes X_j in the ordering, an arc from X_j to X_i is not allowed. Let $Pred(X_i)$ be the set of nodes that precede X_i in the ordering, We initially set the parents $\mathsf{PA}_i^{\mathbb{G}}$ of X_i to empty and compute $score(X_i, \mathsf{PA}_i^{\mathbb{G}} : \mathsf{D})$. Next we visit the nodes in sequence according to the ordering. When we visit X_i, we determine the node in $Pred(X_i)$ that most increases $score(X_i, \mathsf{PA}_i^{\mathbb{G}} : \mathsf{D})$. We "greedily" add this node to PA_i. We continue doing this until the addition of no node increases $score(X_i, \mathsf{PA}_i^{\mathbb{G}} : \mathsf{D})$. Pseudocode for this algorithm follows. The algorithm is called K2 because it evolved from a system named Kutató [Herskovits and Cooper, 1990].

Algorithm 13.1 K2

Input: A set V of n random variables; an upper bound u on the number of parents a node may have; data D.

Output: n sets of parent nodes PA_i, where $1 \leq i \leq n$, in a DAG that approximates maximizing $score\,(\mathbb{G} : \mathsf{D})$.

Procedure $K2$ (V, u, D, **var** PA_i, $1 \leq i \leq n$)
for $i = 1$ **to** n
    $\mathsf{PA}_i^{\mathbb{G}} = \varnothing$;
    $P_{old} = score(X_i, \mathsf{PA}_i^{\mathbb{G}} : \mathsf{D})$;
    $findmore = $ true;
    while $findmore$ **and** $|\mathsf{PA}_i^{\mathbb{G}}| < u$
        $Z = $ node in $Pred(X_i) - \mathsf{PA}_i$ that maximizes
            $score(X_i, \mathsf{PA}_i^{\mathbb{G}} \cup \{Z\} : \mathsf{D})$;
        $P_{new} = score(X_i, \mathsf{PA}_i^{\mathbb{G}} \cup \{Z\} : \mathsf{D})$;
        if $P_{new} > P_{old}$
            $P_{old} = P_{new}$;
            $\mathsf{PA}_i^{\mathbb{G}} = \mathsf{PA}_i^{\mathbb{G}} \cup \{Z\}$;
      else
        $findmore = $ false;
    endwhile
endfor

Neapolitan [2004] analyzes the algorithm. Furthermore, he shows an example in which the algorithm was provided with a prior order and learned a DAG from 10,000 cases sampled at random from the ALARM Bayesian network [Beinlich et al., 1989]. The DAG learned was identical to the one in the ALARM network except that one edge was missing.

You might wonder where we could obtain the ordering required by Algorithm 13.1. Such an ordering could possibly be obtained from domain knowledge such as a time ordering of the variables. For example, we might know that in patients, smoking precedes bronchitis and lung cancer and that each of these conditions precedes fatigue and a positive chest X-ray.

When a model searching algorithm need only locally recompute a few scores to determine the score for the next model under consideration, we say the algorithm has **local scoring updating**. A model with local scoring updating is considerably more efficient than one without it. Clearly, the K2 algorithm has local scoring updating.

13.2.7.2   An Algorithm without a Prior Ordering

Next we present a straightforward greedy search algorithm that does not require a time ordering. The search space is again the set of all DAGs containing the n variables, and the set of DAG operations is as follows:

1. If two nodes are not adjacent, add an edge between them in either direction.

2. If two nodes are adjacent, remove the edge between them.

3. If two nodes are adjacent, reverse the edge between them.

All operations are subject to the constraint that the resultant graph does not contain a cycle. The set of all DAGs that can be obtained from $\mathbb{G}$ by applying one of the operations is called $\mathsf{Nbhd}(\mathbb{G})$. If $\mathbb{G}' \in \mathsf{Nbhd}(\mathbb{G})$, we say $\mathbb{G}'$ is in the **neighborhood** of $\mathbb{G}$. Clearly, this set of operations is **complete** for the search space. That is, for any two DAGs $\mathbb{G}$ and $\mathbb{G}'$, there exists a sequence of operations that transforms $\mathbb{G}$ to $\mathbb{G}'$. The reverse edge operation is not needed for the operations to be complete, but it increases the connectivity of the space without adding too much complexity, which typically leads to a better search. Furthermore, when we use a greedy search algorithm, including edge reversals often seems to lead to a better local maximum.

The algorithm proceeds as follows: We start with a DAG with no edges. At each step of the search, of all those DAGs in the neighborhood of our current DAG, we "greedily" choose the one that maximizes $score\,(\mathbb{G} : \mathsf{D})$. We halt when no operation increases this score.

Note that in each step, if an edge to X_i is added or deleted, we need only re-evaluate $score(X_i, \mathsf{PA}_i : \mathsf{D})$. If an edge between X_i and X_j is reversed, we need only reevaluate $score(X_i, \mathsf{PA}_i : \mathsf{D})$ and $score(X_j, \mathsf{PA}_j : \mathsf{D})$. Therefore, this algorithm has local scoring updating. The algorithm follows:

Algorithm 13.2 DAG Search

>   **Input:** A set V of n random variables; data D.
>   **Output:** A set of edges E in a DAG that approximates maximizing $score\,(\mathbb{G} : \mathsf{D})$.
>
>   **Procedure** DAG_Search (V, D, **var** E)
> $\mathsf{E} = \varnothing$; $\mathbb{G} = (\mathsf{V}, \mathsf{E})$;
>   **do**
>   **if** any DAG in $\mathsf{Nbhd}(\mathbb{G})$ increases $score\,(\mathbb{G} : \mathsf{D})$
>   modify E based on the one that increases $score\,(\mathbb{G} : \mathsf{D})$ most;
>   **while** some operation increases $score\,(\mathbb{G} : \mathsf{D})$;

A problem with a greedy search algorithm is that it could halt at a candidate solution that locally maximizes the objective function rather than globally maximizes it (see [Xiang et al., 1996]). One way of dealing with this problem is iterated hill-climbing. In iterated hill-climbing, local search is done until a local maximum is obtained. Then the current structure is randomly perturbed, and the process is repeated. Finally, the maximum over local maxima is used. Other methods for attempting to avoid local maxima include simulated annealing [Metropolis et al., 1953], best-first search [Korf, 1993], and Gibb's sampling [Neapolitan, 2004].

13.2.7.3 Searching over DAG Patterns

Next we present an algorithm that searches over DAG patterns. First, we discuss why we might want to do this.

Why Search over DAG Patterns?   Although Algorithms 8.1 and 8.2 find a DAG $\mathbb{G}$ rather than a DAG pattern, we can use them to find a DAG pattern by determining the DAG pattern gp representing the Markov equivalence class to which $\mathbb{G}$ belongs. Because $score(gp : \mathsf{D}) = score(\mathbb{G} : \mathsf{D})$, we have approximated maximizing $score(\mathsf{D}, gp)$. However, as discussed in [Neapolitan, 2004], there are a number of potential problems in searching for a DAG instead of a DAG pattern. Briefly, we discuss two of the problems. The first is efficiency. By searching over DAGs, the algorithm can waste time encountering and rescoring DAGs in the same Markov equivalence class. A second problem has to do with priors. If we search over DAGs, we are implicitly assigning equal priors to all DAGs, which means that DAG patterns containing more DAGs will have higher prior probability. For example, if there are n nodes, the complete DAG pattern (representing no conditional independencies) contains $n!$ DAGs, whereas the pattern with no edges (representing that all variables are mutually independent) contains just one DAG. On the other hand, Gillispie and Pearlman [2001] show that an asymptotic ratio of the number of DAGs to DAG patterns equal to about 3.7 is reached when the number of nodes is only 10. Therefore, on average, the number of DAGs in a given equivalence class is small, and perhaps our concern about searching over DAGs is not necessary. Contrariwise, in simulations performed by Chickering [2001], the average number of DAGs in the equivalence classes over which his algorithm searched were always greater than 8.5 and in one case was 9.7×10^{19}.

When performing model selection, assigning equal priors to DAGs is not necessarily a serious problem, as we will finally select a high-scoring DAG that corresponds to a high-scoring DAG pattern. However, as discussed in [Neapolitan, 2004], it can be a more serious problem in the case of model averaging (See Section 13.2.8).

The GES Algorithm   In 1997, Meek developed an algorithm called **Greedy Equivalent Search (GES)**, which searches over DAG patterns and has the following property: If there is a DAG pattern faithful to P, as the size of the data set approaches infinity, the limit of the probability of finding a DAG pattern faithful to P is equal to 1. In 2002 Chickering proved this is the case. We describe the algorithm next.

In what follows we denote the equivalence class represented by DAG pattern gp by **gp**. GES is a two-phase algorithm that searches over DAG patterns. In the first phase, DAG pattern gp' is in the neighborhood of DAG pattern gp, denoted $\mathsf{Nbhd}^+(gp)$, if there is some DAG $\mathbb{G} \in \mathbf{gp}$ for which a single edge addition results in a DAG $\mathbb{G}' \in \mathbf{gp}'$. Starting with the DAG pattern containing no edges, we repeatedly replace the current DAG pattern gp by the DAG pattern in $\mathsf{Nbhd}^+(gp)$ that has the highest score of all DAG patterns in $\mathsf{Nbhd}^+(gp)$. We do this until there is no DAG pattern in $\mathsf{Nbhd}^+(gp)$ that increases the score.

The second phase is completely analogous to the first phase. In this phase, DAG pattern gp' is in the neighborhood of DAG pattern gp, denoted $\mathsf{Nbhd}^-(gp)$, if there is some DAG $\mathbb{G} \in \mathbf{gp}$ for which a single edge deletion results in a DAG $\mathbb{G}' \in \mathbf{gp}'$. Starting with the DAG pattern obtained in the first phase,

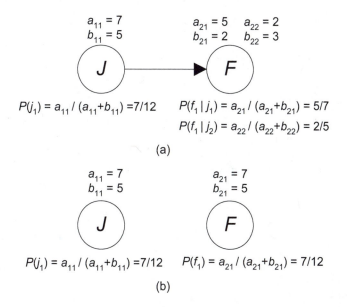

$P(j_1) = a_{11} / (a_{11}+b_{11}) = 7/12$ $P(f_1 | j_1) = a_{21} / (a_{21}+b_{21}) = 5/7$

$P(f_1 | j_2) = a_{22} / (a_{22}+b_{22}) = 2/5$

(a)

$P(j_1) = a_{11} / (a_{11}+b_{11}) = 7/12$ $P(f_1) = a_{21} / (a_{21}+b_{21}) = 7/12$

(b)

Figure 13.4 Updated Bayesian network for learning based on the data discussed in Examples 13.3 and 13.5.

we repeatedly replace the current DAG pattern gp by the DAG pattern in $\mathsf{Nbhd}^-(gp)$ that has the highest score of all DAG patterns in $\mathsf{Nbhd}^-(gp)$. We do this until there is no DAG pattern in $\mathsf{Nbhd}^-(gp)$ that increases the score.

It is left as an exercise to write this algorithm.

Neapolitan [2004] discusses other algorithms that search over DAG patterns.

13.2.8 Model Averaging

Heckerman et al. [1999] illustrate that when the number of variables is small and the amount of data is large, one structure can be orders of magnitude more likely than any other. In such cases, model selection yields good results. However, recall that in Example 13.3 we had few data, we obtained $P(\mathbb{G}_1|D) = .517$ and $P(\mathbb{G}_2|D) = .483$, and we chose (learned) DAG $\mathbb{G}_1$ because it was most probable. Then in Example 13.5 we used a Bayesian network containing DAG $\mathbb{G}_1$ to do inference for Sam. Because the probabilities of the two models are so close, it seems somewhat arbitrary to choose $\mathbb{G}_1$. So, model selection does not seem appropriate. Next, we describe another approach.

Instead of choosing a single DAG and then using it to do inference, we could use the Law of Total Probability to do the inference as follows: We perform the inference using each DAG and multiply the result (a probability value) by the posterior probability of the DAG. This is called **model averaging**.

Example 13.14 Recall that based on the data in Example 13.3, we learned that

$$P(\mathbb{G}_1|D) = .517$$

and

$$P(\mathbb{G}_2|D) = .483.$$

In Example 13.5 we updated a Bayesian network containing $\mathbb{G}_1$ based on the data to obtain the Bayesian network in Figure 13.4 (a). If in the same way we update a Bayesian network containing $\mathbb{G}_2$, we obtain the Bayesian network in Figure 13.4 (b). Given that Sam has never defaulted on a loan ($F = f_2$), we can then use model averaging to compute the probability that Sam is a white-collar worker, as follows:[1]

$$\begin{aligned}
P(j_1|f_1, D) &= P(j_1|f_1, \mathbb{G}_1)P(\mathbb{G}_1|D) + P(j_1|f_1, \mathbb{G}_2)P(\mathbb{G}_2|D) \\
&= (.714)(.517) + (7/12)(.483) = .651.
\end{aligned}$$

The result that $P(j_1|f_1, \mathbb{G}_1) = .714$ was obtained in Example 13.5, although in that example we did not show the dependence on $\mathbb{G}_1$ because that DAG was the only DAG considered. The result that $P(j_1|f_1, \mathbb{G}_2) = 7/12$ is obtained directly from the Bayesian network in Figure 13.4 (b) because J and F are independent in that network.   ∎

Example 13.14 illustrated using model averaging to do inference. The following example illustrates using it to learn partial structure.

Example 13.15 Suppose we have three random variables X_1, X_2, and X_3. Then the possible DAG patterns are the ones in Figure 13.5. We might be interested in the probability that a feature of the DAG pattern is present. For example, we might be interested in the probability that there is an edge between X_1 and X_2. Given the five DAG patterns in which there is an edge, this probability is 1; and given the six DAG pattern in which there is no edge, this probability is 0. Let gp denote a DAG pattern. If we let F be a random variable whose value is *present* if a feature is present,

$$\begin{aligned}
P(F = present|D) &= \sum_{gp} P(F = present|gp, D)P(gp|D) \\
&= \sum_{gp} P(F = present|gp)P(gp|D),
\end{aligned}$$

where

$$P(F = present|gp) = \begin{cases} 1 & \text{if the feature is present in } gp \\ 0 & \text{if the feature is not present in } gp. \end{cases}$$

∎

---

[1] Note that we substitute $P(\mathbb{G}_1|D)$ for $P(\mathbb{G}_1|f_1, D)$. They are not exactly equal, but we are assuming that the data set is sufficiently large that the dependence of the DAG models on the current case can be ignored.

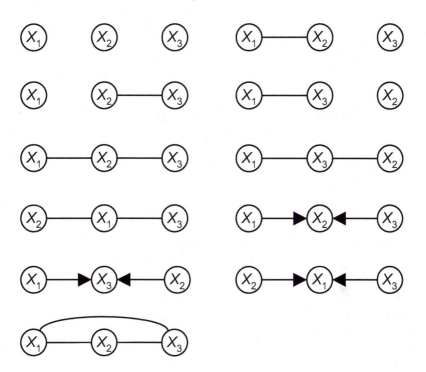

Figure 13.5 The 11 DAG patterns when there are three nodes.

You may wonder what event a feature represents. For example, what event does an edge between X_1 and X_2 represent? This event is the event that X_1 and X_2 are not independent and are not conditionally independent given X_3 in the actual relative frequency distribution of the variables. Another possible feature is that there is a directed edge from X_1 to X_2. This feature is the event that, assuming that the relative frequency distribution admits a faithful DAG representation, there is a directed edge from X_1 to X_2 in the DAG pattern faithful to that distribution. Similarly, the feature that there is a directed path from X_1 to X_2 represents the event that there is a directed path from X_1 to X_2 in the DAG pattern faithful to that distribution.

Given that we are only discussing the relative frequency distribution, these events are ordinarily not of great interest. However, if we are discussing causality, they tell us something about the causal relationships among the variables. For example, recall that in Example 6.16 we mentioned that the proteins produced by one gene have a causal effect on the level of mRNA (called the *gene expression level*) of another gene, and researchers try to learn these causal effects from data. Ordinarily there are thousands of genes (variables), but typically we have at most only a few thousand data items. In such cases, there are often many structures that are equally likely. So, choosing one particular structure is somewhat arbitrary. However, in these cases we are not always interested in learning the entire structure. That is, rather than needing the structure for inference and decision making, we are only interested in learning relationships among some of the variables. In particular, in the gene expression example, we are interested in the dependence and causal relationships between the expression levels of certain genes (see [Lander and Shenoy, 1999]).

13.2.9 Approximate Model Averaging★

As is the case for model selection, when the number of possible DAGs is large, we cannot average over all DAGs. In these situations, we heuristically search for high-probability DAGs, and then we average over them. In particular, in the gene expression example, because there are thousands of variables, we could not average over all DAGs. Approximate model averaging is discussed next.

13.2.9.1 Approximate Model Averaging Using MCMC

Next we discuss how we can heuristically search for high-probability structures and then average over them using the Markov Chain Monte Carlo (MCMC) method.

Recall our two examples of model averaging (Examples 13.14 and 13.15). The first involved computing a conditional probability over all possible DAGs as follows:

$$P(x|y, \mathsf{D}) = \sum_{\mathbb{G}} P(x|y, \mathbb{G}, \mathsf{D}) P(\mathbb{G}|a, \mathsf{D}).$$

The second involved computing the probability a feature is present as follows:

$$P(F = present|\mathsf{D}) = \sum_{gp} P(F = present|gp) P(gp|\mathsf{D}).$$

In general, these problems involve some function of the DAG or DAG pattern and possibly the data and a probability distribution of the DAGs or DAG patterns conditional on the data. If we average over DAG patterns, we can represent the general problem to be the determination of

$$\sum_{gp} f(gp, \mathsf{D}) P(gp|\mathsf{D}), \tag{13.21}$$

where f is some function of gp and possibly D, and P is some probability distribution of the DAG patterns. Although we represented the problem in terms of DAG patterns, we could sum over DAGs instead.

To approximate the value of Expression 13.21 using MCMC, our stationary distribution $\mathbf{r}$ is $P(gp|\mathsf{D})$. Ordinarily we can compute $P(\mathsf{D}|gp)$ but not $P(gp|\mathsf{D})$. However, if we assume that the prior probability $P(gp)$ is the same for all DAG patterns,

$$
\begin{aligned}
P(gp|\mathsf{D}) &= \frac{P(\mathsf{D}|gp) P(gp)}{P(\mathsf{D})} \\
&= k P(\mathsf{D}|gp) P(gp),
\end{aligned}
$$

where k does not depend on gp. If we use Equality 13.17 or 13.18 as our expression for α, k cancels out of the expression, which means that we can use $P(\mathsf{D}|gp)$ in the expression for α. Note that we do not have to assign equal prior probabilities to all DAG patterns. That is, we could use $P(\mathsf{D}|gp)P(gp)$ in the expression for α also.

If we average over DAGs instead of DAG patterns, the problem is the determination of

$$\sum_{\mathbb{G}} f(\mathbb{G}, \mathsf{D}) P(\mathbb{G}|\mathsf{D}),$$

where f is some function of $\mathbb{G}$ and possibly D, and P is some probability distribution of the DAGs. As is the case for DAG patterns, if we assume that the prior probability $P(\mathbb{G})$ is the same for all DAGs, then $P(\mathbb{G}|\mathsf{D}) = kP(\mathsf{D}|\mathbb{G})$, and we can use $P(\mathsf{D}|\mathbb{G})$ in the expression for α. However, we must realize what this assumption entails. If we assign equal prior probabilities to all DAGs, DAG patterns containing more DAGs will have higher prior probability.

As noted previously, when we perform model selection, assigning equal prior probabilities to DAGs is not necessarily a serious problem, because we will finally select a high-scoring DAG that corresponds to a high-scoring DAG pattern. However, in performing model averaging, a given DAG pattern will be included in the average according to the number of DAGs in the pattern. For example, there are three DAGs corresponding to the DAG pattern $X - Y - Z$ but only one corresponding to DAG pattern $X \rightarrow Y \leftarrow Z$. So, by assuming that all DAGs have the same prior probability, we are assuming that the prior probability that the actual relative frequency distribution has the set of conditional independencies $\{I_P(X, Z|Y)\}$ is three times the prior probability that it has the set of conditional independencies $\{I_P(X, Z)\}$. Even more dramatic, there are $n!$ DAGs corresponding to the complete DAG pattern and only one corresponding to the DAG pattern with no edges. So, we are assuming that the prior probability that there are no conditional independencies is far greater than the prior probability that the variables are mutually independent.

This assumption has consequences as follows: Suppose, for example, that the correct DAG pattern is $X : Y$, which denotes the DAG pattern with no edge, and the feature of interest is whether X and Y are independent. Because the feature is present, our results are better if we confirm it. Therefore, averaging over DAG patterns has a better result because, by averaging over DAG patterns, we are assigning a prior probability of $1/2$ to the feature, whereas by averaging over DAGs, we are only assigning a prior probability of $1/3$ to the feature. On the other hand, if the correct DAG pattern is $X - Y$, the feature is not present, which means that our results are better if we disconfirm. Therefore, averaging over DAGs is better.

We see then that we need to look at the ensemble of all relative frequency distributions rather than any one to discuss which method might be "correct." If relative frequency distributions are distributed uniformly in nature and we assign equal prior probabilities to all DAG patterns, then $P(F = present|\mathsf{D})$, obtained by averaging over DAG patterns, is the relative frequency with which we are investigating a relative frequency distribution with this feature when we are observing these data. So, averaging over DAG patterns is "correct." On the other hand, if relative frequency distributions are distributed in nature according to the number of DAGs in DAG patterns and we assign equal prior probabilities to all DAGs, then $P(F = present|D)$, obtained by averaging over DAGs, is the relative frequency with which we are investigating a relative frequency distribution with this feature when we are observing these data. So, averaging over DAGs is "correct." Although it seems reasonable to assume that relative frequency distributions are distributed uniformly in nature, some feel that a relative frequency distribution, represented by a DAG pattern containing a larger number of DAGs, may occur more often because there are more causal relationships that can give rise to it.

13.2.9.2   Algorithms for Approximate Averaging over DAGs

Next we show MCMC algorithms for approximate averaging over DAGs.

Straightforward Algorithm   Our set of states is the set of all possible DAGs containing the variables in the application, and our stationary distribution is $P(\mathbb{G}|D)$, but as noted previously, we can use $P(D|\mathbb{G})$ in our expression for $\boldsymbol{\alpha}$. Recall from Section 13.2.7.2 that $\mathsf{Nbhd}(\mathbb{G})$ is the set of all DAGs that differ from $\mathbb{G}$ by one edge addition, one edge deletion, or one edge reversal. Clearly $\mathbb{G}_j \in \mathsf{Nbhd}(\mathbb{G}_i)$ if and only if $\mathbb{G}_i \in \mathsf{Nbhd}(\mathbb{G}_j)$. However, because adding or reversing an edge can create a cycle, if $\mathbb{G}_j \in \mathsf{Nbhd}(\mathbb{G}_i)$ it is not necessarily true that $\mathsf{Nbhd}(\mathbb{G}_i)$ and $\mathsf{Nbhd}(\mathbb{G}_j)$ contain the same number of elements. For example, if $\mathbb{G}_i$ and $\mathbb{G}_j$ are the DAGs in Figures 13.6 (a) and (b), respectively, then $\mathbb{G}_j \in \mathsf{Nbhd}(\mathbb{G}_i)$. However, $\mathsf{Nbhd}(\mathbb{G}_i)$ contains five elements because adding the edge $X_3 \rightarrow X_1$ would create a cycle, whereas $\mathsf{Nbhd}(\mathbb{G}_j)$ contains six elements. We create our transition matrix $\mathbf{Q}$ as follows: For each pair of states $\mathbb{G}_i$ and $\mathbb{G}_j$, we set

$$q_{ij} = \begin{cases} \dfrac{1}{|\mathsf{Nbhd}(\mathbb{G}_i)|} & \mathbb{G}_j \in \mathsf{Nbhd}(\mathbb{G}_i) \\[2ex] 0 & \mathbb{G}_j \notin \mathsf{Nbhd}(\mathbb{G}_i) \end{cases},$$

where $|\mathsf{Nbhd}(\mathbb{G}_i)|$ returns the number of elements in the set. Because $\mathbf{Q}$ is not symmetric, we use Equality 13.17 rather than Equality 13.18 to compute α_{ij}. Specifically, our steps are as follows:

1. If the DAG at the trial k is $\mathbb{G}_i$, choose a DAG uniformly from $\mathsf{Nbhd}(\mathbb{G}_i)$. Suppose that DAG is $\mathbb{G}_j$.

2. Choose the DAG for trial $k+1$ to be $\mathbb{G}_j$ with probability

$$\alpha_{ij} = \begin{cases} 1 & \dfrac{P(D|\mathbb{G}_j) \times |\mathsf{Nbhd}(\mathbb{G}_i)|}{P(D|\mathbb{G}_i) \times |\mathsf{Nbhd}(\mathbb{G}_j)|} \geq 1 \\[3ex] \dfrac{P(D|\mathbb{G}_j)\,|\mathsf{Nbhd}(\mathbb{G}_i)|}{P(D|\mathbb{G}_i)\,|\mathsf{Nbhd}(\mathbb{G}_j)|} & \dfrac{P(D|\mathbb{G}_j) \times |\mathsf{Nbhd}(\mathbb{G}_i)|}{P(D|\mathbb{G}_i) \times |\mathsf{Nbhd}(\mathbb{G}_j)|} \leq 1 \end{cases},$$

(a) (b)

Figure 13.6 These DAGs are in each other's neighborhoods, but their neighborhoods do not contain the same number of elements.

and to be $\mathbb{G}_i$ with probability $1 - \alpha_{ij}$.

A Simplification It is burdensome to compute the sizes of the neighborhoods of the DAGs in each step. Alternatively, we could include DAGs with cycles in the neighborhoods. That is, $\mathsf{Nbhd}(\mathbb{G}_i)$ is the set of all graphs (including ones with cycles) that differ from $\mathbb{G}_i$ by one edge addition, one edge deletion, or one edge reversal. It is not hard to see that then the size of every neighborhood is equal $n(n-1)$. We therefore define

$$q_{ij} = \begin{cases} \dfrac{1}{n(n-1)} & \mathbb{G}_j \in \mathsf{Nbhd}(\mathbb{G}_i) \\[2mm] 0 & \mathbb{G}_j \notin \mathsf{Nbhd}(\mathbb{G}_i) \end{cases}.$$

If we are currently in state $\mathbb{G}_i$ and we obtain a graph $\mathbb{G}_j$ that is not a DAG, we set $P(\mathsf{D}|\mathbb{G}_j) = 0$ (effectively making r_j zero). In this way, α_{ij} is zero, the graph is not chosen, and we stay at $\mathbb{G}_i$ in this step. Because $\mathbf{Q}$ is now symmetric, we can use Equality 13.18 to compute α_{ij}. Notice that our theory was developed by assuming that all values in the stationary distribution are positive, which is not currently the case. However, Tierney [1996] shows that convergence also follows if we allow 0 values as discussed here.

Neapolitan [2004] develops a similar method that averages over DAG patterns.

13.3 Constraint-Based Structure Learning

Next we discuss a quite different structure learning technique called **constraint-based learning**. In this approach, we try to learn a DAG from the conditional independencies in the generative probability distribution P. First, we illustrate the constraint-based approach by showing how to learn a DAG faithful to a probability distribution. This is followed by a discussion of embedded faithfulness.

13.3.1 Learning a DAG Faithful to P

Recall that $(\mathbb{G}, P)$ satisfies the faithfulness condition if all and only the conditional independencies in P are entailed by $\mathbb{G}$. After discussing why we would

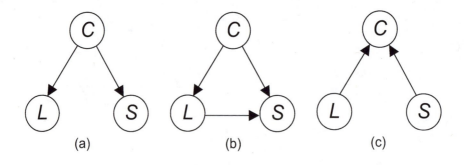

Figure 13.7 If the only conditional independency in P is $I_P(L, S|C)$, then P satisfies the Markov condition with the DAGs in (a) and (b), and P satisfies the faithfulness condition only with the DAG in (a).

want to learn a DAG faithful to a probability distribution P, we illustrate learning such a DAG.

13.3.1.1   Why We Want a Faithful DAG

Consider again the objects in Figure 5.1. In Example 5.23, we let P assign 1/13 to each object in the figure, and we defined these random variables on the set containing the objects:

Variable	Value	Outcomes Mapped to This Value
L	l_1	All objects containing an A
	l_2	All objects containing a B
S	s_1	All square objects
	s_2	All circular objects
C	c_1	All black objects
	c_2	All white objects

We then showed that L and S are conditionally independent given C. That is, using the notation established in Section 5.2.2, we showed that

$$I_P(L, S|C).$$

In Example 6.1, we showed that this implies that P satisfies the Markov condition with the DAG in Figure 13.7 (a). However, P also satisfies the Markov condition with the complete DAG in Figure 13.7 (b). P does not satisfy the Markov condition with the DAG in Figure 13.7 (c) because that DAG entails $I_P(L, S)$ and this independency is not in P. The DAG in Figure 13.7 (b) does not represent P very well because it does not entail a conditional independency that is in P, namely $I_P(L, S|C)$. This is a violation of the faithfulness condition. Of the DAGs in Figure 13.7, only the one in Figure 13.7 (a) is faithful to P.

   If we can find a DAG that is faithful to a probability distribution P, we have achieved our goal of representing P succinctly. That is, if there are DAGs faithful to P, then those DAGs are the smallest DAGs that include P (see [Neapolitan, 2004]). We say *DAGs* because if a DAG is faithful to P, then clearly any Markov-equivalent DAG is also faithful to P. For example, the DAGs $L \rightarrow C \rightarrow S$ and $S \leftarrow C \leftarrow L$, which are Markov equivalent to the DAG $L \leftarrow C \rightarrow S$, are also faithful to the probability distribution P concerning the objects in Figure 5.1. As we shall see, not every probability distribution has a DAG that is faithful to it. However, if there are DAGs faithful to a probability distribution, it is relatively easy to discover them. We discuss learning a faithful DAG next.

13.3.1.2   Learning a Faithful DAG

We assume that we have a sample of entities from the population over which the random variables are defined, and we know the values of the variables of interest for the entities in the sample. The sample could be a random sample, or it could be obtained from passive data. From this sample, we have deduced the conditional independencies among the variables. A method for deducing conditional independencies and obtaining a measure of our confidence in them is described in [Spirtes et al., 1993; 2000] and [Neapolitan, 2004]. Our confidence in the DAG we learn is no greater than our confidence in these conditional independencies.

Example 13.16 It is left as an exercise to show that the data shown in Example 13.1 exhibit this conditional independency:

$$I_P(Height, Wage|Sex).$$

Therefore, from these data we can conclude, with a certain measure of confidence, that this conditional independency exists in the population at large. ∎

Next we give a sequence of examples in which we learn a DAG that is faithful to the probability distribution of interest. These examples illustrate how a faithful DAG can be learned from the conditional independencies if one exists. We stress again that the DAG is faithful to the conditional independencies we have learned from the data. We are not certain that these are the conditional independencies in the probability distribution for the entire population.

Example 13.17 Suppose V is our set of observed variables, $V = \{X, Y\}$, and the set of conditional independencies in P is

$$\{I_P(X, Y)\}.$$

We want to find a DAG faithful to P. We cannot have either of the DAGs in Figure 13.8 (a). The reason is that these DAGs do not entail that X and Y are independent, which means the faithfulness condition is not satisfied. So, we must have the DAG in Figure 13.8 (b). We conclude that P is faithful to the DAG in Figure 13.8 (b). ∎

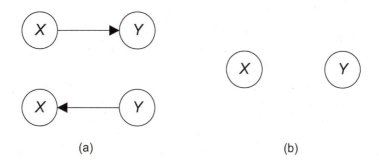

(a)   (b)

Figure 13.8 If the set of conditional independencies is $\{I_P(X, Y)\}$, we must have the DAG in (b), whereas if it is $\varnothing$, we must have one of the DAGs in (a).

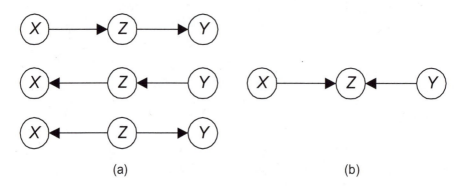

(a)   (b)

Figure 13.9 If the set of conditional independencies is $\{I_P(X, Y)\}$, we must have the DAG in (b); if it is $\{I_P(X, Y|Z)\}$, we must have one of the DAGs in (a).

Example 13.18 Suppose $V = \{X, Y\}$ and the set of conditional independencies in P is the empty set

$$\varnothing.$$

That is, there are no independencies. We want to find a DAG faithful to P. We cannot have the DAG in Figure 13.8 (b). The reason is that this DAG entails that X and Y are independent, which means that the Markov condition is not satisfied. So, we must have one of the DAGs in Figure 13.8 (a). We conclude that P is faithful to both the DAGs in Figure 13.8 (a). Note that these DAGs are Markov equivalent.   ∎

Example 13.19 Suppose $V = \{X, Y, Z\}$, and the set of conditional independencies in P is

$$\{I_P(X, Y)\}.$$

We want to find a DAG faithful to P. There can be no edge between X and Y in the DAG owing to the reason given in Example 13.17. Furthermore, there must

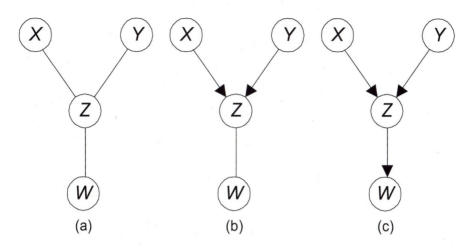

Figure 13.10 If the set of conditional independencies is $\{I_p(X, \{Y, W\}), I_P(Y, \{X, Z\})\}$, we must have the DAG in (c).

be edges between X and Z and between Y and Z owing to the reason given in Example 13.18. We cannot have any of the DAGs in Figure 13.9 (a). The reason is that these DAGs entail $I_P(X, Y | Z)$, and this conditional independency is not present. So, the Markov condition is not satisfied. Furthermore, the DAGs do not entail $I_P(X, Y)$. So, the DAG must be the one in Figure 13.9 (b). We conclude that P is faithful to the DAG in Figure 13.9 (b).   ∎

Example 13.20 Suppose $V = \{X, Y, Z\}$ and the set of conditional independencies in P is

$$\{I_P(X, Y | Z)\}.$$

We want to find a DAG faithful to P. Owing to reasons similar to those given before, the only edges in the DAG must be between X and Z and between Y and Z. We cannot have the DAG in Figure 13.9 (b). The reason is that this DAG entails $I(X, Y)$, and this conditional independency is not present. So, the Markov condition is not satisfied. So, we must have one of the DAGs in Figure 13.9 (a). We conclude that P is faithful to all the DAGs in Figure 13.9 (a). ∎

We now state a theorem whose proof can be found in [Neapolitan, 2004]. At this point your intuition should suspect that it is true.

Theorem 13.5 If $(\mathbb{G}, P)$ satisfies the faithfulness condition, then there is an edge between X and Y if and only if X and Y are not conditionally independent given any set of variables.

Example 13.21 Suppose $V = \{X, Y, Z, W\}$ and the set of conditional independencies in P is

$$\{I_p(X, Y), \quad I_P(W, \{X, Y\} | Z)\}.$$

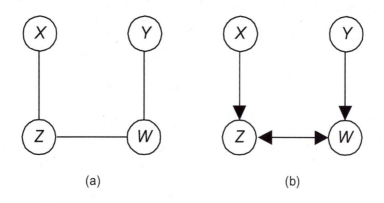

(a)   (b)

Figure 13.11 If the set of conditional independencies is $\{I_P(X, \{Y, W\}),$ $I_P(Y, \{X, Z\})\}$ and we try to find a DAG faithful to P, we obtain the graph in (b), which is not a DAG.

We want to find a DAG faithful to P. Owing to Theorem 13.5, the links (edges without regard for direction) must be as shown in Figure 13.10 (a). We must have the directed edges shown in Figure 13.10 (b) because we have $I_p(X, Y)$. Therefore, we must also have the directed edge shown in Figure 13.10 (c) because we do not have $I_P(W, X)$. We conclude that P is faithful to the DAG in Figure 13.10 (c). ∎

Example 13.22 Suppose $V = \{X, Y, Z, W\}$ and the set of conditional independencies in P is

$$\{I_P(X, \{Y, W\}), \quad I_P(Y, \{X, Z\})\}.$$

We want to find a DAG faithful to P. Owing to Theorem 13.5, we must have the links shown in Figure 13.11 (a). Now, if we have the chain $X \to Z \to W$, $X \leftarrow Z \leftarrow W$, or $X \leftarrow Z \to W$, then we do not have $I_P(X, W)$. So, we must have the chain $X \to Z \leftarrow W$. Similarly, we must have the chain $Y \to W \leftarrow Z$. So, our graph must be the one in Figure 13.11 (b). However, this graph is not a DAG. The problem here is that there is no DAG faithful to P. ∎

Example 13.23 Suppose we have the same vertices and conditional independencies as in Example 13.22. As shown in that example, there is no DAG faithful to P. However, this does not mean we cannot find a more succinct way to represent P than using a complete DAG. P satisfies the Markov condition with each of the DAGs in Figure 13.12. That is, the DAG in Figure 13.12 (a) entails

$$\{I_P(X, Y), \quad I_P(Y, Z)\}$$

and these conditional independencies are both in P, whereas the DAG in Figure 13.12 (b) entails

$$\{I_P(X, Y), \quad I_P(X, W)\}$$

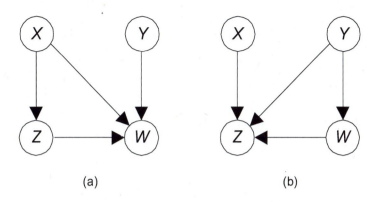

(a)   (b)

Figure 13.12 If the set of conditional independencies is $\{I_P(X, \{Y, W\}),$ $I_P(Y, \{X, Z\})\}$, P satisfies the Markov condition with both these DAGs.

and these conditional independencies are both in P. However, P does not satisfy the faithfulness condition with either of these DAGs because the DAG in Figure 13.12 (a) does not entail $I_P(X, W)$, whereas the DAG in Figure 13.12 (b) does not entail $I_P(Y, Z)$.

Each of these DAGs is as succinct as we can represent the probability distribution. So, when there is no DAG faithful to a probability distribution P, we can still represent P much more succinctly than we would by using the complete DAG. A structure learning algorithm tries to find the most succinct representation. Depending on the number of alternatives of each variable, one of the DAGs in Figure 13.12 may actually be a more succinct representation than the other because it contains fewer parameters. A constraint-based learning algorithm could not distinguish between the two, but a score-based one could. See [Neapolitan, 2004] for a complete discussion of this matter. ∎

13.3.2 Learning a DAG in which P Is Embedded Faithfully

In a sense, we compromised in Example 13.23 because the DAG we learned did not entail all the conditional independencies in P. This is fine if our goal is to learn a Bayesian network that will later be used to do inference. However, another application of structure learning is *causal learning*, which is discussed in the next section. When we are learning causes it would be better to find a DAG in which P is embedded faithfully. We discuss embedded faithfulness next.

Definition 13.2 Suppose we have a joint probability distribution P of the random variables in some set V and a DAG $G = (W, E)$ such that $V \subseteq W$. We say that (G, P) satisfy the **embedded faithfulness condition** if all and only the conditional independencies in P are entailed by G, restricted to variables

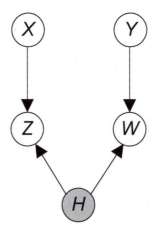

Figure 13.13 If the set of conditional independencies in P is $\{I_P(X, \{Y, W\}), I_P(Y, \{X, Z\})\}$, then P is embedded faithfully in this DAG.

in V. Furthermore, we say that P is embedded faithfully in $\mathbb{G}$.♦

Example 13.24 Again suppose $\mathsf{V} = \{X, Y, Z, W\}$ and the set of conditional independencies in P is

$$\{I_P(X, \{Y, W\}), \quad I_P(Y, \{X, Z\})\}.$$

Then P is embedded faithfully in the DAG in Figure 13.13. It is left as an exercise to show this. By including the hidden variable H in the DAG, we are able to entail all and only the conditional independencies in P restricted to variables in V. ∎

13.4 Application: MENTOR

To illustrate Bayesian network learning, we present the details of one large-scale application.

Mani et al. [1997] developed MENTOR, a system that predicts the risk of mental retardation (MR) in infants. Specifically, the system can determines the probabilities of the child later obtaining scores in four different ranges on the Raven Progressive Matrices Test, which is a test of cognitive function. The probabilities are conditional on values of variables such as the mother's age at time of birth, whether the mother had recently had an X-ray, whether labor was induced, etc.

13.4.1 Developing the Network

The structure of the Bayesian network used in MENTOR was created in the following three steps:

Table 13.3 The Variables Used in MENTOR

Variable	What the Variable Represents
MOM_RACE	Mother's race classified as White or non-White.
MOMAGE_BR	Mother's age at time of child's birth categorized as 14–19 years, 20–34 years, or ≥ 35 years.
MOM_EDU	Mother's education categorized as ≤ 12 and did not graduate high school, graduated high school, and $>$ high school.
DAD_EDU	Father's education categorized same as mother's.
MOM_DIS	Yes if mother had one or more of lung trouble, heart trouble, high blood pressure, kidney trouble, convulsions, diabetes, thyroid trouble, anemia, tumors, bacterial disease, measles, chicken pox, herpes simplex, eclampsia; no otherwise..
FAM_INC	Family income categorized as $< \$10,000$ or $\geq \$10,000$.
MOM_SMOK	Yes if mother smoked during pregnancy; no otherwise.
MOM_ALC	Mother's alcoholic drinking level classified as mild (0–6 drinks per week), moderate (7–20), or severe ($>$20).
PREV_STILL	Yes if mother previously had a stillbirth; no otherwise.
PN_CARE	Yes if mother had prenatal care; no otherwise.
MOM_XRAY	Yes if mother had been X-rayed in the year prior to or during the pregnancy; no otherwise.
GESTATN	Period of gestation categorized as premature (≤ 258 days), or normal (259–294 days), or postmature (≥ 295 days)..
FET_DIST	Fetal distress classified as yes if there was prolapse of cord, mother had a history of uterine surgery, there was uterine rupture or fever at or just before delivery, or there was an abnormal fetal heart rate; no otherwise.
INDUCE_LAB	Yes if mother had induced labor; no otherwise.
C_SECTION	Yes if delivery was a caesarean section; no if it was vaginal.
CHLD_GEND	Gender of child (male or female).
BIRTH_WT	Birth weight categorized as low < 2500 g) or normal (≥ 2500 g).
RESUSCITN	Yes if child had resuscitation; no otherwise.
HEAD_CIRC	Normal if head circumference is 20 or 21; abnormal otherwise.
CHLD_ANOM	Child anomaly classified as yes if child has cerebral palsy, hypothyroidism, spina binfida, Down's syndrome, chromosomal abnormality, anencephaly, hydrocephalus, epilepsy, Turner's syndrome, cerbellar ataxia, speech defect, Klinefelter's syndrome, or convulsions; no otherwise.
CHILD_HPRB	Child's health problem categorized as having a physical problem, having a behavior problem, having both a physical and a behavioral problem, or having no problem.
CHLD_RAVN	Child's cognitive level, measured by the Raven test, categorized as mild MR, borderline MR, normal, or superior.
P_MOM	Mother's cognitive level, measured by the Peabody test, categorized as mild MR, borderline MR, normal, or superior.

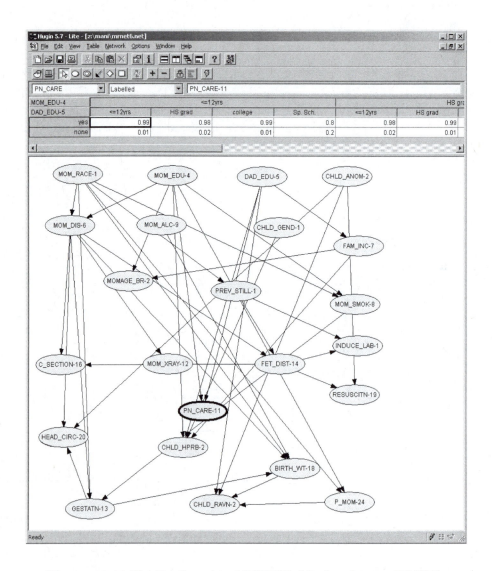

Figure 13.14 The DAG used in MENTOR (displayed using HUGIN).

1. Mani et al. [1997] obtained the Child Health and Development Study (CHDS) data set, which is the data set developed in a study concerning pregnant mothers and their children. The children were followed through their teen years and included numerous questionnaires, physical and psychological exams, and special tests. The study was conducted by the University of California at Berkeley and the Kaiser Foundation. It started in 1959 and continued into the 1980's. There are approximately 6000 children and 3000 mothers with IQ scores in the data set. The children were either 5 years old or 9 years old when their IQs were tested. The IQ test used for the children was the Raven Progressive Matrices Test. The mothers' IQs were also tested, and the test used was the Peabody Picture Vocabulary Test.

   Initially, Mani et al. [1997] identified 50 variables in the data set that were thought to play a role in the causal mechanism of mental retardation. However, they eliminated those with weak associations to the Raven score, and finally used only 23 in their model. The variables used are shown in Table 13.3.

   After the variables were identified, they used the CB algorithm to learn a network structure from the data set. The **CB** Algorithm, which is discussed in [Singh and Valtorta, 1995], uses the constraint-based method to propose a total ordering of the nodes, and then uses a modified version of Algorithm 9.1 (K2) to learn a DAG structure.

2. Mani et al. [1997] decided they wanted the network to be a causal network. So next they modified the DAG according to the following three rules:

   (a) Rule of Chronology: An event cannot be the parent of a second event that preceded the first event in time. For example, CHILD_HPRB (child's health problem) cannot be the parent of MOM_DIS (mother's disease).

   (b) Rule of Commonsense: The causal links should not go against common sense. For example, DAD_EDU (father's education) cannot be a cause of MOM_RACE (mother's race).

   (c) Domain Rule: The causal links should not violate established domain rules. For example, PN_CARE (prenatal care) should not cause MOM_SMOK (maternal smoking).

3. Finally, the DAG was refined by an expert. The expert was a clinician who had 20 years experience with children with mental retardation and other developmental disabilities. When the expert stated there was no relationship between variables with a causal link, the link was removed and new ones were incorporated to capture knowledge of the domain causal mechanisms.

The final DAG specifications were input to HUGIN [Olesen et al., 1992] using the HUGIN graphic interface. The output is the DAG shown in Figure 13.14.

After the DAG was developed, the conditional probability distributions were learned from the CHDS data set using the techniques shown in Chapters 6 and 7. After that, they too were modified by the expert, resulting finally in the Bayesian network in MENTOR.

13.4.2 Validating MENTOR

In actual clinical cases, the diagnosis of mental retardation is rarely made after only a review of history and physical examination. Therefore, we cannot expect MENTOR to do more than indicate a risk of mental retardation by computing the probability of it. The higher the probability the greater the risk. Mani et al. [1997] showed that, on average, children who were later determined to have mental retardation were found to be at greater risk than those who were not. MENTOR can confirm a clinician's assessment by reporting the probability of mental retardation.

Mani et al. [1997] also compared the results of MENTOR with the judgments of an expert. The expert was in agreement with MENTOR's assessments (conditional probabilities) in seven of the nine cases.

13.5   Software Packages for Learning

Based on considerations such as those illustrated in Section 13.3.1, Spirtes et al. [1993, 2000] developed an algorithm that finds the DAG faithful to P from the conditional independencies in P when there is a DAG faithful to P. Spirtes et al. [1993, 2000] further developed an algorithm that learns a DAG in which P is embedded faithfully from the conditional independencies in P when such a DAG exists. These algorithms have been implemented in the Tetrad software package [Scheines et al., 1994], which can be downloaded for free from www.phil.cmu.edu/projects/tetrad/.

The Tetrad software package also has a module that uses the GES algorithm along with the BIC score to learn a Bayesian network from data.

Other Bayesian network learning packages include the following:

- Belief Network Power Constructor (constraint-based approach),

  www.cs.ualberta.ca/~jcheng/bnpc.htm.

- Bayesware (structure and parameters), www.bayesware.com/.

- Bayes Net Toolbox, bnt.sourceforge.net/.

- Probabilistic Net Library, www.eng.itlab.unn.ru/?dir=139.

13.6   Causal Learning

In many, if not most, applications the variables of interest have causal relationships to each other. For example, the variables in Example 13.1 are causally

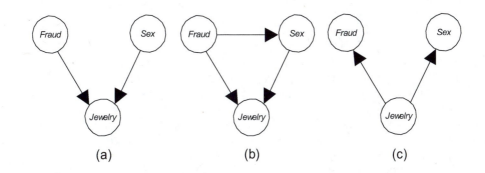

Figure 13.15 If the only causal relationships are that *Fraud* and *Sex* have causal influences on *Jewelry*, then the causal DAG is the one in (a). If we make the causal Markov assumption, only the DAG in (c) is ruled out if we observe $I_P(Fraud, Sex)$.

related in that sex has a causal effect on height and may have a causal effect on wage. If the variables are causally related, we can learn something about their causal relationships when we learn the structure of the DAG from data. However, we must make certain assumptions to do this. We discuss these assumptions and causal learning next.

13.6.1   Causal Faithfulness Assumption

Recall from Section 6.3.2.2 that if we assume the observed probability distribution P of a set of random variables V satisfies the Markov condition with the causal DAG G containing the variables, we say we are making the **causal Markov assumption**, and we call (G, P) a **causal network**. Furthermore, we concluded that the causal Markov assumption is justified for a causal graph if the following conditions are satisfied:

1. There are no hidden common causes. That is, all common causes are represented in the graph.

2. There are no causal feedback loops. That is, our graph is a DAG.

3. Selection bias is not present.

Recall the discussion concerning credit card fraud in Section 6.1. Suppose that both fraud and sex do indeed have a causal effect on whether jewelry is purchased, and there are no other causal relationships among the variables. Then the causal DAG containing these variables is the one in Figure 13.15 (a). If we make the causal Markov assumption, we must have $I_P(Fraud, Sex)$.

Suppose now that we do not know the causal relationships among the variables, we make the causal Markov assumption, and we learn only the conditional independency $I_P(Fraud, Sex)$ from data. Can we conclude that the causal DAG must be the one in Figure 13.15 (a)? No, we cannot because P

also satisfies the Markov condition with the DAG in Figure 13.15 (b). This concept is a bit tricky to understand. However, recall that we are assuming that we do not know the causal relationships among the variables. As far as we know, they could be the ones in Figure 13.15 (b). If the DAG in Figure 13.15 (b) were the causal DAG, the causal Markov assumption would still be satisfied when the only conditional independency is $I_P(Fraud, Sex)$, because that DAG satisfies the Markov condition with P. So, if we make only the causal Markov assumption, we cannot distinguish the causal DAGs in Figures 13.15 (a) and 13.15 (b) based on the conditional independency $I_P(Fraud, Sex)$. The causal Markov assumption only enables us to rule out causal DAGs that contain conditional independencies that are not in P. One such DAG is the one in Figure 13.15 (c).

We need to make the causal faithfulness assumption to conclude that the causal DAG is the one in Figure 13.15 (a). That assumption is as follows: If we assume that the observed probability distribution P of a set of random variables V satisfies the faithfulness condition with the causal $\mathbb{G}$ containing the variables, we say we are making the **causal faithfulness assumption**. If we make the causal faithfulness assumption, then if we find a unique DAG that is faithful to P, the edges in that DAG must represent causal influences. This is illustrated by the following examples.

Example 13.25 Recall that in Example 13.19 we showed that if $V = \{X, Y, Z\}$ and the set of conditional independencies in P is

$$\{I_P(X, Y)\},$$

the only DAG faithful to P is the one in Figure 13.9 (b). If we make the causal faithfulness assumption, this DAG must be the causal DAG, which means we can conclude that X and Y each cause Z. This is the exact same situation as that illustrated earlier concerning fraud, sex, and jewelry. Therefore, if we make the causal faithfulness assumption, we can conclude that the causal DAG is the one in Figure 13.15 (a) based on the conditional independency $I_P(Fraud, Sex)$. ∎

Example 13.26 In Example 13.20 we showed that if $V = \{X, Y, Z\}$ and the set of conditional independencies in P is

$$\{I_P(X, Y|Z)\},$$

all the DAGs in Figure 13.9 (a) are faithful to P. So, if we make the causal faithfulness assumption, we can conclude that one of these DAGs is the causal DAG, but we do not know which one. ∎

Example 13.27 In Example 13.21 we showed that if $V = \{X, Y, Z, W\}$ and the set of conditional independencies in P is

$$\{I_p(X, Y), \quad I_P(W, \{X, Y\}|Z)\},$$

the only DAG faithful to P is the one in Figure 13.10 (c). So, we can conclude that X and Y each cause Z and Z causes W. ∎

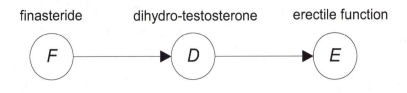

finasteride   dihydro-testosterone   erectile function

Figure 13.16 Finasteride and erectile function are independent.

When is the causal faithfulness assumption justified? It requires the three conditions mentioned previously for the causal Markov assumption plus one more, which we discuss next. Recall from Section 7.2.1 that the causal relationships among finasteride (F), dihydro-testosterone (D), and erectile dysfunction (E) have clearly been found to be those depicted in Figure 13.16. However, as discussed in that section, we have $I_P(F, E|D)$. We would expect a causal mediary to transmit an effect from its antecedent to its consequence, but in this case it does not. As also discussed in Section 7.2.1, the explanation is that finasteride cannot lower dihydro-testosterone levels beyond a certain threshold level, and that level is all that is needed for erectile function. So, we have $I_P(F, E)$.

The Markov condition does not entail $I_P(F, E)$ for the causal DAG in Figure 13.16. It only entails $I_P(F, E|D)$. So, the causal faithfulness assumption is not justified. If we learned the conditional independencies in the probability distribution of these variables from data, we would learn the following set of independencies:

$$\{I_P(F, E), \quad I_P(F, E|D)\}.$$

There is no DAG that entails both these conditional independencies, so no DAG could be learned from such data.

The causal faithfulness assumption is usually justified when the three conditions listed previously for the causal Markov assumption are satisfied and when we do not have unusual causal relationships, as in the finasteride example. So, the causal faithfulness assumption is ordinarily justified for a causal graph if the following conditions are satisfied:

1. There are no hidden common causes. That is, all common causes are represented in the graph.

2. There are no causal feedback loops. That is, our graph is a DAG.

3. Selection bias is not present.

4. All intermediate causes transmit influences from their antecedents to their consequences.

13.6.2   Causal Embedded Faithfulness Assumption

It seems that the main exception to the causal faithfulness assumption (and the causal Markov assumption) is the presence of hidden common causes. Even in

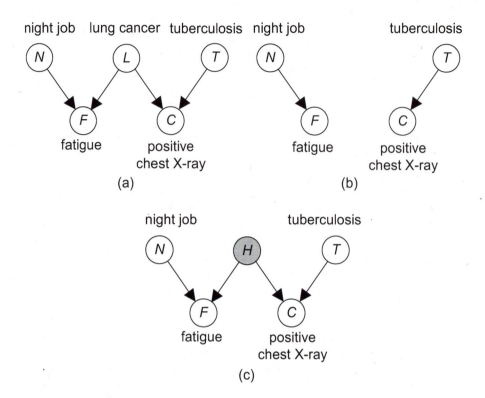

Figure 13.17 If the causal relationships are those shown in (a), P is not faithful to the DAG in (b), but P is embedded faithfully in the DAG in (c).

the example concerning sex, height, and wage (Example 13.1), perhaps there is a genetic trait that makes people grow taller and also gives them some personality trait that helps them compete better in the job market. Our next assumption eliminates the requirement that there are no hidden common causes. If we assume that the observed probability distribution P of a set of random variables V is embedded faithfully in a causal DAG containing the variables, we say that we are making the **causal embedded faithfulness assumption**. The causal embedded faithfulness assumption is usually justified when the conditions for the causal faithfulness assumption are satisfied, except that hidden common causes may be present.

   Next we illustrate the causal embedded faithfulness assumption. Suppose that the causal DAG in Figure 13.17 (a) satisfies the causal faithfulness assumption. However, we only observe V $= \{N, F, C, T\}$. Then the causal DAG containing the observed variables is the one in Figure 13.17 (b). The DAG in Figure 13.17 (b) entails $I_P(F, C)$, and this conditional independency is not entailed by the DAG in Figure 13.17 (a). Therefore, the observed distribution $P(V)$ does not satisfy the Markov condition with the causal DAG in Figure 13.17 (b), which means the causal faithfulness assumption is not warranted.

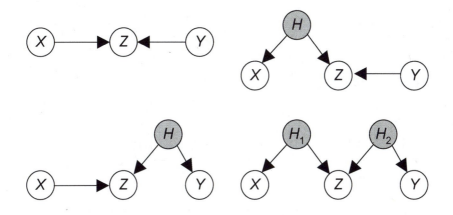

Figure 13.18 If we make the causal embedded faithfulness assumption and our set of conditional independencies is $\{I_P(X,Y)\}$, the causal relationships could be the ones in any of these DAGs.

However, $P(V)$ is embedded faithfully in the DAG in Figure 13.17 (c). So, the causal embedded faithfulness assumption is warranted. Note that this example illustrates a situation in which we identify four variables and two of them have a hidden common cause. That is, we have not identified lung cancer as a feature of humans.

Let's see how much we can learn about causal influences when we make only the causal embedded faithfulness assumption.

Example 13.28 Recall that in Example 13.25, $V = \{X, Y, Z\}$, our set of conditional independencies was
$$\{I_P(X,Y)\},$$
and we concluded that X and Y each caused Z while making the causal faithfulness assumption. However, the probability distribution is embedded faithfully in all the DAGs in Figure 13.18. So, if we make only the causal embedded faithfulness assumption, it could be that X causes Z, or it could be that X and Z have a hidden common cause. The same holds for Y and Z. ∎

While making only the more reasonable causal embedded faithfulness assumption, we were not able to learn any causal influences in the previous example. Can we ever learn a causal influence while making only this assumption? The next example shows that we can.

Example 13.29 Recall that in Example 13.27, $V = \{X, Y, Z, W\}$ and our set of conditional independencies was

$$\{I_P(X,Y), \quad I_P(W, \{X,Y\}|Z)\}.$$

In this case the probability distribution P is embedded faithfully in the DAGs in Figures 13.19 (a) and 13.19 (b). However, it is not embedded faithfully in the

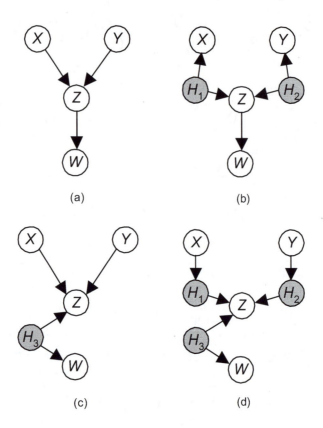

Figure 13.19 If our set of conditional independencies is $\{I_P(X,Y),$ $I_P(W,\{X,Y\}|Z)\}$, then P is embedded faithfully in the DAGs in (a) and (b) but not in the DAGs in (c) and (d).

DAGs in Figure 13.19 (c) or 13.19 (d). The reason is that these latter DAGs entail $I_P(X,W)$, and we do not have this conditional independency. That is, the Markov condition says X must be independent of its nondescendents conditional on its parents. Because X has no parents, this means that X must simply be independent of its nondescendents, and W is one of its nondescendents. If we make the causal embedded faithfulness assumption, we conclude that Z causes W.   ∎

Example 13.30 Recall that in Example 13.23, $V = \{X,Y,Z,W\}$, our set of conditional independencies was

$$\{I_P(X,\{Y,W\}),\quad I_P(Y,\{X,Z\}),$$

and we obtained the graph in Figure 13.20 (a) when we tried to learn a DAG faithful to P. We concluded that there is no DAG faithful to P. Then in Example 13.24 we showed that P is embedded faithfully in the DAG in Figure

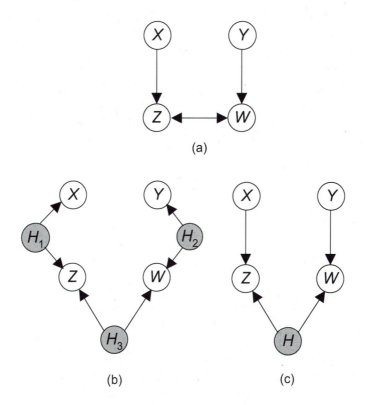

Figure 13.20 If our set of conditional independencies is $\{I_P(X, \{Y, W\}),$ $I_P(Y, \{X, Z\})$, we can conclude that Z and W have a hidden common cause.

13.20 (c). P is also embedded faithfully in the DAG in Figure 13.20 (b). If we make the causal embedded faithfulness assumption, we conclude that Z and W have a hidden common cause. ∎

13.6.3 Application: College Student Retention Rate

Next we show a real application of using the theory just discussed to learn causal influences. First, however, we review the edges in a causal graph.

When using a software package to learn causal influences, the graph learned has several different types of edges, with each indicating a different conclusion about the causal relationship between the variables connected by the edge. Different packages may denote these edges differently. Below is the notation used here.

Edge	Causal Relationship
$X - Y$	X causes Y or (exclusive) Y causes X; or X and Y have a hidden common cause.
$X \rightarrow Y$	X causes Y or X and Y have a hidden common cause; and Y does not cause X.
$X \rightarrowtail Y$	X causes Y.
$X \leftrightarrow Y$	X and Y have a hidden common cause.

In the above, when we do not denote an "or" as exclusive, it is not exclusive. There is one additional restriction. If we have the chain $X - Y - Z$, we cannot have two causal edges with their heads at node Y. For example, we could not have node X causing node Y and nodes Y and Z having a hidden common cause.

The example now follows. Using the database collected by the *U.S. News and World Report* magazine for the purpose of college ranking, Druzdzel and Glymour [1999] analyzed the influences that affect university student retention rate. By "student retention rate" we mean the percent of entering freshmen who end up graduating from the university at which they initially matriculate. Low student retention rate is a major concern at many American universities, as the mean retention rate over all American universities is only 55%.

The database provided by the *U.S. News and World Report* magazine contains records for 204 U.S. universities and colleges identified as major research institutions. Each record consists of over 100 variables. The data were collected separately for the years 1992 and 1993. Druzdzel and Glymour [1999] selected the following eight variables as being most relevant to their study:

Variable	What the Variable Represents
$grad$	Fraction of entering students who graduate from the institution
$rejr$	Fraction of applicants who are not offered admission
$tstsc$	Average standardized score of incoming students
$tp10$	Fraction of incoming students in the top 10% in high school
$acpt$	Fraction of students who accept the institution's admission offer
$spnd$	Average educational and general expenses per student
$sfrat$	Student/faculty ratio
$salar$	Average faculty salary

Druzdzel and Glymour [1999] used Tetrad II [Scheines et al., 1994] to learn causal influences from the data. Tetrad II allows the user to specify a temporal ordering of the variables. If variable Y precedes X in this order, the algorithm assumes there can be no path from X to Y in any DAG in which the probability distribution of the variables is embedded faithfully. It is called a temporal ordering because in applications to causality if Y precedes X in time, we would assume X could not cause Y. Druzdzel and Glymour [1999] specified the following temporal ordering for the variables in this study:

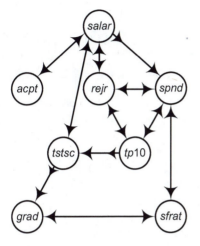
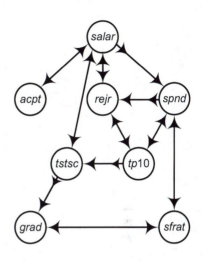
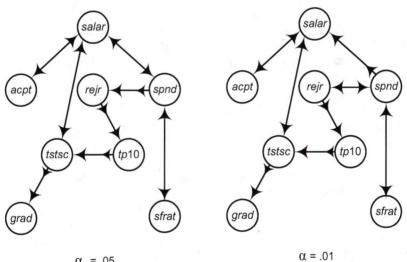

Figure 13.21 The graphs Tetrad II learned from *U.S. News and World Report*'s 1992 database.

>spnd, sfrat, salar
>rejr, acpt
>tstsc, tp10
>grad

Their reasons for this ordering are as follows: They believed the average spending per student (*spnd*), the student/teacher ratio (*sfrat*), and the faculty salary (*salar*) are determined based on budget considerations and are not influenced by any of the other five variables. Furthermore, they placed rejection rate (*rejr*) and the fraction of students who accept the institution's admission offer (*acpt*) ahead of average test scores (*tstsc*) and class standing (*tp10*) because the values of these latter two variables are only obtained from matriculating students. Finally, they assumed the graduate rate (*grad*) does not cause any of the other variables.

Tetrad II allows the user to enter a significance level. A significance level of α means the probability of rejecting a conditional independency hypothesis, when it is true, is α. Therefore, the smaller the value of α is, the less likely we are to reject a conditional independency, and therefore the sparser our resultant graph. Figure 13.21 shows the graphs which Druzdzel and Glymour [1999] learned from the 1992 database, provided by *U.S. News and World Report*, using significance levels of .2, .1, .05, and .01.

Although different graphs were obtained at different levels of significance, all the graphs in Figure 13.21 show that the average standardized test score (*tstsc*) has a direct causal influence on graduation rate (*grad*), and no other variable has a direct causal influence on *grad*. The results for the 1993 data base were not as overwhelming, but they too indicated *tstsc* to be the only direct causal influence of *grad*.

To test whether the causal structure may be different for top research universities, Druzdzel and Glymour [1999] repeated the study using only the top 50 universities according to the ranking of *U.S. News and World Report*. The results were similar to those for the complete database.

These results indicate that although factors such as spending per student and faculty salary may have an influence on graduation rates, they do so only indirectly by affecting the standardized test scores of matriculating students. If the results correctly model reality, retention rates can be improved by bringing in students with higher test scores in any way whatsoever. Indeed, in 1994, Carnegie Mellon changed its financial aid policies to assign a portion of its scholarship fund on the basis of academic merit. Druzdzel and Glymour [1999] noted that this resulted in an increase in the average test scores of matriculating freshman classes and an increase in freshman retention.

13.7   Class Probability Trees

Recall that Bayesian networks represent a large joint distribution of random variables succinctly. Furthermore, we can use a Bayesian network to compute the conditional probability of any variable(s) of interest given values of some other variables. This is most useful when there is no particular variable that is our target, and we want to use the model to determine conditional probabilities of different variables depending on the situation. However, in some applications there is a single target variable, and we are only concerned with the probability of the values of that variable given values of other variables. In situations like this, we can certainly model the problem using a Bayesian network. However, there are other techniques available for modeling problems that concentrate on a target variable. Standard parametric statistical technical techniques include linear and logistic regression [Anderson et al., 2007]. The machine learning community developed a quite different method, called **class probability trees**, for handling discrete target variables. This method, which we discuss next, makes no special assumptions about the probability distribution.

13.7.1 Theory of Class Probability Trees

Suppose we are interested in whether an individual might buy some particular product. Suppose further that income, sex, and whether the individual is mailed a flyer all have an influence on whether the individual buys, and we articulate three ranges of income, namely low, medium, and high. Then our variables and their values are as follows:

Target Variable	Values
Buy	$\{no, yes\}$

Predictor Variables	Values
$Income$	$\{low, medium, high\}$
Sex	$\{male, female\}$
$Mailed$	$\{no, yes\}$

There are $3 \times 2 \times 2 = 12$ combinations of values of the predictor variables. We are interested in the conditional probability of Buy given each of these combinations of values. For example, we are interested in

$$P(Buy = yes | Income = low, Sex = female, Mailed = yes).$$

We can store these 12 conditional probabilities using a class probability tree. A **complete class probability tree** has stored at its root one of the predictors (say $Income$). There is one branch from the root for each value of the variable stored at the root. The nodes at level 1 in the tree each store the same second predictor (say Sex). There is one branch from each of those nodes for each value of the variable stored at the node. We continue down the tree until all predictors are stored. The leaves of the tree store the target variable along with the conditional probability of the target variable given the values of the predictors in the path leading to the leaf. In our current example there are 12 leaves, one for each combination of values of the predictors. If there are many predictors, each with quite a few values, a complete class probability tree can become quite large. Aside from the storage problem, it might be hard to learn

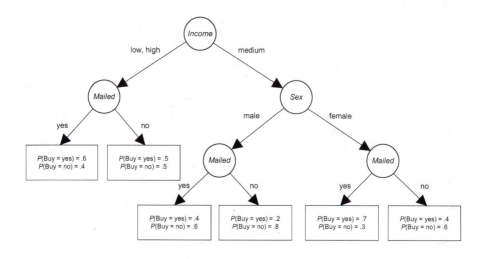

Figure 13.22 A class probability tree.

a large tree from data. However, some conditional probabilities may be the same for two or more combinations of values of the predictors. For example, the following four conditional probabilities may all be the same:

$$P(Buy = yes | Income = low, Sex = female, Mailed = yes)$$

$$P(Buy = yes | Income = low, Sex = male, Mailed = yes)$$

$$P(Buy = yes | Income = high, Sex = female, Mailed = yes)$$

$$P(Buy = yes | Income = high, Sex = male, Mailed = yes).$$

In this case we can represent the conditional probabilities more succinctly using the class probability tree in Figure 13.22. There is just one branch from the *Income* node for the two values *low* and *high* because the conditional probability is the same for these two values. Furthermore, this branch leads directly to a *Mailed* node because the value of *Sex* does not matter when *Income* is *low* or *high*.

We call the set of edges emanating from an internal node in a class probability tree a **split**, and we say there is a split on the variable stored at the node. For example, the root in the tree in Figure 13.22 is a split on the variable *Income*.

To retrieve a conditional probability from a class probability tree, we start at the root and proceed to a leaf following the branches that have the values on which we are conditioning. For example, to retrieve $P(Buy = yes | Income = medium, Sex = female, Mailed = yes)$ from the tree in Figure 13.22, we proceed to the right from the *Income* node, then to right from the *Sex* node, and, finally, to the left from the *Mailed* node. We then retrieve the conditional probability value .7. In this way, we obtain

$$P(Buy = yes | Income = medium, Sex = female, Mailed = yes) = .7.$$

The purpose of a class probability tree learning algorithm is to learn from data a tree that best represents the conditional probabilities of interest. This is called **"growing the tree."** Trees are grown using a greedy one-ply lookahead search strategy and a scoring criterion to evaluate how good the tree appears based on the data. The classical text in this area is [Breiman et al., 1984]. Buntine [1993] presents a tree learning algorithm that uses a Bayesian scoring criterion. This algorithm is used in the IND Tree Package [Buntine, 2002], which comes with source code and a manual.

13.7.2 Application to Targeted Advertising

Suppose we have some population of potential customers such as all individuals living in a certain geographical area or all individuals who are registered users of Microsoft Windows. In targeted advertising we want to mail (or present in some way) an advertisement to a given subpopulation of this population only if we can expect to increase our profit by so doing. For example, if we learn we can expect to increase our profit by mailing to all males over the age of 30 in some population, we should do so. On the other hand, if we cannot expect to increase our profit by mailing to females under 30, we should not do so. First, we obtain an equality that tells us whether we can expect to increase our profit by mailing an advertisement to members of some subpopulation. Then we show how to use this inequality along with class probability trees to identify potentially profitable subpopulations. Finally, we show some experimental results.

13.7.2.1 Calculating Expected Lift in Profit

We can distinguish the following four types of potential customers:

Customer Type	Does Not Receive Ad	Receives Ad
Never-Buy	Won't buy	Won't buy
Persuadable	Won't buy	Will buy
Anti-Persuadable	Will buy	Won't buy
Always-Buy	Will buy	Will buy

A never-buy customer will not buy no matter what; a persuadable customer will buy only if an advertisement is received; an anti-persuadable customer will buy only if an advertisement is not received (such a customer is perhaps aggravated by the advertisement, causing the customer to reverse the decision to buy); and an always-buy customer will buy regardless of whether an advertisement is received. An advertisement is wasted on never-buy and always-buy customers, while it has a negative effect on an anti-persuadable customer. So the ideal mailing would send the advertisement only to the persuadable customers. However, in general, it is not possible to identify exactly this subset of customers. So we make an effort to come as close as possible to an ideal mailing.

In some subpopulation let N_{Never}, N_{Pers}, N_{Anti}, and N_{Always} be the number of people with behaviors never-buy, persuadable, anti-persuadable, and always-buy, and let N be the total number of people in the subpopulation. Furthermore, let c denote the cost of mailing (or in some way delivering) the advertisement to a given person, let r_u denote the profit obtained from a sale to an unsolicited customer, and let r_s denote the profit from a sale to a solicited customer. The reason r_s may be different from r_u is that we may offer some discount in our advertisement. Now suppose we pick a person at random from the subpopulation and mail that person the advertisement. We have

$$P(Buy = yes|Mailed = yes) = \frac{N_{Pers} + N_{Always}}{N}, \qquad (13.22)$$

where we are also conditioning on the fact that the person is in the given subpopulation without explicitly denoting this.

So the expected amount of profit received from each person who is mailed the advertisement is

$$\left(\frac{N_{Pers} + N_{Always}}{N}\right) \times (r_s - c) + \left(1 - \frac{N_{Pers} + N_{Always}}{N}\right) \times (-c)$$

$$= \frac{N_{Pers} + N_{Always}}{N} \times r_s - c.$$

Similarly,

$$P(Buy = yes|Mailed = no) = \frac{N_{Anti} + N_{Always}}{N}, \qquad (13.23)$$

and the expected amount of profit received from each person who is not mailed the advertisement is

$$\frac{N_{Anti} + N_{Always}}{N} \times r_u.$$

We should mail the advertisement to members of this subpopulation only when the expected profit received from a person who is mailed the advertisement exceeds the expected profit received from a person who is not mailed the advertisement. So we should mail the advertisement to members of the subpopulation only if

$$\frac{N_{Pers} + N_{Always}}{N} \times r_s - c > r_u \times \frac{N_{Anti} + N_{Always}}{N},$$

or equivalently,

$$\frac{N_{Pers} + N_{Always}}{N} \times r_s - \frac{N_{Anti} + N_{Always}}{N} \times r_u - c > 0.$$

We call the left side of this last inequality the **expected lift in profit (ELP)** that we obtain by mailing a person the advertisement. Owing to Equality 13.22, we can obtain an estimate of $(N_{Pers} + N_{Always})/N$ by mailing many people in the subpopulation the advertisement and seeing what fraction buy. Similarly, owing to Equality 13.23, we can obtain an estimate of $(N_{Anti} + N_{Always})/N$ by not mailing the advertisement to a set of people and see what fraction of these people buy.

We developed the theory using N_{Never}, N_{Pers}, N_{Anti}, and N_{Always} to show the behavior in the subpopulation that results in the probabilities. The relevant formula in deciding whether or not to mail to a person in a subpopulation is simply

$$ELP =$$

$$P(Buy = yes|Mailed = yes)r_s - P(Buy = yes|Mailed = no)r_u - c, \quad (13.24)$$

where the conditional probabilities are obtained from data or from data along with prior belief. We mail to everyone in the subpopulation if $ELP > 0$, and we mail to no one in the subpopulation if $ELP \leq 0$.

13.7.2.2   Identifying Subpopulations with Positive ELPs

Next, we show how to use class probability trees to identify subpopulations that have positive $ELPs$.

First, we take a large sample of individuals from the entire population and obtain data on the target variable Buy, the indicator variable $Mailed$, and n other indicator variables $X_1, X_2, \ldots, X_n$ for members of this sample. The n other indicator variables are attributes such as income, sex, salary, etc. Next, from these data we grow a class probability tree using a tree growing algorithm as discussed at the end of Section 13.7. For example, suppose $n = 2$, $X_1 = Sex$, and $X_2 = Income$. We might learn the class probability tree in Figure 13.22.

Once we learn the tree, we can calculate the ELP for every subpopulation. The next examples illustrate this.

Example 13.31 Suppose

$$
\begin{aligned}
c &= .5 \\
r_s &= 8 \\
r_u &= 10,
\end{aligned}
$$

and we are investigating the subpopulation consisting of individuals with medium income who are male using the tree in Figure 13.22. We follow the right branch from the root of the tree and then the left branch from the Sex node to arrive at the $Mailed$ node corresponding to this subpopulation. We then find for this subpopulation that

$$
\begin{aligned}
ELP &= P(Buy = yes|Mailed = yes)r_s - P(Buy = yes|Mailed = no)r_u - c \\
&= .4 \times 8 - .2 \times 10 - .5 = .7.
\end{aligned}
$$

Because the ELP is positive, we mail to this subpopulation.   ∎

Example 13.32 Suppose the same values of c, r_s, and r_u as in the previous example, and we are investigating the subpopulation consisting of individuals with low income who are female. We follow the left branch from the root to arrive at the *Mailed* node corresponding to this subpopulation. We then find for this subpopulation that

$$
\begin{aligned}
ELP &= P(Buy = yes | Mailed = yes)r_s - P(Buy = yes | Mailed = no)r_u - c \\
&= .6 \times 8 - .5 \times 10 - .5 = -.7.
\end{aligned}
$$

Because the *ELP* is negative, we do not mail to this subpopulation. Notice that for members of this subpopulation there is an increased probability of buying if we mail them the advertisement (.6 versus .5). However, owing to the cost and profits involved, the *ELP* is negative.   ■

In general, the goal of a tree growing algorithm is to identify a tree that best represents the conditional probability of interest. That is, the scoring criterion evaluates the predictive accuracy of the tree. So a classical tree growing algorithm would attempt to maximize the accuracy of our estimate of $P(Buy | Mailed, X_1, X_2, \ldots, X_n)$ for all values of the variables. However, in this application we want to maximize expected profit, which is determined by the *ELP*. Notice in Equality 13.24 that the *ELP* will be 0 if $P(Buy = yes | Mailed = yes) = P(Buy = yes | Mailed = no)$. So if in some path from the root to a leaf there is no split on *Mailed*, the value of the *ELP* at the leaf will be 0. It seems a useful heuristic would be to modify the tree growing algorithm to force a split on *Mailed* on every path from the root to a leaf. In this way for every subpopulation we will determine that either the *ELP* is positive (and therefore we should definitely mail), or the *ELP* is negative (and therefore we should definitely not mail). One way to implement this heuristic would be to modify the algorithm so that the last split is always on the *Mailed* node. Chickering and Heckerman [2000] developed a tree growing algorithm with this modification.

Chickering and Heckerman [2000] performed an experiment applying the method just described. The experiment concerned deciding which subpopulations of Windows 95 registrants to mail an advertisement soliciting for an MSN subscription. Regardless of the subscription rate, they found we can expect to benefit by doing targeted advertising as described above rather than simply mailing to everyone. The reason is that the method seems to identify persuadable individuals who would buy only if they are sent an advertisement and anti-persuadable individuals who are turned off by the advertisement.

13.8   Discussion and Further Reading

In Section 8.8 we showed applications of Bayesian networks. Next we present applications specifically concerned with learning Bayesian networks from data.

13.8.1   Biology

1. Friedman et al. [2000] developed a technique for learning causal relationships among genes by analyzing gene expression data. This technique is

a result of the "Project for Using Bayesian Networks to Analyze Gene Expression," which is described at www.cs.huji.ac.il/labs/compbio/expression.

2. Friedman et al. [2002] formulated a method for phylogenetic tree reconstruction. The method is used in SEMPHY, which is a tool for maximum likelihood phylogenetic reconstruction. More on it can be found at http://www.cs.huji.ac.il/labs/compbio/semphy/.

3. Friedman and Koller [2003] created an approximate model averaging technique using MCMC for analyzing gene expression data.

4. Segel et al. [2005] constructed a module network approach to analyzing gene expression data.

5. Fishelson and Geiger [2002, 2004] developed a Bayesian network model for genetic linkage analysis and an inference algorithm for that model.

6. Jiang [Jiang et al., 2010], [Jiang et al., 2011a], [Jiang et al., 2011b] modeled the relationships among a phenotype and genes using a Bayesian network, and applied Bayesian network scoring criteria to learning the genetic basis of diseases from GWAS data sets.

7. The text *Probabilistic Methods for Bioinformatics* [Neapolitan, 2009] discusses many of the applications to biology just mentioned.

13.8.2 Business and Finance

1. Breeze et al. [1998] learned Bayesian network models for collaborative filtering from several data sets. Collaborative filtering concerns learning an individual's interests based on the interests of similar individuals.

2. Sun and Shenoy [2006] learned a bankruptcy prediction Bayesian network from data.

13.8.3 Causal Learning

Applications to causal learning can be found in [Spirtes et al., 1993; 2000], [Glymour and Cooper, 1999], and [Neapolitan, 2004].

13.8.4 Data Mining

Margaritis et al., [2001] developed NetCube, a system for computing counts of records with desired characteristics from a database, which is a common task in the areas of decision support systems and data mining. The method can quickly compute counts from a database with billions of records.

13.8.5 Medicine

Herskovits and Dagher [1997] learned from data a system for assessing cervical spinal-cord trauma.

13.8.6   Weather Forecasting

Kennett et al. [2001] learned from data a system which predicts sea breezes.

EXERCISES

Section 13.2

Exercise 13.1 Suppose we have the two models in Figure 13.1 and the following data:

Case	J	F
1	j_1	f_1
2	j_1	f_1
3	j_1	f_1
4	j_1	f_1
5	j_1	f_1
6	j_1	f_2
7	j_2	f_2
8	j_2	f_2
9	j_2	f_2
10	j_2	f_1

1. Score each DAG model using the Bayesian score and compute their posterior probabilities, assuming that the prior probability of each model is .5.

2. Create a data set containing 20 records by duplicating the data in the table one time, and score the models using this 20-record data set. How have the scores changed?

3. Create a data set containing 200 records by duplicating the data in the table 19 times, and score the models using this 200-record data set. How have the scores changed?

Exercise 13.2 Suppose we have a Markov chain with the following transition matrix:
$$\begin{pmatrix} 1/5 & 2/5 & 2/5 \\ 1/7 & 4/7 & 2/7 \\ 3/8 & 1/8 & 1/2 \end{pmatrix}.$$

Determine the stationary distribution for the chain.

Exercise 13.3 Suppose we have the distribution $\mathbf{r}^T = (\ 1/9 \quad 2/3 \quad 2/9\ )$. Using the Metropolis-Hastings method, find a transition matrix for a Markov chain that has this as its stationary distribution. Do it both with a matrix $\mathbf{Q}$ that is symmetric and with one that is not.

Exercise 13.4 In Example 13.14, we computed $P(j_1|f_1, \mathsf{D})$ using model averaging. Use the same technique to compute $P(j_1|f_2, \mathsf{D})$.

Exercise 13.5 Assume that we have the models and data set discussed in Exercise 13.1. Using model averaging, compute the following:

1. $P(j_1|f_1, \mathsf{D})$ when D consists of our original 10 records.

2. $P(j_1|f_1, \mathsf{D})$ when D consists of 20 records.

3. $P(j_1|f_1, \mathsf{D})$ when D consists of 200 records.

Exercise 13.6 Assume that there are three variables X_1, X_2, and X_3, and that all DAG patterns have the same posterior probability $(1/11)$ given the data. Compute the probability of the following features being present given the data (assuming faithfulness):

1. $I_p(X_1, X_2)$

2. $\neg I_p(X_1, X_2)$

3. $I_p(X_1, X_2|X_3)$ and $\neg I_p(X_1, X_2)$

4. $\neg I_p(X_1, X_2|X_3)$ and $I_p(X_1, X_2)$.

Section 13.3

Exercise 13.7 Suppose $V = \{X, Y, Z, U, W\}$ and the set of conditional independencies in P is

$$\{I_P(X, Y) \quad I_P(\{W, U\}, \{X, Y\}|Z) \quad I_P(U, \{X, Y, Z\}|W)\}.$$

Find all DAGs faithful to P.

Exercise 13.8 Suppose $V = \{X, Y, Z, U, W\}$ and the set of conditional independencies in P is

$$\{I_P(X, Y) \quad I_P(X, Z) \quad I_P(Y, Z) \quad I_P(U, \{X, Y, Z\}|W)\}.$$

Find all DAGs faithful to P.

Exercise 13.9 Suppose $V = \{X, Y, Z, U, W\}$ and the set of conditional independencies in P is

$$\{I_P(X, Y | U) \qquad I_P(U, \{Z, W\} | \{X, Y\}) \qquad I_P(\{X, Y, U\}, W | Z)\}.$$

Find all DAGs faithful to P.

Exercise 13.10 Suppose $V = \{X, Y, Z, W, T, V, R\}$ and the set of conditional independencies in P is

$$\{I_P(X, Y | Z) \qquad I_P(T, \{X, Y, Z, V\} | W)$$

$$I_P(V, \{X, Z, W, T\} | Y) \qquad I_P(R, \{X, Y, Z, W\} | \{T, V\})\}.$$

Find all DAGs faithful to P.

Exercise 13.11 Suppose $V = \{X, Y, Z, W, U\}$ and the set of conditional independencies in P is

$$\{I_P(X, \{Y, W\} | U) \qquad I_P(Y, \{X, Z\} | U)\}.$$

1. Is there any DAG faithful to P?

2. Find DAGs in which P is embedded faithfully.

Section 13.6

Exercise 13.12 If we make the causal faithfulness assumption, determine what causal influences we can learn in each of the following cases:

1. Given the conditional independencies in Exercise 13.7

2. Given the conditional independencies in Exercise 13.8

3. Given the conditional independencies in Exercise 13.9

4. Given the conditional independencies in Exercise 13.10

Exercise 13.13 If we make only the causal embedded faithfulness assumption, determine what causal influences we can learn in each of the following cases:

1. Given the conditional independencies in Exercise 13.7

2. Given the conditional independencies in Exercise 13.8

3. Given the conditional independencies in Exercise 13.9

4. Given the conditional independencies in Exercise 13.10

5. Given the conditional independencies in Exercise 13.11

Exercise 13.14 Using Tetrad (or some other Bayesian network learning algorithm), learn a DAG from the data in Table 13.1. Next learn the parameters for the DAG. Can you suspect any causal influences from the learned DAG?

Exercise 13.15 Create a data file containing 120 records from the data in Table 13.1 by duplicating the data nine times. Using Tetrad (or some other Bayesian network learning algorithm), learn a DAG from this larger data set. Next learn the parameters for the DAG. Compare these results to those obtained in Exercise 13.14.

Exercise 13.16 Suppose we have the following variables:

Variable	What the Variable Represents
H	Parents' smoking habits
I	Income
S	Smoking
L	Lung cancer

and the following data:

Case	H	I	S	L
1	Yes	30,000	Yes	Yes
2	Yes	30,000	Yes	Yes
3	Yes	30,000	Yes	No
4	Yes	50,000	Yes	Yes
5	Yes	50,000	Yes	Yes
6	Yes	50,000	Yes	No
7	Yes	50,000	No	No
8	No	30,000	Yes	Yes
9	No	30,000	Yes	Yes
10	No	30,000	Yes	No
11	No	30,000	No	No
12	No	30,000	No	No
14	No	50,000	Yes	Yes
15	No	50,000	Yes	Yes
16	No	50,000	Yes	No
17	No	50,000	No	No
18	No	50,000	No	No
19	No	50,000	No	No

Using Tetrad (or some other Bayesian network learning algorithm), learn a DAG from these data. Next learn the parameters for the DAG. Can you suspect any causal influences from the learned DAG?

Exercise 13.17 Create a data file containing 190 records from the data in Exercise 13.16 by duplicating the data nine times. Using Tetrad (or some other Bayesian network learning algorithm), learn a DAG from this larger data set. Next learn the parameters for the DAG. Compare these results to those obtained in Exercise 13.16.

Section 13.7

Exercise 13.18 Retrieve the following probability from the tree in Figure 13.22:

$$P(Buy = yes | Income = medium, Sex = male, Mailed = no).$$

Exercise 13.19 Retrieve the following probability from the tree in Figure 13.22:

$$P(Buy = yes | Income = low, Mailed = yes).$$

Exercise 13.20 Suppose

$$
\begin{aligned}
c &= .6 \\
r_s &= 7 \\
r_u &= 9.
\end{aligned}
$$

1. Compute the ELP for the subpopulation consisting of individuals with medium income who are male using the tree in Figure 13.22. Should we mail to this subpopulation?

2. Compute the ELP for the subpopulation consisting of individuals with medium income who are female using the tree in Figure 13.22. Should we mail to this subpopulation?

3. Compute the ELP for the subpopulation consisting of individuals with low income using the tree in Figure 13.22. Should we mail to this sub-population?

Chapter 14

More Learning

In this chapter, we discuss two specialized types of learning: namely, unsupervised learning and reinforcement learning.

14.1 Unsupervised Learning

Unsupervised learning concerns trying to find hidden structure in data. **Clustering**, which involves the discovery of categories from data, is a basic form of unsupervised learning, and one in which we have achieved a good deal of success. We discuss clustering first.

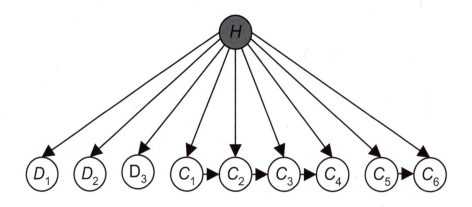

Figure 14.1 An example of a DAG model used in Autoclass.

14.1.1   Clustering

The cluster learning problem is as follows: Given a collection of unclassified entities and features of those entities, organize those entities into categories that in some sense maximize the similarity of the features of the entities in the same category. Like supervised learning, in clustering we have a training set consisting of data items whose attributes are values of predictors (features of the entities), but there is no attribute for a target variable representing the category. We not only do not know the category of each entity, we do not even know the number of categories. As an example, suppose that we arrive at an unexplored island, and we observe many different plants that we have previously never seen. We might decide that we would like to group them into categories based on their observed characteristics. As another example, we may observe the spectra of hundreds of thousands of stars, and want to group them according to their characteristics.

Cheeseman and Stutz [1996] developed **AutoClass** to address the cluster learning problem. Next we discuss AutoClass.

Autoclass models this problem using the DAG model in Figure 14.1. The root in that DAG is a hidden variable. When learning a DAG model, a **hidden variable** in the DAG is a hypothesized variable for which we have no observable data. In Figure 14.1, the hidden variable is discrete, and its possible values correspond to the underlying categories of entities. The model assumes that the features represented by discrete variables (in the figure D_1, D_2, and D_3), and sets of features represented by continuous variables (in the figure $\{C_1, C_2, C_3, C_4\}$ and $\{C_5, C_6\}$) are mutually independent given H. Given a data set containing values of the features, Autoclass searches over variants of this model, including the number of possible values of the hidden variable, and it selects a variant so as to approximately maximize the posterior probability of the variant. The Expectation-Maximization (EM) Algorithm is used to estimate the posterior probability of each model. See [Neapolitan, 2004] for a discussion of the EM Algorithm and [Cheeseman and Stutz, 1996] for the details of AutoClass. The AutoClass software is available as freeware at http://directory.fsf.org/project/autoclass/.

Example 14.1 Cheeseman and Stutz [1995] applied AutoClass to a 1024×1024 array of pixels, where each pixel recorded seven spectral intensities from a 30-m square ground patch. Their test image was a 30-km square region in Kansas, which means there were a total of 1,000,000 pixels. The image was taken by the LandSat/TM satellite in August, 1989. The goal of the investigation was to find categories in the 1,000,000 pixels.

Instead of treating each spectral value independently within a category, they allowed the values to be correlated with each other with separate correlations for each category. The model did not take into account the spatial correlation of neighboring pixels.

The best classification had 93 categories, and these categories were classified to produce a meta-classification. Each pixel was assigned to its most probable category, and then two-dimensional distributions of the resultant categories were plotted. Many categories exhibited immediate interpretations such as roads, rivers, valley bottoms, valley edges, and fields of particular crops. Other categories with many fewer members contained pixels with a mixture of basic types. For example, a pixel partially falling on a highway and partially falling on surrounding grass resulted in a mixed pixel. When there were enough of these mixed pixels with roughly the same mixing proportion, they formed a category of their own. In the mixed pixel case the categories are not very meaningful, but the majority of the categories were composed of pure pixels of a single type.

14.1.2   Automated Discovery

Another quite different and not as successful area of unsupervised learning involves **automatic discovery**. Researchers in automatic discovery endeavors to develop algorithms that discover properties or laws such as those in mathematics and science from data.

In 1977, Doug Lenat [Davis and Lenat, 1982] developed **Automated Mathematician (AM)**. AM was empowered with a large body of heuristics and by modifying LISP programs was able to discover the natural numbers, arithmetic, and several elementary concepts in number theory. However, it failed to discover anything advanced. Lenat [1983] developed **EURISKO** to address some of the problems in AM. EURISKO tries to learn new heuristics. Lenat and Brown [1984] discuss why AM and EURISKO appeared to work. Other efforts at automatic discovery of mathematical concepts appear in [Sims, 1987] and [Cotton et al., 2000].

As another example of automated discovery, Langley et al. [1987] describe BACON, which attempts to learn scientific laws from data. For example, BACON discovered Kepler's laws of planetary motion form the distances between planets and information about the planets' orbits around the sun.

14.2   Reinforcement Learning

In **reinforcement learning** the algorithm interacts with an environment by producing a sequence of actions $a_1, a_2, ..., a_t$ over time. These actions affect the environment, which results in a reward or punishment r_t in each time slot t. The goal of the algorithm is to learn to act in a way that is likely to maximize some utility measure in the future. The reinforcement need not literally be a reward or punishment; rather, it can be any feedback that is useful for determining future actions. Genetic Algorithms, which were introduced in Chapter 9, are very similar to reinforcement learning algorithms. However, in the case of reinforcement learning, the algorithm can recall and use what it has learned in all previous time slots, whereas in the genetic algorithms the decisions concerning each generation are based only on information about individuals in that generation. Reinforcement learning is related to decision analysis, which we discussed in Chapter 8. Indeed, the second method we present for reinforcement learning is based on influence diagrams. First, we present a method that is based on slot machines, known as one-armed bandits.

14.2.1   Multi-Armed Bandit Algorithms

As discussed in Chapter 8, we often make decisions in the hope of maximizing some expected reward. Sometimes the results of these decisions not only include reward, but also knowledge on which we can base future decisions. For example, Hardwick and Stout [1991] describe the following situation. When performing clinical trials researchers allocate patients to treatments so that the trial goals may be achieved and the costs are kept at a minimum. Traditionally, subjects are allocated up front to groups in equal or predetermined proportions. However, these researchers note that this practice lacks the flexibility to incorporate other desirable design goals. They suggest that adaptive design, in which allocation strategies may depend on data observed during the trial, would be more flexibility. As another example, Awerbuch and Kleinberg [2004] note that minimal delay routing is a fundamental task in networks. Uncertainty about the network delays may make the current routing choices sub-optimal; so an algorithm can analyze the traffic patterns and keep adapting its choice of routing paths to improve performance.

The multi-armed bandit problem [Robbins, 1952] is a generalization of these two problems. The one-armed bandit is a name give to a slot machine, which is a gambling device with a lever. The gambler inserts a certain fee in the slot machine, pulls a lever, and then receives a certain reward according to some distribution. In the **multi-armed bandit problem**, there are k levers. Initially, the gambler knows nothing about the levers, but through repeated trials can learn which ones tend to be more rewarding.

Concretely, the k-armed bandit problem is as follows. We have a set of k real probability distributions $\{p_1, p_2, ...p_k\}$. In sequence, we choose an integer i such that $1 \leq i \leq k$. A value (reward) is chosen at random according to distribution p_i. This process is repeated N times. The objective is to maximize the sum of the values (total reward).

As noted above, reinforcement learning algorithms are very similar to genetic algorithms. Like genetic algorithms, strategies for solving the k-armed bandit problem include combining exploitation with exploration (See Section 9.2.1). In the current context, by **exploitation** we mean to exploit knowledge already obtained about levers that look good, while by **exploration** we mean looking for new levers without regard for how good they currently appear.

Next we present several strategies for using exploitation/exploration to solve the k-armed bandit problem.

1. ε-Greedy Strategy: First, the mean value of the rewards obtained for all levers is computed based on the previous rounds. A lever chosen at random according to the uniform distribution is pulled with probability ε; otherwise the lever with the highest mean value is pulled. The choice of ε is left to the user. The process is started by choosing a lever at random according to the uniform distribution.

2. ε-First Strategy: For the first εN rounds, the lever pulled is chosen a random according to the uniform distribution, where N is the total number of rounds. The mean values of the rewards for all levers based on these rounds is then computed. The lever with highest mean value is pulled during the remaining $(1 - \varepsilon)N$ rounds.

3. ε-Decreasing Strategy: This strategy is like the ε-Greedy Strategy except the value of ε decreases for each round. That is, $\varepsilon_t = \min[1, \varepsilon/t]$ for $t = 2, 3, ...N$.

4. ε-LeastTaken Strategy: The least-taken lever is pulled with a probability of $4\varepsilon/(4 + m^2)$, where m is the number of times the least taken lever has already been pulled. Otherwise, the lever with the highest mean value is pulled.

Vermoral and Mohri [2005] discuss more complex strategies. Furthermore, they develop a new strategy called POKER.

The **regret** ρ for a given strategy after all N rounds is defined to be the difference associated with an optimal strategy and the sum of the rewards obtained using the strategy. That is,

$$\rho = N\mu^* - \sum_{i=1}^{N} r_t,$$

where μ^* is the expected value of the probability distribution p_i that has the largest expected value, and r_t is the reward actually received in round t. A strategy is said to be a **zero-regret strategy** if its average regret per round tends to 0 with probability 1 as N approaches infinity. Vermoral and Mohri [2005] show that POKER is a zero-regret strategy.

Vermoral and Mohri [2005] compared the performance of POKER, the four strategies presented here, and other strategies discussed in their paper using the following two experiments.

Table 14.1 Comparisons of Performance of Several Bandit Strategies

Strategy	R-100	R-1000	R-10,000	N-130	BN-1300
POKER	.787	.885	.942	203	132
ε-Greedy, .05	.712	.855	.936	733	431
ε-Greedy, .10	.740	.858	.916	731	453
ε-Greedy, .15	.746	.842	.891	715	474
ε-First, .05	.732	.906	.951	735	414
ε-First, .10	.802	.893	.926	733	421
ε-First, .15	.809	.869	.901	725	411
ε-Decreasing, 1	.755	.805	.851	738	411
ε-Decreasing, 5	.785	.895	.934	715	413
ε-Decreasing, 10	.736	.901	.949	733	417
ε-LeastTaken, .05	.750	.782	.932	747	420
ε-LeastTaken, .10	.750	.791	.912	738	432
ε-LeastTaken, .15	.757	.784	.892	734	441

For the R-experiment, bigger numbers are better (rewards), and for the N-experiments, smaller numbers are better (punishments).

In the first experiment, they simulated 1000 levers, where the reward associated with each lever was normally distributed. The means and standard deviations were drawn uniformly from the interval $(0, 1)$. They then generated a data set containing 10,000 rounds, and they evaluated the strategies using 100 rounds, 1000 rounds, and all 10,000 of the rounds. They computed the average reward per round for each strategy. This process was repeated 10,000 times and the averages over all 10,000 trials was computed.

The second experiment concerns the real-world problem known as the **Content Distribution Network Problem (CDN)** [Krishnamurthy et al., 2001]. The problem is to retrieve data through a network with several redundant sources available. For each retrieval, one source is selected, and the algorithm then waits until the data are retrieved. The objective is to minimize the sum of the delays over all retrievals. To simulate this problem, they used the home pages of over 700 universities as sources. The universities represent the levers. The home page for each university was retrieved every 10 minutes for 10 days, resulting in 1300 rounds. For each retrieval, the retrieval latency in milliseconds was recorded. This latency was the punishment. The strategies were evaluated using 130 rounds and all 1300 rounds. They computed the average latency (punishment) per round for each strategy.

For both experiments, the process was repeated 10,000 times and the averages over all 10,000 trials was computed. Table 14.1 shows the results for POKER and the four strategies presented here. For the R-experiments, bigger numbers are better because they represent rewards, whereas for the N-experiments smaller numbers are better because they represent punishments. Vermoral and Mohri [2005] include results for some other strategies. Interesting is that all the strategies perform similarly for the R-experiments, but POKER does much better for the N-experiments (which are real-world). This results remains true when we include the additional results in [Vermorel and Mohri, 2005].

14.2.2 Dynamic Networks★

Dynamic Bayesian networks model relationships among random variables that change over time. Dynamic Influence diagrams model sequential decision making based on observing variables over time. So the latter can be used for reinforcement learning. Before discussing dynamic influence diagrams and their application to reinforcement learning, we present Dynamic Bayesian networks.

14.2.2.1 Dynamic Bayesian Networks

After developing the theory, we present an example.

Formulation of the Theory Bayesian networks do not model temporal relationships among variables. That is, a Bayesian network only represents the probabilistic relationships among a set of variables at some point in time. It does not represent how the value of some variable may be related to its value and the values of other variables at previous points in time. In many problems, however, the ability to model temporal relationships is very important. For example, in medicine it is often important to represent and reason about time in tasks such as diagnosis, prognosis, and treatment options. Capturing the dynamic (temporal) aspects of the problem is also important in artificial intelligence, economics, and biology. Next, we introduce dynamic Bayesian networks, which do model the temporal aspects of a problem.

First, however, we need to define a random vector. Given random variables $X_1, \ldots, X_n$, the column vector

$$\mathbf{X} = \begin{pmatrix} X_1 \\ \vdots \\ X_n \end{pmatrix}$$

is called a **random vector**. A **random matrix** is defined in the same manner. We use $\mathbf{X}$ to denote both a random vector and the set of random variables that comprises $\mathbf{X}$. Similarly, we use $\mathbf{x}$ to denote both a vector value of $\mathbf{X}$ and the set of values that comprises $\mathbf{x}$. The meaning is clear from the context. Given this convention and a random vector $\mathbf{X}$ with dimension n, $P(\mathbf{x})$ denotes the joint probability distribution $P(x_1, \ldots, x_n)$. Random vectors are called **independent** if the sets of variables that comprise them are independent. A similar definition holds for conditional independence.

Now we can discuss dynamic Bayesian networks. We assume that changes occur between discrete time points, which are indexed by the non-negative integers, and we have some finite number T of points in time. Let $\{X_1, \ldots, X_n\}$ be the set of features whose values change over time, let $X_i[t]$ be a random variable representing the value of X_i at time t for $0 \le t \le T$, and let the random vector $\mathbf{X}[t]$ be given by

$$\mathbf{X}[t] = \begin{pmatrix} X_1[t] \\ \vdots \\ X_n[t] \end{pmatrix}.$$

For all t, each $X_i[t]$ has the same space that depends on i, and we call it the space of X_i. A **dynamic Bayesian network** is a Bayesian network containing the variables that comprise the T random vectors $\mathbf{X}[t]$ and is determined by the following specifications:

1. An initial Bayesian network consisting of (a) an initial DAG $\mathbb{G}_0$ containing the variables in $\mathbf{X}[0]$ and (b) an initial probability distribution P_0 of these variables.

2. A transition Bayesian network, which is a template consisting of (a) a transition DAG $\mathbb{G}_\rightarrow$ containing the variables in $\mathbf{X}[t] \cup \mathbf{X}[t+1]$ and (b) a transition probability distribution $P_\rightarrow$, that assigns a conditional probability to every value of $\mathbf{X}[t+1]$ given every value $\mathbf{X}[t]$. That is, for every value $\mathbf{x}[t+1]$ of $\mathbf{X}[t+1]$ and value $\mathbf{x}[t]$ of $\mathbf{X}[t]$, we specify

$$P_\rightarrow(\mathbf{X}[t+1] = \mathbf{x}[t+1] | \mathbf{X}[t] = \mathbf{x}[t]).$$

Because for all t each X_i has the same space, the vectors $\mathbf{x}[t+1]$ and $\mathbf{x}[t]$ each represent values from the same set of spaces. The index in each indicates the random variable that has the value. We showed the random variables above; henceforth we do not show them.

3. The dynamic Bayesian network consisting of (a) the DAG composed of the DAG $\mathbb{G}_0$ and for $0 \le t \le T-1$ the DAG $\mathbb{G}_\rightarrow$ evaluated at t and (b) the following joint probability distribution:

$$P(\mathbf{x}[0], \ldots \mathbf{x}[T]) = P_0(\mathbf{x}[0]) \prod_{t=0}^{T-1} P_\rightarrow(\mathbf{x}[t+1] | \mathbf{x}[t]). \qquad (14.1)$$

Figure 14.2 shows an example. The transition probability distribution entailed by the network in Figure 14.2 is

$$P_\rightarrow(\mathbf{x}[t+1] | \mathbf{x}[t]) = \prod_{i=0}^{n} P_\rightarrow(x_i[t+1] | \mathsf{pa}_i[t+1]),$$

where $\mathsf{pa}_i[t+1]$ denotes the values of the parents of $X_i[t+1]$. Note that there are parents in both $\mathbf{X}[t]$ and $\mathbf{X}[t+1]$.

Owing to Equality 14.1, for all t and for all $\mathbf{x}$,

$$P(\mathbf{x}[t+1] | \mathbf{x}[0], \ldots \mathbf{x}[t]) = P(\mathbf{x}[t+1] | \mathbf{x}[t]).$$

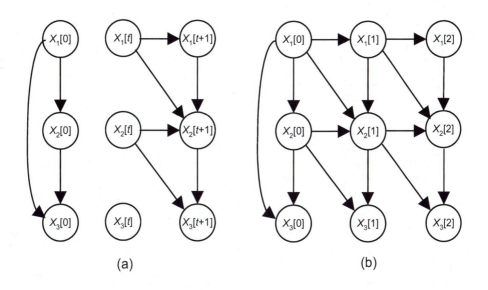

Figure 14.2 Prior and transition Bayesian networks are in (a). The resultant dynamic Bayesian network for $T = 2$ is in (b). Note that the probability distributions are not shown.

That is, all the information needed to predict a world state at time t is contained in the description of the world at time $t-1$. No information about earlier times is needed. Owing to this feature, we say the process has the **Markov** property. Furthermore, the process is **stationary**. That is, $P(\mathbf{x}[t+1]|\mathbf{x}[t])$ is the same for all t. In general, it is not necessary for a dynamic Bayesian network to have either of these properties. However, they reduce the complexity of representing and evaluating the networks, and they are reasonable assumptions in many applications. The process need not stop at a particular time T. However, in practice, we reason only about some finite amount of time. Furthermore, we need a terminal time value to properly specify a Bayesian network.

Probabilistic inference in a dynamic Bayesian network can be done using the standard algorithms discussed in Chapter 3. However, because the size of a dynamic Bayesian network can become enormous when the process continues for a long time, the algorithms can be quite inefficient. There is a special subclass of dynamic Bayesian networks in which this computation can be done more efficiently. This subclass includes dynamic Bayesian networks in which the networks in different time steps are connected only through non-evidence variables. An example of such a network is shown in Figure 14.3. The variables labeled with an E are the evidence variables and are instantiated in each time step. We lightly shade nodes representing them.

An application that uses a dynamic Bayesian network like the one in Figure 14.3. is shown in the next subsection. Presently, we illustrate how updating can be done effectively in such networks.

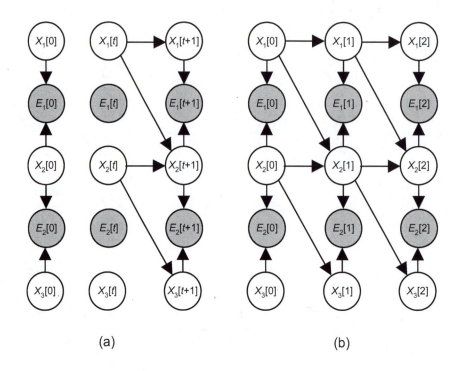

(a)   (b)

Figure 14.3 Prior and transition Bayesian networks, in the case where the networks in different time slots are connected only through non-evidence variables, are in (a). The resultant dynamic Bayesian network for $T = 2$ is in (b).

Let $e[t]$ be the set of values of the evidence variables at time step t, and let $f[t]$ be the set of values of the evidence variables up to and including time step t. Suppose for each value $\mathbf{x}[t]$ of $\mathbf{X}[t]$ we know

$$P(\mathbf{x}[t]|\mathbf{f}[t]).$$

We want to now compute $P(\mathbf{x}[t+1]|\mathbf{f}[t+1])$. First, we have

$$
\begin{aligned}
P(\mathbf{x}[t+1]|\mathbf{f}[t]) &= \sum_{\mathbf{x}[t]} P(\mathbf{x}[t+1]|\mathbf{x}[t],\mathbf{f}[t])P(\mathbf{x}[t]|\mathbf{f}[t]). \\
&= \sum_{\mathbf{x}[t]} P(\mathbf{x}[t+1]|\mathbf{x}[t])P(\mathbf{x}[t]|\mathbf{f}[t]). \quad (14.2)
\end{aligned}
$$

Using Bayes' theorem, we then have

$$
\begin{aligned}
P(\mathbf{x}[t+1]|\mathbf{f}[t+1]) &= P(\mathbf{x}[t+1]|\mathbf{f}[t],\mathbf{e}[t+1]) \\
&= \alpha P(\mathbf{e}[t+1]|\mathbf{x}[t+1],\mathbf{f}[t])P(\mathbf{x}[t+1]|\mathbf{f}[t]) \\
&= \alpha P(\mathbf{e}[t+1]|\mathbf{x}[t+1])P(\mathbf{x}[t+1]|\mathbf{f}[t]), \quad (14.3)
\end{aligned}
$$

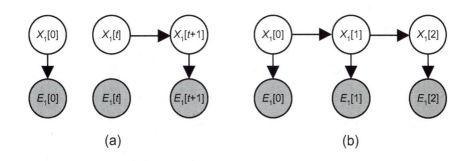

Figure 14.4 Prior and transition Bayesian networks for a hidden Markov model are in (a). The resultant dynamic Bayesian network for $T = 2$ is in (b).

where α is a normalizing constant. The value of $P(\mathbf{e}[t+1]|\mathbf{x}[t+1])$ can be computed using an inference algorithm for Bayesian networks. We start the process by computing $P(\mathbf{x}[0]|\mathbf{f}[0]) = P(\mathbf{x}[0]|\mathbf{e}[0])$. Then at each time step $t+1$ we compute $P(\mathbf{x}[t+1]|\mathbf{f}[t+1])$ using Equalities 14.2 and 14.3 in sequence. Note that to update the probability for the current time step we only need values computed at the previous time step and the evidence at the current time step. We can throw out all previous time steps, which means we need only keep enough network structure to represent two time steps.

A simple way to view the process is shown next. We define

$$P'(\mathbf{x}[t+1]) \equiv P(\mathbf{x}[t+1]|\mathbf{f}[t]),$$

which is the probability distribution of $\mathbf{X}[t+1]$ given the evidence in the first t time steps. We determine this distribution at the beginning of time step $t+1$ using Equality 14.2, and then we discard all previous information. Next we obtain the evidence in the time step $t+1$ and update P' using Equality 14.3.

A **hidden Markov model** is a dynamic Bayesian network such that in each times step there is a single unobserved variable and a single evidence variable, and the only edges include an edge from each unobserved variable to the evidence variable in its time step and an edge to the unobserved variable in the following time step. Figure 14.4 shows a hidden Markov model.

An Example: Mobile Target Localization We show an application of dynamic Bayesian networks to mobile target localization, which was developed by Basye et al. [1992]. The **mobile target localization problem** concerns tracking a target while maintaining knowledge of one's own location. Basye et al. [1992] developed a world in which a target and a robot reside. The robot is supplied with a map of the world, which is divided into corridors and junctions. Figure 14.5 shows a portion of one such world tessellated according to this scheme. Each rectangle in that figure is a different region. The state space for the location of the target is the set of all the regions shown in the figure, and the state space for the location of the robot is the set of all these regions augmented with four quadrants to represent the directions the robot

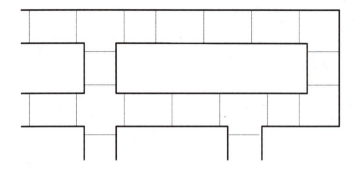

Figure 14.5 Tessellation of corridor layout.

can face. Let L_R and L_A be random variables whose values are the locations of the robot and the target, respectively.

Both the target and the robot are mobile, and the robot has sensors it uses to maintain knowledge of its own location and to track the target's location. Specifically, the robot has a sonar ring consisting of eight sonar transducers, configured in pairs pointing forward, backward, and to each side of the robot. Each sonar gives a reading between 30 and 6000 mm, where 6000 means 6000 or more. Figure 14.6 shows one set of readings obtained from the sonars upon entering a T-junction. We want the sensors to tell us what kind of region we are in. So we need a mapping from the raw sensor data to an abstract sensor space consisting of the following: corridor, T-junction, L-junction, dead-end, open space, and crossing. This mapping could be deterministic or probabilistic. Basye et al. [1992] discuss methods for developing it. Sonar data are notoriously noisy and difficult to disambiguate. A sonar that happens to be pointed at an angle of greater than 70 degrees to a wall will likely not see the wall. So we will assume the relationship is probabilistic. The robot also has a forward-pointing camera to identify the presence of its target. The camera can detect the presence of a blob identified to be the target. If it does not detect a suitable blob, this evidence is reported. If it does find a suitable blob, the size of the blob is used to estimate its distance from the robot, which is reported in rather gross units, that is, within 1 meter, between 2 and 3 meters, etc. The detection of a blob at a given distance is only probabilistically dependent on the actual presence of the target at that distance. Let E_R be a random variable whose value is the sonar reading, which tells the robot something about its own location, and E_A be a random variable whose value is the camera reading, which tells the robot something about the target's location relative to the robot. It follows from the previous discussion that E_R is probabilistically dependent on L_R and E_A is probabilistically dependent on both L_R and L_A. At each time step, the robot obtains readings from its sonar ring and camera. For example, it may obtain the sonar readings in Figure 14.6, and its camera may inform it that the target is visible at a certain distance.

The actions available to the robot and the target are as follows: travel

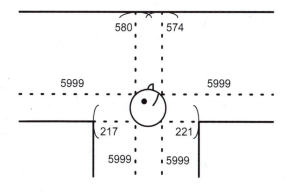

Figure 14.6 Sonar readings upon entering a T-junction.

down the corridor the length of one region, turn left around the corner, turn around, etc. In the dynamic Bayesian network model, these actions are simply performed in some preprogrammed probabilistic way, which is not related to the sensor data. So the location of the robot at time $t + 1$ is a probabilistic function of its location at time t. When we model the problem with a dynamic influence diagram in Section 14.2.2.2, the robot will decide on its action based on the sensor data. The target's movement could be determined by a person or be preprogrammed probabilistically.

In summary, the random variables in the problem are as follows:

Variable	What the Variable Represents
L_R	Location of the robot
L_A	Location of the target
E_R	Sensor reading regarding location of robot
E_A	Camera reading regarding location of target relative to robot

Figure 14.7 shows a dynamic Bayesian network that models this problem (without showing any actual probability distributions). The prior probabilities in the prior network represent information initially known about the location of the robot and the target. The conditional probabilities in the transition Bayesian network can be obtained from data. For example, $P(e_A|l_R, l_A)$ can be obtained by repeatedly putting the robot and the target in positions l_R and l_A, respectively, and seeing how often reading e_A is obtained.

Note that although the robot can sometimes view the target, the robot makes no effort to track the target. That is, the robot moves probabilistically according to some scheme. Our goal is for the robot to track the target. However, to do this it must decide on where to move next based on the sensor data and camera reading. As mentioned above, we need dynamic influence diagrams to produce such a robot. They are discussed next.

14.2.2.2 Dynamic Influence Diagrams

Again, we first develop the theory and then we give an example.

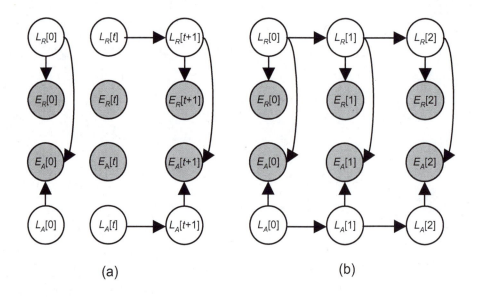

(a)   (b)

Figure 14.7 The prior and transition Bayesian networks for the mobile target mobilization problem are in (a). The resultant dynamic Bayesian network for $T = 2$ is in (b).

Formulation of the Theory To create a **dynamic influence diagram** from a dynamic Bayesian network, we need only add decision nodes and a value node. Figure 14.8 shows the high-level structure of such a network for $T = 2$. The chance node at each time step in that figure represents the entire DAG at that time step, and so the edges represent sets of edges. There is an edge from the decision node at time t to the chance nodes at time $t+1$ because the decision made at time t can affect the state of the system at time $t+1$. The problem is to determine the decision at each time step that maximizes expected utility at some point in the future. Figure 14.8 represents the situation where we are determining the decision at time 0 that maximizes expected utility at time 2. The final utility could, in general, be based on the earlier chance nodes and even the decision nodes. However, we do not show such edges to simplify the diagram. Furthermore, the final expected utility is often a weighted sum of expected utilities independently computed for each time step up to the point in the future we are considering. Such a utility function is called **time-separable**.

In general, dynamic influence diagrams can be solved using the algorithm presented in Section 8.2.2. The next section contains an example.

An Example: Mobile Target Localization Revisited After we present the model, we show some results concerning a robot constructed according to the model.

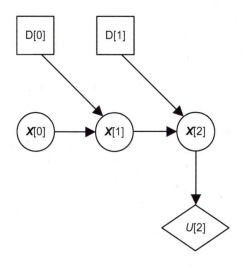

Figure 14.8 The high-level structure of a dynamic influence diagram.

The Model Recall the robot discussed in Section 14.2.2.1. Our goal is for the robot to track the target by deciding on its move at time t based on its evidence at time t. So now we allow the robot to make a decision $D[t]$ at time t of which action it will take, where the value of $D[t]$ is a result of maximizing an expected utility function based on the evidence in time step t . This evidence is the "reward" that is analyzed in order to try to maximize future reward. The future reward is to be close to the target.

We assume there is error in the robot's movement. So the location of the robot at time $t + 1$ is a probabilistic function of its location at the previous time step and the action taken. The conditional probability distribution of L_R is obtained from data, as discussed at the end of Section 14.2.2.1. That is, we repeatedly place the robot in a location, perform an action, and then observe its new location.

The dynamic influence diagram, which represents the decision at time t and in which the robot is looking three time steps into the future, is shown in Figure 14.9. Note that there are crosses through the evidence variable at time t to indicate their values are already known. We need to maximize expected utility using the probability distribution conditional on these values and the values of all previous evidence variables. Recall that at the end of Section 14.2.2.1 we called this probability distribution P', and we discussed how it can be obtained. First, we need to define a utility function. Suppose we decide to determine the decision at time t by looking M time steps into the future. Let

$$\mathsf{d}_M = \{d[t], d[t+1], \ldots d[t+M-1]\}$$

be a set of values of the next M decisions including the current one, and let

$$\mathsf{f}_M = \{e_R[t+1], e_A[t+1], e_R[t+2], e_A[t+2], \ldots e_R[t+M], e_A[t+M]\}$$

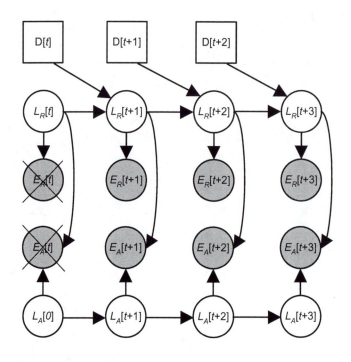

Figure 14.9 The dynamic influence diagram modeling the robot's decision of which action to take at time t.

be a set of values of the evidence variables observed after the decisions are made. For $1 \leq k \leq M$, let d_k and f_k, respectively, be the first k decisions and evidence pairs in each of these sets. Define

$$U_k(\mathsf{f}_k, \mathsf{d}_k) = -\min_u \sum_v dist(u, v) P'(L_A[t + k] = v)|\mathsf{f}_k, \mathsf{d}_k), \qquad (14.4)$$

where $dist$ is the Euclidean distance, the sum is over all values v in the space of L_A, and the minimum is over all values u in the space of L_A. Recall from the beginning of Section 14.2.2.1 that the robot is supplied with a map of the world. It uses this map to find every element in the space of L_A. The idea is that if we make these decisions and obtain these observations at time $t + k$, the sum in Equality 14.4 is the expected value of the distance between the target and a given location u. The smaller this expected value is, the more likely it is that the target is close to u. The location $\breve{u}$ that has the minimum expected value is then our best guess at where the target is if we make these decisions and obtain these observations. So the utility of the decisions and the observations is the expected value for $\breve{u}$. The minus sign occurs because we maximize expected utility.

We then have

$$EU_k(\mathsf{d}_k) = \sum_{\mathsf{f}_k} U_k(\mathsf{f}_k, \mathsf{d}_k) P'(\mathsf{f}_k | \mathsf{d}_k). \qquad (14.5)$$

This expected utility only concerns the situation k time steps into the future. To take into account all time steps up to and including time $t + M$, we use a utility function that is a weighted sum of the utilities at each time step. We then have

$$EU(\mathsf{d}_M) = \sum_{k=1}^{M} \gamma_k EU_k(\mathsf{d}_k), \qquad (14.6)$$

where γ_k decreases with k to discount the impact of future consequences. Note that implicitly $\gamma_k = 0$ for $k > M$. Note further that we have a time-separable utility function. We choose the decision sequence that maximizes this expected utility in Equality 14.6, and we then make the first decision in this sequence at time step t.

In summary, the process proceeds as follows: In time step t the robot updates its probability distribution based on the evidence (sensor and camera readings) obtained in that step. Then the expected utility of a sequence of decisions (actions) is evaluated. This is repeated for other decision sequences, and the one that maximizes expected utility is chosen. The first decision (action) in that sequence is executed, the sensor and camera readings in time step $t + 1$ are obtained, and the process repeats. Notice that the robot develops a plan as discussed in Section 4.2.2, but the plan is not necessarily carried out beyond the first action. That is, in the next time slot a new plan is developed.

The computation of $P'(\mathsf{f}_k | \mathsf{d}_k)$ in Equality 14.5 for all values of f can be quite expensive. Dean and Wellman [1991] discuss ways to reduce the complexity of the decision evaluation.

Result: Emergent Behavior   Basye et al. [1992] developed a robot using the model just described, and they observed some interesting, unanticipated emergent behavior. By **emergent behavior** we mean behavior that is not purposefully programmed into the robot, but emerges as a consequence of the model. For example, when the target moves toward a fork, the robot stays close behind it, because this will enable it to determine which branch the target takes. However, when the target moves toward a cul-de-sac, the robot keeps fairly far away. Basye et al. [1992] expected it to remain close behind. By analyzing the probability distributions and results of the value function, they discovered that the model allows for the possibility that the target might slip behind the robot, leaving the robot unable to determine the location of the target without additional actions. If the robot stays some distance away, regardless of what action the target takes, the observations made by the robot are sufficient to determine the target's location. Figure 14.10 illustrates the situation. In time step t, the robot is close to the target as the target is about to enter the cul-de-sac. If the robot stays close, as illustrated by the top path, in time step $t + 1$ it is just as likely that the target will slip behind the robot as it is that the target will move up the cul-de-sac. If the target does slip behind the robot, it will no

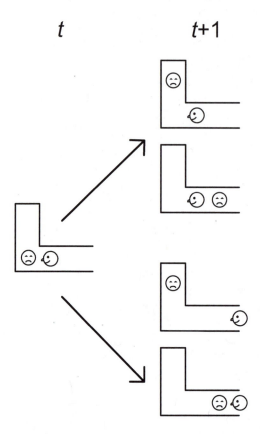

Figure 14.10 Staying close to the target may not be optimal.

longer be visible. However, if the robot backs off, as illustrated by the bottom path, the robot will be able to determine the location of the target regardless of what the target does. When considering its possible observations in time step $t+1$, the observation "target not visible" would not give the robot a good idea as to the target's location. So the move to stay put is less valued than the move to back off.

Large-Scale Systems The method used to control our robot could be used in a more complex system. For example, an autonomous vehicle could use a vision-based, lane-position sensor to keep it in the center of its lane. The position sensor's accuracy would be affected by rain and an uneven road surface. Also, both rain and a bumpy road could cause the position sensor to fail. Clearly, sensor failure would affect the sensor's accuracy. Two time steps in a dynamic influence diagram, which models this situation, appears in Figure 14.11. This figure was based on a figure in [Russell and Norvig, 1995].

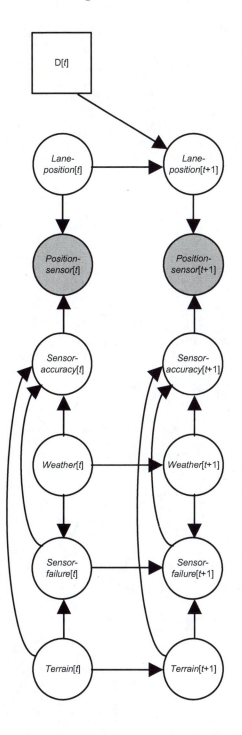

Figure 14.11 Two time steps in a dynamic influence diagram, which models the decision faced by an autonomous vehicle.

14.3   Discussion and Further Reading

Markov Decision Processes (MDP) [Bellman, 1957] were developed to model decision making under uncertainty. **Partially Observable Markov Decision Processes (POMDP)** [Kaelbling et al., 1998] are a generalization of MDPs. Traditionally, MDPs have been used in machine learning to model reinforcement learning [Meuleau and Bourgine, 1999]. However, it turns out that POMDPs are mathematically equivalent to Dynamic Bayesian networks but do not provide the intuitive graphical framework. Vermoral and Mohri [2005] note that the multi-armed bandit problem is actually a one-state MDP.

EXERCISES

Section 14.1

Exercise 14.1 Either obtain or develop data concerning some entities you wish to classify. For example, the data could concern the spectra of many stars. Download AutoClass at http://directory.fsf.org/project/autoclass/, and use AutoClass to classify the entities.

Exercise 14.2 Suppose we have five levers and the following sequence of rewards for the levers:

round	lever 1	lever 2	lever 3	lever 4	lever 5
1	4	2	8	1	12
2	3	5	7	10	8
3	5	7	6	3	15
4	6	4	8	20	6
5	2	9	3	6	12
6	8	8	4	8	14
7	7	10	3	10	12
8	3	2	6	4	10
9	1	14	3	8	9
10	5	3	5	15	14
11	3	8	6	8	20
12	2	5	8	21	8
13	5	15	3	10	10
14	6	2	4	7	9
15	1	4	5	5	15

Apply the ε-Greedy Strategy, the ε-First Strategy, the ε-Decreasing Strategy, and the ε-LeastTaken Strategy to these levers and this sequence of rewards. Use $\varepsilon = .3$ for the ε-Greedy, the ε-First, and the ε-LeastTaken Strategies. Use $\varepsilon = 3$ for the ε-Decreasing Strategy.

Section 14.2

Exercise 14.3 Assign parameter values to the dynamic Bayesian network in Figure 14.7, and compute the conditional probability of the locations of the robot and the target at time 1 given some evidence at times 0 and 1.

Exercise 14.4 Assign parameter values to the dynamic influence diagram in Figure 14.9, and determine the decision at time 0 based on some evidence at time 0 and by looking 1 time into the future.

Part V

Language Understanding

Chapter 15

Natural Language Understanding

You may have had the experience of calling a utility or credit card company with the hope of talking to an operator. Sometimes this scenario plays out as follows. When an automated message asks you what you would like to do, you answer, "Talk to an operator." Then after being led in circles for quite a while, the system hangs up on you. However, if things worked properly, the system would "understand" your query and take the action of routing you to an operator. This chapter concerns the development of algorithms that accomplish such tasks.

We do not pursue the question of what it means to understand language or how humans have come to understand language. You are referred to a text such as [Pinker, 2007] for a discussion of these matters. Rather, we take a pragmatic, operational approach. We assume that we have some knowledge base concerning known facts about the domain of discourse. For example, if the domain of discourse is the blocks world in Section 4.2.2, then the knowledge base might contain the fact on(**a**,**b**), which means block **a** is on block **b**. We need to make the knowledge base understand our sentences in the sense that a declarative sentence can be interpreted as a concept that can be added to the knowledge base, and a question can be converted to a query that can be presented to the knowledge base, which can then be answered. For example, in the blocks world if you tell the system, "The block labeled **c** is on the table," the system should understand this sentence and add on(**c**,table) to the knowledge base. If you ask the system, "What block is on block **b**," the system should understand this question and answer **a** if on(**a**,**b**) is in the knowledge base. In the credit card domain, if you ask, "What is the balance on my account," the system should understand this query, look up your balance, and report it to you. The "answer" can be an action. For example, if you ask "Can I speak to an operator," the system should answer by routing you to an operator.

There are several steps involved in understanding a declarative sentence (or question). They are as follows:

1. **Parsing**: This step analyzes the syntactic structure of the sentence by verifying that it is syntactically correct, and by identifying the linguistic components and relationships such as subject, verb, and object. Parsing produces a **parse tree** that represents these relationships.

2. **Semantic Interpretation**: This step produces a representation of the meaning of the sentence from the parse tree. We call this representation a **concept**.

3. **Contextual Interpretation**: This step incorporates the concept into the knowledge base.

The relationships among these steps are shown in Figure 15.1. We discuss each step in turn.

15.1   Parsing

The sentence is parsed using a **grammar**, which is set of rules that determine the composition of clauses, phrases, and words in a language. We present our grammars using **Backus-Naur Form** (**BNF**). A BNF grammar consists of the following:

1. A set of **terminal symbols**. These are the words in the language such as "block", "on", "speak", and "operator".

2. A set of **nonterminal symbols**. These symbols represent linguistic concepts that categorize phrases in the language such as *NounPhrase* and *VerbPhrase*.

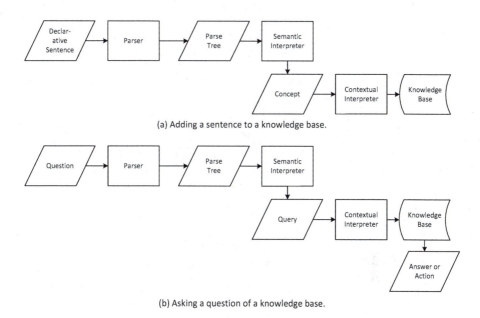

(a) Adding a sentence to a knowledge base.

(b) Asking a question of a knowledge base.

Figure 15.1 Steps in adding a sentence to a knowedge base and in asking a question of a knowledge base.

3. A **start symbol**. This symbol represents the entire string being parsed. For the English language, it is *Sentence*.

4. A set of **derivation rules**. The nonterminal symbol on the left in these rules can be substituted by the terminal and nonterminal symbols on the right. For example, if we write "*Noun* → block," then a *Noun* can be substituted by block.

5. The "|" denote "or".

Such a grammar is a **context-free grammar** (**CFG**), which means that there may only be one nonterminal symbol on the left in each rule. Table 15.1 shows a simple CFG grammar.

A grammar is in **Chomsky normal form** if every rule is of the form $A \leftarrow B\ C$ or $D \leftarrow$ word, where A, B, C, and D are nonterminals and "word" is a terminal. The context-free grammar in Table 15.1 is not in Chomsky normal form because of rules 2, 3, 6 and 10 through 15. It is possible to show that every context-free grammar can be transformed into a grammar that is in Chomsky normal form.

The terminals are the words in the language, and the set of all of them is called the **lexicon**. The grammar in Table 15.1 shows a very small lexicon for illustration. Most grammars we would actually use would have a much larger lexicon. A **legal sentence** is a string of symbols that can be derived using a sequence of these rules. A **derivation** must start with the start symbol

Table 15.1 A CFG

1	$Sentence \rightarrow NounPhrase\ VerbPhrase$
2	$Sentence \rightarrow NounPhrase\ Aux\ VerbPhrase$
3	$Sentence \rightarrow Sentence\ Conj\ Sentence$
4	$NounPhrase \rightarrow Article\ Noun$
5	$NounPhrase \rightarrow Adj\ Noun$
6	$NounPhrase \rightarrow Article\ Adj\ Noun$
7	$NounPhrase \rightarrow Noun$
8	$VerbPhrase \rightarrow Verb\ NounPhrase$
9	$VerbPhrase \rightarrow Verb$
10	$Noun \rightarrow$ man | monkey | book | right | left | help
11	$Verb \rightarrow$ read | reads | love | loves | left | help
12	$Article \rightarrow$ a | an | the
13	$Adj \rightarrow$ fat | big | right
14	$Aux \rightarrow$ can | may
15	$Conj \rightarrow$ and | or

Sentence, perform a sequence of substitutions by applying the rules, and end up with the sentence being parsed.

Example 15.1 Suppose we want to derive the following sentence:

the monkey reads a book.

The following is a derivation of this sentence using the grammar in Table 15.1.

		Rule
Sentence	$\rightarrow NounPhrase\ VerbPhrase$	1
	$\rightarrow Article\ Noun\ VerbPhrase$	3
	$\rightarrow$ the $Noun\ VerbPhrase$	9
	$\rightarrow$ the monkey $VerbPhrase$	7
	$\rightarrow$ the monkey $Verb\ NounPhrase$	5
	$\rightarrow$ the monkey reads $NounPhrase$	8
	$\rightarrow$ the monkey reads $Article\ Noun$	3
	$\rightarrow$ the monkey reads a $Noun$	9
	$\rightarrow$ the monkey reads a book	7

∎

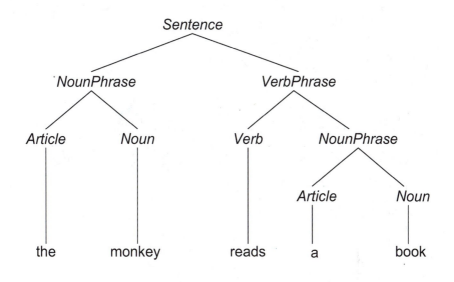

Figure 15.2 A parse tree.

A derivation can be represented by a **parse tree**. Each non-leaf in the tree contains the nonterminal symbol on the left of a rule used in the derivation, and each of its children contains one of the terminal or nonterminal symbols on the right of the rule. Each leaf contains a terminal symbol. The root of the tree is the start symbol *Sentence*. Figure 15.2 shows the parse tree corresponding to the derivation just shown.

15.1.1 Recursive Parser

In the derivation just shown, we simply proceeded in sequence successfully applying rules until we derived the sentence. However, suppose we have the following more complex sentence:

the monkey can read and the man can love.

Using the grammar in Table 15.1, we could try parsing the sentence using Rules 1, 3, 9, 7, and 5 (as done in Example 15.1) in sequence to arrive at "the monkey *Verb NounPhrase*." However, we would then fail because "can" is not a verb. We could then try Rule 6 instead of Rule 5 and again fail. At that point, we could go back and apply Rule 2 and eventually arrive at "the monkey can read." However, we would not have parsed the entire sentence. We could then back up again and start with Rule 3, which would finally lead us to a parse of the entire sentence. This procedure suggests using a backtracking technique for parsing that can be implemented using recursion. The following is such an algorithm.

Algorithm 15.1 Parse
  Input: A phrase to be parsed.
  Output: True if the phrase can be parsed and False otherwise.

  Function *Parse(level, symbol, phrase)*;
  if *symbol* is a terminal
      if *symbol* = first word in *phrase*;
          remove first word in *phrase* from *phrase*;
          return True;
      else
          return False;
  else
      success = False;
      rule = first rule for *symbol*;
      while *rule* ≠ null and not *success*
          string = right side of rule;
          phrasenew = *phrase*;
          symbolnew = first symbol in *string*;
          success = True;
          while *symbolnew* ≠ null and *success*
              success = *parse(level + 1, symbolnew, phrasenew)*;
              symbolnew = next symbol in string;
          endwhile
          if *level* = 1 and *phrasenew* ≠ *null*
              success = False;
          rule = next rule for *symbol*;
      endwhile
      phrase = *phrasenew*;
      return *success*;
  endelse

The global call to function *Parse* is as follows:

success = *Parse*(1, *Sentence*, *phrase*);

The value of variable *phrase* in the top-level call is the sentence we are parsing. For example, it would be "the monkey reads the book" if that is the sentence we are parsing. The purpose of the variable *level* is to enable us to perform a check in the top-level call as to whether there are more words in the sentence than the ones arrived at with a successful parse. Otherwise, a sentence such as "the monkey reads the book man may a love" would successfully parse. The value of the variable *string* is the right side of a rule. For example, if we are applying the rule "*Sentence ← NounPhrase VerbPhrase*," the value of *string* would be "*NounPhrase VerbPhrase*." Using a given rule, we recursively try to parse each symbol in *string* until we reach the end of the string, which we denote with the value "null." If they all are successfully parsed, the value of

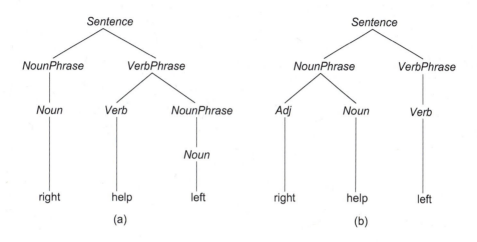

Figure 15.3 Two parse trees for the sentence "right help left".

success is true. However, it is switched to false if it is the top-level call and there are more words left to be parsed.

The value of function *Parse* is true if a successful parse is obtained and false otherwise. The function does not produce a parse tree. However, it can be readily modified to produce such a tree as follows. When a successful parse of a symbol is obtained, the function returns a pointer to a node containing that symbol. The symbol is then made a child of the symbol at the previous level. The pointer returned in the top-level call points to the root of the tree. It is left as an exercise to write this modification.

15.1.2 Ambiguity

Consider the following sentence, which might appear as a headline in the newspaper:

  right help left.

This sentence could mean that the political right helped the political left, or it could mean the correct hired workers (the right help) left the premises. The difficulty is that the word "right" is both a noun and an adjective, the word "help" is both a verb and a noun, and the word "left" is both a noun and a verb. Using the grammar in Table 15.1, we can parse the sentence in the two different ways shown in Figure 15.3. When a sentence can be parsed in more than one way, we say the sentence has **syntactic ambiguity**. There are many, more amusing forms of syntactic ambiguity, but many of them require a more complex grammar that allows preposition phrases. Table 15.2 shows such a grammar without the lexicon. Words that are *Prepositions* are words such as "by", "of", and "to".

Table 15.2 A CFG that Allows Prepositional Phrases (without the lexicon).

1	*Sentence → NounPhrase VerbPhrase*
2	*Sentence → NounPhrase Aux VerbPhrase*
3	*Sentence → Sentence Conj Sentence*
4	*NounPhrase → Article Noun*
5	*NounPhrase → Adj Noun*
6	*NounPhrase → Article Adj Noun*
7	*NounPhrase → Noun*
8	*NounPhrase → NounPhrase PP*
9	*PP → Preposition NP*
10	*VerbPhrase → Verb NounPhrase*
11	*VerbPhrase → Verb*
12	*VerbPhrase → Verb NounPhrase PP*
13	*VerbPhrase → Verb PP*

Example 15.2 The following are more syntactically ambiguous sentences:

Teacher strikes idle kids.

Two sisters reunited after 18 years in checkout counter.

The lady hit the man with an umbrella.

Joe and Sam are hunting dogs.

Finally, we have the old Groucho Marx joke:

I once shot an elephant in my pajamas. How he got into my pajamas, I'll never know. ■

The modification suggested for Algorithm 15.1 produces the first parse that the algorithm finds. It is left as an exercise to write another modification that produces all parses of a sentence.

Another type of ambiguity is **lexical ambiguity**, which arises when a word or phrase has more than one meaning. Consider this sentence:

I deposited my money in the bank.

This sentence could mean that I put my money in a financial institution, which is the usual meaning. However, it could also mean that I put it next to a river. Notice that the sentence allows only one parse; the ambiguity is in the meaning of the word "bank".

Table 15.3 A Simple Grammar

1	$S \rightarrow A\,B$
2	$A \rightarrow A\,C$
3	$B \rightarrow C\,B$
4	$A \rightarrow$ x $\mid$ y
5	$B \rightarrow$ x
6	$C \rightarrow$ x

Example 15.3 The following are other examples of lexical ambiguity:

Prostitutes appeal to governor.

President seeks arms.

Francisco put the mouse on the desk.

Jim likes his new pen. ∎

Yet a third type of ambiguity occurs in the following sentence:

I love it when I stub my toe.

There is only one way to parse the sentence and there is no word in the sentence that has more than one meaning. However, the speaker could be a masochist and really love stubbing a toe, but more likely the speaker is being facetious. Without further context it is impossible to know which is the case. This is an example of **semantic ambiguity**.

15.1.3   Dynamic Programming Parser

At the beginning of Section 15.1.1 we discussed parsing the sentence "the monkey can read and the man can love" using the grammar in Table 15.1. We noted that we could try parsing the sentence first starting with Rule 1, then backing up and starting with Rule 2, and finally backing up and starting with Rule 3. This procedure is precisely what Algorithm 15.1 does. In the process, the phrase "the monkey" is repeatedly parsed over and over. Often, recursive algorithms have this problem, namely that the same subinstance is reevaluated. When this happens, we can often obtain a more efficient algorithm using dynamic programming. In dynamic programming, we solve small subinstances first, store the result, and later, when we need the result, look it up instead of recomputing it. Often, an array or table is used to store the results. John Cocke, Daniel Younger, and Tadeo Kasami developed the **CYK dynamic programming algorithm** for the parsing problem. The algorithm requires the grammar to be in Chomsky normal form, which is not a problem because, as noted earlier, and context-free grammar can be converted to one that is in Chomsky normal form. We discuss this algorithm next. Our discussion is based on a similar discussion in [Allison, 2007].

Suppose we have the simple grammar in Table 15.3, and we want to parse the sentence

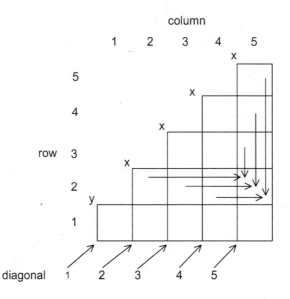

Figure 15.4 A table for constructing the solution to parsing the sentence "y x x x x."

y x x x x.

We develop an $n \times n$ table where n is the number of words in the sentence ($n = 5$ in this example), and we construct our solution in the lower-right part of the table. Such a table T appears in Figure 15.4. We construct the solution by filling in diagonals 1, 2, 3, 4, and 5 in sequence. The sentence appears on the edges of diagonal 1. The values for diagonal 1 are computed directly from the words in the sentence. For each of the other diagonals, the value for $T[i, j]$ is determined from the elements in row i that are left of $T[i, j]$ and the values in column j that are above $T[i, j]$. For example, suppose that we are determining the value of $T[2, 5]$. Figure 15.4 shows how that value is determined from values in row 2 and column 5. The far-left item in row 2 (the one in column 2) is combined with the closest item in column 5 (the one in row 3). Then the next item in row 2 (the one in column 3) is combined with the next item in column 5 (the one in row 4). Finally, the closest item in row 2 (the one in column 4) is combined with the farthest item in column 5 (the one in row 5). The results of all these combinations determines the value of $T[2, 5]$.

Next we walk through the algorithm using the sentence "y x x x x," show how the values are combined, and along the way explain why this results in the solution finally appearing in $T[1, 5]$.

To determine the values in diagonal 1 we visit each array slot in that diagonal in sequence. When visiting the first one ($T[1, 1]$), we find a "y" on it edge (see Figure 15.5 (a)). We then look at the rules in grammar and see which nonterminals can yield a "y". The only such nonterminal is A; so we place an

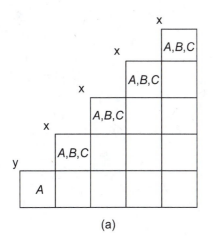

(a)

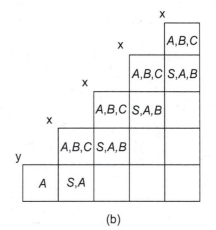

(b)

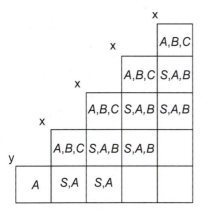

(c)

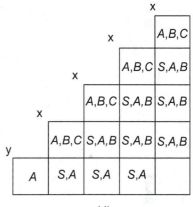

(d)

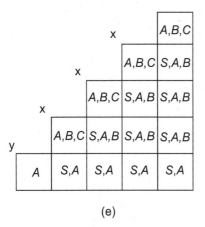

(e)

Figure 15.5 The array values determined when the CYK algorithm parses "y
x x x x."

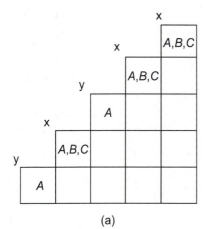

(a)

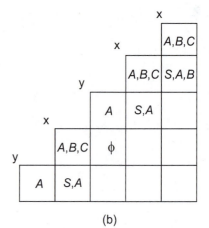

(b)

(c)

(d)

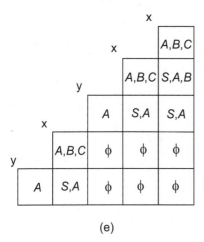

(e)

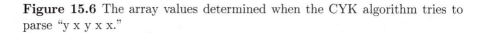

Figure 15.6 The array values determined when the CYK algorithm tries to parse "y x y x x."

A in the $T[1,1]$. We then visit the next array slot ($T[2,2]$), we find an "x" on its edge, and see from the rules that A, B, and C can all determine an "x". So we place A, B, and C all in $T[2,2]$. In the same way, A, B, and C are placed in the remaining array slots in diagonal 1. The result appears in Figure 15.5 (a). Note that these array slots now contain the values that could possibly be in the nodes directly above the leaves (terminals) in the parse tree.

Next we determine the values in diagonal 2. The value of the first one ($T[1,2]$) is determined as follows. We investigate the values in the array slot on its left ($T[1,1]$) and in the array slot above ($T[2,2]$), and look for rules that have precisely one nonterminal from each of these array slots on its right side. For each such rule we find, we place the nonterminal on its left side in $T[1,2]$. For example, we place S in $T[1,2]$ because we have the rule $S \leftarrow A\ B$, and A is in $T[1,1]$ while B is in $T[2,2]$. We place an A in $T[1,2]$ owing to the rule $A \leftarrow A\ C$. We now know that the sentence "y x" can be derived as an S and as an A. The remainder of diagonal 2 is completed in the same way. That is, the values in each array slot are determined from the values in the slot to its left and in the slot above it. Figure 15.5 (b) shows the result.

The completion of diagonal 3 is done in the same way, but is a little more complicated. Look again at Figure 15.4. It shows that three pairs of array slots are used to determine the values in $T[2,5]$, which is in diagonal 4. Similarly, two pairs of array slots are used to determine the values in diagonal 3. To determine the values in $T[1,3]$, we investigate $T[1,1]$ with $T[2,3]$ and $T[1,2]$ with $T[3,3]$. These investigations enable us to place an S and an A in $T[1,3]$. We now know that the sentence "y x x" can be derived as an S or as an A. Diagonals 4 and 5 are completed in the same way. Because S appears in $T[1,5]$, we know that we can derive the sentence "y x x x x" as an S, which means it is a legal sentence.

Suppose now that we want to parse the sentence

y x y x x.

Figure 15.6 shows the steps in the parsing of this sentence. Notice that there is a ϕ in array slot $T[2,3]$. This is because there is no rule whose left-hand side consists of A, B, C followed by A. This means that it is not possible derive the sentence "x y" as any nonterminal. Note that this does not necessarily mean that we cannot derive "y x y x x" because possibly we could derive "y x" as a nonterminal, "y x x" as a nonterminal, and these two nonterminals as an S. However, this is not the case because we end up with a ϕ in $T[1,5]$, which means $S \notin T[1,5]$ and the sentence is not legal.

It is left as an exercise to write the CYK algorithm and show that its time complexity is $\theta(mn^3)$, where m is the number of rules and n is the number of words in the sentence. Furthermore, the algorithm can be extended by storing pointers to parse tree nodes in the array slots (or in a second array). All possible parse trees (which might be exponential in number) can then be retrieved from the array. It is also left as an exercise to write this extension.

15.1.4   Probabilistic Parser

If we write the CYK algorithm as suggested at the end of the last section, we can retrieve all possible parse trees for a given sentence. However, our goal is ordinarily to retrieve the most likely parse tree or the several most likely parse trees. This matter is addressed by using a **probabilistic context-free grammar** (**PCFG**). Table 15.4 shows a PCFG.

Each rule in a PCFG has a probability associated with it. The probabilities for the rules for the a given category sum to 1. For example, there are three rules for *Sentence*, namely Rules 1, 2, and 3. We have that

$$P(\text{Rule 1}) + P(\text{Rule 2}) + P(\text{Rule 3}) = .6 + .25 + .15 = 1.$$

This means, for example, that if a string is a *Sentence*, then it has a .6 probability of being a *NounPhrase* followed by a *VerbPhrase*. For a category that is substituted by a terminal, we have written the set of all substitutions as one rule. So it is the probabilities in this one rule that sum to 1. For example, in Rule 12,

$$P(\text{a}) + P(\text{an}) + p(\text{the}) = .4 + .2 + .4 = 1.$$

This means, for example, that given that the word is an Article, it has a .4 probability of being an "a". Of course, we have used a very small lexicon for the sake of example. In an actual application there would be many more words (perhaps approaching the entire dictionary), and each word would have a much smaller probability.

Figure 15.7 shows the parse trees in Figure 15.3 with probabilities from Table 15.4 added. We make independence assumptions similar to those in a Bayesian network. Namely, we assume, for example, that the $P(\text{right}|Noun) = .15$ regardless of the values of other nodes in the parse tree. Call the parse tree in Figure 15.7 (a) $Parse_a$ and the one in Figure 15.7 (a) $Parse_b$. Given our assumptions, we have the following:

$$P(Parse_a) = .15 \times .3 \times .2 \times .15 \times .3 \times .8 \times .65 = 2.11 \times 10^{-4}$$

$$P(Parse_b) = .2 \times .1 \times .3 \times .1 \times .2 \times .65 = 7.8 \times 10^{-5}.$$

So we choose $Parse_a$ because it is more probable. Because these are the only two parses of the sentence "right help left", the probability of the sentence is $2.11 \times 10^{-4} + 7.8 \times 10^{-5} = 2.89 \times 10^{-4}$.

To find the most probable parse from the array of pointers produced by the CYK algorithm, we can simply find all the parse trees and choose the most probable one. However, if we only want the most probable one (or few most probable ones), we can search the space of all parse trees using a best-first search algorithm called A* [Dechter and Pearl, 1985].

The parse with the highest probability is not necessarily the sensible one. Consider again this sentence.

I shot an elephant in my pajamas.

Table 15.4 A PCFG

1	$Sentence \rightarrow NounPhrase\ VerbPhrase$	[.65]
2	$Sentence \rightarrow NounPhrase\ Aux\ VerbPhrase$	[.25]
3	$Sentence \rightarrow Sentence\ Conj\ Sentence$	[.1]
4	$NounPhrase \rightarrow Article\ Noun$	[.3]
5	$NounPhrase \rightarrow Adj\ Noun$	[.3]
6	$NounPhrase \rightarrow Article\ Adj\ Noun$	[.1]
7	$NounPhrase \rightarrow Noun$	[.3]
8	$VerbPhrase \rightarrow Verb\ NounPhrase$	[.8]
9	$VerbPhrase \rightarrow Verb$	[.2]
10	$Noun \rightarrow$ man [.2] | monkey [.2] | book [.2] | right [.15] | left [.15] | help [.1]	
11	$Verb \rightarrow$ read [.25] | reads [.1] | love [.25] | loves [.1] | left [.1] | help [.2]	
12	$Article \rightarrow$ a [.4] | an [.2] | the [(.4]	
13	$Adj \rightarrow$ fat | [.4] | big [.4] | right [.2]	
14	$Aux \rightarrow$ can [.5] | may [.5]	
15	$Conj \leftarrow$ and [.5] | or [.5]	

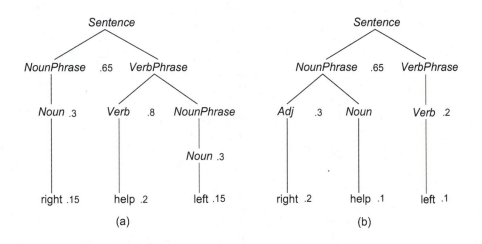

Figure 15.7 Two parse trees for the sentence "right help left" with probabilities.

Depending on the probabilities in the PCFG, the parse that entails that the elephant is wearing the pajamas could easily have a higher probability than the other parse. The parser would need to recognize that the phrase "elephant in x" is unlikely when $x = $ pajamas.

Two parses of a given sentence can even have the same probability regardless of the actual probability values. Consider this sentence:

dogs in houses and cats like humans.

It is left as an exercise to show that the two parses of this sentence use the same set of rules and clearly contain the same words. So the probabilities of the two parses must be identical.

15.1.5 Obtaining Probabilities for a PCFG

The most straightforward way to learn the probabilities for a PCFG is to learn them from a **treebank**, which is a collection of correct parse trees. For example, the well-known Penn treebank [Marcus et al., 1993] contains $3,000,000$ words along with their parts of speech, and parse trees containing the words. It was developed using efforts by experts along with automation.

Example 15.4 Suppose we have the grammar in Table 15.2, and we want to learn the probability for this rule:

$NounPhrase \rightarrow NounPhrase\ PP$

If there are $200,000$ occurrences of $NounPhrase$ in the parse trees in the treebank, and $10,000$ of them point to $NounPhrase\ PP$, then the probability of this rule is estimated to be

$$\frac{10000}{200000} = .05.$$

Suppose now that we have a data set consisting of unparsed sentences instead of a treebank. The **inside-outside algorithm** uses the **expectation-maximization (EM)** method to not only learn the probabilities but also the rules themselves from such a data set. See [Lari and Young, 1990] or [Manning and Schuetze, 2003] for a discussion of the inside-outside algorithm, [Neapolitan, 2004] for an introduction to the EM method in the Bayesian network domain, and [McLachlan and Krishnan, 2008] for complete coverage of the EM method.

15.1.6 Lexicalized PCFG

The difficulty with PCFG is that they are indeed context free. So the probability of a given word does not depend on the other words in the sentence. This problem was mentioned at the end of Section 15.1.4. Here is a simple example. Consider these two verb phrases parsed as a verb followed by a noun:

demands quiet.

Table 15.5 A Simple LPCFG

1	$S \to NP(n) \, VP(v)$	$P_1(n, v)$	$P_1(\text{man,demands}) = .01, \ldots$
2	$NP(n) \to Art(a) \, N(n)$	$P_2(a, n)$	$P_2(\text{the,man}) = .03, \ldots$
3	$NP(n) \to N(n)$	$P_3(n)$	$P_3(\text{quiet}) = .6, \ldots$
4	$VP(v) \to V(v) \, NP(n)$	$P_4(v, n)$	$P_4(\text{demands,quiet}) = .02,$ $P_4(\text{sleeps,quiet}) = .00001, \ldots$
5	$VP(v) \to V(v)$	$P_5(v)$	$P_5(\text{demands}) = .00001,$ $P_5(\text{sleeps}) = .06, \ldots$

sleep quiet.

The probabilities of the phrases will depend only on the probabilities of the individual words. The fact that an intransitive verb such as "sleep" would almost certainly not be followed by a noun in a verb phrase is not modeled. So if we parsed the sentence "when I sleep quiet rooms help," the parse tree that treated "quiet" as a noun would not be determined to be extremely improbable.

This difficulty is addressed by a **lexicalized PCFG** (LPCFG). In such a grammar we are able to focus on patterns of words occurring together. Table 15.5 shows a simple LPCFG. If a phrase can be parsed by a given category, we call the **head** of the phrase the word that is most important to the category. For example, if the category is a noun phrase and the phrase is "the man", the head of the phrase is "man". If the category is a verb phrase and the phrase is "demands quiet", the head of the phrase is "demands". For brevity in what follows, we replace *Sentence* by S, *NounPhrase* by NP, etc. The notation $NP(n)$ is used to denote a phrase categorized as a noun phrase whose head is n. Using this notation, Table 15.5 shows a simple LPGFG. The probability $P_1(n, v)$ is defined for every noun and verb in the lexicon. We store the probability of each such pair. For example,

$$P_1(man, demands) = .01.$$

Because these are all the ways an S can be formed, these probabilities sum to 1. The probabilities $P_2(a, n)$ is defined for every article and noun pair, and the probability $P_3(n)$ is defined for every noun. Because these are all the ways an NP can be formed, the sum of all values of $P_2(a, n)$ and $P_3(n)$ sum to 1. The other probabilities in the grammar are similarly defined.

Figure 15.8 shows the parse tree obtained using the grammar in Table 15.5 to parse the following sentence:

the man demands quiet.

If we call this parse *Parse*, we have that

$$P(Parse) = .6 \times .02 \times .3 \times .01 = 3.6 \times 10^{-5}.$$

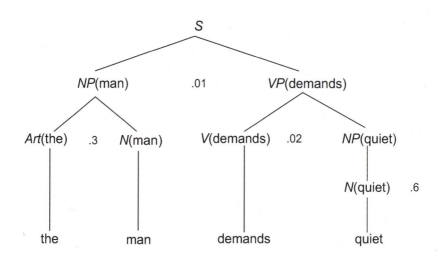

Figure 15.8 A parse tree obtained using a LPCFG.

Because this is the only parse of the sentence, this is also the probability of the sentence.

Consider now the following sentence:

the man sleeps quiet.

Because P_4(sleeps,quiet) = .00001, this sentence will have a much smaller probability.

A problem with LPCFG is that they require many more probabilities than PCFG. One way to handle this problem is to estimate the $P_4(v, n)$ for a rare (v, n) tuple by a probability that depends only on v.

The LPCFG we have shown is very simple. There are a number of ways of developing and learning LPCFGs. You are referred to the following texts and papers: [Charniak, 1993], [Charniak, 1997], [Manning and Schuetze, 2003], [Collins, 1997].

15.2 Semantic Interpretation

Parsing produces a tree that represents the linguistic components of a sentence such as the subject, verb, and object, and their relationships. The next step, namely **semantic interpretation**, represents the meaning of the sentence from the parse tree. By *meaning* we mean a statement that can be added to the knowledge base or a query that can be presented to the knowledge base. For example, suppose the domain of discourse is the blocks world in Section 4.2.2. Suppose further that the sentence is "block **a** is situated on block **b**." Then the semantics of the sentence is on(**a**,**b**), and the semantic interpretation of the sentence must derive this logical formula from the sentence.

Table 15.6 A grammar augmented with semantics

1	$S(pred(obj)) \rightarrow NP(obj)\ VP(pred)$
2	$NP(obj) \rightarrow Block(obj)$
3	$VP(pred(obj)) \rightarrow Verb(pred)\ NP(obj)$
4	$Block(\mathbf{a}) \rightarrow \mathbf{a}$
5	$Block(\mathbf{b}) \rightarrow \mathbf{b}$
6	$Verb(\lambda y\ \lambda x\ on(x,y)) \rightarrow$ on

In Figure 15.1 we depicted the semantic interpretation as a step that follows parsing for the sake of clarity. However, it could proceed along with parsing. Next we show a way to do them simultaneously.

For the sake of simplicity, suppose our sentence is follows:

$$\mathbf{a}\ \text{on}\ \mathbf{b}.$$

Based on this sentence, we should derive the logical statement on($\mathbf{a}$,$\mathbf{b}$). Table 15.6 shows a simple grammar for this domain augmented with semantics. The terminal are "$\mathbf{a}$", "$\mathbf{b}$", and "on". The semantics (meaning) of the terminals "$\mathbf{a}$" and "$\mathbf{b}$" are the logical terms "$\mathbf{a}$" and "$\mathbf{b}$". Because in general a noun part (NP) could be something other than a block, we have Rule 2, namely $NP(obj) \rightarrow Block(obj)$. The variable obj represents the semantics or meaning of a constituent of the sentence. So using Rule 4 we can obtain $Block(\mathbf{a})$, and then using Rule 2 we can obtain $NP(\mathbf{a})$. The difficulty is deriving "on $\mathbf{b}$". The semantic interpretation of this phrase is neither a term, nor a predicate, nor a logical sentence. However, we can consider "on $\mathbf{b}$" a predicate that, when combined with a term (in this case $\mathbf{a}$), yields a logical sentence. To accomplish this, we represent "on $\mathbf{b}$" a predicate as follows:

$$\lambda x\ on(x, \mathbf{b}).$$

This is λ-notation, and it represents an unnamed function of x. We can apply the function to "$\mathbf{a}$" as follows:

$$on(\mathbf{a},\mathbf{b}) = \lambda x\ on(x, \mathbf{b})\ (\mathbf{a}).$$

So when we apply Rule 1 with obj having the value $\mathbf{a}$ and $pred$ having the value $\lambda x\ on(x,\mathbf{b})$, we obtain the derivation

$$S(on(\mathbf{a},\mathbf{b})) = S(\lambda x\ on(x, \mathbf{b})\ (\mathbf{a})) \rightarrow NP(\mathbf{a})\ VP(\lambda x\ on(x, \mathbf{b})).$$

In the same way, the verb "on" is represented as the following predicate:

$$\lambda y\ \lambda x\ on(x, y).$$

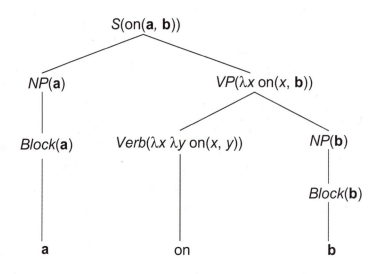

Figure 15.9 A derivation of the semantic interpretation $on(\mathbf{a},\mathbf{b})$ from the sentence "**a** on **b**".

Applying this predicate to "**b**" we have the following:

$$on(x,\mathbf{b}) = \lambda y \lambda x \; on(x,y) \; (\mathbf{b}).$$

Figure 15.9 shows the parse tree deriving the semantic interpretation $on(\mathbf{a},\mathbf{b})$ from the sentence "**a** on **b**".

We have shown how to hard-code semantic interpretations into the parse tree. Zelle and Mooney [1996] developed CHILL, which is a program that learns semantic interpretations from examples.

15.3   Concept/Knowledge Interpretation

Semantic interpretation of a sentence produces a unit of information such as the logical statement $on(\mathbf{a},\mathbf{b})$. In the final step, **concept/knowledge** or **contextual interpretation**, the item of information is incorporated into the knowledge base. For example, suppose our world or knowledge base consists of two rooms, Room 1 and Room 2; Room 1 has a table and the blocks in that room are situated on the table as shown on the left in Figure 15.10; and Room 2 has no table and the blocks in that room are situated as shown on the right in Figure 15.10. If our semantic interpretation is $on(\mathbf{a},\mathbf{b})$, how do we know whether to place block **a** on block **b** in Room 1 or Room 2? Linguists handle the problem using the notion of a **situation**, which is a particular set of circumstances in the world. The situation keeps track of everything that has happened so far. In the current example, the situation includes not only the placement of the various blocks in the rooms, but also that the robot is currently in Room 1. So

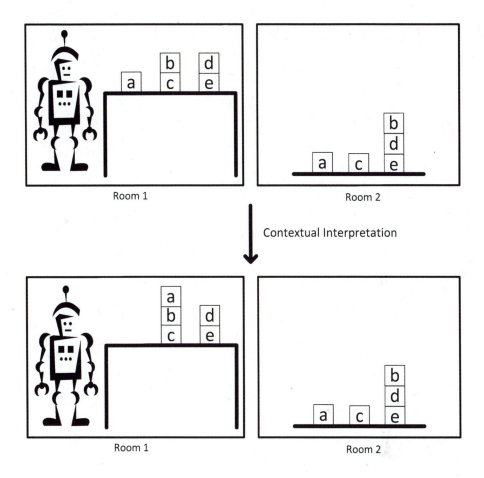

Figure 15.10 In the current situation, the robot is in Room 1.

the contextual interpretation of $on(\mathbf{a},\mathbf{b})$ is to place block $\mathbf{a}$ on block $\mathbf{b}$ in Room 1.

15.4   Information Extraction

We close with an application of language understanding, namely information extraction. An **information extraction** system takes as input a body of text, and extracts from it facts concerning pre-specified topics of interest. Figure 15.11 shows an example of how such a system proceeds. The purpose of this particular system is to extract information relative to the domain of natural disasters. The desired information is represented by a **template** that contains the precise attributes we want to retrieve. In this case they are as follows: Event, Date, Time, Location, Damage, Estimated Losses, and Injuries. In the example in Figure 15.11, the text consists of a paragraph that might appear

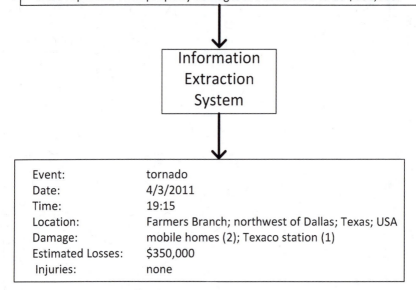

April 4 Dallas – Early last evening a tornado swept through an area northwest of Dallas, causing extensive damage. Witnesses confirm that the twister occurred without warning at approximately 7:15 pm and destroyed two mobile homes. The Texaco station at 102 Main street, Farmers Branch, Texas, was also severely damaged, but no injuries were reported. Total property damages are estimated to be $350,000.

Information
Extraction
System

Event:	tornado
Date:	4/3/2011
Time:	19:15
Location:	Farmers Branch; northwest of Dallas; Texas; USA
Damage:	mobile homes (2); Texaco station (1)
Estimated Losses:	$350,000
Injuries:	none

Figure 15.11 An example of an information extraction system in the domain of natural disasters.

in the local newspaper about an earthquake in Dallas, and the information extracted consists of all the information about the earthquake.

After discussing the various useful applications of information extraction, we present an architecture for an information extraction system.

15.4.1   Applications of Information Extraction

Today information extraction often concerns mining desired facts from information appearing on the Web. Applications involve monitoring newspapers and other articles to learn details of natural disasters, terrorist events, political affairs, business ventures, scientific discoveries, etc. Another application involves summarizing free-form patient records to extract symptoms, test results, treatments, and diagnoses. Yet another application concerns the automatic classification of documents such as legal documents.

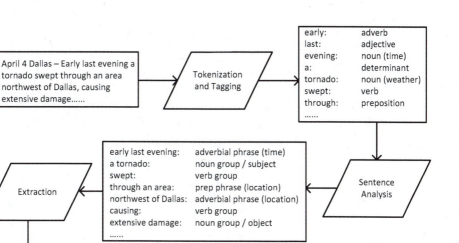

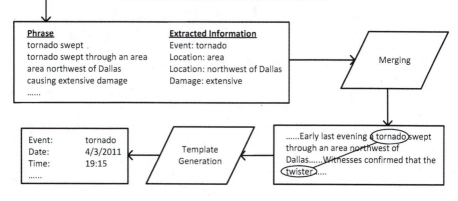

Figure 15.12 Architecture for an Information Extraction System.

15.4.2 Architecture for an Information Extraction System

Various approaches have been tried in the development of an information extraction system. At one extreme, systems were developed that simply performed keyword matching with no linguistic analysis at all. At the other extreme, systems processed the text using all the natural language understanding techniques developed in this chapter, including syntactic analysis, semantic interpretation, and contextual interpretation.

Cardie [1997] described what evolved as a standard architecture for an information extraction system. That architecture appears in Figure 15.12. We discuss each component of the architecture in turn.

1. **Tokenization and tagging**: In this step each word is disambiguated or tagged regarding its part of speech.

2. **Sentence analysis**: This stage performs syntactic analysis and finds and labels semantic entities relevant to each extraction topic. For example,

in the natural disaster domain, the system identifies events, locations, names, injury expressions, time expressions, and money expressions. The goal of sentence analysis in an information extraction system is not to produce a complete parse tree as is the case in a standard natural language understanding program. Rather, the system does **partial parsing**, which involves only developing as much structure as is needed to accomplish the information extraction task. A partial parser looks for fragments of recognizable texts such as noun groups and verb groups.

3. **Extraction**: In the extraction phase, the system concentrates on identifying the information that is relevant to the particular domain. For example, in the natural disaster domain, it identifies events (tornado) and locations ("area" and "northwest of Dallas").

4. **Merging**: In the merging phase, the system tries to resolve whether different entities discovered in the text are the same entity. For example, in the text concerning the tornado in Dallas, the system might resolve that "tornado" and "twister" refer to the same entity. The purpose here is to enable the system to associate information in two different statements with one entity. For example, in the case of the tornado, we have the text "a tornado swept...causing excessive damage," and "the twister occurred without warning....and destroyed two mobile homes." Once we identify that "tornado" and "twister" are the same entity, we know that the tornado caused excessive damage and destroyed the two mobile homes.

5. **Template Generation**: In the template phase, the extracted information is mapped to attributes required by the template.

Cardie [1997] discusses algorithms for implementing the architecture just presented.

15.5 Discussion and Further Reading

There is much more to the field of natural language understanding than the introduction provided here, both at theoretical and algorithmic levels. Two popular texts on the subject are [Allen, 1995] and [Jurafsky and Martin, 2009]. The former text had long been the standard, while the latter one is more current in that it covers the advances in statistical techniques that have occurred recently. Natural language understanding is a sub-field of **natural language processing (NLP)** , which concerns both understanding natural language input and producing natural language output. The latter text mentioned above, namely [Jurafsky and Martin, 2009], covers both aspects of NLP.

EXERCISES

Section 15.1

Exercise 15.1 Show that any context-free grammar can be transformed into a grammar in Chomsky normal form.

Exercise 15.2 Using the CFG in Table 15.1, parse these sentences and show the resultant parse trees:

1. A big man loves the monkey.

2. The fat monkey can read the right book.

3. The man loves the left and the monkey loves the right.

Exercise 15.3 Modify Algorithm 15.1 so that it produces a parse tree.

Exercise 15.4 Implement Algorithm 15.1 and use it to parse the sentences in Exercise 15.2

Exercise 15.5 Show two different parse trees for each of the sentences in Example 15.2.

Exercise 15.6 Using the grammar in Table 15.3, show the table produced by the CYK algorithm when parsing each of the following sentences:

1. y y x x x

2. x x y x x

3. x y y y y.

Exercise 15.7 Implement the CYK algorithm.

Exercise 15.8 Show that the time complexity of the CYK algorithm is $\theta(mn^3)$, where m is the number of rules and n is the number of words in the sentence.

Exercise 15.9 Using the PCFG in Table 15.4, compute probabilities of the sentences in Exercise 15.2.

Exercise 15.10 Using the LPCFG in Table 15.5, obtain the parse tree and compute the probability of this sentence:

The man sleeps quiet.

Section 15.2

Exercise 15.11 Augment the grammar in Table 15.1 with semantics, and use the augmented grammar to obtain semantics for the sentences in Exercise 15.2.

Bibliography

Aczel and Sounderpandian, 2002   Aczel, A., and J. Sounderpandian, *Complete Business Statistics*, McGraw-Hill, New York, 2002.

Allen, 1995   Allen, J., *Natural Language Understanding*, Benjamin/Cummings, 1995.

Allison, 2007   Allison, C.. "Practical Computation Theory," *The Journal of Computing Sciences in Colleges*, Vol. 22, No. 10, 2007.

Amarel, 1968   Amarel, S., "On Representations of Problems of Reasoning About Actions," in Michie, D. (Ed.): *Machine Intelligence 3*, Elsevier/North-Holland, 1968.

Anderson et al., 2007   Anderson, D., D. Sweeney, and T. Williams, *Statistics for Business and Economics*, South-Western, 2007.

Ash, 1970   Ash, R. B., *Basic Probability Theory*, Wiley, 1970.

Baldassarre et al., 2007   Baldassarre, G., et al., "Self-Organized Coordinated Motion in Groups of Physically Connect Robots," *IEEE Transactions on Systems, Man, and Cybernetics, Part B: Cybernetics*, Vol. 37, No. 1, 2007.

Banzhaf et al., 1998   Banzhaf, W. P. Nordin, R.E. Keller, and F.D. Francone, *Genetic Programming An Introduction*, Morgan Kaufmann, 1998.

Basye et al., 1992   Basye, K., T. Dean, J. Kirman, and M. Lejter, "A Decision-Theoretic Approach to Planning, Perception and Control," *IEEE Expert*, Vol. 7, No. 4, 1992.

Bauer et al., 1997

Bauer, E., D. Koller, and Y. Singer, "Update Rules for Parameter Estimation in Bayesian Networks," in Geiger, D., and P. Shenoy (Eds.): *Uncertainty in Artificial Intelligence; Proceedings of the Thirteenth Conference*, Morgan Kaufmann, 1997.

Beckers et al., 1992

Beckers, E., S. Ceria, and G. Cornuéjols, "Trails and U-turns in the Selection of the Shortest Path by the Ant Lasius Nifwe," *Journal of Theoretical Biology*, Vol. 159, 1992.

Beinlich et al., 1989

Beinlich, I. A., H. J. Suermondt, R. M. Chavez, and G. F. Cooper, "The ALARM Monitoring System: A Case Study with Two Probabilistic Inference Techniques for Belief Networks," *Proceedings of the Second European Conference on Artificial Intelligence in Medicine*, London, 1989.

Bell, 1982

Bell, D.E., "Regret in Decision Making Under Uncertainty," *Operations Research*, Vol. 30, No. 5, 1982.

Bellman, 1957

Bellman, R., "A Markovian Decision Process." *Journal of Mathematics and Mechanics*, Vol. 6, No. 4, 1957.

Benson, 1995

Benson, S., "Active Model Learning and Action Execution in a Reactive Agent," *Proceedings of the 1995 International Joint Conference in Artificial Intelligence* (IJCAI), 1995.

Bentler, 1980

Bentler, P. N., "Multivariate Analysis with Latent Variables," *Review of Psychology*, Vol. 31, 1980.

Bernardo and Smith, 1994

Bernado, J., and A. Smith, *Bayesian Theory*, Wiley, New York, 1994.

Bilmes, 2000

Bilmes, J.A., "Dynamic Bayesian Multinets," in Boutilier, C. and M. Goldszmidt (Eds.): *Uncertainty in Artificial Intelligence; Proceedings of the Sixteenth Conference*, Morgan Kaufmann, 2000.

Boden, 1977

Boden, M.A., *Artificial Intelligence and Natural Man*, Basic Books, 1977.

Brachman and Levesque, 2004   Brachman, R.J., and H.J. Levesque, *Knowledge Representation and Reasoning*, Morgan Kaufmann, 2004.

Breder, 1954   Breder, C.M., "Equations Descriptive of Fish Schools and Other Animal Aggregations," *Ecology*, Vol. 35, 1954.

Breese et al., 1998   Breese, J., D. Heckerman, and C. Kadie, "Empirical Analysis of Predictive Algorithms for Collaborative Filtering," in Cooper, G.F., and S. Moral (Eds.): *Uncertainty in Artificial Intelligence; Proceedings of the Fourteenth Conference*, Morgan Kaufmann, 1998.

Breiman et al., 1984   Breiman, L., J. Friedman, R. Olshen, and C. Stone, *Classification and Regression Trees*, Wadsworth and Brooks, 1984.

Brooks, 1981   Brooks, R.A., "Symbolic Reasoning Among 3-D Models and 3-D Images," *Artificial Intelligence*, Vol. 17., No. 1–3, 1981.

Brooks, 1991   Brooks, R.A., "Intelligence without Representation," *Artificial Intelligence*, Vol. 47, 1991.

Buchanan and Shortliffe, 1984   Buchanan, B.G., and E.H. Shortliffe, *Rule-Based Expert System*, 1984.

Bulmer, 2003   Bulmer, M., *Francis Galton: Pioneer of Heredity and Biometry*, Johns Hopkins University Press. 2003.

Buntine, 1993   Buntine, W., "Learning Classification Trees," in Hand, D.J. (Ed.): *Artificial Intelligence Frontiers in Statistics: AI and Statistics III*, Chapman & Hall/CRC, 1993.

Buntine, 2002   Buntine, W., "Tree Classification Software," *Proceedings of the Third National Technology Transfer Conference and Exposition*, Baltimore, MD, 2002.

Burnell and Horvitz, 1995   Burnell, L., and E. Horvitz, "Structure and Chance: Melding Logic and Probability for Software Debugging," *Communications of the ACM*, Vol. 38, No. 3, 1995.

Campo et al., 2010   Campo, A., et al., "Artificial Pheromone for
                                      Path Selection by a Foraging Swarm of Ro-
                                      bots," *Biological Cybernetics*, Vol. 103, No.
                                      5, 2010.

Cardie, 1997   Cardie, C., "Empirical Methods in Informa-
                                      tion Extraction," *AI Magazine*, Vol. 18, No.
                                      4, 1997.

Chalmers, 1996   Chalmers, D., *The Conscious Mind: In
                                      Search of a Fundamental Theory*, Oxford
                                      University Press, 1996.

Charniak, 1993   Charniak, E., *Statistical Language Learning*,
                                      MIT Press, 1993.

Charniak, 1997   Charniak. E, "Statistical Parsing with a
                                      Context-Free Grammar and Word Statis-
                                      tics," *Proceedings of the Fourteenth National
                                      Conference on Artificial Intelligence (AAAI
                                      1997)*, 1997.

Cheeseman and Stutz, 1996   Cheeseman, P., and J. Stutz, "Bayesian
                                      Classification (Autoclass): Theory and Re-
                                      sults," in Fayyad, D., G. Piatetsky-Shapiro,
                                      P. Smyth, and R. Uthurusamy (Eds.): *Ad-
                                      vances in Knowledge Discovery and Data
                                      Mining*, AAAI Press, 1996.

Chib, 1995   Chib, S., "Marginal Likelihood from the
                                      Gibbs Output," *Journal of the American
                                      Statistical Association*, Vol. 90, No. 432,
                                      1995.

Chickering, 2001   Chickering, D., "Learning Equivalence
                                      Classes of Bayesian Networks," Technical
                                      Report # MSR-TR-2001-65, Microsoft Re-
                                      search, Redmond, WA, 2001.

Chickering, 2002   Chickering, D., "Optimal Structure Identifi-
                                      cation with Greedy Search," *Journal of Ma-
                                      chine Learning Research*, Vol. 3, 2002.

Chickering and Heckerman, 1997   Chickering, D., and D. Heckerman, "Effi-
                                      cient Approximation for the Marginal Like-
                                      lihood of Bayesian Networks with Hidden
                                      Variables," Technical Report # MSR-TR-
                                      96-08, Microsoft Research, Redmond, WA,
                                      1997.

Christensen et al., 2009   Christensen, L.M. , H. Harkema , P.J. Haug, J.Y. Irwin, and W.W. Chapman, "ONYX: A System for the Semantic Analysis of Clinical Text," *Proceedings of the Workshop on BioNLP*, Boulder, CO, June 04–05, 2009.

Clemen, 1996   Clemen, R.T., *Making Hard Decisions*, PWS-KENT, 1996.

Collins, 1997   Collins, M., "Three Generative, Lexicalised Models for Statistical Parsing," *Proceedings of the 35th Annual Meeting of the Association for Computational Linguistics*, 1997.

Collins and Quillan, 1969   Collins, A., and M.R. Quillian, "Retrieval Time From Semantic Memory," *Journal of Verbal Learning and Verbal Behavior*, Vol. 8, 1969.

Cooper, 1990   Cooper, G. F., "The Computational Complexity of Probabilistic Inference Using Bayesian Belief Networks," *Artificial Intelligence*, Vol. 42, No. 2–3. 1990.

Cooper and Herskovits, 1992   Cooper, G. F., and E. Herskovits, "A Bayesian Method for the Induction of Probabilistic Networks from Data," *Machine Learning*, Vol. 9, 1992.

Cotton et al., 2000   Cotton, S., A. Bundy, and T. Walsh, "Automatic Invention of Integer Sequences," *Proceedings of AAAI-2000*, MIT Press, 2000.

Cozman and Krotkov, 1996   Cozman, F., and E. Krotkov, "Quasi-Bayesian Strategies for Efficient Plan Generation: Application to the Planning to Observe Problem," in Horvitz, E., and F. Jensen (Eds.): *Uncertainty in Artificial Intelligence; Proceedings of the Twelfth Conference*, Morgan Kaufmann,1996.

Dagum and Chavez, 1993   Dagum, P., and R. M. Chavez, "Approximating Probabilistic Inference in Bayesian Belief Networks," *IEEE Transactions on Pattern Analysis and Machine Intelligence*, Vol. 15, No. 3, 1993.

Dagum and Luby, 1993   Dagum, P., and M. Luby, "Approximating Probabilistic Inference in Bayesian Belief Networks Is NP-hard," *Artificial Intelligence*, Vol. 60, No. 1, 1993.

Davis and Lenat, 1982

Davis, R., and D.B. Lenat, *Knowledge-based Systems in Artificial Intelligence*, McGraw-Hill, 1982.

Dean and Wellman, 1991

Dean, T., and M. Wellman, *Planning and Control*, Morgan Kaufmann, 1991.

Dechter and Pearl, 1985

Dechter, R. and J. Pearl, "Generalized Best-First Search Strategies and the Optimality of A*," *Journal of the ACM*, Vol. 32, No. 3, 1985.

de Finetti, 1937

de Finetti, B., "La prévision: See Lois Logiques, ses Sources Subjectives," *Annales de l'Institut Henri Poincaré*, Vol. 7, 1937.

Delgrande and Schaub, 2003

Delgrande, J., and T. Schaub, "On the Relation Between Reiter's Default Logic and its (major) Variants," *Proceedings of the Seventh European Conference on Symbolic and Quantitative Approaches to Reasoning with Uncertainty*, 2003.

Demirer et al., 2006

Demirer, R., R. Mau, and C. Shenoy, "Bayesian Networks: A Decision Tool to Improve Portfolio Risk Analysis," *Journal of Applied Finance*, Vol. 6, No. 2, 2006.

Dempster et al., 1977

Dempster, A, N. Laird, and D. Rubin, "Maximum Likelihood from Incomplete Data via the EM Algorithm," *Journal of the Royal Statistical Society B*, Vol. 39, No. 1, 1977.

DePuy et al., 2005

DePuy, G.W., R.J. Moraga, and G.E. Whitehouse, "Meta-RaPS: A Simple and Effective Approach for Solving the Traveling Salesman Problem," *Transportation Research Part E*, Vol. 41, No. 2, 2005.

Diez and Druzdzel, 2002

Diez, F.J., and M.J. Druzdzel, "Canonical Probabilistic Models for Knowledge Engineering," Technical Report IA-02-01, Dpto. Inteligencia Artificial, UNED, Madrid, 2002.

Dorigo and Gambardella, 1997

Dorigo, M., and L.M. Gambardella, "Ant Colonies for the Traveling Salesperson Problem," *Biosystems*, Vol. 43, 1997.

Dorigo et al., 1996

Dorigo, M., V. Maniezzo, and A. Colorni, "The Ant System: by a Colony of Cooperating Agents," *IEEE Transaction on Systems, Man, and Cybernetics*, Part B, Vol. 26, No. 1, 1996.

Doyle, 1979

Doyle, J., "A Truth Maintenance System," *Artificial Intelligence*, Vol. 12, No. 3, 1979.

Druzdzel and Glymour, 1999

Druzdzel, M.J., and C. Glymour, "Causal Inferences from Databases: Why Universities Lose Students," in Glymour, C., and G.F. Cooper (Eds.): *Computation, Causation, and Discovery*, AAAI Press, 1999.

Duda et al., 1976

Duda, R.O., P.E. Hart, and N.J. Nilsson, "Subjective Bayesian Methods for Rule-Based Inference Systems," Technical Report 124, Stanford Research Institute, 1976.

Durbin and Willshaw, 1987

Durbin, R., and D. Willshaw, "An Analogue Approach to the Traveling Salesperson Problem Using an Elastic Net Method," *Nature*, Vol. 326, 1987.

Edelman, 2006

Edelman, G.M., *Second Nature: Brain Science and Human Knowledge*, Yale University Press, 2006.

Edelman, 2007

Edelman, G.M., "Learning In and From Brain-Based Devices," *Science*, Vol. 318, No. 5853, 2007.

Eells, 1991

Eells, E., *Probabilistic Causality*, Cambridge University Press, 1991.

Farnsworth et al., 2004

Farnsworth, G.V., J.A. Kelly, A.S. Othling, and R. J. Pryor, "Successful Technical Trading Agents Using Genetic Programming," Technical Report # SAND2004-4774, Sandia National Laboratories, Albuquerque, NM, 2004.

Feigenbaum et al., 1971

Feigenbaum, E.A., B.G. Buchanan, and J. Lederberg, "On Generality and Problem Solving: A Case Study Using the Dendral Program, in Meltzer, B., and D. Mitchie (Eds.): *Machine Intelligence 6*, Edinburgh University Press, 1971.

Feller, 1968

Feller, W., *An Introduction to Probability Theory and its Applications*, Wiley, New York, 1968.

Fikes and Nilsson, 1971

Fikes, R.E., and N.J. Nilsson, "STRIPS: A New Approach to the Application of Theorem Proving to Artificial Intelligence," *Artificial Intelligence*, Vol. 3, No. 2, 1971.

Fishelson and Geiger, 2002

Fishelson, M., and D. Geiger, "Exact Genetic Linkage Computations for General Pedigrees," *Bioinformatics*, Vol. 18 (supplement 1), 2002.

Fishelson and Geiger, 2004

Fishelson, M., and D. Geiger, "Optimizing Exact Genetic Linkage Computation," *Journal of Computational Biology*, Vol. 11, No. 2–3, 2004.

Fogel, 1994

Fogel, D.B., "Evolutionary Programming in Perspective: The Top-Down View," in Zurada, J.M., R.J. Marks II, and C.J. Robinson (Eds.): *Computational Intelligence: Imitating Life*, IEEE Press, 1994.

Frazer, 1958

Fraser, A.S., "Monte Carlo Analyses of Genetic Models," *Nature*, Vol. 181, 1958.

Freedman et al., 2007

Freedman, F., R. Pisani, and R. Purves, *Statistics*, W.W. Norton & Co., 2007.

Friedman et al., 2000

Friedman, N., M. Linial, I. Nachman, and D. Pe'er, "Using Bayesian Networks to Analyze Expression Data," in *Proceedings of the Fourth Annual International Conference on Computational Molecular Biology*, 2000.

Friedman et al., 2002

Friedman, N., M. Ninio, I Pe'er, and T. Pupko, "A Structural EM Algorithm for Phylogenetic Inference," *Journal of Computational Biology*, Vol. 9, No. 2, 2002.

Friedman and Koller, 2003

Friedman, N., and K. Koller, "Being Bayesian about Network Structure: A Bayesian Approach to Structure Discovery in Bayesian Networks," *Machine Learning*, Vol. 50, No.1, 2003.

Fung and Chang, 1990

Fung, R., and K. Chang, "Weighing and Integrating Evidence for Stochastic Simulation in Bayesian Networks," in Henrion, M., R. D. Shachter, L. N. Kanal, and J. F. Lemmer (Eds.): *Uncertainty in Artificial Intelligence 5*, North-Holland, 1990.

Galán et al., 2002

Galán, S.F., and F. Aguado, F.J. Díez, and J. Mira, "NasoNet, Modeling the Spread of Nasopharyngeal Cancer with Networks of Probabilistic Events in Discrete Time," *Artificial Intelligence in Medicine*, Vol. 25, No. 3, 2002.

Gambardella and Dorigo, 1995

Gambardella, L.M., and M. Dorigo, "Ant-Q: a Reinforcement Learning Approach to the Traveling Salesperson Problem," in Prieditis, A., and S. Russell (Eds.): *Proceedings of ML-95, 12th International Conference on Machine Learning*, Morgan Kaufmann, 1995.

Geiger and Heckerman, 1994

Geiger, D., and D. Heckerman, "Learning Gaussian Networks," in de Mantras, R.L., and D. Poole (Eds.): *Uncertainty in Artificial Intelligence; Proceedings of the Tenth Conference*, Morgan Kaufmann, 1994.

Gelernter, 1959

Gelernter, H., "Realization of a Geometry Theorem-Proving Machine," *Proceedings of International Conference on Information Processing*, UNESCO, 1959.

Geman and Geman, 1984

Geman, S., and D. Geman, "Stochastic Relaxation, Gibb's Distributions and the Bayesian Restoration of Images," *IEEE Transactions on Pattern Analysis and Machine Intelligence*, Vol. 6, 1984.

Gilks et al., 1996

Gilks, W.R., S. Richardson, and D.J. Spiegelhalter (Eds.): *Markov Chain Monte Carlo in Practice*, Chapman & Hall/CRC, 1996.

Gillispie and Pearlman, 2001

Gillispie, S.B., and M.D. Pearlman, "Enumerating Markov Equivalence Classes of Acyclic Digraph Models," in Koller, D., and J. Breese (Eds.): *Uncertainty in Artificial Intelligence; Proceedings of the Seventeenth Conference*, Morgan Kaufmann, 2001.

Glymour, 2001   Glymour, C., *The Mind's Arrows: Bayes Nets and Graphical Causal Models in Psychology*, MIT Press, 2001.

Glymour and Cooper, 1999   Glymour, C., and G. Cooper, *Computation, Causation, and Discovery*, MIT Press, 1999.

Goertzel and Pennachin, 2007   Goertzel, B., and C. Pennachin, *Artificial General Intelligence*, Springer, 2007.

Goldstone and Janssen, 2005   Goldstone, R.L., and M.A. Janssen, "Computational Models of Collective Behavior," *Trends in Cognitive Sciences*, Vol. 9, No. 9, 2005.

Goodwin, 1982   Goodwin, J., "An Improved Algorithm for Non-Monotonic Dependency Net Update," Technical Report LITH-MAT-R-82-23, Department of Computer Science and Information Science, Linköping University, Linköping, Sweden, 1982.

Griffiths et al., 2007   Griffiths, J. F., S. R. Wessler, R. C. Lewontin, and S. B. Carroll, *An Introduction to Genetic Analysis*, W. H. Freeman and Company, 2007.

Hamilton, 1971   Hamilton, W.D., "Geometry for the Selfish Herd," *Journal of Theoretical Biology*, Vol. 31, 1971.

Harnad, 2001   Harnad, S. "What's Wrong and Right About Searle's Chinese Room Argument," in Bishop, M., and J. Preston (Eds.): *Essays on Searle's Chinese Room Argument*, Oxford University Press, 2001.

Hartl and Jones, 2006   Hartl, D. L., and E. W. Jones, *Essential Genetics*, Jones and Bartlett, 2006.

Hanks and McDermott, 1987   Hanks, S., and D. McDermott, "Nonmonotonic Logic and Temporal Projection," *Artificial Intelligence*, Vol. 33, No. 3, 1987.

Hardwick and Stout, 1991   Hardwick, J.P., and Q.F. Stout, "Bandit Strategies for Ethical Sequential Allocation," *Computing Science and Statistics*, Vol. 23, 1991.

Hastings, 1970

Hastings, W.K., "Monte Carlo Sampling Methods Using Markov Chains and their Applications," *Biometrika*, Vol. 57, No. 1, 1970.

Hebb, 1949

Hebb, D., *The Organization of Behavior*, Wiley, 1949.

Heckerman, 1996

Heckerman, D., "A Tutorial on Learning with Bayesian Networks," Technical Report # MSR-TR-95-06, Microsoft Research, Redmond, WA, 1996.

Heckerman and Meek, 1997

Heckerman, D., and C. Meek, "Embedded Bayesian Network Classifiers," Technical Report MSR-TR-97-06, Microsoft Research, Redmond, WA, 1997.

Heckerman et al., 1992

Heckerman, D., E. Horvitz, and B. Nathwani, "Toward Normative Expert Systems: Part I The Pathfinder Project," *Methods of Information in Medicine*, Vol. 31, 1992.

Heckerman et al., 1994

Heckerman, D., J. Breese, and K. Rommelse, "Troubleshooting Under Uncertainty," Technical Report MSR-TR-94-07, Microsoft Research, Redmond, WA, 1994.

Heckerman et al., 1999

Heckerman, D., C. Meek, and G. Cooper, "A Bayesian Approach to Causal Discovery," in Glymour, C., and G.F. Cooper (Eds.): *Computation, Causation, and Discovery*, AAAI Press, 1999.

Heppner and Grenander, 1990

Heppner, F., and U. Grenander, "A Stochastic Nonlinear Model for Coordinated Bird Flocks," in Kasner, S. (Ed.): *The Ubiquity of Chaos*, AAAS Publications, 1990.

Herskovits and Cooper, 1990

Herskovits, E. H., and G. F. Cooper, "Kutató: An Entropy-Driven System for the Construction of Probabilistic Expert Systems from Databases," in Shachter, R. D., T. S. Levitt, L. N. Kanal, and J. F. Lemmer (Eds.): *Uncertainty in Artificial Intelligence; Proceedings of the Sixth Conference*, North-Holland, 1990.

Herskovits and Dagher, 1997

Herskovits, E.H., and A.P. Dagher, "Applications of Bayesian Networks to Health

Care," Technical Report NSI-TR-1997-02, Noetic Systems Incorporated, Baltimore, MD, 1997.

Hey and Morrone, 2004

Hey, J.D., and A. Morone, "Do Markets Drive Out Lemmings-or Vice Versa?," *Economica, London School of Economics and Political Science*, Vol. 71, No. 284, 2004.

Hogg and Craig, 1972

Hogg, R. V., and A. T. Craig, *Introduction to Mathematical Statistics*, Macmillan, 1972.

Holland, 1975

Holland, J., *Adaptation in Natural and Artificial Systems*, University of Michigan Press, 1975.

Horvitz et al., 1992

Horvitz, E., S. Srinivas, C. Rouokangas, and M. Barry, "A Decision-Theoretic Approach to the Display of Information for Time-Critical Decisions: The Vista Project," *Proceedings of SOAR-92*, Houston, TX, 1992.

Huang et al., 1994

Huang, T., D. Koller, J. Malik, G. Ogasawara, B. Rao, S. Russell, and J. Weber, "Automatic Symbolic Traffic Scene Analysis Using Belief Networks," *Proceedings of the Twelfth National Conference on Artificial Intelligence (AAAI94)*, AAAI Press, 1994.

Hume, 1748

Hume, D., *An Inquiry Concerning Human Understanding*, Prometheus, 1988 (originally published in 1748).

Iversen et al., 1971

Iversen, G. R., W. H. Longcor, F. Mosteller, J. P. Gilbert, and C. Youtz, "Bias and Runs in Dice Throwing and Recording: A Few Million Throws," *Psychometrika*, Vol. 36, 1971.

Jadbabaie et al., 2003

Jadbabaie, A., J. Lin, and A.S. Morse, "Coordination of Groups of Mobile Autonomous Agents Using Nearest Neighbor Rules," *IEEE Transactions on Automatic Control*, Vol. 48, 2003.

Jensen et al., 1990

Jensen, F., S. Lauritzen, and K. Olesen, "Bayesian Updating in Causal Probabilistic Networks by Local Computations," *Computational Statistics Quarterly* 4, 1990.

Jensen, 2001

Jensen, F.V., *Bayesian Networks and Decision Graphs*, Springer-Verlag, New York, 2001.

Jiang et al., 2010

Jiang, X., M.M. Barmada, R.E. Neapolitan, S. Visweswaran, and G.F. Cooper, "A Fast Algorithm for Learning Epistatic Genomic Relationships," *AMIA 2010 Symposium Proceedings*, 2010.

Jiang et al., 2011a

Jiang, X., R.E. Neapolitan, M.M. Barmada, and S. Visweswaran, "Performance of Bayesian Network Scoring Criteria for Learning Genetic Epistasis," *BMC Bioinformatics*, Vol. 12, No. 89, 2011.

Jiang et al., 2011b

Jiang, X., S. Visweswaran, and R.E. Neapolitan, "Mining Epistatic Interactions from High-Dimensional Data Sets Using Bayesian Networks," in Holmes, D. and L. Jain (Eds.): *Foundations and Intelligent Paradigms-3*, Springer-Verlag, 2011.

Joereskog, 1982

Joereskog, K. G., *Systems Under Indirect Observation*, North Holland, 1982.

Jurafsky and Martin, 2009

Jurafsky, D., and J. Martin, *Speech and Language Processing*, Prentice Hall, 2009.

Kaelbling et al., 1998

Kaelbling, L.P., M.L. Littman, and A.R. Cassandra, "Planning and Acting in Partially Observable Stochastic Domains," *Artificial Intelligence*, Vol. 101, 1998.

Kahneman and Tversky, 1979

Kahneman, D., and A. Tversky, "Prospect Theory: An Analysis of Decision Under Risk," *Econometrica*, Vol. 47, 1979.

Katz, 1997

Katz, E.P., "Extending the Teleo-Reactive Paradigm for Robotic Agent Task Control Using Zadehan (fuzzy) Logic," *Proceeding of IEEE International Symposium on Computational Intelligence in Robotics and Automation* (CIRA'97), 1997.

Kemmerer et al., 2002

Kemmerer, B., Mishra, S., and P. Shenoy, "Bayesian Causal Maps as Decision Aids in Venture Capital Decision Making," *Proceedings of the Academy of Management Conference*, 2002.

Kennedy and Eberhart, 1995   Kennedy, J., and R.C. Eberhart, "Particle Swarm Optimization," *Proceedings of the IEEE Conference on Neural Networks IV*, IEEE Service Center, New York, 1995.

Kennedy and Eberhart, 2001   Kennedy, J., and R.C. Eberhart, *Swarm Intelligence*, Morgan Kaufmann, 2001.

Kennett et al., 2001   Kennett, R., K. Korb, and A. Nicholson, "Seabreeze Prediction Using Bayesian Networks: A Case Study," *Proceedings of the 5th Pacific-Asia Conference on Advances in Knowledge Discovery and Data Mining - PAKDD*, Springer-Verlag, New York, 2001.

Kenny, 1979   Kenny, D. A., *Correlation and Causality*, Wiley, 1979.

Kerrich, 1946   Kerrich, J. E., *An Experimental Introduction to the Theory of Probability*, Einer Munksgaard, 1946.

Klein et al., 2000   Klein, W.B., C.R. Stern, G.F. Luger, and D. Pless, "Teleo-Reactive Control for Accelerator Beam Tuning," *Artificial Intelligence and Soft Computing: Proceedings of the IASTED International Conference*, IASTED/ACTA Press, 2000.

Koehler, 1998   Koehler, S. *Symtext: a Natural Language Understanding System for Encoding Free Text Medical Data*, Ph.D. dissertation, University of Utah, 1998.

Korf, 1993   Korf, R., "Linear-Space Best-First Search," *Artificial Intelligence*, Vol. 62, 1993.

Koza, 1992   Koza, J., *Genetic Programming*, MIT Press, 1992.

Krishnamurthy et al., 2001   Krishnamurthy, B., C. Wills, and Y. Zhang, "On the Use and Performance of Content Distribution Networks," *ACM SIGCOMM Internet Measurement Workshop*, 2001.

Lander and Shenoy, 1999   Lander, D. M., and P. Shenoy, "Modeling and Valuing Real Options Using Influence Diagrams," School of Business Working Paper No. 283, University of Kansas, 1999.

Langley et al., 1987   Langley, P., H.A. Simon, G.L. Bradshaw, and J.M. Zytkow, *Scientific Discovery: Computational Explorations of the Creative Processes*, MIT Press.

Lari and Young, 1990   Lari, K., and S. Young, "The Estimation of Stochastic Context-Free Grammars Using the Inside-Outside Algorithm," *Computer Speech and Language*, Vol. 4, 1990.

Latané, 1981   Latane, B., "The Psychology of Social Impact," *American Psychologist*, Vol. 36, 1981.

Lauritzen and Spiegelhalter, 1988   Lauritzen, S. L., and D. J. Spiegelhalter, "Local Computation with Probabilities in Graphical Structures and Their Applications to Expert Systems," *Journal of the Royal Statistical Society B*, Vol. 50, No. 2, 1988.

Lenat, 1983   Lenat, D.B., "EURISKO: A Program that Learns New Heuristics," *Artificial Intelligence*, Vol. 21, No. 1-2, 1983.

Lenat, 1998   Lenat, D.B., " From 2001 to 2001: Common sense and the mind of HAL," in Stork D.G. (Ed.): *Hal's Legacy: 2001 as Dream and Reality*, MIT Press, 1998.

Lenat and Brown, 1984   Lenat, D.B., and J.S. Brown, "Why AM and Eurisko Appear to Work," *Artificial Intelligence*, Vol. 23, No. 3, 1984.

Leung et al., 2004   Leung, K.S., H.D. Jin, and Z.B. Xu, "An Expanding Self-Organizing Neural Network for the Traveling Salesman Problem," *Neurocomputing*, Vol. 62, 2004.

Li, 1997   Li, W., *Molecular Evolution*, Sinauer Associates, 1997.

Li and D'Ambrosio, 1994   Li, Z., and B. D'Ambrosio, "Efficient Inference in Bayes' Networks as a Combinatorial Optimization Problem," *International Journal of Approximate Inference*, Vol. 11, 1994.

Lifschitz, 1994   Lifschitz, V., "Circumscription," In Gabbay, D., C. J. Hogger, and J. A. Robinson (Eds.): *Handbook of Logic in Artificial Intelligence*

	and Logic Programming, Volume 3: Non-monotonic Reasoning and Uncertain Reasoning, Oxford University Press, 1994.
Lindley, 1985	Lindley, D.V., *Introduction to Probability and Statistics from a Bayesian Viewpoint*, Cambridge University Press, London, 1985.
Lindsay et al., 1980	Lindsay, R. K., B. G. Buchanan, E.A. Feigenbaum, and J. Lederberg, *Applications of Artificial Intelligence for Organic Chemistry: The Dendral Project*, McGraw-Hill, 1980.
Lugg et al., 1995	Lugg, J. A., J. Raifer, and C. N. F. González, "Dehydrotestosterone Is the Active Androgen in the Maintenance of Nitric Oxide-Mediated Penile Erection in the Rat," *Endocrinology*, Vol. 136, No. 4, 1995.
Mani et al., 1997	Mani, S., S. McDermott, and M. Valtorta, "MENTOR: A Bayesian Model for Prediction of Mental Retardation in Newborns," *Research in Developmental Disabilities*, Vol. 8, No.5, 1997.
Manning and Schuetze, 2003	Manning, C., and Schuetze, H., *Foundations of Statistical Natural Language Processing*, MIT Press, 2003.
Marcus et al., 1993	Marcus, P., B. Santorini, and M. Marcinkiewicz, "Building a Large Annotated Corpus of English: The Penn Treebank," *Computational Linguistics*, Vol. 19, No. 2, 1993.
Margaritis et al., 2001	Margaritis, D., C. Faloutsos, and S. Thrun, "NetCube: A Scalable Tool for Fast Data Mining and Compression," *Proceedings of the 27th VLB Conference*, Rome, Italy, 2001.
McCarthy, 1958	McCarthy, J., "Programs with Common Sense," *Symposium on Mechanization of Thought Processes*. National Physical Laboratory, Teddington, England, 1958.
McCarthy, 1980	McCarthy, J., "Circumscription–A Form of Non-Monotonic Reasoning," *Artificial Intelligence*, Vol. 13, 1969.

McCarthy, 2007   McCarthy, J., From Here to Human-Level AI, *Artificial Intelligence*, Vol. 171, No. 18, 2007.

McCarthy and Hayes, 1969   McCarthy, J., and P. J. Hayes, "Some Philosophical Problems From the Standpoint of Artificial Intelligence, *Machine Intelligence*, Vol. 4, 1969.

McCorduck, 2004   McCorduck, P., *Machines Who Think*, A. K. Peters, Ltd., 2004.

McCulloch and Pitts, 1943   McCulloch, W., and W. Pitts, "A Logical Calculus of the Ideas Immanent in Nervous Activity, *Bulletin of Mathematical Biophysics*, Vol. 5, 1943.

McDermott, 1982   McDermott, J., "A Rule-Based Configurer of Computer Systems," *Artificial Intelligence*, Vol. 19, No. 1, 1982.

McDermott and Doyle, 1980   McDermott, D., and J. Doyle, "Nonmonotonic Logic 1," *Artificial Intelligence*, Vol. 13, 1980.

McLachlan and Krishnan, 2008   McLachlan, G. J., and T. Krishnan, *The EM Algorithm and Extensions*, Wiley, 2008.

Meek, 1995   Meek, C., "Strong Completeness and Faithfulness in Bayesian Networks," in Besnard, P., and S. Hanks (Eds.): *Uncertainty in Artificial Intelligence; Proceedings of the Eleventh Conference*, Morgan Kaufmann, 1995.

Meek, 1997   Meek, C., "Graphical Models: Selecting Causal and Statistical Models," Ph.D. dissertation, Carnegie Mellon University, 1997.

Metropolis et al., 1953   Metropolis, N., A. Rosenbluth, M. Rosenbluth, A. Teller, and E. Teller, "Equation of State Calculation by Fast Computing Machines," *Journal of Chemical Physics*, Vol. 21, 1953.

Meuleau and Bourgine, 1999   Meuleau, N., and P. Bourgine, "Exploration of Multi-State Environments: Local Measures and Back-Propagation of Uncertainty," *Machine Learning*, Vol. 35, No. 2, 1999.

Meystre and Haug, 2005   Meystre, S., and PJ Haug, "Automation
                                of a Problem List Using Natural Language
                                Processing," *BMC Medical Informatics and
                                Decision Making*, Vol. 5, No. 30, 2005.

Minsky et al., 2004   Minsky, M.L., P. Singh, and A. Sloman,
                                "The St. Thomas Commonsense Sympo-
                                sium: Designing Architectures for Human-
                                Level Intelligence, *AI Magazine*, Vol. 25, No.
                                2, 2004.

Minsky, 2007   Minsky, M.L., *The Emotion Machine: Com-
                                monsense Thinking, Artificial Intelligence
                                and the Future of the Human Mind*, Simon
                                and Schuster, 2007.

Montes de Oca et al., 2011   Montes de Oca, M.A., T. Stützle, K. Van
                                den Enden, and M. Dorigo, "Incremental
                                Social Learning in Particle Swarms," *IEEE
                                Transactions on Systems, Man, and Cyber-
                                netics, Part B: Cybernetics*, Vol. 41, No. 2,
                                2011.

Morjaia et al, 1993   Morjaia, M., F. Rink, W. Smith, G. Klemp-
                                ner, C. Burns, and J. Stein, "Commercial-
                                ization of EPRI's Generator Expert Moni-
                                toring System (GEMS)," in *Expert System
                                Application for the Electric Power Industry*,
                                EPRI, Phoenix, AZ, 1993.

Neal, 1992   Neal, R., "Connectionist Learning of Belief
                                Networks," *Artificial Intelligence*, Vol. 56,
                                1992.

Neapolitan, 1989   Neapolitan, R. E., *Probabilistic Reasoning in
                                Expert Systems*, Wiley, 1989.

Neapolitan, 1996   Neapolitan, R. E., "Is Higher-Order Uncer-
                                tainty Needed?" in *IEEE Transactions on
                                Systems, Man, and Cybernetics Part A: Sys-
                                tems and Humans*, Vol. 26, No. 3, 1996.

Neapolitan, 2004   Neapolitan, R. E., *Learning Bayesian Net-
                                works*, Prentice Hall, 2004.

Neapolitan, 2009   Neapolitan, R. E., *Probabilistic Methods for
                                Bioinformatics*, Morgan Kaufmann, 2009.

Neapolitan and Jiang, 2007   Neapolitan, R. E., and X. Jiang, *Probabilis-
                                tic Methods for Financial and Marketing In-
                                formatics*, Morgan Kaufmann, 2007.

Neapolitan and Naimipour, 2010 Neapolitan, R. E., and K. Naimipour, *Foundations of Algorithms*, Jones and Bartlett, 2010.

Nease and Owens, 1997 Nease, R.F., and D.K. Owens, "Use of Influence Diagrams to Structure Medical Decisions," *Medical Decision Making*, Vol. 17, 1997.

Nefian et al., 2002 Nefian, A.F., L.H. Liang, X.X. Liu, X. Pi. and K. Murphy, "Dynamic Bayesian Networks for Audio-Visual Speech Recognition," *Journal of Applied Signal Processing, Special Issue on Joint Audio Visual Speech Processing*, Vol. 11, 2002.

Newell and Simon, 1961 Newell, A., and H. Simon, "GPS, a Program that Simulates Human Thought," in Building, H. (Ed.): *Lerenede Automaten*, R. Oldenbourg, 1961.

Newell, 1981 Newell, A., "The Knowledge Level," *AI Magazine*, Summer, 1981.

Nicholson, 1996 Nicholson, A.E., "Fall Diagnosis Using Dynamic Belief Networks," *Proceedings of the 4th Pacific Rim International Conference on Artificial Intelligence (PRICAI-96)*, Cairns, Australia, 1996.

Nillson, 1991 Nillson, N.J., "Logic and Artificial Intelligence," *Artificial Intelligence*, Vol. 47, 1991.

Nillson, 1994 Nillson, N.J., "Teleo-Reactive Programs for Agent Control," *Journal of Artificial Intelligence Research*, Vol. 1, 1994.

Norwick et al., 1993 Norwick, S.M., M.E. Dean, D.L. Dill, and M. Horowitz, "The Design of a High-Performance Cache Controller: A Case Study in Synchronous Synthesis," *Integration, the VLSI Journal*, Vol. 15, No. 3, 1993.

Ogunyemi et al., 2002 Ogunyemi, O., J. Clarke, N. Ash, and B. Webber, "Combining Geometric and Probabilistic Reasoning for Computer-Based Penetrating-Trauma Assessment," *Journal of the American Medical Informatics Association*, Vol. 9, No. 3, 2002.

Olesen et al., 1992   Olesen, K. G., S. L. Lauritzen, and F.
                           V. Jensen, "aHUGIN: A System Creating
                           Adaptive Causal Probabilistic Networks," in
                           Dubois, D., M. P. Wellman, B. D'Ambrosio,
                           and P. Smets (Eds.): *Uncertainty in Arti-
                           ficial Intelligence; Proceedings of the Eighth
                           Conference*, Morgan Kaufmann, 1992.

Olmsted, 1983   Olmsted, S.M., "On Representing and Solv-
                           ing Influence Diagrams," Ph.D. disserta-
                           tion, Dept. of Engineering-Economic Sys-
                           tems, Stanford University, California, 1983.

Onisko, 2001   Onisko, A.,"Evaluation of the Hepar II Sys-
                          tem for Diagnosis of Liver Disorders," *Work-
                          ing Notes on the European Conference on
                          Artificial Intelligence in Medicine (AIME-
                          01): Workshop Bayesian Models in Medi-
                          cine*," Cascais, Portugal, 2001.

Partridge, 1982   Partridge, B., "The Structure and Function
                          of Fish Schools," *Scientific American*, Vol.
                          246, No 6, 1982.

Pearl, 1986   Pearl, J., "Fusion, Propagation, and Struc-
                          turing in Belief Networks," *Artificial Intelli-
                          gence*, Vol. 29, 1986.

Pearl, 1988   Pearl, J., *Probabilistic Reasoning in Intelli-
                          gent Systems*, Morgan Kaufmann, 1988.

Pearl, 2000   Pearl, J., *Causality: Models, Reasoning,
                          and Inference*, Cambridge University Press,
                          2000.

Pearl et al., 1989   Pearl, J., D. Geiger, and T. S. Verma, "The
                          Logic of Influence Diagrams," in Oliver,
                          R.M., and J. Q. Smith (Eds.): *Influence
                          Diagrams, Belief Networks and Decision
                          Analysis*, Wiley, 1990. (a shorter version
                          originally appeared in *Kybernetica*, Vol. 25,
                          No. 2, 1989.)

Pham et al [2002]   Pham, T.V., M. Worring, A. W. Smeulders,
                          "Face Detection by Aggregated Bayesian
                          Network Classifiers," *Pattern Recognition
                          Letters*, Vol. 23. No. 4, 2002.

Piaget, 1966   Piaget, J., *The Child's Conception of Phys-
                          ical Causality*, Routledge and Kegan Paul,
                          1966.

Pinker, 2007

Pinker, S., *The Stuff of Thought: Language as a Window into Human Nature*, Viking, 2007.

Potvin, 1993

Potvin, J.Y., "The Traveling Salesperson Problem: A Neural Network Perspective," *ORSA Journal on Computing*, Vol. 5, No. 4, 1983.

Pradhan and Dagum, 1996

Pradhan, M., and P. Dagum, "Optimal Monte Carlo Estimation of Belief Network Inference," in Horvitz, E., and F. Jensen (Eds.): *Uncertainty in Artificial Intelligence; Proceedings of the Twelfth Conference*, Morgan Kaufmann, 1996.

Quinlan, 1983

Quinlan, J.R., "Learning Efficient Classification Procedures and their Application to Chess Endgames," in Michalski. R.S., J.G. Carbonell, and T.M. Mitchell (Eds.), *Machine Learning – An Artificial Intelligence Approach*, Tioga, 1983.

Quinlan, 1986

Quinlan, J.R., "Induction of Decision Trees," *Machine Learning*, Vol. 1, No. 1, 1986.

Quinlan, 1987

Quinlan, J.R., "Simplifying Decision Trees," *International Journal of Man-Machine Studies*, Vol. 27, No. 3, 1987.

Rechenberg, 1994

Rechenberg, I., *Evolution Strategies*, in Zurada, J.M., R.J. Marks II, and C.J. Robinson (Eds.): *Computational Intelligence: Imitating Life*, IEEE Press, 1994.

Reiter, 1980

Reiter, R., "A Logic for Default Reasoning," *Artificial Intelligence*, Vol. 13, 1980.

Reiter, 1991

Reiter, R., "The Frame Problem in the Situation Calculus: A Simple Solution (Sometimes) and a Completeness Result for Goal Regression," in Lifschitz, V. (Ed.): *Artificial Intelligence and Mathematical Theory of Computation: Papers in Honor of John McCarthy*, Academic Press.

Reynolds, 1987

Reynolds, C.W., "Flocks, Herds, and Schools: A Distributed Behavioral Model," *Computer Graphics*, Vol. 21, No. 4, 1987.

Robbins, 1952

Robbins, H., "Some Aspects of the Sequential Design of Experiments," *Bulletin of the American Mathematical Society*, Vol. 58, No. 5, 1952.

Robinson, 1977

Robinson, R. W., "Counting Unlabeled Acyclic Digraphs," in Little, C. H. C. (Ed.): *Lecture Notes in Mathematics, 622: Combinatorial Mathematics V*, Springer-Verlag, 1977.

Rosenschein, 1985

Rosenschein, S.J., "Formal Theories of Knowledge in AI and Robotics," *New Generation Computing*, Vol.3, No. 4, 1985.

Royalty et al., 2002

Royalty, J., R. Holland, A. Dekhtyar, and J. Goldsmith, "POET, The Online Preference Elicitation Tool," *Proceedings of AAAI Workshop on Preferences in AI and CP*, 2002.

Ruhnka et al., 1992

Ruhnka, J.C., H.D. Feldman, and T.J. Dean, "The 'Living Dead' Phenomena in Venture Capital Investments," *Journal of Business Venturing*, Vol. 7, No. 2, 1992.

Russell and Norvig, 1995

Russell, S., and P. Norvig, *Artificial Intelligence A Modern Approach*, Prentice Hall, 1995.

Salmon, 1997

Salmon, W., *Causality and Explanation*, Oxford University Press, 1997.

Savage, 1954

Savage, L.J., *Foundations of Statistics*, Wiley, New York, 1954.

Scheines et al., 1994

Scheines, R., P. Spirtes, C. Glymour, and C. Meek, *Tetrad II: User Manual*, Erlbaum, 1994.

Searle, 1980

Searle, J.R., "Mind, Brains, and Programs," *Behavioral and Brain Sciences*, Vol. 3, 1980.

Segal et al., 2005

Segal, E., D. Pe'er, A. Regev, D. Koller, and N. Friedman, "Learning Module Networks," *Journal of Machine Learning Research*, Vol. 6, 2005.

Shachter, 1986

Shachter, R. D. "Evaluating Influence Diagrams," *Operations Research*, Vol. 34, 1986.

Shachter and Peot, 1990   Shachter, R. D., and M. Peot, "Simulation Approaches to General Probabilistic Inference in Bayesian Networks," in Henrion, M., R. D. Shachter, L. N. Kanal, and J. F. Lemmer (Eds.): *Uncertainty in Artificial Intelligence 5*, North-Holland, 1990.

Shannon, 1948   Shannon, C.E., "A Mathematical Theory of Communication," *The Bell System Technical Journal*, Vol. 27, 1948.

Shaparau et al., 2008   Shaparau, D., M. Pistore, and P. Traverso, "Fusing Procedural and Declarative Planning Goals for Nondeterministic Domains," *Proceedings of the Twenty-Third AAAI Conference on Artificial Intelligence*, Chicago, IL, 2008.

Shenoy, 2006   Shenoy, P., "Inference in Hybrid Bayesian Networks Using Mixtures of Gaussians," in Dechter, R., and T. Richardson (Eds.): *Uncertainty in Artificial Intelligence: Proceedings of the Twenty-Second Conference*, AUAI Press, 2006.

Shepherd and Zacharakis, 2002   Shepherd, D.A., and A. Zacharakis, "Venture Capitalists' Expertise: A Call for Research into Decision Aids and Cognitive Feedback," *Journal of Business Venturing*, Vol. 17, 2002.

Shiller, 2000   Shiller, R.J., *Irrational Exuberance*, Princeton University Press, 2000.

Simon, 1957   Simon, H., *Models of Man: Social and Rational*, Wiley, 1957.

Sims, 1987   Sims, M.H., "Empirical and Analytic Discovery in IL," *Proceedings of the 4h International Machine Learning Workshop*, Morgan Kaufmann, 1987.

Singh and Valtorta, 1995   Singh, M., and M. Valtorta, "Construction of Bayesian Network Structures from Data: A Brief Survey and an Efficient Algorithm," *International Journal of Approximate Reasoning*, Vol. 12, 1995.

Spirtes et al., 1993; 2000   Spirtes, P., C. Glymour, and R. Scheines, *Causation, Prediction, and Search*,

Springer-Verlag, New York, 1993; second edition, MIT Press, 2000.

Srinivas, 1993

Srinivas, S., "A Generalization of the Noisy OR Model," in Heckerman, D., and A. Mamdani (Eds.): *Uncertainty in Artificial Intelligence; Proceedings of the Ninth Conference*, Morgan Kaufmann, 1993.

Strutt and Hall, 2003

Strutt, J.E., and P.L. Hall, *Global Vehicle Reliability: Prediction and Optimization Techniques*, Wiley, 2003.

Sun and Shenoy, 2006

Sun, L., and P. Shenoy, "Using Bayesian Networks for Bankruptcy Prediction: Some Methodological Issues," School of Business Working Paper No. 302, University of Kansas, Lawrence, KS, 2006.

Süral et al., 2010

Süral, H., N.E. Özdemirel, I Önder, and M.S. Turan, "An Evolutionary Approach for the TSP and the TSP with Backhauls," in Tenne, Y., and C.K. Goh (Eds.): *Computational Intelligence in Expensive Optimization Problems*, Springer-Verlag, 2010.

Szolovits and Pauker, 1978

Szolovits, P., and S.G. Pauker, "Categorical and Probabilistic Reasoning in Medical Diagnosis," *Artificial Intelligence*, Vol. 11, 1978.

Tatman and Shachter, 1990

Tatman, J.A., and R.D. Shachter, "Dynamic Programming and Influence Diagrams," *IEEE Transactions on Systems, Man, and Cybernetics*, Vol. 20, No. 2, 1990.

Tierney, 1996

Tierney, L., "Introduction to General State-Space Markov Chain Theory," in Gilks, W. R., S. Richardson, and D. J. Spiegelhalter (Eds.): *Markov Chain Monte Carlo in Practice*, Chapman & Hall/CRC, 1996.

Torres-Toledano and Sucar, 1998

Torres-Toledano, J.G and L.E. Sucar, "Bayesian Networks for Reliability Analysis of Complex Systems," in Coelho, H. (Ed.): *Progress in Artificial Intelligence - IBERAMIA 98*, Springer-Verlag, Berlin, 1998.

Turing, 1950 — Turing, A., "Computing Machinery and Intelligence," *Mind*, Vol. 59, 1950.

Tversky and Kahneman, 1981 — Tversky, A., and D. Kahneman, "The Framing of Decisions and the Psychology of Choice," *Science*, Vol. 211, 1981.

Valadares, 2002 — Valadares, J. "Modeling Complex Management Games with Bayesian Networks: The FutSim Case Study," *Proceeding of Agents in Computer Games, a Workshop at the 3rd International Conference on Computers and Games (CG'02)*, Edmonton, Alberta, Canada, 2002.

van Lambalgen, 1987 — van Lambalgen, M., "Random Sequences," Ph.D. thesis, University of Amsterdam, 1987.

VanLehn et al., 2005 — VanLehn, K., C. Lynch, K. Schulze, J.A. Shapiro, R. Shelby, L. Taylor, D. Treacy, A. Weinstein, and M. Wintersgill, "The Andes Physics Tutoring System: Lessons Learned," *International Journal of Artificial Intelligence and Education*, Vol. 15, No. 3, 2005.

Vermorel and Mohri, 2005 — Vermorel, J., and M. Mohri, "Multi-Armed Bandit Algorithms and Empirical Evaluation," *European Conference on Machine Learning*, 2005.

Vicsek et al., 1995 — Vicsek, T., A. Czir´ok, E. Ben-Jacob, and O. Shochet, "Novel Type of Phase Transition in a System of Self-Driven Particles," *Physical Review Letters*, Vol. 75, 1995.

von Mises, 1919 — von Mises, R., "Grundlagen der Wahrscheinlichkeitsrechnung," *Mathematische Zeitschrift*, Vol. 5, 1919.

Williams et al., 2003 — Williams, B., M. Ingham, S. Chung, and P. Elliot, "Model-based Programming of Intelligent Embedded Systems and Robotic Space Explorers," *Proceedings of IEEE Special Issue on Modeling and Design of Embedded Software*, 2003.

Winograd, 1972 — Winograd, T., "Understanding Natural Language," *Cognitive Psychology*, Vol. 3, No. 1, 1972.

Winston, 1973   Winston, P., "Progress in Vision and Robot-
                                       ics," M.I.T. Artificial Intelligence TR-281,
                                       1973.

Wright, 1921   Wright, S., "Correlation and Causation,"
                                       Journal of Agricultural Research, Vol. 20,
                                       1921.

Xiang et al., 1996   Xiang, Y., S. K. M. Wong, and N. Cercone,
                                       "Critical Remarks on Single Link Search in
                                       Learning Belief Networks," in Horvitz, E.,
                                       and F. Jensen (Eds.): *Uncertainty in Artifi-
                                       cial Intelligence; Proceedings of the Twelfth
                                       Conference*, Morgan Kaufmann, 1996.

Yob, 1975   Yob, G., "Hunt the Wumpus," *Creative
                                       Computing*, Vol. 1, No. 5, Sep-Oct 1975.

Zadeh, 1965   Zadeh, L., "Fuzzy sets," *Information and
                                       Control*, Vol. 8, No. 3, 1965.

Zell and Mooney, 1996   Zell, J., and R. Mooney, "Learning to
                                       Parse Database Queries Using Inductive
                                       Logic Programming," *Proceedings of AAAI-
                                       96*, MIT Press, 1996.

Index